# Omnibus I

# OMNIBUS I

## Biblical and Classical Civilizations

General Editor **DOUGLAS WILSON**
Managing Editor **G. TYLER FISCHER**

Veritas Press

Veritas Press, Lancaster, Pennsylvania
©2005 by Veritas Press
800-922-5082
www.VeritasPress.com
ISBN-13: 978-1-932168-42-6
ISBN-10: 1-932168-42-7

Printed in the United States of America.

For the Detweiler clan, who have brought vision and friendship in equal measure.

—DOUGLAS WILSON

For Emily, whose love, support and longsuffering made this work possible. May your children rise up and call you blessed, adding their voices of praise to mine. *Amore fidelis.*

—G. TYLER FISCHER

# TABLE OF CONTENTS

Preface . . . . . . . . . . . . . . . . . . . . . . . . . . . . . . . . ix

Publisher's Preface . . . . . . . . . . . . . . . . . . . . . . xi

Introduction . . . . . . . . . . . . . . . . . . . . . . . . . . . . 1

## PRIMARY BOOKS FIRST SEMESTER

Genesis *Stuart W. Bryan* . . . . . . . . . . . . . . . . . . 7

Exodus *Peter J. Leithart* . . . . . . . . . . . . . . . . . 23

Epic of Gilgamesh *Ben Merkle* . . . . . . . . . . . . . 37

Code of Hammurabi *William S. Dawson* . . . . . . . . 51

First and Second Samuel *Peter J. Leithart* . . . . . . . . 67

First and Second Kings *Peter J. Leithart* . . . . . . . . . . 81

Odyssey *Douglas Wilson* . . . . . . . . . . . . . . 95

Histories *N.D. Wilson* . . . . . . . . . . . . . . . . 123

Oresteia *Michael Metzler and Toby Sumpter* . . . . . . . 151

Plutarch's Lives *William C. Michael* . . . . . . . . . . . 163

## PRIMARY BOOKS SECOND SEMESTER

Theban Trilogy *G. Tyler Fischer* . . . . . . . . . . . . . 179

The Last Days of Socrates *Doug Jones* . . . . . . . . . 195

The Early History of Rome *Natali H. Miller* . . . . . . . 213

Luke and Acts *Gregg Strawbridge* . . . . . . . . . . . . 235

Aeneid *Douglas Wilson* . . . . . . . . . . . . . . . . . 247

The Twelve Caesars *Brent Harken* . . . . . . . . . . . . 269

Julius Caesar *Jared Miller* . . . . . . . . . . . . . . . . 291

Revelation *Randy Booth* . . . . . . . . . . . . . . . . . 309

## SECONDARY BOOKS FIRST SEMESTER

Chosen by God *Gregg Strawbridge* . . . . . . . . . . . . 327

Till We Have Faces *G. Tyler Fischer* . . . . . . . . . . . 339

The Magician's Nephew *Douglas Wilson* . . . . . . . . 355

The Lion, the Witch and the
      Wardrobe *Douglas Wilson* . . . . . . . . . . . . . . . 367

The Horse & His Boy *Douglas Wilson* . . . . . . . . . . . 381

Prince Caspian: The Return to Narnia
      *Douglas Wilson* . . . . . . . . . . . . . . . . . . . 391

The Voyage of the *Dawn Treader* *Douglas Wilson* . . 403

Isaiah *Jerrold W. Owen* . . . . . . . . . . . . . . . . . 415

Jeremiah *Gregg Strawbridge* . . . . . . . . . . . . . . . 427

Minor Prophets *J.C. Evans* . . . . . . . . . . . . . . . . 437

## SECONDARY BOOKS SECOND SEMESTER

The Silver Chair *Douglas Wilson* . . . . . . . . . . . . . 449

The Last Battle *Douglas Wilson* . . . . . . . . . . . . . . 461

The Best Things in Life *William S. Dawson* . . . . . . . 473

The Unaborted Socrates *William S. Dawson* . . . . . . 487

Galatians *Douglas Wilson* . . . . . . . . . . . . . . . . . 501

Romans *Bruce Etter* . . . . . . . . . . . . . . . . . . . . 511

James *Bruce Etter* . . . . . . . . . . . . . . . . . . . . . 525

The Eagle of the Ninth *Deborah Erb* . . . . . . . . . . . 535

The Screwtape Letters *O. Woelke Leithart* . . . . . . . 551

The Holiness of God *G. Tyler Fischer* . . . . . . . . . . 563

Appendix I Reading Schedule . . . . . . . . . . . . . . . . 575

Appendix II Timeline . . . . . . . . . . . . . . . . . . . . . 577

Index . . . . . . . . . . . . . . . . . . . . . . . . . . . . . . . 599

# PREFACE

One of the most obvious questions that Christians might ask about a curriculum like this one is, "Why study this stuff?" The question can be asked for different reasons. Perhaps a concerned parent is attracted to the rigor of a "classical and Christian approach," and yet has thumbed through a couple of the texts and is taken aback by some of the material. "It was this kind of gunk," he thinks, "that chased us out of the government school." Or perhaps the question is asked by the student himself when he "hits the wall." The rigor that is built into this course of study is signifi- cant, and about a third of the way through the year, a student might be asking all sorts of pointed questions. "Why are you making me do this?" is likely to be one of them. The student may be asking because of his workload, but if he points to the nature of the material, the question still needs a good answer. It is a good question, and everyone who is involved in teaching this course needs to have the answer mastered.

G.K. Chesterton said some- where that if a book does not have a wicked character in it, then it is a wicked book. One of the most pernicious errors that has gotten abroad in the Christian community is the error of *sentimentalism*—the view that evil is to be evaded, rather than the more robust Christian view that evil is to be conquered. The Christian believes that evil is there to be fought, the dragon is there to be slain. The sentimentalist believes that evil is to be resented.

My wife and I did not enroll our children in a classical Christian school so that they would never come into contact with sin. Rather, we wanted them there because we wanted to unite with like-minded Christian parents who had covenanted together to deal with the (inevitable) sin in a consistent, biblical manner. We fully expected our children to encounter sin in the classroom, on the playground and in the

curriculum. We also expected that when they encoun- tered it, they would see it dealt with in the way the Bible says sin should be dealt with.

A classical Christian school or a home school following the classical Christian curriculum must never be thought of as an asylum. Rather, this is a time of basic training; it is boot camp. Students are being taught to handle their weapons, and they are being taught this under godly, patient supervision. But in order to learn this sort of response, it is important that students learn it well. That is, setting up a "straw man" paganism that is easily demolished equips no one. All that would do is impart a false sense of security to the students—until they get to a secular college campus to encounter the real thing. Or, worse yet, if they continue the path into a soft, asylum-style Christian college and then find themselves addressing the marketplace completely unprepared.

If this basic training is our goal, and it is, then we should make clear what one potential abuse of the Omnibus curriculum might be. This curriculum was written and edited with the assumption that godly oversight and protection would accompany the student through his course of work. It was written with the conviction that children need teachers, flesh and blood teachers, who will work together with them. It was also written with the assumption that many of these teachers need the help and the resources that a program like this can supply. But we also believe that, if a seventh-grader is simply given this material and told to work through it himself, the chances are good that the student will miss the benefit that is available for those who are taught.

The Scriptures do not allow us to believe that a record of sinful behavior, or of sinful corruption, is inherently corrupting. If it were, then there are many stories and accounts in the Bible itself that would have to be excluded. But if we ever begin to think our children need to be protected "from the Bible," this should bring us up short. Perhaps we have picked up false notions of holiness somewhere. In short, there is no subject that this curriculum will raise in the minds of seventh-grade students that would not *also* be raised when that student reads through his Bible, cover to cover. It is true that this curriculum has accounts of various murders, or examples of prostitution, or of tyranny from powerful and cruel kings. But we can find all the same things in the book of Judges.

So the issue is not the *presence* of sin, but of the *response* to that sin. What we have sought to do throughout—in the introductory worldview essays, the questions and exercises, and in the teachers' materials—is provide a guideline for responding to all the various worldviews that men outside of Christ come up with. This program, we believe, will equip the student to see through pretences and lies that other Christian children, who have perhaps been too sheltered, are not able to deal with.

Of course, there is a limit to this, as we have sought to recognize. There *are* certain forms of worldliness and corruption that would overwhelm a student's ability to handle it, no matter how carefully a parent or teacher was instructing them. And while children differ in what they can handle, in our experience with many students of this age, we believe that the content of this curriculum is well within the capacity of Christian children of this age group. But again, this assumes godly oversight and instruction. The challenge here is two-fold. The rigor of the curriculum can seem daunting, but we have sought to provide direction and balance with regard to the demands of the material. The second concern is the question of false worldviews, paganism and just plain old-fashioned sin, which we have addressed above.

As our students work their way through this material, and in the years of the Omnibus program that will

follow, we want them to walk away with a profound sense of the *antithesis*. What we mean by this is that right after Adam and Eve fell in the Garden, God gave His first messianic promise (Gen. 3:15). But along with this promise, He also said that there would be constant antipathy between the seed of the woman and the seed of the serpent. This is what we mean by the antithesis, and we want our students to come to share in that godly antipathy. The fear of the Lord is to hate evil (Ps. 97:10; Prov. 8:13). In every generation, in all movements (whether of armies or philosophies), in all schools of literature, the men and women involved are either obeying God or disobeying Him. They are either trusting Him or they are not trusting Him. All students are learning to love God, or they are not learning to love God.

But when they love and trust Him, they must do so in the face of conflict. Jesus was the ultimate seed of the Woman, and yet when He came down and lived among us, He faced constant opposition from "broods of vipers." It is not possible to live in this world faithfully without coming into conflict with those who have no desire to live faithfully. The task of every Christian parent bringing children up to maturity in such a world is to do it in *a way that equips*. False protection, precisely because it does not equip, leaves a child defenseless when the inevitable day comes when that artificial shelter is removed. True protection equips. We do not want to build a fortress for our students to hide in; we want to give them a shield to carry—along with a sword.

Students who have faithfully worked through this course of study will not be suckers for a romanticized view of ancient paganism offered up by Hollywood. They have read Suetonius, and they have worked through a Christian response to true paganism. They are grateful that Christ came into this dark world, and they know *why* they are grateful.

—*Douglas Wilson*

# PUBLISHER'S PREFACE

Have you ever stopped to think what the President of the United States in the year 2040 is doing right now? What about the next Martin Luther or John Calvin? I'll tell you what I hope they are doing. I hope they just finished reading this sentence!

There is no doubt in my mind that classical Christian education and the rigorous study of the greatest works of Western Civilization is a tool to create leaders like no other—godly leaders who understand that this is God's world, Christ inherited it, and we are to take dominion of it to His glory.

Many have begun down the path of studying this material and have not persevered—in their minds it was too hard, too salacious for Christian ears, too unrealistic, too much to grasp, the books were too old or some other "too." Be assured, like the Scriptures say in the Parable of the Sower, the work you do will *bear fruit a hundredfold* if you stick with it. In the lives of our own children we have already seen tremendous benefit and really have just barely scratched the surface.

Our goal with this text is to make the work easier for you. This text should make approaching *Omnibus*, and other material not previously encountered, come alive in a way that instills confidence, and it should convey a sense that young students (and teachers) can handle it.

We have done all we could to make this text a stand-alone guide for reading, studying and understanding these great books. A couple reference books will prove beneficial as resources for this year as well as the following years. *Western Civilization* by Jackson Spielvogel and *History of Art for Young People* by H.W. Janson and Anthony F. Janson are the two main ones. If you have previously used our *Veritas Press History and Bible Curriculum*, you will want to keep the flashcards from them handy, too.

May you be blessed as you dig in and study the hand of God at work in the past and prepare for His use of you in the future.

—*Marlin Detweiler*

**ADVISORY TO TEACHERS AND PARENTS**

In the course of history there has been much fluctuation on what has been deemed age appropriate for young students. And for those of us alive today, there remains great variation as to what is considered age appropriate. The material we have created and the books we have assigned address numerous subjects and ideas that deal with topics (including sex, violence, religious persuasion and a whole host of other ideas) that have been the subject of much discussion of whether they are age appropriate. The judgment we applied in this text has been the same as we apply to our own children.

In the creation of this program we have assumed that it will be used by students in seventh grade and above. Furthermore, we have assumed that there is no part of the Bible deemed inappropriate to discuss with a seventh-grade student. Therefore, the material assumes that the student knows what sex is, that he understands the existence of violence, that he understands there are theological and doctrinal differences to be addressed and that he has the maturity to discern right and wrong.

The worldview we hold and from which we write is distinctly protestant and best summarized in the *Westminster Confession of Faith*. The Bible is our only ultimate and infallible rule of faith and practice.

We encourage you to become familiar with the material that your students will be covering in this program in order to avoid problems where you might differ with us on these matters.

# INTRODUCTION

Knowing *why* we ought to study the books in *Omnibus I: Biblical and Classical Civilizations* is a good first step. It leads, of course, to another monumental question: "*How* are we going to do this?" While from the outside the "Great Books" might seem imposing (stack them up and just look at the height of the pile!), the *Veritas Press Omnibus Curriculum* is going to enable you to unlock the treasure chest of ideas contained in these works. This curriculum is going to make it not only doable, but enjoyable.

Before you start, however, there are a few terms that you need to understand clearly. First among them is the term *omnibus*. This Latin term means "all encompassing" or "everything." So in a very loose sense, the Omnibus is where we talk about everything. All of the important ideas are set on the table to explore and understand. In a more technical sense, however, this Omnibus focuses our attention on the ideas, arguments and expressions of the Western Canon which have also become known as the *Great Books* of Western Civilization. Thus, Omnibus is the study of the Great Books, leading to the analysis of the *Great Ideas*—the ideas that have shaped Western Civilization.

This definition leads, of course, to the next set definitions that we must consider. What are the Great Books and the Great Ideas? Even though all these concepts are linked, they can be distinguished.

Simply put, the Great Books are those books that have guided and informed thinking people in Western Civilization. They are the books that have stood the test of time. They come from many sources, starting with the Hebrews and Greeks and extending to their Roman, European and colonial heirs. These books represent the highest theological and philosophical contemplations, the most accurate historical record and the most brilliant literary tradition that have come down to us from our forefathers.[1] The use of the term *Great Books* today has been linked to the work of the late Mortimer Adler, University of Chicago professor and editor of the *Great Books of Western Civilization Series* for Encyclopedia Britannica. The set of books which he edited has been a great source of light, and his work an inspiration, to those involved in this project.

Adler, however, did not compile the list of the Great Books for *Omnibus I*. This curriculum is produced by protestants, so you might note that we sprinkle in less Aristotle and Aquinas and more Calvin and Lewis. We consulted a number of sources, and then, in good Western style, argued about which books to include. On most lists there was great overlap. No one omits Plato, Aristotle, Augustine or Aquinas, for example.

This book is the first of six in the entire curriculum. We use this material and recommend using it for seventh grade. It can certainly be used by older students but probably not younger ones. The completed curriculum will likely look something like this:

| TITLE | PERIOD | YEARS | EMPHASIS |
|---|---|---|---|
| Omnibus I | Ancient | Beginning–A.D. 70 | Logic |
| Omnibus II | Medieval | 70–1563 | Logic |
| Omnibus III | Modern | 1563–Present | Logic |
| Omnibus IV | Ancient | Beginning–A.D. 70 | Rhetoric |
| Omnibus V | Medieval | 70–1563 | Rhetoric |
| Omnibus VI | Modern | 1563–Present | Rhetoric |

The list of books in the Ancient and Medieval years is fairly settled. The list of modern period books that we use is more flexible, but we are confident that our choices will stand the test of time. Thus the list of books that we use is what we are calling the Great Books.

A distinction must be made at this point between Primary and Secondary books. The list of Primary Books for each year is what might be termed the traditional Great Books. For this seventh-grade year, *Omnibus I,* you will find authors like Homer, Plato and Sophocles on the list. The Secondary Books are ones that give balance to our reading (balance in the general areas of Theology, History and Literature).[2] In the secondary list you will find works such as *The Chronicles of Narnia* and *The Holiness of God.*

All of these books inform us on the *Great Ideas,* which are, simply put, the main thoughts discussed in the Great Books. In a very real sense books become great because of their wise, timeless and effective dealing with great ideas. There are certain ideas that recur or cause great and intense thinking. They set the path for orthodoxy and for further growth in understanding. These ideas affect all areas of life. They include concepts like the Trinity or ask questions like "What is the nature of the soul?" These questions have caused an immense amount of thinking, and we are well served by seeking to gain understanding in these areas.

But how are we to gain access to these ideas? This happens as we join in what is sometimes called the *Great Conversation.* Perhaps the most wondrous aspect of the Great Books is that they are inescapably related. They must not be viewed as a pile of unrelated things, but as a long, continual search for truth or an extended discussion. These books speak to each other. They answer each other.

An example will be helpful. At the time of the Reformation, in the early sixteenth century, many ideas were being discussed and many people were divided. One scholar who had been critical of the Roman Church was Desiderius Erasmus. He was perhaps the most educated scholar in the history of the West and was responsible for the production of the edition of the Greek New Testament that sparked biblical scholarship in his day. While he had much to criticize about the abuses of the Popes of his day, Erasmus was not going to leave the Roman communion. To distance himself from Protestantism he penned his work, *On the Freedom of the Will,* spelling out his beliefs on this topic. This book, however, elicited a response from Martin Luther, who wrote his classic work, *On the Bondage of the Will.* The two minds were firing ideas and assertions back and forth at each other. The rest of the world watched this battle and learned. A Frenchman named John Calvin followed in Luther's path and took some of Luther's ideas even further. The Counter-Reformation was the Roman Catholic response, hardening the position of the Roman Church. In the eighteenth century John Wesley, credited for founding the Methodist Church, sought some middle ground. As you might know, vigorous history-making discussion ensued. But this discussion stretches back into the ancient past. It begins with the pens of Moses (well, maybe not a pen for him) and unknown scribes writing about Gilgamesh. It is augmented by the poets and philosophers who set the agenda for future discussion as they sat around and discussed ideas in Athens.[3] This discussion poured out of the minds of men like Augustine, who battled Donatists and Pelagians in his day. It saw the great schools of the Middle Ages take positions in debates and dueling works.

The pattern of entering into this discussion is to listen, learn and then to speak. Just as in the past, you will be made ready to enter into this discussion by reading the discussion from the beginning, and then you will next learn by engaging in this ongoing discussion. When you finish the *Omnibus,* you will be equipped to stand on the shoulders of your forefa-thers, looking further, reaching higher and adding to the wisdom of the past. Most well-educated men in the distant past knew this material. They understood the value of knowing it. And they were humble enough to know the process, that is, that they needed to earn the right to be heard. Today, many think all opinions are equally valid and equally important.

Sadly, in our day, few have listened so as to be prepared to speak. The common phenomenon of ignoring virtually all of this knowledge of the past is perhaps the greatest tragedy of the "modern" world. In our great haste to move "forward" we have divorced ourselves from this massive amount of wisdom that is a treasure of inestimable value. Modern man gropes for answers that exist and are his by right, but he refuses to learn from those who went before him, and in failing to do so, makes the same mistakes all over again.

The goal or destination of this course is to learn to reason well and communicate winsomely. The Great Books are the path along which we are going to run to reach that destination. There are any number of paths to reach this goal. We think that this is the best path.

What better way is there to learn to argue and speak or write than to study the greatest arguments and the most winsome rhetoric? Who could be better teachers than Moses, Jesus, Dante, Virgil and Milton?

As a distinctly Christian program, however, we have to consider our destination, our path and the manner in which we run in light of God's revelation. We do not learn logic and rhetoric simply to become more competent than our peers. We do it to take dominion in the name of Jesus Christ. We do not choose the path of the Great Books without recognizing that all of the material that we come into contact with along that path must be sifted and evaluated by the inscripturated word of God. Nothing can be allowed to roam free outside of Christ. Every thought must be taken captive, every writer critiqued by Christ.

This program aims to cultivate and produce students who are culturally literate. This means becoming connected to and knowledgeable of the great traditions and thoughts of our forefathers. This should always be done simply out of consideration of the Fifth Commandment, which tells us to honor our father and mother. Our culture has rejected this eminently sensible idea in favor of the novelty of constant rebellion, which comes with the obvious punishment of reinventing the wheel every generation. This sort of insanity continues to infect many, and our culture finds itself lost in the woods.

Finally, you should know a little about the people heading up this project. The publishers are Marlin and Laurie Detweiler, the founders of Veritas Press. They have been involved in the genesis of this and many other products in the realm of classical Christian education and have been instrumental in the founding of both The Geneva School in Orlando, Florida and Veritas Academy in Lancaster, Pennsylvania. The editors are Douglas Wilson and G. Tyler Fischer. Douglas is the pastor of Christ Church in Moscow, Idaho, and Senior Fellow of Theology at New St. Andrew's College. Among his many books is *Recovering the Lost Tools of Learning*, which is the foundational work of the resurgent classical

Christian schooling movement, and he founded Logos School in Moscow, Idaho. Ty is the headmaster at Veritas Academy in Lancaster, Pennsylvania. During his tenure there the Omnibus was begun and has continued to develop. Ty is also the author of the *Veritas Press Bible Curriculum* for grammar school.

Many writers from across the country have worked to produce the material contained in this program. Some of particular note are Dr. Peter Leithart, the pastor of Trinity Church, Moscow, Idaho, and a Senior Fellow of Theology and Literature at New St. Andrews; and Douglas Jones, Senior Fellow of Philosophy at New St. Andrews. Many other notable men and women have made contributions and have produced this material.

We hope that God blesses your work in Omnibus, and we pray that He would help all of us to remember much that never should have been forgotten. *Kyrie Eleison.*

*—G. Tyler Fischer*
Ash Wednesday, A.D. 2005

## NOTES

1  This certainly is not meant to denigrate any other literary tradition in the world. This Omnibus goes out of its way to introduce books from other traditions as they have become meaningful in the West. This Omnibus, however, is produced by heirs of the Christian West for use by the future heirs of that glorious tradition, so we look to the West. We also do believe that it is the most glorious of traditions, and would invite those skeptical to simply take, read and compare. We also believe that the first step in appreciating other cultures—which is a common theme today—is to first appreciate our own.

2  To seek to maintain balance between the three disciplines that are covered comprehensively, each book has received a value of ten points that has been divided among the disciplines of Theology, History and Literature. So, the *Odyssey* is rated 2.2.6 (i.e., its ten points are divided into a score of 2 for Theology, 2 for History and 6 for Literature). This score, although somewhat artificial, allows us to maintain a balance in the subject matter and to produce grades for each of these three disciplines (Theology, History and Literature) which is particularly important for transcripts. See the Teacher's Edition for more information on grading. The entire listing of books with their respective point values is included in Appendix 1.

3  It is interesting that the play *Clouds* by Aristophanes makes fun of Socrates. So, the great minds not only debated each other, they teased each other as well.

# PRIMARY BOOKS

First Semester

# GENESIS

*We live in a world shattered,*
   *Each step reechoes the cracking of broken glass,*
*Shards removed at first from aching feet*
*but then ... finally ... tolerated,*
*Longing to recover the tranquil garden of gentle grass.*

Some days you might not feel it, but I bet that often you do. I call it "the longing." Often, it is felt most on days that are either best or worst. It happens when the world seems almost perfect (like a warm day at the shore with tall waves to ride and lavender sunsets), or when horror surrounds you (like hearing of the death of a friend). You long for the day at the beach to never end. You long for your friend to rise from the casket. You long for ... it.

Many have explained "the longing" in different ways. My favorite explanation came from the poet Dante Alighieri. He said that winds blew out from the top of the Mountain of Purgatory on the opposite side of the world and made us long for "it." (Don't get me wrong, there is no mountain in the Pacific like this, but I still like the story.) The Garden of Eden was set at the top of this mountain. These winds carried the scent of the Earthly Paradise out over the world. Each

night this brought back to us memories of a land that only a few humans had ever seen but that all of us somehow yearn for, the land of Eden. This sweet smell made us long to go back into the garden with God, with peace. This is what we long for in the best and worst of times.

Many centuries ago our first father began a sad journey, the journey of his exile. His path leads through the years to you ... to today. As our father first stepped out of the garden into a world cursed and fighting against him, he knew he had shattered the world.

He carried with him, however, one glimmer of hope. He was promised that someday, Someone, a Seed would come and open the gates of the garden again. He could go back home again then. This is where the longing started.

You stand at the beginning of another journey. Before you is the first book of the Bible, Genesis. In it and the many other books you will be studying are wonders that you can not now imagine. Come along for the journey. Our destination is set. We hope to see our ancestral home once more, but first we have to figure out how we got here.

In this detail from the fresco in the Sistene Chapel, we look back
to the dawn of Time and see the creation of the sun and moon.

# GENERAL INFORMATION

## Author and Context

Both Jewish and Christian scholars have historically maintained that Moses was the author of Genesis. While this has been questioned by modern scholarship, Mosaic authorship or editorship is quite reasonable. First, Moses was certainly capable of writing the book, educated as he was in all the learning of the Egyptians (Acts 7:22). Second, the text of Genesis is structured around ten sections[1] which begin with the Hebrew word *toledoth,* "These are the generations of . . ." (2:4; 5:1; 6:9; 10:1; 11:10; 11:27; 25:12; 25:19; 36:1; 37:2). It is likely that these were written sources which the author edited and compiled into their present form. As a prince in Egypt, Moses would have had access to such written records, whether among the Egyptians or the Israelites. Third, and most significant, both Jesus and the apostles assume that Moses was the author (e.g., Matt. 8:4; Mark 7:10; John 1:17; 7:22; Acts 3:22; Rom. 10:5; etc.). Since Jesus was omniscient, that is He knew everything and the apostles wrote under the inspiration of the Spirit, the conclusion that Moses was the author follows quite naturally.[2]

Abraham welcomes heavenly visitors to a meal.

Growing up in the Egyptian court during the New Kingdom in Ancient Egypt, Moses (c. 1526–1406 B.C.) would have been exposed to one of the most sophisticated, wealthy, and powerful kingdoms the earth had yet seen. Under the tutelage of his adoptive mother, most likely the powerful Hatshepsut, Moses could have become a major player in Egyptian history. However, he considered the "reproach of Christ greater riches than the treasures of Egypt" (Heb. 11:26) and numbered himself with the people of God, leading them out of bondage, revealing to them the precious law of God, and bringing them to the brink of the Promised Land.

## Significance

Genesis is a masterpiece. Using a wide variety of literary genres (writing styles) and techniques, Genesis successfully acquaints the sons of Israel with their fathers and enables them to see both their faithfulness and weakness. As a result, it enables the Israelites to depart from Egypt knowing their role in God's plan. Despite their own weakness, God would use them to bless the nations if they would but love and serve Him. The same holds true today for us who are the sons of Abraham by faith (Rom. 4:16, 17).

The word *Genesis* means beginnings. Nearly all ideas, events, and themes developed later in the Bible have their beginning in this book. The frequent references to God as Creator (e.g., Ps. 8; 19; Isa. 40:28; Rom. 1:25) drive us back to Genesis. The ubiquitous or ever present nature of sin which prompts the fall of Israel again and again (Deut. 27:9-26; Judg. 2:11-23; 2 Kings 17:7-20; 24:1-5) receives its explanation in the Fall. Our hope for deliverance from corruption bases itself upon the repeated promises in Genesis—the Seed of the woman who would crush the serpent's head (3:15), the Descendant of Abraham through whom all the families of the earth would be blessed (12:3; 22:18), the Lamb of God who would take away the sin of the world (22:13,14), and the Ruler who would arise from the tribe of Judah (49:8-12).

The significance of Genesis is not limited to the biblical text. Throughout history, Genesis has shaped the thinking and imagination of millions. Writers have imitated its stories. Scientists have used and abused the creation account. Artists and musicians have sought to capture its passion and emotion. It is hard to overestimate the influence of Genesis.

## Main Characters

The major character who pervades Genesis is the Triune God of heaven and earth, Yahweh. In the beginning He speaks the world into existence, creating all things "very good." After the Fall, He repeatedly evaluates the works of the sons of men. Eventually He chooses a people for Himself and preserves them from certain destruction despite their foolishness and treachery.

The other characters are divisible according to the two main sections of the book. Chapters 1 through 11 discuss the early history of the world, known as primeval history. During this period the major figures are Adam and Eve, the first couple, Cain and Abel, the first siblings, and Noah and his three sons, Shem, Ham, and Japheth, the founders of a new humanity following the flood.

The second section of the book, chapters 12 through 50, chronicles the beginning of God's redemptive (the way He would save a people) program through a single family. The three patriarchs—Abraham, Isaac, and Jacob—figure largely in this story. Associated with them are a variety of other fascinating characters. With Abraham, we see his wife Sarah, his nephew Lot, his wife's maid-servant Hagar, his child Ishmael, and his promised son Isaac. With Isaac we witness his wife Rebekah and his sons Esau and Jacob. With Jacob, renamed Israel, we meet his brother Esau, his uncle Laban, his wives Leah and Rachel, and his twelve children, the founders of the twelve tribes of Israel. Noteworthy among them are Judah and Joseph who play pivotal roles in the last portion of the book.

## Summary and Setting

Interestingly enough, Genesis has two different historical settings. First, it has the original setting in which the events occurred: the Fertile Crescent and Egypt from creation until the death of Joseph around 1805 B.C., the lion's share of the material spanning from the call of Abraham in 2091 B.C. (12:4) to the death of Jacob around 1859 B.C. (49:33ff). Second, it has the setting in which it was finally written: Israel was either still in the land of Egypt or had just departed under the leadership of Moses and the time was around 1446 B.C.

The book of Genesis treats its story like a chef peeling an onion. Starting with a broad focus upon the world at large, the book gradually, by removing one layer after another, highlights the selection of the twelve tribes of Israel as God's chosen people. The book begins with the universe as it bursts upon the scene, new and fresh from its Creator's hands but soon twisted by man's rebellion. This rebellion reaps horrendous consequences. Brother is set against brother and in time all men rise up in rebellion against God. Yet in the midst of this rebellion, God works to fulfill His promise to bring forth a Seed of the woman who would crush the serpent (Gen. 3:15). He delivers Noah and his family from judgment and brings them safely through the deluge. God then covenants with Noah, promising never again to destroy the earth in such a fashion but to provide a stable environment in which His Gospel promise would be fulfilled.

As the book progresses, its focus narrows step by step. God's promised deliverance will not come through Ham and Japheth but through Shem. Yet it will not come through all of Shem's descendants but only through those of Terah, the father of Abraham. And to Abraham the gospel promise is reissued, "in you all the families of the earth shall be blessed" (Gen. 12:3; cf. Gal. 3:8).

But God has not finished narrowing the scope of his redemptive purpose. Not all of Abraham's children shall be incorporated into God's plan—Ishmael is passed over and the story focuses upon Isaac, whose life is redeemed by the ram which God provides in the thicket. Then Esau is left behind and the story of Jacob becomes paramount. Jacob is renamed Israel and his sons, the sons of Israel, become the twelve tribes through whom God's redemptive purposes for the world will be fulfilled.

The sons of Israel, however, fail to perceive their role in the plan of God. They quarrel and complain and treat their brother Joseph treacherously, selling him into slavery in Egypt. But God's promises cannot be thwarted. He uses their jealousy and spite to change their character and preserve them in the land of Egypt; they meant it for evil, but God intended it for good (50:20). And so the book ends, awaiting the fulfillment of God's promise to lead His people to the promised land (50:24, 25; cf. 15:12–16).

## Worldview

J.R.R. Tolkien's superb *The Lord of the Rings* epic never fails to stir my imagination. It has spawned whole industries. Book stores are lined with "Tolkien like" material (much of which deserves as little attention as it receives). Hollywood produced three blockbuster movies based on Tolkien's epic. When these movies came out they caused quite a stir, and many people were so inspired by them that they actually picked up the books and began to read. Or, better yet, perhaps they picked up the books first and read them before they went to see the movies.

But imagine for a moment that you did watch the first movie and were so inspired by what you saw that you picked up *The Fellowship of the Ring* and began to read Tolkien's tale. Let us pretend that you were so excited that you decided to skip the prologue with its extended discourse on the history of hobbits and jump right into Chapter 1. You would, of course, immediately bump into Bilbo Baggins. And as you

Scripture tells of a flaming sword outside of the garden to keep out Adam and Eve.

read, you would find that Bilbo is not your typical hobbit. It seems that Bilbo has had some odd adventures, has actually been out of the Shire and is now fabulously rich as a result. You pause in your reading. "I'd like to know about that adventure," you say to yourself. Suppressing this desire, however, you press on—you want to read about Sauron and Isengard. But the desire continues to increase as tantalizing details from the past leak out—a magic ring, a wizard, frozen trolls, the House of Elrond, and the son of Gloin. You get a nagging feeling that you are missing an important piece of the puzzle. "Will I never have any peace?" you ask yourself. So you decide to glance at the Prologue. And there you find mention of an earlier book, *The Hobbit,* where many of these tantalizing details are discussed. Heaving a great sigh, you decide to become a true Tolkien aficionado. You close *The Fellowship of the Ring* and go to the store where you pick up a copy of *The Hobbit* and you begin to read at the beginning.

The point of this vignette is to illustrate that the first book of a series often sets the stage for the entire set. Frequently it reveals key information without which the other books are cryptic or make no sense. What is the basic story line or plot? Who are the major characters? The heroes? The villains? What problems do the characters face? How will they overcome these problems? The answers to these and other questions are often provided in the first book.

So it is with the Bible. The book of Genesis sets the stage for the entire book—both Old and New Testaments and for all of life. Without an understanding of Genesis the reader of Deuteronomy, the Psalms, or Matthew is going to be at a loss to understand fully what is being discussed. On the contrary, the man or woman who knows Genesis will both understand and enjoy the latter books much more.

To understand this "introduction" to the Bible and to all of life, one must understand the main characters and the main problem that faces these characters.

The reward for this grand epic, however, is unlike reading the *Rings* trilogy or *The Hobbit.* Much more is at stake; much more can be gained because this epic is the story of your race. The great problem set forth in Genesis is your great problem, and to grasp God's answer to this problem at Calvary you must understand Genesis.

## God Is Personal

The great main character of this story is the Lord God of heaven and earth, Who is unlike any other being.

One of the interesting aspects of God's personhood is that He interacts with Himself. This indicates that God is Triune—He is three persons in one nature. While the full revelation of the Triune character of God comes in the New Testament, Genesis contains at least two clear allusions to this central biblical doctrine. First, within the first three verses of Chapter 1 we have all three persons of the Trinity mentioned: God, the Spirit of God, and the Word of God. Second, God refers to Himself in the plural, "Let Us make man . . ." (1:26), "Behold the man has become like one of Us . . ." (3:22), "Let Us go down . . ." (11:7). Some have argued that this use of the plural is the "plural of majesty" as when a queen says, "We would like crumpets with our tea." Others have argued that this is a reference to other heavenly beings such as angels. However, in the light of later revelation it seems that the most reasonable explanation is that this is a foreshadowing of the Triune character of God.

Genesis not only reveals the Triune nature of God, it also assumes that there is only one true God. In the context of Egyptian culture and belief, the opening chapter of Genesis is revolutionary. The Egyptians associated the various portions of creation with a multitude of different deities who each had their respective sphere(s) of authority. Genesis overthrows this entire way of

## CREATION MYTHS

Many in academia refer to Genesis as a creation myth. While the Bible is not "mythological," there are creation myths from vastly diverse cultures and civilizations.

The Sumerians held that the primeval sea existed first and within that the heaven and the earth were formed. The stars, planets, sun and moon were formed between heaven and earth. The Babylonian story is similar: "When in the height heaven was not named, and the earth beneath did not yet bear a name, and the primeval Apsu, who begat them, and chaos, Tiamut, the mother of them both their waters were mingled together, and no field was formed, no marsh was to be seen; when of the gods none had been called into being, and none bore a name, and no destinies were ordained; then were created the gods in the midst of heaven . . ."

There are several creation myths in Hinduism. One myth tells of Brahma sitting in a lotus flower, floating and tossing on the sea. He lifted up his arms and calmed the wind and the ocean. Then he split the lotus flower into three. He stretched one part into the heavens, another part into the earth, and with the third part he created the skies.

In ancient Egypt several versions of creation emerged. In one there was the swirling watery chaos from which arose Atum, the primordial god represented in the form of a human and a serpent. He created the gods, then men were created from his tears. In another myth, the god Ptah is the supreme deity and creator of Atum: "He who made all and created the gods . . . who gave birth to the gods, and from whom every thing came forth, foods, provisions, divine offerings, all good things."

There have been many reports from missionaries in the last century that pre-literate tribes often have "sacred narratives" which are quite similar to, and provide a kind of echo for, the truth of Biblical creation.

In Hinduism, Brahma is the supreme god whose essence pervades the entire universe.

thinking by tracing the origin of everything to the creative power of the God of Abraham, Isaac, and Jacob. The gods of Egypt, Moses declares in Genesis 1, are mere idols (cf. Ps. 115:1-8).

## God is Sovereign

Like all good epics, the history of the world has a producer and director.

As the Creator of all, the God of Genesis is also the Lord of all, or Sovereign. This means, first, that God is distinctly different from His creation. While God has existed from eternity, the world began to exist when God called it into being. God created the world *ex nihilo*, out of nothing (cf. Rom. 4:17; Heb. 11:3). While God is not dependent on anything for His own existence, all of creation depends on Him.

God's sovereignty extends over all the earth. The God of Scripture is immanently involved in His creation, not passively and distantly watching all that transpires. The creation is His and He does with it as He sees fit. He destroys the earth with a flood, He confuses the tongues at Babel, He destroys Sodom and Gomorrah, He turns Lot's wife into a pillar of salt, He chooses Jacob rather than Esau. The list could go on, but the point is the same: God acts in the world as He sees fit.

God's sovereignty would be frightening if it were not simultaneously revealed that God is holy, righteous, and good. His sovereignty is the power to do all those things which He wants to do. Of course, all that He wants to do is good and right because He is Goodness and Righteousness. When Abraham was informed of the coming destruction of Sodom and Gomorrah, he feared for the lives of the righteous within the city and asked, "Shall not the Judge of all the earth deal justly?" The ensuing conversation between God and Abraham reveals that God does indeed deal justly and mercifully with sinners.

God's goodness, however does not make Him too lax and indulgent to visit calamity on his enemies. Cain is cast out for murder, the earth is flooded because of man's wickedness, languages are confused because of pride, Sodom and Gomorrah

> So the LORD said, "I will destroy man whom I have created from the face of the earth, both man and beast, creeping thing and birds of the air, for I am sorry that I have made them."

are incinerated for their debauchery, and two of Judah's sons are killed for their "evil."

While God condemns ungodliness, He promises to bless those who love Him and keep His commandments. God's treatment of those who serve Him is in sharp contrast to pagan deities who may or may not be favorably disposed to those who seek their aid. The gods are foremost man's enemies. In contrast, the God of Abraham, Isaac, and Jacob always works for the good of those who love Him and keep His commandments. He never punishes the godly for following in His paths. Thus, He takes Enoch to himself, He preserves the life of Noah, He rewards the faithfulness of Abraham, and He blesses the integrity of Joseph.

## God is Covenantal

This God who is unique and sovereign is also love.

The reason God works for the good of His people is because He loves them. This love is demonstrated by the fellowship God has with His people. First, He communicates with them. He does not leave them ignorant of Himself and His standards; He reveals Himself via direct revelation, blessings, dreams, prophecies, angelic visitations. Second, He establishes a clearly defined relationship (or covenant) with them, promising to bless them if they will but love and serve Him but threatening to chastise and even destroy them should they rebel. We see this in His relationship with Adam (2:15-17), in His covenant with Noah and his offspring (9:8-17), and in His covenant with Abraham and his descendants (17:1-14).

In His covenant with Adam[3] God gives clearly defined privileges, expectations, and consequences. He grants that Adam and Eve can eat from any tree in the garden, presumably even from the tree of life. However, God restricts them from the tree of the knowledge of good and evil. He warns them that if they eat of its fruit, they "will surely die." Adam and Eve despise the Word of the Lord and listen to the word of the serpent. As a result, God demonstrates His faithfulness—He fulfills His word of judgment, and mankind becomes subject to death and decay.

After the Fall, God sets in motion a plan to save His ruined creation. His plan, much like Tolkien's *Hobbit,* involves some strange choices. We might expect God to immediately wipe out the wicked or raise up some army of the righteous. God often, however, chooses the few and the obscure, just as Tolkien calls on the frightened and apprehensive Bilbo to do great things and to set in motion the actions far beyond his imagination. So God looks at times to single families like Noah and his children. God calls Abraham to be the father of many nations. Ironically, when God first comes to Abraham he is an idol worshipper who has been unable to have any children. What irony!

God's covenant with Noah likewise stresses God's faithfulness. While we are accustomed to think of the regularity of the seasons as a matter of scientific necessity, Genesis presents this regularity as a testimony of God's faithfulness. Why does the sun rise each morning? Why does winter turn to spring? Why do birds fly? Apples fall from trees? Why do cows moo? The answer, according to Genesis, is because God is faithful—He orchestrates both the mundane and the spectacular events in the world (cf. Ps. 104; Col. 1:17).

God's covenant with Abraham shines brighter than the sun. Again and again God manifests His determination to fulfill His promises in the life of Abraham and His descendants. Nowhere is this portrayed more forcefully than in Genesis 15. It was a common practice in the Ancient Near East to establish covenants by slaying an animal, cutting the animal in two and then placing the two pieces opposite one another. The participants of the covenant would then walk through the pieces as they recited the terms of the covenant. The action symbolized the covenanters' vow either to fulfill the terms of the covenant or to become like the divided animal—dead. The remarkable part of Genesis 15 is that, though there are two parties to the covenant, God and Abraham, only one of them walks through the pieces. God, symbolized by the flaming pot, passes through the pieces and thus declares to Abraham—either I will fulfill my promise to grant you a son or I will die. The latter of course is impossible. What follows? God will certainly grant a son. What a testimony of God's faithfulness![4]

This testimony continues throughout Genesis as God fulfills His promises despite the foibles, trickery, and treachery of men. He blesses the faithful efforts of His people and makes them successful. Likewise, God turns the evil actions of His own people to *their* eventual good. While not excusing sin, Genesis emphasizes that God is faithful and does whatever is necessary to fulfill His promises.

Then Noah built an altar to the LORD, and took of every clean animal and of every clean bird, and offered burnt offerings on the altar.

## God is Merciful

As in Tolkien's epic where the weaknesses of even a hobbit like Bilbo is eventually unmasked, the biblical characters prove that they are sinners in need of grace. During his adventure, as you might remember, Bilbo finds a "precious" magic ring. Eventually, he begins to fall under its powers, and we see his weakness. In the same manner, the biblical heroes all have feet of clay. Noah falls into drunkenness. Sarah laughs at God's promise of an heir. Abraham seeks to fulfill God's promise in his own strength by fathering Ishmael. Isaac tries to bless Esau instead of Jacob. The patriarchs even sell their brother, Joseph, into slavery. All are in need of mercy.

Genesis emphasizes the mercy of God alongside His covenantal faithfulness. Though Adam and Eve rebel against Him, He does not completely disown them but promises to deliver them from the craft of the serpent (3:15), provides them with clothing to cover their shame and symbolize their forgiveness (3:21), and expels them from the garden lest they live forever in their fallen state (3:22-24). Though God destroys the world in a great deluge, He "remembers" (8:1) Noah and delivers Him. Though Sarai is brought into the harem of Pharaoh, God delivers her and preserves her to bear the promised child (12:10-20). The God of Genesis is a God who delights to show mercy.

## Man Reflects the Image of God

The other main character in Genesis is mankind. Man begins his time on earth as a true and righteous reflector of God's glory. Man is like a mirror reflecting back to God the wonder of His own glorious love.

Originally, man was made in the image of God. What is he as the image of God? First, he is personal. Just as God speaks, acts and judges, so man speaks, acts and judges. He has the capacity to think and reason. He can analyze and assess.

Second, like God, man is initially sovereign, but in a limited way. He is sovereign, first, in the sense that he is a mini-creator. Many creatures are like God in this way. Beavers make dams; birds make nests; bumble bees make honey. But man has the unique ability to create, not simply things that he needs, but frivolous things—things which have no apparent link to his needs—bookshelves, video games, sculptures, and Oreos. The reason man can and should create such things is because God did. God did not need the universe; He created it because He wanted to. It delighted Him. And just as there is a fundamental distinction between God and the universe, there is also a distinction between the things man makes and man himself.[5]

Man is also sovereign because God has invested man with authority over the creatures of the earth.

"Then God said, 'Let Us make man in Our image, according to Our likeness; and let them rule over the fish of the sea ....' And God said to them, 'Be fruitful and multiply, and fill the earth, and subdue it; and rule over the fish of the sea ...'" (1:26, 28).

Like God, man is covenantal. God created man to live not in isolation from but in relation to God and other creatures. Man always lives *coram Deo,* before the face of God. God walks in the garden and finds Adam when he is trying to cover his sin (3:8-11). God "comes down" to see what the men of a particular region are

Isaac is shown mercy and a ram is given for the sacrifice to God.

doing (11:7; 18:21). All men are in a covenantal relationship with God. Some men acknowledge this relationship, and others choose to suppress it (e.g., 19:9 cf. Rom. 1:18–32), but everyone is accountable to God. Man also lives in relationship with other people. In the opening chapters of Genesis, the covenant of marriage is created by God as a perpetual statute (2:24). Sons are identified in relation to their fathers and nations in relation to their father, or patriarch (10:1ff). Man is responsible to see that justice is upheld and to hold perpetrators of injustice, notably murder, accountable (9:6). Man always exists in covenantal relation with other people—in the family, the church, and the state. Third, Adam himself bore a special covenantal relationship to the entire creation. Adam was appointed by God as the head of creation. When Adam sinned against the Lord, the earth was plunged into ruin and decay and all of Adam's descendants were born in a state of moral corruption. In other words, man is born into sin and born a sinner.

## Man is a Distorted Reflection

"Now the serpent was more cunning than any beast of the field which the LORD God had made."

obey. This expectation of obedience recurs again and again in Genesis. When God looked down upon the earth prior to the Flood, He "saw that the wickedness of man was great on the earth, and . . . the Lord was sorry that He had made man on the earth, and He was grieved in His heart" (6:5, 6). As a result, He judges man for his disobedience with the great deluge. God expected that His law would be obeyed. However, as a result of the Fall, man no longer had the capacity to do good on his own initiative. Following the Flood, God declares that "the intent of man's heart is evil from his youth" (8:21). By nature man ought to be holy, righteous and good, but he is not.

Early in the story of Genesis, however, Adam, the righteous mirror reflecting God's glory, is shattered by sin. As a sinner man no longer perfectly bears the image of God, but he still bears God's image.

This fall into sin creates the great problem for the human race. Adam was created "very good." Sin, however, made man love evil and commit sin. For now, because he is created in the image of God, there are certain things which man is but other things he ought to be but is not.

Man ought to be holy, righteous, and good. God created man to joyfully receive His commands and obey them. He told Adam and Eve to abstain from the fruit of the tree of the knowledge of good and evil. When they disobeyed, He visited them with death and cast them out of the garden. He demanded that they

Also man ought to be faithful both to God and to other men. Just as God is faithful to fulfill his covenantal obligations and promises, man ought to fulfill his. Sadly, this does not happen. Beginning in the opening chapters of Genesis, man turns against his sovereign Lord. Although God created man to live in fellowship with Him, man rejected this relationship. As a result, man's covenantal faithfulness to other men is also undermined. Isaac endeavors to avoid the Word of the Lord and give the blessing to Esau, forcing Rebekah and Jacob to resort to trickery in order to fulfill God's prophecy. Laban treacherously betrays Jacob, forcing him to work for seven years and then failing to give Rachel in fulfillment of his promise. By nature, therefore, man is a covenant breaker, always with respect to God and frequently with respect to other men.

Finally, man ought to be merciful just as God is merciful. God extends grace to those who are undeserving or weak. Ought not his creatures then do the same? But in Genesis we learn that this is not the case. Jealous of Joseph's favor in the eyes of their father, the sons of Israel plot to kill their brother. Their mercy consists in a decision not to kill their innocent sibling but to sell him into slavery to some Midianite traders. This was their idea of mercy! The book is full of examples of man's cruelty to men. By nature man ought to be merciful, but he is not.

## Man is a Restored Image-Bearer

The problem of sin must be solved and the shattered mirror of man must be restored. Fortunately, Genesis does not leave us with what man ought to be by nature but is not. It leads us on to what man can be by grace. This basic distinction is set up in the garden, when God establishes a dichotomy between the seed of the serpent and the Seed of the woman. The seed of the serpent are those who build up the kingdom of Satan and rebellious man. The Seed of the woman is ultimately Christ and also, in Him, those who build up the kingdom of God and redeemed man.

This redemption follows a basic pattern. First, God extends his grace to a man. Second, He speaks a word to him, expecting that he will receive His word and believe it. Third, the man responds by approaching him via blood sacrifice as an acknowledgement of his sin (this pattern can be seen as early as Genesis 4 with Abel). Finally, the faithful man demonstrates his faith and gratitude by living in obedience to God's law.

This pattern is evident throughout Genesis: *See Chart 1.*

Genesis sets the stage for the greatest epic, the real history of the world in which God redeems Adam's fallen race through Christ. God's story sets the stage for all future history. It also sets the pattern for all great stories throughout history. As we recall Tolkien's *Hobbit,* we see that he echoes Genesis in many ways. The insignificant, like Bilbo of Bag End, are called to become great players in the history of their imaginary world. This, of course, repeats the pattern of the patriarchs, who are called to important roles in the history of God's saving plan.

*The Hobbit* also leaves us with the same sense as Genesis. Both end leaving us in a state of hope and expectation mixed with foreboding. What will become of the Ring? What will happen to Bilbo? We haven't seen the last of Gollum, have we? Now, we are ready to dive into the *Fellowship* with new understanding. In a similar way, Genesis leaves us with the expectation that God will bring about great things through the family of Abraham. We hope that we will again enter the garden. We long for the Seed of the woman to appear. This expectation, however, is mixed with foreboding of coming slavery and the fact that the problems of the Fall have still left the world in pieces as we leave the book. God's original creative act has been distorted and corrupted, but God Himself has not been thwarted.

—*Stuart W. Bryan*

## For Further Reading

Spielvogel, Jackson. *Western Civilization.* Fifth Edition. Belmont, Calif.: Wadsworth/Thomson Learning, 2003. 1–33.

*Veritas Press Bible Cards: Genesis through Joshua.* Lancaster, Pa.: Veritas Press. 1, 2, 5, 9, 17.

Jordan, James. *Primeval Saints.* Moscow, Idaho: Canon Press, 2001.

Leithart, Peter J. *A House for My Name: A Survey of the Old Testament.* Moscow, Idaho: Canon Press, 2000. Pages 17–70.

Sméagol— or Gollum— from Tolkien's epic *The Lord of the Rings*

### Chart 1: PATTERNS OF OBEDIENCE

|  | NOAH | ABRAHAM | JACOB |
|---|---|---|---|
| God's Man | 6:8 | 12:1 | 25:23 |
| God's word to the man | 6:13 | 12:1–3 | 28:13–15 |
| Man's sacrifice for sin | 8:20–22 | 12:7, 13:4 | 33:20 |
| Man's obedience | 6:22 | 15:6 | 35:2 |

# SESSION I: PRELUDE

## The Mystery of Michelangelo's *Creation of Man*

This is the famous fresco painting by Michelangelo that is on the ceiling of the Sistine Chapel. It shows the creation of man spoken of in Genesis. This, of course, shows a very unbiblical picture of God. He is not a grey haired old man. The cherubim are not pudgy little babies. This, however, is not the controversial part. Look behind God. One character is not like the others. Just under God's left arm is a beautiful woman (who is not like the c h e r u b s ).

Artists and art h i s t o r i a n s dispute her identity.

*Write a paragraph explaining who she is (Hint: on another part of*

Detail of Eve from *The Temptation and Expulsion*.

*the ceiling Eve is pictured but she does not look like this woman).*[6]

*Discuss or list short answers to the following questions:*

## *Comprehension Questions*

1. When and by whom was Genesis written?
2. What does the word *Genesis* mean?
3. How would one divide Genesis into a two part outline?
4. What purpose does the word *toledoth* serve in Genesis? What does it mean?
5. Make a list of the things we learn about God from the book of Genesis.
6. Why did the Fall introduce a distinction between what man is as the image of God and what man ought to be?
7. What is a covenant? With whom did God enter into covenants in Genesis?

### READING ASSIGNMENT:
Genesis 1:1–11:26 (*This reading is the Toledoth 1–5 mentioned in the Author and Context section.*)

# SESSION II: DEBATE
Genesis 1:1–11:26

## A Question to Argue

How long did it take God to create the world?

*Read the three views of Creation held by Christians in the church today outlined below. Then discuss or write short responses to the objections to each view, thinking through how advocates of each view would seek to defend their position.*

### THE HISTORIC SEVEN 24-HOUR DAYS POSITION.

This view takes Genesis literally. It states that God created the world in six days. Each day was a 24-hour period. It holds that this creation happened in the order set forth in Scripture and that God rested the Seventh Day. This view also holds that all death was the result of the Fall. This pattern of work and rest set up the weekly paradigm that we are all to follow.

### THE DAY-AGE POSITION.

This position asserts that the "days" in Genesis are not 24-hour days, but that each Day represents an age that could have been years or even millennia long. It bases its interpretation of the Hebrew word *yom* (day) on verses like Psalm 90:4 and 2 Peter 3:8. It looks at the Sabbath rest of God on the Seventh day as His rest from His creative activity which continues to this day. This view does believe that animal death occurred before the Fall.

### THE FRAMEWORK POSITION.

This view believes that the seven days of creation are not to be taken as literal, twenty-four hour days, but are instead figurative, topical descriptions of God's creation of the world. As evidence they point to the fact that there is a pattern in Genesis 1 in which God creates realms in days 1–3 (light and dark in the

heavens, the sky and sea, and dry land) and their rulers in days 4–6 (sun and moon to "rule" the day and night, birds and fish to rule the sky and sea, animals and finally man to rule the dry land). This view asserts that the Genesis language offers snapshots of the divine creativity, but that this language is by nature metaphorical. The chief thing not to be taken literally according to the framework position is the chronological sequence. This view does not, however, commit to any specific time frame for creation; neither does it commit itself to any specific order of events. It also allows for the possibility of death in all but man (who bears God's image) before the Fall and points to the Sabbath as God's eternal enthronement over creation, and the eternal rest to which all creation ultimately points and is fulfilled in Christ.

## Objections

### OBJECTIONS TO THE SEVEN 24-HOUR DAYS POSITION:

1. How can you know that days 1–3 are "normal 24-hour days" if the sun and moon had not yet been created?
2. How can you hold this view since modern science has found that the earth is about 4 billion years old?

### OBJECTIONS TO THE DAY-AGE POSITION:

1. In the few Old Testament passages in which the words *day* or *days* are not to be taken literally (normal 24-hour days), doesn't the context determine this meaning? What in the context of Genesis 1 tells us that *day* does not mean what it normally means (i.e., a normal 24-hour day)?
2. Isn't your view just an attempt to force the conclusions of modern science into the biblical text?

### OBJECTIONS TO THE FRAMEWORK POSITION:

1. It can be said that the language of Genesis 1 points

to a poetic structure (i.e., Realms on Days 1–3 and Rulers on Days 4–6). While this seems clear, why does this pattern prove that the language is figurative? Or, put another way, why couldn't God have done his creative work in a poetic pattern?

2. Do you think that this complicated theory is really what God was trying to convey with the language of Genesis 1 or is this just another attempt to make our Bibles fit the conclusions of modern science?

*Write a paragraph promoting which view of creation you think is correct.*

**READING ASSIGNMENT:**
Genesis 11:27–37:1 *(Toledoth 6–9)*

# SESSION III: DISCUSSION
Genesis 11:27–37:1

## A Question to Consider

Should someone ever be punished or rewarded for the actions of another?

*Discuss or list short answers to the following questions:*

### Text Analysis

1. What one prohibition did God give to Adam in Genesis 2?
2. Why did Eve disobey God and eat the forbidden fruit?
3. Why did Adam eat? (See 1 Timothy 2:14 if you need some clarification)
4. What punishments resulted from Adam's sin?
5. What curse does the ground receive because of Adam?
6. What curse do Adam and Eve receive because of Adam's sin?

7. How do we know that this curse is carried on to their children?

### Cultural Analysis

1. In athletic events, if one player does something wrong (e.g., drops an easy fly ball in the bottom of the ninth inning, allowing two runs to score and his team to lose), is it fair for his whole team to be punished for it (i.e., lose the game)?
2. If a child robbed a store, what would our culture say about sending the parents of that thieving child to jail?
3. Why does our culture react differently in these circumstance? Is this biblical?

### Biblical Analysis

*Read Romans 5 and 1 Corinthians 15:20–22 thoughtfully out loud. These passages can be difficult to understand so make sure you have your Bibles open while you discuss it.*

1. In both of these passages to what is Adam's sin compared?
2. In Romans 5:12, why did death spread to all men?
3. In Romans 5:13–14 how were the sins of those that lived between Adam and Moses different than (not in the likeness of) Adam's sin?
4. What does Romans 5:18–19 make clear about Adam's sin?
5. In 1 Corinthians 15:22, what happen to all men in Adam?

## SUMMA

*Write an essay or discuss this question, integrating what you have learned from the questions above.*
Is it righteous to punish or reward some people for the actions of another? What does culture believe and what does Scripture teach?

**READING ASSIGNMENT:**
Genesis 37:2–50:26 *(Toledoth 10)*

*Chart 2:* **PARTS OF A COVENANT**

| ASPECT OF COVENANT | NOAH | ABRAHAM |
|---|---|---|
| Promise | Never again shall all flesh be cut off by the waters of the flood; never again shall there be a flood to destroy the earth. (9:11) | I will be a God to you and your children (17:7). You will receive a Seed (15:5). Your descendants will be like the stars (15:5). You will receive a land (12:8). I will bless the world through you (12:3). |
| Law | Protecting the image of God seems closely related to this covenant. (9:1–7) | Walk before me and be blameless (17:1) |
| Blessing | Food, multiplication and safety. (9:1–4) | Seed, land, wealth, blessing to the world. *See above.* |
| Sign | Rainbow (9:13 ff) | Circumcision (17:9 ff) |

| ASPECT OF COVENANT | SCRIPTURE REFERENCE | QUESTION |
|---|---|---|
| Promise | John 17:1–3, Matt. 28:20 | What does Christ pray for? What does He promise for His Church? |
| Law | Rom. 13:9, Gal. 3:13–14; | What is this Law in this passage the same as? What does this tell you about God's rules of righteousness? |
| Blessing | Rom. 4:12–14; 1 Pet. 2:4–5 | Whose blessings has the Church inherited? How has this promise expanded? If we are what 1 Pet. 2:4–5 says, is the Church still his people? |
| Sign | Matt. 28:19; I Cor. 11:24–26 | What are the signs of the New Covenant? How do they relate to the sign of Circumcision and Passover given to Israel? |

# SESSION IV: ANALYSIS
Genesis 37:2–50:26

## A Question to Consider

What is a covenant?

*Discuss or list short answers to the following questions:*

### Text Analysis

*Reread: Genesis 9:1–17 and Genesis 15*
1. According to the similarities of these passages, what is a covenant?
2. One theologian has said that God's covenant is basically a relationship (or bond) of life or death significance ruled over by God.[7] What do you see in these two passages that supports this view?

### Biblical Analysis

What are the essential parts of a covenant?
*Answer the questions in Chart 2.*

# SESSION V: DISCUSSION

## A Question to Consider

Can God accomplish His will by using sinful people in the process?

*Discuss or list short answers to the following questions:*

### Text Analysis

1. Does God ordain that sinful actions take place? Consider Genesis 45:4–8; 50:19, 20; Exodus 4:21; Matthew 26:54; Luke 22:22; Acts 2:23; 4:28.
2. Does this remove man's responsibility for his sin? Consider the above passages, Ecclesiastes 7:29 and Romans 9:19–26.

### Biblical Analysis

1. What does it mean that God is sovereign? Consider the following Scriptures:
   • He accomplishes His will (Ps. 115:3; 135:5-7;

Rembrandt Harmenszoon van Rijn. *Jacob Blessing the Sons of Joseph*. 1656. Oil on canvas. Staatliche Kunstsammlungen, Kassel, Germany.

Dan. 4:17, 34, 35; Eph. 1:11)
- He brings about trivial things (Ex. 34:24; Prov. 16:1, 9, 33)
- Calamity is under His rule (Isa. 45:7; Lam. 3:37, 38)

## SUMMA

*Write an essay or discuss this question, integrating what you have learned from the questions above.*

How can God accomplish His purposes through the sinful actions of human beings and still be holy, just, and good?

## OPTIONAL SESSION

### Analyzing the Art

*Begin class by analyzing this painting by Rembrandt.*

1. Who are the characters in this painting?
2. Where in Genesis is this scene described?
3. What is Joseph endeavoring to do with Jacob's hand?
4. Does Rembrandt capture the emotion which the biblical text ascribes to Joseph at this point? What emotion is portrayed?
5. Which of the boys appears the more pious? Why?
6. What event does this blessing recall from Jacob's own life?
7. Rembrandt's painting changes a number of things in the biblical text, both by addition and omission. Can you identify them? Why do you suppose he did this?

## ENDNOTES

1   Technically there are eleven sections. The two toledoth sections about Esau have been combined (36:1–8 and 36:9–37:1).

2   The identification of Moses as the primary author of Genesis does not exclude some later editorial revisions or additions. For instance, Genesis 11:31 associates Ur with the tribe of the Chaldeans, a group of people who did not emerge until after Moses' death. For a fuller treatment of Mosaic authorship consult Raymond B. Dillard and Tremper Longman, III, *An Introduction to the Old Testament* (Grand Rapids, MI: Zondervan, 1994) pp. 38-48.

3   Some people are uncomfortable describing Adam's relationship with God as a covenant. However, Scripture explicitly identifies this relationship as a covenant (Hos. 6:7), and all the elements of a covenant are present: privileges, expectations, blessings, consequences, etc. For a fuller treatment, see O. Palmer Robertson, *The Christ of the Covenants* (Phillipsburg, NJ: Presbyterian & Reformed, 1980) chapter 5.

4   Hebrews 6:13–20 discusses this passage in Genesis 15 and uses it to encourage us to trust in God's faithfulness through His Son, our Lord Jesus Christ.

5   This point is related to the Nicene Creed's statement that Jesus was *genitum non factum* (begotten, not made). Jesus is the only begotten Son of God, meaning of course that Jesus has the same nature as God Himself (Jesus is divine). We are adopted sons of God. We do not have His nature because we are creatures. Nevertheless, through Christ, we receive all the benefits that He as the Son of God deserves. For example, we shall inherit the earth.

6   For a fascinating discussion of this question, see James Romaine's chapter on Creativity in: Ned Bustard, ed. *It was Good: Making Art to the Glory of God* (Baltimore: Square Halo Publishing, 2000) pp. 159-201.

7   O.P. Robertson, *Christ of the Covenants* (Phillipsburg, NJ: Presbyterian and Reformed Publishing, 1980) pp. 3-15. This gives the definition for covenant, saying that it is a bond in blood sovereignly administered. For the adventurous student or the inquisitive parent this chapter of this book does a great job explaining covenants.

# EXODUS

Freedom is one of the most important ideas in the modern world. The great revolutions that started the modern world proclaimed liberty and freedom: The slogan of the French Revolution was "Liberty, Equality, and Fraternity," and the Declaration of Independence claims that men are endowed by their Creator with the rights to "life, liberty, and the pursuit of happiness."

Some of the greatest wars in modern history have been waged to secure freedom. The Union fought the Confederacy in the Civil War to preserve the union and to free slaves, and America entered World War II to liberate Europe from the Nazis. During the second half of the twentieth century, many millions in Eastern Europe were enslaved to a cruel Soviet system, until the Soviet Union broke into pieces in the 1980s and 1990s. Throughout the Southern Hemisphere, the twentieth century was the century of freedom. In Africa, Asia, and Latin America, peoples that had been subjected to European nations fought for freedom, and often succeeded.

Freedom is especially important in American culture and politics. Everyone in American politics says they favor liberty and everyone in American politics accuses his opponents of enslaving Americans. Liberals say that we should throw off the chains of traditional morality and society so that we can be truly free. Without freedom to abort babies and pursue a homosexual lifestyle, Americans would be slaves. Conservatives say that liberal laws make the government too big and make people slaves.

But what is freedom? Is freedom the same as "liberty?" Is there any difference between freedom and "license?" Does freedom mean being able to do anything? Are there several different kinds of freedom? Is freedom equal for all people? Is freedom compatible with authority?

Scripture has clear answers to these questions, and Exodus, the story of a slave people being freed from slavery, is one of the most important books of the Bible for addressing these questions.

The Great Pyramid of Giza existed during the Exodus. It was the world's tallest structure for more than 43 centuries, and remains the world's largest compass—each side is oriented to north, south, east, and west.

## GENERAL INFORMATION

### Author and Context

Who wrote Exodus? Many scholars today believe that Exodus, like Genesis, Leviticus, Numbers, and Deuteronomy, is patched together from several different books. These "source" books are known as the "Jahwist" or J book ("Jahweh" or "Yahweh" is one way to write the Hebrew name of God), the "Elohist" or E book ("Elohim" is another name for God), the Deuteronomist or D book, and the "Priestly" or P book. The names are supposed to tell us what is unique in each book. The "J" book uses the name "Jahweh" a lot, and the "P" book has a lot to say about priests and their activities.

This is not correct and is a foolish idea. Exodus mentions that Moses writes portions of the book (Exodus 17:4; 24:4; 34:4, 27-29), and the Ten Words (or Ten Commandments) were written by God Himself (Exodus 32:15-16). Most of Exodus 20-40 comes straight from God's mouth, and Moses only records what He hears God say. Exodus is written by someone who took part in the events that the book talks about. The author was an eyewitness to the plagues and the exodus, and the author actually wrote down God's words as He spoke on Mount Sinai.

### Significance

The book of Exodus is a cornerstone of the Bible. It tells about the story of Israel's birth as a nation, and of the Lord's covenant with Israel. Over and over again throughout the Bible, this story is told and replayed. When David goes into Philistia to escape from Saul and then returns to become king, he has gone through an exodus. Israel later is taken captive to Babylon, but returns in what Isaiah describes as a new exodus. Jesus goes into the grave, but death "passes over" and He rises to new life, leaving "Egypt" behind.

Exodus is also a key book in the history of Christendom. Many of the law codes of the early Middle Ages were based on the Mosaic laws of Exodus 20-23, and even in the early colonial period, the Puritans tried to design their laws and government after a biblical model. Moses is one of the greatest figures in history, honored by Jews as the founder of Israel, as well as by Christians and Muslims as a great prophet. In the modern world, Moses has been studied by many writers. Sigmund Freud, the founder of psychology, wrote a book called Moses and Monotheism and political thinker Michael Walzer has studied the Exodus to gain insight into politics.

### Summary and Setting

When did Moses live? When did the events in Exodus take place? We know from the Bible that the Exodus happened 480 years before Solomon began to build the temple (1 Kings 6:1). Solomon begins to build the temple in 967 B.C., and that means that the Exodus took place in 1447 B.C.

Yet, many today believe that the Exodus took place much later, in the thirteenth century, between 1270 and 1250 B.C., rather than in the fifteenth century. This conclusion is partly based on the names of the

While bathing in the Nile, the pharaoh's daughter—possibly Hatshepsut—found a Levite's son floating in a basket made with bulrushes and tar. The princess named the baby Moses, which means "to draw out" because she drew him out of the water.

cities in Exodus 1:11: Israel works to build Pithom and Ramses, and these cities are built by Seti I (1308-1290 B.C.) or Ramses II (1290-1224 B.C.). This is called the "late date" theory.

But there are problems with this later date, especially for those who believe the Bible contains accurate dates and chronologies. If the late date is correct, then 1 Kings 6:1 is not accurate. Often, it is said that this is a merely symbolic number, since it is the product of 12 and 40, the number of Israel (12) multiplied by the length of a generation (40 years). But the numbers in the Bible are both literal and symbolic (e.g., the 40 days of the Flood, 40 years of Israel's wandering, 40 days of

Jesus' temptation, etc.). Chronological issues are discussed later in more detail. It is a fascinating question, but one that is too complicated to figure out here.

Moses is the main character in Exodus, but to understand what Moses does, we need to remember why Israel goes to Egypt in the first place.

Israel goes into Egypt at the end of Genesis, when Jacob takes his family from Canaan to Egypt because of a famine. Israel is in Egypt for four generations (Exodus 6:14ff). According to Genesis 15:16, the Lord told Abraham that his seed would be strangers for that length of time. So, when Exodus begins, the four generations are nearly passed. Israel has been prospering and multiplying in Egypt. They are "fruitful, increased greatly, multiplied exceedingly, became numerous, and filled the land" (Exodus 1:7).

Suddenly everything changes (1:8). A new king arises who does not know Joseph and does not care about Israel. This Pharaoh is also afraid of Israel because they are multiplying so fast. He fears that if a nation invades Egypt, the Hebrews will switch sides and fight against him (vv. 9-10). And he fears that they are "spreading out," taking over land that belongs to the Egyptians (v. 12). So, the Pharaoh makes life very hard for the Israelites, forcing them to make bricks without straw, then making them slaves, and then trying to kill

their male children.

Pharaoh's plan does not work. Even though Pharaoh makes the Israelites work harder and harder and tries to kill all their sons, the midwives save many of the boy babies so that "the people multiplied and became very mighty" (1:20). More importantly, the Lord is working to raise up a deliverer to bring Israel out of slavery into rest. That deliverer is Moses.

Like many boys of his time, Moses has to be saved from Pharaoh, and he is saved by his mother, Jochebed. Jochebed puts her "beautiful son" in a basket and lines it with pitch, where he is found by Pharaoh's daughter, who takes him into Pharaoh's house and raises him there. When he grows up, he kills an Egyptian who is beating a Hebrew slave (Exodus 2:11-15). Stephen the martyr calls this an act of "vengeance on behalf of the oppressed" (Acts 7:24), and that is a good thing to do. Moses is hoping that killing the Egyptian will be the beginning of Israel's deliverance from Egypt (Acts 7:25). Nothing in the Bible says that Moses is guilty of murder. The next day, though, Moses gets his first taste of how the Israelites will treat their savior. He tries to stop a fight between two Israelites, as he stopped the fight between the Egyptian and the Israelite the day before. But the Israelites do not want him to be ruler and judge over them (Exodus 2:14). Moses sees that Israel isn't ready to leave Egypt, and so he flees to Midian for forty years.

While Moses is in Midian, he marries Zipporah, the daughter of Jethro, and takes care of Jethro's animals on the "mountain of God," Mount Horeb (Exodus 3:1). There he sees the burning bush, and God speaks to him from the bush and tells him he must return to Egypt to deliver Israel. Though he objects, Moses obeys and announces to Israel that the Lord is going to deliver the people. Moses tells Pharaoh that Yahweh, the God of Israel considers Israel his son, and demands that Pharaoh let his son go (4:22–23).

As the Lord had told Moses, Pharaoh hardens his heart and refuses to let the people go. "Who is Yahweh?" he asks (5:2). Yahweh responds by showing who He is. He brings ten plagues against Egypt, plagues that get worse and worse for Egypt (Exodus 5–11). Meanwhile, the Lord protects Israel from the plagues, dividing between Israel and Egypt. Finally, the Lord sends the final plague, the killing of the firstborn of Egypt. The Israelites stay safe from the angel of death by killing a lamb or goat and spreading its blood on the doorposts of their houses (Exodus

*"The sight of the glory of the LORD was like a consuming fire on the top of the mountain in the eyes of the children of Israel. So Moses went into the midst of the cloud and went up into the mountain."*

12–13). This is the Passover, when the angel of death "passed over" the people of Israel.

Seeing all the firstborn of Egypt dying, Pharaoh finally agrees to let Israel go (Exodus 12:31–32). After Israel gets a short start, Pharaoh changes his mind, gathers his chariots, and begins to chase down Israel in order to force them to come back to Egypt. Israel is stuck between Pharaoh's army and the Sea of Reeds. The Lord makes a way of escape for Israel by sending a wind that blows back the sea and opens up dry land. Israel passes through the sea in safety, but when Pharaoh tries to get through the sea he and all his army are drowned (Exodus 14).

From there, Israel moves toward Mount Sinai, where the Lord has called them to meet with Him. Along the way, the people complain that there is no food or drink, and the Lord miraculously provides bread (manna) from heaven and water from a rock (Exodus 16–18).

When Israel gets to Mount Sinai, God "cuts" a covenant with His people in a ceremony that is like a wedding. God promises to provide all good things for His bride, and His people take an oath to obey and honor Him. If His people don't keep the covenant promise that they make, God threatens to bring all kinds of bad things—diseases, famine, drought, death (Leviticus 26; Deuteronomy 28).

The wedding service goes from Exodus 19–24, with Moses officiating. He goes up on the mountain to hear the Lord's word, and then brings it back down to the people. The Husband's part of the wedding service begins with the Lord reminding His bride of what He has done for her (Exodus 20:1–2). Then Yahweh tells Israel how they are to live as His holy people (Exodus 20–23). When Moses brings these words to the people, they say, basically, "I do": "All the words which the Lord has spoken we will do!" (Exodus 24:3). The wedding ceremony ends with a wedding reception, a feast in the Lord's presence (Exodus 24:9–11). Now that Yahweh and Israel are married, Yahweh decides to move in with His bride. Most of the rest of Exodus is about the kind of house He wants Israel to build for Him (Exodus 25–40).

In Exodus 20–23, the Lord tells Israel how they are to live as His servants. Many of these laws are based on the exodus. For example, the Sabbath day is the seventh day of the week, and it is a time when all Israelites stop working and rest. They do this to follow

The first record of a man being filled by the Spirit of God is an artist named Bezalel. *"And I have filled him with the Spirit of God, in wisdom, in understanding, in knowledge, and in all manner of workmanship, to design artistic works . . ."* Here Bezalel is crafting the altar for burnt offering.

God's example in creation, since He rested on the seventh day (Exodus 20:8–11). Resting on the Sabbath is also a reminder of the Exodus (Deuteronomy 5:12–15). When Israel is in Egypt, they are slaves and are not allowed to rest. By rescuing them from Pharaoh, Yahweh gives His people rest, and so every week they are reminded that they were slaves and that they should give rest (Deuteronomy 5:15).

The rest of Exodus is concerned with the house of God, the tabernacle. The tabernacle is not merely canvas, but has walls made of wooden boards that are set in sockets on the ground (Exodus 26:15ff). Three layers of curtains cover the wooden frame, and the inner layer is a beautiful curtain with figures of cherubim woven into it. The doorway of the tabernacle is to the east, so that anyone who wants to enter the tabernacle has to move from east to west (Numbers 1:53; 3:23, 29, 35, 39).

Within the tent are two rooms. The first is the Holy Place and the second is the Most Holy Place or "Holy of Holies." The courtyard makes a third area. Each "room" of the Lord's house has furniture in it. In the courtyard is a bronze altar. All the animal offerings are burned on this altar and blood of most animals is poured out here. Also in the courtyard is the bronze laver filled with water, set between the altar and the tent (Exodus 30:17–21). Priests wash their hands and feet in the water from the laver every time they enter the Holy Place.

In the Holy Place are three pieces of furniture. On the North side is a table made of wood and overlaid with gold (Exodus 25:23–30). Twelve loaves of Shewbread or "bread of the presence" are on the table, and are replaced each Sabbath day (Leviticus 24:5–9). To the South is a lampstand of pure gold that looks like an almond tree, with branches and bulbs (Exodus 25:31–40). On the West side, in front of the veil that separates the Holy Place and the Most Holy Place is the golden altar of incense (Exodus 30:1–10).

The Most Holy Place contains only one piece of furniture, the ark of the covenant, a box of wood covered inside and out with gold. The cover of the ark is pure gold, and has golden cherubim stretching over the top of it (Exodus 25:10–22).

In the middle of the tabernacle section of Exodus is the story of the golden calf. Israel becomes impatient waiting for Moses to come back from the mountain, and they ask Aaron to make them a god who will go before Israel as Moses has done. When Moses comes down from the mountain, he sees Israel worshiping the golden calf, and breaks the tablets of the law, as a symbol of the broken covenant between God and Israel.

The glory of God that fills the Most Holy Place and makes the tabernacle holy comes from the top of Sinai (Exodus 19:16; 24:17; 40:34–38).

## Artistic Design

Try telling your little brother this story: "See Jack sit. See Jack sit and sit and sit. See Jack sit and do nothing. See him sit and sit and sit all day. The end." If your little brother is smart, he will never ask you to tell him a story again.

Stories always tell about change. If you tell a story where nothing changes, you are telling a bad story. When you think about the change that takes place in a story, it is usually helpful to ask what specific things have changed. And a good way to get an idea of what is changing in the story is to look at the beginning and end of the story. At the beginning of Robinson Crusoe, Robinson survives a shipwreck on a desert island; at the end of the story, he leaves the island. The story tells how his situation changes from the beginning to the end.

When we think about Exodus this way, we can see how things change for Israel during the book. At the beginning of Exodus, Israel is serving Pharaoh by building storage cities (1:11). When we come to the end of the book, Israel is still busy building, but they are building the tabernacle for their new King, Yahweh (Exodus 35–40). At the beginning of the book, the Egyptian Pharaoh is killing Israelite babies; but Pharaoh himself is killed in the middle of the book (Exodus 14). When the book begins, Pharaoh says that Israel belongs to him. Yahweh says that Israel belongs to Him (4:23; 8:1), and at the end of the book Israel is serving a new Master. At the beginning of the book, Israel has no rest. At the end of the book, the Lord tells Israel to take a day of rest every week and He Himself rests in the tabernacle. At the beginning of the book, Israel is in slavery; by the end of the book they are free servants of God. The story of Exodus could be titled "From Slavery to Sabbath," or "From Serving Pharaoh to Serving God."

Think about how this is different from some other ways of telling the exodus story. Exodus does not end like the movie Prince of Egypt, with Israel crossing through the Sea. If it ended there, it would be a story of Israel being delivered from Pharaoh. But Israel passes through the sea in Exodus 14, and there are forty chapters in the book. The end of the story happens at Sinai.

The book of Exodus is not the first "exodus" story in the Bible. God displays His power and shows that idols are powerless by saving His people from their enemies. The stories that tell about God rescuing His people are called "exodus stories." The story of Jacob is an exodus story: He goes out of the land, spends time with Laban who treats him badly, and then returns to the land wealthier than before. And Jacob is not the first patriarch to leave the land and return. Abram leaves twice, and his first exodus in Genesis 12 reminds us of what happens to Israel later on in history (Genesis 12:10–20). Like a preview at the movie theater, the exodus of Abram is a preview of the exodus of Israel. Long before Israel goes to Egypt, God is the God of exodus, the God who delivers His people from slavery.

Another important design of the book is the connection between Moses as the "head" of Israel and Israel as the "body" of Moses. Everything that happens to Moses early in the book of Exodus later happens to Israel. Moses is saved through the water, and the whole nation will be saved through the sea. Jochebed places Moses in the "reeds" along the river (Exodus 2:3), and he will bring Israel through the "Sea of Reeds" (Exodus 13:18). Moses flees to Midian, where he spends forty years (compare Acts 7:23 with Exodus 7:7), just as Israel will have to spend forty years in the wilderness because of her rebellion (Numbers 13). While Moses is among the Midianites, Yahweh appears to him in a burning bush on Mount Horeb (Exodus 3:1–2), just as the Lord will appear at Horeb to the whole nation after the exodus. Moses is the head of Israel, and whatever happens to the head will happen to the body.

## Worldview

He is a pillar of the community. The foundations of our society are crumbling. We have to defend our gates against the barbarians. We should establish stronger walls to protect our children against pornography. The economy is caving in. Everyone should be actively engaged in building our community.

All of these expressions assume a common metaphor: That a society or group of people is like a building or a house. Important people in a group are "pillars," since they carry the burdens of the group on their shoulders. Every group is based on certain beliefs and practices that serve as a foundation. A community is something to be built, and once it's built it has to be protected.

We not only think of society as a building, but we also think of our lives as construction projects. When we are young, we may draw out a "blueprint" of what we are going to do when we grow up. Education helps to establish the "foundation" for a career, and a career is something to be built on that foundation. Marriage and family too are like a house to be built, decorated, protected, and expanded.

The similarity between houses and societies, between our lives and a building, are not random. In fact, Scripture speaks a lot about the design of God's houses, the tabernacle and the temple. About a third of exodus is concerned with the tabernacle, and three long chapters in Kings describe the temple (1 Kings 6-8). There is even more information about the temple in Chronicles, and in Ezra Israel returns from exile to rebuild the temple. Ezekiel 40-48 is a great vision of the future temple, and Jesus spends a lot of His ministry attacking the corruptions of Herod's temple (cf. Matthew 24). Revelation, the final book of the Bible, is largely about the fall of the temple and city of Jerusalem, and God's creation of a new city (Revelation 17-22).

In the New Testament, Paul says that the people who make up the church form a "holy temple," a building where God lives. As Jesus said, people can build their houses on a rock, in which case the house will last, or they can build a house on sand, in which case the house is doomed (Matthew 7:24-27).

The tabernacle portion of Exodus develops this analogy in detail. The tabernacle has many different levels of meaning. Fundamentally, it is a house, God's

house. Israel is living in tents, and so Yahweh agrees to live in a tent alongside them. In God's house, there is a "kitchen," the courtyard where God's food is cooked, a "dining room" or "living room" in the Holy Place, and the "throne room" of the Most Holy Place. The tabernacle is also like Sinai, a building made like a holy mountain. When Israel leaves the mountain, they take the mountain with them. Like the tabernacle, Sinai is divided into three zones. The people are encamped at the foot of Sinai, but they may not even touch it (Exodus 19:20-25). Elders and priests ascend partway to feast in God's presence (Exodus 24:1-8), but only Moses enters the cloud on the top of the mountain. Similarly, in the tabernacle, the people may only enter the courtyard, and are not allowed to touch the altar. Priests work in the Holy Place, but are not allowed to enter the Most Holy Place, where only the High Priest, a permanent "Moses" may enter. If the tabernacle is like Sinai, every time a priest enters the tabernacle, it is like climbing up God's mountain.

The tabernacle is not only a picture of Sinai, but also a picture of the people of God. The New Testament tells us that the church is the temple of God, and in the Old Testament the tabernacle is a picture of the people of God. As the holy things of the tabernacle are "gathered at the throne of God," so also the holy people are arranged around God's throne. Like Sinai and the tabernacle, Israel is divided in three groups. Most of the people of Israel are not priests; the descendants of Aaron are all priests; and one of the priests is the High Priest. So, the house of Israel is like the house of the Lord, and the house of the Lord is a picture of the house of Israel. This is why the blood of the animal offerings is always sprinkled or thrown on some piece of furniture in the tabernacle, never on the people.[1] This seems odd at first. How can blood make a sinner clean if the blood is never put on him? The answer is that the tabernacle is a picture of Israel, and

| *Chart 1:* **ARRANGEMENT OF THE TABERNACLE** | | |
|---|---|---|
| **UNIVERSE** | **EARTH** | **TABERNACLE AREA** |
| Heaven | Land of Eden | Most Holy Place (throne of God) |
| Firmament | Garden | Holy Place (lampstand) |
| Land | Eastern land | Courtyard (altar) |
| Sea | Other lands | Outside the courtyard |

## TOMBS OF GIZA

These royal tombs belonged to the leading kings of the Fourth Dynasty, the early part of the Pyramid Age. The Great Pyramid, the tomb of Pharaoh Cheops (also known as Khufu), is on the right, and next in size is Khafre's on the left. In front of the pyramids is a temple, where food, drink, and clothing were placed for use by the dead pharaoh. These temples, like the pyramids, were built on the desert plateau above, while the royal town was in the valley below. For convenience the temple was connected with the town below by a covered gallery or corridor of stone, seen here descending in a straight line from the temple of Khafre and ending below, just beside the Sphinx, in a large oblong building of stone, called a valley-temple. It was a splendid structure of granite, serving as temple and entrance way to the great corridor from the royal city. The pyramids are surrounded by tombs of the queens and the great lords of the age. At lower left is an unfinished pyramid, showing the inclined ascents up which the stone blocks were dragged. These ramps were built of sun-dried brick and were removed after the pyramid was completed. Sometimes we fail to make historic connections. Are there buildings in your town that were seen by past generations? Of course there are. When we see the Great Pyramid we must realize that the Hebrews enslaved in Egypt would have been living and working around this pyramid.

so putting blood on the tabernacle is counted as putting blood on the sinner. When the priest puts blood on the altar, God accepts the sinner as clean.

The tabernacle is not only a picture of Israel but of the whole world. The world is a "three-story house," the heavens are divided between the "highest heavens" and the "firmament," and earth is also divided into several areas. With these things in mind, we can understand the arrangement of the tabernacle, as demonstrated in Chart 1.

Let's look at one of these connections. A number of things in the tabernacle remind us of the garden of Eden. Like the garden, it has a doorway on the east side (Genesis 3:24). The cherubim in the tabernacle curtains and above the ark remind us of the garden (Exodus 26:31–37). When a priest enters the Holy Place, he looks at the veil that has cherubim on it, and is reminded over and over of the cherubim with the flaming sword in Genesis 3. Like the

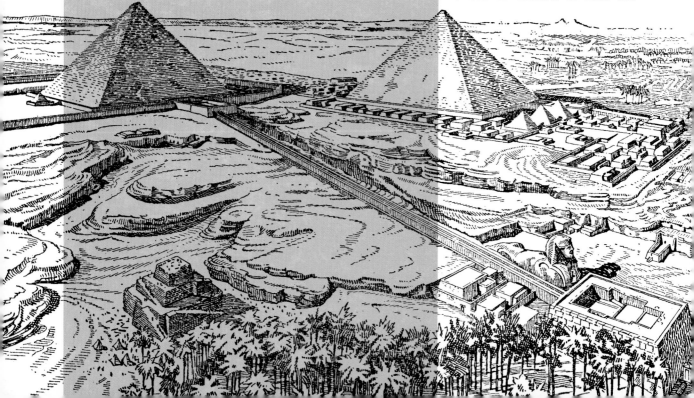

garden and land of Eden, the tabernacle is mostly off limits.

The fact that the world is a house means that our work in the world is like building and decorating a great building. We take the raw materials that God gives us, and with those we build a "house" out of the world for God to live in.

Thinking about our life as a construction project helps us to address questions about freedom that we thought about at the beginning of this study guide. It helps in two major ways. First, Exodus makes it clear that complete freedom is never a biblical goal. Israel is not freed from Egypt so that they can do whatever they please. They are freed from Egypt so they can work on the Lord's house. They are freed from Pharaoh so they can become slaves to another King.

Second, the process of building itself shows the reality and limits of freedom. If we want to build a house that stands, we need to pay attention to the kinds of materials we use and how we put them together. In one sense we are free to make a house from anything we want, and to slap it together in any way we please. But if we make walls from Jello or put the foundation in quicksand, it won't last very long. If we use thumb tacks and cellophane tape for the framing, the house will not stand. We have to find materials that can be made into a house, and put those materials together in a way that will actually stand as a house. Our freedom is limited by the materials, and our freedom is limited by what we want to build.

—*Peter J. Leithart*

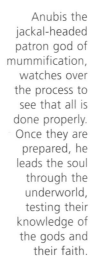

Anubis the jackal-headed patron god of mummification, watches over the process to see that all is done properly. Once they are prepared, he leads the soul through the underworld, testing their knowledge of the gods and their faith.

# SESSION I: PRELUDE

## A Question to Consider

What does it mean to be free? How can we be free?

*From the General Information above answer the following questions:*
1. Who wrote Exodus?
2. How do we know who wrote the book?
3. What do the letters J, E, D, and P stand for?
4. When did Moses live?
5. How do we know?
6. What are the alternative dates for the exodus?

### *Optional Activities*

Watch *Prince of Egypt* or *The Ten Commandments* and explain how the story is different from the biblical account. This involves not only noticing differences of detail, but differences in the overall shape of the story.

Do some research on Egyptian religion. How do the plagues in the story of the Exodus strike at the core of Egyptian religious beliefs?

 READING ASSIGNMENT: Exodus 1–15

## For Further Reading

Spielvogel, Jackson. *Western Civilization*. Fifth Edition. Belmont, Calif.: Wadsworth/Thomson Learning, 2003. 16–27.

Janson, H.W. & Janson, Anthony F. *History of Art for Young People*. Sixth Edition. New York: Harry N. Abrams, 2003. 48–63.

*Veritas Press Bible Cards: Genesis through Joshua*. Lancaster, Pa: Veritas Press. 18–24.

# SESSION II: DISCUSSION

## A Question to Consider

Do we have free will? What does "free will" mean?

*Discuss or list answers to the following questions:*

### Text Analysis

1. What does Yahweh tell Moses about how Pharaoh will react to his demands? See Exodus 4:21.
2. What is Pharaoh's first reaction when Moses tells him that he comes from Yahweh?
3. Who hardens Pharaoh's heart? See Exodus 8:15 and 9:12.
4. What makes Pharaoh harden his heart?
5. Why does God let this all happen?

### Cultural Analysis

1. What does our culture believe concerning free will? What do modern people believe about free will?
2. How does modern science deal with the question of free will? For example, think of the science of genetics or brain research.
3. According to modern science, what causes alcoholism? What causes homosexuality? What does this say about free will?

### Biblical Analysis

1. What do the rest of the Scriptures say about free will? Does the Bible teach that we have freedom to do whatever we want?
2. Does God force people to sin? Is he the one who invented or created sin?
3. How does Paul apply the story of Pharaoh in Romans 9?

## Application

1. Should we be frightened to think that God hardens hearts? Why or why not?
2. If God has mercy on whom He wills, and hardens whom He wills, why should we pray or do evangelism? Shouldn't we just wait for God to act?

## SUMMA

*Write an essay or discuss this question, integrating what you have learned from the questions above.* Do we have free will?

This fresco is opposite *The Temptation of Christ* on the wall of the Sistine Chapel, and both deal with the theme of temptation. Botticelli brought together seven episodes from the life of Moses reading the painting from right to left. Moses strikes an Egyptian overseer and then flees to the Midianites. There he chases off a group of shepherds who were harassing the daughters of Jethro at the well. He meets with God in the burning bush (top left), then leads the Israelites out of slavery.

## Optional Activities

*Study the passage below from Martin Luther's treatise,* The Bondage of the Will. *Answer the questions that follow.*

"For if we believe it to be true that God foreknows and foreordains all things; that He cannot be deceived or obstructed in His foreknowledge and predestination; and that nothing happens but at His will (which reason itself is compelled to grant); then, on reason's own testimony, there can be no 'free-will' in man, or angel, or in any creature. So, if we believe that Satan is the prince of this world, ever ensnaring and opposing the kingdom of Christ with all his strength, and that he does not let his prisoners go unless he is driven out by the power of the Divine Spirit, it is again apparent that there can be no 'free-will.'"

1. What does Luther mean by *foreknowledge?*
2. How does foreknowledge differ from *foreordaining* or *predestination?*
3. Why does Luther reject the idea of *free will?*
4. How can people who are slaves of the devil be freed from him?

*David Rohl, a British Egyptologist, has challenged the traditional chronology of Egyptian history. He accepts the traditional dating of the Exodus (1447 B.C.), but argues that ancient historians are mistaken to identify the Pharaoh of the Exodus as Ramses II. Read the summary of Rohl's new chronology found at the time of this printing at members.aol.com/_ht_a/judeoroots/rohl.htm, and answer the following questions:*

1. What mistake did Champollion make?
2. How does this mistake affect the chronology of the ancient world?
3. According to Rohl's new chronology, who is the Pharaoh Shishak who attacks Jerusalem after the reign of Solomon?
4. According to Rohl, who was the Pharaoh during the time of David?
5. What evidence supports Rohl's conclusion about the Pharaoh during David's time?

*Not all scholars accept Rohl's new chronology. Read the following paragraphs from J.G. van der Land (taken from an article posted at the time of this printing at www.bga.nl/en/discussion/echroroh.html), and answer the questions that follow:*

"The big shifts proposed by Rohl would lead to apparent solutions to a few problems, but would give rise also to insoluble problems concerning the history of Israel and Biblical data."

"Pharaoh Seti I (1294–1279 B.C.), the father of Rameses II, would become a contemporary of King Solomon (972–931 B.C.) and would have led his army through the latter's kingdom several times, capturing cities on his way."

"The Late Bronze period too would be moved forward some 350 years, to end around 850 B.C. The Philistines settled in Ashkelon and Ashdod only after Late Bronze. The proposed new chronology would place this event about a century after king Solomon, despite the fact that both cities had already been inhabited for over a century before Solomon (1 Sam.6:17)."

1. What is van der Land's main criticism of Rohl's theory?
2. What did Seti I do?
3. Why is this a problem for Rohl's theory?
4. What is van der Land's point regarding the Late Bronze age?

### READING ASSIGNMENT:
Exodus 16–24

# SESSION III: DISCUSSION

## A Question to Consider

What are the appropriate punishments for crimes like theft, murder, or adultery? Should we try to apply the laws of the Old Testament in our own day?

*Discuss or list answers to the following questions:*

## Text Analysis

1. Under the law of Moses, what happens to a person who strikes or curses a father and mother?
2. What is the punishment for kidnapping?
3. What is the punishment for a man who causes a pregnant woman to go into premature labor? What does this say about abortion?
4. Why are there different punishments for different sorts of killing?
5. What are the rules for animals that harm human beings?
6. What is the penalty for theft? Why?
7. How are the Israelites supposed to treat strangers, orphans, and the poor? Why?

## Cultural Analysis

1. What does our culture think of the death penalty? What are the arguments against the death penalty? Are they valid arguments?
2. How are thieves punished in our society? Is this a good idea?
3. Should the government pay special attention to the poor? Or to the rich?
4. Should we attempt to apply the laws of Moses to our own government and laws?

## Biblical Analysis

1. There are a number of crimes that are punished by death in the Old Covenant. But many Christians believe that the death penalty should not be used in the New Covenant. Do you agree with this? What does Romans 13 have to say about this?
2. How was a murderer punished in ancient Israel (Numbers 35)? How can we apply this practice today? Should we?

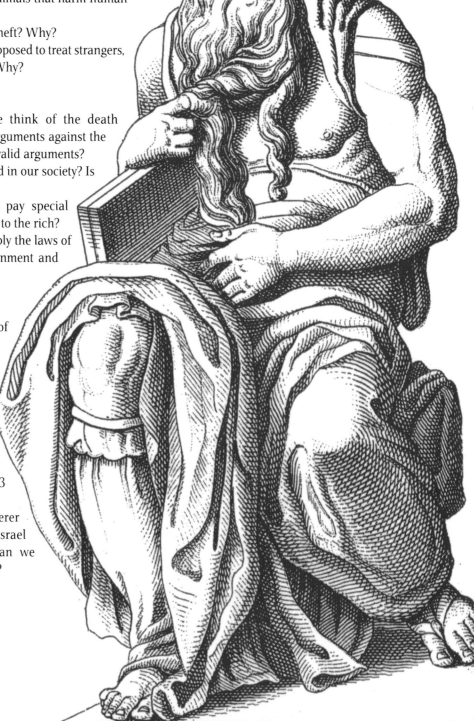

## SUMMA

*Write an essay or discuss this question, integrating what you have learned from the questions above.* Should we try to apply the laws of the Old Testament in our own day especially concerning the punishment of criminals?

**READING ASSIGNMENT:** Exodus 25–40

# SESSION IV: RECITATION

## Comprehension Questions

*Answer the following questions for factual recall:*

1. What do the Hebrew midwives do to protect the Hebrew children? Are their actions good?
2. Why does Moses say he cannot lead the people from Egypt?
3. What name does the Lord give Himself? What does it mean?
4. What is the first plague? Why is this significant?
5. What do you think happens to Egypt's farming during the plagues?
6. Who eats the Passover meal?
7. What do the Hebrews call the bread that they find in the wilderness? What does the word mean?
8. How does Israel know that the Lord has come down on Mount Sinai?
9. What is the penalty for theft according to the law of Moses?
10. What are the rules for owning and releasing slaves?
11. How many festival days is Israel supposed to observe?
12. Describe the tabernacle and its furniture.
13. What does the clothing of the high priest look like?
14. Why does Israel want Aaron to make a golden calf?
15. What does Moses do when he sees Israel worshiping an idol?
16. What does the Lord say He is going to do because of the golden calf? How does Moses respond to that?
17. Who are Bezalel and Oholiab? What do they do?
18. Who puts the tabernacle together?
19. What happens when the tabernacle is finished?

## Lateral Thinking

*Discuss the following questions or answer them in a short essay.*

1. Some Christians today believe that the Exodus story shows that God is on the side of the poor and oppressed. Does the Exodus story teach this? In what sense?
2. In the discussion above, we looked at some other Bible stories that were like the story in Exodus. Can you find other "exodus narratives" in the Bible? Look at 1 Samuel 21–2 Samuel 6 and Matthew 1–7.

## Optional Activities

*Examine the drawing opposite based on Michaelangelo's sculpture called* Moses *and answer the following questions:*

1. What does Moses have in his hand?
2. What event from Exodus is this picture showing? How can you tell?
3. Why is Moses seated?
4. What is coming out of Moses' head? Why are they there?

# SESSION V: EVALUATION

## Possible Review Questions

*Answer the questions from the recitation in Session III.*

## Evaluation

1. What is the situation for Israel at the beginning of Exodus?
2. Summarize the early life of Moses.
3. Describe some of the plagues, and their effect on Egypt.
4. What happened at Passover?
5. How did Israel behave in the wilderness?
6. What happened at Mount Sinai?
7. Describe the tabernacle.
8. Why did Israel ask Aaron to make a golden calf?
9. What did Moses do when he saw the golden calf?
10. What happens at the end of Exodus?

*Demonstrate your understanding of the themes of Exodus by answer the following questions in complete sentences. Answers should be a paragraph or two. 10 points per answer.*

1. Describe the overall story-line of Exodus.
2. What does Exodus teach about the relationship of Moses and Israel?
3. Why is there so much emphasis on the tabernacle in Exodus?
4. Discuss some of the details of the Mosaic law. Is it a just system? Is it excessively harsh?

*Answer two of the following three questions. These questions will require more substantial answers. 12 points per answer.*

1. Describe the leadership qualities of Moses. Give specific examples of how Moses leads Israel.
2. What does the book of Exodus teach about freedom?
3. What does the book of Exodus teach us about God?

# OPTIONAL SESSION: ACTIVITY

*Assign a panel of students to serve as judges, and bring the following cases to them. They must render a verdict on the basis of the laws of Exodus 20–23.*

1. Judy has a Doberman that usually stays in a fenced yard. One day, the Doberman got loose, and chased the mailman back to his truck. Along the way, the Doberman bites the mailman's leg. He brings his complaint to the judges, and asks them to make Judy pay for his stitches.
2. Larry borrows a lawnmower from Jerry. While Larry is mowing, the mower breaks down. Should Larry pay Jerry to fix the mower?

## ENDNOTES

1   Exodus 24:8 looks like an exception, since the text says that Moses sprinkled blood on the people. But verse 4 makes it clear that there are 12 pillars in front of Moses "for the people," and it is most likely that the pillars were sprinkled as a symbol of cleansing the people. After all, Moses was standing in front of hundreds of thousands of people, and they could not all be sprinkled by the blood of a few bulls.

# EPIC OF GILGAMESH

"So now, who can gather the gods on your behalf, Gilgamesh?"

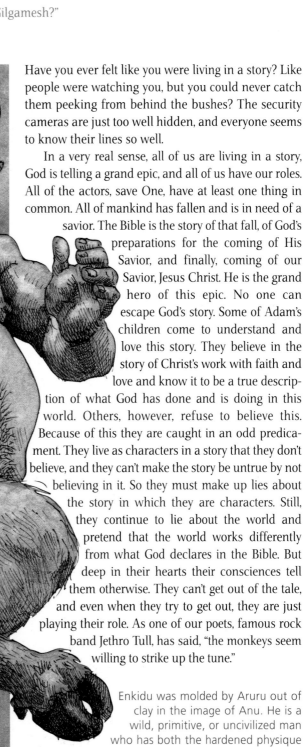

Have you ever felt like you were living in a story? Like people were watching you, but you could never catch them peeking from behind the bushes? The security cameras are just too well hidden, and everyone seems to know their lines so well.

In a very real sense, all of us are living in a story, God is telling a grand epic, and all of us have our roles. All of the actors, save One, have at least one thing in common. All of mankind has fallen and is in need of a savior. The Bible is the story of that fall, of God's preparations for the coming of His Savior, and finally, coming of our Savior, Jesus Christ. He is the grand hero of this epic. No one can escape God's story. Some of Adam's children come to understand and love this story. They believe in the story of Christ's work with faith and love and know it to be a true description of what God has done and is doing in this world. Others, however, refuse to believe this. Because of this they are caught in an odd predicament. They live as characters in a story that they don't believe, and they can't make the story be untrue by not believing in it. So they must make up lies about the story in which they are characters. Still, they continue to lie about the world and pretend that the world works differently from what God declares in the Bible. But deep in their hearts their consciences tell them otherwise. They can't get out of the tale, and even when they try to get out, they are just playing their role. As one of our poets, famous rock band Jethro Tull, has said, "the monkeys seem willing to strike up the tune."

Enkidu was molded by Aruru out of clay in the image of Anu. He is a wild, primitive, or uncivilized man who has both the hardened physique and virtue of Ninurta, the god of war; the long hair of Ninursa, goddess of corn; and the hairy body of Samuqan, god of cattle.

When Christians tell stories, they tell stories that picture to us the world that God created. C.S. Lewis does this very well in his *Chronicles of Narnia*. Even though Aslan is not Jesus Christ, he still teaches us about Jesus. He is a sort of Christ figure in that he shows us a small picture of what Christ has done for us. Lewis understood that mankind has fallen and that the salvation God offers us in the person of Jesus Christ is our only hope. And so the story that he tells gives a small picture of man's fallen condition and of God's cure for this fallen condition.

Pagans, who live outside of a covenant with the

Gilgamesh fights the bull, aided by his friend Eabani. This image is from a Babylonian seal of the time of Sargon I.

God of the Bible, frequently have Christ figures as well, even though their overall stories are lies. They know that mankind is fallen, but in their unbelief they must invent their own ways to solve man's fallen condition. And so pagans have false christs in their stories, men who attempt to drag men out of their fallen condition without recognizing the saving work of Jesus Christ. History is full of these wicked men. Hitler thought that he could remake mankind and reverse the curse by changing the genetic makeup of the world. He thought that he could save the world if only he could make everyone white. Acts 12:20–24 tells the story of Herod Agrippa who thought that his ability to supply the people of Tyre and Sidon with bread qualified him as a messiah. God struck him

down for his presumption, and he was eaten from the inside out by worms. Literature is also full of these sorts of men. Tolkien's Saruman thought that his machines from Orthanc could remake the world and usher in a new age. Tolkien, a Christian, had him learn a similar lesson to that of Herod Agrippa. These are always false christs, and Gilgamesh is the story of one of the pagan world's most famous false christs.

# GENERAL INFORMATION

## Significance

The *Epic of Gilgamesh* is one of the oldest stories known to man. Because of this, reconstructing the actual story is difficult. Our oldest fragments of the story come from excavations of the ancient nation Sumer. The capital of Sumer was the city Ur, not far from the city of Uruk, where Gilgamesh had been king. The story of Gilgamesh appears to have been quite popular in Ur around 2150–2000 B.C. It is quite interesting that this is roughly the same time that the biblical patriarch Abraham was growing up in the city of Ur. It is quite likely that Abraham was told the story of Gilgamesh a number of times as he grew up and that the gods who appear in Gilgamesh are gods that were being worshipped all around Abraham throughout his childhood. In fact, the Bible tells us that Abraham was saved from a family that was immersed in pagan worship. "And Joshua said to all the people, 'Thus says the LORD God of Israel: 'Your fathers, including Terah, the father of Abraham and the father of Nahor, dwelt on the other side of the River in old times; and they served other gods.''" (Josh. 24:2) Since Abraham was from Ur, the "other gods" of which Joshua is speaking would almost certainly be the gods of the story *Gilgamesh*. To a certain extent, the *Epic of Gilgamesh* is the story of the world that all Christians have been saved out of.

Although Sumer was wiped out by the Elamites

around 2000 B.C. (perhaps this has something to do with why Abraham was leaving Ur), the various stories of Gilgamesh were preserved in the literature of many Mesopotamian cities, particularly Babylon and Ninevah. Both of these city states used a language called Akkadian, Akkadian uses the writing system called cuneiform, where clay tablets are written on instead of paper and a small carved stick is used to write instead of a pen. The author presses wedge shapes into the clay while it is still wet and then bakes the clay to preserve his marks.

Many of these clay tablets full of Akkadian writing have been discovered throughout Mesopotamia and as far away as modern day Turkey, where the Hittites had their own version of cuneiform. Some of these Akkadian tablets go as far back as 2000 B.C. and some are as recent as 100 B.C. From these a number of tablets have been discovered relating various stories about Gilgamesh.

The first discovery of the story of Gilgamesh was made in 1839 by a young Englishman named Austen Henry Layard, while excavating the ruins of Ninevah, the ancient capital of Assyria. When Ninevah was destroyed in 612 B.C., as the Babylonian empire wiped out the Assyrians, it appears that an entire library of cuneiform texts was buried in the rubble of Ninevah. Around 700–650 B.C. the Assyrian kings Sennacherib and then Assurbanipal had built the royal library and had ordered that copies of all the great works of literature be placed in it, including

## FLOOD MYTHS

Stories of the Flood can be found all the way from the ancient Middle East to South America to the Pacific Islands. They almost all say: *Once upon a time there was a worldwide flood, sent by God as a judgment. But there was one righteous man warned of the flood. By building a boat they survived the flood along with the animals. After this flood their boat landed on a high mountain.*

There are many striking parallels between the biblical Flood account and ancient Sumerian, Babylonian, Assyrian and Phoenician accounts. For the Christian student of ancient and classical literature, these provide a wondrous glimpse of these amazing past civilizations. The *Epic of Gilgamesh* is one such example from the ancient library of Ninevah, recovered by archeologists in the nineteenth century. The *Epic* actually says, *"Lay upon the sinner his sin; lay upon the transgressor his transgression."* It is intriguing that the Genesis account does not mention Noah's preaching, though in 2 Peter 2:5 it says "Noah" was "a preacher of righteousness."

Other parallels to the biblical account of the Flood (Gen. 6–9) include many things, such as the extent of flood, its cause, similarities between Noah and Utnapishtim, the ark/boat, similarities in the flood waters, the ark landing on a mountain, blessing following the flood, etc. Even unbelieving scholars admit such shared aspects of the stories. *Gilgamesh*, like other ancient accounts, both preserves and embellishes a cultural memory through a people that did not have the guidance of scriptures. We should appreciate it for what it is, a sacred narrative from an ancient culture. Yet it provides a kind of echo to the true account of Genesis.

Bible critics tend to presuppose that the Genesis account is dependent on these ancient myths since some of these predate the time of Moses (c. 1528–1409 B.C.) and the writing of Genesis. The *Gilgamesh* tablets date to around 650 B.C., but fragments of the Flood story have been found on tablets dated around 2,000 B.C. In answer to this, note that any kind of dependence this or other accounts have certainly has not been demonstrated. Critical scholarship has its own pre-commitments. Of course, it is an elementary fallacy of logic to suppose that something is truer because it is older. Such critics have more confidence in their own fallible ideas which are ever changing, than the sure Word of God which abides forever.

the story of Gilgamesh. In the rubble of this library Austen Henry Layard was the first to read the story of Gilgamesh in well over two thousand years.

It took some work to learn how to translate this strange language. But when archeologists were finally able to read the story of Gilgamesh they discovered another story of Noah's Flood, whose similarity was beyond coincidence. Since that first discovery, the *Epic of Gilgamesh* has continued to surprise its readers with the light that it sheds on the ancient world.

Ninsun was a Sumerian goddess known for her wisdom. She was the wife of the deified king Lugulbanda and mother of the great hero Gilgamesh. In the *Epic* she counsels her son and interprets his dreams. Also known as "Lady Wild Cow" and referred to as "Wild-Cow Ninsun," she was the city goddess of Kullab and the embodiment of the best in bovines.

The text that forms the backbone to the current translation of *Gilgamesh* comes from this ancient Ninevah library. However, being almost 3000 years old, many of the tablets are damaged, leaving large gaps at many places. Many of these gaps can be filled in with what we know from other older tablets. But even with the help of these other tablets, much of *Gilgamesh* must be filled in by the translator. Because of this, many translations can vary widely since many translators take a great deal of liberty with how they fill in the gaps.

## Main Characters

The central character is, of course, Gilgamesh. To say the least, he comes from an interesting family. He is a famous king of the city Uruk and is described as being two parts god and one part man. His mother is Ninsun, a Sumerian goddess from whom he received his partial divinity. She is often called "lady wild cow." His father is Lugalbanda, who was King of Uruk before Gilgamesh.

He has interesting friends. The story revolves around Gilgamesh's friendship with Enkidu, a wild man who was created by the mother goddess Aruru as a rival and friend for Gilgamesh. He is raised in the wild and lives with animals, eating in the fields with them until he is tamed by a prostitute named Shamhat. Shamhat, used here as a proper name, was a term to describe the prostitutes that staffed the temple to Ishtar.

He goes on thrilling quests, beginning with a fight with Huwawa,[1] guardian of the Pine Forest. His face is usually made out of intestines, and he is said to be a terrible giant.

He has to face his greatest fear. After the death of Enkidu, Gilgamesh becomes overwhelmed by the dread of death. He hears of a man named Utnapishtim the Faraway. The story of Utnapishtim is the early Sumerian/Babylonian equivalent of the story of Noah and the Flood. After the flood Utnapishtim was granted eternal life by the gods. He is called the Faraway because he lives on the other side of the waters of death.

The gods, Annunaki, are a mysterious group. They are the great ones who once lived with the host of heaven, but they fell through some sort of disobedience and are now the judges of the world. Anu is the sky god, the god of Uruk, Gilgamesh's city, and father of Ishtar. While Anu tends to be far off, Enlil is his breath and is near to man. Ea is the god of fresh water and wisdom. Shamash is the sun god (in Hebrew the word for sun is shemesh) and the great omniscient judge. Ishtar was worshipped along with Anu in the temple at Uruk. She is the goddess of war and love and her wrath can be terrible as Gilgamesh discovers. (The biblical character Esther probably gets her name from Ishtar, as does the Christian holiday Easter.[2])

## Summary and Setting

The story is packed with action. It begins with the introduction of Enkidu to Gilgamesh. At last Gilgamesh has found someone mighty enough to be worthy of his friendship. The two set out on a number of adventures. This starts with their victory over Huwawa (i.e., intestine face) the guardian of the great pine forest. After Huwawa's death, the goddess Ishtar attempts to woo mighty Gilgamesh. When he rejects the goddess, she is so angry that she sends the Bull of Heaven to seek vengeance. But again the friends triumph. The death of the Bull causes such a stir amongst the gods that it is decided that either Enkidu or Gilgamesh must die. Enkidu gets the short straw and Gilgamesh mourns his terrible loss. He begins to fear his own mortality and searches for a way to escape death. He travels to Utnapishtim, survivor of the flood, to see if he can help him find eternal life. Utnapishtim tries to help and sends him on an errand which, if successful, could bring him eternal life. However, despite his incredible power, Gilgamesh finally discovers the limits of his own mortality.

The dividing line between history and myth has always been difficult to draw. How much of the Epic of Gilgamesh actually happened? Many historians are now willing to grant that there was at one time a king of Uruk named Gilgamesh. Uruk is now modern Warka in central Iraq. A list of the kings of Uruk from around 2000 B.C. lists Gilgamesh as the fifth king of Uruk, putting him as king around 2150 B.C. In many inscriptions he is credited with having built the walls of Uruk and many other cylinder seals picture him wrestling with wild animals.

Some have attempted to connect Gilgamesh with Nimrod of the Bible (Gen. 10:8–12). The brief description that the Bible gives of Nimrod is similar to the character of Gilgamesh, and many take the biblical account as crediting Nimrod with the founding of the town of Erech, which was most likely Uruk. However, Gilgamesh was said to have built the walls of Uruk, not to have founded the city. This and other discrepancies make the connection between Gilgamesh and Nimrod questionable. So, Gilgamesh is likely not Nimrod.

## Worldview

Have you ever wandered through a graveyard to read the epitaphs on the gravestones? Some of them are fairly straightforward, citing the person's name, birth date and the date he passed away. Others may have a phrase on them, perhaps something chosen by the deceased. Still other epitaphs pass into an entirely different class. They let you know in a few brief phrases something of the character of the person buried there. For example:

*She lived with her husband 50 years*
*and died in the confident hope of a better life.*

Or, for the flipside of the marriage:

*Here lies my wife*
*Here let her lie*
*Now she has peace*
*And so do I.*

If you were to write your own epitaph, what would it be? It certainly can be hard to think of one simple phrase or short rhyme which could sum up the importance of your life to people who live hundreds of years later. Perhaps those you leave behind would not think an epitaph could serve you, and they would erect a statue. There's certainly a lot more room on a big statue to write things of importance from your life. Think of the many stones left with the recorded exploits of military conquerors such as those of Roman emperors, or more recent examples such as the *l'Arc de Triomph* in Paris. These structures certainly clearly convey the importance victory held to the people who erected them.

But if you really want to leave a legacy, something which conveys not just one important idea, but perhaps your whole philosophy-a story is the best way to go. Here the only limit to what you convey to following generations is the amount of paper (or papyrus or stone tablets) you are willing to use. In this case—your legacy should be safe, right? Well perhaps not. When a story is written, too often the next generation feels the necessity to embellish the bits they feel are important. What may have started as biography gets turned into legend. Why? Perhaps because men search for a savior, a super-human, a man who started out similar to them but then became so much more. Such may be the case with Gilgamesh. As the history of this king evolved into legend and myth, it reveals a great deal about what was important to the

people living at the time, what they believed and also what they struggled with.

Let's take a moment to recall the central character of the *Epic of Gilgamesh*. He is a hero in the pagan sense. He is part man and part god. There is no one equal to him. He has his way with everything and everyone. Gilgamesh is, in the pagan world, the greatest man alive. But Gilgamesh has a problem. His problem is a problem that all men have, although it doesn't become clear to him until the death of Enkidu. The problem that Gilgamesh faces, that all of the children of Adam must face, is that he is still mortal and must someday die. How we face death, that is, the answer that we have for death, is one of the great factors which distinguishes Christianity from all other faiths. Gilgamesh is ancient Babylon's best chance at a bridge between heaven and earth. Given their worldview, he is their only possible savior.

As you read the *Epic of Gilgamesh* continue thinking of the ways in which Gilgamesh attempts to be a savior and of the ways in which he falls short. Can you think of other characters in novels that you have read recently that play a similar role as Gilgamesh? Since he is a false messiah, the fact that he fails is no surprise. Of course he fails. There is only one Messiah and there can be no substitute. Despite all of his efforts, mankind is left entirely dead in sin, and death still comes to everyone.

This problem, the mortality of man, is the central theme to the *Epic of Gilgamesh*. But as Christian readers we must remember that the problem that Gilgamesh confronts is a problem that the Bible has confronted and answered. And since Gilgamesh does not give the answer that the Bible provides, we must know that Gilgamesh teaches lies. As Christians, when we come to literature like Gilgamesh, we are called to be literary critics. We need to be able to discern the truth of God (even in pagan works) and be able to guard ourselves against the subtleties of their lies. That being said—let's dive into Gilgamesh's world to see what legacy they were creating–what was of central importance to them and what they wanted to pass on. At the same time, we need to contrast it to the Christian faith.

## The Gods

One of the most striking elements in the *Epic of Gilgamesh* is its portrayal of the nature of the gods. The author of *Gilgamesh* is attempting to teach his audience about the gods and what mankind can expect from them. But what the Babylonians could expect from their gods and what we can expect from our God are two very different things.

The gods that Gilgamesh interacts with are not creator gods. One of the foundational truths about the God of the Bible is that He is the God Who created *ex nihilo*. He created out of nothing. He spoke, and there it was. When God wants to establish His authority over mankind, He needs to merely point to His work as Creator. Why does God get to be in charge of us? Because He made us, and nobody made Him. But the gods of Gilgamesh are as created as Gilgamesh himself is. Each has sprung from an earlier god.[3] The reason they are "in charge" is merely because they are stronger than everyone else. But this is not a very reliable way to establish your position, as every bully eventually learns; somebody bigger always comes along. If you read the *Enuma Elish* you will read the story of how Marduk (a new god) slew Tiamat (one of the older gods) and created the world from her body. Marduk becomes the new head of the Babylonian gods. But if a newly created god can overthrow one of the older gods, then this new god can also be overthrown. None of the gods in *Gilgamesh* is truly supreme the way the Christian God is. As you read through *Gilgamesh*, ask yourself, which god is in charge of everything? Which god can be relied on at all times? Is there a god whose work never fails? There is none. As we are taught in Isaiah 44:6 "'Thus says the Lord, the King of Israel, And his Redeemer, the Lord of hosts: 'I am the First and I am the Last; Besides Me there is no God.'" Which Babylonian god can make this claim?

Not only are the gods subject to the whims of other gods, but they are subject to their own unbridled passions. A good example of this might be Ishtar who is infamously capricious, which her treatment of Gilgamesh demonstrates. One moment she is fawning all over Gilgamesh and begging him to be her lover. The next moment she is boiling over with anger and sending the Bull of Heaven to seek revenge on Gilgamesh and Enkidu. Gilgamesh is aware of her unstable nature and points this out to her when she makes her advances. "Which of your lovers did you ever love forever?" he asks and then proceeds to list all of the lovers that Ishtar has forsaken. Ishtar represents very well the love of the Babylonian gods, fleeting and unpredictable. Gilgamesh knows that this sort of love is not a love that can be depended on.

The fact that the gods are susceptible to whims reveals another problem with the Babylonian pantheon: they are not bound by any sense of morality. They may feel that some things should not be done or other things should be done. But they are not bound by these feelings. The gods are just as guilty of terrible crimes as the men are. Men rape, but so do the gods. Men murder, but so do the gods. Men steal, but so do the gods. When the gods send the great flood to destroy mankind, it is not like the true God's destructive flood, aroused by a righteous anger at the wickedness of mankind. It is because the gods are sick of all the noise and clamor that mankind has been making. Can you imagine the epitaph for humanity that these gods could have written?

*The human race made such a din,*
*For peace and quiet we did them in.*
*So now take heed, avoid their fate,*
*Bite your tongue or be fish bait.*

## The Men

Psalm 115:8 tells us how men who worship false gods will eventually become like the false gods whom they worship. Next we should look to see how the men in this story begin to imitate the god of the story. How do the men in *Gilgamesh* become like their gods?

Let's begin with the question of morality. Since there is a lack of morality amongst the gods themselves, the men who worship these gods also lose all sense of morality. When Gilgamesh is introduced, he is described as such a great man that he can take any woman he wants, no matter whose wife she is. Enkidu is created as a companion to Gilgamesh because the men of Uruk are complaining to the gods that Gilgamesh is taking all of their wives and daughters. Although this sounds horrible to us, in the story of Gilgamesh, *it is proof of his greatness.*

The lack of moral standards for either the gods or the men informs us about the kind of world in which Gilgamesh lives. Take a moment to reconsider the creative work of the Triune God. God spoke into nothing, creating all that is with the power of His Word. Since all that is comes directly from Him, everything in this world reflects part of His character. There is absolutely nowhere that we can go, nothing that we can speak of, no private imagination that does not find itself completely dependent on the Triune God of Abraham, Isaac and Jacob. Consider the consequences of this. What room in your house can you hide in and expect God's word to not have something to say about your conduct? What continent can you run to and expect God's word to have no instructions for your life? What vocation can you take on and yet not need to consider how God would have you pursue it? As Paul said in another context, "There is none. No, not one."

But is this the world that Gilgamesh lives in? Is this the god whom he serves? Not at all. As with most pagan systems, piety consists of regular sacrifice and little more. What worship does Gilgamesh offer up to Shamash? Is it a life of total devotion, considering how each action conforms to the word of Shamash? Not at all. He offers regular sacrifice and little more. This is the difference between a Creator God and a demon god. The Creator God is the rightful king and can therefore require complete obedience in all areas of life from His subjects. The demon god is little more than a mob boss, pumping his subjects for frequent protection money, but without the ability (or desire) to seek for anything more.

## Salvation

Gilgamesh's lack of confidence in Ishtar's love demonstrates the position that men were in under the rulership of these gods. How can man be saved when the gods can't be trusted? Abraham abandoned the world of these gods to meet a different sort of God, a God who introduced himself with a covenant. Genesis 15 records God's covenant with Abraham. In this passage, the sacrifices are divided in half and then a smoking pot (representing God's Spirit) passes through the animal halves. This was a common but significant ceremony in the ancient world. Frequently, when a covenant was made between two men the covenant would be sealed by having the two men walk between the animal halves. In doing so, the two men were saying that, if either of them broke the covenant, then what was done to the sacrifices (being chopped in half) would be done to that man. As God passed through the animal halves he was communicating to Abraham that he was making a sure covenant, one that He would never break. The author of Hebrews refers to this promise (Heb. 6:13–20) and tells us that God did this so that we could have a hope for our salvation which is "both sure and steadfast."

The gods of Gilgamesh are not covenanting gods; they are capricious gods. Because of this lack of covenant, Gilgamesh can

never be at peace. As the story concludes we find Gilgamesh standing in despair, knowing that death has taken Enkidu, that death will come for Gilgamesh as well and that there is nothing that can be done about it. Though Gilgamesh has tried to build a great city, one that will be a great legacy behind him, it does nothing to soften the horror of his future death. As Christians we can see that the story of Gilgamesh tells the truth about the lack of hope for mankind outside of the covenanting God of the Bible. Gilgamesh is a fallen man, fallen in Adam, without the salvation that the God of the Bible offers. His situation is without hope. As far as that goes, The *Epic of Gilgamesh* tells the truth.

But, regardless of how true it is, it is only half of the truth, because, though it tells us the truth of man's hopeless condition outside of Christ, it does not tell us about God's provision for our salvation inside of Christ. The *Epic of Gilgamesh* is a picture of the terrible hopelessness from which we are spared when we find ourselves in the mercy of Jesus Christ. For a Christian, reading *Gilgamesh* can be likened to dreaming a terrible nightmare. Whatever happened in the dream is swept away in the morning as the light pours in, and you realize that although the evil encountered in your dreams may be real somewhere else, for you it is only a dream.

When you complete your reading of *Gilgamesh,* think for a moment about how fortunate you are to be spared from all these lies.

For those who believe and love the God of the Bible, there is a God in heaven who always hears you. There is a God in heaven who has covenanted with you and will not allow you to be lost. There is a God in heaven whose concern for His children was so great that He sent His Son to come and die for them. That Son rose again from the dead, ascended into heaven, and now sits on a throne in heaven to prove to us that the underworld has been conquered and holds no power over us anymore. And that Father and that Son have sent the Holy Spirit to guide, strengthen, comfort and cheer us. The Spirit is God's pledge to us of our salvation. And when we see all this, reading the *Epic of Gilgamesh* leads us to pure gratitude for our salvation. Our epitaph can be:

> *Deserving death and the horrors of hell,*
> *Because of Christ now all is well.*
> *God has promised to ransom me*
> *And now from death I am set free.*

## For Further Reading

Spielvogel, Jackson. *Western Civilization.* Fifth Edition. Belmont, CA: Wadsworth/Thomson Learning, 2003. 8–16.

*Veritas Press Bible Cards: Genesis through Joshua.* Lancaster, Pa.: Veritas Press. 4, 5, 8.

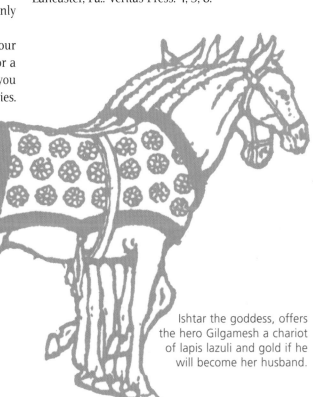

Ishtar the goddess, offers the hero Gilgamesh a chariot of lapis lazuli and gold if he will become her husband.

# SESSION I: PRELUDE

## A Question to Consider

What does it mean to be a savior?

*Discuss or list short answers to the following questions:*

### Discussion

1. When someone says that Jesus is his Savior, what does he mean?
2. Can you list any stories that have saviors in them?
3. Could a story by a writer who is not a Christian have a savior? Why or why not?
4. If a story by a writer who is not a Christian tried to have a savior, in what ways would that savior fall short of Jesus Christ?
5. Who was Gilgamesh?
6. When did he live?
7. How did we get the text of *Gilgamesh?*
8. Where does the story of *Gilgamesh* overlap with the Bible?

## Optional Activity

Find a copy of the *Enuma Elish* and read about the origins of the Babylonian gods. How are these gods different from the God of the Bible? What does this difference mean for you and for the ancient Babylonians?[4]

 **READING ASSIGNMENT:**
Tablets 1–5

# SESSION II: DISCUSSION
Tablets 1–5

## A Question to Consider

What does it mean to be a friend?

*Discuss or list short answers to the following questions:*

### Text Analysis

1. What do we learn about friendship from the *Epic of Gilgamesh?* What was Gilgamesh like in the beginning of the story?
2. What was Enkidu like when we first meet him?

3. What changes Enkidu?
4. What changes Gilgamesh?

### Cultural Analysis

1. What does our culture believe about friendship? Where do we see friendship in our culture today?
2. How have perversions like homosexuality destroyed friendship in our culture?

### Biblical Analysis

1. What do the Scriptures teach concerning friendship? What aspects of friendship do David and Jonathan display in I Samuel 18?
2. How is the friendship of David and Jonathan superior to that of Gilgamesh and Enkidu?
3. How does 2 Samuel 1 show both the strength and the vulnerability of David's love for Jonathan?

### Application

1. What does the Bible call us to?

## SUMMA

*Write an essay or discuss this question, integrating what you have learned from the questions above.*
What does it mean to be a friend?

## Optional Activity: *Progymnasmata*

Classical training in rhetoric included preparatory writing exercises called the *progymnasmata*. These exercises in composition introduced the beginning student to basic forms and techniques that would then be used and combined when practicing more advanced exercises and speeches. One of these progymnasmata was called a *chreia,* or "saying exercise," and was simply a concise exposition of some memorable saying or deed.

A chreia has eight paragraphs. The first is the *Panegyric* which is a paragraph in which you praise the person who uttered the wise saying. The second is called the *Paraphrastic.* In this short paragraph you put the saying into your own words. This paragraph often begins with something like: "When Saint Augustine said that evil was the deprivation of good he meant that . . ." In the third paragraph, called *From the Cause,* you explain the motivation of the person. The fourth paragraph is called *From the Contrary,* and in it you explain what would have happened if the opposite of the saying or action had occurred. For example, "If Diogenes had not struck the inept teacher, bad education would have continued." In the fifth paragraph, called the Analogy, you liken the saying or action to something else, usually something more concrete and easier to understand. The sixth paragraph is similar to the fifth. It is called *Example*, and in it you show the wisdom of the saying or deed by pointing your reader to a specific instance in which this wisdom was demonstrated. The *Analogy* is different from the *Example* in that it is about a general practice (e.g., "Education is like a harvest: you work hard and reap great reward.") whereas the *Example* is about a specific person, place or thing (e.g., "Erasmus studied many things and became a learned man."). The seventh paragraph is called the *Testimony of the Ancients*. Here you quote a sage person from the past who testifies to the truth of the saying. Finally, in the eighth paragraph called the Epilogue, you sum up the chreia.

Write a chreia on these words spoken by Gilgamesh: "Who is the mortal able to enter heaven? Only the gods can live forever. The life of man is short."

I. Panegyric
  • Praise the person who uttered the wise saying
II. Paraphrastic
  • Put the saying into your own words
III. From the Cause
  • Explain the motivation of the speaker
IV. From the Contrary
  • Explain the consequences if the opposite of the saying or action had occurred
V. Analogy
  • Liken the saying or action to something else
VI. Example
  • Point the reader to a specific instance in which the wisdom of the saying was demonstrated

VII. Testimony of the Ancients
  • Quote a sage person from the past who testifies to the truth of the saying
VIII.   Epilogue
  • Summarize your previous paragraphs

READING ASSIGNMENT:
Tablets 6, 7

# SESSION III: REFLECTION
Tablets 6, 7

## A Question to Consider

How is Gilgamesh like Jesus Christ? How is he not?

## *Discussion*

How does this epic reveal Gilgamesh's savior qualities?

1. What is the significance of Gilgamesh's mixed parentage?
2. How is this similar to the mixed parentage of Jesus Christ?
3. How is Gilgamesh's nature different from that of Jesus?
4. How important is righteousness to Gilgamesh? How does this compare to Jesus?
5. How does Gilgamesh use his power? In particular, how does Gilgamesh use his partial divinity? How does this compare to Christ?
6. If you lived in the ancient world and were raised with stories like *Gilgamesh,* of heroes who were part god and part man, what would you expect the Messiah prophesied by the Bible to be like? How surprised would you be to meet Jesus?

## *Cultural and Biblical Analysis*

1. What does a Christian hero look like? What biblical figures most model for us Christian heroism?
2. Think of at least three hero figures from books that you have recently read or movies you have recently seen. Is the heroism of these men a Christian heroism or a pagan heroism?
3. Are there any attributes in pagan heroes that Christians can admire? Is there anything dangerous in admiring pagan heroes?

## *Application*

It is important that we don't use two different standards of morality when we move from doing our homework and going out to a movie with friends. Understanding what we are being taught in a story and maintaining a Christian understanding of how to interpret the story is essential. The Babylonians were being taught about how to think about the world when they were entertained with the story of *Gilgamesh.* What are you being taught by your entertainment? Do you believe it? Are you thinking like a Christian as you read books, watch movies, listen to music, etc.?

## SUMMA

*Write an essay or discuss this question, integrating what you have learned from the questions above.*

Why do all "saviors" fall short of the real Savior, Jesus Christ?

## Optional Activity

Write and act out a short play recounting Gilgamesh and Enkidu's encounter with Huwawa. Remember that Huwawa's face is supposed to be drawn with intestines. Did acting out this section of the story change your impression of Gilgamesh? Do you have any more sympathy for Huwawa?

### READING ASSIGNMENT:
Tablets 8–10

Huwawa is a monster in the *Epic of Gilgamesh* who is the guardian of the cedar forests in Lebanon.

## SESSION IV: RECITATION
Tablets 8–10

## Comprehension Questions

*Answer the following questions for factual recall:*

1. Who takes an interest in Gilgamesh after his victory over Huwawa? What sparks this interest? What does that tell us about the gods?
2. How does Gilgamesh react to the advances of Ishtar? What is the evidence that Gilgamesh uses to make his point?
3. Is Gilgamesh innocent of the sins that he accuses Ishtar of?
4. What does Anu think of Ishtar's anger? Does he think it is just? What does Anu do for Ishtar?
5. How does Enkidu react to Ishtar's curses?
6. What does Gilgamesh do with the horns of the Bull of Heaven? How is this similar to his encounter with Huwawa?
7. What do the gods decide must happen to Gilgamesh and Enkidu?

8. What is the reason for the death of Enkidu? Is it because he did something unrighteous?
9. What does Enkidu's dream reveal about the afterlife? Is there any hope for the afterlife?
10. What change does the death of Enkidu work in Gilgamesh's life?
11. How does Gilgamesh honor Enkidu after his death?
12. Which do you think is hardest for Gilgamesh to take, the death of Enkidu or the realization of his own mortality?
13. As Gilgamesh tells of the death of Enkidu to Siduri and Urshanabi, what does he relate as the final sign of the mortality of man?

## Lateral Thinking

1. How many other myths do you know of where the gods become sexually involved with men? Can you think of any biblical parallels? Many think that Genesis 6 tells the story of this sort of interaction. If this was the case, then it was this sort of interaction that brought on the Flood. Why would this kind of sin require such drastic measures as the Flood?
2. Compare the vision of the afterlife communicated in Enkidu's dream to the vision of the afterlife described in other pagan mythologies. How similar is it to the Greek underworld? How do these compare to the biblical description? In addition to Enkidu's dream, you can read Tablet 12, a fragment describing the Babylonian underworld.
3. How does the rotting of Enkidu compare with the biblical description of man's mortality (see Gen. 3:17-19)? Why do you think God decreed that as part of the curse we would all rot after death? What promise has God given us in addition to this curse?

## Optional Activity

Do a quick search on the Internet or in your local library for works on the Akkadian language.[6] What can you learn about the way cuneiform tablets were made? Try looking on Ebay for cuneiform tablets. There are always some for sale in the *Antiquities* section. Most of them are records of sales, but some can get a little more exciting. Can you talk your parents into letting you bid on one?

## READING ASSIGNMENT:
Tablet 11

# SESSION V: ANALYSIS
Tablet 11

## A Question to Consider

How could a written newspaper report of an auto accident be different from an eyewitness account?

### *Discussion*

Some unbelievers have said that the flood story in the *Epic of Gilgamesh* proves that the Bible is just one of the many mythological stories of the ancient world. They propose that the biblical story of Noah developed out of stories like the legend of Utnapishtim.

*Reread Genesis 7 and 8 and fill in the questions in Chart 1. Then discuss or list short answers to the following questions:*
1. Is the *Epic of Gilgamesh* older than the Bible?
2. Why does the biblical story of the Flood make more sense than the flood story in the *Epic of Gilgamesh*?
3. Why should we expect there to be many stories like that of Utnapishtim in the *Epic of Gilgamesh*?

| Chart 1: **THE FLOOD** | | |
|---|---|---|
| QUESTION | NOAH | UTNAPISHTIM |
| How are they pictures of eternal life? | | |
| Why did God (gods) destroy the world? | | |
| Why did one family survive the flood? | | |
| Why was there a sacrifice made after the flood? | | |

# OPTIONAL SESSION

## Possible Review Questions

*All questions from the Comprehension section of Session II and Session IV are fair game, as well as the following concerning Tablet 11.*
1. What is Utnapishtim called?
2. See how many different elements of the story of Utnapishtim and the flood resemble the biblical

account of Noah's Flood.

3. Given what we know of Ishtar, how confident should her vow make Utnapishtim?

4. How does Utnapishtim test Gilgamesh? How does he do?

5. Gilgamesh is given one more chance at immortality. What is it? How does he do this time?

6. Who steals the flower? Is there any significance to this?

7. Why do you think the story ends with a reference to the glory of Uruk?

## Evaluation

*Open book and open Bible. Write one to two sentences on each of the following questions. (2 points each)*

1. Describe the character Gilgamesh as he is introduced to us. Who is he, and what is he like?

2. What is Enkidu like before he is brought into the city, and how is he changed?

3. How is the arrival of Enkidu an answer to the prayers of the people?

5. What is Gilgamesh's major motivation in the seeking out of Utnapishtim?

7. What about the death of Enkidu is most distressing to Gilgamesh?

8. After the great flood, what is Utnapishtim given for his wisdom?

9. What are the two chances at immortality that Utnapishtim gives Gilgamesh?

10. How does Gilgamesh lose the flower named How–the–Old–Man–Again–Becomes–a–Young–Man?

*Demonstrate your understanding of the worldviews set forth in* The Epic of Gilgamesh *by answering the following question in complete sentences. Answers should be a paragraph or two. (10 points each)*

What does *Gilgamesh* say about:

THE GODS

MAN

MORTALITY

SALVATION

THE AFTERLIFE

*Answer the following three questions. These answers should require more substantial answers. (10 points each)*

1. How does the author of *Gilgamesh* set Gilgamesh up to be a type of Savior for the story? How does Gilgamesh succeed, and how does he fail? From reading this epic, how much do you think the early Babylonian pagans understood about the state of mankind?

2. Compare and contrast Shamash with Ishtar. What roles did they play in the epic? In what way do they both fail as gods?

3. Compare the gods of the Babylonian pantheon, collection of gods, with the God of Abraham. You may want to look at Genesis 12, 15, 17 and 22. How does the use of a covenant make Yahweh differ from the Babylonian gods?

## Endnotes

1    No, really this is his name, and there is no evidence that most of the gas stations in New Jersey have any etymological connection to him.

2.   Originally, the pagans had a fertility festival in the spring called Ishtar. When the gospel invaded the pagan world, it conquered the people and, of course, made a wreck of their immoral fertility festivals. Because Christ's resurrection happened in the spring, Christians stole the name of the pagan festival and emptied it of all of its immoral content. (It must have really irked those pagans that all of their original bunny and egg connotations were cleaned up and Christianized.) That is how the pagan celebration of Ishtar became our Easter.

3.   If you can find a copy of the *Enuma Elish*, you can read the story of the generations of the Babylonian gods.

4    At the time of publication, this material can be found at www.gatewaystobabylon.com/myths/texts/classic/enuma.htm, but should be available online by using a search engine of your choice.

5    *This endnote appears only in the teacher's edition.*

6    At the time of publication a description can be found at www.encyclopedia.thefreedictionary.com/Akkadian%20language

# CODE OF HAMMURABI

Teach me, O Lord the way of Your statutes,
And I shall keep it to the end.
Give me understanding and I shall
    keep your law;
Indeed, I shall observe it with my
    whole heart.
Make me walk in the path of
    Your commandments,
For I delight in it.
Incline my heart to your
    testimonies, and not
    to covetousness.
Turn away my eyes from looking at
    worthless things,
And revive me in Your way.
Establish Your word to
    Your servant,
Who is devoted to fearing You.
Turn away my reproach which
    I dread,
For Your judgments are good.
Behold, I long for Your precepts;
Revive me in Your righteousness.
(Psalm 119:33-40)

Hammurabi (c. 1792–1750 B.C.) was a priest-king who united all of Mesopotamia.

Have you ever wished that there weren't so many rules in life—you know, your parents' rules, or church rules, or the government's rules, or even God's rules? Did you ever wonder why we need rules to begin with? Did you ever wonder whether an ad campaign that once proclaimed "No Rules—Just Right!" was *right?* Sure you have! And you're not alone. Most people have at some time or another.

Now imagine playing in a pick-up soccer game with friends. You're playing fullback defending against a player on the opposing team who's dribbling at full speed down the sidelines trying to turn the corner and score a goal. You stop him from turning the corner and force him to dribble over the end line, out of bounds. Having done your jobs, you and your teammates relax for a moment, expecting to get the ball back for a goal kick. Unexpectedly the opposing winger continues to dribble the ball out of bounds behind the goal, then suddenly cuts back on to the field, shoots the ball into the net, and shouts "GOAL!"

while running triumphantly with his hands in the air. Your whole team angrily shouts at him: "That's no goal! You went out of bounds! It's a goal kick! You're breaking the *rules!*" The winger shouts back, "I don't have to follow the rules. Rules are made to be broken. I'm 'creative.' I just made a new move. You guys are just jealous. No rules—just right!"

Or imagine performing the role of Juliet in a presentation of Shakespeare's *Romeo and Juliet.* In the famous "balcony scene" where Romeo and Juliet profess their undying love for each other, your Romeo suddenly veers off script and begins shouting that he really doesn't like you anymore, "it was just a fling, I'm outta here, hope you have a good life," and exits stage left.

What is the problem in these two situations? The problem is that somebody in the game (and somebody in the play) decided not to follow "the rules." If these rule breakers are not punished in some manner, the game or play will be ruined. If everybody made up his own soccer rules (or lines for Romeo and Juliet) then you could never *have* a soccer game (or perform Shakespeare's play). Rules are a necessary part of life. "No rules" doesn't mean freedom or "just right," it means chaos, destruction and ultimately death. (Just ask Outback Steakhouse if "no rules" applies to paying their bill after you eat their steak!) The issue is not whether there are rules, but whose rules they are and how we should follow them.

Laws are formal rules enacted or decreed (commanded) by an authority to govern social relationships. Just as there is no soccer game without soccer rules, there is no society without laws. And laws are required not just in our current sinful

This is a stele that stands nearly eight feet high on which the laws of Hammurabi are engraved, extending entirely around the shaft and occupying over 3,600 lines. Above is a fine relief showing King Hammurabi standing at the left, receiving the laws from the Sun-god on the right.

world. Remember in your reading of the book of Genesis how God set Adam and Eve in the Garden of Eden and gave them certain rules, requiring them to "tend and keep" the Garden and permitting them to eat the fruit of every tree in the Garden, "but of the tree of the knowledge of good and evil you shall not eat." (Gen. 2:15–17). Likewise, even in the New Heavens and New Earth after the return of our Lord Jesus Christ, and His final judgment, there will be rules for awesome praise and worship in the glory of the Lord. The difference in the New Heavens and Earth is that the rules will be written on our hearts by the grace of God, and we will never break them!

The book you are about to read is a translation of old Babylonian case laws (commonly called the "Code") of Hammurabi, written or collected by a pagan king of ancient Babylonia, with comments and a comparison of some similar laws from the Bible. In building the first great Babylonian empire, Hammurabi conquered most of Mesopotamia, including the cities and land of the *Epic of Gilgamesh*, the previous book in your Primary Omnibus reading. Hammurabi lived in the eighteenth century B.C., a couple hundred years after Gilgamesh, king of Uruk and a few hundred years *before* the Exodus of God's people from Egypt.

Because Hammurabi's empire worshipped the same unreliable pagan gods as Gilgamesh (no doubt the Gilgamesh story was told to Hammurabi when he was growing up), Hammurabi decided that one way to glorify his accomplishments, make his empire permanent and demonstrate his divine wisdom for all to see, was to publish his legal decisions and judgments throughout the land. In reading Hammurabi's Code (we will call it "the Code") we will learn some important things about why and how pagan kings made rules and tried to establish justice and order in their kingdoms, why they were unsuccessful, why external laws by themselves are not sufficient to establish a godly life or society, and why justice depends on the righteousness of the triune God of the Bible.

## GENERAL INFORMATION

### Author and Context

In 1905 professor W. W. Davies edited an English translation of the *Code of Hammurabi*. He notes some comparisons with the laws of Moses from the Bible and comments on many of the laws to make their meaning clearer. In the 1890s scholars already knew much about the great King Hammurabi, and a three volume book on the letters and inscriptions of the king was published in 1900. The Code, however, was not discovered until early in 1902, unexpectedly, during a dig by French archeologist M. deMorgan in ancient Susa (biblical Shushan), Persia (present day Iran). During the time of Hammurabi, Persia was called Elam. Since the Code is in Babylonian script and language, and Hammurabi was king of Babylonia, scholars did not suspect that such a code would be found in Persia. (Either Hammurabi controlled Elamite territory, or the Code was brought back to Susa when the Elamites conquered Babylon later in the twelfth century B.C.).

The Code was discovered on three pieces of a large, black stone (usually called a "stele") approximately eight feet tall, five to six feet wide (slightly tapered) and rounded at the top. Both sides of the stone monument are covered with the inscription of

the laws. The top third or so of the monument, above the inscription of the laws, is a large engraved picture showing Hammurabi humbly and reverently standing before Shamash, the sun god of Sippar, the ancient city that founded the Hammurabi dynasty. The god is sitting on his throne and delivering the divine code to Hammurabi. The text of the monument underneath the picture is divided into three main parts: a lengthy Prologue saying where the laws came from, why the king who gave them is so great and why you had better pay attention to them; the 282 laws (of which we have 247, the other 35 having been "erased" by damage to the surface of the stone); and an Epilogue restating where these laws came from, and declaring them to be justice and light which no future kings must ever change.

Despite Hammurabi's bragging about his achievements in the Code's Prologue, his empire was very shaky and unstable. In order to keep and grow his empire he had to fight wars almost continually. Several times he double-crossed city-states that had been his allies, and many times he broke agreements he made with other kings. The last four years of his reign were relatively quiet, and he concentrated on his lawgiving (this is when he produced the Code) and enlarging the religious centers and temples in his empire. Even then, however, he was building many defensive fortifications for his cities, expecting future attacks against his empire. Soon after Hammurabi's death his empire began falling apart, and the region broke up into several smaller, competing kingdoms. No "super power" empire appeared again until the great and terrible Assyrian empire in the early 700's B.C., the empire which conquered the northern Kingdom of Israel in 722 B.C.

### Significance

Why do we care about these four thousand-year-old case laws anyway? There are several reasons. One is that they are one of the oldest and largest collections of non-biblical laws of which we have actual copies from ancient times. They demonstrate how the ancient pagan societies and kingdoms that "went their own way" after Noah and God's dispersing of the peoples at Babel were very sophisticated and smart people with a highly developed understanding of the need for rules of justice and order.

A second reason we read the Code is because it shows us how ancient pagan societies tried to bring order and justice to their lands without having the laws that God delivered to His chosen people.

A third reason is that they show how a great pagan king attempted to control his kingdom, demonstrating his self-proclaimed divine wisdom through just laws, in an attempt to create a kingdom which lasts forever.

## Main Characters

Not much is known about the personal life or personality of Hammurabi. Documents that we have, including signed letters of Hammurabi, indicate that he had a powerful personality, was a good military strategist, broke alliances or agreements whenever he thought he could increase his empire by doing so, and he did not like to delegate work (that is, he was always personally involved in negotiations and diplomacy, or in making decisions on appeals made to him from his subjects, rather than letting the people who worked for him handle these matters). This latter observation leads historians to believe that one reason his empire was so fragile and did not last long after his death was that he refused, or did not know how, to construct an effective government bureaucracy to manage his vast empire. Thus, the whole empire depended on him as "the great man" who ran things by the force of his personality. He did have organizational skills, since he produced many large public works including temples to the gods and huge canal projects. Typical of most ancient kings, who were the celebrities of their day, his ego and vanity knew no limits (he had a very *big* head").

## Summary and Setting

Babylon was a setting in which many gods were worshiped and served. We do not have room to give a detailed account of all of the gods mentioned in the Code. Here are the main ones:

Lord of heaven An (or Anu) is the chief god (although he had divine parents too), and with his wife Ki was the father and creator of numerous gods and demons. He was the chief god of Uruk and its temple called Eanna.

Enlil is lord of the atmosphere, who sends rains and destructive storms and was creator of the pickaxe,

the key technological tool of Mesopotamian farmers and builders (Mesopotamian buildings were made out of baked mud bricks). Enlil was associated with the city of Nippur.

Enki is the manager of the earth's productivity, and god of artists and craftsmen. He was associated with the city of Eridu.

Ishtar (Inanna in Sumerian) is queen of heaven, a prostitute and the goddess of love and war, the chief female deity (the Hebrew Ashtoreth and the Greek Astarte represent the same goddess, widely worshiped in the ancient world).

Nanna or Sin is the moon god, who measures and illuminates the night. His chief centers of worship were Ur and Haran, both places associated with Abraham. "And Terah took his son Abram and his grandson Lot, the son of Haran, and his daughter-in-law Sarai, his son Abram's wife, and they went out with them from Ur of the Chaldeans to go to the land of Canaan; and they came to Haran and dwelt there." (Gen. 11:31). Nanna is often represented as a bull, such as the famous harp with a carved bull whose beard is made of lapis lazuli, found at Ur and now at the Museum of Archeology at the University of Pennsylvania in Philadelphia (which would make a great field trip if you are close to Philadelphia).

Shamash or Utu is the sun god, widely known in the ancient middle east (Beth-shemesh is the "house of the sun god," Joshua 15:10). As the god of the penetrating light that goes everywhere, he was judge and defender of justice. His sacred cities were Sippar and Larsa, and his symbol was the sun disk. In Ezekiel 8:16, apostate Israelite men in Jerusalem were worshipping Shamash with their back to God's Temple.

Nergal is the god of the underworld who is responsible for fever, plague and the scorching summer heat on earth. His wife, Ereshkigal, was the sister and underworld rival of Ishtar or Inanna. In Mesopotamian mythology, because of some mean things Ereshkigal did when Inanna and her consort Dumuzi (Tammuz in Hebrew) once visited her, Dumuzi was forced to live in the underworld part of every year, and thus became known as the dying and reviving god (like Persephone in the Greek myths). In Ezekiel 8:14, at the same time that some Hebrew men were worshipping Shamash, some Hebrew women were worshipping pagan gods by ritually lamenting Tammuz' death.

The Code is divided into three basic sections: 1) the Prologue, 2) the list of case laws, and 3) the Epilogue. In some ways the Prologue and Epilogue are the most important parts because they establish what Hammurabi was trying to do by publishing the Code, and why he was trying to do this.

## Worldview

Remember the soccer winger who dribbled out of bounds behind the goal, then back onto the field to score a "goal?" He made up his own rules, and his "goal" of course would not count in any real soccer match. Obviously, if everyone made up their own rules, or changed the rules whenever they felt like it, there could be no soccer game. Everyone would be doing something different, and it would not look like soccer at all. Similarly, if the actors do not closely follow the lines of Romeo and Juliet, it is impossible to have the play *Romeo and Juliet* at all.

Now, imagine you are playing in a soccer game officiated by a referee. This time you are dribbling the ball toward your opponent's goal. A defending player tries to steal the ball from you, but misses and fouls you

The pagan festival of Easter originated as the worship of the Babylonian goddess, Ishtar. Easter was not considered a "Christian" festival until the Council of Nicaea in 325 A.D. decreed that "Easter" should be celebrated on the first Sunday, after the full moon, on or after the vernal equinox. Many pagan customs were then absorbed into the Christian holiday of Easter. The egg was an emblem of rebirth, and the rabbit was a pagan symbol of fertility. Christian missionaries extended the dominion of Christ to the celebrations of pagan cultures and replaced the older festivals with the celebration of the Resurrection.

instead. The foul, however, does little to stop your progress and you continue toward the goal. The referee waves his arm signaling "play on" and you continue to dribble closer to unload a strong shot on goal. Stop and consider: Why didn't the referee stop the match and give the defender who fouled you the usual penalty for breaking the rules? The answer is that the foul rule is intended to prevent the defender from unfairly impeding the dribbler's progress. In this case, even though the foul was committed, you continued on and your progress was not significantly impeded. Calling the penalty in this situation would have harmed you because play would have stopped just when you had gained an advantage (by beating the defender who fouled you). Thus the rule was *not* enforced because enforcement would not have served the purpose of the rule—to prevent unfair impeding of the dribbler.

In this sense the soccer rules and rules of life are similar. The rules God gives us Himself, as well as those from the authorities (like our parents) that He gives us, are there for a purpose, and the purpose is not the rules themselves. Just as the soccer rules were created not as an end in themselves (the winner of the game is not the team that follows the most rules, but the team that scores the most goals), but to permit the playing of the game, so life's rules are not the end or purpose for which we live, but a means which permits us to live godly lives and have a godly society. The purpose or end of a soccer game is to play the game and

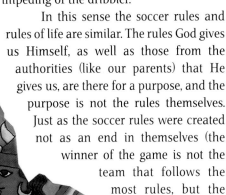

score the most goals. The purpose or end of life, both individually and for society, is to live to the glory of God and enjoy Him forever.

Remember when Jesus was out walking through some grain fields on the Sabbath? His disciples were hungry, and they pulled off some heads of grain to eat. The Pharisees complained to Jesus that His disciples were doing "what is not lawful on the Sabbath." Jesus then asked the Pharisees why they didn't remember the story of David when he was a refugee running from Saul, how, needy and hungry, he and his men went into the house of God and ate the showbread, "which is not lawful to eat except for the priests." Jesus then told the Pharisees, "The Sabbath was made for man, and not man for the Sabbath. Therefore the Son of Man is also Lord of the Sabbath." Jesus, who did not come to abolish the law, but to fulfill it (Matt. 5:17) shows us that the law is given not as an end in itself, but for life in Christ.

People who are being disobedient (unbelievers or Christians) will not see this purpose and thus often twist the law or make bad laws. (Remember, any man-made law that conflicts with God's laws is by definition a bad law). God has made us for Himself. When we rebel against Him we "naturally" misinterpret or misapply God's laws or seek to make different laws of our own. As sinners we have a tendency to disobey in one of two ways: we either refuse to obey any laws that we do not agree with (this is called *antinomianism* by theologians—*anti* is against and *nomos* is law in Greek) or we try to perfectly obey the external letter of God's laws (as we interpret the letter) for the purpose of "earning" salvation or our own glory (called "legalism" by theologians). Both of these sins reflect an unbiblical view of the purpose of the law.

The Bible tells us we can neither avoid the consequences of ignoring God's law nor earn salvation or glory by keeping the letter of the law. These things are simply impossible to accomplish. As rebellious creatures first created and loved by the Creator, we deserve the just wrath of God. Only God can save us, through the blood atonement of Jesus Christ that provides both for God's justice *and* His mercy. When God does a great work in us by changing our hearts to follow Jesus, He gives us His Spirit, Who gives us the ability to desire and follow His laws because we love Him and know that this is best for us and everybody else. Only with such a changed heart can David say in Psalm 119:20 "My soul breaks with longing for Your judgments at all times."

Jesus tells us that He, the Son of Man, is the Lord and giver of the law, thus reminding us that 1) laws always have a personal source, and 2) laws are a reflection of the character of their source. All law codes reveal something about the worldview of the people who make the laws, including what they assume about God, man, justice, and the purpose of the law. In the case of Hammurabi, we know a lot about the gods that he said gave him the authority to make the Code.

*God*

Earlier we learned that the top of the stele containing the Code has a large picture of Hammurabi standing before Shamash, the Babylonian sun god, seated on his throne delivering the Code to the Babylonian king. In the lengthy Prologue and Epilogue Hammurabi declares to the world and his subjects that he rules like the sun god over the people, giving "light to the land" and promoting the "welfare of mankind." Hammurabi actually claims the authority to "cause justice," destroy the wicked, and prevent oppression in his god-like status. Like the Greeks later on, and like all pagan peoples that God let "go their own way" from the time of Noah to the time of Christ, the ancient Mesopotamian peoples were polytheistic, meaning they had many gods. As we saw above, the gods of the Mesopotamian cities that were strongest, or conquered other cities, became the most important gods because the people believed that they were the most powerful gods. When Babylon became the preeminent city in southern Mesopotamia, thanks in large part to Hammurabi, the patron or hometown god of Babylon, Marduk, was regarded as the supreme ruler among the gods. This is the same Marduk who is the top god of the Babylonian empire of Nebuchadnezzar over one thousand years later. The prophet Jeremiah then prophesied (Jer. 50:2) that when the Lord brings judgment on Babylon, even Marduk (spelled Merodach in the New King James version) will be terrified. As with all the pagan gods throughout history, ancient and modern, they are man-made "no gods" (or demons worshipped as if they were real gods) whom the living God will destroy for good on the final "day of the Lord." On that day, all the nations will worship the one true God and Savior, Jesus Christ (See Jer. 10:11; Zeph. 2:11).

Like all pagan gods, Hammurabi's gods were thought of as supermen. They were stronger and more powerful than men, but not all-powerful and sovereign over the universe like the triune God of the Bible. They behaved in all the bad ways men behave. Different gods seemed to have responsibility for different parts of life or different parts of the land, representing the people's understanding of different parts of nature (like the sun and storm gods) and culture (like the technology and judging gods). The gods continually fought against each other for position and power. They were amoral gods, who raped, killed and were unfaithful just like men. They were untrustworthy like men, which may explain why

there were so many gods. If one failed, you tried the next one, hoping he or she would not fail. For example, the inscription on a statue of the god Nabu (son of Marduk), set up in the Mesopotamian city of Nimrud in the 700's B.C., ends with the words "Wait on Nabu; do not trust in another god."

The gods' only interest in men seemed to be for their ability to do the hard work on the earth necessary for feeding, caring for and worshipping them in the temples of the land. They may or may not show favor or mercy to a man at any particular time, and they never made a covenant with man or gave man any written rules by which to live and relate to the gods. Like the Egyptian and Greek gods, the Mesopotamian gods, although very powerful, were unreliable and ultimately subject to "fate" like men. In short, they were not in control of the world like the creator God of the Bible. Because the Mesopotamian gods did not have the power, goodness, or desire to change men's hearts and live in a loving relationship with them, it was impossible for such gods to give men laws for the purpose of life in the true, biblical sense, for which men were created.

This situation left the Mesopotamians with no guidance on how to build a just and orderly society among sinners. Just like their gods, the king who was strongest made the rules—until a stronger king shoved him out of the way and brought his own rules. When Hammurabi became the strongest king, he imposed his will by force and then claimed that all the gods had given him the authority to rule and "cause justice" in the land. He knew that, like soccer, you can't play the game of life

One of the numerous clay-tablet letters of Hammurabi, the king of Babylon. The writing, done while the clay was still soft, shows signs of the speed with which the king's secretary took down the king's dictation over four thousand years ago. This particular letter orders a local governor to hear the appeal of an official who thinks himself unjustly defeated in law.

without rules. One of the ways he proclaims his justice is by publishing his Code of laws throughout the empire so that all the people would submit to him and all the cities would have the same rules. Then they all would be playing the "game of life" under his rules. Hammurabi the man sought to become, and effectively was, the 'god' of his empire. Unfortunately for him and his empire, he had no power to change men's hearts and give them life. So the only purpose of his laws was to glorify himself and help keep control of his people.

Unlike Hammurabi and his powerless gods, our triune God is the sovereign creator and sustainer of the universe. The Father has given His Son, Jesus Christ, all power in Heaven and Earth, and Jesus, through the Holy Spirit working in the church is building His eternal kingdom, which will never fail. Christians are part of that glorious kingdom building because of His gracious covenant. Unlike Hammurabi, who had neither the power or goodness to bring real salvation to life, Christians will never have to worry about Christ's kingdom collapsing or failing.

## Man

The Code assumes two things about the nature of man that appear inconsistent. On the one hand, Hammurabi assumes "great" men like himself can attain divine status through "great" deeds such as conquering cities and empires, ruling vast numbers of people and establishing justice through great judgments like the Code. The Code assumes there is no absolute separation between all men and the gods, but rather a great "chain of being" from the lowliest human being to the greatest god. The gods are simply supermen who live forever, and "great" men may hope to become gods. On the other hand, the laws of the Code assume that "ordinary" men can and will do many "wrong" things and that it is necessary to stop them from doing such things by laws and punishments in order to bring justice and peace to society. But without any power to change people on the inside, real justice and peace are impossible. Imagine people who want to play soccer but will not play by the rules. The rules by themselves will not enable them to play the game. Only a change in the people themselves, giving them the ability and desire to play by the rules will enable them to play the game.

Scripture tells us that there is a *permanent* gulf between the uncreated, sovereign, all-powerful, all-knowing Triune God and his creatures made in His image—man. This is known as the "Creator/ creature distinction" that can never be changed. Even when we are with the Lord in the eternal state, and by the grace of God without sin, we will not be gods, but sanctified men. The Bible also tells us that *all* men, from kings to beggars, are sinners subject to God's just wrath who can only be saved by the mercy and grace of God through the atonement of Jesus Christ. The main purpose of God's laws is to show sinners their need for Christ and give God's people the rules that help them live for the glory and enjoyment of God. Without God's laws we could not know how to live for His glory, just like we could not know how to play soccer without knowing the soccer rules.

## Salvation

Since Mesopotamian religion taught that man was made to serve the gods and work for the gods, the Babylonians did not consider or admit that sin was the problem in life. They thought their problems were caused by not knowing or understanding the plan of the gods—so they always strove to find out or divine (from which we get divination) what those plans were. Since there are a lot of things to understand about life, the number of gods they consulted continually expanded. They arranged their social life around working for and soliciting the favors of the gods, and they arranged their rules around providing the order and control necessary for their society to function. Thus, marriage was for procreation and social control, not for love. Similarly, perversions and prostitution were permitted, sometimes even encouraged by the gods, and was even permitted for married people as long they stayed married. To the extent people were thought of as good or bad, it was not an ethical consideration as in Christianity, but whether they were functioning in the proper manner in their role in society and with respect to worship of the gods. Given their confused view of the world, their thinking was very practical—they sought to obey or manipulate their unpredictable gods and environment in order to obtain security and prosperity. The Code reflects this on a society-wide scale—it is an attempt to come up with wise judgments that will keep order and prosperity in the larger society. As a result of this unreal view of man, Babylonian society never understood the root cause of its problems—the failure to acknowledge and give thanks to the creator God who actually created and sustained them—in short, its sin and need for repentance.

Hammurabi boldly claims to be "the salvation-bringing shepherd" of his people, apparently because he now considers himself divine. Through his domination and conquering spirit he mistakenly

chief judge of the empire. Of course, his attempts at salvation fail. Hammurabi dies without God and, in fact, his great justice does not bring any real peace or safety to his people. Most of his lifetime his people were at war, and shortly after his death his empire began to unravel.

As part of his hopeless quest for salvation, Hammurabi's publication of his case laws reflect two different but related motives natural to our sinful human condition. First, Hammurabi wants to declare and justify his own power and greatness in building the Babylonian empire. This is simply the old pagan desire for self-glorification, a vivid contrast to our savior Jesus' desire to glorify His Father rather than Himself. It was only in His giving glory to His Father that real glory reflected back to Jesus. The vast majority of Hammurabi's Code statements focus on "me" and what "I" am and did, with a token nod to the gods who let him "do his own thing." There are many ways in which Hammurabi sought glorification during his reign, including conquering every city in sight (including those of his "friends") and building all kinds of monuments and statues to himself (one of which is specifically referred to in the Code). The Code is another way in which he sought self-glorification. As far as we can tell today, the Code was not a body of laws enacted for his government to follow. That is, neither Hammurabi, nor any of his councilors or other authorities made these into laws like our Congress in the United States enacts laws. (No Code laws are ever referred to in the numerous legal documents that still exist from Hammurabi's time, and they do not represent a comprehensive legal code). Rather, the Code is a collection of actual or theoretical cases judged by Hammurabi or his judges, written in the Mesopotamian style of learned or "scientific" treatises

Code 263: If he lose an ox or sheep intrusted to him, he shall compensate the owner, ox for ox, sheep for sheep.

believes he has the power to bring salvation to himself and his people. (By the time of Hammurabi, the great kings of Mesopotamia, like the Pharaohs, and later the Roman Emperors, were exalted as divinity). He seeks to bring salvation to his people through the supposed permanent order and justice he brings as

his desire to bring about peace and justice without God was pure folly.

The Bible tells us that salvation is possible *only* through Jesus Christ, who is the way, the truth and the life. No man comes to the Father but through Jesus. And those Gentiles who lived before Jesus came were responsible to look *forward* to His coming, as Melchizedek and Jethro did. No matter how just or good external human laws may seem, they are powerless to bring about true peace and justice without Jesus Christ.

## Source of Justice

Although Hammurabi implies in the picture at the top of the stele that the sun god gave him the code of laws, he says repeatedly in the Prologue and Epilogue that *he, Hammurabi,* created the laws and is responsible for law and justice in the land. "I rule and give light to the land," "I put law and justice in the mouth of the people," "The just rules which Hammurabi, the wise king, established." Clearly, Hammurabi is the creator of the rules, not the gods. Although Hammurabi claims to be commissioned by the various gods to bring justice to the land, he brings no words or laws from the gods. His gods are mute—speechless—because they are not like the true God. So he has to create the laws himself.

Now contrast this situation with that of Moses. At Sinai, where the Lord first gave the people of Israel the Ten Commandments, Moses went "up to God" and the Lord "called to him from the mountain."

"Thus you shall say to the house of Jacob, and tell the children of Israel: "You have seen what I did to the Egyptians, and how I bore you on eagles' wings and brought you to Myself. Now therefore, if you will indeed obey My voice and keep My covenant, then you shall be a special treasure to Me above all people; for all the earth is Mine. And you shall be to Me a kingdom of priests and a holy nation.' These are the words you shall speak to the children of Israel." (Ex. 19:3-6)

Then at Mount Sinai God gave the Ten Commandments directly to the people of Israel—"And God spoke all these words, saying . . ." (Ex. 20:1-17) After the frightened people heard the word of the Lord from the mountain, they pleaded with *Moses* to give them God's word, because they were too afraid to hear it directly from the Lord. The Lord told

("If such and such happens, then this shall be the result.") Hammurabi published the Code so all the peoples could see the great wisdom of the god-like man who brought order and justice, as he lets everyone know over and over in the Prologue and Epilogue.

Second, Hammurabi wants to keep order and power in his empire. It is possible that he even desired to bring more peace, justice and prosperity to his people and thought his "wise" case laws would help him do so. Although his desire for peace and justice was not wrong in itself,

Moses the exact words to say when delivering His case laws to the people, telling Moses, "Thus you shall say to the Children of Israel." (Ex. 20:18–23:33) Likewise the Lord gave word for word instructions to Moses regarding holiness laws and the building of the Ark of the Covenant and His tabernacle as recorded in Exodus and Leviticus. Repeatedly the books state "And the Lord spoke to Moses" and "Then the Lord said to Moses." Repeatedly the Lord instructs Moses "speak to the children of Israel," "command the children of Israel," and repeatedly Moses tells the people "This is the thing which the Lord commanded." Likewise, when Moses talks to the people near the end of his life, before they are to enter the Promised Land, Deuteronomy tells us that "Moses spoke to the children of Israel according to all that the Lord had given him as commandments to them."

This contrast is complete. Hammurabi is making up the rules like the "creative" soccer player in our game. His rules are made to work in his favor. On the one hand the power-hungry man and empire builder Hammurabi proceeded to assert that *he* was lord and the savior of his people, the creator of justice and the Code. On the other hand God, the Lord of Heaven and Earth who redeemed His people with mighty historical works, chose Moses, who was living a quiet life in the desert and did not want the job, to be His spokesman before the mighty Pharaoh, led His people out of bondage, and explicitly revealed His laws and commandments, pursuant to a covenant established by Him with Moses and His people.

### What About the Similarities?

Since Hammurabi is pagan and his gods are demons or empty idols, why are some of the case laws in the Code similar to some in the Mosaic law, given to us directly by the true God? For example, Law 14 says that a kidnapper shall be put to death for such a crime, as does Exodus 21:16. There are many applications of the "eye for an eye" (*lex talionis*) principle in Laws 196–214. These closely parallel Exodus 21:18–27. (There are other similarities, as well as many dissimilarities, but no evidence of borrowing or direct influence of Code laws on Mosaic law. The tone of the Mosaic law is obviously more humane than that of the Babylonian law.) So how do we explain the similarities? Although pagans suppress the knowledge of the true God (Rom. 1), they do not suppress many of the obvious or observed truths of God's world, because they desire the obvious benefits derived from those truths. Most pagans, even if they desire to fly, acknowledge gravity and don't jump off the top of high mountains for fear of death. And many pagans will obey a law of God if they think there is some benefit in doing so. Similarly, pagans responsible for making laws and judging legal cases cannot expect to keep order while ignoring the realities of human nature in god's world. Through experience in the world they learn that in order to keep peace and prevent violence in their kingdoms, laws prohibiting bad behaviors and oppression of the weak by the strong are necessary. When pagans establish laws similar to God's laws it does not mean that pagans have the right motive or goal for such laws. They are trying to write the rules to favor themselves so they can dribble the ball behind the goal, kick it in and claim that they have scored. For Christians, such laws are part of God's covenant relationship with the world and His people. They are motivated by gratitude and obedience to God for His covenant mercy and grace. By contrast, pagans desire peace and justice *without* acknowledging or submitting to God—a desire that is ultimately unattainable. True peace and justice among men is impossible while men are in rebellion against God, because men can have no peace within themselves or with each other until they are reconciled with God. And only God can reconcile men to himself, through the blood atonement of Jesus Christ.

—*William S. Dawson*

## For Further Reading

Spielvogel, Jackson. *Western Civilization.* Fifth Edition. Belmont, Calif.: Wadsworth/Thomson Learning, 2003. 8–16.

*Veritas Press History Cards: Old Testament and Ancient Egypt.* Lancaster, Pa.: Veritas Press. 19.

*Veritas Press Bible Cards: Genesis through Joshua.* Lancaster, Pa.: Veritas Press. 4, 5, 8.

## SESSION I: PRELUDE

### Questions to Consider

1. Why are laws necessary? How do we know when laws are just?
2. Do you think the laws of a country or kingdom have anything to do with the God or gods that are worshipped in that country or kingdom? Why or why not?
3. Why do you think God gave specific laws to Moses rather than let Moses and the Hebrew elders make their own laws? Why do you think Hammurabi's gods let him make the laws rather than give him specific laws?
4. Why do you think both Moses and Hammurabi wrote their laws down and published them so that everybody could see them?

*After reading the General Information, answer the following questions:*

1. Who was Hammurabi?
2. When did he live?
3. How did we get the text of the *Code of Hammurabi?*
4. Where does the *Code of Hammurabi* have some parallels in the Bible?

### Optional Activity

If you are near an archaeology museum that houses ancient material, take a trip and study the material that has been found in Mesopotamia, such as steles, and clay tablets and small and large statues of the gods. The two best museums in the country for this material are the University of Chicago and the University of Pennsylvania (UPenn, in Philadelphia) archaeology museums. UPenn has a replica of the *Code of Hammurabi* stele and a large collection of Sumerian/Babylonian artifacts, many from the famous Ur excavation site. Look up the location of other ancient archaeology museums on the internet.

READING ASSIGNMENT:
Prologue and Laws 1–49

## SESSION II: ACTIVITY

Prologue and Laws 1–49

### Hammurabi on Trial

*In a group setting, divide into two teams. Both teams have ten minutes to record their answers to Case I below. The teams are to first judge the case using the* Code of Hammurabi. *Secondly, judge the case biblically. The teams may use their Bibles but must work from memory with regards to the Code. After ten minutes each team will present its findings to the teacher, who will decide which team came closest to the correct answer. Repeat with the other cases. The teacher may give hints to help the teams, but hints should be counted against the team when deciding a winner.*

*A writing alternative to this activity for individuals is provided as an option to accomplish the same learning. Answer at least two of the cases in writing, one paragraph for the Code and one for the Bible. As above, only your Bible may be used, not the Code. The time limit is fifteen minutes per case.*

### Case I

Roy is walking down the road and sees smoke coming from Ray's home. He runs over to the house and tries to find out if anyone is inside. Seeing no one he begins to leave, when over in the den he spies a beautiful vase (it is worth the equivalent of $1000). Imagining that it will be priceless some day (he was right although off by a couple thousand years), he slips the vase into the leg of his trousers (or whatever the ancient version of trousers was). As he scrambles from the burning house he sees Ray sobbing as he watches his house burn. After making sure that Ray is ok, Roy begins to limp away (that vase was heavier than he thought!). Suddenly, the vase slips out and everyone sees it. There is a moment of awkward silence. What should be done to the thieving Roy?

### Case II

Reuben, an Israelite, finds himself enslaved to a wicked Moabite master, Enosh, when his village was overrun when he was a child. One night, Enosh commands Reuben to go and steal grain from a neighbor who is out of town. Reuben goes out according to his master's will, but instead of carrying out the theft, he flees for Israel. Arriving in the hill country of Ephraim without any money, he becomes the servant of Elihu, a fellow Israelite. One day, Enosh arrives and finds Reuben serving as a servant in Elihu's house. He demands that Reuben be returned and Elihu be punished. What should be done?

## Case III

Mark is running low on cash. As he is walking home, he sees two enclosures full of animals (pigs, goats, cows and sheep). He figures that with all of these animals the owners would not miss one of each. So, he steals a pig, a goat, a sheep and a cow from each farm—eight animals in all. Later, he is caught. As it turns out, one of the fenced-in areas belonged to God (they were the property of the Temple), the other belonged to a freeman. What should be done with the poverty-stricken Mark?

 **READING ASSIGNMENT:** Laws 50–194

# SESSION III: RECITATION
Laws 50–194

## Comprehension Questions

*Answer these questions for factual recall:*

1. According to Hammurabi, which gods gave Marduk "dominion over mankind?"
2. Why did the gods "call" Hammurabi, "the exalted prince, a god-fearing man," to do?
3. What are some of the "accomplishments" achieved by Hammurabi in his long list set forth in the Prologue?
4. Can you distinguish the two basic categories of accomplishments that Hammurabi lists in his Prologue?
5. At the end of the Prologue, what does Hammurabi say Marduk sent him to do?
6. What was a prevalent practice in ancient Babylonia that is addressed by the first couple of laws in the Code?
7. What did the Babylonians employ to test the guilt or innocence of those suspected or charged with sorcery or witchcraft?
8. Laws 3–5 address what kind of problems with respect to legal proceeding?

9. Why does Law 7 prohibit buying things from the son or slave of any person without a witness or contract?
10. What was the major difference between the fugitive slave laws of Babylon and those of the Hebrews?
11. What type of property are Laws 27–41 concerning in general?
12. Law 48 says that a man in debt whose fields are destroyed because of flood or lack of water does not have to pay his creditor interest for that year. What was the symbolic act he was to perform to show that he did not have to pay interest that year?
13. What besides money could a debtor pay in interest to a creditor?

## Lateral Thinking

*Discuss the following questions or answer one in a short essay:*

1. Compare and contrast the Prologue of the Code with Exodus 19:1–24 introducing the Ten Commandments?
2. Compare and contrast who the ultimate source of law and justice is in the Code and in the Mosaic law?
3. Compare and contrast Hammurabi's Prologue statement that he "put law and righteousness in the mouth of the people" with God's promise to Jeremiah that "I will put My law in [His peoples'] minds, and write it on their hearts" (Jer. 31:33)?

## Optional Activity

Draw up a legal "code" for your house rules in the form of the laws in the Code, such as: "If a son or daughter go out of the house at any time before doing their daily chore(s) that son or daughter shall perform all the house chores on the following day."

 **READING ASSIGNMENT:** Laws 195–282 and Epilogue

## SESSION IV: DISCUSSION
Laws 195–282 and Epilogue

## A Question to Consider

Have you ever been involved in a situation where you thought a decision or action was unjust? What made you think it was unjust?

*Discuss or list short answers to the following questions:*

### Text Analysis

1. What do laws have to do with justice?
2. Who is the source of justice in the Code? Who is the source of justice in the Bible?
3. What is the major difference between the two different sources of law in the Code and in the Bible?
4. Does this mean that none of Hammurabi's laws are just?
5. How is justice related to mercy?

### Cultural Analysis

1. How is justice understood in our culture?
2. What does our culture consider the source of justice?
3. How does our culture perceive mercy?

### Biblical Analysis

1. What does the Bible say is justice?
2. What does the Bible say is the only source of justice?
3. What does the Bible say is our responsibility with respect to justice?
4. What does the Bible say about mercy?

### Application

How should God's justice and mercy affect us?

## SUMMA

*Write an essay or discuss this question, integrating what you have learned from the material above.*

How was God able to reconcile justice and mercy (that is, be merciful by forgiving us while still exacting rightful punishment for wrongdoing) when no other religion or culture (including our own) has been able to accomplish this?

## SESSION V: ACTIVITY
### The Hammurabi Mêlée

*In a group setting, divide into two teams. Both teams have ten minutes to record their answers to Case I below. The teams are to first judge the case using the* Code of Hammurabi. *Secondly, judge the case biblically. The teams may use their Bibles but must work from memory with regards to the Code. After ten minutes each team will present its findings to the teacher, who will decide which team came closest to the correct answer. Repeat with the other cases. The teacher may give hints to help the teams, but hints should be counted against the team when deciding a winner.*

*A writing alternative to this activity for individuals is provided as an option to accomplish the same learning. Answer at least two of the cases in writing, one paragraph for the Code and one for the Bible. As above, only your Bible may be used, not the Code. The time limit is fifteen minutes per case.*

### Case I

Ben is drinking at the bar and gets drunk. When Sheila, the pregnant bar maid, asks Ben to leave and refuses to serve him any more fermented fig juice (or whatever they drank back then), he gets angry with her and punches her. Unfortunately, this causes her to go into labor and her child is stillborn. Just after delivering the dead child, Sheila dies of internal bleeding caused by Ben's punch. What punishment should Ben receive?

### Case II

Sam has a mean bull named Ferdinand. This bull is known to gore anyone that comes near him, except Sam. Sam does not keep Ferdinand away from others, but leaves him in an open field. One day Larry, a freeborn man, is walking through the field not knowing that Ferdinand is near. Ferdinand attacks and kills Larry. What should be done to Ferdinand? What should be done to Sam?

### Case III

Kate is murdered, but no one knows who the murderer is. A couple of days later Roger comes forward and says that he saw Kevin kill Kate with a lead pipe. A search is made for the pipe (in all of the rooms, even the study with the secret passage) and nothing is found. Kevin denies that he has done anything wrong. What should be done?

# Optional Session

## Possible Review Questions

*All questions from the Comprehension section of Session III may be used as review questions.*

## Evaluation

*Open book and open Bible. Write one to two sentences on each of the following questions. (3 points each)*

1. In his Code, who does Hammurabi claim to be?
2. With his mighty exploits, Hammurabi made glad the heart of which god?
3. When Marduk sent Hammurabi "to rule over men," what does Hammurabi say he did?
4. What is Hammurabi's major motivation in publishing his Code?
5. What do the majority of the case laws in the Code deal with?
6. Who is the god who became the premier deity in the Mesopotamian pantheon of gods as a result of Hammurabi's empire building and patronage?
7. Why does Hammurabi enlist the assistance of Shamash in support of his Code?
8. What is the major difference between Hammurabi's Prologue and the Old Testament introductions to Moses' deliverance of the laws to the Hebrews?
9. What is the main difference between Hammurabi's curses on those who do not follow his Code and the curses God sets out in Deuteronomy against those who do not obey His laws?
10. Why does Hammurabi invoke the curses of so many gods on future "princes" who desecrate or otherwise do not follow his Code?

*Demonstrate your understanding of the worldviews set forth in The* Code of Hammurabi *by answering the following question in complete sentences. Answers should be a paragraph or two. (10 points each)*

1. What does the Code assume about the gods?
2. How did these gods assist Hammurabi in bringing order and justice to his empire?
3. What is the Code's assumption about the nature of man?
4. Compare and contrast the assumptions of the Code and the Bible about who will provide salvation for the people.

# FIRST AND SECOND SAMUEL

The year is 2067, and the United States of America no longer exists.

In Washington, D.C., the Constitution has been discarded, and the President has declared herself Queen. She begins persecuting her opponents—mainly Christians—who oppose abortion rights, secular education, homosexual marriage, and government control of religion. The queen establishes the worship of "JesAllaYahBuddKrish" (JAYBuK for short) as the official religion of what is now called "Red America," with centers of worship at the National Cathedral in Washington and at St. John the Divine in New York City. It is widely rumored that the queen is insane and that she runs around the White House frothing at the mouth in an eighteenth-century sleeping gown.

Not all Americans—if we can still call them that—go along with these changes. Some have banded together in northern Idaho, working out plans to restore the Constitution, decentralize power, and get things back to the ancient, happy, sane days of 2004. Some groups in Idaho begin stockpiling weapons to launch an assault on Washington. Other former Americans have fled to South Sea islands. Several thousand climb up into the Rockies around Colorado Springs. They think of themselves as the "true America," and begin to plan for the future, knowing that they can never go back to the old America.

If this happened, where would you be? Would you be among the people wanting to go back to the old ways? Would you go along with the Red America? Would you be in the Rockies planning for a new America? Suppose your group took over control of the U.S. How would you act then? Would you attack and destroy all the other Americans? Would you try to win them over to your side? How?

You may never have to make decisions like this. But you are faced with changing circumstances all the time, and you have to decide how to react to them. We need to gain wisdom from Scripture about how to respond to such changes. Do we accept all changes? Do we try to "turn back the clock?" Do we try to take advantage of the changes that take place? How are we to do this?

First and Second Samuel cover a period of rapid and radical change in Israel's history. These changes take place on many different levels. Politically, Israel moves from government by judges to rule by a king. In terms of worship, like in the scenario above, the Mosaic tabernacle was destroyed and never rebuilt, and 2 Samuel ends looking ahead to Solomon's temple. First and Second Samuel describes the change from the Mosaic covenant, which was laid out in the Pentateuch (Genesis through Deuteronomy), to the Davidic covenant (cf. 2 Sam. 7). By the end of 2 Samuel, Israel is a very different nation than she was at the beginning of 1 Samuel. Few books of the Bible are more useful to us as we try to respond in a godly way to the changes around us.

## GENERAL INFORMATION

### Author and Context

First and Second Samuel are two separate books in our Bibles, but they are really two parts of a single book. The book was divided into two parts when the Old Testament was translated into Greek (the Greek translation is called the *Septuagint*), probably because the book was too long to fit onto a standard sized scroll.

Samuel ministered before the LORD, even as a child, wearing a linen ephod. Moreover his mother used to make him a little robe, and bring it to him year by year when she came up with her husband to offer the yearly sacrifice. And Eli would bless Elkanah and his wife, and say, "The LORD give you descendants from this woman for the loan that was given to the LORD." And the LORD visited Hannah, so that she conceived and bore three sons and two daughters. Meanwhile the child Samuel grew before the LORD.

But the story is one story. At the end of 1 Samuel, Saul dies at the battle of Gilboa. That is a good way to end a book—with the tragic death of one of the main characters. But the story of David is far from over. David is introduced in the middle of 1 Samuel and quickly becomes a hero. We know that he is going to become king (1 Sam. 16:1, 13; 25:30-31), but at the end of 1 Samuel he has not become king yet. With respect to Saul, 1 Samuel comes to an ending; with respect to David, the story of 1 Samuel is unfinished. We need 2 Samuel to finish David's story.[1]

The book has had a number of different names. Greek and Russian Orthodox Christians call the book First and Second Kingdoms, and Roman Catholic Bibles sometimes use the titles First and Second Kings. In Hebrew and in English, the book is named for Samuel, but the prophet Samuel could not have written the whole book, since he dies before Saul (1 Sam. 25:1). Samuel may have written down some parts of the book, but Jewish tradition says that the book was written by Gad and Nathan, prophets in David's court. Those are pretty good guesses, but we cannot be sure who wrote the book.

## Significance

The most important thing about any book of the Bible is what it tells us about Jesus (Luke 24:26-27, 44-49). This is especially clear in the life story of David, who is one of the greatest Old Testament "types" or "foreshadowings" of Jesus.

Generally, we can see parallels between Jesus and David in the way that David deals with Saul. Saul spends a lot of his reign persecuting David, and David has several opportunities to kill Saul (1 Sam. 24, 26). In every case, David refuses to lift his hand against the Lord's anointed. He suffers patiently and does good to Saul in spite of Saul's sins against him. Eventually, David inherits the kingdom. As Jesus said, David's life shows the sufferings and the glory of the Anointed One.

We can also examine the terms of what is called the "Davidic covenant," which are described in 2 Samuel 7. In some ways, the promises to David are nothing new. Yahweh promised to give Abram a "great name" (Gen. 12:2), and He reiterates that promise to David (2 Sam. 7:9). God promised a land to Israel (15:7–21), and He promises David a place for Israel to rest (vv. 10–11). Before the Davidic covenant, these promises had been given to the house of Abram in general, but after David they were specifically given to the house of David. David was *the* seed of Abram who would bring blessing to the nations.

The designation of David's son as a "son of God" (v. 14) is also an important new thing in the covenant with David. Prior to David, the phrase "son of God" language was used primarily for Israel as a whole. At the Exodus, Moses came to Pharaoh with the demand, "Israel is My son; let him go" (Ex. 4:22–23). With the Davidic covenant, however, the national identity of the "son" of God is focused in the single person of the Davidic king. The blessings and curses of Deuteronomy 28 depend on the obedience or disobedience of the king.

We can see this already in David's life, which follows the pattern of the history of Israel:

| ISRAEL | DAVID (2 Samuel) |
| --- | --- |
| Exodus from Egypt | Exodus from Philistia |
| War with Canaanites | War with Ishbosheth (3:1–4:12) and Philistines, 5:17–25 |
| Conquest of land | Conquest of Jerusalem, 5:6–10 |
| Yahweh rules the land | David rules the land, 5:1–5 |
| Ark at Shiloh, Josh. 18:1 | Ark in Jerusalem, 6:1–19 |

First and Second Samuel has a central place in Western culture, mainly because it is our main source for the life of David. The Psalms of David have been the basis for Christian prayer and worship for centuries, and many medieval Psalters were illustrated with pictures of David. Medieval kings frequently tried to emulate David. Charlemagne thought of himself as a "new David," and the

Jonathan said to David, "Go in peace, since we have both sworn in the name of the LORD, saying, 'May the LORD be between you and me, and between your descendants and my descendants, forever.'" Rembrandt Harmensz Van Rijn captures this emotional scene in *David's Farewell to Jonathan*, the most famous painting in the collection of Russian Tsar Peter the Great. The canvas was bought at auction in 1716 to be hung in Monplaisir Palace, according to the instructions of the tsar. Many details mentioned in the biblical account are represented in the piece, including the sword given by the prince to David, as well as the arrows used to give signal. In the painting Rembrandt gave Jonathan his own features but gave David more feminine characteristics, possibly an allusion to the loss he felt due to the early death of his wife Saskia, whom he loved and to whom he was deeply devoted.

Carolingian kings who followed Charlemagne[2] often had themselves depicted in art to bring out resemblances to David. Renaissance painters and sculptors saw David as a symbol of political freedom. David has a prominent place in the Bible, and he is also one of the most famous kings in history.

Saul is Israel's first king. He is a Benjamite and son of a man named Kish who is from the Benjamite town of Gibeah. He starts out as a good and faithful king, but quickly falls into sin and loses the kingdom. He declines into madness and paranoia. His story is a somewhat tragic story of spoiled hopes.

In *David with the Head of Goliath* the artist painted himself as the beheaded Philistine. A master in the use of *chiaroscuro* (the interplay of light and dark parts in a pictorial work of art), Caravaggio understood his need for divine mercy —he had been arrested often, imprisoned, and in 1606, was even charged with murder.

## Main Characters

First and Second Samuel focus on three major characters: Samuel, Saul, and David. Samuel is the hero of the first part of Samuel. Born miraculously to a barren woman, Samuel grows up around the tabernacle in Shiloh, and becomes a prophet and a judge. He is also the Lord's instrument for anointing Saul and David as kings. He initiates the main actions of the book.

After Saul falls, David takes center stage. He begins as Saul's musician and armor-bearer and rises to prominence by killing the Philistine giant Goliath. Saul becomes jealous and seeks to kill him, but David shrewdly stays alive and takes over the kingdom after Saul's death. The rest of Samuel is about the reign of David, which is marked by David's sins, conflicts in his house and civil wars in his kingdom.

## Summary and Setting

The story of 1 & 2 Samuel concentrates on three men. First, there is the prophet Samuel. As a boy, he serves with Eli the high priest at the tabernacle at Shiloh, and during that time Yahweh appears to him and calls him to be a prophet. As a prophet, Samuel tells Eli that the house at Shiloh will be destroyed and that the family of Eli will lose the priesthood (1 Sam. 3:10–18), and he sets up something new in Israel—a monarchy, rule by a king.

The first king of Israel is Saul, a Benjamite. He starts out well, fighting heroically to deliver the city of Jabesh-gilead from the Ammonites and showing meekness toward some of his own people who had to that point not recognized his rule (1 Sam. 11). But, like Adam, Saul falls. First, he sins by offering a sacrifice without waiting for Samuel (1 Sam. 13); then he sins by attacking his son Jonathan, who has led Israel to victory over the Philistines (1 Sam. 14); finally, he sins by refusing to kill the Amalekite king Agag (1 Sam. 15). Because of his sins, the kingdom is torn from him and given to another man.

Yahweh tells Samuel to go anoint another king in the house of Jesse of Bethlehem (1 Sam. 16), and that young man who is the new king-designate is David, from the tribe of Judah. David proves himself by defeating the Philistine giant Goliath, and by serving as a commander in Saul's army. David's success makes Saul insanely jealous, and Saul begins to attack David and seek ways to kill him. David now has to fight the Israelite "giant" (1 Sam. 10:23). Saul chases David around Israel, while David tries to evade him. David eventually flees from Saul's house and even out of the land of Israel. He finds safety with the Philistine king Achish, who gives him the town of Ziklag as a base. At the end of 1 Samuel, Saul dies in battle with the Philistines. David's actions toward Saul provide another example of 1 & 2 Samuel's teaching about change. Even though David is anointed king, he does not take things into his own hands. He avoids confronting Saul and refuses to fight him. Instead, he waits on God to give him the kingdom. David is a great example of faith, a man who trusts that God will keep His promises.

David immediately becomes king over the tribe of Judah, his own tribe, in Hebron, while Saul's son Ishbosheth (whose name means "Man of shame")

rules the other tribes. After a period of civil war, David becomes king over the whole of Israel. After seven years in Hebron, David conquers Jerusalem and moves his capital, and the ark of Yahweh, to that city. He conquers nations surrounding Israel, defeats the Philistines and brings peace to Israel. In many ways, David is a great and successful king.

Much of 2 Samuel, though, tells about David's sins and failures as a king and a father. He commits adultery with Bathsheba, and then arranges her husband's murder to cover it up. He repents when the prophet Nathan confronts him, but the consequences of his sin continue through the rest of his reign (2 Sam. 11–12). Amnon, one of David's sons, rapes David's daughter (and Amnon's half-sister) Tamar. To avenge her honor, Tamar's full brother, Absalom, kills Amnon, and then flees the land (2 Sam. 13). David eventually brings Absalom back to the land, and Absalom immediately begins to conspire to seize the throne from David (2 Sam. 15). Absalom's rebellion is successful for a time, forcing David from Jerusalem and driving him out of Israel east of the Jordan River. Joab, David's army commander, defeats Absalom's forces, and restores David to the throne (2 Sam. 19). But the end of David's reign is marked by turmoil and trouble. David limps to the end of his life.

Now a certain man saw it and told Joab, and said, "I just saw Absalom hanging in a terebinth tree!"

## Artistic Design

Whoever wrote 1 & 2 Samuel, it is clear that he wrote it very carefully. The writer organized his history in order to bring out certain themes. For example, there are three poetic sections in the book. The first is the song of Hannah, Samuel's mother, who sang a hymn to praise God for giving her a son (1 Sam. 2:1–10). The second is David's lament after the death of Saul and Jonathan (2 Sam. 1:17–27), right in the middle of the book. At the end of 2 Samuel there are two poems of David, one a long Psalm praising God for delivering His king (2 Sam. 22:1–51; cf. Psalm 18) and the other a brief poem describing a righteous ruler (2 Sam. 23:1–7). Each poem is about one of the principal characters in the book: Samuel, Saul and David. Each poem, also, is about kingship.

Another sign of the artistic design of the book is the fact that the story begins and ends with stories about the house of Yahweh.[3] At the beginning of the story, the tabernacle of Moses is at Shiloh, where it was established in the days of Joshua (Joshua 18:1; 1 Sam. 1:3). Because of the sins of the priests of God, God judges the tabernacle and lets the Philistines capture the ark (1 Sam. 4–6). God's house is torn apart, and the tabernacle is never put back together again. At the end of 2 Samuel, however, David builds an altar on a threshing floor in Jerusalem and offers sacrifice in order to stop a plague (2 Sam. 24:18–25). That same threshing floor becomes the site for Solomon's Temple (2 Chron. 3:1). In the middle of the book of Samuel, David brings the ark into Jerusalem and pitches a tent to house it (2 Sam. 6:12–19).

The story of Yahweh's house highlights the teaching in 1 & 2 Samuel on the issue of change. After the Mosaic tabernacle is torn down, it seems natural to put it back together again. Samuel never tries to do that, and neither does David. They know that God is planning something else. Yahweh does not want them to go back to the Mosaic tabernacle; He wants them to prepare for the Temple of Solomon.

## Worldview

Suppose you step into a river today and then step into the river at the very same spot tomorrow. Have you stepped into the same river? Heraclitus, one of the earliest Greek philosophers, said "No." You never step into the same river twice. The river may still be called the Nile or the Chattahoochee, but the water you stepped in yesterday is not the same water you step in today. And you have changed, both physically and mentally. You are older, and some of the cells of your body have sloughed off during the night. You are feeling better or worse than you did the day before.

First and Second Samuel, as we see above, is about change in Israel's politics, religion, worship and relation to the nations surrounding her. Israel is not the same Israel at the end of the book as they were at the beginning. Israel's history moves on, further down the stream toward the climax of her history in Jesus.

Then Saul said to his armorbearer, "Draw your sword, and thrust me through with it, lest these uncircumcised men come and thrust me through and abuse me." But his armorbearer would not, for he was greatly afraid. Therefore Saul took a sword and fell on it.

## Fathers and Sons

Relations between fathers and sons are important themes throughout the Old Testament. The book of Genesis is largely concerned with the clans and families of the patriarchs, and family struggles and dramas are frequent.

Nearly every major character in 1 & 2 Samuel has rebellious sons. Eli, the high priest at Shiloh at the beginning of 1 Samuel, is father to Hophni and Phinehas, whose sins against God and the people are "very great" (1 Sam. 2:17). Eli attempts to control his sons (1 Sam. 2:23–25), but his efforts are weak and ineffective. Eli is not wicked as his sons are, but his family loses the priesthood because he gives more honor to his sons than he gives to Yahweh (1 Sam. 2:29). Between the father and the son, the river flows on, and Israel is not the same.

Samuel comes into Eli's house as an adopted son, and he is a completely different character from Hophni and Phinehas. Yet, Samuel too fails as a father (1 Sam. 8:3). Though the Bible never blames Samuel for the state of his sons, he clearly fails to pass on his "ways."

David's sons are worse than all the rest. Amnon rapes his sister; Absalom murders Amnon and conspires to overthrow his father; Adonijah follows Absalom's example and attempts to take the throne away from Solomon (1 Kings 1–2). There are three key factors in understanding David's failure as a father. First, contrary to the law for kings (Deut. 17:16–17), David gathers wives here and there as he makes his way to the throne. 2 Samuel 3:2–5 lists six sons, each of whom has a different mother. A family like this is like a barrel of explosives waiting for a spark.

Second, David's sons often repeat his sins. Especially with regard to women, David's sons imitate their father's sins. When the sons imitate David's sins, however, they go a step further. David does not rape Bathsheba; he uses his position as king to seduce her, but does not actually force her. Amnon's rape of

In the spring, at the time when kings go off to war, David remained in Jerusalem. One evening he got up from his bed and from his roof he saw a woman bathing. The woman was very beautiful, and David sent someone to find out about her.

Tamar is worse than David's sin with Bathsheba, but in a sense Amnon's sin exposes the truth about David's original sin with Bathsheba. When Absalom takes over Jerusalem, he follows Ahitophel's advice and sleeps with David's concubines in a tent set up on the roof of the palace (2 Sam. 16:20–23).

Finally, David does nothing about Amnon and Absalom. When he hears that Amnon has raped Tamar, David "was very angry," but he does nothing to punish Amnon (2 Sam. 13:21). After Absalom kills Amnon, David foolishly forgives Absalom and allows him to return to the land (2 Sam. 14). David, a great warrior and a vigorous king, is strangely passive in dealing with the sins of his sons. As the book flows on toward the end, the river begins to sweep more and more things away.

When we look at the theme of fathers and sons in the book of Samuel, one striking fact stands out. Eli, Samuel, and David are all righteous men with unrighteous sons. But Saul, an unrighteous king, has an exemplary son, Jonathan. Jonathan is a courageous warrior who is willing to take risks to gain victory (1 Sam. 14). More impressive than that, he is incredibly humble. If David becomes king, Jonathan, of course, will not. Instead of opposing David, however, Jonathan willingly bows to Yahweh's choice, and acknowledges David as the true prince of Israel (1 Sam. 18:3–4).

The theme of fathers and sons in 1 & 2 Samuel shows how difficult it is for sinners to maintain faithfulness over time, over generations. Faithful fathers sometimes have unfaithful sons who undo everything their fathers have accomplished. Through all the changes that take place in our lives, we must work diligently so that one thing stays the same from generation to generation: we must work hard to ensure that our children keep to the Lord's ways.

## Politics

Israelite politics during this period are also in flux. Much of the story of 1 & 2 Samuel is concerned with Israelite politics, and particularly with the question of kingship. Some passages of 1 & 2 Samuel seem to be opposed to Israel having a king at all. When Samuel grows old, the elders of Israel ask for a king like the nations. Samuel is not pleased by this, but having a king is not wrong in itself. Jacob speaks of the "scepter" of the tribe of Judah (Gen. 49:10), and Moses tells Israel what kind of king they are to have (Deut. 17:14–20).

Though it is not wrong for Israel to have a king, Israel sins in asking for a king in this particular way and at this particular time. In

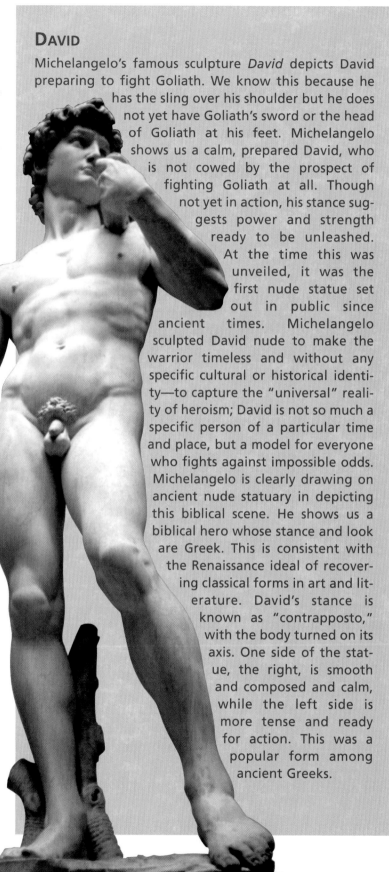

## DAVID

Michelangelo's famous sculpture *David* depicts David preparing to fight Goliath. We know this because he has the sling over his shoulder but he does not yet have Goliath's sword or the head of Goliath at his feet. Michelangelo shows us a calm, prepared David, who is not cowed by the prospect of fighting Goliath at all. Though not yet in action, his stance suggests power and strength ready to be unleashed. At the time this was unveiled, it was the first nude statue set out in public since ancient times. Michelangelo sculpted David nude to make the warrior timeless and without any specific cultural or historical identity—to capture the "universal" reality of heroism; David is not so much a specific person of a particular time and place, but a model for everyone who fights against impossible odds. Michelangelo is clearly drawing on ancient nude statuary in depicting this biblical scene. He shows us a biblical hero whose stance and look are Greek. This is consistent with the Renaissance ideal of recovering classical forms in art and literature. David's stance is known as "contrapposto," with the body turned on its axis. One side of the statue, the right, is smooth and composed and calm, while the left side is more tense and ready for action. This was a popular form among ancient Greeks.

1 Samuel 8:7, the Lord reveals to Samuel that Israel has asked for a king because they reject the Lord as their king. Israel has a king, and His name is Yahweh. He will fight for them, if they will but serve Him faithfully (1 Sam. 7). But Israel does not want this One to be king over them.

This passage gives us an interesting perspective on political change. Israel's desire for a king like the other nations was sinful, yet Yahweh planned for Israel to have a king. Even changes that come from sinful motives can be part of God's design for moving the world to a new order.

Though the Lord is displeased with the request, He tells Samuel to give the people what they ask for. But he also tells Samuel to warn the people about the "custom" of the king (1 Sam. 8:11). Samuel delivers one basic message: "You want a king like the nations, so you will get a king like the nations." Throughout Samuel's speech, the key word is "take," which is repeated six times (vv. 11, 13, 14, 15, 16, 17). The king will exalt himself to be equal with God, demanding, as God does, a tenth of Israel's increase (v. 17). Israel might as well go back to Egypt, for their king will treat them the same as Pharaoh did, taking everything important from them.

But 1 Samuel 8 is not the only passage in the book that deals with kingship. Near the end of 2 Samuel is a brief poem that describes the ideal king (2 Sam. 23:1-7). David writes that a king who rules in righteousness is one who rules in the fear of God (v. 3), and Yahweh compares such a ruler to the light of the morning sun (see Gen. 1:16). The king brings light out of darkness; he brings morning. The sun also brings fertility from the earth, causing vegetation to shoot up. Sunshine and rain make the land flourish like a fruitful garden (see Ps. 72:1-7). Under the light and warmth of a righteous king, the land becomes a land of milk and honey.

Is 1 & 2 Samuel in favor of monarchy? Or opposed to it? Neither. The issue is not monarchy itself. The issue is whether the king rules well, in the fear of Yahweh.

In addition to these passages about kingship, 1 & 2 Samuel include a lot of instruction about the nature of politics and the challenges of ruling well. First, David's relationship to Joab is worth noting. The first time we see Joab, he is involved in a violent incident that ends with Abner, the commander of Saul's armies, killing Asahel, Joab's brother (2 Sam. 2:13-32).

Shortly after, Joab takes revenge by killing Abner (2 Sam. 3:6-30). Much later, after David replaces Joab for killing Absalom (2 Sam. 19:13), Joab murders his replacement, Amasa (2 Sam. 20:4-13).

Given all this, we are left wondering why David would tolerate such as man as his commander. There are two main reasons. First, Joab is a "son of Zeruiah," and 1 Chronicles 2:16 tells us that Zeruiah is David's sister. Joab and his brothers are David's nephews, and that family connection forces David to tolerate their wickedness. Second, Joab knows all about David's affair with Bathsheba and his plot to kill Uriah. Joab is the one who gives the order for troops to withdraw from Uriah, leaving him exposed and vulnerable (2 Sam. 11:14-25). Joab has some dirt on David, and that gives Joab far more power than he should have.

First and Second Samuel also illustrate the importance of gifts, symbols and dramatic actions to political leadership. Politics is not all about brute power. It is about symbolism. For example: No doubt many in Israel believe that David has been trying to overthrow Saul. Nabal certainly considers David a rebel (1 Sam. 25:10). But David publicly chants a lament for Saul, where he describes Saul as "beloved and pleasant," "swifter than eagles" and "stronger than lions" (2 Sam. 1:23). This makes people think again about David's relationship to Saul. They will realize that David is not a rebel, but a faithful servant who honors Saul in life and in death. David does something similar after Joab murders Abner (2 Sam. 3:31-36).

Absalom shares his father's knack for impressing the people. He begins his conspiracy against David by getting a chariot and horses and hiring fifty men to run before him everywhere he goes (2 Sam. 15:1). Every time the people of Jerusalem see Absalom go by in his yellow stretch Hummer, surrounded by smartly-dressed Secret Service agents, they will know he is somebody important. He also wins over the people by treating them as equals to himself, even superiors. When an Israelite comes to Absalom, Absalom does not let him bow: "He would put out his hand and take hold of him and kiss him" (2 Sam. 15:5). Absalom runs around with an entourage like a rock star, but also wants people to think he is just a "regular guy."

Finally, 1 & 2 Samuel shows that love, expressed in giving gifts, is central to political leadership. The most dramatic example of this occurs at the end of 1 Samuel. David has been living in Philistine territory in

Ziklag and is among the Philistine troops that are going out to confront Saul at Gilboa (1 Sam. 29). When some Philistines object to David's presence in their army, he returns to Ziklag to find that Amalekite raiders have attacked his camp, plundered his goods and kidnapped his wives. He pursues them, defeats them in battle, and gets back all his goods (1 Sam. 30:1–25). Instead of keeping all the plunder for himself or for the men who fought with him, David shares it with the men who kept the baggage (1 Sam. 30:21–25) and then distributes the plunder to cities throughout Israel. This is an act of justice, since much of the Amalekite plunder was originally taken from these cities. But David's gifts are also a means for winning over portions of Israel to him. Instead of threatening them, he wins them over with kindness, with a gift. And by doing this, David also demonstrates that he will not be a king like the kings of the nations; he will not be a king who takes, but one who gives (see also 1 Sam. 31:11–13 with 2 Sam. 2:4–7; 2 Sam. 9).

—*Peter J. Leithart*

## For Further Reading

Leithart, Peter J. *A Son to Me.* Moscow, Idaho: Canon Press, 2003.

*Veritas Press Bible Cards: Judges through Kings.* Lancaster, Pa.: Veritas Press. 40–55.

# SESSION I: PRELUDE

## A Question to Consider

How should we respond to religious change? Cultural change? Political change?

*Discuss or list short answers to the following questions:*

1. Why is the book of Samuel divided into two books? When was it divided?
2. How can you tell that the story of 1 & 2 Samuel is a single story?
3. Who wrote Samuel? What are the other titles for the book?

The Dome of the Rock is an Islamic shrine situated on Mt. Moriah where Abraham worshiped the Lord after almost sacrificing his son and where David sacrificed to God. David's son Solomon would build the Temple on this spot. It has been under Muslim control since the times of the Crusades. The Dome of the Rock was built by the Muslim ruler Abd el-Malik in the late seventh century.

4. Give some illustrations of the books' artistic design.

5. Who are the main characters in 1 & 2 Samuel? What are the main events?

## READING FOR SESSION II:
Reading for Session II: 1 Samuel 1–14

# SESSION II: DISCUSSION
1 Samuel 1–14

## A Question to Consider

How should we respond to change?

*Discuss or list short answers to the following questions:*

### Text Analysis

1. What is the condition of Israel at the time as a result of Eli's wicked sons? (1 Sam. 1–4)
2. What political changes occur during the period that 1 & 2 Samuel describes? Worship changes?
3. What is Samuel's role in these changes?
4. Why did the tabernacle system at Shiloh fall apart? Why was the priesthood taken from Eli's family?
5. What is the relationship of Eli's sin and God's plan? In other words, did God want Israel to have a king and build a temple in which to worship God even though they resulted from Eli's sin?
6. What happened to the ark when it was brought back into the land? For advanced students: Why is this significant?
7. Why did the people want to change the political system? Was this good or bad? Why?

### Cultural Analysis

1. What kinds of political, cultural, and religious changes has our culture been experiencing recently? (Think about how a war affects our political system or how questions about biotechnology such as cloning might change our world.)
2. How have Christians responded to these changes? How have secularists (non-Christians) responded?
3. What form of government do we have in our country today? Is monarchy a good or bad form of government? What are the pluses and minuses of monarchy?

4. Assess this argument: If God controls everything (Eph. 1:3–14; Rom. 9:1–24), then all the changes that take place in the world are from Him. Therefore, we should accept and submit to whatever happens. Whatever happens must be right.

## SUMMA

*Write an essay or discuss this question, integrating what you have learned from the material above.*
How should we respond to change?

## Optional Activity

For advanced students: Samuel Rutherford's *Lex Rex* (1644) is a classic text in Christian political thinking. Have a student study questions 30–32 of the treatise, and summarize how Rutherford uses stories of David in his discussion.[4]

## READING FOR SESSION III:
1 Samuel 15–31

# SESSION III: RECITATION
1 Samuel 15–31

## Comprehension Questions

*Answer these questions for factual recall:*

1. What are the sins of Hophni and Phinehas?
2. What happens when the ark is taken into Philistia? What do these events mean?
3. Whom does Saul fight in his first battle? Is that battle successful?
4. What is Saul's first sin?
5. What is David's first job when he entered Saul's service?
6. How does David get a reputation as a great warrior?
7. How does Saul react to David's popularity?
8. Where does David go when he flees from the land of Israel?
9. What does David do when he has a chance to kill Saul?
10. What is the story of Nabal about, and what is it doing in 1 Samuel?

## Optional Activity

*John Dryden (1631–1700) wrote a poem about Absalom entitled* Absalom and Achitophel. *Read the abridged poem below and answer the following questions:*

**ABSALOM AND ACHITOPHEL** | John Dryden
In pious times, ere priestcraft did begin,
Before polygamy was made a sin;
When man on many multiplied his kind,
Ere one to one was cursedly confined;
When nature prompted, and no law denied,
Promiscuous use of concubine and bride;
Then Israel's monarch after heaven's own heart,
His vigorous warmth did variously impart
To wives and slaves; and, wide as his command,
Scattered his Maker's image through the land.
Michal, of royal blood, the crown did wear,
A soil ungrateful to the tiller's care:
Not so the rest; for several mothers bore
To godlike David several sons before.
But since like slaves his bed they did ascend,
No true succession could their seed attend.
Of all the numerous progeny was none
So beautiful, so brave, as Absalon;
Whether inspired by some diviner lust,
His father got him with a greater gust;
Or that his conscious destiny made way,
By manly beauty, to imperial sway.
Early in foreign fields he won renown,
With kings and states, allied to Israel's crown;
In peace the thoughts of war he could remove,
And seemed as he were only born for love.
Whate'er he did, was done with so much ease,
In him alone 'twas natural to please;
His motions all accompanied with grace,
And paradise was opened in his face.
With secret joy indulgent David viewed
His youthful image in his son renewed;
To all his wishes nothing he denied,
And made the charming Annabel his bride.
What faults he had,—for who from faults is free?
His father could not, or he would not see.
Some warm excesses, which the law forbore,
Were construed youth that purged by boiling o'er;
And Amnon's murder, by a specious name,
Was called a just revenge for injured fame.
Thus praised and loved, the noble youth remained,
While David undisturbed in Sion reigned.
But life can never be sincerely blest;
Heaven punishes the bad, and proves the best.
The Jews, a headstrong, moody, murmuring race,
As ever tried the extent and stretch of grace;
God's pampered people, whom,
    debauched with ease,
No king could govern, nor no God could please;
Gods they had tried of every shape and size,
That godsmiths could produce, or priests devise;
These Adam-wits, too fortunately free,
Began to dream they wanted liberty:
And when no rule, no precedent was found,
Of men, by laws less circumscribed and bound;
They led their wild desires to woods and caves,
And thought that all but savages were slaves.
They who, when Saul was dead, without a blow,
Made foolish Ishbosheth the crown forego;
Who banished David did from Hebron bring,
And with a general shout proclaimed him king;
Those very Jews, who at their very best,
Their humour more than loyalty exprest,
Now wondered why so long they had obeyed
An idol monarch, which their hands had made;
Thought they might ruin him they could create,
Or melt him to that golden calf,—a State.
But these were random bolts; no formed design,
Nor interest made the factious crowd to join:
The sober part of Israel, free from stain,
Well knew the value of a peaceful reign;
And, looking backward with a wise affright,
Saw seams of wounds dishonest to the sight;
In contemplation of whose ugly scars,
They curst the memory of civil wars.
The moderate sort of men, thus qualified,
Inclined the balance to the better side;
And David's mildness managed it so well,
The bad found no occasion to rebel.
But when to sin our biassed nature leans,
The careful devil is still at hand with means,
And providently pimps for ill desires;
The good old cause, revived, a plot requires.
Plots, true or false, are necessary things,
To raise up commonwealths, and ruin kings.

1. How does Dryden describe David?
2. How does Dryden describe David's attitude toward Absalom?
3. Research John Dryden's life. Was his poem directed at anyone in his own time? How is Dryden's poem a satire? Discuss the uses of satire.

 **READING FOR SESSION IV:**
2 Samuel

# SESSION IV: RECITATION
2 Samuel

## Comprehension Questions

*Answer these questions for factual recall:*

1. How does war break out between Saul's house and David's?
2. Describe the transport of the ark into Jerusalem.
3. How does David attempt to cover up his sin with Bathsheba?
4. Who is Nathan? What does Nathan do?
5. Who is Amnon and what does he do? How is this related to David's sin?
6. Who is Absalom, and what does he do?
7. Who is Ahitophel? Why does he hang himself?
8. Who is Mephibosheth? Who is Ziba? What does Ziba do?
9. Why does David have to kill several members of Saul's house?

# SESSION V: DISCUSSION

## A Question to Consider

What are the characteristics of a great political leader?

*Discuss or list short answers to the following questions:*

## Text Analysis

1. How does David work to secure the approval of the people of Israel?
2. Describe some ways that David uses drama and symbolism to make him a favorite of the people, thereby strengthening himself politically?
3. Give some examples of situations where David's kindness and love are politically expedient (i.e., helped him become more popular toward becoming a political leader).
4. What does the story of Bathsheba tell us about the connection of private sin and public office?
5. How does David's failure to control his family affect his rule as king?

6. Discuss the symbolism of the poem in 2 Samuel 23:1-7. What does this tell us about the importance of having good rulers?

## Cultural Analysis

1. How do our present leaders measure up to David as a political leader? Do they meet the description of leaders in 2 Samuel 23:1-7?
2. Give some examples of how today's political leaders try to secure power by the use of symbols, gestures and drama. Think particularly about how the media is used in political campaigns.
3. What is the difference between securing power by giving gifts and securing power by bribery? Was David engaged in bribery with the cities of Israel? Why or why not? Is bribery always wrong?

## Biblical Analysis

1. Compare and contrast David as king to some of the other great kings in Israel's history. How does his reign compare to Solomon's (1 Kings)? Hezekiah's (2 Kings 18, 19)? Josiah's (2 Kings 21-23)?
2. Examine Romans 13:1-7. What does this passage tell us about political powers?

## SUMMA

*Write an essay or discuss this question, integrating what you have learned from the material above.* What are the qualities of a great political leader?

### ENDNOTES
1  Since our Bibles divide the book of Samuel into two books, I need to refer to passages in "1 Samuel" and "2 Samuel."
2  Charlemagne or "Charles the Great" was the king of the Franks who established a Frankish Christian empire in the eighth and early ninth century. The "Carolingian" kings were those that followed him in succession.
3  "Yahweh" is the name of God in the Old Testament. In most English Bibles, the Hebrew word is translated as "LORD," but that is not a good translation. "Yahweh" is a personal name, like Peter or Sam or Emily, not a title like *Lord, King* or *Sir.*
4  It is available online at the time of publication at: www.constitution.org/sr/lexrex.htm.
5  *This endnote appears only in the teacher's edition.*

# FIRST AND SECOND KINGS

The history of the world is about the rise and fall of nations. Nations become powerful and wealthy for a time, but eventually they lose power and influence. Some simply disappear from the globe. A few modern nations can claim roots in the ancient world—Egypt for instance—but many of the people and nations that the Bible talks about vanished long ago into dust and ruins.

Percy Bysshe Shelley, the English Romantic poet, reflected on this in his famous poem, "Ozymandias":

*I met a traveler from an antique land*
*Who said: Two vast and trunkless legs of stone*
*Stand in the desert. Near them, on the sand,*
*Half sunk, a shattered visage lies, whose frown,*
*And wrinkled lip, and sneer of cold command,*
*Tell that its sculptor well those passions read,*
*Which yet survive, stamped on these lifeless things,*
*The hand that mocked them, and the heart that fed,*
*And on the pedestal these words appear:*
*"My name is Ozymandias, King of Kings:*
*Look upon my works, ye Mighty, and despair!"*
*Nothing beside remains. Round the decay*
*Of that colossal wreck, boundless and bare*
*The lone and level sands stretch far away.*

Despite his boasts, nothing remains of Ozymandias's kingdom but the fragments of a monument amid endless tracks of sand.

But *why* do nations rise and fall? Can we determine why some nations become powerful? Can we understand why they eventually collapse?

First and Second Kings is the story of the rise and fall of Israel, and the story of Israel includes the story of the rise and fall of two nations within Israel—the Northern Kingdom of Israel and the Southern Kingdom of Judah. Studying this book will help us to understand why Ozymandias and other proud leaders like him ended up the way they did.

## GENERAL INFORMATION

### Author and Context

The books we call 1 and 2 Kings were originally one book. Like 1 and 2 Samuel and 1 and 2 Chronicles, Kings was divided into two books in the Septuagint, the Greek translation of the Old Testament. The book was divided in two probably because the book was too long to fit on just one scroll. In Greek and Russian Orthodox churches, these books are known as "Third and Fourth Kingdoms," following "First and Second Kingdoms" (the books we call 1 and 2 Samuel).

As with 1 and 2 Samuel, the story of 1 and 2 Kings is a single story. This is clear in a number of ways. First, one of the main events early in the book is the building and dedication of the Temple (1 Kings 6–8). The last event of 2 Kings is the destruction of the Temple and the exile of Judah (2 Kings 25). So, Kings is about the Temple built and the Temple destroyed.

Another sign that the book tells a unified story is the fact that the book begins and ends with a united kingdom of Israel. Under Solomon, all the tribes are part of one kingdom (1 Kings 1–11). Jeroboam takes ten of the tribes out of the house of David and establishes

David charged Solomon to keep God's commandments as written in the Law of Moses, so that the LORD would fulfill His word: "If your sons take heed to their way, to walk before Me in truth with all their heart and with all their soul . . . you shall not lack a man on the throne of Israel."

the Northern Kingdom (1 Kings 12). For most of 1 and 2 Kings, the story goes back and forth between Israel (the Northern Kingdom) and Judah (the Southern Kingdom). Eventually, Josiah reunites the kingdom. One of Josiah's most important acts is to destroy the shrine at Bethel (2 Kings 23:15–20), which had been a center of idolatrous worship for the kingdom of Israel (1 Kings 12:29). First and Second Kings moves from the glory of a united kingdom, through a division, to reunion, and then to destruction. It is one sustained story.

No one knows for sure who wrote 1 and 2 Kings. We know that the writer was alive at the time of Judah's exile in Babylon. He describes Nebuchadnezzar's invasions of Judah and his attack on Jerusalem (2 Kings 25). But he does not describe the return from exile under Cyrus the Persian. The last scene of 2 Kings is about Jehoiachin, Josiah's grandson and a later king of Judah (2 Kings 25:27–30). In this, Kings differs from 1 and 2 Chronicles, which ends with the decree of Cyrus that gives Israel permission to return to their land (2 Chronicles 36:22–23). From this, we can see that Kings was written during the exile and not after the exile ended.

## Significance

All Scripture speaks about Jesus, and 1 and 2 Kings is no exception. Jesus is the Greater Solomon, who rules in wisdom and does not turn away from His Father. John the Baptist is another Elijah, and Jesus is another Elisha, performing miracles of healing. Even Jehu, who overthrows the dynasty of Omri in a bloodbath, is like Jesus. When Jehu is acclaimed king, his soldiers lay their garments in his path (2 Kings 9:13), as the Jews of Jerusalem do when Jesus enters Jerusalem centuries later.

The book of Kings explains why Israel and Judah ended in exile. The exile in Babylon is one of the great events of Israel's history. Israel is taken from Egypt to inherit the land promised to Abraham, and for centuries Israel remains in the land, despite recurrent sins and rebellions. Finally, Yahweh has had enough. The land spews Judah out into Babylon. This is the most devastating event in Israel's history. Even in the time of Jesus, Jews remember the exile and many think that it has never ended. According to the New Testament, Jesus brings the final end of Israel's exile by delivering His people from sin.

## Main Characters

First Kings begins with the story of David's death and the establishment of Solomon as king in Israel (chaps. 1–2). In a dream, Yahweh, the God of Israel, offers Solomon a gift of his choice, and Solomon chooses wisdom (3:1–15). Solomon displays his wisdom by giving wise judgments (3:16–28), organizing the kingdom (chap. 4), entering alliance with Hiram of Tyre (chap. 5), and overseeing the building of the Temple (chaps. 6–8). Yet Solomon breaks all the laws of kingship from Deuteronomy 17: He accumulates gold (1 Kings 10:14), horses and chariots (10:26–29), and wives (11:1–8). His wives turn him away from Yahweh, and because of that Yahweh gives a portion of the kingdom to Solomon's adversary, Jeroboam (11:26–40; chap. 12).

Jeroboam sets up golden calves at Bethel and Dan and establishes a sinful new form of worship for the Northern tribes (12:25–33). A prophet prophesies that the altar at Bethel will be destroyed by Josiah (13:1–5), but Jeroboam does not repent of his idolatry. Throughout the history of the Northern Kingdom, the kings lead Israel in idolatrous worship and ignore prophets.

Because of Jeroboam's idolatry, his dynasty does not last very long, and neither does the dynasty that follows. When the dust clears, Omri, a former general, has taken control of the North, and he establishes the strongest dynasty in the history of Israel (1 Kings 16:15–28). His son, Ahab, is a powerful king, but a wicked one. Like Jeroboam, he continues to worship golden calves and, with the help of his wife, Jezebel, establishes Baal worship in the land and rebuilds the city of Jericho (16:29–34). During his reign, Ahab fights often with the Arameans (or Syrians).

During Ahab's reign, Yahweh raises up one of the greatest prophets in Israel's history, Elijah. He challenges Ahab's idolatry and cruelty as a ruler and calls the people to repent of their sins. Elisha follows and works to establish the "sons of the prophets" throughout the land of Israel. Elisha is particularly known for his miracles, which are like the miracles of Jesus.

Ahab will not listen to Elijah, and his sons will not listen to Elisha. Yahweh therefore commissions Jehu, an army commander, to overthrow the house of Ahab (2 Kings 9–10). The house of David has become closely allied with the house of Ahab. When Jehu

So King Solomon answered and said, "Give the first woman the living child, and by no means kill him; she is his mother." And all Israel heard of the judgment which the king had rendered; and they feared the king, for they saw that the wisdom of God was in him to administer justice.

destroys the house of Ahab, he kills many in the house of David, and for a time Athaliah, the daughter of Ahab and Jezebel, sits on David's throne (2 Kings 11). Through Jehoiada, a faithful priest, Yahweh preserves Joash, a Davidic prince, from Athaliah and restores the dynasty of David to the throne (2 Kings 11–12).

Jehu destroys the house of Ahab, but he does not turn from idolatry (2 Kings 10:29–31). His dynasty lasts only a few generations before being cut off. From that point, Israel rapidly degenerates to chaos, and in 722–721 B.C. the Assyrians invade and conquer Samaria (2 Kings 17).

When Samaria falls, it is a warning to the Southern Kingdom. Judah also worships idols, so Judah also is in danger. Some kings of Judah do take the warnings seriously, and during the century after the fall of Samaria, Judah has some of its best kings. The first of these is Hezekiah. He is the first king to get rid of the places of worship on the "high places." A "high place" is a place of worship on a mountain or hill. According to Deuteronomy 12, the Temple is supposed to be the only place where the people of Yahweh worship. But through most of Judah's history, the kings set up high places elsewhere (e.g., 1 Kings 14:23). Because of his faithfulness, the Lord protects Hezekiah from the Assyrians (2 Kings 18–19; Isa. 36–37).

Manasseh follows Hezekiah, and undoes everything his father did. Manasseh is the Ahab of the Southern Kingdom, setting up idols in God's house (21:4) and filling Jerusalem with innocent blood (21:16).

After the brief reign of Manasseh's son Amon, Josiah comes to the throne at the age of eight, and there is another great change in Judah. Like Hezekiah, Josiah purges the land of idols, removes the high places, and thus starts to turn Judah back to the Lord. He also reunites Israel and Judah, so that, like David and Solomon, he rules over a single kingdom (2 Chron. 35:16–19). During his reign, the priests find the book of the law in the Temple, and when the law is read, Josiah and all Judah repent and renew the covenant with the Lord.

*Chart 1:* **THE KINGS IN KINGS**

**THE UNITED MONARCHY**

| DATES | |
| --- | --- |
| 1020–1000 | Saul |
| 1000–961 | David |
| 961–922 | Solomon |

**THE DIVIDED KINGDOMS**

| DATES | ISRAEL (Northern) | JUDAH (Southern) | DATES |
| --- | --- | --- | --- |
| 922–901 | Jeroboam I | Rehoboam | 922–915 |
| | | Abijah | 915–913 |
| | | Asa | 913–873 |
| 901–900 | Nadab | | |
| 900–877 | Baasha | | |
| 877–876 | Elah | Jehoshaphat | 873–849 |
| 876 | Zimri/Tibni | | |
| 876–869 | Omri | | |
| 869–850 | Ahab | | |
| 850–849 | Ahaziah | Jehoram | 849–843 |
| 849–843 | Joram (Jehoram) | Ahaziah | 843 |
| 843–815 | Jehu | Athaliah | 843–837 |
| 815–802 | Jehoahaz | Joash | 837–800 |
| 802–786 | Jehoash (Joash) | Amaziah | 800–783 |
| 786–746 | Jeroboam II | Uzziah (Azariah) | 783–742 |
| 746–745 | Zachariah | Jotham (co–regent) | 750–742 |
| 745 | Shallum | Jotham (king) | 742–735 |
| 745–737 | Menahem | | |
| 737–736 | Pekahiah | | |
| 736–732 | Pekah | Ahaz | 735–715 |
| 732–724 | Hoshea | | |
| 721 | **FALL OF ISRAEL** | | |
| | | Hezekiah | 715–687 |
| | | Manasseh | 687–642 |
| | | Amon | 642–640 |
| | | Josiah | 640–609 |
| | | Jehoahaz | 609 |
| | | Jehoiakim (Eliakim) | 609–598 |
| | | Jehoiachin (Jeconiah) | 598–597 |
| | | Zedekiah (Mattaniah) | 597–586 |
| | | **FALL OF JUDAH** | 586 |

Yahweh promises to wait before bringing the final judgment against Jerusalem and Judah (2 Kings 22:14–20).

Despite Josiah, the Lord is still angry over the sins of Manasseh (2 Kings 23:26–27; 24:4). By this time, Babylon and Egypt are fighting about who will control Judah. Several kings of Judah rebel against Babylon, and Babylonian armies make three invasions into Judah. Finally, Nebuchadnezzar decides to teach Judah a lesson, and so he returns and captures the city, breaking down its walls and destroying Solomon's Temple. And so Judah goes the way of Israel into exile.

## Summary and Setting

First and Second Kings cover about four centuries of Israel's history, from the end of David's reign (around 960 B.C.) to the fall of Jerusalem to Nebuchadnezzar and the Babylonians (586 B.C.). Chart 1 plots the reigns of the kings during these years. The chronology of this period is a complicated area of study, so some of these dates may not be exact, but this gives a good idea of the sequence of events.

## Artistic Design

Much of Kings is divided into sections that summarize the reign of an individual king. A good illustration of the basic pattern comes from 1 Kings 15:

**BEGINNING OF THE REIGN:**
"In the eighteenth year of King Jeroboam . . . Abijam became king over Judah" (v. 1).
**LENGTH OF THE REIGN:**
"He reigned three years in Jerusalem" (v. 2).
**THE GODLINESS OR UNGODLINESS OF THE KING:**
"he walked in all the sins of his father" (v. 3).
**EVENTS OF THE REIGN:**
"And there was war between Rehoboam and Jeroboam all the days of his life." (v. 6).
**SOURCE FOR MORE DETAILS:**
"Now the rest of the acts of Abijam . . . are they not written in the Book of the Chronicles of the Kings of Judah?" (v. 7).
**DEATH NOTICE:**
"And Abijam slept with his fathers and they buried him in the city of David" (v. 8).
**SUCCESSOR:**
"and Asa his son became king in his place" (v. 8).

The big picture of the book of Kings also has an artistic design. This becomes clear when we consider the life of Omri, the father of Ahab and the founder of the most important dynasty in the history of the Northern Kingdom. In many ways, Omri's life is like the life of David:

The king before Omri is Zimri. Zimri's reign lasts only a week, and he dies by setting fire to the king's house in Tirzah and letting it burn down over him (1 Kings 16:18). This reminds us of Saul's suicide (1 Sam. 31:3–4).

Prior to becoming king, Omri serves as "commander of the host" (1 Kings 16:16), a position similar to David's under Saul (1 Sam. 18:13).

As commander, Omri fights Philistines (1 Kings 16:15–16). David makes his reputation as a warrior by fighting the Philistine giant Goliath and by killing his "ten thousands" of Philistines (1 Sam. 17; 18:6–7, 20–30).

After Zimri's death, Omri fights a civil war against Tibni ben-Gineath and eventually prevails (1 Kings 16:21–22). This is like "long war" between David and Ishbosheth of the house of Saul (2 Sam. 3:1).

Both David and Omri have two capitals during their reigns. After defeating Ishbosheth, David remains in Hebron for seven-and-a-half years (2 Sam. 5:5) before conquering Jerusalem and making it his capital (2 Sam. 5:6–16). After conquering Tibni, Omri retains the capital at Tirzah for six years (1 Kings 16:23) before purchasing Samaria (v. 24).

David conquers his capital, while Omri buys his. But Omri's purchase of the hill of Shemer is like David's purchase of the threshing floor of Araunah in Jerusalem (2 Sam. 24:18–25).

Omri's reign is like David's. But Omri worships idols and is "more wicked than all who were before him" (1 Kings 16:25–26). Omri is a "new David," but he is more like a photo negative of David.

We can also examine the similarities between Jeroboam and David. Jeroboam's life story is found in 1 Kings 11:

Jeroboam begins as a servant to Solomon (1 Kings 11:26–28), as David is to Saul.

A prophet, Ahijah, tells Jeroboam he will be king

## CANAANITE MYTHOLOGY

*2 Kings 17:16: So they left all the commandments of the LORD their God, made for themselves a molded image and two calves, made a wooden image and worshiped all the host of heaven, and served Baal.*

Readers are often perplexed by how quickly the Israelites abandoned the true God for idol worship. How could they sacrifice to mere fertility gods when they knew Yahweh? A brief overview of Canaanite mythology may help to explain things.

The Bible makes it clear that incomplete obedience led to this chronic problem. At his death, Joshua told Israel that their failure to completely drive out the Canaanites would become a snare to them (Josh. 23:12–13). One of the main snares would be that the Israelites would fall into idolatrous worship of other gods. This type of senseless worship was a punishment visited by God on His people when they turned away from Him. One of the first instances of this rebellion occurs at the foot of Mt. Sinai while Moses is receiving the Ten Commandments. At the foot of the mountain Aaron makes a golden calf for the people to worship. This foolishness leads to further wickedness, because worshiping idols makes people like the idols that they worship. Thus, it is only after the worship of the golden calf that the Israelites are called a "stiff-necked" people (they are stiff-necked like cattle). Idolatrous paganism was often associated with wild parties and sexual immorality, and often Israel was seduced into idolatry through intermarriage (Num. 25). The pagan gods offered a veritable cornucopia of deities.

The gods and goddesses that cause most of the trouble in 1 and 2 Kings are Baal and Asherah. The word *baal* means "lord" and was used for the Canaanite god Hadad. The son of Dagon, consort of Anat, and brother and lover of Asherah, Baal was the main Canaanite god of sky, weather, and fertility. Baal statues often depict him wearing a conical hat with horns that conveys the strength and fertility associated with bull imagery. In one hand he holds a club that represents his military strength and in the other a stylized lightning bolt which symbolizes his role as a storm god. In Greek mythology, Baal would be the parallel of Zeus. Baal's daughters were Pidray, the maid of light, Tallay, the maid of rain, and Arsay, the maid of floods.

Baal's consort, Asherah, was the fertility, love and war goddess. In Greece she would be similar to Aphrodite and in Mesopotamia she would be known as Ishtar. Asherah was represented by an unshaped pole of wood or a naked, curly-haired goddess riding a lion and holding lilies and serpents. It was in her temple that the Philistines hung Saul's armor.

There were two other main gods in Canaanite mythology. Mot was the god of death and sterility. Yam was the chaotic god of the sea. The Canaanite myths describe the struggles of Baal, the god of fertility, with these representatives of the forces of chaos, death, and sterility.

While it might seem almost comical to us that people would worship these weird gods, we must not be so easily duped. Man's heart is an idol-making factory, and our compromises today, although more subtle, are just as damnable. Today, we too often find Christians preoccupied with power, wealth or some other insidious idol that receives their devotion.

over ten tribes (1 Kings 11:29–39). Samuel the prophet anoints David while Saul is still king (1 Samuel 16).

After Solomon learns that Jeroboam is going to be king, he tries to kill Jeroboam (1 Kings 11:40), as Saul tries to kill David (1 Sam. 18:10-11).

Jeroboam flees to Egypt for safety (1 Kings 11:40), as David flees to Philistia (1 Sam. 27:1).

After Solomon's death, Jeroboam takes control of a part of the kingdom (1 Kings 11:42; 12:1-24). David returns to the land after Saul's death and rules Judah and then the rest of the tribes.

Jeroboam is like Solomon because he builds a high place (like the Temple) and establishes a new way of worship for the Northern tribes (1 Kings 12:25-33).

The beginning of the united kingdom of Israel is like the beginning of the Northern Kingdom of Israel and both are like the beginning of the major dynasty of the Northern Kingdom.

The end of the Omride dynasty is similar to the end of the Southern Kingdom of Judah. Jehu, who destroys the Omrides, moves from the destruction of a royal house to the destruction of a house of worship, the house of Baal in Jerusalem (2 Kings 10:18-36). Likewise, 2 Kings 25 says that the Chaldeans slaughter the sons of Zedekiah and take him into exile (vv. 1-7), and then describes the destruction of the house of Yahweh in Jerusalem (vv. 8-17). Following Jehu, there is not a Davidic king in Jerusalem. After seven years of Athaliah's reign, Joash, a descendant of David, is restored to the throne in Jerusalem (2 Kings 11). There is a revival of David's dynasty. Likewise, after the Babylonians destroy the Temple, there is no Davidic king in Judah.

There are also parallels between the fall of the Northern Kingdom and the fall of the South, that is, between the fall of Jeroboam's kingdom and the fall of the kingdom of David. Hoshea, the last king of Israel, rebels against the Assyrian king (2 Kings 17:1-4a), leading the Assyrians to invade Israel, besiege Samaria, and take Israel into exile (17:5-6). After the Northern king falls, a temple is destroyed: Josiah destroys the shrine at Bethel (2 Kings 23). Finally, after the North falls, Hezekiah leads a revival of Judah (2 Kings 18:1-8). At the very end of Kings, this all happens again. Jehoiakim of Judah rebels against Babylon (2 Kings 24:1), leading the Babylonians to invade Judah, besiege Jerusalem, and take Judah into exile (24:10-17). Nebuchadnezzar kills kings and

destroys Solomon's Temple. But then we read of Jehoiachin, who is brought out of prison in Babylon and given a place at the table of King Evil-Merodach (2 Kings 25:27-30).

These stories show one of the major themes of Kings: Yahweh punishes the guilty, but He is faithful to His promises to David. Nations fall when they reject Yahweh. But Yahweh's promises and word are victorious. Even when the Davidic dynasty looks dead, Yahweh raises it from the dust.

## Worldview

The nations of the world can seem to be like plants. They are usually rooted in the ground, confined to one place. Their customs seem to grow as naturally as acorns do on oaks. This is true in some sense, and Jesus compared His own kingdom to a mustard plant that grows from a small seed. This is why some people think of nations going through "infancy," "youth," and "old age," before they "die."

In the Bible, though, nations are often compared to buildings and houses than to plants. This gives us a different picture of the nation. Houses don't grow "naturally;" they have to be built. Nations are the same way. People work to make nations. They don't grow and prosper without human beings working. Nations rise like a house, because they are built; and nations lose power and prosperity when they are not maintained, or when they are broken down. Human beings build and tear down nations; ultimately, God builds and destroys them.

What is necessary to build a nation? And why does God break down nations? These questions are answered in 1 and 2 Kings.

### *Word of God: Prophecy*

First, the word of God builds a nation, provided the nation responds to it with faith and obedience. Prophecy and the word of God are important issues in 1 and 2 Kings. At the center of the book is a long section about two of the greatest prophets of Israel, Elijah and Elisha, and there are other prophets mentioned throughout the book: Ahijah (1 Kings 11), the "man of God from Judah" (1 Kings 13), Micaiah (1 Kings 22), Isaiah (2 Kings 19), and Huldah the prophetess (2 Kings 22:14).

Many events happen as a fulfillment of the word

of God. Abiathar the priest is removed from his office to fulfill the word spoken against Eli (1 Kings 2:27). Jeroboam's son Abijah dies according to the word of the prophet Ahijah (1 Kings 14:18), and the house of Jeroboam is destroyed to fulfill another prophecy of Ahijah (1 Kings 15:29). When Hiel the Bethelite loses a son because he rebuilds Jericho, it fulfills a prophecy of Joshua, spoken centuries before (1 Kings 16:34; Joshua 6:26).

The words of Elijah and Elisha are especially powerful. Elijah's word stops the rain (1 Kings 17:1) and keeps the widow's jar of oil full (1 Kings 17:16). All that he speaks against Jezebel and the house of Ahab comes to pass (2 Kings 10:10, 17). Elisha's word multiplies loaves of bread (2 Kings 4:44), and he predicts a sudden decline in the price of flour in Samaria during a siege (2 Kings 7:1).

From Kings, we see that the word of the Lord is the most powerful force in history. The word of Yahweh shapes history. When nations respond to the word of Yahweh with faith and obedience, they are prosperous. When they resist and rebel against the word of God, they fall.

Through their prophetic word, Elijah and Elisha seek to restore Israel and move Israel into a new covenant. Elijah's life follows the story of Israel very closely. Like Jacob and his sons, Elijah is driven out of the land by a famine (1 Kings 17:1-4). In the wilderness, Elijah receives food from ravens. In a Passover scene, he raises the widow's son from the dead (vv. 8-24). Finally, he returns to the land. Elijah's life is an exodus, return, and conquest. By doing this, Elijah is bringing Israel into a new covenant, what some call the "remnant covenant."

Accepting the word of God is like giving a house a regular coat of paint, and repairing the damage done by weather. Refusing the word of God is like pulling out the cornerstone of a large building. It cannot stand.

### Idolatry

If the word of God builds nations, idolatry tears them apart. When nations worship things built by their own hands, they will eventually be torn by the hand of the Lord.

First and Second Kings illustrate this by recording the history of Israel in particular. Kings is designed to answer the question, Why are Israel and Judah in exile? The main answer is that they go into exile because they refuse to listen to the prophets (2 Kings 17:13-14). And the specific sin that the prophets attack is idolatry.

Idolatry is the chief sin of both the Northern and Southern Kingdoms, though it takes different forms. In the Southern Kingdom, the main problem is "high places." Not until Hezekiah's reign are the high places torn down (2 Kings 18:4).

In the north, Israel worships golden calves. Jeroboam says that Israel is worshiping the God who brought Israel from Egypt through golden calves (1 Kings 12). He is breaking the Second Commandment, which says that we are not to worship even the true God by using images or statues. The Northern Kingdom continues in this sin for its whole history (cf. 15:29-30; 15:34; 16:19; 16:26). The Second Commandment warns that those who hate God by worshiping Him through images will be punished to the third or fourth generations. And this is what happens to the kings of Israel. Only Jehu's dynasty lasts longer than four generations.

The theme of idolatry helps us answer the question we asked at the beginning of this study. Nations rise and fall depending on whom and how they worship. If a people worship the true God in His way, they prosper. If they worship idols, or worship the Lord falsely, they will fall.

### The Temple

Solomon's Temple symbolizes Israel, and the tearing down of the Temple means an end to the nation. The temple is one of the big issues in Kings. Good kings in Judah are ones that attack idolatry, remove false gods, and restore the temple. Solomon, the most glorious king of all, builds the temple. Joash, Hezekiah, and Josiah, three of the greatest kings of the Southern Kingdom, all work to rebuild the Temple when it breaks down.

Solomon's Temple is not exactly like the Tabernacle. Though the Tabernacle is beautiful, the Temple is more beautiful still. The Tabernacle has a bronze laver in the courtyard, but the Temple has a bronze "sea," decorated with gourds and resting on the backs of twelve oxen, along with ten water stands of bronze, set up in the courtyard, with five on each side (7:27-39). On either side of the door are two huge bronze pillars, Jachin and Boaz (7:15-22), with capitals formed like lilies and a collar of chains and pomegranates around the base of the capital.

The walls of the Holy Place and Most Holy Place are covered with cedar wood, and gourds, flowers, cherubim and palm trees are carved into it (1 Kings 6:29). Gold covers over the cedar (vv. 21–22), and even the floor of the Temple is gold (v. 30), replacing the dirt floor of the Tabernacle. In place of the veils of the Tabernacle, Solomon makes doors for the two rooms of the Temple (vv. 31–32). In the Most Holy Place, Solomon places two giant cherubim of olive wood, which are overlaid with gold (vv. 23–28). The Tabernacle has a single golden lampstand, but Solomon's Temple has ten golden lampstands, five on each side of the Holy Place, all of pure gold (7:49).

One of the main differences between the Tabernacle and the Temple is that the king's house is part of the Temple area. First Kings 6:1 begins the record of the building of the Lord's house, and this does not end until 7:51, which says that "all the work that King Solomon performed in the house of the Lord was finished." Between 6:1 and 7:51, though, the writer tells not only about the Temple but about Solomon's palace and other buildings that Solomon built for himself (7:1–8). The description of Solomon's palace comes right in the middle of this passage that is talking about building the "house of Yahweh." This means that Solomon's house and the Temple are both part of something called the "house of Yahweh."

Nothing like this has happened in Israel before. Priests serve in the Tabernacle, but there is no king's tent beside the tent of King Yahweh. But Solomon lives "in" the Lord's house, as prince over Israel.

Before the end of Kings, however, both the "house" that is Israel and the house that is in Israel are destroyed, taken into exile. Because Israel did not build on the word of God, but instead worshiped what they had built and in high places that they built, the Lord tears down the nation.

—*Peter J. Leithart*

## For Further Reading

Spielvogel, Jackson. *Western Civilization*. Fifth Edition. Belmont, Calif.: Wadsworth/Thompson Learning, 2003. 30–42.

*Veritas Press Bible Cards: Judges through Kings.* Lancaster, Pa.: Veritas Press. 59–64.

*Veritas Press Bible Cards: Chronicles through Malachi.* Lancaster, Pa.: Veritas Press. 65–73.

Leithart, Peter J. *A House For My Name*. Moscow, Idaho: Canon Press, 2000. 196–211.

 READING ASSIGNMENT: 1 Kings 1–11

Herod the Great rebuilt many fortresses and temples during his reign, but his most notable achievement was the building of the third Temple. It was begun in 20 B.C. and finished in A.D. 63—over fifty years after his death. On the south side he ordered a triple colonnade to be built that was called the Royal Portico—because it was the site where Solomon was crowned.

# SESSION I: PRELUDE
1 Kings 1–11

## A Question to Consider

Why do nations become strong and prosperous? Why do they become weak?

*Discuss or list short answers to the following questions:*

1. What are some of the other names for 1 and 2 Kings?
2. How can we tell that 1 and 2 Kings is one book with one story?
3. Who wrote Kings? What can we know about the author of Kings?
4. What time period does Kings cover?

## Optional Activity

*In 1622 the Flemish painter, Frans Francken II, crafted an oil painting entitled* The Idolatry of Solomon—*a popular theme for art made in Protestant countries at that time. Examine the painting (on the internet at http://www.getty.edu/art/collections/objects/oz656.html) and answer the following questions.*

1. Solomon is the old man with the long robe at the center of the painting. Who is pointing to the idol? Why is this significant? (Hint: See 1 Kings 11)
2. The right side of the painting is full of women. What was Francken trying to show?
3. Several men stand near the bottom on the left of the painting. Who do you think they are? How can you tell? (Hint: How well are they dressed?)
4. Can you tell what these men think about Solomon's actions? Why is it important that they are standing? (Hint: How does their posture compare with Solomon's?)
5. At the top left is a grove of trees leading to a building. What do you think that building is? Why is it in the picture? (Hint: How prominent is it?)
6. Francken was a native of Antwerp, in the area known then as Flanders.

A Judean king gives tribute to his Persian overlord.

Flemish painting had a long tradition of excellence, and Antwerp was one of the centers of art. It was also a place of religious conflict during the Reformation. When Francken was four years old (in 1585), the city fell to a Spanish army that was punishing the city for destroying images in the churches (this is called "iconoclasm"). How is this background important for understanding the painting? (Hint: How might this painting be used to bolster one side of the Reformation debate, especially concerning the Second Commandment? For a primer on the Protestant side of the debate read questions 49–52 in the Westminster Shorter Catechism.)

READING ASSIGNMENT:
1 Kings 12 – 2 Kings 4

# SESSION II: RECITATION
1 Kings 12–2 Kings 4

## Comprehension Questions

*Answer these questions for factual recall.*

1. What does Solomon do to remove Abiathar, Joab, and Shimei?
2. Describe Solomon's prayer at the Temple dedication.
3. What is the Queen of Sheba's reaction to Solomon's kingdom?
4. What does Jeroboam ask from Solomon's son, Rehoboam? What is Rehoboam's response?
5. What happens to the "man of God from Judah?"
6. How does Omri become king?
7. Who is Jezebel?
8. What does Elijah do for the widow of Zarephath?
9. What happens at Mount Carmel?
10. What happens in the battles with the Arameans?
11. Who is Naboth? What does Ahab do to him?
12. Describe Elijah's departure. What does Elisha do?
13. What does Elisha do for the Shunammite woman?

 **READING ASSIGNMENT:**
2 Kings 5–18

# SESSION III: DISCUSSION
2 Kings 5–18

## A Question to Consider

What do 1 and 2 Kings teach us about the rise and fall of nations?

*Discuss or list short answers to the following questions:*

### *Text Analysis*

1. How does Solomon secure his kingdom?
2. What kind of wisdom does Solomon ask for?
3. Why does he want this wisdom?
4. What is Solomon's first wise act?
5. What is the condition of Israel during Solomon's reign?
6. Why does Solomon lose part of his kingdom?

### *Cultural Analysis*

1. What nations have declined in power during the latter half of the twentieth century? What happened to them?
2. What are America's prospects for the future? What signs are there that we are going to increase in power and wealth? What signs that we are going to decline?

### *Biblical Analysis*

1. Study Leviticus 26 and Deuteronomy 28. How are the principles in those chapters reflected in the story of Kings?
2. Solomon asks for "wisdom to know good and evil" (1 Kings 3:9), using the same phrase that described the tree in the garden in Genesis 2–3. How are these two passages connected? What kind of wisdom is being offered in 1 Kings 3?
3. Examine the first chapter of Proverbs. What does that chapter say about wisdom? How does this wisdom help to build a nation?

### *Application*

In 1 Kings 3, two prostitutes come to Solomon with conflicting stories. There is no way to prove which story is true, since there were no witnesses other than the two women. Yet Solomon finds a way to discover who is telling the truth. How does this story illustrate how biblical wisdom operates?

Solomon was the wisest man of his time, and he continuously warns in Proverbs about the dangers of the "strange woman." Yet he loved foreign women who led him astray into idolatry. What does his story teach us? What does it tell us about the rise and fall of kings?

### SUMMA

*Write an essay or discuss this question, integrating what you have learned from the material above.*
Why do nations rise and fall?

 **READING ASSIGNMENT:**
2 Kings 19–25

# SESSION IV: DISCUSSION
2 Kings 19–25

## A Question to Consider

How should we respond when our nation comes under the judgment of God?

*Discuss or list short answers to the following questions:*

### Text Analysis

1. Look at the opening verses of Jeremiah 1. When did Jeremiah live? What is happening in Judah at the time?
2. Study Jeremiah 27 and 29. What does this chapter tell us about God's purposes for Nebuchadnezzar?
3. How do the different kings at the end of the kingdom of Judah react to Jeremiah's advice? Examine 2 Kings 24–25 to find out.
4. What is the result of the kings' actions?
5. Why does Kings emphasize the destruction of the Temple?
6. Why does Kings take so much space to describe the two great pillars that Nebuchadnezzar cut?

### Cultural Analysis

1. Study Romans 1:18–32. What are the signs that America is a nation under judgment?
2. How are Jeremiah 27 and 29 relevant to our situation? Is Jeremiah's situation the same as ours? Should we try to follow his counsel? How?
3. What does Psalm 115:1–8 tell us about the effects of idolatry? Can you apply that to the contemporary world?

### Biblical Analysis

1. Examine the chronological information in the first chapters of Daniel, and compare it to 2 Kings 24–25. What does this tell you? Why is this important?
2. Jeremiah gives more detail about the governorship of Gedaliah and his murder. Write a summary of the events recorded in Jeremiah 40–41.[1]

### SUMMA

*Write an essay or discuss this question, integrating what you have learned from the material above.*

How should we respond when God's judgment falls on our culture?

Michelangelo's Jeremiah sits brooding among the prophets on the Sistine Chapel—his head is hanging, his beard repeating the downward movement, his left hand is inert, and the verticals in the drapery around his legs direct the eyes downward. The composition of the figure underscores Jeremiah's dejection at the word of prophecy he must bring to God's people.

## Optional Activity

*Read the poem below and answer the questions that follow.*
**THE COMING OF SENNACHERIB** | George Gordon, Lord Byron

The Assyrian came down like the wolf on the fold,
And his cohorts were gleaming in purple and gold;
And the sheen of their spears was like stars on the sea,
When the blue wave rolls nightly on deep Galilee.

Like the leaves of the forest when Summer is green,
That host with their banners at sunset were seen:
Like the leaves of the forest when Autumn hath blown,
That host on the morrow lay withered and strown.

For the Angel of Death spread his wings on the blast,
And breathed in the face of the foe as he passed;
And the eyes of the sleepers waxed deadly and chill,
And their hearts but once heaved, and for ever grew still!

And there lay the steed with his nostril all wide,
But through it there rolled not the breath of his pride;
And the foam of his gasping lay white on the turf,
And cold as the spray of the rock-beating surf.

And there lay the rider distorted and pale,
With the dew on his brow, and the rust on his mail:
And the tents were all silent, the banners alone,
The lances unlifted, the trumpet unblown.

And the widows of Ashur are loud in their wail,
And the idols are broke in the temple of Baal;
And the might of the Gentile, unsmote by the sword,
Hath melted like snow in the glance of the Lord!

1. What events is Byron describing?
2. Why do you think he mentions "Galilee" in the first stanza?
3. What does the contrast of summer and autumn in the second stanza suggest?
4. Looking at the last stanza, how does Byron understand the conflict between Sennacherib and Israel?

# Session V: Activity

## The Black Obelisk of Shalmanezer III

*On the right is one of the most important archeological finds from ancient Nineveh, the Assyrian capital, the "black obelisk of Shalmanezer III." It was discovered in 1846 and is in the British Museum. The six-foot obelisk mentions Jehu and actually depicts Jehu bringing tribute to the Assyrians. Answer the following questions about the obelisk:*

1. Jehu is called *Ja'ua abal Humri*, "Jehu son of Omri." From Scripture we know that Jehu was not a descendant of Omri. Why does the obelisk identify him as such?
2. What does this identification say about Omri? How does that fit with the biblical portrait of Omri?
3. Israel was known as the "land of Omri" long after the Omride dynasty ended. What does this identification say about the Assyrian view of Israel?

Shalmanezer III's limestone obelisk contains in bas-relief the earliest surviving picture of an Israelite, with the inscription: "The tribute of Jehu, son of Omri: I received from him silver, gold, a golden bowl, a golden vase with pointed bottom, golden tumblers, golden buckets, tin, a staff for a king [and] spears."

## OPTIONAL SESSION

### Possible Review Questions

*Answer the questions from the Recitation in Session II.*

### Evaluation

*All tests and quizzes are to be given with an open Bible. Write one or two sentences on each of the following questions. (2 points each)*

1. How did Solomon gain wisdom? How did he display it?
2. Discuss the division of the kingdom following Solomon's reign.
3. What were the sins of Ahab? How did he die?
4. What happened at Mount Carmel?
5. Who was Jehu and what did he do?
6. How did Joash survive to return to the throne of David?
7. Why did the Northern Kingdom fall? Who conquered them?
8. What did the priests find in the Temple during the reign of Josiah? What effect did that discovery have?

*Demonstrate your understanding of the themes of 1 and 2 Kings by answering two of the following four questions in complete sentences. Answers should be a paragraph or two. (10 points per answer)*

1. Describe the standard form that Kings uses to summarize a king's reign. What important events do not follow this standard form?
2. Discuss the parallels between Omri, Jeroboam, and David. Why are these parallels significant?
3. What does 1 and 2 Kings teach about the power of the word of God's prophets?
4. Why did Israel and Judah fall before Assyria and Babylon? What does Kings teach about the rise and fall of nations?

*Answer one of the following two questions. These questions will require more substantial answers than the prior essays. (12 points per answer)*

1. Jesus said that the entire Old Testament speaks of Him. How does the book of Kings teach about Jesus?
2. What are the common features of the reigns of the three great later kings of Judah—Joash, Hezekiah, and Josiah? What achievements do they have in common? How are they similar in their failures?

### ENDNOTE:

1   At the time of publication the web site, MyJewishLearning.com, is offering this summary.

# ODYSSEY

The *Odyssey* is one of the most appreciated and loved classical works.

Although it is set in an ancient world, unknown to us, the themes of the poem have been accessible to readers ever since the poem was first composed, down to the present. Who does not understand the glory of coming home? And who does not derive satisfaction from reading about someone who comes home and puts everything right again?

(or chanting) in the courts of rulers and princes. All of this contributes to Mark Twain's joke that we now know that the works of Homer were not by him, but rather were the work of another blind, Greek poet with the same name. Although the dating of his life is also uncertain, we may tentatively place him in the eighth century B.C., which would make him a contemporary of the prophet Isaiah.

All this said, a few things must be noted about the form of this story. The *Odyssey* is an epic poem. But what does this mean? An epic is an extended

## GENERAL INFORMATION

### Author and Context

We know very little about Homer, other than the general time in which he lived, and the fact that he was a great poetic genius. He was blind, as many ancient poets were, and that is about all we can say. At the same time, some educated specula- tions are possible. He may have been a Greek from Ionia because of his apparent ignorance of how the Dorians in the Peloponnese lived. He is likely to have resembled the bards in the *Odyssey*, who earned their way by singing

Aiolos is the Greek god of the winds who lived on the floating island of Aiolia. He kept the mighty winds of the world in vast caves on the island and let them out as soft breezes, gales, or what- ever the major gods desired. When Odysseus visited the god, Aiolos gave him a bag holding all the contrary winds so that he might reach Ithaka with a fair wind.

narrative poem, which usually recounts the history or legendary history of the deeds of a national hero. Examples of primary epic would be Homer and *Beowulf*. Examples of secondary epic, or "spin-off" epic, would be Virgil and Milton. Secondary epic aims at a loftier style, but the audience is usually not sitting in a great hall after the battle, but rather is all by himself in an armchair with a book.

Epic poetry is formulaic poetry. Because it is long, and with a settled meter, the recurrence of certain phrases should not really be a

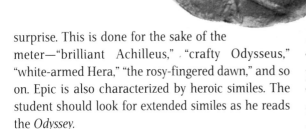

"A man of constant sorrow," Odysseus faced many trials and troubles as he traveled back to Ithaka and Penelope. He saw his men eaten by a Cyclops, turned into swine, snatched by Scylla. Finally, after his men unwisely killed the cattle of Helios and were wiped out, Odysseus mourned alone—as illustrated in this impression made from an ancient belt buckle.

surprise. This is done for the sake of the meter—"brilliant Achilleus," "crafty Odysseus," "white-armed Hera," "the rosy-fingered dawn," and so on. Epic is also characterized by heroic similes. The student should look for extended similes as he reads the *Odyssey*.

The meter in Homer is *dactylic hexameter*. This is the basic *heroic line* for the epic in the original Greek. This is very difficult to make work in English although some have tried it. This is (roughly) what it would sound like metrically in English. This is an example of dactylic hexameter:

> *strawberry strawberry strawberry*
> *strawberry strawberry jam pot*

This kind of epic poetry is *court* poetry. Remember that epic poetry was oral, meant to be *heard* in a great hall of a great king, in the midst of a great feast. Just as Shakespeare's plays were written to be *seen*, not read, so epic poetry was composed to be *heard*, not read.

## Significance

The central organizing principle of any culture is the religion of that culture. In a certain sense, we may say that *culture is religion externalized*. This means that what we see in culture is the outworking or practice of that culture's religion. But the "carrier" of religion is language, and the standardizing "carrier" of language is literature. This is why, for example, Homer's *Iliad* had the same kind of impact on ancient Greek culture that the King James Version of the Bible had on 17th century English-speaking peoples. It helped to shape the Greeks into a people, and the *Odyssey*, a companion epic to the *Iliad*, had the same shaping force. Not only was this the case for the Greeks, but because of the position of the Greeks in the history of Western culture, the *Odyssey* has had a continuing effect down to the present.

## Main Characters

The main characters in this work are Odysseus, the hero who is making his way back to Ithaka, his son, Telemachos, and his faithful wife, Penelope. Penelope is being pressured by a host of suitors, and one of the principal suitors is named Alcinous. Gods and goddesses who are important to the story are Zeus, Poseidon, Kalypso, and Circe.

## Summary and Setting

After ten years of fighting at Troy, Odysseus has sought to return home. He is detained in many different ways, and when the *Odyssey* opens he is on the island of Kalypso, ten years *after* the fall of Troy.

The first portion, Books 1–4, of the *Odyssey* is called the *Telemachy*, and this section shows how his son Telemachos is coming of age. He is old enough to understand the evil of his mother's suitors, but not quite old enough to do anything about it. He is on the brink of coming of age. This is very important, for in another sense, the same thing can be said about Odysseus.

When Kalypso gets the word from Hermes, who was sent by Zeus, Kalypso helps Odysseus build a raft and sends him off. Poseidon is the god who is out to get Odysseus, and so he stirs up a great storm. Odysseus washes ashore in the land of the Phaiakians, the princess of whom is Nausikaa. Odysseus is prevailed upon to tell them the story of his travels, and so in a flashback, he recounts what has happened to him—the Lotus-eaters, the Cyclops, the Sirens and the last disastrous incident with the cattle of Helios.

After this brief sojourn with the Phaiakians, they help him to return home to Ithaka, where he finds great uncertainty—the suitors pillaging his house, his faithful wife Penelope holding them off and his son ready to fight. He disguises himself as a beggar, giving the suitors ample time to repent, and then, in a dramatic conclusion, he kills them all.

The setting of this story is twenty years after the fall of Troy. This would place it around 1100 B.C., or shortly before the time of King David, during the period of the judges in the Bible. This would make Hector, Achilleus and Odysseus contemporaries with the prophet Samuel.

In this portion of a famous Florentine fresco, princess Nausikaa discovers Odysseus while her handmaidens play in the background. This piece was created in the 1500's by the painter and scholar Alessandro Allori.

## Worldview

Have you ever engaged in shadow boxing? Shadow boxing is when someone practices his fighting skills without having a real opponent there. While it can be good for developing reflexes, at the same time, shadow boxing is a good metaphor for an exercise in futility (1 Cor. 9:26). Someone who really fights is encountering an *actual* opponent, one who can fight back. Someone who is shadow boxing does not need to worry about getting hit.

Now when it comes to the spiritual warfare that existed in biblical times, too many Christians assume that this was a time of shadow boxing. Since all the gods and goddesses of antiquity were myths, believed in only by superstitious people, the victory of the Christian faith was in some sense a triumph over nothing. But as we will see, this is too simplistic. The apostles and evangelists who preached the gospel in the Greco/Roman world were not shadow boxing. But to get some idea of what they were doing, we have to understand the world of the *Odyssey*.

Classical literature is a body of literature existing between Homer's *Iliad* and the fall of Rome in 410 A.D., a literature which has shaped those cultures, and which has stood the critical test of time, surviving down to the present. This includes, but is not limited to, Homer's *Iliad* and *Odyssey*, Hesiod's *Theogony*, plays by Aeschylus, Sophocles, Euripides and Aristophanes, lyric poets such as Sappho and Pindar, Virgil's *Aeneid*, Ovid's *Metamorphoses*, and the poetry of Horace and Catullus. The basic worldview exhibited in this litera-ture is that of paganism, which we must be careful to understand in the light of our faith in the triune God of Scripture. We believe in the God of the Bible, but the world represented in the *Odyssey* is that of pagan polytheism.

So the first great question for us to consider is the matter of gods and the only God. The student should always remember that the religion seen in the *Odyssey* is the kind of religion that is continually resisted in the pages of the Bible. The true God of Scripture is a warrior who does battle with the gods represented in pagan literature, and He is a warrior who overcomes them. But we must understand the nature of this conflict. It was not shadow boxing.

There are two basic options. One is that we understand the Creator/creature distinction, with the

triune God on one side and all of creation on the other. This means that there is an infinite difference between the God who is the uncreated Creator of all things and all other creatures, who rely on God for their life and existence. God lives "beyond" the world and is fundamentally different from all creatures. The other idea is called "the great chain of being." In this chain all beings are similar and no great chasm exists. The only differences between beings are ones ending in the letters *er*. So we could say comparing an angel to an amoeba, that the angel is strong*er*. If we compare a parrot to a condor, we could say that the parrot is the small*er* or that the parrot perhaps is the gabbi*er* (if it has been taught to speak). Unfortunately, in this type of system everything runs (or mushes) all together—including "humanity" and "deity." It does not matter how high the staircase goes if each step is just eight inches higher than the previous one.

In the latter case, certain entities, like gods, are farther up the chain than we are, but they are basically operating within the same "world." The world is nothing but an extended staircase, and there is nothing "outside" the staircase. When asked what is beyond that world, the pagan unbeliever would deny that anything is, or he would simply claim that he doesn't know (known as *agnosticism*).

For the pagan unbeliever, beings which are significantly higher on the chain of being can readily be dubbed gods or goddesses. Thus rebellious celestials (i.e., demons) or angels are identified as deities, and the uncreated God beyond them all is ignored or minimized. But for the Christian believer, such celestial beings are identified as principalities, powers, thrones, demons, etc. In the Bible the existence of such beings is not denied, but the claims made on their behalf (that they are gods in the same class as the true God) are rejected. Their existence is real; their claims are not. Think of it this way. If a man walked up to you on the street and claimed to be

"Hear me, Poseidon . . . grant that Odysseus, who styles himself Sacker of Cities and son of Laertes, may never reach his home in Ithaka. But if he is destined to reach his native land, to come once more to his own house and see his friends again, let him come late, in evil plight, with all his comrades dead, in someone else's ship, and find troubles in his household," said Polyphemos, the son of Poseidon and Thoosa. This vase painting depicts the *cyclops* (literally meaning "round eye") being blinded by Odysseus.

divine, you could dispute this without denying that man's existence.

Now the Bible does not reserve the use of the word *god* for God alone. God alone is the Most High God, and God alone is the Creator. But the Bible frequently uses the word *gods* to describe creatures on our side of the Creator/creature divide.

> God stands in the congregation of the mighty; He judges among the gods . . . I said, "You are gods, and all of you are children of the Most High. But you shall die like men, and fall like one of the princes." Arise, O God, judge the earth; for You shall inherit all nations (Ps. 82:1, 6–8).

Jesus interprets this psalm as referring to gods, and not simply to the "mighty."

> Jesus answered them, "Is it not written in your law, 'I said, "You are gods"'? If He called them gods, to whom the word of God came (and the Scripture cannot be broken), do you say of Him whom the Father sanctified and sent into the world, 'You are blaspheming,' because I said, 'I am the Son of God'?" (John 10: 34–36).

We also see this elsewhere in Scripture. "Among the gods there is none like You, O Lord; nor are there any works like Your works" (Ps. 86:8). "Oh, give thanks to the God of gods! For His mercy endures forever" (Ps. 136:2).

The Scriptures also show us how these gods have particular national loyalties. There are particular gods behind particular nations. "When the Most High divided their inheritance to the nations, when He separated the sons of Adam, He set the boundaries of the peoples according to the number of the children of Israel" (Deut. 32:8). For "children of Israel" some manuscripts have "sons of God." The Septuagint, the ancient version of the Old Testament translated from Hebrew into Greek, has "angels of God." God divided up the nations in accordance with the number of a certain kind of angel.

In another passage, the god of Babylon is treated as more than a creation of Babylonian imagination. "I will punish Bel in Babylon, and I will bring out of his

mouth what he has swallowed; and the nations shall not stream to him anymore. Yes, the wall of Babylon shall fall" (Jer. 51:44).

And here is yet another example. "Now when the Pharisees heard it they said, 'This fellow does not cast out demons except by Beelzebub, the ruler of the demons'" (Matt. 12:24). We can identify this ruler of the demons as the god of Ekron, a city of Philistia. "Now Ahaziah fell through the lattice of his upper room in Samaria, and was injured; so he sent messengers and said to them, "Go, inquire of Baal-Zebub, the god of Ekron, whether I shall recover from this injury" (2 Kings 1:2).

So throughout the Old Testament we see a celestial and angelic government over the nations of men (an "Angelocracy," if you will). The gods of the various nations are closely identified with those nations. For example, angelic beings stand behind the nations of Persia (Dan. 10:13) and Tyre (Ezek. 28:11–16). General statements are made in which God is *contrasted* with these beings, and He is seen as being in another category entirely. God was sovereign over such celestials then, but He exercised His sovereignty over and through them.

> "What am I saying then? That an idol is anything, or what is offered to idols is anything? Rather, that the things which the Gentiles sacrifice they sacrifice to demons and not to God, and I do not want you to have fellowship with demons" (1 Cor. 10:19–20).

Paul does not say that the Gentiles sacrifice to nonexistent beings, but rather to demons masquerading as gods. And Acts gives us another very striking example. "Now it happened, as we went to prayer, that a certain slave girl possessed with a spirit of divination met us, who brought her masters much profit by fortune-telling (Acts 16:16). The original here says that the girl was possessed by the spirit of a python, which meant that she was devoted to the god Apollo (who in myth had killed a python at Delphi). So nothing is plainer than that for the biblical writers, the idols were *real* in one sense (i.e., not imaginary) and *not* real in another (i.e., not what they purported to be). And this is why the fight with them was not shadow boxing.

Thus, we as modern Christians have no reason to dismiss Zeus, Aphrodite, Thor, Odin, Hadad-Rimmon, Bel-Marduk, or any other ancient deity as a completely

Crafty Odysseus knew that there was more than one way to "skin a city." His ingenious plan of building the Trojan Horse led the Greeks to victory.

made-up being. This is important for the student to remember in reading works like the *Odyssey*.

At the same time, it is not this way anymore—because Christ came into this dark, pagan world. The New Testament speaks of this frequently.

> Now is the judgment of this world; *now the ruler of this world will be cast out.* And I, if I am lifted up from the earth, will draw all peoples to Myself. This He said, signifying by what death He would die (John 12:31–33).

The celestials were, in some significant sense, mediators and princes. But in the Christian aeon, or age, God has established just one Prince . . . and He is one of us, a *man*. In Odysseus we see a good example of man in Adam. And the period of the New Testament is the time of transition between the reign of the celestial princes, and the dominion of man *in Christ*.

> "For He has not put the world to come, of which we speak, in subjection to angels. [Thus intimating that the old world *was* subject to angels.] But one testified in a certain place, saying: 'What is man that You are mindful of him . . .' For in that He put all in subjection under him, He left nothing that is not put under him. But now we do not yet see all things put under him. But we see Jesus, who was made a little lower than the angels, for the suffering of death crowned with glory and honor, that He, by the grace of God, might taste death for everyone" (Heb. 2:5–9).

The author of Hebrews did not yet see the promise made to mankind fulfilled. Nevertheless, he did see the fulfillment as centered in Christ.

But an important distinction is necessary. God, by definition, has always exercised sovereign control over the world. The hair on every head has *always* been numbered (Luke 12:6–8). But in the accomplished mission of Christ, the cross and resurrection, God established a new *mediatorial* rule in the world. Christ as the eternal Word of God has always been sovereign. But in the Incarnation, God has established His Son as a new mediatorial Prince, and we are seated and enthroned in the heavenly places in Christ.

So the spiritual conflict that Christ won when He came into the world was not shadow boxing. We must remember the power of the conquering cross. This is how the New Testament describes it over and over again. If we miss this, we are missing a central part of the impact of the gospel. In the following quotation, note especially the italics. "However, we speak wisdom among those who are mature, yet not the wisdom of this age, nor of the rulers of this age, *who are coming to nothing.* But we speak the wisdom of God in a mystery, the hidden wisdom which God ordained before the ages for our glory, which none of the rulers of this age knew; for had they known, they would not have crucified the Lord of glory. But as it is written: 'Eye has not seen, nor ear heard, nor have entered into the heart of man the things which God has prepared for those who love Him'" (1 Cor. 2:9). What did these rulers not know? They did not know the cross would topple them and glorify the saints. Jesus said, ". . . of judgment, because the ruler of this world is judged" (John 16:11). Paul exults in this conquest: "Having disarmed principalities and powers, He made a public spectacle of them, triumphing over them in it" (Col. 2:15). In the ancient world, a "triumph" included a public humiliation of the defeated enemy after the battle was over.

What was the point of the cross? ". . . that through death He might *destroy him* who had the power of death, that is, the devil . . ." (Heb. 2:14). What Satan offered Christ in the temptation, Christ refused. But Christ refused because He planned to knock him down and take the kingdoms of men from him. "No one can enter a strong man's house and plunder his goods, unless he first binds the strong man. And then he will plunder his house" (Mark 3:27). So who is now the God of this world? ". . . and from Jesus Christ, the faithful witness, the firstborn from the dead, *and the ruler over the kings* of the earth . . ." (Rev. 1:5; 11:15; Heb. 6:5). We cannot study ancient literature safely without becoming aware of what the cross accomplished.

Now this may be all very interesting, but what relevance does it have to the *Odyssey*? As the apostle Paul might have put it, much in every way. The study of classical literature and the *Odyssey* in particular, is a tremendous help in understanding the "backdrop" assumptions which the inhabitants of the Greco/Roman world had, and which we as moderns no longer have. Their fundamental assumptions about the world around them were shaped by works such as the *Iliad* and *Odyssey*, while that of moderns tends to be shaped by popular movies, books, and dumb songs by Alanis Morissette.

For example, in this you are going to read an ancient account of a "descent" into Hades, the realm of the departed dead. Having this understanding, you will read the biblical accounts of *Christ's* conquest of Hades differently. In other words, how do we define such terms when the scriptural accounts and classical accounts of various things overlap? People who do not know the classical world do not really know the Bible. And knowledge of the classical world is impossible without knowledge of classical literature.

In summary, worldview thinking helps us identify what can be appreciated in classical literature and what must be rejected. Some Christians are tempted to be superficial in what they reject. Some of what the student will read will conflict with biblical standards—of course. Why read it then? The student must learn not to apply *pietistic* standards—rather he should apply *biblical* standards. Pietistic standards tend to be "sweety-nice," or moralistic. In contrast, biblical standards are *moral,* not moralistic.

Always remember while reading works like this, that *this is the world* into which Christ came. You should be able to see the ancient pagan assumptions that Christ has removed forever. You should not see them in order to adopt them, but rather to *consciously* reject them. At the same time, there is much that may be appreciated and loved. In God's common grace, pagans have been able to produce literature of unbelievable beauty. That beauty can and should be appreciated. Once understood and appreciated, it may be successfully appropriated and put to good use in the service of the kingdom of God. Good writers are not only good

"Beware of Greeks bearing gifts!" said the priest of Troy, Laocoon, before he and his sons were pulled into the sea by the Python.

readers, they are also readers *who read good writing.*

At the same time, many students may exhibit a typical Christian reaction to some elements of this story. "Fine, fine. Odysseus takes his sweet time sleeping with goddesses across the Mediterranean, while his faithful wife Penelope is at home all by herself, fighting off the suitors. And *then,* when Odysseus is good and ready, he comes home. What a toad." This objection to the immorality is all very well and good, as well as the objection to the double standard for men and women, but much more is involved in all of this. Homer is presenting to us a transition from one world to another. How so? He is seeking to lay a foundation for the city of man. The city of man attempts to build a lasting civilization apart from the triune God of the Bible.

The world of the *Iliad* is that of a warrior caste, which fights, takes plunder, seizes beautiful women, lives for honor, and is not concerned, really, with a humdrum existence. The mentality is that of Achilleus, valuing a short and glorious life over a long and inglorious one. (Achilleus is offered glory and a short life if he fights in Troy or a long life without glory if he avoids the conflict—he chooses glory.) But Odysseus represents a transition from this era to the next era, which Homer is representing as a coming of age (remember Telemachos!), as a growing up. Odysseus' first adventure after the fall of Troy is a military raid on the Cicones. Odysseus is still in his adventurous, head-cracking mode. But ten years of getting home changes him completely.

Now Odysseus had not wanted to go to war in the first place. And when the war was over, he genuinely wanted to get back home. This means he provides good raw material for this transition. But what about Circe and Kalypso? What about *them?* Notice what Odysseus wants to get away from, and what he finally rejects in the end. He is promised immortality, and a life of sexual paradise with a goddess—but no descendants, no issue—no civilization. The question here is not "another woman" besides Penelope. The issue is another kind of life, which Odysseus rejects, in favor of *human* life with Penelope.

Before Odysseus goes home, he goes to Hades first. While there, he is promised that he will die. He is not to die in battle in the mode of the *Iliad,* but will die peacefully, in the mode of the *Odyssey.* He learns from Teiresias that he must accommodate himself to the maturity of peace. He has chosen to live and die as a mortal, and this means he rejects the life of freebooting piracy. As one writer put it, no more "adventures, sexual escapades, no more honor won in war."[1] Odysseus' men died because they could not learn this lesson. They continued their life as pirates, and that is why they died. Odysseus survived *because he had learned how to restrain himself.*

So there are two maturations. The book begins with Telemachos coming of age, and concludes with Telemachos standing with his father in the battle with the suitors, and then with the relatives of the suitors. At the same time, Odysseus represents the coming of age for Greek culture—the transition from the "Viking" period to the civilized period, and we see in Homer the self-consciousness of the transition. This civilization is pagan and humanistic, but it is a *civilization* that Homer is seeking to commend to us. We as Christians do not reject it because it is a city, but because it is merely the city of man.

Another important issue is the difference between tragedy and comedy. We must first note and contrast a more recent Christian view of tragedy and comedy with the ancient Hellenistic view. Aristotle held that tragedy was about the fall of a noble human being. His fall must not be so deserved that the audience cheers, but neither must it be so undeserved that the audience is furious with the author. The tragic hero must deserve it because of a tragic flaw (the word Aristotle uses for this is *hamartia,* the New Testament word for *sin*), and yet he must be a sympathetic character. The most common flaw among the Greek nobles about whom the tragedies were composed was *hubris,* pride. For the classical theorists the point of comedy was *to ridicule vice.* In doing this it was often depicted, and it was frequently risqué, but the point was consistently a moral one. But too often moderns use comedy simply to ridicule virtue.

Dante, an author from the 13th century, reflects the change that the Christian faith brought to these two terms. He held that tragedy was a story with a sad ending and a comedy was a story with a happy one. In this definition the *Odyssey* is a comedy. And, after the resurrection of Jesus, all true stories are ultimately comedies.

In conclusion, the student reading the *Odyssey* should come to understand another world, but he does this without ceasing to inhabit his own world, the world of the Christian faith. We see through other eyes without relinquishing our own. Two comments by C.S. Lewis help to make this point. "I had much rather know what I should feel like if I adopted the beliefs of Lucretius than how Lucretius would have felt if he had never entertained them."[2]

"But in reading great literature I become a thousand men and yet remain myself. Like the night sky in the Greek poem, I see with a myriad eyes, but it is still I who see. Here, as in worship, in love, in moral action, and in knowing, I transcend myself; and am never more myself than when I do."[3]

So, put on your gloves; get into the boxing ring; and let's get to work.

—Douglas Wilson

## For Further Reading

Leithart, Peter J. *Heroes of the City of Man.* Moscow, Idaho: Canon Press, 1999. 147–169.

Spielvogel, Jackson. *Western Civilization.* Fifth Edition. Belmont, Calif.: Wadsworth/Thomson Learning, 2003. 50–62.

"Kalypsoed?" The goddess Athene "hides" Odysseus from his enemies by disguising him as a beggar—as shown in this Roman sculpture. This enables Odysseus to plan his revenge and to see which of his "friends" are truly loyal to him.

# SESSION I: PRELUDE

## Introduction to Greek Meter

In the essay above, we noted that epic poetry was written in a meter that is called *dactylic hexameter.* The purpose of this exercise is to help the student get an understanding of this rhythm down into his bones.

A line of epic poetry is called hexameter because it is made up of six metrical "feet." Those feet are (for the most part) dactyls. The example that was used above was this one:

*strawberry strawberry strawberry
strawberry strawberry jam pot*

The word *strawberry* is one dactylic foot, and all the feet are dactylic except for the last one. This means that strawberry conforms to the metrical pattern *DAH da da.* We say *STRAWberry,* not *strawBERey* or *strawberRY.* So a dactylic foot has three syllables, with the accent on the first one.

You can remember this more easily if you know that the word *dactylos* is the Greek word for *finger.* And if you look at your forefinger, where it joins to the hand, you see that you have (or should have) one long joint, and then two short ones. There it is, right on your hand—*DAH da da.*

If you want to hear examples of dactylic hexameter being read, you may find it at the Veritas Press website at www.veritaspress.com/store/ SL_Resource_Download.asp.

In the following exercise, list ten English words that are *dactyls.* The first two are given for you. As you do this, try to avoid overuse of berries like *blueberry.*

### EXERCISE 1

1. blueberry
2. pentagon
3. 
4. 
5. 
6. 
7. 
8. 
9. 
10.

Now string five of your words along in one line, ending with our emphatic *jam pot*. This is a line of dactylic hexameter. Not quite like Homer, but we are getting there!

*Telegraph telephone Joshua portable*
*blueberry jam pot*

Now in the next exercise, there are ten lines of poetry from various poets writing in English. Three of these lines are made up of dactyls and the others are not. Identify which three are dactylic. Please note that none of the lines are long enough to be hexameter. You are just looking for the kind of feet, and not how many feet there are.

## Exercise 2
1. In Xanadu did Kubla Khan
2. Once upon a midnight dreary, while I pondered weak and weary
3. This is the forest primeval. The murmuring pines and the hemlocks
4. Look on my works, ye mighty and despair
5. The outlook wasn't brilliant for the Mudville nine that day
6. The nox was lit by lux of luna and twas a nox most opportuna
7. Leaped like the roe, when he hears in the woodland . . .
8. The sea was wet as wet could be, the sands were dry as dry.
9. When voices of children are heard on the green
10. Speaks, and in accents disconsolate answers . . .

## Exercise 3
Write ten lines of poetry on a heroic theme, using dactylic hexameter. The heroic theme does not have to be from the ancient world of the Greeks—try writing about Aragorn and Gandalf if you like. As you write, you should have the rhythm *DAH da da DAH da da* in your mind.

## Exercise 4
Epic is also characterized by heroic similes. The student should look for extended similes as he reads the *Odyssey*. The best way to describe a heroic simile is that it is a simile which looks as though it has changed the subject. An ordinary simile says something like:

The "cloud was like a cow."

A heroic simile looks like it has (almost) changed the subject. It would say something like:

The "cloud was like a cow that had been bellowing all night from hunger, and which, in the early morning hours, kicked down the door of the stall, attacking the farmer coming out with his milk pail, the same farmer who had forgotten to feed the cow the night before."

Such similes are called heroic because they are found in heroic epics, and not because the subject matter of the simile is necessarily noble or high-flown. Many of Homer's similes are quite earthy. As you are reading the *Odyssey*, identify and copy three heroic similes.

## Optional Exercise A
The basic kinds of feet in English meter are iambic, anapestic, trochaic, and dactylic. We have already covered the dactylic, but if you would like, you may go through the previous exercise and identify the other kinds of feet that are there.

An iambic foot goes *da DAH.*
A trochaic foot goes *DAH da*
An anapestic foot goes *da da DAH*

1. Iambic
2. Trochaic
3. Dactylic
4. Iambic
5. Iambic
6. Iambic
7. Dactylic
8. Iambic
9. Anapestic
10. Dactylic

Now it has to be emphasized that English dactylic hexameter can only *approximate* what dactylic hexameter was like in ancient Greek. This is because in English we mark meter by means of accented and unaccented syllables. In the ancient world, it was done by means of long and short syllables. In fact, we call vowels *long* and *short,* even to this day, because long vowels used to be like a half note in music, and short vowels were like a quarter note. In other words, a long *a* and short *a* took different lengths of time to say. Today that is not the case (unless you are from

Texas). In short, we put the emphasis on STRAW in STRAWberry, but *straw* doesn't take up significantly more time. But imagine if straw took a second to say, and then the two syllables of berry took up one second total. So this is just our approximation of the ancient meter, but it is nevertheless a decent approximation.

## Optional Exercise B

Take the three examples of dactylic verse you found in Exercise 3, and try to say them while giving two seconds to each accented syllable, and less than a second to each unaccented syllable. You may want to close the door to your bedroom while doing this so your mother won't think you are going crazy.

### READING ASSIGNMENT:
Book 1 and Book 8, lines 486–534

A sixth-century vase painting shows the goddess Athene inspecting the Trojan Horse. She had suggested the ruse to Odysseus as a way for his army to gain entry into the enemy's city.

## SESSION II: ACTIVITY
Book 1 and Book 8, lines 486–534

Odysseus is the main character of the *Odyssey*. During this book we learn a lot about him, but some of his most striking characteristics are announced in the first lines of the book, when Homer tells us:

Tell me, Muse, of the
man of many ways,
who was driven
far journeys, after he
had sacked Troy's
sacred citadel.
(Book 1, lines 1 and 2)

In the *Odyssey*, Odysseus will furnish us plenty of evidence that he is a "man of many ways." This means that he is a cunning person who gains victory with his mind rather than brute force. We will see this throughout the *Odyssey*, but ancient readers would have come to the presentation of the *Odyssey* with a detailed understanding of the Trojan War and Odysseus's crucial role in it. In some senses Odysseus single-handedly, or maybe it would be better said "single-mindedly," wins the Trojan war. This battle had lasted ten years with great warriors having died on both sides. The stalemate seemed endless, but then Odysseus came up with his most famous "way." He had the Greeks build a giant horse and leave it on the beaches at Troy. This was a "gift" to the Trojans announcing the Greek intention of ending the fruitless war and heading home. When the Trojans finally ventured outside the city they found the horse and an abandoned Greek soldier, Sinon, who explained the meaning of the horse to them. It was a trophy of their victory, he said.

Having defeated the Greeks the Trojans rejoiced and began a great celebration. Still, some had questions about the horse. Laocoon, a priest who is devoured by a snake while warning the Trojans, and Cassandra, a prophetess who always seems to be right but is never heeded, both warn of the danger of the horse, but the Trojans ignore their warnings because of the crafty plan of Odysseus and because the gods had blinded them.

Even with the warning and the sounds that were heard coming from the huge horse, the Trojans took the bait and brought the horse into the city. A huge party began. Late that evening Odysseus and about fifty Greeks slipped out of the hollow horse, opened the gates of the city for their comrades who had been hidden just out of sight and began the destruction of Troy. (A detailed account of this story is told by Aeneus in Book 2 of the *Aeneid*.) After ten years of war, Troy fell in one night because of the crafty Odysseus. Now that's a man of "many ways."

The fame of Odysseus's strategy at Troy has endured through the ages. Today in sports, trick plays are often termed *Trojan Horses,* and seemingly harmless bits of data that sack the Ilium of your computer's hard drive are called *Trojan Horses.* Even modern singers allude to this story: Jakob Dylan (Bob's son), the lead singer of the Wallflowers in their tune *Bringing Down the Horse,* says, "Maybe it was the first of mistakes when we held on too loosely and opened the gates."[4]

*Discuss or list short answers to the following questions:*
1. What is the basic theme of this book?
2. What kind of man is Odysseus and how does the story of the Trojan Horse prove this?
3. In light of what he did to Troy, why is it ironic that Odysseus wants to go home, settle down and build civilization?
4. What does this transition in Odysseus tell us about him?

As you have seen already in the *Odyssey* you will encounter a robust adventure, monsters included. But behind all this you will learn of the contrast between a life of pillaging and looting and a life of civilization. At the same time, you will contrast the civilization found in the city of man with the civilization found in the city of God.

## Activity

### OPTION 1
**DRAW A SCENE OF THE FALL OF TROY**

Draw a scene about the Trojan Horse or about Laocoon being attacked by the python. Groups may want to paint on a large sheet of paper on the wall to create a poster that can be a constant reminder of Odysseus's craftiness. If you draw your scene carefully in miniature, you can make your own personal Odysseus bookmark that will consistently remind you of the "man of many ways." Perhaps you can draw the Trojan Horse on one side and after you have finished reading the *Odyssey* draw another episode from this book chronicling Odysseus's cunning. Laminate it and you will have your *Odyssey* bookmark ready for your next reading of this great story.

### OPTION 2
**WRITING TEN LINES OF YOUR OWN DACTYLIC HEXAMETER ABOUT THE FALL OF TROY**

Use what you have learned in Session I to write ten lines about the story of the Trojan Horse or Laocoon. If you write it out in your best handwriting (or calligraphy if you are able), on a slender piece of stiff paper you can make your own *Odysseus* bookmark. Remember, as you write, you should have the rhythm *DAH da da DAH da da* in your mind.

## Optional Activities

Memorize the first ten lines of the *Odyssey.*

 READING ASSIGNMENT: Books 2 and 3

# SESSION III: DISCUSSION
Books 2 and 3

## A Question to Consider

What do warriors on the high seas and lawless motorcycle gangs have in common?

*Discuss or list short answers to the following questions:*

### Text Analysis

1. The Greek word *kleos* refers to "heroic fame." The word *nostos* refers to the idea of "return." Achilleus knows that for him it is one or the other. But Odysseus does not have to choose. What is different about the circumstances of these two heroes' situations?
2. Odysseus is exiled on the island of Ogygia with Kalypso. Does he really want to be there?
3. The Greek word *metis* refers to cunning or craftiness. How does this word describe Odysseus?
4. How is Telemachos in a strange situation?
5. The Greek word *kaluptein* is related both to Kalypso's name and to one of the names for the book of Revelation, or the Apocalypse (the Unveiling). The word means "to hide." How is Kalypso hidden, and how must Odysseus become "unhidden" in the course of this story?
6. Why is it interesting that Zeus brings up the story of Agamemnon in the first book of the *Odyssey*?
7. What does Athene tell Telemachos?

### Cultural Analysis

1. Why are "family values" important to the survival of any civilization?
2. What can be learned of Penelope's suitors' behavior who are consuming Odysseus's wealth? How does their behavior compare to those today in our culture who consume more than they earn?
3. How does Odysseus' view of sexual purity differ from the Christian view?
4. Why does Telemachos have to go away from Ithaka?

### Biblical Analysis

1. Look up the following verses in the Bible: 2 Samuel 22:27; Psalm 18:26; Psalm 64:6; Luke 16:8. Are Christians supposed to be shrewd? If they are, should they be shrewd the same way Odysseus is?

2. Telemachos is coming of age. In our culture, we do not really have any "rite of passage" for young men. What do you think would be a good time to do this, and what sort of thing should we do?
3. In light of the Fifth Commandment, what responsibility does a son have for his mother when his father is away? What example does Telemachos provide for us?

## SUMMA

 *Write an essay or discuss this question, integrating what you have learned from the material above.*
What causes civilizations to grow and mature?

## Optional Activity

In a dictionary of mythology, look up Odysseus, and make a list of all the other things he was known for in the ancient world. What else did he do? Make particular note of things recorded about him in the *Iliad*.

**READING ASSIGNMENT:**
Book 4

# SESSION IV: RECITATION
Book 4

*Answer these questions for factual recall.*

## Comprehension Questions

1. What god was trying to prevent Odysseus from making it home?
2. Why?
3. What goddess is trying to help Odysseus?
4. Does Telemachos receive Athene willingly?
5. What does this tell us about him?
6. Whom does Telemachos visit first?
7. Whom does he visit second?
8. Does he threaten the suitors before he goes?
9. How does he amaze Penelope his mother?
10. What story does Nestor tell Telemachos?
11. Is Helen a sympathetic character in the *Odyssey*?
12. What do Menelaos and Odysseus have in common?
13. What do the suitors want to do with Telemachos?
14. How is Kalypso persuaded to release Odysseus?
15. What happens after Odysseus builds his raft?

Odysseus again is saved by the gods. This time Hermes, the messenger god, gives him herbs that will keep Circe's potion from turning Odysseus into a beast.

### READING ASSIGNMENT:
Books 5 and 6

## SESSION V: DISCUSSION
Books 5 and 6

### A Question to Consider

When are people allowed to remarry?

*Discuss or list short answers to the following questions:*

### Text Analysis

1. How did Penelope avoid marrying one of the suitors?
2. What did she not do?
3. Is she being true to Odysseus?
4. Why is Penelope so hopeful about the return of Odysseus?

### Cultural Analysis

1. Why do few people demonstrate the faithfulness of Penelope in our culture today?

2. Penelope is waiting on Odysseus and is the picture of faithfulness in waiting. Can people also make a mistake by not marrying again?

3. In our culture, what usually determines whether someone marries again after a marriage is broken by divorce or death?

### Biblical Analysis

1. Who is allowed to remarry? (See 1 Cor. 7)

2. Would it have been biblically allowable for Penelope to remarry? Would it have been wise?

### Application

Choose your spouse carefully. Odysseus and Penelope did. While both of them have flaws, Odysseus is a talented man who is able to make his way across the world to get back to his family. He also makes the difference in the Greek victory over the Trojans. Penelope is resourceful as well. She trusts in her husband and holds out in faith, waiting for her husband to return, and she is beautiful too. A woman like this is very desirable.

### SUMMA

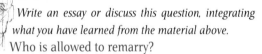 *Write an essay or discuss this question, integrating what you have learned from the material above.* Who is allowed to remarry?

 **READING ASSIGNMENT:** Books 7 and 8

# SESSION VI: DISCUSSION
Books 7 and 8

## A Question to Consider

Should immortality ever be rejected or sought?

*Discuss or list short answers to the following questions:*

### Text Analysis

1. How long does Kalypso want Odysseus to stay with her on her island?

2. What is Odysseus's life like with Kalypso?

3. How does all of this make him feel?

4. What inconsistency in Zeus does Kalypso point out when she receives the message to let Odysseus go?

### Cultural Analysis

1. What does our culture hold out as the ideal life (how do professional athletes and rock stars live)?

2. What similarities does Odysseus's life with Kalypso have with what is considered ideal today?

3. How is Odysseus's life better than a rock star's?

4. Why do rock stars and professional athletes often take recreational drugs and even kill themselves?

### Biblical Analysis

1. What does God do with the Tree of Life when Adam and Eve fall (Gen. 3:22–24)? Why?

2. How is Adam's life in the garden (Gen. 2) and our lives on the New Earth (Rev. 22) different from the vision of paradise painted by Homer?

### SUMMA

 *Write an essay or discuss this question, integrating what you have learned from the material above.* When should immortality be rejected?

**READING ASSIGNMENT:** Book 9

# SESSION VII: DISCUSSION
Book 9

## A Question to Consider

What do you love most about home?

*Discuss or list short answers to the following questions:*

### Text Analysis

1. In the first part of this work, we learned how the identity of Odysseus was hidden by Kalypso. He is gradually becoming known. How is this accomplished in Books 7 & 8 of the *Odyssey*?

2. Why is the suggested marriage to Nausikaa (in Book 7) significant?

3. Why does Odysseus change his mind and end up participating in the athletic competition?

4. Why is it apparent that Odysseus is no ordinary man?

## Cultural Analysis

1. How does our culture love home?
2. On the other hand, how does our culture despise home?
3. What temptations can our culture present concerning dropping out of the real world and into an unreal one (like that of the Phaiakians or Kalypso)?

## Biblical Analysis

1. How is the Bible a trip from home (Gen. 2) to home (Rev. 22)?
2. How does the Bible encourage a real life with real children and spouses rather than a Kalypso-like escape (See Ps. 128, and Prov. 7:10–27)?
3. How does Christ overcome Satan's temptation to gain the world without sacrificing Himself (Luke 4)? What is His weapon?

## Application

Is your life at home one in which the gospel is shown forth? Do you lay down your life for other family members? If not, why not start today by finding something that you can do for someone else. Try to pick the chore that they hate doing the most (it might be cleaning their room or taking out the trash) and just do it for them even though they have not asked. Do it in secret if you can, but if you get "caught" explain your lesson from

the *Odyssey*. Hopefully, your action will be even more fuel poured on the living sacrifice of your family.

## SUMMA

*Write an essay or discuss this question, integrating what you have learned from the material above.* What should we love about home?

## Optional Activity

Memorize lines 234–250 in Book XII of the *Odyssey*.

**READING ASSIGNMENT:**
Book 10

# SESSION VIII: DISCUSSION
Book 10

## A Question to Consider

What does your family do when you wish to demonstrate hospitality to guests?

Odysseus incurred Poseidon's enmity when he blinded his son Polyphemos. Poseidon then made Odysseus wander the sea for ten years, before he was allowed to return to Ithaka. In this third century mosaic from Constantinople the sea god is shown with his wife, Amphitrite. It was told that Amphitrite calmed stormy seas while travelling in a boat made of mussels. She was the daughter of Nereus and Doris—one of the fifty sea goddesses known as the Nereids. Poseidon fell in love with the beautiful Amphitrite, but she resisted his advances. So Poseidon sent out all of his sea creatures to search for her. A dolphin found Amphitrite and pleaded with her to consider Poseidon's proposal. She agreed, and they were wed. Poseidon rewarded the dolphin by making it a constellation.

*Discuss or list short answers to these questions:*

## Text Analysis

1. Give examples of how hospitality has been breached in this world that Homer is describing?
2. Where must Odysseus go before returning home?
3. Does Odysseus trust Circe?
4. What happens to Elpenor?
5. Is Odysseus able to govern or restrain his men?
6. What are some of his men turned into on Circe's island, and why is this significant?
7. What does it mean to you that Circe and Kalypso seem to be more dangerous than evil?
8. What is the parallel between the suitors on Ithaka and the men with Odysseus?

## Cultural Analysis

1. How has hospitality broken down in our culture?
2. What happens in our culture when true hospitality is given?
3. Where could Christians find open opportunities for hospitality in our culture today?

## Biblical Analysis

1. How do we know that being hospitable is important to God (1 Pet. 4:9, 1 Tim. 3:2)?
2. Why does God always instruct His people to be hospitable to those who are strangers (Ex. 22:21–22)?
3. What added motive do believers have to show hospitality (Heb. 13:2)?
4. When has this happened in the past (Gen. 18, Judg. 11)?

## Application

1. Consider how often Odysseus is offered things which he refuses. Why is Odysseus especially careful about accepting gifts? How is this pattern a good example?
2. Telemachos is not with his father, but he is like him. Odysseus's men are with him, but they are not like him. What does this tell us?
3. What responsibility do we have to restrain our curiosity?

## SUMMA

*Write an essay or discuss this question, integrating what you have learned from the material above.* Why is hospitality so important?

READING ASSIGNMENT:
Book 11

# SESSION IX: ACTIVITY
Book 11

## The Journey of Odysseus

*On the map provided see if you can trace Odysseus's journey. Compare each reference below with the labeled locations on the map. Once you have looked up the passage in your book, on a separate sheet of paper write the name of the location and give a two sentence summary of Odysseus's adventure there. Repeat the process until you reach the Phaiakians. Note: not all of Odysseus's landfalls are recorded here, and, since Homer did not provide a map, many of these locations are conjecture.*

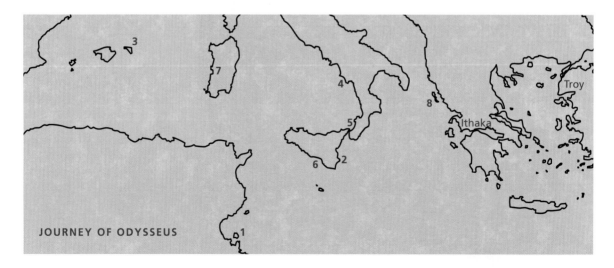

JOURNEY OF ODYSSEUS

1. BOOK 9, 82
2. BOOK 9, 106FF
3. BOOK 10, 135
4. BOOK 12, 39
5. BOOK 12, 85
6. BOOK 12, 260
7. BOOK 12, 448
8. BOOK 5, 35

### READING ASSIGNMENT:
Books 12 and 13

# SESSION X: WRITING
Books 12 and 13

## Comprehension Questions

*Write an answer to two of the following four essays. Your answer should be a paragraph or two written very carefully.*

1. How does the behavior of Polyphemos compare to a biblical view of hospitality? How should Christians be radically different from Polyphemos?
2. Later in the year you will read how in the *Aeneid*, Aeneas goes down into Hades. But in this description, it would be more accurate to say that Hades comes up to Odysseus. Discuss how this happens, and why you might think it had to happen this way.
3. In the Bible, what is Hades like? Look up Psalm 16:10, Acts 2:27, Luke 16:23, and Revelation 20:14 and discuss.
4. Discuss the importance of authority and loyalty to it. How does disregard of authority get Odysseus's crew in trouble? How might pagan and Christian views of authority differ?

## Optional Activity

If you are near a body of water, plan out your own *Odyssey*. Use canoes, kayaks or charter a vessel. If you wish to go all out, plan a family vacation to the Mediterranean and visit some of the places where Odysseus sojourned. If any goddesses entice you, say *no*. Don't eat the sun cattle. One of the most vivid memories I have of my time in the Navy was the time our boat visited Ithaka. It was a very strange sensation to sit offshore on a modern submarine and look at the land that Odysseus spent ten years longing for.

# SESSION XI: ACTIVITY
## The Slap Game
### FOR GROUPS

Put your copy of the *Odyssey* on your desk or table. When a question is asked, the first person to raise his hand and slap his book gets a chance to answer. If you answer correctly you receive 10 points. If you miss, the teacher should ask a new question.

### FOR INDIVIDUALS

See how many characters you can identify in a row without making a mistake. You get one point per correct answer. But your points for answering the second consecutive question correctly are doubled (i.e., 2 points, then 4, then 8).

## Comprehension Questions

*Briefly identify the following characters or peoples.*

1. Alkinoos
2. Demodokos
3. Euryalos
4. Ares and Aphrodite
5. The Kikonians
6. The Lotus Eaters
7. Polyphemos
8. Poseidon
9. Aiolos
10. The Laistrygones
11. Circe
12. Hades
13. Elpenor
14. Skylla and Charybdis
15. The Cattle of Helios
16. Kikonians
17. Teiresias
18. The Sirens

*Practice it again. Can you run the table and get them all correct?*

### READING ASSIGNMENT:
Book 14

## SESSION XII: DISCUSSION
Book 14

### A Question to Consider

When is it right to make fun of someone?

*Discuss or list short answers to the following questions:*

### Text Analysis

1. What does Polyphemos do to Odysseus and his men?
2. How does Odysseus dull Polyphemos's senses?
3. How do Odysseus and his men escape?
4. Why do the other Cyclopes fail to come to the aid of Polyphemos?
5. How does Odysseus get past the boulder?
6. When did Odysseus taunt the Cyclops?
7. Why did he taunt Polyphemos?
8. How does the taunting of Polyphemos cause Odysseus a number of problems?

### Cultural Analysis

1. When do we see taunting in our culture?
2. How is the "trash talk" of a professional athlete like Odysseus's insulting of Polyphemos?
3. How is it unlike Odysseus?

### Biblical Analysis

1. Why does the Psalmist taunt the ungodly in Psalm 137? How is this different from most of the verbal jabs in our culture?
2. How does God taunt the pagans in Isaiah 44?
3. Why would Paul taunt death in 1 Cor. 15:55?
4. What does Christ do with His enemies in Eph. 4:8?

### Application

But when do you know that you are taunting rightly? Most of the time we wish to sinfully attack our brother, but we can learn to be righteous in this from Christ. He did insult, but His holy words went in different directions than ours often do. Christ could have attacked the sinners that crowded around Him: tax gatherers and prostitutes. He, however, called the *Pharisees* "a brood of vipers," "sons of the devil" and "whitewashed tombs." He attacked those who oppressed and fleeced God's people. The next time you read through the Gospels, pay careful attention to Christ's insults and ask yourself the following questions:
1. Do your insults center on what angered Christ?
2. Where do you fall short?

### SUMMA

 *Write an essay or discuss this question, integrating what you have learned from the material above.* When is it right to taunt people?

 **READING ASSIGNMENT:** Book 15

## SESSION XIII: ANALYSIS
Book 15

### Women of the *Odyssey*

*Complete Chart 1.*

### Optional Activity

In Scripture, God uses many metaphors to tell us about the Church. She is a temple, she is a body, she is a bride. While some of the metaphors have no gender, a bride is distinctly feminine. When we consider Penelope, Kalypso and Circe, which is the Church most like and why? All three of these women exhibit power and strength. Whose power and strength is most like the Church's?

**READING ASSIGNMENT:** Books 16 and 17

## SESSION XIV: DISCUSSION
Books 16 and 17

### A Question to Consider

If you had enough money would you stop school, never pursue a career and live leisurely as if you were always on vacation for the rest of your life? Should you?

*Discuss or list short answers to the following questions:*

## Text Analysis

1. In Book 14 of the poem, Odysseus begins his return to reality. Just as he was asleep on the beach of the Phaiakians, so they leave him asleep on the beach at Ithaka. How is this significant?

2. Peter Leithart, who has written wisely on many ancient works, comments, "[Odysseus] is no longer 'nobody,' stripped of glory; he has begun his ascent. This return to glory is also a return to humanity." The *Odyssey* is a preeminent story of return. Why is this return home so satisfying?

3. What happens to the Phaiakians as a result of them helping Odysseus?

4. This portion of the poem contains a number of contrasts and setbacks. Where do you find them?

5. Why is it so important for Odysseus to come home?

## Cultural Analysis

1. Where do we see people serving pleasure in our culture?

2. How does our culture view people who have devoted themselves to pleasure?

3. What would the reaction of people be to someone who won the lottery, quit his job and decided to live on the beach sipping drinks with little umbrellas in them for the rest of his life?

## Biblical Analysis

1. What does Galatians 5:15–17 tell us about serving our own lusts?

2. What does 1 Corinthians 6:20 tell us about our motivation to not be ruled by our passions and lusts?

## Summa

*Write an essay or discuss this question, integrating what you have learned from the material above.*

How should we balance pleasure and "real life?"

---

*Chart I:* **WOMEN OF THE *ODYSSEY***

| | PENELOPE | KALYPSO | CIRCE |
|---|---|---|---|
| Who are they? | She is the faithful wife of Odysseus and the mother of Telemachos. | A goddess who rules an island. | A witch/goddess who rules an island and turns her visitors into animals. |
| What household task do we see them perform? | | | |
| Are they beautiful? | | | |
| Are they surrounded by animals? | | | |
| Does Odysseus love them? | | | |
| How do they relate to men? | | | |
| What do they offer Odysseus? | | | |
| Why does Odysseus leave them? | | | |
| Does he do this willingly? | | | |

# SESSION XV: DISCUSSION

## A Question to Consider

How important is it to be a loyal person?

*Discuss or list short answers to the following questions:*

### Text Analysis

1. How does Telemachos display his loyalty to Odysseus?
2. How does Penelope show herself to be loyal?
3. Is Odysseus's dog loyal?
4. How does Odysseus know that Eumaios, his swineherd, is loyal?
5. How is the goatherd different?

### Cultural Analysis

1. Does our culture consider loyalty important?
2. Where do you see disloyalty in the corporate or business world?
3. Where do you see disloyalty in the covenantal and marriage life of our culture?

### Biblical Analysis

1. Read Psalm 78. What kind of loyalty does Israel show toward God?
2. In light of Psalm 78, what do we see concerning God's loyalty?
3. What does Romans 7:2 tell us about loyalty in marriage? What part of the traditional wedding ceremony does Romans 7:2 foreshadow?

## SUMMA

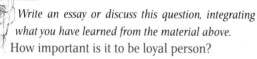

*Write an essay or discuss this question, integrating what you have learned from the material above.* How important is it to be loyal person?

READING ASSIGNMENT: Book 18

# SESSION XVI: RECITATION

Book 18

*In a group setting the teacher should orally quiz the students with these questions, looking for opportunities to introduce other questions as the students' answers open doors to deeper, probing questions. Working individually, answer the questions mentally and check yourself against the answers provided in the teacher's material.*

## The Game: *Overcome the Obstacles*

DIRECTIONS: The goal of this game is to answer consecutive questions correctly concerning the *Odyssey*. Questions rotate from student to student, or, if you have enough students, divide up into teams. Questions alternate between teams. The first question that a team answers correctly earns them one point. If they answer a second consecutive question correctly, they earn two more points. Each consecutive correct answer makes the next question worth more. If you miss a question, you go back to the first level. Each level represents one of the obstacles that Odysseus overcame. If you make it all the way to Ithaka, earn a bonus and start again. It is not necessary to use all the questions, but the first ten are most critical.

| LEVEL | POINTS |
| --- | --- |
| Troy | 1 |
| Polyphemos's Cave | 2 |
| Circe | 3 |
| The Cattle of Helios | 4 |
| Skylla and Charybdis | 5 |
| Kalypso | 6 |
| The Suitors | 7–10 |

**COMPREHENSION QUESTIONS**

*Briefly identify the following characters or peoples.*

1. Athene
2. Eumaios
3. Theoklymenos
4. Antinoos
5. Amphinomos
6. Melanthios
7. Argos
8. Iros
9. Eurymachos
10. Telemachos
11. What god was trying to prevent Odysseus from making it home?
12. Why?
13. What goddess is trying to help Odysseus?
14. How does Telemachos receive Athene?
15. What does this tell us about him?
16. Whom does Telemachos visit first?
17. Whom does he visit second?

18. Does he threaten the suitors before he leaves Ithaka?
19. How does he amaze Penelope his mother?
20. What story does Nestor tell Telemachos?
21. Is Helen a sympathetic character in the Odyssey?
22. What do Menelaos and Odysseus have in common?
23. What do the suitors want to do with Telemachos?
24. How is Kalypso persuaded to release Odysseus?
25. What happens after Odysseus builds his raft?
26. Who is Penelope?
27. Who is Telemachos?
28. Who is Menelaos?
29. Who is Helen?
30. Who is Poseidon?
31. Who is Athene?
32. Who is Nestor?
33. Who is Kalypso?
34. Who is Nausikaa?
35. Who is Hermes?
36. Who is Alkinoos?
37. Who is Demodokos?
38. Who is Euryalos?
39. Who are Ares and Aphrodite?
40. Who are the Kikonians?
41. Who are the Lotus Eaters?
42. Who is Polyphemos?
43. Who is Poseidon?
44. Who is Aiolos?
45. Who are the Laistrygones?
46. Who is Circe?
47. What is Hades?
48. Who is Elpenor?
49. Who are Skylla and Charybdis?
50. What are the cattle of Helios?
51. What is Aiaia?
52. Who is Teiresias?
53. Who are the Sirens?

## Optional Activity

With some of your friends or classmates, write a short play about the reunion of Odysseus with Telemachos, and Odysseus with Penelope. Once you are happy with the wording of the play, assign parts and act it out.

### READING ASSIGNMENT:
Book 19

# SESSION XVII: WRITING
Book 19

## Progymnasmata

Classical training in rhetoric included preparatory writing exercises called the *progymnasmata.* These exercises in composition introduced the beginning student to basic forms and techniques that would then be used and combined when practicing more advanced exercises and speeches. One of these progymnasmata was called the *encomium,* a composition written to praise an individual. This writing exercise expounds the virtues of a specific person (e.g., Joe is a strong warrior), but does not talk about virtue in a general sense (e.g., strength in war is admirable).

An encomium has six parts. The *Prologue* comes first. It introduces the topic and, at the end of the paragraph, states or implies the opinion of the writer. The second part of this exercise is a paragraph called *Description of Heritage* about the person in question. The writer looks for ways to praise the person on account of his family history. For instance, if a person comes from righteous parents, then highlight the fact that he learned his righteous habits at home and added to the glory of the family name. Next comes a paragraph called *Description of Upbringing.* The point is to show how the person profited from a good education or overcame a bad one. The most powerful part of the encomium comes next: the *Description of Deeds.* In this section the writer praises the excellencies of the mind, body and fortune of the subject. For example, the writer praises the practice of philosophical virtue, the way the person looked and his wealth, influence or social stature. Since Christianity has transformed our society it seems out of place to dwell on physical appearance or possessions, so instead the paragraph should concentrate on the actions and motives of the subject. This can be especially powerful if his life demonstrates a pattern. Next is a *Comparison* of the subject to someone else to portray him in a favorable light. The final paragraph is an *Exhortation* or *Prayer* in which others are called on to imitate this person's example.

*Write an encomium on the following statement:* Odysseus demonstrated self-control. *Use the following outline as the structure for your composition, making each part one paragraph long.*

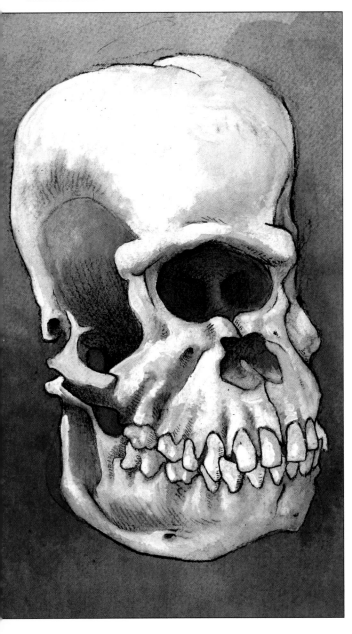

Where does one dig up the idea for a myth? Some think that the ancient Greeks found fossils that inspired stories of the one-eyed giants, like Polyphemos. On February 5, 2003, *National Geographic News* reported the discovery of the tusk, several teeth, and some bones of a *Deinotherium giganteum* on the Greek island Crete. A distant cousin of the elephant, this mammal—the second-largest ever to walk the earth—stood fifteen feet tall at the shoulder, and had tusks that were over four feet long. The supposed eye socket was formed from an extremely large nasal opening in the center of the skull.

V.  Comparison
   • Portray the person favorably to someone else
VI. Exhortation or Prayer
   • Call upon others to imitate this person's example

READING ASSIGNMENT:
Books 20 and 21

# SESSION XVIII: DISCUSSION
Books 20 and 21

## A Question to Consider

If someone were stealing from you, how should you treat them?

*Discuss or list short answers to the following questions:*

### Text Analysis

1. We have previously considered the importance of hospitality. How is this reinforced at the return of Odysseus?
2. The entire book is about Odysseus being "unkalypsoed" or revealed out of hiddenness. How is all of Ithaka "unkalypsoed?"
3. Odysseus and Telemachos make plans to deal with the suitors. Why do we not have any doubts about the propriety of this?
4. Why do Odysseus and Telemachos return to the house separately?
5. What is significant about Melanthios?
6. What is the point of Argos?
7. Odysseus is dressed like a beggar. Why do you think he actually begs from the suitors?
8. What does the boxing match with Iros tell us?

I.  Prologue
   • Introduce the topic
   • State your opinion
II. Description of Heritage
   • Praise the person on account of his family history
III. Description of Upbringing
   • Show how the person profited from his education
IV. Description of Deeds
   • Praise the excellencies of his actions and motives

## Cultural Analysis

1. Why is it important that a culture practice the Golden Rule (i.e., "do as you would be done by")?
2. Applying the Golden Rule is not always easy. How does it apply to our treatment of the alien and stranger in our midst?

## Biblical Analysis

1. What kind of justice does the Bible demand concerning thieves? (Ex. 22:1–5)
2. How is this justice "merciful" (especially when compared to Odysseus's)?
3. Are there cases of stealing where the thief might pay with his life?
4. What would the Bible say about "jail time" for a thief?

## Application

1. When was the last time you showed kindness to a bum that might have been an angel (Heb. 13:2)?
2. When you were a guest at someone else's house, did you conduct yourself like the suitors? Were your hosts thinking about stringing a bow?
3. What care should we take in "testing" others? Is that ever appropriate?

## SUMMA

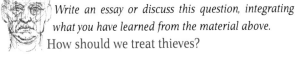

*Write an essay or discuss this question, integrating what you have learned from the material above.* How should we treat thieves?

## Optional Activities

Take a bow and arrow and set up the kind of target that Odysseus shot through. Line up *two* small circles in a straight line, and try to get some idea how hard it was for Odysseus to shoot through the holes in twelve axe heads. Or draw an image of the suitors and find a local archery range or an area where it is safe to shoot arrows and aim high. It is time to bring a little justice—Ithaka style. Try to find an archery expert who will let you attempt to string a long bow. Also, if you want to add even more to the event, hold a weaving contest with the girls. The winners are crowned Penelope and Odysseus.

### READING ASSIGNMENT:
Books 22 and 23

# SESSION XIX: REVIEW
Books 22 and 23

## Comprehension Questions

*Discuss or list short answers to the following questions:*

1. When Telemachos leaves Menelaos and Helen, she gives him a gift of a wedding garment. Why is this significant?
2. Is it sub-Christian to show hospitality on the chance that you might be entertaining an angel? This is a question about motives. Does the Bible prohibit any thought of reward, or does the Bible encourage it?
3. In the book of Romans, Paul tells us not to take revenge, because "vengeance is Mine, saith the Lord" (Rom. 12–13). Is Odysseus violating the spirit of this passage in what he is preparing to do (Books 19–20)?

### READING ASSIGNMENT:
Book 24

*Note: Tomorrow's class will be an Evaluation. To prepare for this test you should review your earlier answers to the questions in previous lessons.*

# SESSION XX: EVALUATION
Book 24

## Comprehension Questions

Grammar

*Briefly identify the following characters, things, or peoples with one or two sentences. (2 points each)*

1. Argos
2. Telemachos
3. Athene
4. Theoklymenos
5. Antinoos

Logic

*Questions should be answered with a paragraph or two. (10 points each)*

1. Narrate the basic outline of the story of the *Odyssey*.
2. Describe and evaluate Odysseus's character

overall—his intelligence, justice, courage, perseverance, etc.—drawing from everything you know of him in this epic as well as the *Iliad* (if you have read it). Whatever your assessment is, be prepared to defend it.

A fifth-century terra-cotta relief depicting Odysseus disguised as an old beggar, finally returning to his distressed Penelope.

Lateral Thinking

*This essay challenges you to take concepts and ideas learned in the* Odyssey *and see the connections that these ideas have in other works that we have read this year. Write up to a 1,000 word essay on one of the three questions. This answer is worth 15 points.*

1. This story is one of return and cleansing. What other stories follow this same structure?
2. Will Odysseus end his days as a seafarer?
3. When Odysseus dies, what does he have to look forward to?

# OPTIONAL SESSION A: ACTIVITY

## O Brother, Where Art Thou?

View the movie *O Brother, Where Art Thou?* The movie is based on the *Odyssey*. Write down as many parallels (however loose you might believe them to be) to this poem. Do you think the parallels work?

# OPTIONAL SESSION B: DISCUSSION

## A Question to Consider

Are you ever justified in killing someone for stealing from you? When? When can you fight back?

*Discuss or list short answers to the following questions:*

### Text Analysis

1. The final stage for the cleansing of the house has arrived. What is significant about Odysseus and

Telemachos removing the armor from the hall?

2. Why are the suitors to be considered less than dogs?

3. Penelope sets up a contest to determine whom she will marry. What is significant about the contest?

4. What dramatic effect does Homer accomplish by postponing the revealing of Odysseus to Penelope?

## Cultural Analysis

1. What does our culture do to thieves?

2. Why does our culture fail to bring justice to criminals, especially thieves?

## Biblical Analysis

1. What is the biblical punishment for kidnapping, or man-stealing (Ex. 21:16)?

2. What is the normal biblical punishment for stealing (Ex. 22:1)?

3. Why does Odysseus not follow this injunction of Exodus 22:1 (besides the fact that he has never heard it) and demand restitution from the suitors?

4. Why does our culture tend to ignore Exodus 22:1?

## SUMMA

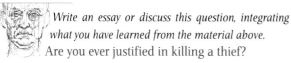 *Write an essay or discuss this question, integrating what you have learned from the material above.*
Are you ever justified in killing a thief?

# OPTIONAL SESSION C: DISCUSSION

## A Question to Consider

What does fidelity in marriage mean? What if your husband or wife had been missing for 20 years?

*Discuss or list short answers to the following questions:*

## Text Analysis

1. Is there any reason to believe that Penelope has been at all tempted by the suitors? Read the section on the geese again (Book 19, 535–550). What is Penelope's reaction when an eagle kills them all?

2. Not only are the suitors killed, but so are the serving women. Does this seem just or unjust? Why or why not?

3. How is the test of the bed in Book 23, lines 173–230 actually a two-way test?

4. Is there any symbolic significance to the construction of the marital bed of Odysseus and Penelope?

5. Arriving in Hades, what is Amphimedon's complaint?

6. What is the significance of Agamemnon's praise of Penelope?

7. When the suitors are killed, does this mean that Odysseus's troubles are over?

8. Does Penelope believe that Odysseus has taken his revenge when she hears about the death of the suitors?

## Cultural Analysis

1. Odysseus is lucky in his homecoming. The caprice or whim of the gods has turned, and now events favor him. Compare the pagan "hope" that their luck may turn with the Christian confidence that all things work together for good (Rom. 8:28). What impact would these two beliefs, widely held, have on any given society?

2. Odysseus reveals himself to Laertes while he is farming. Some of the proofs he gives of his identity have to do with the identity of the fruit trees and so on. Why might this have great significance?

3. We noted earlier that Odysseus exhibits sexual self-control but not sexual purity with Kalypso and Circe. Compare this with his treatment of his own serving maids. Is this an example of the ancient double standard? Or was the problem that Odysseus had with the servants more a matter of the disorder involved than with the morality of it?

4. Discuss how a culture of personal revenge might function or not function.

## Application

1. Have you ever thought of taking revenge upon someone? What ought to hinder you in this? What should your thoughts be on it?

2. Odysseus does what he does because he comes home and finds everything in a disorderly and chaotic state. If he were to visit your bedroom,

would he be tempted to pull out his bow and start shooting people?

3. When you have received discipline for some wrongdoing, do you respond the way the suitors did (complaining even in Hades), or do you accept it fully as a lesson from the Lord?

## SUMMA

*Write an essay or discuss this question, integrating what you have learned from the material above.* What does fidelity mean?

## ENDNOTES

1   William Wyatt, "The Education of Everyman," *Chronicles,* September, 1997, pp. 19-22.

2   C.S. Lewis, *A Preface to Paradise Lost* (London: Oxford University Press, 1942 ), p. 64.

3   C.S. Lewis, *An Experiment in Criticism* (London: Cambridge University Press, 1961), p. 141.

4   Dylan, Jakob. *Invisible City.* The Wallflowers. On the album *Bringing Down the Horse.* 1996. Interscope Records. This citation should not be considered a blanket endorsement of the Wallflowers, this album or song. It is meant to prove the point that the fame of Odysseus's guile still captivates us today.

5   *This endnote appears only in the teacher's edition.*

# HISTORIES

Whether you know it or not you are on a ride down a river. The river is called Western Civilization. There are other rivers, but this one is yours … and it's a great river—you are very fortunate. Long ago the West became Christian. The waters of the river, however, stretch back even further. The headwater flowed by a beach called Marathon and through a bay called Salamis. Herodotus of Halicarnassus records some of the beginning of this great river. Christ came long ago and purified the waters of the river. Sadly, today the water is polluted. It was a new river back then, and because of this newness it was full of wonder. Looking back on this beginning, many have been inspired. The writings of America's founding fathers and the architecture of our great buildings point back to the city of Athens, and that city was possible because of the greed of great kings, the courage of a rag-tag bunch of divided city-states and a tight bay where a great armada could not move. All of this and much more awaits in one of the greatest stories ever told.

## GENERAL INFORMATION
## Author and Context

Five centuries before Christ's birth, global power was held and dominated by the Persian Empire. Rome was nothing; Greece was a collection of poor and fundamentally bitter city-states. Unconquered kingdoms remained in Africa (particularly the long-lived Ethiopians), but the continent had already been circumnavigated. The migration of mankind that eventually formed early Britain had not yet occurred, and on any map that portion of the world would have been functionally blank as men at that time did not yet use the phrase "Here be dragons" to designate the unknown. If other histories are to be believed, it was primarily inhabited by giants.

To Persia, Egypt was a province of the Persian Empire, the pharaoh, merely a governor. Persia was strength, but it was also greed, and to the Persian mind no land ought to remain free of its rule. Virtually

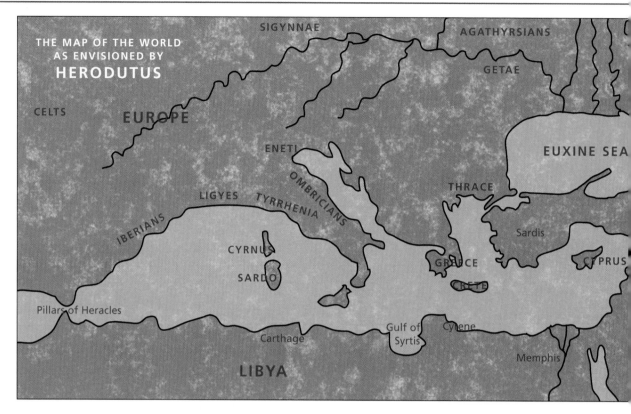

THE MAP OF THE WORLD
AS ENVISIONED BY
**HERODUTUS**

SIGYNNAE

AGATHYRSIANS

GETAE

CELTS

EUROPE

ENETI

EUXINE SEA

OMBRICIANS

LIGYES

TYRRHENIA

THRACE

IBERIANS

Sardis

CYRNUS

GREECE

CYPRUS

SARDO

CRETE

Pillars of Heracles

Gulf of
Syrtis

Cyrene

Carthage

Memphis

**LIBYA**

all lands were required to send "earth and water"—signs of submission—to the king they believed to be the king of kings.

It was in this time that Herodotus was born in Halicarnassus (484 B.C.), now the Turkish city of Bodrum. He died in 425 B.C. at the age of 59. He came into the world at roughly the time of the Persian Wars, and grew up to document the course and cause of the bloodshed and, incidentally, the birth of something else: the West. It was in the Persian Wars that the heritage that western man now takes for granted first found strength and overthrew Persia.

Little is known of Herodotus. He was probably exiled by a tyrant named Lygdamis, who ruled Halicarnassus. He then moved to the island of Samos and finally to Thurii in Southern Italy. While he probably did not visit all the places that he wrote about, it seems that he did venture out to Athens, Egypt, Scythia and Cyrene.

## Significance

What Herodotus did in writing his *Histories* cannot be over emphasized. He is the first modern historian. In fact, the word history comes first from his usage. Of course others recounted history in the way we think of it, and Herodotus freely quotes Homer authoritatively—after all Homer was the historian of the Trojan War. But he also takes issue with him where he believes that mistakes were made or poetic license taken. Poetry was not considered non-historical in the way that we would think of it. It was the medium in which history was passed on and was no doubt more memorable to its students than our history books. What Herodotus did was to compile the accounts and stories—firsthand and hearsay—of what caused, occurred in and resulted from the Persian Wars. The *Histories* are most likely a collection of lectures or recitals that he would give in Athens and other places in his capacity as a factual story-teller. The compilation of his stories is the first like it, to be followed not too long after by the work of Thucydides that laid out the course of the Peloponnesian War between Athens and Sparta. Herodotus is notorious for his tangents, but his tangents demonstrate much wisdom. He seems to be the first to have realized, or at least to have collected, many small stories and tales that, when placed together, communicate a unified whole.

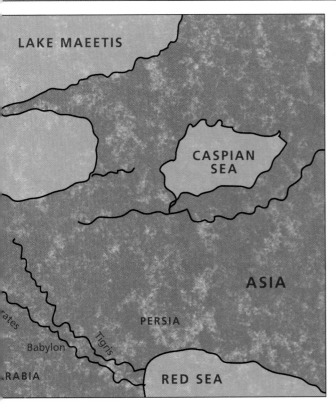

LAKE MAEETIS

CASPIAN SEA

ASIA

PERSIA

Babylon

Tigris

ARABIA

RED SEA

## Main Characters

Herodotus tells a story in which there are many great characters, and he communicates honestly about them, warts and all. Some of the characters of chief importance are the great Persian kings: Cyrus, Darius, and, of course, Xerxes. Of these, Xerxes stands out in importance, because it is he who actually leads the great army into Greece seeking revenge for Marathon. Xerxes is a great but foolish king who gets a little obsessive about Greece, even rebelling and punishing the wind and the sea when it acts disagreeably.

On the Greek side, we meet men of equally great standing with equally striking flaws. Leonidas sets standards for bravery that might be unmatched in all of history. Themistocles, the great strategist who eventually sinks the Persian fleet, also is a politician whose services are for sale to the highest bidder and a man who actually aids the enemy if it seems in his interest.

The most striking thing about the characters in Herodotus is how many of them there are. It seems that there is an endless assortment of stories to be told and no lack of odd and appealing or gross and appalling characters to fill them.

## Summary and Setting

Herodotus has been called the "Father of History." He is generally credited with being the first person to write with a cause and effect way of looking at the world. Substantially gone are the references to the gods directing the affairs of men as is routinely seen in Homer's epic poetry. Of course, as Christians we would want to challenge this on two counts. First, inspired history was being written in Scripture well before the days of Herodotus. And secondly, while it was good for Herodotus to exclude the gods as directing the affairs of men, it is not good to do the same thing with the living God.

Herodotus tells us his goal immediately. He wishes to tell us the cause of the hostilities between the invading barbarians and the Greeks. In the first six books Herodotus discusses the various cultures and conquests that went into the creation of the Persian Empire. He is setting the stage and introducing all the players and all of their stories before letting the action begin, though there is plenty of action in the first six books. In books seven, eight, and nine we read of the actual invasions of Greece by Xerxes, then king of Persia.

Herodotus documents the rise of the Persian Empire (circa 550 B.C.) and its great defeat at the hands of the Greeks in the Persian War (circa 500-480 B.C.). Herodotus lived in the aftermath of Greek victory. Athens, having played a major and glorious role in the war, now entered into a highly rational era in which human reason served as the highest authority, the type of era that frequently follows victory (or defeat) in a major conflict. Having passed through fire, cultures frequently change and revolt against former or traditional ways of doing things. In the case of Athens, this revolt—and the following conflict with other Greek city-states—made them what they are generally thought to have been: a cultural center for the arts, philosophy, and politics. Contemporaries that Herodotus may have met during the time he spent in Athens most likely included Sophocles and Euripides, Pericles, the famed general, even Socrates and perhaps Hippocrates (often thought to be the founding father of medicine). Some plays by the comic playwright, Aristophanes, even poke fun of and mock the newly rational Athens, first basking in victory over Persia, then in dominance among Greeks.

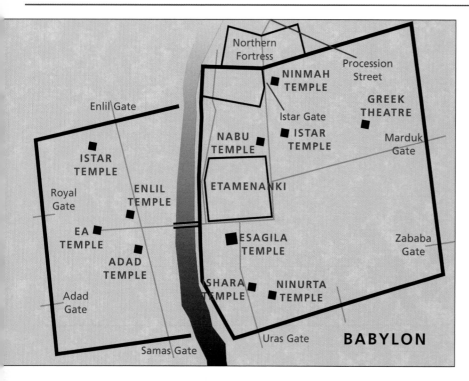

Map of Babylon showing: Northern Fortress, Enlil Gate, NINMAH TEMPLE, Procession Street, Istar Gate, GREEK THEATRE, ISTAR TEMPLE, NABU TEMPLE, Marduk Gate, ISTAR TEMPLE, Royal Gate, ENLIL TEMPLE, ETAMENANKI, EA TEMPLE, ESAGILA TEMPLE, Zababa Gate, ADAD TEMPLE, SHARA TEMPLE, NINURTA TEMPLE, Adad Gate, Uras Gate, BABYLON, Samas Gate

## Worldview
### The World of Herodotus

Life is not a symphony. It is not a painting, and it is not a loud sweater. But, in some sense, it is like all of these things. A symphony is a single item, a unit. So is a painting and so is a sweater, no matter how tacky it may be. They are each singular but are made up of a number of seemingly unrelated items. The violins seem to have nothing in common with or related to the percussion, and the horns are a group given to much independence. But when all of them are working together under an arrangement by Vivaldi, a new thing comes into existence, and it sounds like something aptly called Spring. The same is true of every brush stroke of an artist, every shadow and shift in color that makes up a Rembrandt. Black and brown and golds—not related, but in Rembrandt's hands they become a windmill, cliff and sea. And, of course, in your grandmother's hands, strands of green, red and brown yarn become a reindeer with places for your head and arms.

Herodotus is not your grandmother, and he is more like Rembrandt than Vivaldi. God the Father, Author from before time, is the one who laid out the color and structure of History. Herodotus, like Rembrandt, is one who was able to see and record the many elements and stories that came together to make History the single story that it is.

All of creation imitates the Creator, and the Creator is both One and Many—both one-in-three and three-in-one. This is quite a mystery, yet one that is before us all the time. All events in history carefully and meticulously contribute to a single story carrying out the grand will of God. Each member of the Trinity, Father, Son and Holy Spirit acts in ways that might seem like an unharmonious cacophony to the untrained ear, but these many sounds come together into one beautiful masterpiece. The story of mankind mirrors this aspect of its Creator. Nothing could be more chaotic than human history, and yet it is all woven and interwoven, threads crossing and weaving, into a single plot-line. The story is one of defeat, fall and death and victory, glory and resurrection.

Initially, this might not seem too dire a concern, but it was a problem for pagans (both ancient and modern ones). Their philosophers either believed that the world was all made up of one thing (Thales, a well-known Greek philosopher thought that everything was water—even though he admitted that some things do not look or feel much like water), or they claimed that the world was made up of a collection of unrelated things. One group affirmed the unity; the other sided with diversity. They knew no God who was both One and Many, but they were confronted by a world that screamed this fact. There was a lot of head scratching.

Apart from Christianity no philosophy or worldview adequately explains or describes the world and stories in which we live. Cultures, and the gods that rule them, ricochet from the One to the Many. It is only in the Trinity that the two ideas find unity, because God is both One and Many. He is singular and plural, and He, like a conductor or an author, shatters things into pieces only to bring them into harmony, or resolution.

In modern times we can see cultures pursue both the One and the Many. In the early- and mid-twentieth century every one tried to be the same: cubicles were created in tall and sky-scraping glass boxes. Why? To eliminate diversity. Everything was to be the same. Everything must be one. Products were advertised and sold based on the fact that "everyone else is already wearing this." During and after the 1960's, post-modernity has tried to change things, though not effectively. Diversity is lauded and praised, but everyone must conform to it. Buildings are designed to look as if they are falling down, or wearing their structures on the outside. Artists fling paint at canvas in a hopeless quest for pure chaos, pure non-conformity. Even restaurants attempt to decorate by screwing objects randomly to the ceiling or walls. Our culture bounces back and forth because neither the One alone, nor the Many alone, can maintain logical consistency or represent the created reality.

The world in which Herodotus lived was different from ours. He lived before Christ. The rebellious thrones, dominations, principalities and spiritual powers that ruled over the world then had not yet been bound by Christ. (Col. 2:15) In other words, characters like Zeus and a lot of other mythological characters were real demonic beings exercising authority over mankind. Paul says that these false gods were demons (1 Cor. 10:19–21). A plurality of voices, addressing man, proclaimed what was good or evil and overthrew nations and men. Many of these wicked demons who were proclaimed to be gods were attempting to claim supremacy and attempting to gain as much worship from men as they could. Of course all of these were within the divine plan of God, functioning simply as characters in the story, but Christ had not yet bound the strong man (Mark 3:26, 27).

Many modern secularists laugh at Herodotus or believe that his stories were folk tales. They think that he is naïve or crazy for what he believed actually happened in history. He refers to flying serpents, donkey unicorns and to a woman who gave birth to a lion cub. He describes peoples like the long-lived

This glazed brick relief depicting a royal guardsman was found in the palace of Darius I at Susa.

Ethiopians and the strength their god or gods had given them. They laugh because it is obvious that Herodotus believed in the gods and believed that they really did things. He did not believe everything he was told. He believed the gods were real, but he was just as convinced of the lying nature of man. But he believed far more than most modern people would ever believe about strange matters.

Christians should take Herodotus seriously. They, of all people, should know that angels rebelled against God and were cast down. It should not surprise us that wicked spiritual entities would meddle in and seek to rule the affairs of men. We should not look down on Herodotus for believing the stories he believes, but we should appreciate the fact that we do not stand where he did. The strong man has been bound, and we live in a world increasingly dominated by the effects of the Christian faith, but most of all, by the rule of Jesus Christ, Who conquered death and sits at the right hand of His Father, waiting for the remainder of His enemies to be made a footstool. Enemies remain, but they are not the enemies Herodotus knew.

Herodotus was a polytheist—he believed in many gods. With many gods it is difficult to slip into the folly of modernity and pursue Oneness, though it was done, and by Greeks. When we read the Histories, we should hear the terrible music of the gods. Herodotus knew many gods and these gods speak with many voices and leave Herodotus in a land where there are many truths (or, as we might say, no real truth). The stories are full of tangents and tacked on genealogies. A character may be introduced, and then that character's father may require an introduction, and, as it turns out, that man's father had a gold goat that had once belonged to a pharaoh who had it made and thrown into the Nile to stop a pestilence. Of course, we must also learn how the pestilence came about. Egypt is introduced, a whole country, not merely a man, and so we must hear its story rewinding in what seems like a story that is never going forward but always trying to find the beginning.

But Herodotus was not a consistent polytheist. His story-telling is not a mere conglomeration of facts and anecdotes, the stream of consciousness reminiscences of a senile Greek. All of it comes together; all of it contributes to a greater tale, a greater story. Out of the "many" truths and pile of assorted stories, comes "one" great tale. All of it has a destination. Herodotus is repeating a large portion of one of God's stories, and he is trying to fit as much of it in as possible. God used a man named Croesus to bring about the destruction of Lydia at the hands of Cyrus the Persian. God drove Cambyses the Incestuous mad and sent him across the desert to find and conquer the long-lived Ethiopians, only to turn back when his men grew so hungry that they drew lots to pick one out of every ten to be eaten. God, never One to be stingy when it comes to creating villains, desperadoes to be eventually overthrown, did not hold back in shaping the character of the Scythians, men who would drink from the skulls of the enemies, and line the skulls of any relatives they had killed with gold, a cup for feast days. In the tale of Persia, the Scythians were the only people to bring fear to the Persians. They were not defeated, though they did not stand as the Greeks did. The Scythians, those villains, would live on in wickedness to be truly defeated only by the gospel. The world was very different before Christ.

Herodotus was aware of the multitude of threads and histories that go on in any nation. But he was equally aware that those many threads all come together into a single story. All of the many have a single unity of purpose, a single plot made up of millions. Herodotus did not know what that unity was. He did not know Christ or even the true overarching story that is all of history, but he was not a consistent Greek. He did not simply hand himself over to the noise of many voices, or the judgments of many gods, as do some of the characters he describes. Nor did he unify the story as some Greeks did through an appeal to the Fates, three feminine Greek deities who supposedly governed all things. He saw the world boiling through its action, unified and diverse. And when he saw it, he wrote it down.

## The Image of God, Persian and Greek

Apart from the four Persian emperors, any leading characters are hard to identify. Men crop up, are given histories and then die on the battlefield or win gloriously. Then, not to leave threads untied, Herodotus adds that this legendary hero went on to receive bribes later in life, was exiled and died at sea, or some equivalent end. Nearly every character is revealed to have been, at some point, a villain or criminal and in need of serious civil punishment. The

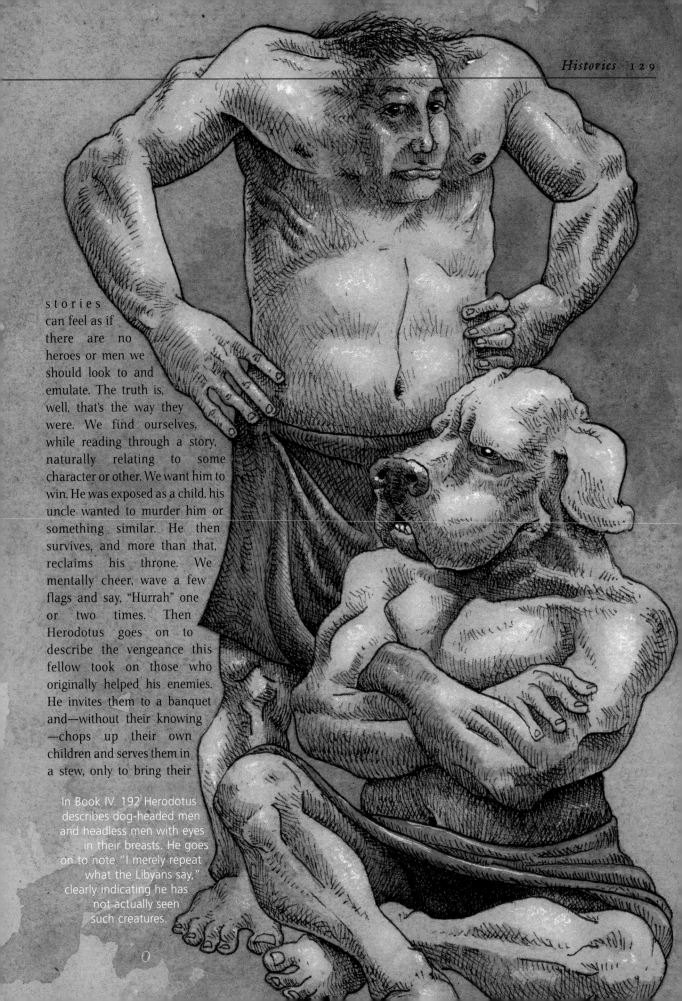

stories
can feel as if
there are no
heroes or men we
should look to and
emulate. The truth is,
well, that's the way they
were. We find ourselves,
while reading through a story,
naturally relating to some
character or other. We want him to
win. He was exposed as a child, his
uncle wanted to murder him or
something similar. He then
survives, and more than that,
reclaims his throne. We
mentally cheer, wave a few
flags and say, "Hurrah" one
or two times. Then
Herodotus goes on to
describe the vengeance this
fellow took on those who
originally helped his enemies.
He invites them to a banquet
and—without their knowing
—chops up their own
children and serves them in
a stew, only to bring their

In Book IV. 192 Herodotus
describes dog-headed men
and headless men with eyes
in their breasts. He goes
on to note "I merely repeat
what the Libyans say,"
clearly indicating he has
not actually seen
such creatures.

*Chart 1: Timeline*

This timeline notes the extensive overlap between familiar biblical stories and the events recorded by Herodotus. Isn't it fascinating to realize that this is the world in which Daniel lived?

| DATE (approximate) | EVENT | REFERENCE |
|---|---|---|
| 931 B.C. | Israel divides into two kingdoms. | 1 Kings 12, 2 Chron. 10 |
| 800 | Jonah takes an unusual route to preach repentance to the Assyrian capital of Ninevah. | Jonah |
| 722 | Israel falls to Assyria. The southern kingdom of Judah still stands. | 2 Kings 17 |
| 701 | God kills 185,000 Assyrians, answering King Hezekiah's prayer. | 2 Kings 19, 2 Chron. 32 |
| 601 | Daniel and friends taken captive to Babylon, where he serves at court. He also serves at the Persian court after Babylon is conquered. | Daniel |
| 586 | Judah falls to Nebuchadnezzar, king of Babylon. The Temple is destroyed. Final deportation of the Jews to Babylon. | 2 Kings 24–25, 2 Chron. 36 |
| 560–547 | Croesus, the king of Lydia, conquers coastal Ionia where many Hellenic (Greek) communities have been established. | Hist. I. 25–28 |
| 547 | The Persian king, Cyrus, overthrows Croesus. | Hist. I. 76–92 |
| 539 | Babylon falls to Persia. Cyrus, king of Persia, allows Jews to return and rebuild Jerusalem. | Ezra 1–5, Neh. 1–6 |
| 522 | Darius I seizes the Persian throne from the one pretending to be Smerdis. | Hist. III. 61–88 |
| 520 | The Temple is rebuilt in Jerusalem. | Ezra 6 |
| 516 | Esther made queen of Persia. | Esther |
| 499 | Persia attacks the Greek island of Naxos in the Aegean Sea. | Hist. V. 28–34 |
| 496 | Sophocles the playwright is born. | NA |
| 494 | The Ionian revolt is ended by Persia destroying Miletus in Asia Minor. Persian dominance of the Hellenistic cities in Ionia is restored. | Hist. VI. 18–21 |

heads out under dishes at the end of the meal. The *Histories* are full of this sort of story demonstrating both the depravity of man and the horror of paganism.

Man is made in the image of God, but he will shape himself in the image of any god he worships. In the pre-Christian cultures involved in these stories, there is very little pure nobility or virtue, and when it appears that a man is virtuous, it is most likely not that he is actually noble but because Herodotus has left things out for the sake of space. This is fundamentally because there were no noble gods. The gods worshiped in this period of history were petty liars, greedy for themselves and completely lacking in any self control. At times they would assist those who worshiped them, at others they would lie and trick their supplicants into wrongdoing so that they might destroy them or see them destroyed. They would

| DATE *(approximate)* | EVENT | REFERENCE |
| --- | --- | --- |
| 490 | Under Darius I, Persia invades Greece, and the Persian Wars and forty years of war begins. The Athenians and Plataeans win the battle of Marathon. | Hist. VI. 95–120 |
| 486 | Darius I dies. Xerxes, his son, succeeds him. | Hist. VII. 4 |
| 484 | Herodotus is born in Halicarnossos, a Greek colony in Asia Minor controlled by Persia. The playwright Euripides is also born. | NA |
| 481 | The Greek city states send representatives to Corinth, where they decide to unite against the Persian invasion. | Hist. VII. 145 |
| 480 | Xerxes' Persian troops annihilate the troops of King Leonidas of Sparta at Thermopylae. Persians severely damage and actually occupy Athens. Greek naval troops dominate the Persians in the straits of Salamis, near Athens. This battle is the first great naval conflict to be recorded in history. | Hist. VII. 198–239 |
| 479 | The Greeks defeat the Persians by land at Plataea and by sea at Mycale. This marks the end of the most intensive fighting of the Persian Wars. | Hist. IX. 31–107 |
| 478 | The Delian League, an alliance of Greek cities under the leadership of Athens, is formed. This association is intended for protection from future attacks, to avenge the destruction caused by Persia and to regain Greek cities still under Persian control. | NA |
| 472 | Aeschylus's tragedy *Persians* is staged. | NA |
| 470 | Socrates is born. | NA |
| 464 | Herodotus begins to travel, enabling him to write aspects of *Histories* from a firsthand viewpoint. | NA |
| 461 | Pericles begins his rise to power in Athens. | NA |
| 460 | Thucydides, the historian of the Peloponnesian War, is born. | NA |
| 458 | Aeschylus stages the *Oresteia*, his trilogy. | NA |

betray those who served them.

When we read the story of a hero like Themistocles, using brilliant naval strategy to resist the invading Persians, we should not be at all surprised to later discover that he was only in it for himself, took bribes and partook in many other activities that would get him crossed off any modern-day hero list. That is because what it means to be a hero now is no longer defined by ancient heroic codes which seemed to consist primarily in raping more of their women than they raped of yours. What it means to be noble and heroic is now defined by the cross. We must understand this difference to understand Herodotus.

Just as Herodotus is able to write more like a Trinitarian than he actually was (because the world he was watching is Trinitarian), so many of these men actually did display courage, bravery and forms of nobility. But it always breaks down somewhere. The desperately outnumbered Spartans made an absolutely spectacular stand against the Persians in a high mountain pass, killing thousands upon thousands of the Persian "Immortals" and others. But they were homosexuals and even taught the Persians new forms of perversion. The men we find ourselves cheering for—the protagonists or heroes—are actually introducing their enemies—the antagonists—to the finer delicacies of perversion. When we read of the nomadic Scythian cavalry that ducked and dodged the Persian forces into madness, and we find ourselves enjoying such bold and clever fighters, we need to remember that behind these men, stretched on wicker-like frames mounted vertically on the back of Scythian saddles, were the hides of men, flayed and tanned, that their clothes were also frequently of human skin and that the notches in their ears showed how many kings they had lived under.

What is a Christian to do when reading such things? How is it profitable at all? First, we should read the stories of such men and learn from them. These men corrupted the image of God that they bore, and yet they bear it sometimes better than we. Spartan perverts were men corrupted, but bold. They are not bolder than a man who bears the image of God faithfully, a man like King David, or Saint Boniface. David would destroy them and bring the evidence to Saul (1 Sam. 18:27). Boniface would laugh at them and pull their human sacrifices off of the altar, mocking their gods. The Scythians and the Spartans did not fear death, and death for them should have been feared. David and Boniface feared it even less, because even that enemy would be conquered. But we, we in this time, living in our First World countries, we have a very soft faith. If we met a Scythian dressed in human hide and drinking from the skull of his father, we would be afraid. He would be braver, bolder and more capable of looking into Death's eye and smirking. The Scythian—for all of his wickedness and immorality—is still frequently a better man, a man more clearly communicating the image of the true God, even though he worshiped a lesser and fallen deity who destroyed and damned him. A Scythian, or a Spartan, was at least a man worth converting, a man who would certainly serve a meaningful faith as well as he served a worthless king. In contrast, in our softness we tend to value God's kingdom very little.

There are very few true protagonists. We should look at Greek and Persian alike and see their wickedness, follies and strengths. We should learn the patterns of God's story and apply it to our day and age. Why was Xerxes, with all of the millions and millions marching and sailing into Greece, doomed to lose? How do we, from our perspective in history, know that he is going to lose before he ever does? Because this is how God writes stories. If you ever look about yourself and find that your country is a Goliath, towering over a small enemy, be afraid. God enjoys letting giants grow, giants like Persia, or our own country, but He always fells them, and He always fells them with something small or petty, a stone, or a ragged bunch of impoverished Greeks with schizophrenic gods. It is a curious thought to consider what God will use to rein in our present predominant unrighteousness.

Perhaps the most fundamental understanding we should gain from reading the stories Herodotus tells is gratitude. We should look around and see the worst of our enemies shaping themselves after the images of their gods. Idols, after Christ's conquest, are silly things. Nations can no longer offer themselves up

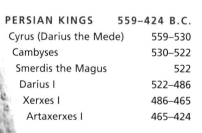

| PERSIAN KINGS | 559–424 B.C. |
|---|---|
| Cyrus (Darius the Mede) | 559–530 |
| Cambyses | 530–522 |
| Smerdis the Magus | 522 |
| Darius I | 522–486 |
| Xerxes I | 486–465 |
| Artaxerxes I | 465–424 |

The relief shown here is of a young Xerxes, who became king of Persia at the death of his father, Darius the Great.

to false gods given names like Zeus or Ares and be shaped in their image. Those gods are weak now. Though Germany tried to rebuild Babylon with its Third Reich, it was doomed to a short life because the era of deities dominating, protecting and fighting for a nation (at least successfully) is over. Gods no longer find pet favorites among men and decide that they should rule the world. The idols of today's idolaters are deafer, dumber and blinder than they have ever been. There will never be another Darius or Xerxes. And, thanks to the gospel and the overthrow of the old spiritual order, now we have flush toilets and air conditioning to boot.

## The Cross

The Christian faith has reshaped the world. Modern secularists chalk it up to the evolutionary process (though they rarely admit it). Society is better now because we have evolved or learned from our past. Religion, some would even say, is just another tool we use to push ourselves further up the chain of being. We have fewer cannibals in this country than were in ancient Persia because we are growing out of it, not because of the now-ingrained and residual moral compass that comes from living in a society that has been greatly influenced by the gospel. We have fewer people (at least in this country) who climb onto the tallest chair and announce that they are now as good as a god and everyone should bow down. That is what Zeus did. According to legend Zeus announced that he had overthrown his father and was now in charge. The idea of conquest for conquest's sake was perfectly normal. All the gods tried it and all of them jockeyed for power amongst themselves. Tyranny was an assumption, and the early democracy that came out of Athens after the Persian Wars was not much better.

Now leaders both Christian and pagan know that you have got to go kiss babies, put on a pair of overalls and drive a combine and throw your arms around strange, sweaty voters if you want to get elected to power. Of course most of them are just pretending, but you have to serve, to lower yourself, to become humble in order to be lifted up. This, now so ingrained in us that we do it hypocritically, would have been wildly foreign to any city-state or country described in Herodotus. The most noble people Herodotus mentions (and we don't get a close enough look to discover their dirt most times) were the long-

lived Ethiopians, and they chose their kings based on who was tallest and had strength proportionate to their height. Most people in those times just grabbed an axe, bribed or blackmailed a few followers and went about assassinating important people until they were the only ones left. One man Herodotus tells us about really wanted to be a tyrant (not something you could tell people nowadays), and so he hatched a plan, and boy was it revolutionary. He decided to be honest. Not because he really was, but because he knew people would begin coming to him to judge matters. And they did. Eventually he convinced them all to make him tyrant, and they did, and the first thing he did was to build himself a large palace and pass a law that no one was allowed to ever see the tyrant. The gospel and the example of Christ have changed a lot of things.

But moderns, though they believe evolution can change man, do not believe that evolution can weed out a bunch of Greek, Persian and Egyptian gods. All spiritual aspects of the *Histories*, in their view, must be discarded. Also anything that might make men then just as intelligent or as capable as we are. The existence of any gods would destroy their framework of materialism. The existence of sophisticated societies thousands of years ago does not overthrow evolution, but it is discouraging to those who believe in evolution.

Should we believe Herodotus? He says much about gods, the existence of flying serpents and snakes with wings. Could this all be true? Christians must not fall into the trap of rejecting strange stories because they cannot be experienced today. The world was different before Christ. The gods do not play the role that they once did because those demons have been thrown down. Men have changed because of the direct influence of the gospel or the social influence of the gospel directly influencing those around them. The world we see in the *Histories* is not a different world. It is not a world that never existed. It is a depressing world full of nations and men that love death and can truly love nothing else. It is a world that required a Savior. The incarnation, crucifixion and resurrection did not take place in a quiet middle-class neighborhood. It occurred right in the middle of a world completely mad, chasing after many wicked gods. Christ was born into the world Herodotus describes and He brought the many threads and

The tomb of Cyrus the Great. This memorial rises more than 35 feet above the windy plain at Murghab. This extraordinary leader, also known as Darius the Mede, allowed the Jewish people to return to Jerusalem to rebuild the temple during the time of Ezra and Nehemiah.

voices together into one purpose. He was born in that world. He has made it this world, and He is far from done. There remain many idols to topple, many knees will still bow. But the death blow has been struck, the former kings of the world have been overthrown and Another rules in justice and mercy.

Christians should not read Herodotus and believe him to be some ancient Greek with a bizarre imagination. They should read him and see in the strengths of his characters men who, by a kind common grace, still retained some humanity, some image of the Creator. In these same men they should see wickedness as long as they remained apart from Grace. They should not disbelieve in the world Herodotus describes; they should see a world apart from Christ.

Herodotus was a master, but he was writing only in imitation of the reality God wrote. He was, like Vivaldi or Rembrandt, or even your grandmother, seeing patterns and relationships that others did not see. Aspects of his stories are beautiful. Aspects are ugly and false. There is a bit of the misshapen reindeer on his sweater, but most of it is Rembrandt. All of it should lead us away from a simplistic understanding of reality. When we read Herodotus, we should see both the individual elements and the painting they create. We should hear the symphony.

—N. D. Wilson

## For Further Reading

Ezra 1; Isaiah 44:24–45:25; Daniel 5, 6

Spielvogel, Jackson. *Western Civilization.* Fifth Edition. Belmont, Calif.: Wadsworth/Thomson Learning, 2003. 62–66

*Veritas Press History Cards: New Testament, Greece and Rome.* Lancaster, Pa: Veritas Press. 13.

*Veritas Press Bible Cards: Judges through Kings.* Lancaster, Pa: Veritas Press. 63, 64.

*Veritas Press Bible Cards: Chronicles through Malachi and Job.* Lancaster, Pa: Veritas Press. 73–90.

# Session I: Prelude

## A Question to Consider

If you were going to write a great work of history how would you do it? What would you avoid at all costs?

*From the General Information above answer the following questions:*

1. What was the name of the culture that was "birthed" and found strength in winning the Persian Wars?
2. Why was Herodotus nicknamed "The Father of History?"
3. What was the goal of Herodotus in writing the *Histories?*
4. What was the importance of Persia in the ancient world?
5. When was the rise of the Persian Empire? At what war were they defeated? When? By whom?
6. How is the world of Herodotus different from our world? What major historic event made the change?
7. It is said that Herodotus writes of many events that weave together into one great story. To what Christian understanding can we relate this ancient writer's method and understanding?

 **Reading Assignment:**
Book I. 1–94

# Session II: Discussion
Book I. 1–94

## A Question to Consider

What can cause a small insignificant event to escalate into a very large conflict?

*Discuss or list short answers to the following questions:*

### Text Analysis

1. Why does Herodotus start with telling of women-stealing? Would it have been better to start some other way?
2. Describe Croesus's dream about the death of his son?

3. What steps did Croesus take to stop the dream from becoming reality? How did it become a reality anyway?
4. For what reason might we expect Croesus to be doomed from the start? Was it fair?

### Cultural Analysis

How would the United States respond if the president's daughter were kidnapped?

### Biblical Analysis

1. Name a biblical story where a dream of a fatality or major calamity became a reality.
2. Our sense of fairness is violated by Croesus being punished for the sins of his family four generations back. Is such an occurrence right or wrong biblically speaking? Why?

# Summa

 *Write an essay or discuss this question, integrating what you have learned from the material above.*
What is a right response by an individual who has been wronged?

**Reading Assignment:**
Book I. 95–216

# Session III: Discussion
Book I. 95–216

## A Question to Consider

What do prostitution, body piercing and tattoos have in common?

*Discuss or list short answers to the following questions:*

### Text Analysis

1. In ancient Babylon every woman was required to serve as a prostitute at the temple to Aphrodite at least once in her life. Why would a fallen deity be interested in such worship?
2. What would make women of Babylon, particularly the wealthy and the nobility, submit to such a demeaning practice? Social pressure? Tradition? Or were there actually *gods* who would exact

punishment on those who failed to serve as commanded?

3. As you have read so far do you get the impression that these ancient peoples loved their gods?

### Cultural Analysis

1. What do you think a person is saying with body piercings and tattoos? Is it fundamentally different from Babylonian activities (apart from being voluntary)?

2. First Corinthians 6:19 says "Do you not know that your body is a temple of the Holy Spirit, who is in you, whom you have received from God?" If the body is a temple how are Christians to keep it holy?

### Biblical Analysis

1. What could man possibly have that would cause demons to resent us enough that they would require destructive types of worship? (Hint: Gen. 1:27)

2. What should a Christian, a Daniel (who lived in this very kingdom), have done if living in such a culture?

3. What is the connection between Cyrus from Herodotus's writings and Darius the Mede in Scripture? (Hint: Compare Book I. 178–191 and Dan. 5:31.)[1]

4. How is it helpful to see connections between works like Herodotus and Scripture?

### SUMMA

*Write an essay or discuss this question, integrating what you have learned from the material above.* What does worship of false gods do to its worshipers?

## SESSION IV: RECITATION
Book I

### Comprehension Questions

*Answer these questions for factual recall.*

1. Who did the Persians say started the conflict between the Greeks and their enemies?
2. Who did the Phoenicians say started the conflict?
3. How did Croesus's great-great-grandfather become king?
4. What question did Croesus ask Solon?
5. Why did Croesus want to attack Persia?
6. How did Lydia and its capital city, Sardis, fall?
7. What advice did Croesus give his conqueror about looting that earned him a place as a counselor?
8. What infant was to be killed by Harpagus?
9. How was he spared?
10. How was his true identity eventually exposed?
11. The king now knew Harpagus had failed to have the king's grandson killed. What did the king do to Harpagus in response? How did Harpagus respond?
12. How old was a Persian son before his father would see him?

King Croesus of Lydia is here depicted on the funeral pyre to which he had been condemned when captured by King Cyrus. Herodotus reports that rain sent by Apollo extinguished the fire, saving his life. Afterward, he became Cyrus's advisor.

13. Does Herodotus think this was a good practice?
14. How did Cyrus die?
15. Whose fault was the loss Cyrus experienced?
16. What did the Massagetae think was the best way to die?

## Optional Activity

Read C.S. Lewis's essay "Xmas and Christmas: A Lost Chapter of Herodotus"[2] from *God in the Dock*, and then go to the mall or some other place where people gather. Write an essay describing the culture you see there. Cover all the aspects that Herodotus would. Whom do these people worship and how? Are they noble? Are they free men or slaves? How do they dress? By what names do they call their gods, and to what purpose do they live? Are they attractive? What is the architecture like? What size is the building, and how was it made? Attempt to see the practices of our culture for the first time through eyes not only from another country but from another time and serving other gods.

# SESSION V: WRITING

## Outline of Book I
### *with Biblical Integration*

*Copy the list below, which includes dates and references from the* Histories, *Book I, and the Bible. Fill in the blanks under "Event" from the list given below the chart by looking up the given reference.*

| DATE | BOOK | EVENT |
|------|------|-------|
| Unknown | Hist. I. 1–5 | _____ |
| c. 700 B.C. | Isaiah 44:24–45:13 | _____ |
| c. 586 B.C. | 1 Kings 24–25 | _____ |
| c. 560–547 B.C. | Hist. I. 6–29 | _____ |
| c. 547 B.C. | Hist. I. 46–91 | _____ |
| c. 539 B.C. | Daniel 5 | _____ |
| c. 539 B.C. | Hist. I. 178–191 | _____ |
| c. 538 B.C. | Daniel 6, Ezra 1 | _____ |
| c. 530 B.C. | Hist. I. 204–216 | _____ |

1. Daniel thrown into the lion's den, yet prospers, while the Jews are freed by Cyrus to return home and rebuild the Temple

2. Babylon/Belshazzar's fall to Darius the Mede/Cyrus announced by Daniel the day before it occurs when he interprets MENE, MENE, TEKEL, UPHARSIN

3. Cyrus follows the advice of Croesus when attacking the Massagetae where he and much of his army are destroyed

4. Croesus of Lydia established as king of Lydia and controlled numerous Greek lands from Sardis

5. Isaiah prophesies of Cyrus (a gentile) defeating Babylon and freeing the Jews long before Judah had even been taken captive

6. Jerusalem is destroyed along with the Temple, and Judah is taken captive by Babylon when Nebuchadnezzar was its king

7. Cyrus's first capture of Babylon

8. Conflict between Greeks and non-Greeks established

9. Cyrus, the Persian King, overthrows Croesus

### READING ASSIGNMENT:
Book II. 1–98

# SESSION VI: DISCUSSION
Book II. 1–98

## A Question to Consider

Do you believe in flying snakes?

*Discuss or list short answers to the following questions:*

### *Text Analysis*

1. Herodotus describes the bone-yard of flying snake skeletons that he visited. He claims to have seen them firsthand. Do you believe him? Why or why not?

2. Would you find it embarrassing to admit that you believed in flying snakes? Is it embarrassing to believe in dinosaurs? What does this tell us about who we're afraid of and who we want to respect us?

3. Read Job 39:9–12 in the King James Version. Then read the same passage in the New International Version. What is the difference? Why would translators decide that it must not be talking about a unicorn?

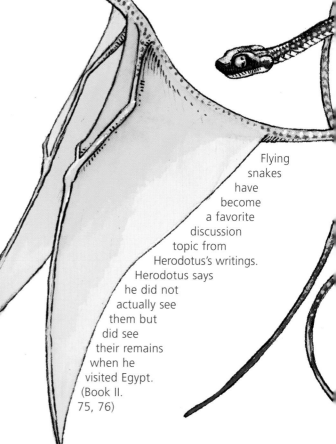

**KING JAMES VERSION**
Will the unicorn be willing to serve thee, or abide by thy crib? Canst thou bind the unicorn with his band in the furrow? or will he harrow the valleys after thee? Wilt thou trust him, because his strength is great? or wilt thou leave thy labour to him? Wilt thou believe him, that he will bring home thy seed, and gather it into thy barn?

**NEW INTERNATIONAL VERSION**
"Will the wild ox consent to serve you? Will he stay by your manger at night? Can you hold him to the furrow with a harness? Will he till the valleys behind you? Will you rely on him for his great strength? Will you leave your heavy work to him? Can you trust him to bring in your grain and gather it to your threshing floor?

Flying snakes have become a favorite discussion topic from Herodotus's writings. Herodotus says he did not actually see them but did see their remains when he visited Egypt. (Book II. 75, 76)

4. Why would Herodotus lie about having seen the bones of winged Arabian snakes that had been killed flying into Egypt? Why would he seem to take it for granted that his reader would be familiar with winged water snakes already?

## Application

### AGREE OR DISAGREE?

Christians today have allowed themselves to be bullied or duped into a secular mind-set. Evangelism is a top priority and Christians sharing their faith do not want to be laughed at. What chance is there that someone will convert to a religion that seems silly? We want Christianity to be taken seriously by secularists and atheists, so we tailor it to their views and opinions. They do not believe in dragons, so we say that it's a crocodile (the fire-breathing bit was just for effect). They don't believe in unicorns, so we translate it wild ox (after all, an ox from the side looks like he has just one horn). But the truth is that disbelief in these things is quite recent for mankind. Herodotus wouldn't bat an eye at these passages in Job. We are willing to believe in dinosaurs—because the secularists do—but not in what the Bible tells us, because that's embarrassing. When Herodotus tells us he saw a flying snake—and he has no motivation to be lying—well then, the man might well have seen a flying snake.

## SUMMA

*Write an essay or discuss this question, integrating what you have learned from the material above.*

What does Herodotus teach us about the animals of the ancient world?

READING ASSIGNMENT:
Book II. 99–182

# SESSION VIII: DISCUSSION
Book III. 1–66

## A Question to Consider

How does pride affect us? When is it ever satisfied?

*Discuss or list short answers to the following questions:*

### Text Analysis

1. Why did Cambyses invade Egypt? Will pride ever let a man stop?
2. How did the Ethiopian king answer the Persian spies? Was this wisdom or folly?
3. What lesson should be learned from Cambyses' death?

### Cultural Analysis

1. Where do we see sinful pride in our culture?
2. Where do we see examples of humility in our culture?
3. Why is pride such a problem in our culture?

### Biblical Analysis

1. What does Proverbs 16:18 say about pride?
2. What happened to the proud leaders of the people who rejected Christ (Matt. 27:15–26; Rev. 14:17–20)?[3]
3. How does Christ define true humility (Matt. 20:28)?

### Application

Look for areas in which you have influence. When God gives you influence and even responsibility, you need to ask if you are using it for His glory.

## SUMMA

*Write an essay or discuss this question, integrating what you have learned from the material above.*

What is the connection between leadership and humility?

READING ASSIGNMENT:
Book III. 67–160

# SESSION VII: RECITATION
Book II. 99–182

## Comprehension Questions

*Answer these questions for factual recall.*

1. Who did the Egyptians think were the oldest people?
2. How did they test this?
3. What did they learn?
4. What did the small snakes sacred to Zeus have that was distinctive? What was done with them when they died?
5. Why does Herodotus think the Trojan War lasted so long?
6. Why did the man thieving one of the pyramids have to behead his brother?
7. What, in the end, was this man's reward?
8. Why are we talking about Egypt? What is going to happen to it?
9. What is the most interesting fact of the story that Herodotus gives us about Egypt?

READING ASSIGNMENT:
Book III. 1–66

# SESSION IX: RECITATION
Book III

## Comprehension Questions

*Answer these questions for factual recall.*

1. Why does Herodotus think the Egyptian skulls were tough?
2. What metal was common to the Ethiopians?
3. What were the signs of Cambyses' insanity?
4. Why did he murder his brother, Smerdis?
5. How did Cambyses die?
6. Who pretended to be Smerdis?
7. How was the usurper discovered?
8. Why was it important to Darius and the others that the Magus be overthrown?
9. How did Indian men get gold from the ground?
10. Why does Herodotus think that the world was not overrun by the tiny, dappled, winged snakes and vipers?
11. How did the Arabians obtain cinnamon?
12. What scheme was devised for Darius to capture Babylon?

This 2,500-year-old, two-foot tall, green basalt statue depicts Ubjahorresne, an Egyptian dignitary. The hieroglyphics express his support for King Cambyses, who had conquered Egypt.

# SESSION X: WRITING PROJECT

## Writing a History

Herodotus is quite famous, maybe infamous, among scholars and devotees for his start-stop-starts, meanderings, rabbit trails and other distractions to what we might think is the main point, the important issue to the matters about which he writes.

This betrays a bias that we twenty-first-century readers have adopted toward the study of history. We have an expectation that history should be told from start to finish, beginning to end. Some find his constant back-tracking annoying. Maybe our mind-set is the problem and not his work. Maybe he has the right idea. We certainly remember more when history is told with such a visual and cultural backdrop.

You are to choose a topic that you would enjoy and historically document it in the same way or style that Herodotus uses to document the events leading up to the Persian Wars. Make sure it's trivial. Something like a certain bicycle, or the car your family drives, or your teacher. Think about where you would begin in your history. How far back should you go? Make connections and run down rabbit trails to make the story more interesting and understandable. Try to keep the story short—one page will be fine. Think quality, not quantity.

READING ASSIGNMENT:
Book IV. 1–142

# SESSION XI: DISCUSSION
Book IV. 1–142

## A Question to Consider

Does reciprocating violence (where one group attacks another and then the first group seeks revenge) have an end? Is there a way Christians should try to stop the cycle of violence between nation states, or perhaps we should just seek to totally destroy the enemies of the Triune God?

*Discuss or list short answers to the following questions:*

### Text Analysis

1. Hearkening back to Book I, what was the first offense the Greeks said the Persians committed against them?
2. For what reason did Darius attack the Scythians?
3. How did the Ionians prove to be fickle (wavering back and forth) in determining whose orders they would follow?

### Cultural Analysis

1. Cite a present day instance of a long-standing conflict with ancient grievances. Do you think ancient grievances are the causes of present conflict, or are they excuses after the fact?
2. In response to the 9/11 attack and destruction of the World Trade Center, we have destroyed the Saddam Hussein regime in Iraq and the Taliban rule of Afghanistan. As of this writing we have not stopped yet. How is this different or the same as Darius growing angry with the Athenians?

### Biblical Analysis

1. How might Darius, if behaving as a Christian, have responded to the Scythians instead of seeking revenge as indicated in Book IV. 1?
2. How can Darius's attack on the Scythians be justified in light of God's Word, which says, "Vengeance is Mine; I will repay" (Deut. 32:35)?

## SUMMA

*Write an essay or discuss this question, integrating what you have learned from the material above.*
How should we respond when we are wronged?

**READING ASSIGNMENT:**
Book IV. 143–205

The Persian infantryman was not as well equipped as his heavily-armored Greek adversary. His head was protected with merely a cloth hat, and his torso was covered with iron scales worn beneath a decorative tunic. His shield was made of wicker, and his spear was much shorter than that wielded by a hoplite.

# SESSION XII: RECITATION
Book IV

## Comprehension Questions

*Answer these questions for factual recall.*

1. What did the Scythian men find upon their return home?
2. How did the army overthrow their rebellious step-children?
3. What practice often associated with American Indians did the Scythians actually pioneer?
4. How did the Scythians bury their kings?
5. How does Herodotus think the Scythians bathed? What were they really doing?

6. What strategy did the Scythians adopt against Darius?
7. What Scythian tactic nearly destroyed Darius and the Persian army?
8. How did the Persians escape?
9. What were the strangest creatures that lived in Libya, according to what the inhabitants tell Herodotus?
10. How did Pheretime die?
11. What moral does Herodotus draw from this?

**READING ASSIGNMENT:**
Book V. 1–78

# SESSION XIII: DISCUSSION
Book V. 1–78

## A Question to Consider

Has the modern era brought us a greater fear of death than past eras?

*Discuss or list short answers to the following questions:*

### Text Analysis

1. What did the Trausi tribe of the Thracians believe about life and death?
2. What did the wives of a Crestonian tribesman do upon his death?
3. Why were ancient people so willing to face death willingly?

### Cultural Analysis

1. Should Christians be willing to die for something they consider worthwhile?
2. In relation to our current foreign conflicts, the American people seem very afraid of taking casualties. Why is this? Have we been spoiled by success in war?
3. What would a nation full of Christians unafraid of death look like? How would it change our country?

### Biblical Analysis

1. Why should Christians not fear death (especially in light of John 11:25)?
2. Why are we then still afraid?

### Application

There is something respectable about men willing to live boldly, to risk their lives to attain something. In Herodotus they frequently risk their lives for something foolish, but we do not do it at all. Do you know anyone who has risked his life for something? What was it? But rather than being unafraid of death, the ancients may have simply despised life. When Christians live full and beautiful lives and are still willing and unafraid to lay them down, then we will be more potent than any Persia.

### SUMMA

 *Write an essay or discuss this question, integrating what you have learned from the material above.* How should we face death?

### Optional Activity

If you have a father or a grandfather who fought in a war, talk to him about how he viewed death while he was fighting. Who did he know that died, and what did they die doing?

**READING ASSIGNMENT:**
None, but do the interview portion of the Session XIV activity.

# SESSION XIV: ACTIVITY

## Interview

*Find a veteran of a recent war (World War II, Korea, Vietnam, Iraq, etc.) and ask him these questions and some questions of your own. Write down the answers.*

1. In which war did you fight?
2. Were you in danger of being killed?
3. Did you believe you were fighting for a worthy cause so as to risk your life? Why or why not?

4.  What makes a war important enough to risk your life?
5.  What advice would you offer a young person today about why a war is fought? When it should be fought? And when it should be avoided?

*Compare the answers given to the interview questions. How did the responses compare to what you learned in Session XIII on matters of death and war?*

**READING ASSIGNMENT:**
Book V. 79–126

# SESSION XV: RECITATION
Book V

## Comprehension Questions

*Answer these questions for factual recall.*
1.  How did Histiaeus instruct Aristagoras to rebel against Darius?
2.  What trick did Alexander, son of Amyntas, play that ends in the death of their Persian guests?
3.  What did Aristagoras do when King Cleomenes first refused his proposal to assist in attacking Persia?
4.  What does Herodotus say is the reason Athenians were the finest fighters in the world?
5.  How many ships did the Athenians contribute?
6.  Did the Athenians continue to support the Ionians?
7.  What did Darius instruct a servant to tell him three times before each dinner?
8.  How did Aristagoras die?

**READING ASSIGNMENT:**
Book VI. 1–69

## SESSION XVI: WRITING

More history should be written in the style of Herodotus. The story-telling and cultural backdrop works like a painting, with all the canvas being important. History ought to feel more like time spent around a campfire than in a science lab.

For each of the five items listed below, write two or three cleverly phrased sentences that might be the beginning of a fictional account that Herodotus would be pleased to finish for you:

1. YOUR SCHOOL OR FAMILY
2. THE AMERICAN WAR FOR INDEPENDENCE
3. NOAH'S FLOOD
4. YOUR FATHER'S EMPLOYMENT
5. WORLD WAR II

When you have completed the sentences for each topic, pick one and expand the idea into a complete thought of no more than a paragraph or two.

READING ASSIGNMENT:
Book VI. 70–140

## SESSION XVII: RECITATION
Book VI

## Comprehension Questions

*Answer these questions for factual recall.*

1. Why did the Ionians lose at sea?
2. What happened to Histiaeus when he was captured and taken to Sardis?
3. How did Greece respond to Darius's demand for earth and water?
4. How many kings did the Spartans have?
5. What happened at Marathon?
6. Who was sent from the Athenian commanders at the Battle of Marathon to seek help from the Spartans?
7. What were the casualties?
8. How did Epizelus lose his sight?
9. Why did many Greek men gather for an extended period at the home of Cleisthenes, the ruler of Sicyon?

## Optional Activity

Research the origin of the modern day marathon races. When was the first "commemorative" marathon run? What is true and what is legend?

READING ASSIGNMENT:
Reading Assignment: Book VII. 1–99

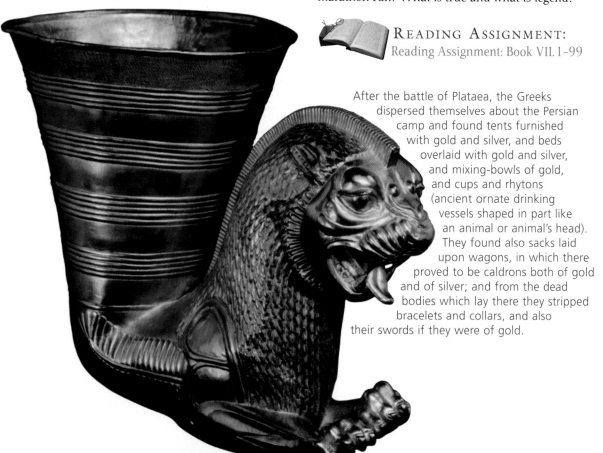

After the battle of Plataea, the Greeks dispersed themselves about the Persian camp and found tents furnished with gold and silver, and beds overlaid with gold and silver, and mixing-bowls of gold, and cups and rhytons (ancient ornate drinking vessels shaped in part like an animal or animal's head). They found also sacks laid upon wagons, in which there proved to be caldrons both of gold and of silver; and from the dead bodies which lay there they stripped bracelets and collars, and also their swords if they were of gold.

# SESSION XVIII: DISCUSSION
Book VII. 1–99

## A Question to Consider

Are dreams meaningful?

*Discuss or list short answers to the following questions:*

### Text Analysis

1. When Xerxes took the throne he first wanted to invade Greece, but then he was convinced not to attack. A dream convinced him to resume his plan to attack. What would you have advised Xerxes to do? Why?
2. Which of Xerxes' advisors stood alone advising against attacking Greece? How did Xerxes convince him to agree that attacking the Greeks should be done?

### Cultural Analysis

1. What is the modern-day scientific explanation of dreams?
2. What is a modern-day psychological belief about dreams?

### Biblical Analysis

1. Xerxes' gods were not trustworthy, but what would you do if you received a recurring dream telling you to do something?
2. Do the Scriptures affirm that God gives dreams to people?
3. Does this mean that every dream is a message from God?

## SUMMA

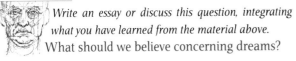 *Write an essay or discuss this question, integrating what you have learned from the material above.* What should we believe concerning dreams?

 READING ASSIGNMENT:
Book VII. 100–188

# SESSION XIX: DISCUSSION
Book VII. 100–188

## A Question to Consider

Is a war between nations or civilizations actually a war between their gods?

*Discuss or list short answers to the following questions:*

### Text Analysis

1. Xerxes was repeatedly commanded in a dream to invade Greece. But at the outset of his invasion he saw the omen of the eclipse, and a horse gave birth to a hare. Dreams pushed him one way, and omens seemed to foretell his destruction. Did Xerxes have a correct choice available to him?
2. Did the Athenians seek the gods for direction regarding the Persian attack?
3. Does Herodotus seem to believe the oracle of Delphi is a source of prophetic truth?

### Cultural Analysis

1. Throughout the *Histories* we hear of many consulting the oracle of Delphi. To what modern phenomenon would this compare?
2. Does our society value spiritual and prophetic sources as much as the ancients did? Why or why not?
3. How should our society respond to spiritual and prophetic sources?

### Biblical Analysis

1. What are some reasons God leads people to war as found in Scripture?
2. Who are believers to follow into battle?

### Application

Idols will always betray their servants. Obeying a commandment from Zeus is no comfort. It is no promise of safety. Obeying God is always a position of strength. Before Christ came the only path of righteousness was to war against the gods. The only way to war against the gods was to serve God rightly beneath harsh masters, as did Joseph, Daniel and the three cast into the fiery furnace. We must be good citizens of our country, but we cannot be ruled by our country's idols.

## SUMMA

*Write an essay or discuss this question, integrating what you have learned from the material above.*
Is a war between nations really a war between their gods?

## Optional Activity

Keep a notebook with you over the course of a couple days. Every odd thing you see write down as an omen (a crow pecking a policeman, a smiley face in your eggs, etc.). When you have collected enough examples, analyze them and foretell your own doom. Then give the list of omens to a friend and see what he comes up with. Trying this should help you to see the folly of fortune-telling and the desperation of people that practice this hopeless activity, because they do not know the true God.

**READING ASSIGNMENT:**
Book VII. 189–239

# SESSION XX: RECITATION
Book VII

## Comprehension Questions

*Answer these questions for factual recall.*
1. What made Xerxes angry at the Hellespont?
2. What did he do to it?
3. What did Xerxes do to Pythius when he was asked for a favor?
4. Xerxes wept watching his men march by. Why?
5. What is Herodotus' interpretation of the omen of the horse giving birth to a hare?
6. How many men were in Xerxes' infantry (land army) alone?
7. How did Xerxes count his men?

8. What did the Sargatians have in common with the American cowboy?
9. How many ships were in the Persian fleet?
10. What did Demaratus say to Xerxes about the Spartans that made Xerxes laugh?
11. How many people does Herodotus think Xerxes must have led up to Thermopylae?
12. What did Xerxes do to the Spartan commander who held out so long at Thermopylae?

**READING ASSIGNMENT:**
Book VIII. 1–83

# SESSION XXI: WRITING

Using various resources, excluding *Histories* by Herodotus, write a brief essay answering this question: What are the greatest highlights of the Persian War? This detailed essay should at least contain a paragraph a piece about each of the main combatants and a paragraph apiece on the battles of Marathon and Salamis, including names, dates and places.

**READING ASSIGNMENT:**
Book VIII. 84–144

# SESSION XXII: RECITATION
Book VIII

## Comprehension Questions

*Answer these questions for factual recall.*
1. Why did Themistocles carve messages onto rocks around watering holes?
2. What did Xerxes do to make the battlefield of

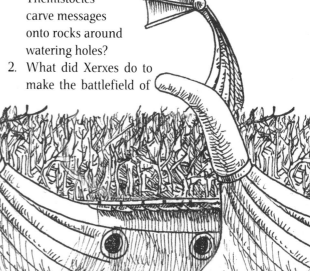

Thermopylae look like a victory?

3. What did the oracle say that convinced the Athenians to abandon Athens?
4. What strategy did Themistocles use to defeat the Persians?
5. How did the Athenians defeat the Persian navy?
6. What size army did Xerxes leave in Greece with Mardonius?
7. Was Themistocles a noble man?

 **READING ASSIGNMENT:**
Book IX. 1–64

# SESSION XXIII: DISCUSSION
Book IX. 1–64

## A Question to Consider

Is the future certain? Can it be known?

*Discuss or list short answers to the following questions:*

### Text Analysis

1. When Mardonius was defeated, what many Persians had been expecting all along came to pass. What ultimately brought about the downfall of the Persians? Was it anything the Greeks did?
2. The world would be a very different place if the Persians had enslaved the Athenians. As it was, the Athenian culture had time to grow and become attractive to many before being destroyed. Was Greek culture to be preferred?
3. Any number of things could have happened to prevent Xerxes from invading Greece, breaking his own power and putting Athenian culture on a firm footing in Greece. What strategies would you offer in hindsight that might have produced a Persian victory?

### Cultural Analysis

1. Does our culture believe that the future is certain?
2. What are some examples of ways in which our culture seems to confess that the future is certain?
3. What are some of the ways in which our culture seems to profess that the future is not certain?

### Biblical Analysis

1. What does the Bible teach about the certainty of the future?
2. What does Proverbs 16:33 tell us about the settled nature of the future?

### Application

God used the rise of Greek culture to spread the gospel. Eventually Alexander advanced Greek culture by conquest. The New Testament is written in Greek, which was as prevalent then as English is today. Many men understood it, and translations of Scripture were not immediately necessary. Thus the gospel spread through the Mediterranean world.

### SUMMA

 *Write an essay or discuss this question, integrating what you have learned from the material above.* How certain is the future?

**READING ASSIGNMENT:**
Book IX. 65–122

To cross the Hellespont, a mile-wide waterway, it was necessary for Xerxes' army to make a bridge. His clever men placed hundreds of his 120-foot-long vessels side by side, parallel to the Hellespont banks, and strung cables of papyrus and flax upon which they laid planks. This combination pontoon and suspension bridge allowed his entire army to cross.

## SESSION XXIV: DISCUSSION AND ACTIVITY

*Answer the following questions:*

1. What explanation can we make of inaccurate anatomical descriptions in the *Histories?* Would we be willing to consider that evolution modified creatures over the past 2,500 years and that Herodotus's descriptions are accurate? Why or why not?

2. Some things Herodotus himself disbelieves (like headless men in Libya) but mentions to us anyway. What explanation could be given for descriptions of the hippo as having a horse's mane and tail and hoofed feet, the crocodile having no tongue, and ants the size of foxes (the structure of which science claims to be impossible)?

3. Science tells us that no woman would ever give birth to a lion cub (as Herodotus claims happened in Sardis), no horse would give birth to a hare and that no gods bred with women (as Herodotus claims happened in Sparta). What do you tell science?

### Math Project

Modern scientists and historians tell us that the logistics involved in a march of one to two million men make Herodotus's claim about the size of Xerxes' army impossible. Based on your own eating and drinking habits, estimate how much food, in pounds, and water, in gallons, Xerxes' army would have consumed in a day. A week. A year. Do you think Herodotus's numbers are credible? Would rivers actually have been drunk dry?

The Istar Gate, over 75 feet high, was the main entrance to Babylon. King Nebuchadnezzar had the original built and dedicated it to the goddess Ishtar. This reproduction shows well the dragons and bulls that symbolized Babylonian deities.

## SESSION XXV

Chart 2 seeks to establish similarities between the Persian War and World War II. Can you think of others?

*Discuss or list short answers to the following questions:*

1. Was World War I really the first world war?

2. What caused the Persians during the Persian Wars and Nazi Germany during World War II to think they were superior and had the right to dominate the world? What is the lesson to be learned?

### Application

With all the differences between ancient times and today, men are still of the same nature and sin against each other in the same ways. There are far more patterns and repetitions in the actions of men than we realize. God likes certain plot-lines, and He reuses them.

# OPTIONAL SESSION A: WRITING

More history should be written in the style of Herodotus. History ought to feel more like time spent around a campfire than in a science lab. We get more of a feel for the context and backdrop. We feel like we have looked at a painting rather than a written outline.

Pick a historic topic that you have studied, one in which you know people who witnessed it or maybe even one you witnessed personally. Write in the style of Herodotus, taking side roads and painting backgrounds. Try to develop the skill of having the reader understand more than just the names dates and places, but be able to share the insights of the first hand observers meaningfully.

Topics for which eyewitnesses are available might include:

THE COLD WAR

INVENTION OF THE COMPUTER

LIBERALISM AND ITS INFLUENCE IN THE CHURCH

THE VIETNAM WAR

WAR WITH IRAQ

9/11 ATTACKS ON THE WORLD TRADE CENTERS

# OPTIONAL SESSION B: DISCUSSION

## A Question to Consider

What is the purpose of understanding history?

*Discuss or list short answers to the following questions:*

## Text Analysis

1. What is the primary reason for studying history?
2. The Persians thought they were the greatest nation in the world. Are we the greatest nation? Do we think the same?
3. What does reading Herodotus tell us about the personality of God?

## Cultural Analysis

1. Many times our assumption is always that we are wiser and have more insight into ancient events than the ancients. Is this a legitimate assumption? Why?
2. Is it arrogant to disbelieve men who wrote near to the time the actual events took place? Do we have a better perspective 2,500 years later?
3. How do you react to reading Herodotus? What does that tell you about your own personality?

---

*Chart 2:* WORLDS AT WAR

| PERSIAN WARS | WORLD WAR II |
|---|---|
| **Superiority of a Race** | |
| The Persians believed that they were a superior race and had the right to subjugate the races around them. | The Germans believed that they were a superior race and had the right to eliminate or rule other races. |
| **Standing Against the Foe** | |
| The Greeks at Thermopolyae stood against an incredible force and held out for such a long time that the rest of Greece was given more time to prepare for the Persians. This eventually led to the defeat of the Persians at Salamis. | During the Battle of Britain, the people of Britain held out against the great German onslaught. This allowed the Allies to prepare, and eventually America entered the war and turned the tide against Germany. |
| **City-States vs. Allies** | |
| Athens is the city-state that actually beat the Persians. This victory was aided by the ability of the Spartans to hold out against the Persians at Thermopolyae. | The analogy might be a bit stretched, but America was like Athens. The British were like Sparta and the French were like any conquered city-state. |

## Biblical Analysis

1. Why did God rehearse the history of Israel in Psalm 78?
2. What relationship do the sacraments of the Passover and the Lord's Supper have to history?

## Application

Many people claim that history repeats itself. This is true as long as those in the present think that they are above or outside history. We do not have the same idols, but we are still men and have the same temptations to pride and arrogance. We still desire to rule reality without being ruled from above. History tells us about man, but it also tells us about what God does to man.

## SUMMA

 *Write an essay or discuss this question, integrating what you have learned from the material above.* What is the purpose of history?

## ENDNOTES

1   See Jordan, James B. 1995. Daniel: Historical & chronological comments (V). Biblical Chronology 7:4, (www.biblical horizons.com/ch).

2   At the time of publication this essay may be found at http://www-personal.umich.edu/~dunlapg/Xmas_and_ Christmas.html.

3   The Romans destroyed Jerusalem in A.D. 70. See Josephus's *Jewish Wars* 3.10.9 in Whiston, William, trans. *The New Complete Works of Josephus.* Grand Rapids, Mich.: Kregel Publications, 1999.

# ORESTEIA

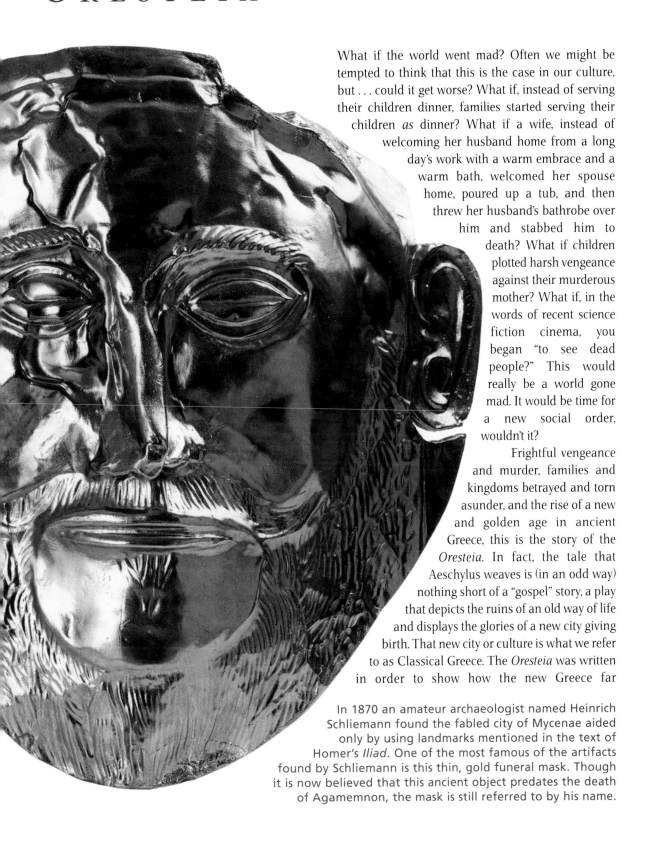

What if the world went mad? Often we might be tempted to think that this is the case in our culture, but . . . could it get worse? What if, instead of serving their children dinner, families started serving their children *as* dinner? What if a wife, instead of welcoming her husband home from a long day's work with a warm embrace and a warm bath, welcomed her spouse home, poured up a tub, and then threw her husband's bathrobe over him and stabbed him to death? What if children plotted harsh vengeance against their murderous mother? What if, in the words of recent science fiction cinema, you began "to see dead people?" This would really be a world gone mad. It would be time for a new social order, wouldn't it?

Frightful vengeance and murder, families and kingdoms betrayed and torn asunder, and the rise of a new and golden age in ancient Greece, this is the story of the *Oresteia*. In fact, the tale that Aeschylus weaves is (in an odd way) nothing short of a "gospel" story, a play that depicts the ruins of an old way of life and displays the glories of a new city giving birth. That new city or culture is what we refer to as Classical Greece. The *Oresteia* was written in order to show how the new Greece far

In 1870 an amateur archaeologist named Heinrich Schliemann found the fabled city of Mycenae aided only by using landmarks mentioned in the text of Homer's *Iliad*. One of the most famous of the artifacts found by Schliemann is this thin, gold funeral mask. Though it is now believed that this ancient object predates the death of Agamemnon, the mask is still referred to by his name.

surpassed the old one. Athene, the Greek goddess of wisdom, was ushering in enlightenment and prosperity. Under her kindly rule, a new sort of community was being formed, and this new city, ruled by its citizens—a Democracy—would give peace and justice to the land.

The *Oresteia* is a three part tragedy. Not the sort of tragedy that might make your mother cry, mind you. It is a tragedy in one of the oldest senses of the word: a serious drama that makes the audience feel sorry or scared for the heroes. At the end, however, a solution is presented, and we are left feeling quite relieved. In this sense, you might describe a winning chess match as a tragedy: serious and heated, but having cornered your opponent's king, you breathe a huge sigh of relief.

Aeschylus starts his story where many ancient writers and playwrights begin theirs, with Homer. Beginning at the end of the Trojan War, Aeschylus takes his audience all the way up to the rise of the Athenian Democracy. Although it probably seems rather odd, this tragedy is not only not very sad, to the contrary, it ends on a rather comic note. This is the case in at least two different ways. First, Aeschylus ends the *Oresteia* comically in the technical or literary sense: Everything ends happily. Praises are sung about the greatness of Athens, and everyone seems contented, like after three helpings of Thanksgiving dinner. Second, the story is truly comic in the regular sense of the word—it's downright funny. Aeschylus tries to tell a story about redemption, a story that shows how peoples' disastrous lives could be mended and healed through the Athenian Democracy. But for Christians, this "gospel" is highly amusing. Even though many modern, unbelieving scholars and their disciples still think that brokenness and guilt can be fixed through a political system, we know that true salvation is found in the Lord Jesus. When we consider this and watch the *Oresteia* unfold, it becomes more than a little difficult to stifle our laughter. Yet this comic element is also a powerful portrayal of pagan man yearning for true salvation. Therefore, a careful study of the *Oresteia* shows how God prepared the world for the coming of Christ, the true gospel story, and how His Kingdom has brought new life and salvation to the world.

Athene, as represented by this beautiful statue that was taken from the Acropolis, is the goddess after whom Athens gets its name. Athene is the virgin goddess of wisdom and the arts and also the goddess of war. When Zeus saw that his first wife, Metis, was pregnant, he swallowed her to prevent the birth. Metis died through this extreme abortion, but Athene sprang, fully grown and armored, from the head of Zeus. She is one of only three gods who can resist the charms and spells of Aphrodite.

# GENERAL INFORMATION

## Author and Context

Aeschylus was a Greek celebrity. Having been born at the end of the sixth century B.C. and living until 456 or 455 B.C, he fought in the Persian wars (remember Herodotus?) as a young man, was involved in politics, and led a highly successful career in the arts as a playwright. With these credentials there is no doubt that Aeschylus was at least well-known, if not a hero, to many. Fame and fortune, however, are never guarantees of being remembered. Only seven of his plays still exist out of the seventy plays he originally wrote.

Aeschylus wrote the *Oresteia* in order to defend and celebrate a way of life that had been developing for over two hundred years. He was writing, looking back at Greek life as someone might look back and study the history of America from our day. One of the most significant parts of this Greek culture was found in its *polis. Polis* is a Greek word that describes the culture, government and community of Greece all rolled into one. Often this term is simply translated "city," which is a good translation if one knows his Greek history well. Otherwise, we are tempted to think only of big buildings, highways, parking lots and lots of traffic. But before 700 B.C., the Greek community was more agrarian, meaning that most people lived in only very small communities. These miniature kingdoms were ruled by chiefs or local kings of some sort. But around 700, a radical change began to ripple through the lands of Greece. People began moving and living in larger communities closer together. This was done for protection, food and (presumably) enjoyment. Thus the cultural center moved from the "house" (*oikos*) to the "city" (*polis*). But addresses were not the only things that changed. One of the most significant changes was how a community was recognized. When the cultural center had been the "house," the most sacred bond of community had been "blood," such as the bond of blood between a parent and a child or between siblings. But the move from oikos to polis (house to city) displaced those central bonds of blood and in their place put the more public bond of covenant or contract, such as the bond between citizens and rulers.[1] This change, while not occurring overnight, was nevertheless a radical shift in the communities and culture of the Greek people.

And it is this shift that provides the overarching structure of redemption throughout the *Oresteia*. Agamemnon, the war-lord of Argos, and his oikos (house) is cursed until his son, Orestes, finds refuge in Athens' law courts. The "gospel" that Aeschylus preaches presents salvation as something to be found not in the house but in the city. The family (and every kingdom that is built upon it) is cursed, but in the democracy of the city of Athens, Aeschylus sees a remedy and a cure. The polis had been developing for two hundred years, but it was during Aeschylus's days that Athens saw democracy firmly established for the first time. Pericles (who ruled Athens during its golden age) ended a long chaotic flux between the rule of the aristocracy (the rich and mighty) and the rule of the tyrant. Pericles, the general and politician, supported Aeschylus's plays and even produced (directed the chorus) some of Aeschylus's works. At the end of the Oresteia, the goddess Athene offers her city freedom from both tyranny and chaos.

## Significance

The *Oresteia* was Aeschylus's last work we know of, written two years before his death. It is a trilogy presented in three plays: *Agamemnon, The Libation Bearers* and *The Eumenides*. Like all of Aeschylus's works, the Oresteia is pioneering. It is his version of tragedy that defined and paved the way for much of later classical tragedy. The *Oresteia*, it should be pointed out, was (and is) a play: something to be performed, acted and sung. It is likely that this form of poetry was a direct growth from different kinds of religious music that preceded it, although unfortunately we no longer have the original musical score. Many of these tragedies were written and performed publicly at annual competitions. Just like we have the Oscars, they would award prizes for the best shows, and Aeschylus won first prize thirteen times. Talk about a star.

The *Oresteia* shows how Greek thinking changed dramatically over the course of several hundred years. The heroes of the old Greek culture had been the fierce warriors and vindictive gods of Homer, but in the new Greece, the heroes would be philosophers, poets, statesmen, orators and gods that seem (on the surface) quite a bit more tame.

## Main Characters

In the first play, *Agamemnon,* the bloodthirsty Clytaemnestra is the central character. She is the wife of Agamemnon, the king of Argos. Agamemnon himself is necessary for the plot, but only in so far as his wife has someone to kill. The play opens with Agamemnon absent, still journeying back to his land of Argos from his final victory at Troy, and, before the play closes, Agamemnon is already dead (talk about a small role!). The world of this first play is barbaric and crude; it presents the characters as trapped under the weight of the curse that binds the house of Atreus (Agamemnon's father). Agamemnon is led on to slaughter, "netted" with his royal robe and stabbed to death by Clytaemnestra. The chorus is the comic relief, listening to the cries of their king being murdered, playing guessing games and trying to decide what to do, if anything at all. Clytaemnestra's lover, Aegisthus, arrives at the close, cheers her on and defends her deeds.

The second play, *The Libation Bearers,* opens up to a world of action. The main character is Agamemnon's son, Orestes (from whom the trilogy gets its name). He and his sister, Electra, are energetic and passionate. They quickly plot and prepare themselves to avenge the death of their father, and by the close of the second play, Orestes and Electra are motherless and Aegisthus is sleeping with the daisies. But in that old Greece, where blood bonds held people tightest, there is a curse for killing family members, and the Furies (or Eumenides) seek Orestes out. These ugly female deities had the job of carrying out vengeance on those who shed family blood.

The third play, *The Eumenides,* is a processional from the depths of the earth to the high court of Athens. Gods and goddesses begin making dramatic performances in the world of men. Athene is now the main character, and Apollo plays a significant role as well. Orestes and Clytaemnestra are the only actors present from the first two plays. The Furies come in as full personalities and dominate the stage; their transformation in this play provides Aeschylus with the title: "Eumenides," meaning the "kindly ones."

## Summary and Setting

As already mentioned, the *Oresteia* is a retelling and continuation of Homer and the darker legends surrounding his stories. Setting the stage for the *Oresteia* is the curse on the house of Atreus. A brief retelling of this strange and bloody tale will help a first reading of the *Oresteia:*

Once upon a time there was a man named Tantalus of Lydia, the true founder of the house of Atreus. Tantalus, being a rather odd fellow, decided to serve his son as dinner for the gods. Apparently less than pleased with the menu, the gods sent Tantalus to Hades and brought his son, Pelops, back to life. Pelops, however, being no better than his father, murdered an older man in order to marry the older man's daughter. Continuing the family tradition, Pelops's sons, Atreus and Thyestes, added to the mess. Thyestes seduced Atreus' wife and in return, Atreus murdered Thyestes' children and fed them to Thyestes. For some reason, serving children as dinner was becoming a rather common practice. Thyestes fled with his one surviving child, Aegisthus,

Bronze masks like this were used in Greek drama to suggest character and mood. This is a mask depicting tragedy.

and cursed the house of Atreus. Aegisthus thus grew up as an exile, banished from the house. Atreus had two sons, Agamemnon and Menelaus. Agamemnon married Clytaemnestra and Menelaus married Helen. And as the well-known story goes, Agamemnon and Menelaus spent a decade warring against Troy in order to avenge Paris's seduction of Helen. Having a lot to live up to with such infamous ancestors, Agamemnon joined the circus when, at the beginning of the Trojan War, he sacrificed his virgin daughter Iphigeneia to the gods in return for a good sailing wind. After Agamemnon got his winds and left for Troy, Aegisthus returned from exile, stole Agamemnon's wife, Clytaemnestra, and made himself at home.

Most of these events are mentioned throughout the course of the *Oresteia*, but the opening setting of the *Oresteia* begins with Agamemnon's return from the successful toppling of Troy. Aegisthus, Agamemnon's cousin, had moved in with Clytaemnestra, and she, as you may imagine, having last seen her husband slaying their daughter, had spent ten long years awaiting and carefully planning his "welcome home party."

## Worldview

If you could be transported back in time and had the opportunity to find yourself strolling through an ancient Israelite city, you might walk by the gate of the city and see sitting as judges the old men of the community. They might be deciding disputes between shepherds or farmers, they could be discussing the law amongst themselves, or you might see another very curious thing. You might see a man taking off his shoe and giving it to another man. If you had seen some curious scene like this, what would you think they might be doing? Would you take the shoe from the man if he offered it to you? Would it depend on how old or smelly the shoe was? Would you think it was just a funny tradition?

The reason you might see a scene like this in ancient Israel is because God instructed the men of Israel to do this very thing whenever they were redeeming land or making other exchanges. (Ruth 4:7; cf. Deut. 25:5–10) In ancient Israel, the Promised Land was a sacred gift from God to His people, and therefore God gave careful instructions regarding how it would pass from generation to generation.

Sometimes because of misuse, neglect or misfortune land had to be sold out of the family, but God always made provision for the land to return to its original owner, particularly through the institution of Jubilee. Every fifty years all lands that had changed hands were required to be returned to their original owners, people who had been sold into slavery were freed and it was a great year of rest and liberty (Lev. 25:10ff). But in the between times, God also provided for His people by giving them opportunities to redeem themselves, their land or their family members. Part of the ceremony could involve this funny ritual of taking off your shoe and giving it to your neighbor.

This little history of Israel may seem completely unrelated to the *Oresteia*, but keep reading and the connection will become clear.

The *Oresteia* is a gospel story, as said earlier, and this means that it is a story about redemption. But what is redemption? And what does it mean to be redeemed? In ancient Israel, a man who was first in line to redeem a plot of land might give you (the second in line) his shoe, and then you would redeem the land. To redeem a plot of land would mean that you would be buying back the land and returning it to the family it originally belonged to. Redeeming a person meant that you bought them from their slave master and returned them free to their family. In the *Oresteia*, the lands and realm of Agamemnon need to be redeemed. The land is in slavery, in bondage to a curse. Blood has been shed unjustly, and the guilt haunts the house of Atreus. They are bound and unable to be freed. But as the story unfolds, Aeschylus presents a redemption to his audience. While the ancient laws and gods demanded blood for blood, and the Furies pursued Orestes to uphold this "justice" in the lands, Orestes is saved out of this torment through Athene's law court in Athens. You might now have an inkling that someone came along and gave Orestes their shoe. But sadly, Aeschylus is not as creative as that. The redemption of the house of Atreus occurs at the end of the trilogy when Orestes, accused by the Furies for the blood of his mother, stands trial in Athens. Athene, the Greek goddess of wisdom, does some fancy rhetoric and gets Orestes off the hook (quite literally!).

However, Aeschylus, it must be said, offers a pale and sickly redemption in the end. For a power-hungry god and tormenting demons, he offers a manipulative goddess who bribes the demons to keep them happy.

For the indecisive chorus of elders who cannot save their king when he is being murdered, he offers an indecisive jury divided equally over the verdict concerning Orestes. For the driving dance of the Furies full of hatred, rage and lust, he offers the arid, timeless and equally inhuman illusion of peace and justice in the Athenian law court. But Aeschylus is to be praised for identifying the real problems that people face in their lives and families and knowing that the solution must be found in a new kind of community. He knows that the family is under a curse and, apart from divine intervention, is doomed to a bloody end. This is what the Bible teaches as well. In Adam, all men are under the curse of sin (Rom. 3:23, 5:18–19). And that curse flows down through generations. It is a family curse. Everyone related to Adam has it in their blood. And everyone is related to Adam.

Unless a new cultural center is created our "house" is doomed. Every *oikos* is under the wrath and curse of God because of our sin, originating in Adam. Aeschylus knew that what man needs so very much is a *polis*. Sinful mankind needs a city! That does not mean that a street light and post office are the solution to the world's problems. But we do need a new kind of community. Unless the world is re-organized and our families are remade, unless we are recreated and refashioned into a new humanity, we, like the house of Atreus, will feed our children to demon-gods and kill one another ceaselessly, even though we may not do it literally anymore.

Aeschylus knew we needed a city, but the best he could offer was the city of Athens, run by a democratic vote of the people and overseen by the goddess Athene, who kept a mob of blood thirsty

The Erinyes, or, euphemistically, Eumenides ("the Kindly Ones") punish crimes that are not within the reach of human justice. The Eumenides were conceived when Uranus's spilled blood hit Gaia's body, and are therefore older than any of the Olympians. There are three Furies—Tisiphone the Avenger, Megara the Jealous, and Alecto the Unresting. They live in Darkness but travel the Earth constantly in search of sinners.

Furies at bay by promising them honor and glory. Unfortunately, like Aeschylus, there are many moderns who believe that the solutions to the problems of the family are found in a political institution. They believe if the government is organized in a particular way and certain laws are passed people will enjoy peace and prosperity. These modern day Athenians think that the curse of sin can be removed by a vote. This is, of course, an extremely funny idea, but sadly there are many Christians that act like this is true. Christians in our day are faced with a truly enormous crisis. Like ancient Greece there is a Trojan War going on in America and all over the world. Ultimately, the battle is over the Bible and whether or not the standards that God gives us to live by are good and just and lovely. Many Christians recognize that this battle is taking place. Often it is referred to as a "war of worldviews" or a "culture war." Even the newspapers and news stations on television know about the war. Many of the great battles are over children and families. Should they be raised by the government and their schools? Should a parent be allowed to take the life of an unborn child? What is marriage? What are the roles of men and women? These questions and many more are the scenes of great battles in our day. But many Christians, after recognizing these as the issues, then become like Aeschylus and talk and act like the solution to these and other questions can be found in the right kind of government and the right sort of laws. Of course, God is very interested in seeing righteous governments with just laws in every state and country in the world. But laws and politics are not God's answer to corrupt families and kingdoms. As Aeschylus ultimately shows in the *Oresteia*, laws and governments always flow out of a particular kind of worship and religion. In the case of Athens, goddess worship and the honoring of demons (1 Cor. 10:20) were the foundations of the Athenian Democracy. The kind of government we have always emerges from the god that we serve.

Abraham, even though he lived long before Aeschylus, also knew that he and his family needed a city. The writer of Hebrew says, ". . . for he waited for the city which has foundations, whose builder and maker is God." (Heb. 11:10) He goes on to say that we, as New Testament Christians, have come to that city (12:22). What is that city? What is that *polis*? Is it different from Aeschylus's picture?

The city of God which we have come to is the Christian Church. This is the city that Abraham looked for. It is the New Jerusalem coming down out of heaven (Rev. 21:2). We are the new Israel, a holy nation, a kingdom of priests, and the commonwealth of God (1 Pet. 2:9, Eph. 2:12–22). Aeschylus was right to see the need for a city, but his city was founded on the worship and appeasement of demons. In Christ, God is building a new city, His Church, which is founded on the worship of the Triune God. It is from this city where rivers of life and peace and justice flow.

In the *Oresteia*, we are not left with a great confidence in the Athenian law system either. The law of the gods and the power of the Furies have been made clear throughout the plays: "Blood will have blood," but in Athene's court, as Peter Leithart has remarked, "or maybe not, or maybe sometimes."[2] Remember in the end, Athene (oddly enough) casts the deciding vote for the split jury. When the Furies react with their usual poison and angst, Athene essentially *bribes* them! What kind of justice is this? Persuasion and bribery are presented as the badges of honor and foundations of justice. If the Furies submit to the judgment of the court and go in peace, they will be given status, respect, power and riches in the city.

Ultimately, there is no foundation for the Athenian court. Athens has not found true peace or justice; rather these counterfeits depend "on an alliance with the powers of darkness."[3] This city is still built on the same foundations as the house of Atreus. It has only managed to make a truce for the time being. The curse is still there. Bloodshed will continue. Justice always breaks out in the end.

But in the Church, justice has been found and delivered. We are the people who have been delivered from the curses on our houses, and real satisfaction has been made. The Athenian court declares Orestes innocent on some kind of bizarre technicality, insisting that "The mother is no parent of that which is called her child, but only nurse of the new-planted seed that grows. The parent is he who mounts." (*Eumenides* 658–660) That is to say, Orestes did not really kill his mother; he merely killed the woman who happened to carry his father's child. She was only a nurse, not *really* a blood relative, so the Furies cannot harm Orestes. This is sort of like declaring a bank robber innocent of theft by renaming the bank the "public library." It was not really a bank you see?

The Herod Atticus Theater in Athens as it stands today. This is typical of the theaters that would have been used for plays by Aeschylus.

So he could not have robbed a bank. Therefore he is innocent. Right? Er . . . yeah right.

But in the *polis* of God there is no need for this kind of name game. Our sin and curse was borne by Jesus Christ who is God and man. He was someone both from our family and from outside of our family. He took the curse to himself and bore the penalty and judgment of God, purchasing us with his blood and displaying for Aeschylus and the whole world what true justice is. And on the third day, Jesus rose from the dead for our justification. God's justice is displayed openly for the world to see, and it makes demonic Athens and its indecisive democracy look like a goofy circus. We have come to a city. And it is this city that gives true peace built on the foundation of true justice.

Remember we began not long ago talking about men giving shoes for redemption or something like that, right? Well the point of all that was that true redemption purchases lost land and enslaved people and gives them back with freedom to their original owners and families. That is what the Church is, the Christian *polis*. The Church is the world reconciled and redeemed to God in Jesus. Jesus came

proclaiming a permanent year of Jubilee, and the world, which was under the curse and slavery of sin and evil, has been purchased and redeemed with his blood (Luke 4:18–19, Rev. 5:9). Aeschylus offers us a comic book religion in the end: a truly remarkable story, fearsome violence, real agony, and, at a number of points, real humor. But his redemption and justice are shallow and fake, and the glories of ancient Greece are crumbling ruins today; whereas the Church has God's promise that it will never fall or be destroyed but will overcome the world (Matt. 16:18, 1 John 5:4).

—*Michael Metzler and Toby Sumpter*

## For Further Reading

Spielvogel, Jackson. *Western Civilization.* Fifth Edition. Belmont, Calif.: Wadsworth/Thomson Learning, 2003. 34–37.

*Veritas Press History Cards: New Testament, Greece and Rome.* Lancaster, Pa.: Veritas Press. 3, 6.

Cowan, Louise and Guinness, Os. *Invitation to the Classics,* Grand Rapids, Mich.: Baker Books, 1998. 53–65.

# SESSION I: PRELUDE

## A Question to Consider

Which of the problems or parts of our lives listed below should the government try to help? For each item on the list explain why the government should be involved or why it should not be involved.

1. Crimes such as theft and murder
2. Family problems such as violent marriages and neglect of children
3. Protection against other nations
4. Moral guilt (guilt we feel from sin)
5. Our worship and religion
6. The salvation of the world

*From the General Information above answer the following questions:*
1. Who was Aeschylus?
2. When did he live?
3. What is the difference between tyranny and anarchy?
4. What is democracy?
5. What were the tragedies that Aeschylus usually wrote about?

 **READING ASSIGNMENT:**
Agamemnon

# SESSION II: DISCUSSION
Agamemnon

## A Question to Consider

When is it right to take revenge?

*Discuss or list short answers to the following questions:*

## Text Analysis

1. What is the opening mood of the play? What is the condition of the house of Atreus?
2. Does the return of Agamemnon and the news of the defeat of Troy completely change this mood? Does the problem with the house of Atreus go deeper than the consequences of war? The

watchman desires "redemption." Does he see this redemption come?
3. Is there any character in this first play who is good? Does Aeschylus want us to respect king Agamemnon, his wife or the older wise men?
4. Do the gods give any comfort to the characters' sorrow?
5. Does Clytaemnestra have good reason to kill her husband? Why does she take the matter into her own hands?
6. Could Agamemnon have escaped this fate? Could he have done anything different to save his house from murders and hate?
7. Cassandra is a special holy woman who can speak for the gods. Does she give us reason to think that holiness and closeness to the gods is desirable?

## Cultural Analysis

1. Is the world presented in this first play much like our own today? Is our world better or worse than the world Aeschylus presents to us in this play?
2. Do we practice blood vengeance anymore in any way? The desire for revenge is still with us, but how do people today seek to avenge a wrong done to them?

## Biblical Analysis

1. Does the Bible anywhere allow for blood vengeance as we see in *Agamemnon*?
2. What drives the desire for justice in this first play? Is real justice accomplished? How does it compare to the way Scripture commands us to deal with murder and hate? (Consider James 3:13–18 and Titus 3:3–7)

## Application

Does this first play give us any true wisdom for our own lives?

## SUMMA

 *Write an essay or discuss this question, integrating what you have learned from the material above.*
Is it ever right to take revenge?

**READING ASSIGNMENT:**
The Libation Bearers

# SESSION III: RECITATION

Agamemnon *and* The Libation Bearers

## Comprehension Questions

*Answer these questions for factual recall.*

### Agamemnon:

1. Why is the watchman full of sorrow?
2. What is the curse that haunts the house of Atreus?
3. Why did Agamemnon murder his daughter Iphigeneia?
4. Why does Agamemnon not want to walk across his robes?
5. Compare Cassandra's attitude toward Clytaemnestra with her attitude toward Agamemnon. Does Cassandra show loyalty to Agamemnon?
6. Does Clytaemnestra love Agamemnon? Does Clytaemnestra hate Agamemnon?
7. At the close of the play, who is the new ruler of Argos? Who is the rightful ruler?

### The Libation Bearers:

1. At the opening of this second play, how much time has elapsed since the death of Agamemnon?
2. Why is Electra so happy to see Orestes?
3. Do Orestes and Electra seem to see any justice in the murder of their father?
4. How do Orestes and Electra find the passion, will and power to carry out the murder of their own mother?
5. Who are the "dark gods beneath the earth" that Orestes and Electra appeal to?
6. What is "the law" that the Chorus speaks of?
7. What drives Orestes to Apollo after the murder?
8. At the end of this second play, is there yet any reason to believe that good will "win out in the end?"

READING ASSIGNMENT:
The Eumenides

# SESSION IV: ACTIVITY

## The Trial of Orestes

### Directions

Today we are going to serve as judge and jury as we consider the case that could be laid out against Orestes. To do this, follow these steps:

Elect a judge, a prosecutor (to set forth the Furies' case) and a defense attorney (for Orestes).

All of you will be the witnesses and the jury. List charges that could be made against Orestes and the things that might mitigate or lessen his guilt. The judge should write out the charges on the blackboard for all to see. The prosecuting and defense attorney should write the charges on notebook paper.

The prosecution will then set forth its case. Then the defense will present its case. (Limit the time for each side.)

The jury should then decide whether Orestes is guilty of murder (the purposeful and intentional, unlawful [according to God's law] killing of another human being) or manslaughter (killing of a human in the heat of passion). They can also acquit him on the grounds that the killing of Clytaemnestra was justified (for our case this means that it is a killing that is allowed by God's law).

Your debates should take these facts into account in defense of Orestes:

- CLYTAEMNESTRA COMMITTED ADULTERY AGAINST AGAMEMNON (*Agamemnon* 1654–1661)
- CLYTAEMNESTRA DECEIVED AGAMEMNON AND KILLED HIM (*Agamemnon* 914–1343)
- CLYTAEMNESTRA GAVE AEGISTHUS THE THRONE WHICH RIGHTFULLY BELONGED TO ORESTES (*Agamemnon* 1577–1673)
- AGAINST ORESTES
- HE KILLS HIS MOTHER (*Libation Bearers* 851–971)
- HE DOES THIS NOT AS AN ACT OF PASSION, BUT OUT OF FIRM RESOLVE, AND CONSIDERS IT JUST (*Libation Bearers* 971–1076).

## Optional Activity

### THE TRIAL OF CLYTAEMNESTRA

Have the same kind of trial for Clytaemnestra. Is she guilty of murder, manslaughter or was her killing of Agamemnon justifiable?

# SESSION V: DISCUSSION

## A Question to Consider

Can justice and mercy work together at the same time?

*Discuss or list short answers to the following questions:*

### Text Analysis

1. How does Apollo seek to establish justice?
2. How do the Eumenides seek to establish justice?
3. How does Athene seek to avoid establishing justice?
4. What does Athene do to end the trial?
5. How does Athene keep the Eumenides from destroying Athens because of the verdict?

### Cultural Analysis

1. Where do you see the advocates of justice in our society?
2. Where do you see the advocates of mercy in our society?
3. When we consider "three strike drug" laws where someone committing minor offenses is sent away for life versus the attitude displayed when star athletes are caught using drugs, how does our culture seek to balance justice and mercy?

### Biblical Analysis

1. How has God established both justice and mercy? (Romans 3:21–26)
2. How are the justice and mercy of God both upheld in the Cross? (Rom. 3:26)

## SUMMA

*Write an essay or discuss this question, integrating what you have learned from the material above.*

Why do people have trouble joining justice and mercy? How do they actually work together rightly?

# OPTIONAL SESSION A: REVIEW

## The Eumenides

1. Who are the Furies?
2. Are the gods closer to humans in this last play?
3. Why does Orestes correct Apollo? Does Apollo listen?
4. Where has Athene returned from?
5. Why do the Furies listen to Athene?
6. What is Orestes' defense?
7. How was Orestes purged from his own guilt?
8. Why does Athene not judge the case on her own?
9. Why does Athene decide the case in favor of Orestes?

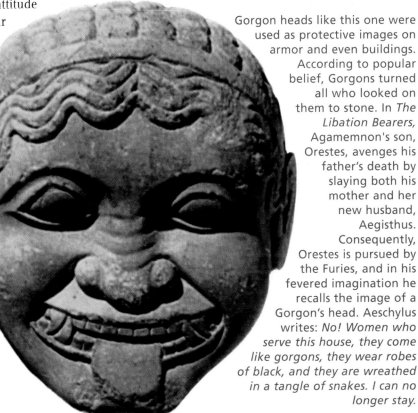

Gorgon heads like this one were used as protective images on armor and even buildings. According to popular belief, Gorgons turned all who looked on them to stone. In *The Libation Bearers*, Agamemnon's son, Orestes, avenges his father's death by slaying both his mother and her new husband, Aegisthus. Consequently, Orestes is pursued by the Furies, and in his fevered imagination he recalls the image of a Gorgon's head. Aeschylus writes: *No! Women who serve this house, they come like gorgons, they wear robes of black, and they are wreathed in a tangle of snakes. I can no longer stay.*

11. How does Athene finally convince the Furies to accept her decision without destroying Athens?

12. Has redemption finally come upon the house of Atreus?

*Answer two of the following three questions:*

1. Could the house of Atreus been saved apart from the government of Athens? Explain and defend your answer.

2. List those aspects of Athene's handling of the guilt of Orestes that are just and those aspects that are unjust.

3. Has our own culture embraced a story of redemption that is similar to the story of the *Oresteia?*

# OPTIONAL SESSION B: WRITING

*Write an essay for one of the following questions:*

1. Jesus came to save and to give Himself to the world. What about the world (particularly the world that we see in the *Oresteia*) needed to be saved? What did Jesus give the world?

2. The Apostle Paul says that civil government is instituted by God to restrain bad men and encourage good men. Does this mean that before Jesus came the governments of the world were good? Did governments acknowledge who gave them their authority to punish evil and encourage good?

## ENDNOTES

1   For a discussion of this shift, see Peter Leithart's *Heroes of the City of Man.* Moscow, Idaho: Canon Press, 1999. 286.

2   Leithart, *Heroes of the City of Man,* 302.

3   Leithart, *Heroes of the City of Man,* 293.

4   *This endnote appears only in the teacher's edition.*

5   Clarence Darrow was the effective barrister who lost the infamous Scopes Monkey Trial. Darrow had represented many people charged with capital crimes. None of them were ever put to death. His main concern was picking the jury by denomination. Of Presbyterians, he says, *"If a Presbyterian enters the jury box and carefully rolls up his umbrella, and calmly and critically sits down, let him go. He is cold as the grave; he knows right from wrong, although he seldom finds anything right. He believes in John Calvin and eternal punishment. Get rid of him with the fewest possible words before he contaminates the others; unless you and your clients are Presbyterians you probably are a bad lot, and even though you may be a Presbyterian, your client most likely is guilty."* At the time of publication you may find more help from Darrow for getting yourself acquitted (should you ever need it) at: www.law.umkc.edu/faculty/projects/ftrials/DAR_JURY.HTM

# PLUTARCH'S LIVES

In this work Plutarch writes brief biographical comparisons between men of ancient Greece and comparable men of ancient Rome. These men were some of the bravest men who had ever lived. They were chosen from among their peers as the most faithful and fearless of men. They were devoted completely to religious study and spiritual preparation. They had been forced by their enemies to hide in caves, flee to desert hideouts and live in disguise for decades. They were devoted to one goal: to die for their faith and glorify their god. The deeds of these martyrs brought the ideas and teachings of their faith into the lives of hundreds of millions of people in every nation. Their spiritual warfare, despite being small in number and, many times, far weaker than their enemies, sometimes overpowered even the most powerful nations.

Such a description like the one above could effectively apply to many groups in history. For example, it could describe both the Christian martyrs of ancient times and Islamic suicide bombers of the twenty-first century. If we listed their virtues, the lists might look very similar. Religious, patriotic, courageous, spiritually-minded, zealous, cunning, selfless, persevering, fearless and heroic

would be suitable adjectives. However, if we were to set a Christian martyr alongside an Islamic martyr and analyze their motives as expressed in their lives and deeds carefully, they will appear very different.

People may share the same virtues but be very different when examined closely. In the *Lives,* the Greek philosopher Plutarch has set many of the greatest men of ancient history side-by-side so that we can consider how the ancient pagans viewed virtue and so we can consider what *true* virtue really is.

## GENERAL INFORMATION

### Author and Context

Plutarch was a Greek—a philosopher, priest and politician—yet lived during the greatest days of the Roman Empire, which confuses some people. He was a citizen of the Roman Empire, but was a Greek, living in Greece—in some ways like a Native American Indian living in the United States. Born in A.D. 46, just fewer than fifteen years after the death and resurrection of Jesus Christ, he lived the majority of his life in the town of Chaeronea of Boeotia, to the north and west of Athens and just east of the famous religious center at Delphi—the belly-button of the earth.[1] His devotion to

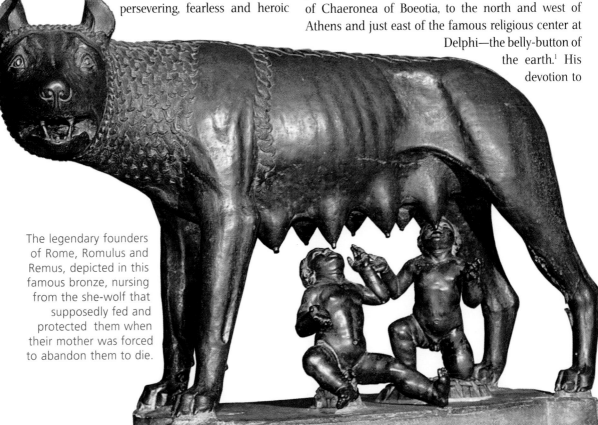

The legendary founders of Rome, Romulus and Remus, depicted in this famous bronze, nursing from the she-wolf that supposedly fed and protected them when their mother was forced to abandon them to die.

philosophical study, his love of peace and quiet and his patriotism suggest that he lacked the selfish ambition that drove most men to pursue the wealth and fame of the Roman Empire. Instead he cherished his Greek background and quiet hometown life. Plutarch enjoyed an active, pleasant life during the more glorious days of the Roman Empire, dying in A.D. 120.

Plutarch agreed with the teaching of Plato and believed that studying philosophy and serving one's country was the most important work of all. He praises such men in an essay he wrote, *On the Education of Children,* that they are:

> Masters of two of the greatest good things that are—a life of public usefulness as Statesmen, and a life of calm tranquility as Students of Philosophy…

With this as his ideal, it should not be a surprise that *all* of the "noble" men studied in the *Lives* are themselves statesmen—generals, senators, law-makers and such. In another essay titled *Can Virtue Be Taught?,* Plutarch argues that every man's life is made up of three basic parts:

- his birth: his parentage & gifts of mind, body and opportunity;
- his education: training & development of his gifts;
- his work: what deeds he performs in his life.

While man has no control over his birth, Plutarch argues that he can be educated to develop all of his gifts and seize enough opportunities to overcome all obstacles of his birth to live virtuously. The key was education, because Plutarch did not believe that man is fallen or evil by nature as Scripture plainly teaches. He believed instead that man simply does not really know what is good and needs to be taught. In our study of *Plutarch's Lives,* we will use these three elements to discuss and judge the virtue of famous men from the ancient world. Keeping these three elements in mind as we read and discuss the book will help us analyze Plutarch's comparisons and compose our own.

## Significance

Plutarch's book was not widely read during his lifetime, nor for the next five hundred years after he died. During his life, his writings were shared among his students and friends, but seem to have had little effect on Romans at large. The book became very popular among students during the Renaissance, when the study of Greek and Roman literature revived throughout Europe, and the study of rhetoric flourished.

*Plutarch's Lives* is studied today for many different reasons. Many students love the biographies for their exciting accounts of the great deeds of famous men. Historians read the work of Plutarch to gather details about the lives and times of these men for writing their own history books. For example, see how Jackson Spielvogel uses excerpts from Plutarch to fill in information about men in his *Western Civilization* textbook.[2] Philosophers read Plutarch's writing for his ideas about life and death, the gods, good and bad, what makes men happy and more. Rhetoric students have studied Plutarch to imitate his writing style. Many of the modern world's greatest writers, philosophers, rulers and historians have been greatly affected by reading *Plutarch's Lives.*

## Main Characters

Plutarch wished to demonstrate that for every great Roman, there was a comparable or superior Greek. To challenge Rome's famous founder Romulus, Plutarch set forward Greece's hero, Theseus. The self-denial and legendary victories of Theseus were far more glorious than the necessity-driven and rather selfish acts of Romulus. The political and religious organization of the early Roman monarch Numa, marvelous as it was, was not far beyond the greatness of the Spartan military state of Lycurgus. The Roman Poplicola received as much of his glory from Solon, who served as his wisest supporter, as any other—indeed, without Solon's example, Poplicola would have been far less appreciated in his time. And lastly, the saving of Rome from the barbarian invaders by Camillus was less historically significant than Themistocles' rescuing of the Western world from the mighty Persians in the fifth century B.C., as was mentioned in Herodotus's *Histories.*

The lives featured by Plutarch include most of the greatest statesmen of classical history, including Julius Caesar, Cicero, Alexander the Great, Nero, Demosthenes and more, though we will examine only the first eight.

## Summary and Setting

Plutarch lived and wrote during the Silver Age of Roman literature, which lasted roughly from A.D. 15 to 160. The earlier, Golden Age, which included such literary giants as Virgil, Ovid, Livy and Horace, ended with the death of Emperor Augustus. The age that followed, though excellent, was forever destined to be second best, surely silver compared to the gold of the previous generation.

As a Silver Age writer, Plutarch wrote with Seneca, Petronius and Tacitus. In the Roman cities, the moral excellence of the Augustan Age was decaying, and the "conservatives," like Tacitus, wrote bitterly and pessimistically of Roman events. Plutarch, on the other hand, being content with country life and beyond the reach of inner city troubles, was far less negative in his writing and thus was considered more enjoyable to many readers. *Plutarch's Lives* compares the lives of the greatest Romans with the greatest Greeks. Living at the time that Roman histories were being written suggesting that this was the nation of nations, destined by the gods for "empire without end," as Virgil wrote, it was Plutarch's belief that Roman achievements were not much greater than those of his beloved Greeks.

## Worldview

In America today, so much ungodly behavior has been publicly accepted and even welcomed that, when we see something not entirely wicked, we call it good.

Christians rejoice to hear that an unmarried teenager wants to deliver her baby and consider it an act of moral courage, because we have heard of so many thousands of mothers choosing to abort pregnancies year after year. We might hear that a certain college assigns students to read the Bible for ancient history and label it a "conservative" school—and we then feel comfortable with this quasi-Christian school. A new movie has only a few curse words and only a couple of "bad parts" (it is not as bad as many *other* movies), so we can watch it. A professional basketball player talks about "God" helping him grab rebounds and becomes the favorite player of thousands of Christian kids who know he must be a "Christian."

This moral relativism, the idea that all criteria of judgment are relative to the individuals and situations involved, can become very difficult to sense. It can be even harder to defend against, because we breathe it in every day, in every place. We may often find ourselves calling things "good" only because they are not as bad as other things. We can grow comfortable with this kind of thinking, and our judgment can easily lose its Christian sense of right and wrong. But God says that the Scriptures are our only measure for these judgments.

The same happens when we read pagan authors like Plutarch

Legend suggests that Theseus killed the half-man, half-bull monster known as the Minotaur. This vase celebrates this heroic exploit that freed Athens from its obligation to pay this creature an annual tribute of seven boys and seven girls, who were sacrificed to him.

Jacques-Louis David painted the *Intervention of the Sabine Women* around 1799. This oil-on-canvas depicts the Sabine women, who had previously been stolen by the Romans to become their wives, defending their new husbands from their former families and countrymen in an attempt to broker peace.

He was a *relatively* good guy—certainly better than the Roman emperor Nero, who burned Christians as torches in his garden for parties. Plutarch was religious, pro-family, certainly supported prayer in school, believed he was not perfect and may have even believed the historical fact that Jesus died on the cross. But he was a pagan—a Platonist idolater who did not know the Father, nor the Son, nor the Holy Spirit, was never baptized, never attended Communion and did not honor the Word of God as "the only rule to direct us how we may glorify and

enjoy Him." Further, the good that he did he took credit for as though he were its source and never thought to give the God of heaven the glory and thanks He deserved. Such thinking has consequences we must carefully understand. We must consider the virtues Plutarch praises—what are they? Are they *Christian?* Should we imitate them?

First of all, Plutarch is working with a pagan worldview. Many of the things you may have learned in Sunday school would likely be quite unfamiliar to him. He does not understand that when God created all things, he said they were all good. He does not know of the Garden of Eden, the serpent, Adam or Eve or the fall of man. He does not understand God's promise to save sinners by sending His Son into the world. He does not believe that Jesus Christ will come again from heaven to judge all men. He does not know of or believe in the Trinity—no concept of the Father, Son and Holy Spirit. He does not embrace the idea that God became man in the incarnation. Because of his religious beliefs, Plutarch is in an entirely different world from Christians, and his ideas and behavior are affected by it.

Second, Plutarch's view that a man can be made good through education is not true—just ask your teachers! Man is corrupted in his heart and mind and despises God's ways. Man not only fails to do the good he does not understand—he also is unable to do the good that he *does* understand and many times chooses to do evil, even when he knows what is good and the happiness doing good will bring to him! Furthermore, the good that he does do never comes close to the perfection God commands, and so all of his works fall short of his duty. He is ultimately accepted by God *only* because God, in Christ, is merciful and desires to forgive and renew His repentant creatures. Education can teach people what is good, true and beautiful, but it cannot make us love those things, or give us the wisdom and strength to do them.

Third, Plutarch's idea of a noble man is one who achieves great things in the world. It is the same view we often find on television, in magazines and around town. He presents men like Theseus and Romulus, founders of the great cities Athens and Rome. He praises Lycurgus as the father of the mighty Spartans. He praises Poplicola as a man of great power who uses his power for good and dies happily. In the eyes of men, these are the great men of the earth—but we know that God does not see as man sees. All these men may indeed appear impressive to other men, but when their lives are studied carefully, we find they are guilty of all kinds of wickedness—envy, hatred, malice, deceit, adultery, murder, divination, greed and even cosmic treason—all in the service of idols. Our Lord's words apply to these pagan heroes and their admirers: *"You are those who justify yourselves before men, but God knows your hearts. For what is highly esteemed among men is an abomination in the sight of God"* (Luke 16:15).

We do not need to guess at what motivates pagan men to do good deeds. We know what sinfully drives us sometimes. In 1 John 2:16 and 17, John teaches us of the vanity of the pagan world—

> For all that is in the world—the lust of the flesh, the lust of the eyes, and the pride of life—is not of the Father but is of the world. And the world is passing away, and the lust of it; but he who does the will of God abides forever.

Man's duty to God is obedience to His commands, relying on His help, for the glory of His name. God's will is summed up by the prophet Micah:

> He has shown you, O man, what is good; And what does the LORD require of you but to do justly, to love mercy, and to walk humbly with your God? (Mic. 6:8)

Jesus summarized all the law and the prophets in two commands: "You shall love the LORD your God with all your heart, with all your soul, with all your strength, and with all your mind, and your neighbor as yourself" (Luke 10:27). If we are faithful to keep this as our test of the lives of pagan men, what good will they prove to be at all? Unfortunately, all too often the Christian believes they are of no good, of no use to study and discards them. Then there are those who fail to distinguish their false virtue and false righteousness with true biblical righteousness—the kind God defines. Measured by God's Law as found in the Ten Commandments, we quickly find many failures in these "noble" men who rarely honor even the least of the Lord's commandments. Ask yourself—if you took out any of the names of the men in Plutarch's stories and put your name in, would your parents or teachers be happy to read what you have done? Yet understanding their form of virtue remains important. They, many times were far more willing to live and die for their beliefs than we, the people of God. Understanding them can prove motivating to us.

Truly, these men have an outward form of religion and goodness, but they appear good only when considered relatively—in comparison with more wicked men and deeds, not when held up to biblical standards. These lives may seem impressive in comparison to your neighbors, but we are not to judge men's deeds by comparing them to what is normal or common. If we think biblically about these great men and ask whether their lives were pleasing to God, we will see that the Bible everywhere argues that their "virtue" is not the real thing. John Calvin explained this very well when he said:

> ... as they have no regard to the end which the divine wisdom prescribes, although from the performance the act *seems* good, yet from the perverse motive it is sin.[3]

David shows his clear sense of the folly of so-called "mighty" men as he rejoices over his fallen enemy—

> "Here is the man who did not make God his strength, but trusted in the abundance of his riches, and strengthened himself in his wickedness. But I am like a green olive tree in the house of God; I trust in the mercy of God forever and ever" (Ps. 52:7–8).

Proof texts could be quoted endlessly because this is one of the basic themes of the whole Bible. But it is sufficient to sum things up by saying simply that because the deeds of the pagan heroes were not done out of faith towards the true and living God, for the ends that He has made known and from the motive of love to God and men, they are not righteous, they are *sin*. We must be faithful to judge them rightly.

—William C. Michael

## For Further Reading

Spielvogel, Jackson. *Western Civilization.* Fifth Edition. Belmont, Calif.: Wadsworth/Thomson Learning, 2003. 75, 134–151.

*Veritas Press History Cards: New Testament, Greece and Rome.* Lancaster, Pa.: Veritas Press. 21, 26.

## Session I: Prelude

### A Question to Consider

What characteristics do virtuous men exhibit? Must virtuous deeds be done from right motives to be good?

*From the General Information above answer the following questions:*

1. What was the Silver Age of Latin literature?
2. Who was Plutarch?
3. Where did Plutarch live? When?
4. Why was Plutarch's choice of dwelling place significant?
5. What philosopher's thought greatly influenced Plutarch?
6. What were some of Plutarch's goals in writing his biographies?
7. What is different about the aims of Plutarch's historical writing with those of Tacitus?
8. What three elements of a man's life does Plutarch want us to consider as we read their biographies? Why are these important?

**Reading Assignment:**
*Plutarch's Lives,* Theseus

## Session II: Discussion
*Plutarch's Lives,* Theseus

### A Question to Consider

What attributes prove most useful and effective for founders of political movements?

*Discuss or list short answers to the following questions:*

### Text Analysis

1. Who was Theseus?
2. What was significant about the birth of Theseus?
3. What was significant about the education and training received by Theseus?
4. How did Theseus's birth and training prove beneficial? What great work(s) did he perform?

### Cultural Analysis

1. What does our culture value in a political leader?
2. What does the story about the childhood of George Washington and the cherry tree tell us about the virtue of some past political leaders?

### Biblical Analysis

1. What does God seek in a political leader? (See 1 Samuel 13:13–15.)

## SUMMA

*Write an essay or discuss this question, integrating what you have learned from the material above.*
What makes a great leader?

READING ASSIGNMENT:
*Plutarch's Lives*, Romulus and The Comparison between Romulus and Theseus

# SESSION III: ANALYSIS

*Plutarch's Lives*, Theseus, Romulus and The Comparison between Romulus and Theseus

*Discuss or list short answers to the following questions:*

1. What are the similarities between Romulus and Theseus? What are the differences?
2. How do the births of some of the great leaders of the Bible compare to those of Theseus and Romulus? (Consider Moses, David and Jesus.)
3. How do the works of Theseus and Romulus compare to the works of Moses and Christ?

READING ASSIGNMENT:
*Plutarch's Lives*, Lycurgus

# SESSION IV: DISCUSSION

*Plutarch's Lives*, Lycurgus

## A Question to Consider

Which is a better government, a *benevolent* monarch (king) or checks and balances among leaders?

*Discuss or list short answers to the following questions:*

## Text Analysis

1. What was the first major governmental change made by Lycurgus? What effect did it have?
2. Why did Lycurgus, as his second major change, redistribute land ownership?
3. Today the term *Spartan* means "simple," "frugal" or "austere," as in a "Spartan diet" or a "Spartan

lifestyle." What other changes did Lycurgus initiate that set the stage for the Spartan culture from which we get the definition above?

## Cultural Analysis

1. What governmental systems of the twentieth century resemble Sparta under Lycurgus?
2. What problems result from such governments? (Hint: Are you motivated to work if someone else will be paid for your effort?)

## Biblical Analysis

1. Is the sharing of resources among the saints in the early church (Acts 4:32–37) the same sharing as

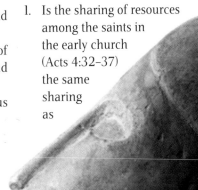

This idealized bust of Themistocles captures the Greek notions of beauty and strength in this brilliant Athenian who led in the victory over the Persians at Salamis.

enacted by Lycurgus?

2. Under Lycurgus the Spartans sought to eliminate the creation and appreciation of things beautiful. What biblical texts would prove this unwise or even wrong?

## SUMMA

*Write an essay or discuss this question, integrating what you have learned from the material above.*

Can you name anyone you think would make a good absolute monarch? Are you more comfortable with the checks and balances approach like that of the United States?

### READING ASSIGNMENT:

*Plutarch's Lives,* Numa Pompilius and The Comparison Between Lycurgus and Numa Pompilius

## SESSION V: WRITING

*Plutarch's Lives,* Lycurgus, Numa Pompilius and The Comparison Between Lycurgus and Numa Pompilius

### Progymnasmata

Remember the writing exercise called an *encomium* in Session XVII of *The Odyssey?* The exercise was part of the *progymnasmata,* a series of exercises used for classical training in writing. You may

Spartans were known as the fiercest of all warriors. This bronze depicts a hoplite, or Spartan soldier, in action.

remember that the encomium praises an individual. A companion exercise, called an *invective* or *vituperation,* condemns an individual, exactly the opposite of an encomium. Another exercise is called a *comparison.* A comparison takes the next step by weighing one individual against another and making a judgment about which one is the greatest. A comparison expounds the virtue of a specific person over and against another (e.g., Joe is a stronger warrior than Ted), but does not talk about virtue in a general sense (e.g., strength in war is admirable).

Although the encomium has six parts, the comparison has five. This is because the fifth part of the encomium (the Comparison) is incorporated into the other parts when writing a comparison. The *Prologue* comes first. It introduces the topic and, at the end of the paragraph, states or implies the opinion of the writer. The second part of this exercise is a paragraph called *Description of Heritage* comparing the persons in question. The writer looks for ways to praise or disparage the subjects on account of their family history. For instance, if a person comes from righteous parents, then highlight the fact that he learned his righteous habits at home and added to the glory of the family name. In a comparison, remember that the two people that you are considering must be viewed in relation to each other. So you might say, "Both Teddy Roosevelt and Franklin Roosevelt came from strong families that taught them tenacity, but Teddy Roosevelt's family did a better job of training him in righteousness."

Next comes a paragraph called *Description of Upbringing*. The point is to show how the individuals profited from good education or overcame faulty education. Again, make sure that you compare the two people in this paragraph. You might say, "Both Washington and Franklin had educations that in many ways were lacking, but Franklin exceeded Washington in this area, because he worked so hard to train himself in the art of language that he became one the nation's most popular writers." The most powerful part of the comparison comes next: the *Description of Deeds*. In this section the writer discusses the excellencies or evils of the mind, body and fortune of the subjects. For example, the writer praises the practice of philosophical virtue, the way the person looked and his wealth, influence or social stature. Since Christianity has transformed our society it seems out of place to dwell on physical appearance or possessions, so instead the paragraph should concentrate on the actions and motives of the subject. This can be especially powerful if his life demonstrates a pattern. Again, comparing the two subjects is critical. In this section, you might say, "Although Grant conquered Lee on the battlefield, Lee's stellar Christian life has outshone all of Grants accomplishments." The final paragraph is an *Exhortation* or *Prayer* in which others are called on to imitate the best in the examples.

*Having read Plutarch's lives of Lycurgus and of Numa and his comparison of them, praise Lycurgus and Numa in close comparison, or praise one and vituperate (find fault with) the other. Be certain not to treat them separately, but together, in parallel fashion.*

I. Prologue
 • Introduce the topic
 • State your opinion
II. Description of Heritage
 • Praise or condemn them on account of their family histories
III. Description of Upbringing
 • Show how the subjects profited from or were hindered by their education
IV. Description of Deeds
 • Praise or disparage the excellencies or evils of their actions and motives
V. Exhortation or Prayer
 • Call upon others to imitate one of the person's examples

READING ASSIGNMENT:
*Plutarch's Lives,* Solon

# SESSION VI: RECITATION

*Plutarch's Lives.* Theseus, Romulus, Lycurgus, Numa Pompilius, Solon

*Discuss or list short answers to the following questions:*
1. To what mythical hero is Theseus compared?
2. What city is Theseus credited with founding?
3. How did Theseus reveal himself to his father after arriving in Athens?
4. What caused Romulus and Remus to be nursed by a wolf and fed by a woodpecker?
5. What ultimately became of Remus?
6. What is the "Rape of the Sabine Women?"
7. Why did Lycurgus redistribute the land of Sparta?
8. Why did Lycurgus demand that war not be waged for a long time with a single enemy?
9. Why did Numa initially turn down the kingship of Rome?
10. Why did Numa forbid all graven images of the deity?
11. Why did Numa create a Roman "Sabbath" day?
12. What was Solon's favorite means of communicating important moral or state matters?

READING ASSIGNMENT:
*Plutarch's Lives,* Poplicola and The Comparison of Poplicola with Solon

# Session VII: Activity
*Plutarch's Lives,* Beginning through Poplicola

## Playing *Draco*

*Read the following[5] then play the game* Draco:

Among other things Solon was known for the changes he made to the laws of Greece. He followed a man named Draco, from whom we get the term *draconian.* Draco was one of the first Athenians about whom we have information. He lived about six hundred years before Christ.

At that time the working people of Athens were very unhappy. One reason for this was that the laws were not written down and the judges were very unfair. They almost always decided in favor of their rich friends. At last everybody in Athens agreed that the laws ought to be written out, and Draco was asked to write them.

Some old laws were so severe that often people had been put to death for very slight offences. Draco changed these severe laws and made new ones a great deal more merciful, and this made the people very fond of him. A story is told about his death, which shows that other people besides the Athenians thought a great deal of him. He went to a theater on an island not far from Athens, and when the audience in the theater saw him they threw him their cloaks and caps to do him honor. Unfortunately, such a pile of cloaks fell on him that he was smothered to death.

Even after the laws had been written down, the people were not happy, because Draco had not changed some laws that bore very hard upon the poor. These were the laws about debts. If a man borrowed money and could not pay it back at the right time, the man who lent the money might take the borrower's house and farm and might even sell him and his wife and children as slaves. On most of the farms near Athens, stone pillars were set up, each of which told that the land on which it stood was mortgaged, or pledged, for a debt. Many of the farmers and their families had been sold as slaves. In time it came to be said that Draco's laws were written in blood.

Happily, a very wise and good man named Solon was then living in Athens, and the Athenians asked him to make a new set of laws. Rich and poor were surprised when they read Solon's new laws. The poor who had lost their farms and houses were to have everything given back to them. Solon thought they had paid so much interest for so many years that their debts should be forgiven. All who had been sold as slaves were to have their freedom, and no one was ever again to be sold for debt. Those debtors who had not lost everything were to be forgiven about a quarter of what they owed.

All this Solon called a "shaking-off of burdens," and thousands of people felt that heavy burdens had indeed been taken from their shoulders. Solon did another good thing for the people. He gave every citizen a vote and all could attend the Assembly of the people, which was like a New England town-meeting. There was a Senate of Four Hundred, which proposed laws, but the people themselves met and passed them. So the people of Athens really made their own laws.

Besides this, every year the Assembly chose nine archons, as the rulers of Athens were called. The chief archon was like the mayor of one of our cities and the others like the aldermen. Under Solon's new laws, Athens soon came to stand in Greece for government by all the people, just as Sparta stood for government by the few.

It remains from the time of Solon to today, that a law too severe or requiring a punishment far exceeding the crime is called *draconian.*

*Draco* is a simpler version of the card game *Mao* for three or more players. The first player to discard all his cards wins the round! Sounds simple, right? But there's more. The rules are selected by and known initially only to one player, named Draco's Enforcer. The winner of each hand is allowed to add a new rule to the game. Each new rule is kept secret, and its effects must then be logically deduced by the other players. The game is played using a standard deck of playing cards, including the Jokers, if you so choose. An additional deck may be necessary for more than five players.

### PLAYING THE GAME

Select the player who will be the first Draco's Enforcer. This individual should, of course, be someone who has an idea how to play the game. He will also be the first dealer.

Draco's Enforcer invents two secret rules or chooses two from the examples provided in the teacher's manual. Do not announce these rules. The other players must deduce them as play proceeds.

Before dealing the cards, Draco's Enforcer should announce the following:

a. "The game is played like *Uno* in the sense that you lay cards from your hand on the discard pile and try to be the first to play all your cards.

b. "There is no talking. Any talking beyond what is required by the rules must be started with the phrase: "Point of order." All players must then lay their cards face down and not touch them until the dealer of that hand calls "End point of order."

c. "I cannot tell you any more of the rules."

Draco's Enforcer shuffles the deck and deals five cards to each player, including himself. Place the leftover cards face down in the middle of the table as the stock pile. Turn the top card over from the stock to begin the discard pile.

Play begins with the player on Draco's Enforcer's left, proceeding clockwise. During a turn the player may either

> **PLAY A CARD** Play a legal card from his hand face up on top of the discard pile.
>
> **DRAW** Instead of playing a card, draw one from the top of the undealt stock pile. This card may not be played on this turn.

Draco's Enforcer is responsible to police whether or not any rule is broken. When a player breaks a rule, the Enforcer is to prompt the transgressor to take back the illegal play and take one penalty card. It is not necessary to go into detail about the incorrect play. He may simply say, "Sorry. That was an incorrect play. Please take a penalty card." Play then moves to the next player.

If the draw pile is exhausted before someone wins the hand, turn the discard pile over to become the stock pile, but leave the last card laid as the first card of the discard pile.

When a player successfully discards his last card, he wins that hand and becomes the dealer for the next hand. He also adds a secret rule to the game and becomes an additional Draco's Enforcer. His new rule and all prior rules are now the rules of the game. Each Draco's Enforcer is responsible for the enforcement of the rules he himself instituted.

The overall winner is the person who has won the most games in a certain time period or is the first to win, say, three games. Pick one for your particular circumstances.

# SESSION VIII: ANALYSIS
*Plutarch's Lives*—Solon, Poplicola and
The Comparison of Poplicola with Solon

*Discuss or list short answers to the following questions:*

1. Who was Solon? Who was Poplicola?
2. What was significant about the births of Solon and/or Poplicola?
3. Describe what is told of the education and training received by Solon? (Plutarch tells us very little of Poplicola's education.)
4. What was important about the lives of Solon and Poplicola? Name several high points or accomplishments of Solon and Poplicola? What great works did they perform?
5. What was one of the most striking laws coming from Solon? What problem did this cause?
6. What was one of the great similarities between Solon and Poplicola?
7. Describe how Plutarch contrasts Solon and Poplicola at the end of their lives.
8. How does Moses' role as lawgiver compare with that of Solon?

 **READING ASSIGNMENT:**
*Plutarch's Lives,* Themistocles

# SESSION IX: DISCUSSION
*Plutarch's Lives,* Themistocles

## A Question to Consider

What is wisdom?

*Discuss or list short answers to the following questions:*

### *Text Analysis*

1. What was Themistocles' main ambition as he entered manhood?
2. In Themistocles' generation, how was "wisdom" defined?
3. What does Plutarch seem to believe is true wisdom? Can you track this opinion throughout the previous readings in Plutarch's work?

## Cultural Analysis

1. Who does our culture regard as "wise?" From whom do Americans seek advice?
2. What does our culture think wisdom to be?

## Biblical Analysis

1. Look up the following passages in the scriptures: Exodus 31:1–11; 1 Kings 4:29–34; Psalm 104:24–34; Proverbs 2; Proverbs 9:10; James 3:13–18. What are some characteristics of wisdom according to the biblical use of the term?
2. Try and boil the data down to a concise definition.
3. How does the biblical definition of wisdom compare with that of Plutarch?

## SUMMA

*Write an essay or discuss this question, integrating what you have learned from the material above.* What is the ultimate test of true wisdom?

## Application

1. Knowing the biblical definition of wisdom, who are we to seek for counsel in our lives?

READING ASSIGNMENT:
*Plutarch's Lives,* Camillus

# SESSION X: WRITING
*Plutarch's Lives,* Themistocles and Camillus

## Progymnasmata

Remember the comparison writing in Session V? Plutarch's comparison of Themistocles and Camillus has been lost over time. This is your opportunity to create one.

*Praise Themistocles and Camillus in close comparison, or praise one and vituperate against (find fault with) the other. Be certain not to treat them separately, but together, in parallel fashion.*

*This is not a report, but an exercise in seeking to argue the equal feats of these great men, or superiority of one over the other. You should have a clearly stated opinion in the comparison, which should be argued through your analysis.*

1. Write a paragraph comparing the births of these two men. Looking back at the lives of Themistocles and Camillus, consider the family each person comes from:

**WHAT PEOPLE?**
**WHAT COUNTRY?**
**WHAT ANCESTORS?**
**WHAT PARENTS?**

2. Write a paragraph comparing the reasons for greatness of these two men.
3. Write a paragraph (or more) comparing the deeds of these two men.
4. Write a paragraph in conclusion. Use an exhortation to the reader to either emulate or not emulate either person

## Optional Assignment

For additional challenge, students should be encouraged to re-write their essay arguing another opinion. For example, if the student wrote that Camillus was greater than Themistocles, the second essay might argue why Themistocles was greater than Camillus.

# OPTIONAL SESSION A: REVIEW

*Discuss or list short answers to the following questions:*
1. Who was Plutarch? When did he live?
2. What famous philosopher influenced Plutarch? Why is this important in understanding Plutarch's opinions regarding virtue and vice?
3. Why does Plutarch consider Theseus to be superior in virtue to Romulus?
4. What does Plutarch consider to be better about Lycurgus than Numa?
5. Why does Plutarch say that Poplicola was more blessed than Solon?
6. What is the significance of Plutarch's statement on page 146: "judgment is to be made of actions according to the times in which they were performed?"
7. How would you define Christian virtue?

8. What is ultimately wrong with pagan virtue?
9. What is wisdom from the perspective of Plutarch? American culture? The Bible?

# OPTIONAL SESSION B: REVIEW

*Discuss or list short answers to the following questions:*
1. During what period did Poplicola live?
2. How does Plutarch compare Poplicola with Solon?
3. During what period did Themistocles live?
4. What enemies did Greece face during the life of Themistocles?

5. During what period did Camillus live?
6. How did Camillus rise to power?

## ENDNOTES

1 Delphi was believed by the ancient Greeks to be the very center of the entire earth. Looking at a map of the Mediterranean region, it is plain that, at that time, according to their understanding they were correct.
2 Spielvogel, Jackson. *Western Civilization.* Fifth Edition. Belmont, Calif.: Wadsworth/Thomson Learning, 2003. 59, 128.
3 Calvin, John. *Institutes of the Christian Religion.* Book III, Sec. 14.
4 *This endnote appears only in the teacher's edition.*
5 Most of this explanation is excerpted from *Famous Men of Greece* originally published in 1904.
6 *This endnote appears only in the teacher's edition.*

# PRIMARY BOOKS
Second Semester

# THEBAN TRILOGY

*What animal walks with four legs in the morning, two at midday and three in the evening?*
—*The Riddle of the Sphinx*

Riddles like this one capture our attention and challenge us to think. What is meant by day? How can a creature change the number of legs on which it walks? Why would it do so? Considering this answer can be frustrating and perplexing. One can only imagine what it would be like if your life and the life of an entire city hung in the balance on your answer. If you answer correctly, you will be a king, the hand of the beautiful widowed queen will be yours, and the city will be saved. If you answer wrongly, you will die and the city will perish. Under that kind of pressure, could you come up with the answer? (If you want, you may take a moment and see if you can answer the riddle. Turn to the endnotes[1] of this chapter to check your answer.)

The story of the *Theban Trilogy* is about the man who discovered the answer to this riddle, received everything he ever could have wished for, and, in the end, wished he had never found the answer.

Oedipus is shown with the Sphinx as he contemplates her riddle.

## GENERAL INFORMATION

### Author and Context

Sophocles, the writer of the *Theban Trilogy*, was one of the greatest dramatists of all time. He was born in a rural area outside of Colonus, a suburb of Athens. Early in life, he showed talent worthy of notice and was selected to lead a chorus of boys at the celebration of the victory over the Persians in the naval battle of Salamis.[2] He learned drama from Aeschylus, but defeated his mentor when he presented his first play during the festival of Dionysus, which was the top dramatic festival in Athens. He produced over 120 plays during his long life. He won the festival as many as twenty times and never finished lower than second place.

Growing up during the "golden age" of Athens (496 B.C.–406 B.C.), Sophocles served in many varied roles. His first fame came as a writer, but he also acted in many of his own plays. He served both as a priest and on the Board of Generals governing Athens. For a time he served as the treasurer of the Delian League.[3]

He is noted as a theatrical innovator. He was the first to introduce the "third actor" into extensive use (plays prior to his employed only two actors changing from one role to another—which led to, among other things, extremely tired actors). He also is credited with being the first playwright to paint scenery. He actually juggled so incredibly well in one of his plays that all Athens was abuzz.

## Significance

The *Theban Trilogy*, and particularly *Oedipus the King*, demonstrates both Sophocles and Greek tragedy at the height of their power and influence. Oedipus's story and the subsequent tales of his cursed children move us, because, unlike many tragic characters, Oedipus's "flaws" are easy to sympathize with, and the horror of his fall which is brought on by his own desire to save his city arouses feelings of pity and horror unparalleled in modern cinema. The shock of understanding Oedipus's secret (even before he does) brings the listener to a massive and purging catharsis, or riddance of bad emotions, where the audience is made to feel both empathy (i.e., to feel the emotions another person is feeling) and pity for a character undergoing a tragic fall. While *Oedipus at Colonus* hints at some peace for his cursed family, *Antigone* brings us back for another round of horrifying tragedy. The Greeks believed that this passionate welling up of feelings was beneficial and was, in fact, the point of writing tragedies. In the *Theban Trilogy*, Sophocles masters this art by setting forth a man who engenders sympathy, is heroic and makes consistent rational and ethical decisions which lead to tragedy that still elicit groans of horror and pity from today's audiences.

For the Greeks, plays like the *Theban Trilogy*, served as important parts of the curriculum of education. Tragic plays, Aristotle argues, are important in teaching us to be human.[4] From them we learn sympathy and can purge ourselves of these passionate emotions without having to go through the tragedies personally.

This 17th-century Poussin painting depicts Apollo with other classical Greek subjects. It is Apollo's oracle that predicts Oedipus will kill his father and marry his mother.

## Main Characters

Oedipus's cursed family composes the main cast of characters. The focal point of the first two plays is the character of Oedipus, born into the ruling family of Thebes, but born under a dark and ominous curse which states that he will kill his father, Laius, and marry his mother, Jocasta (which we all can agree is not the most pleasant of prophecies). Jocasta plays a large role in the play (Laius is not present—you can guess what has happened) as she unwittingly falls victim to the curse and fulfills it by becoming Oedipus's wife. The children of the union of mother and son also play a role in the plays. Chief among them is Antigone. She stands as Oedipus's most loyal child and at times his only comfort in life. Ismene, his other daughter, also visits Oedipus in Colonus and tries to convince Antigone to avoid doom in the final play. Creon, Oedipus's uncle and Jocasta's brother, whose role grows during the trilogy, serves in *Colonus* and *Antigone* as an example of a man corrupted by power as he attempts to guide the destiny of Thebes and control Oedipus and his family. Creon's son Haemon, plays a significant role in the final play.

Two characters from outside of the cursed line of Oedipus should also be mentioned. Teiresias, the blind prophet of ancient lore (who seems to appear in almost every ancient tale), makes appearances both in the first and last plays to reveal hidden things. Theseus, the founder of Athens and slayer of the Minotaur, also plays a role in the second play, befriending and protecting Oedipus and his daughters in *Colonus*.

## Summary and Setting

The trilogy begins in Thebes, a Greek city, in the generations prior to the Trojan War. Thebes, it seems, has fallen under a curse, a curse which can be lifted only if their able King Oedipus gets to the bottom of the problem. The first play, *Oedipus the King*, consists of Oedipus's constant, unrelenting search for answers and his discovery of his own past.

We learn that a number of important events have occurred, however, prior to the beginning of the story. The rulers of Thebes, King Laius and Queen Jocasta, produced a son who was cursed by the gods. This prophecy said that the boy would eventually rise up and murder his father and marry his mother. Horrified, the king and queen commanded that the child be abandoned on a hillside, exposed and left to die.

Many years later troubles in Thebes grew. One day the king, while on a journey, is killed by a traveler that he has insulted. To make matters worse, the Sphinx (a mythical, riddling monster) was holding the city of Thebes captive until a hero could answer her. Into this great need Oedipus stepped, answering the monster, saving the city and winning the heart of its widowed queen. He was made king, and the story opens with him dealing with a curse that has fallen on the city.

One can already see his life unraveling, for the gods' curses cannot be avoided. Oedipus, to his own shock and eye-gouging horror, learns that he has unwittingly fulfilled the curse.

*Oedipus at Colonus*, the second play, continues the story, as the aged, but still-cursed, Oedipus wonders from place to place longing for a quiet death. His only support in this trek is his faithful daughter, Antigone. In Athens at the side of Theseus, the legendary founder of the city, Oedipus finds rest and protection but is disturbed by news of his sons' (Eteocles and Polyneices) squabbles and eventual civil war for the throne of Thebes. Rejecting overtures to join both sides of the battle, Oedipus curses his sons and dies.

In *Antigone*, the third play, the final and ghastly end of the curse is seen. Oedipus's curse has come true and both of his sons have died in battle at each other's hands. Creon, Oedipus's uncle, now takes the throne and provides a large state funeral for Eteocles, but forbids the burial of Polyneices. Antigone, Oedipus's daughter, braves the threats of the power-hungry Creon and gives her brother his burial rites. For this, she wins the admiration of many (even Creon's son Haemon) and condemnation from the state. The play ends with the curse of Oedipus and the pride of Creon bringing ruin and destruction to their families.

## Worldview

Have you ever seen the beautiful plant named the Oleander? Its flowers shoot out in beautiful colors of white, pink and red. Its beauty, combined with it toughness (it needs little water), make it a favorite of many landscapers, who plant it in many areas (some of which are accessible by pets and children). At first glance it is an almost perfect plant. The Oleander, however, has a darker side. On closer examination this "evil side" becomes evident. The Oleander is extremely toxic (1/8 of a leaf can kill an adult man). Its sap can burn and cause blisters. People have even died from burning its sticks in a fire to roast marshmallows and hot dogs.

In many ways the worldview displayed in the *Theban Trilogy* is like the Oleander. At the start of the story, everything seems to be in its place, although a plague has broken out in the city. Its king, the great Oedipus, seems poised to continue to grow in fame by again saving his city from devastation. By the end of the *Trilogy*, however, the poison of the false worldview has worked itself through the family of Oedipus. They lie dead and cursed with lives as shattered as the Oleander is toxic. Like the Oleander, however, there is something good and beautiful that draws the unsuspecting hand toward it. The worldview of the *Theban Trilogy* has some surface similarities to Christianity, but on deeper examination, its worldview leads to destruction and a life of hopelessness.

The harmfulness of this worldview can be seen by examining its view of the gods, man and salvation. Like the God of Christianity, the gods of the *Theban Trilogy* are powerful, controlling and ordaining the future, overcoming the barriers and obstacles set in their path by humans. At first glance this seems good. On closer examination, however, the evil character of these demonic deities can be clearly seen.

Although presented as powerful, the gods of the *Theban Trilogy*, like the Oleander, cannot be trusted. The entire system of Greek deities presents gods that are at odds with, and even at war with, one another. The beauty, serenity and unity of the Trinity is replaced by a multiplicity of gods whose will cannot be clearly known. These gods do not consistently reward piety nor punish sin. In the case of Oedipus, they prove themselves powerful by causing their prophecy to be fulfilled. This horrid oracle claims that Oedipus will kill his father and marry his mother. All of the characters in this story who hear the prophecy take radical steps to avoid these frightful events. These steps involve the attempted murder of an heir to the throne and the flight of a prince from his kingdom. But the vile will of the gods will not be stopped, and none of these actions keep the them from tricking their followers into unknowingly committing this perversity.

Instead of being pleased by piety and virtue, these gods wipe out the "best" that mankind has to offer. Oedipus is a picture of what is most virtuous in man. He demonstrates his courage by defeating the monstrous Sphinx, and winning the throne of Thebes and the hand of her widowed queen. Oedipus is a courageous savior, but the gods, from the time of his birth, are set on poisoning and destroying his family.

Like the deceptive Oleander, which looks like a normal attractive flower, these gods bear some similarity to the true God, but in the end they are seen to be massively different from the true God. Not many of the exact attributes of the gods who torture Oedipus and his family are seen in the *Theban Trilogy*. For the most part, the gods are conspicuously absent. Still, much can be learned of them. They are like the true God in that they display power. They also predict the future and bring their plans to fruition. This, however, is where the likeness ends. The most striking difference is that the gods of Oedipus are almost the moral opposite of the true God. They are unrighteous, unholy and unjust. They use their power to destroy their followers. Virtue, instead of eliciting praise and blessing, brings wrath and destruction from these demonic gods. Their purposes are unknown and unknowable, so these mute gods leave their followers to stumble in darkness, while they themselves place stumbling blocks in the paths of their blind (and blinded) worshipers.

Another telling difference is the lack of anything resembling a covenant between the gods and their followers. Oedipus can never be sure what the gods want. He can never find a place of safety. Even at *Colonus* when death is near, Oedipus has little comfort. The gods rule, but they keep their wishes private and destroy men for their own hidden reasons.

In *Colonus*, Oedipus does refer to the gods as being eternal and unchangeable. From this he draws the conclusion that the gods are the only ones who can be trusted, while man is constantly changing over time. While Oedipus is right to see the weakness of men, his assessment of the divine is certainly questionable. While eternality and immutability (i.e., unchanging nature) mean that the gods could be trustworthy, their actions certainly prove otherwise.

Their attributes, combined with their wretched character, makes the reality that confronts the people of this play even more hopeless. These gods are given the title "immutable and eternal." They are also powerful, but they are wicked. A powerful, wicked god who will last forever and never change truly represents a philosophical "worst case" scenario.

These gods demonstrate themselves to be irrationally wicked. They carefully plot the destruction of Oedipus and his family, causing even sensible actions by the characters who are attempting to avoid patricide (the murder of a parent) and incest to lead to both of these sins. Oedipus's sins did not bring this prophecy to be, for it was uttered over his birth. These gods give no explanation or reason for their hatred of Oedipus. What is worse, even after Oedipus blinds himself, the gods supply no explanation or justification for their horrid actions.

These gods are twisted deities that wreck the lives of their followers for sport. Giving no law or instruction, the hidden gods of the *Theban Trilogy* leave the people to wander in darkness. Oedipus is punished for a sin that he did much to avoid. He tries valiantly to please the gods by avoiding the prophesied defilement. The gods, however, speak in a manner that confuses Laius, Jocasta and Oedipus so much that, not only are they unable to avoid the defilement, they actually cause the very corruption they are hoping to circumvent. The gods' secret will (what they are causing to happen in the world) and their revealed will (what they call people to do and be and avoid) are confused and opaque. They give no clear teaching and lead their followers into disobedience.

The view of man that the *Theban Trilogy* presents is one that shows man to be a slave of the gods, inevitably drawn to accomplish the vile will of the deities who reign supreme. These deities, like the beautiful Oleander, capture the attention of the unsuspecting and draw them into their own harm and destruction.

Man is left with no clear standard of righteousness. There is no law, or objective standard, for Oedipus to follow. He understands that patricide (killing his father) and incest (marrying his mother) are to be avoided, but the gods draw him into these perversions by their trickery. The standard of righteousness communicated to Oedipus is unclear and can be determined only by men thinking through vague utterances of riddling oracles or by applying their own imperfect standards.

The type of human morality that these grisly gods expect remains as hidden as the danger of the Oleander to the

This relief shows dancers and a double flute player. In Greek drama, the performance was set to music and accompanied by dancers.

unsuspecting child. These gods fail to make known what pleases them. They tell them little, and that which they say is unclear and unavoidable. Oedipus stumbles toward his doom and the fulfillment of the prophecy simultaneously. What do these gods want? None of their followers are sure. Their reason for making the prophecy known is not so that Oedipus can avoid it. Try as he might, this proves impossible. The gods delight in showing their destructive powers over their human slaves.

Even more shocking, the gods make no clear entrance into the story to justify themselves or their incomprehensible actions. There is no comfort for Oedipus or Antigone. There is no peace for them, either. They travel through this cursed world as the slaves of mute and vicious gods, only to die hopeless deaths. All the while, the gods are absent, demonstrating that they neither owe nor plan to give a definitive defense of their actions against the family of Oedipus.

Strikingly, in the *Theban Trilogy,* Sophocles demonstrates how a pagan would deal with the problem of predestination. The story of Oedipus shows a man at the mercy of the gods. This man is condemned not for any conscious rebelling against standards of righteousness. He, in fact, spends his life trying to remain righteous and avoid the sins prophesied concerning him. Still, the gods drag him down into wickedness, brokenness and destruction. For their motivation the gods give no answer. They destroy Oedipus because that is what they want to do.

Ironically, the true God often faces charges of unfairness when it comes to the issue of predestination. This

Theseus, friend and chief ally of Oedipus, was depicted on many highly decorated clay pots for freeing Athens from the dreaded Minotaur.

objection comes so naturally to the lips of sinful men that Paul deals with it in Romans 9:19–21, saying,

> You will say to me then, "Why does He still find fault? For who has resisted His will?" But indeed, O man, who are you to reply against God? Will the thing formed say to him who formed it, "Why have you made me like this?" Does not the potter have power over the clay, from the same lump to make one vessel for honor and another for dishonor?

Basically, Paul voices the complaint that sinners make, saying that if God controls all things, how can I be held guilty for my sins? Paul answers by telling men that they do not have the moral standing to even ask God what he is doing. Our relationship to our Creator is likened to the relationship between the potter and the pottery he creates. His rights over it are total and need not be defended.

How then is the true God any different in this than

the Greek gods? Both predestine; both condemn some (it seems that the Greek gods condemn all). The difference, however, is obvious when we consider the distance between creatures and creator and the space between sinners and a holy God. This stark difference does not exist between the Greek gods and their subjects. In Hesiod, one sees that the Greek gods are themselves creations of the natural world.[5] One also sees that they are at least as morally flawed as the people who serve them. They are powerful but not holy. They are massive but not righteous. When a sinful man was faced with the predestination of the Greek gods, he had little hope. These wicked beings did whatever their perverse hearts desired. In the real world, the world of the true God, people face a much different situation. The true God is holy and just. Sinners have no right to question his decisions, because they have no moral equality with Him. He is righteous; He is just. He does not condemn sinners because they failed to jump through some unseen hoop, nor does He punish them in hell because they were straining so hard to do good, while He pushed them into evil. He condemns sinners because they have rebelled against His statutes and justice. They receive only what they deserve. The Greek gods know of no such righteousness.

The original moral and intellectual powers of man are still evident in Oedipus, although they are weakened and twisted. Oedipus demonstrates a great deal of virtue. He is especially blessed with courage and intelligence. He demonstrates a measure of righteousness when he has the courage to face down the terrible Sphinx. In this, Oedipus's intelligence becomes apparent. When everyone else has failed to stop the plague, Oedipus alone is able to solve the riddle and save the city. He also demonstrates his virtue by being willing to leave the people that he supposed to be his mother and father to avoid any possibility of fulfilling the prophecy.

Oedipus knows and understands much truth. His quick mind outwits the Sphinx. He is also able to track down the killer of Laius when given that task.

One might ask, what is the origin of Oedipus's "virtue?" Certainly, his gods are not the source of it. They themselves fail any test of righteousness that could be given to them. By seeking to avoid evil and do good and by consistently demonstrating virtue, Oedipus proves himself to be a virtuous man. At this point, Sophocles, the poet, has a problem. The gods that rule his thinking cannot produce in man the virtue that is needed to make Oedipus a sympathetic hero. Those gods, instead, turn righteousness into a joke, choosing to pull down and destroy those who are the most courageous and skillful. These unpredictable gods could neither keep nor create any stable standards of righteousness and ethics. Sophocles, however, lived in a world where undeniable virtue surrounded him every day. He would have known and looked up to brave men who fought at Marathon and Salamis. The goodness and righteousness of these courageous warriors would have been evident to Sophocles, but the fact that this righteousness did not come from the gods he knew was equally clear.

No doubt unknowingly but wisely, Sophocles borrowed from a biblical worldview to create his tragic tale. In the courageous and righteous actions of Oedipus, Sophocles recognizes the outlines of the law of the true God, which, by God's common grace,[6] still resides, though marred, on the hearts of men. Because of conscience and love of parents, Oedipus flees sin. Because of a love for the truth, Oedipus searches ceaselessly for King Laius's killer. Because of courage, he faces down the dreaded Sphinx. All of these virtues were alive and present in the Greek society of Sophocles' day, although the Greek worldview cannot explain them nor produce them. The God of the Bible, however, gives his gifts liberally even to those who are far from Him. By making Oedipus a virtuous man, Sophocles is inconsistent with his own worldview. This inconsistency, however, makes the story infinitely better. He makes Oedipus a man whom all his audience would recognize as unquestionably good. By demonstrating how the gods wreck this ideal man, he highlights both the vicious evil of the gods and the hopeless condition of man, thus creating a massive catharsis where the sad emotions are purged away.

Unfortunately, Oedipus is most ignorant of that which he should know best. Oedipus (as Teiresias notes in lines 413–415 of *Oedipus the King*) does not understand his own identity. This one bit of ignorance leads him to his own and his family's destruction.

In this marred and imperfect manner, Oedipus clings to a measure of true knowledge, righteousness and reason. Antigone as well shows a measure of righteousness, as she courageously defies the state and Creon to do her duty to her family. All of this is undone by the terrible powers of the gods. By the end of the first play, Oedipus has come to see himself as he really is—a helpless pawn who is trapped by the gods in the sins that he has sought to avoid.

Ironically, by the time he has gouged out his own eyes (upon gaining a clear sight of his life), Oedipus has come to bear the perverse *imago dei*[7] of the gods that he serves. The Greek gods habitually murder or attempt to murder their parents and commit acts of sexual infidelity and depravity. Zeus, the king of the Greek gods, murdered his own father, Cronos, and was involved in so many unsavory adulteries that even listing them would be quite a challenge. The difference between Oedipus and the gods is that he falls into sin unwillingly and accidentally, while the gods rape and murder their adherents for sport and slay and cavort with impunity.

In this story, however, the humans, more than the deities, bear marks of being created by a holy God. In Oedipus, there is much common grace[8] as, in many ways, he defines virtue. The gods, however, bear no such marks. Instead of demonstrating moral righteousness and holiness, they lead their "prey" into temptation and transgression. They deliver Oedipus up to do unknowing evil to himself.

In the case of the Oleander there is a clear distinction between the right and wrong way to treat it. This kind of clear distinction can be called an *antithesis*. This antithesis means that the wise will avoid touching or, especially, eating it. If this law is unknown, however, disaster may result. In the *Theban Trilogy*, there is no antithesis (i.e., clear distinction between sin and righteousness). The main reason for this is that the gods are the worst and yet most powerful beings in the story. Their amorality, or lack of moral absolutes, blurs the lines between righteousness and sin. Is it right to kill one's parents? The gods themselves do it, but they destroy Oedipus by causing him to unwittingly fall into this sin. Is it right to perform the burial rights for a brother? The gods demand it, but when Antigone obeys them, she is left without a protector and the gods allow Creon to destroy her.

Parenthetically, our readers should know that the classics departments of many universities seem to take the side of the gods and seek to find some fault with poor Oedipus. They accuse him of hubris, or inordinate pride. Often, Oedipus and others like him attract the wrath of the gods because they do too much good, solving too many riddles and saving too many cities. They are too good, too beautiful or too courageous. The Greek ideal of perfection, called the "golden mean" (which is based on finding one's place and a balance between extremes), is thereby transgressed and the wrath of the gods is incurred. One has to wonder what motivates the gods to punish people for inordinate goodness or virtue—jealousy? insecurity? Hardly justifiable! This should not be construed as a slight to the intellect of any particular classics professor who takes the side of the evil gods against the beleaguered Oedipus. On the contrary, one would have to have immense cleverness to seriously attempt to justify the wretched actions of these horrid deities.[9] Just so we are clear though, any attempt to justify these gods is futile.

What is even more hopeless for those stuck in this flawed worldview is that the gods never make their will clearly known to anyone. People search for the opinion of prophets and oracles, but the path of blessing always remains unclear. The gods and their will remain hidden except for the troubling prophecies that cannot be avoided.

Wisdom is mocked by these gods. Everyone in the play scrambles to avoid the wrath of the gods being visited upon them. They all take wise steps to avoid destruction, but this is all for naught. Laius trusts that he has killed the child whose birth prophecy says will kill the king himself, but he cannot stop fate. Oedipus flees Corinth to avoid the fulfillment, yet in doing this, he brings the oracle one step closer to completion. Antigone wisely seeks to cover Polyneices body secretly, but all her wisdom comes to nothing, as the destructive plans of the bloodthirsty deities are satisfied. The gods of the *Theban Trilogy* turn wisdom and folly upside down. Those people who take sensible steps, wise steps, to avoid folly are punished

by having the gods transform these wise actions into the very folly that they were hoping to escape.

For those trapped in this awful worldview, the future holds nothing but a grim realization that the world is a garden full of poisonous plants that will destroy them, whenever and for whatever reason they deem appropriate. Imagine that! Nothing is ever safe, and no hope of liberation from the gods of this system could reasonably be expected. This mirrors the lines one might read on a modern bumper sticker saying, "Life is hard and then you die." The future of the family of Oedipus and of the world is bleak. The gods are the unchallenged rulers over all. Their power brings human wisdom crashing down, but their evil attributes and vague revelation mean that man, like Oedipus, faces a future of blind groping, not knowing whether he is pleasing the gods or bringing down a curse on his city and family. These gods cannot be escaped, reasoned with or known, so man must traverse the darkness, hoping for a short life and a quiet death.

After death, however, the picture gets even less clear. The *Theban Trilogy* does not present any extended discourse on the afterlife. Other works, like the *Odyssey,* outline some of the expectation. Achilleus's picture of the land of shades is not flattering, and what is worse, the gods still rule the lands beyond the grave. Oedipus longs for death in *Colonus,* but his hope for peace is not grounded in anything he knows about the gods.

A certain melancholy emerged in Greek art at the end of the fifth century B.C. In this funeral stele we see this exemplified as the young bride selects a necklace to adorn herself for her ultimate husband, Hades.

Neither Oedipus nor Antigone leave life in peace. Oedipus dies knowing that, while his horrible life is coming to an end, the curse is still being fulfilled against his family. He has foreseen the death of Eteocles and Polyneices at each other's hands. Antigone, as well, goes to death by her own hand, and her death is instrumental in the death of Haemon as well. The future of the line of Oedipus, like all of life, withers under the watchful care of these monster gods.

If a young child did eat some of the highly toxic Oleander, he would be taken to the doctor, some antidote would be applied and hopefully he would be saved. Unfortunately, in the case of the poison of this worldview, no known antidote exists. There is no way of salvation or redemption open to Oedipus and his family, only the awful fear that the fulfillment of dreadful prophecies cannot be avoided.

No way of salvation or protection is open to anyone in this tale. No sacrifice for sin presents itself in the work. The whole concept of sin has been muddled by the unrighteous and shadowy behavior of the gods. There is no concept of incarnation (not that anyone would really desire to see an incarnation of these troubling deities). No certain communion exists between the gods and their people. The gods do from time to time give words to people like the Delphic Oracle and Teiresias, but even this is shadowy at best. There is no body that binds the people together like the church. They live in city-states (most of the action takes place in Thebes), but this unity is not connected to any of the gods in any way that yields any hope for Oedipus or his family. There is also no gospel to preach. The gods have not revealed their will, and they punish virtue. There are no sacraments. As Oedipus heads into exile, the possibility of him being cleaned by repentance, faith and baptism (or anything like it) never surfaces. His actions heap shame and scorn upon himself, and his community (as well as his sons) block him out of their minds as this lone exile walks into a life of poverty and wandering. There is no antidote for the poisonous worldview seen in these plays.

At the beginning of the *Trilogy*, the only sign of the awful poison coursing through this worldview is a plague which is crippling the city of Thebes. All other appearances look stable, and hope for relief from the plague seems possible with the riddle-solving King Oedipus at the helm of state. Appearances, however, can be misleading. The king and queen look like a happy couple. The royal line appears stable, with both Eteocles and Polyneices growing into manhood. All of that, however, comes to an end. The gods have other plans. Like the unsuspecting person, drawn in by the beauty of the Oleander, the family of Oedipus is destroyed. The hands of their gods (who should represent the highest good) drip with the blood of innocent people who fruitlessly sought to avoid fulfilling their horrid will. The trick of the gods worked.

The poison had no antidote. The family of Oedipus was destroyed and the worldview of a life under these vicious gods is one of unending hopelessness and pain.

—*G. Tyler Fischer*

## For Further Reading

Leithart, Peter. *Heroes of the City of Man*. Moscow, Idaho: Canon Press, 1999. 305–334.

Cowan, Louise and Guinness, Os, ed. *Invitation to the Classics*. Grand Rapids, Mich.: Baker Books, 1998. 46–50.

Spielvogel, Jackson. *Western Civilization*. Fifth Edition. Belmont, Calif.: Wadsworth/Thomson Learning, 2003. 62–80.

*Veritas Press History Cards: New Testament, Greece and Rome*. Lancaster, Pa: Veritas Press. 6, 9, 13.

# SESSION I: PRELUDE

## A Question to Consider:

Why do bad things happen to good people?

*From the General Information above answer the following questions:*
1. Who was Sophocles?
2. Where did he live and during what period?
3. What innovations in drama did Sophocles make?
4. What was the *Golden Age* of Athens?
5. What was the goal of Greek tragedy?
6. Why was this the goal of Greek tragedy?

## Optional Activity: *Analyze the Art*

*Oedipus and the Sphinx* by Jean Auguste Dominique Ingres[14] (pronounced *ahng*).

*Discuss or list short answers to the following questions:*
1. What is Oedipus doing in this painting?
2. What does this action demonstrate about his character?
3. What is the man in the background doing?
4. Why are there bones and a foot on the rocks beneath Oedipus's feet?
5. Why does Oedipus have his spears down?
6. What is the importance of the buildings in the

background?

7. The riddle of the Sphinx is "What animal walks on four legs in the morning, two at midday, and three in the evening?" What is the answer?

**READING ASSIGNMENT:**
*Oedipus the King*

# SESSION II: DISCUSSION

Oedipus the King

## A Question to Consider

Can you avoid your fate?

*Discuss or list short answers to the following questions:*

### Text Analysis

1. What steps were taken to avoid the fulfillment of the prophecy?
2. How did these steps fail?
3. Why did they fail?
4. Is Oedipus to blame for this tragedy? Are Jocasta and Laius?
5. What role do the gods play in this play?
6. What responsibility do the gods bear for this tragedy?

### Cultural Analysis

1. When the terrorist attack on the World Trade Center occurred in 2001, did the world react in a manner that pointed toward a belief in fate or in our free will?
2. In what way did the American response to that event point toward the "faith" of our country?
3. To whom did America as a people appeal to for protection?

### Biblical Analysis

1. Does the Bible present to us a world in which the future is uncertain or a world in which every occurrence has been planned and is governed by God (Rom. 1, Eph. 1)?
2. Can Christians avoid their "fate" (read Ephesians 1 and 2)? Can unbelievers (see Romans 9)?

3. If this is true, what is the difference between the true God and the gods of the Greeks? (Romans 8:28 and the Gospel accounts of the crucifixion)

## Application

1. How should we approach our life if God is in control and how should we deal with tragedy in our life and in the lives of others?

## SUMMA

*Write an essay or discuss this question, integrating what you have learned from the material above.*

What is wrong with the question, "Why do bad things happen to good people?" (See Romans 3.)

**READING ASSIGNMENT:**
*Oedipus at Colonus*

Sophocles, the great playwright, is shown in this statue reading from one of his tragic plays.

# SESSION III: RECITATION
*Oedipus at Colonus*

## Comprehension Questions

*Answer these questions for factual recall.*

### Oedipus the King

1. What prophecy were Laius and Jocasta given concerning their infant son?
2. What did the herdsman (who was given the task of leaving the baby Oedipus out in the wild to die) do with him?
3. What does Creon discover from the Delphic Oracle?
4. How was it thought that King Laius was killed?
5. For whom does Oedipus call? Why?
6. What is the prophecy of Teiresias?
7. What is Oedipus's reaction to the prophecy?
8. How does Teiresias react to Oedipus's rejection of his prophecy?
9. How does Jocasta seek to prove to Oedipus that all prophets are false?

Athens is the setting for *Oedipus at Colonus,* and the Erechtheum is one of her most famous buildings. It was built between 421 and 405 B.C., just north of the Parthenon. It had spaces dedicated to Athena, Poseidon, Hephaestus, Bute and Erechtheus. Outside the building grew the sacred olive tree, the mythical gift of Athena in her fight with Poseidon.

10. How does this backfire?
11. What bad news does the messenger from Corinth tell Oedipus?

## Oedipus at Colonus

1. Why does Oedipus refuse to move from the "holy ground" in Athens?
2. Who are the Eumenides? Why is it fitting that Oedipus meet death in their sacred grove?
3. What is happening in Argos and Thebes?
4. Why does Creon want Oedipus's body?
5. What does Theseus agree to do for Oedipus?
6. When Oedipus laments the fragile bonds of love and friendship to Theseus, who (ironically) does Oedipus claim are the only ones who can be trusted?
7. How does Sophocles reveal the character of Creon?
8. Who comes from Argos to visit Oedipus?
9. What is Oedipus's reaction to Polyneices' request? Why?
10. Why does Sophocles have Oedipus die in Athens?
11. Who sees the grave of Oedipus?
12. What do Ismene and Antigone ask Theseus to do for them after he refuses to show them their father's grave?

READING ASSIGNMENT:
*Antigone*

# SESSION IV: DISCUSSION
*Antigone*

## A Question to Consider

When is it right to disobey the state?

*Discuss or list short answers to the following questions:*

## Text Analysis

1. What did Creon order?
2. Why did he order that Polyneices not receive proper burial rights?
3. How does he try to ensure that his order is carried out?
4. What does Antigone do? Why?
5. Is Creon forcing Antigone to sin by refusing to let her bury her brother?
6. Is she justified in her disobedience? Why or why not?
7. Is the picture of Antigone that Sophocles paints favorable and sympathetic or not? How do you know?

## Cultural Analysis

1. Do the words of the United States Constitution limit the power of the state?
2. Do our laws limit the power of the state?
3. Do international legislative bodies limit the power of the state?
4. Do the words of the Supreme Court limit the power of the state?
5. Does the Word of God limit the power of the government?
6. Does God Himself limit the power of the U.S. government?
7. What conclusions could we draw from this line of questions?

## Biblical Analysis

1. Read Acts 4:1-31 which describes Peter and John being taken before the Sanhedrin, the Jewish Supreme Court. When do Peter and John refuse to do what their leaders ask them to do?
2. What principle can you draw from their actions?
3. Disobeying the government is often called "Civil Disobedience." In light of the fact that Jesus is the highest authority in all realms of life (including the family, the church and the civil realm of the government), why is this really a misleading name?

## SUMMA

*Write an essay or discuss this question, integrating what you have learned from the material above.*
When is it right to disobey the state?

## Application

Things that we can note about the experience of Peter, John and Antigone:

Note that Peter, John, and Antigone were not out picking a fight with the government. Normally, they were obedient and law-abiding citizens. We should do all that we can to be obedient to our rulers unless and until obedience to them would cause us to be disloyal to our ultimate King, Jesus Christ.

Also note that all of them do not reject the authority of the state in total, but only in the area in which the state has overstepped its bounds. They even willingly accept the punishment that they receive. We should expect the punishments of the state and glory in them if we have to face them for the sake of Christ. Peter and John were thankful to be counted worthy to suffer for the sake of Christ.

If we have to disobey the state in order to obey God, we should pray that we can do it with boldness and thankfulness.

The great difference between Antigone and the Apostles is their attitude toward unjust suffering and persecution. Peter and John suffer in hope and even with joy that they can follow in the footsteps of their Lord and bear witness with their sufferings. Antigone goes to her fate in gloom, having her life (like the lives of all of her family) wrecked by the unseen and capricious deities.

In this fragment of sculpture from the archaic period, Theseus smiles as he carries off Antiope, the queen of the Amazons. She later became so enamoured with her captor that she fought alongside him against her former subjects when they waged war upon Athens.

# SESSION V: WRITING

Classical training in rhetoric included preparatory writing exercises called the progymnasmata. These exercises in composition introduced the beginning student to basic forms and techniques that would then be used and combined when practicing more advanced exercises and speeches. One of these progymnasmata was called a *chreia*, or "saying exercise," and was simply a concise exposition of some memorable saying or deed.

A chreia has eight paragraphs. The first is the *Panegyric* which is a paragraph in which you praise the person who uttered the wise saying. The second is called the *Paraphrastic*. In this short paragraph you put the saying into your own words.

This paragraph often begins with something like: "When Saint Augustine said that evil was the deprivation of good he meant that ..." In the third paragraph, called *From the Cause*, you explain the motivation of the person. The fourth paragraph is called *From the Contrary*, and in it you explain what would have happened if the opposite of the saying or action had occurred. For example, "If Diogenes had not struck the inept teacher, bad education would have continued." In the fifth paragraph, called the *Analogy*, you liken the saying or action to something else, usually something more concrete and easier to understand. The sixth paragraph is similar to the fifth. It is called *Example,* and in it you show the wisdom of the saying or deed by pointing your reader to a specific instance in which this wisdom was demonstrated. The Analogy is different from the Example in that it is about a general practice (e.g., "Education is like a harvest: you work hard and reap great reward.") whereas the Example is about a specific person, place or thing (e.g., "Erasmus studied many things and became a learned man."). The seventh paragraph is called the Testimony of the Ancients. Here you quote a sage person from the past who testifies to the truth of the saying. Finally, in the eighth paragraph called the *Epilogue,* you sum up the chreia.

*Write a chreia on these words spoken by Teiresias: You have your eyes, but do not see where you are in sin, nor where you live, nor whom you live with. Do you know who your parents are?* (Oedipus the King 413–414)

I.   Panegyric
•   Praise the person who uttered the wise saying
II.  Paraphrastic
•   Put the saying into your own words
III. From the Cause
•   Explain the motivation of the speaker
IV.  From the Contrary
•   Explain the consequences if the opposite of the saying or action had occurred
V.   Analogy
•   Liken the saying or action to something else
VI.  Example
•   Point the reader to a specific instance in which the wisdom of the saying was demonstrated
VII. Testimony of the Ancients
•   Quote a sage person from the past who testifies to the truth of the saying
VIII. Epilogue
•   Summarize your previous paragraphs

# OPTIONAL SESSION A

## Review and Evaluation

*Answer the questions from the recitation of Session III on* Oedipus the King *and* Oedipus at Colonus. *Also answer the following questions concerning Antigone:*

1. Why does Creon forbid the burial of Polyneices?
2. Why is Antigone committed to burying her brother (remember *Oedipus at Colonus*)?
3. Do Ismene and Antigone love Polyneices equally?
4. How is Antigone's horrid end like her father's (i.e., what role does her virtue or strength play in her downfall)?
5. What are the similarities and differences between Oedipus and Creon?
6. What irony is involved in the gods' destruction of Antigone?

## Evaluation

### Grammar

*Briefly answer the following questions with one or two sentences (2 points each).*

### OEDIPUS THE KING

1. What is motivating Oedipus to find the killer of King Laius?
2. What is the prophecy of Teiresias?
3. Why is the second herdsman unwilling to tell Oedipus his part in the story?
4. Why do the gods curse Oedipus with this fate?

### OEDIPUS AT COLONUS

1. Why does Creon want Oedipus's body?
2. When Oedipus laments the fragile bonds of love and friendship to Theseus, who (ironically) does Oedipus claim are the only ones who can be trusted?
3. What curse does Oedipus place upon Polyneices?
4. What does Polyneices ask of Antigone? What is her reaction?

### ANTIGONE

1. Why does Creon forbid the burial of Polyneices?
2. How is Antigone's horrid end like her father's (i.e., what role does her virtue or strength play in her downfall)?
3. What irony is involved in the gods' destruction of Antigone?

### Logic

*In this section, demonstrate that you understand the worldview set forth in the* Theban Trilogy. *Do this by answering each question in complete sentences. Answers should be a paragraph or two (10 points per answer).*

What does the *Theban Trilogy* say about:

> GOD
>
> MAN
>
> SALVATION
>
> THE FUTURE

## Lateral Thinking

*This essay challenges you to take concepts and ideas learned in the* Theban Trilogy *and see the connections that these ideas have in other works that we have read this year. Write up to a 1,000-word essay on one of the three questions. This answer is worth 15 points.*

1. Compare and contrast the true God (as He represents Himself in our biblical readings this year) and the gods (as represented by our readings in *Gilgamesh,* the *Code of Hammarabi,* the *Odyssey, Histories* and the *Oresteia Trilogy*).

## Writing

*These essays will test your ability to remember works that you have read this semester, challenging you to relate them to each other.*

1. In 2 Samuel one sees the fall of the house of Saul, Israel's first king. In the *Theban Trilogy* one sees the fall of the house of Oedipus. The gods bring an unavoidable fate upon the hero, as delivered by the prophet Teiresias. Likewise, Saul's house is destroyed by God, whose word is brought to him by God's prophet Samuel. In light of these similarities, what are the differences between how the true God and Greek gods bring calamity?

2. How does the Christian doctrine of predestination differ from the Greek idea of fate as represented in the *Theban Trilogy?*

# OPTIONAL SESSION B

Act out one of the plays (could be multi-day expansion).

These plays are meant to be watched. Working through them as you act them out can be a key to gaining a deeper understanding of the work ... and it's a lot of fun. Be sure to talk about why the characters are doing what they are doing.

## ENDNOTES

1. The answer to the riddle is man. He walks on all fours as an infant, crawling along the ground during the "morning" of his life. At his "midday," man walks on his two feet in the midst of his strength. At the end of his life, man needs a cane, a "third leg," in order to move around. This riddle was given by the Sphinx to Oedipus. As a gift for answering this riddle, Oedipus receives the throne of Thebes and the hand of the beautiful queen. Our story begins years later, during his reign as lord of Thebes.

2. See Spielvogel, Jackson J. *Western Civilization* Fifth Edition. Belmont, Calif.: Wadsworth/Thomson Learning, 2003. 65, and also *Veritas Press History Cards: New Testament, Greece and Rome.* Lancaster, Pa. 13 (*The Persian Wa)r.* For another description of the battle of Salamis, remember: Herodotus, Rawlinson, George, trans. *The Histories,* North Clarendon, Vt.: Everyman Library, 2000. 635–637.

3. Spielvogel, 66–67. *Veritas Press History Cards: New Testament, Greece and Rome,* 14 (*Pericles and the Peloponnesian War*).

4. Aristotle, McKeon, Richard P. ed., *Introduction to Aristotle.* New York: Random House, 1992. 659–712.

5. Hesiod, West, M.L., trans. *Theogony and Works and Days.* New York: Oxford University Press, 1999. 3–33. It is almost comic to see that the whole race of gods is spawned and killed by the same means, patricide and incest, for which the unwitting Oedipus is condemned.

6. *Common grace* is a theological term for the unmerited kindness that God shows to all people. We see this in the blessings that God gives, like rain and food (see Matt. 5:45). "Common grace" can be distinguished from "saving grace," which is the grace that God gives to someone when He regenerates them and saves them.

7. The *imago Dei* refers to the special relationship that God created between Himself and Adam, the crown of His creation. Adam was like his Maker. This means that he was originally righteous and holy. Adam, however, fell from his communion with God, and the image of God became marred and twisted in Adam. Adam became unholy and unrighteous and his works and offspring bore the fallen image of their father. Strikingly, the image that Oedipus bears seems vastly superior to that of the gods.

8. See note 6.

9. If we were of the bolder sort, we might point out that to believe that one has the intelligence to make such a weak argument seem palatable is a case of intellectual hubris. We did, however, want to make it clear that it was not that we have not heard their arguments. We heard; we just do not agree.

10. *This endnote appears only in the teacher's edition.*

11. *This endnote appears only in the teacher's edition.*

12. *This endnote appears only in the teacher's edition.*

13. *This endnote appears only in the teacher's edition.*

14. At the time of this printing, the painting can found at http://www.abcgallery.com/I/ingres/ingres6.html.

15. *This endnote appears only in the teacher's edition.*

# THE LAST DAYS OF SOCRATES

You are breathless, but still you run. Uneven cobblestones throw you off balance, your feet ache, but on you run. Others jostle around you, and you almost stumble, but you can't because it's chasing you. A wave of sharp beats moves over the ancient pavement behind you. You have to run faster. You glance back over your shoulder, and you see them. The bulls are coming. Suddenly, fear overwhelms fatigue, and you rocket ahead of a few competitors. As you round a corner, you cast a look backward. The wall of bulls is steps behind. You search for the bullring ahead of you. You'll never make it. You feel a sharp push in the small of your back, and you almost stumble to the pavement. One beast seems to have his sights set on you. You bail out, diving from the main road to one of the even narrower alleyways. Your body skids along the stones. You are battered, your lungs gasp for oxygen, but at least you are safe. You hear the distant roar of the Pamplona crowd in the distance, as the bulls enter the ring. But you hear another, closer sound behind you in the alleyway. Someone or something is behind you. You slowly turn and face that bull from the street. He followed you. As your eyes meet his, he lowers his head, his sharp horns pointing at you. His right front hoof begins to paw the cobblestones.

Socrates was the son of a sculptor. He was the father of three sons, and he was a legendary drinker. Although no sculptures of him were made in his day, since his death he has always been depicted as an ugly man, due to descriptions of him by his disciple Plato. Socrates was accused of corrupting young minds and, in the end, chose death over exile.

## GENERAL INFORMATION

### Author and Context

Few people in world history have had as much influence as the Greek thinker, Plato. One twentieth-century thinker famously

Socrates was accused of atheism because he called the Greek pantheon of gods into question. Here we see two of those gods, Athena and Apollo, on either side of the kneeling Orestes, with the Furies in the background. The scene is from the third play of Aeschylus's *Oresteia* trilogy and was painted on a fourth-century B.C. Italian vase.

described the history of philosophy as simply "a series of footnotes to Plato"—meaning Plato said all the important stuff, and everyone else was dependent upon him. You have to grasp Plato to understand so much of anything else in Western history.

Plato lived from around 428 to 347 B.C. near the

end of the golden age of Athens (often judged to be from 480 to 430 B.C.). When Plato lived, Homer's writings already held a central place in Greek life; they had been written over three hundred years before Plato's time. When Plato was born, Herodotus had been dead for decades, and Aeschylus, author of the *Oresteia,* had died less than twenty years before.

Plato came from an aristocratic family in Athens, and his father is believed to have descended from the early kings of Athens. His mother may have been related to the famous Athenian lawmaker, Solon (one of the men discussed in *Plutarch's Lives*).

Early in his life, Plato had an interest in politics (statecraft), but he soon became disillusioned. Perhaps this shift occurred near the time he came under the influence of his famous teacher, Socrates. Socrates introduced Plato to the world of philosophy (more on philosophy below). Socrates claimed to pursue truth by means of probing questions and precise answers, and Plato picked up on this style. Socrates claimed to question just about everything (except his pet values), and this got him into trouble with the authorities of his time, and he was finally executed in 399 B.C. Plato started his famous school, the Academy, in 387 B.C., a project sometimes called the first European university; there they taught such subjects as mathematics, political theory, biology, astronomy and philosophy. It was during this later time that Plato wrote his dialogues, including one of the earliest, *Euthyphro.* Throughout these dialogues, Plato inserts Socrates as the key character representing, presumably, his own views as well as Plato's more developed thought.

The *Last Days of Socrates* begins with the *Euthyphro,* in which we find Socrates heading toward the Athenian court preparing to defend himself against accusations that he has corrupted the youth of Athens. The consequences for such a charge are heady. In the second dialogue in the series, the *Apology,* Socrates' defends himself within the Athenian court. The *Apology* moves along as a much more biographical monologue and less of a dialogue, but it serves as Socrates' own statement of his views and situation. The court famously finds Socrates guilty and sentences him to death. Then the *Crito* takes over. Of the four dialogues, the *Crito* is the most political. In it we find Socrates waiting in prison for his execution, sitting around with his friends. The key question of the *Crito* concerns civil disobedience,

whether Socrates ought to disobey the dictate of death and flee Athens, preserving his life. His friends argue he should, but he argues against it. Finally, with the fourth dialogue in the series, the *Phaedo,* we get Socrates' friend Phaedo rehearsing the story of Socrates' last day, the day of Socrates' execution by poison—hemlock. Socrates resigns himself to death and even welcomes it. His friends worry and ask him to explain why he is so serene. He discusses with them why he believes in life after death. The dialogue closes with an account of Socrates' quiet death in prison.

## Significance

Plato wrote about forty dialogues, and the whole collection stands out, in part, because it is not a collection of histories or stories with interesting plots and characters. The dialogues are arguments, sometimes tedious arguments about ideas and definitions and rules. Some think these dialogues were used in the Academy as teaching tools, sort of like logic textbooks to show students how to argue philosophically. They became very famous over the centuries, especially as tools of argumentation.

Philosophers most often characterize philosophy as the pursuit of truth, not by the standard of Scripture, but by means of the standard given by the human mind alone. Where physics studies how matter behaves and biology studies how living things act, philosophy talks about the questions that cannot be discussed in a laboratory, the questions that need to be figured out before any subject starts: What is truth? What counts as knowledge? What is honesty? Why should anyone tell the truth? What standards do we use to prove something in a lab?

The *Euthyphro,* in particular, stands out because it appears to be one of the earliest of Plato's dialogues. It gives readers a good, beginning sense of how both Socrates and Plato thought we ought to pursue truth—questions, answers, definitions, qualifications.

The *Phaedo* stands out because it completes both the four-part series, as well as Socrates' life itself. Unlike many of the other dialogues, these four include just a bit more drama than usual, given their interaction with episodes in Socrates' life. But the *Phaedo* stands out among the four because it aims to give us a dying man's thoughts. We tend to say the most important things when we know we are dying.

## Main Characters

Most of the short Platonic dialogues, like this one, have only a few speakers or "interlocutors," with Socrates always getting the lead. The *Euthyphro* has only two characters, Socrates and the young man Euthyphro. Euthyphro comes to court to prosecute his father, a move that is highly scandalous. In the *Apology*, Socrates finally reaches the Athenian court, and there we learn of his accuser Meletus through Socrates' monologue. The *Crito* shows us Socrates in prison, with his friend Crito by his side. The *Phaedo* gives us more of a mix of characters than the three previous dialogues. The *Phaedo* is actually a dialogue within a dialogue. The opening dialogue begins with Echecrates imploring Phaedo to tell him the story of Socrates' last day. Phaedo takes up this request, and then we hear the main dialogue, made up mostly of Socrates, Simmias and Cebes.

some higher standard of justice.

The *Apology* and the *Crito* have less of a plot than the other dialogues. The *Apology* just gives us Socrates defending himself before the court, and the *Crito* shows us a rather static dialogue between Socrates and his friend. Crito urges Socrates to flee, and Socrates gives his reasons against it.

The *Phaedo* gives us more setting and background, explaining that Socrates' friends visited him every day during his prison wait. Usually executions were carried out swiftly, but a Greek civil celebration had delayed Socrates' execution for nearly a month. When Phaedo arrives that day, he finds Socrates' wife, Xanthippe, and son in a tearful, heartbreaking departure. Soon Socrates falls into conversation with his friends, Cebes and Simmias, who want a new defense, better than in the *Apology*. The dialogue closes with a description of Socrates' final moments, talking to the prison guard and friends and finally drinking the poison.

## Summary and Setting

Keeping in mind that Plato's dialogues are argument exercises, we should not expect a real plot. Readers often get frustrated by trying to read this and his other dialogues as plays. On top of that, most of Plato's dialogues are not intended to give satisfying answers. They are more concerned with the exercise of thinking than with a strong conclusion or an identifiable answer. They just want to get the reader thinking along a certain pattern.

In the *Euthyphro*, we find the character Euthyphro arriving at court to do something scandalous yet apparently very "progressive" and "edgy" for the Greek mind: he has come to prosecute his own father for having unintentionally killed a servant (who happens to be a murderer). Euthyphro breaks with his blood relative to pursue

A mosiac depicting Socrates as he teaches his students.

## Worldview

Have you ever had someone "boss you around?" I am not talking about parents or teachers telling you what to do. They have to; they're your parents and teachers. Sometimes, however, you might run into someone who was not an adult, but still seems to know what is best for you at every turn. They know what games you should play. They know what movies should be watched. They know how much jelly should go on a peanut butter and jelly sandwich. The good news for you if you know someone like this is that many (I did not say all) people outgrow this sort of behavior as they mature, and even those that don't usually become more subtle about it and therefore are less bothersome. What if, however, there was a smart person who never grew out of this type of behavior but instead just became more crafty? It might come to the point where we would say to him (when he was telling us what house we should buy or what church we should attend), "Do you think you're God?"

### Socrates and Autonomy

Here is a quick question to keep asking as you read the *Euthyphro*. What sort of god is most prominent in the dialogue? You might at first think of the numerous Greek gods mentioned there. But polytheism (many-god-ism) is quite secondary. What being with god-like qualities is not so much mentioned but actually dominates the whole discussion? Who gets to frame the whole debate, to quietly dictate what counts as true and false in the universe? That turns out to be Socrates himself (through the authorship of Plato). Socrates takes on all the most important characteristics of a god. Yet it is put in the background and never discussed. That is quite a thing to hide, but it is important for a non-Christian mind like Plato's to hide it.

On the surface, Socrates presents himself as painfully, tediously humble. He pretends to make no claims; he pretends to be a student; he pretends to be ignorant.

But at the same time, he says things like: "Isn't it true that ..." and "are we to say these stories are true?" Who is supposed to be the judge of the answers? Socrates is obviously not asking whether the Trinity reveals something or whether Scripture teaches it. That is outside his universe. Remember, he was born more than 400 years before Jesus.

He is not even answering on the basis of Greek gods. He has already raised himself above them: "when I hear anyone telling stories like these about the gods I somehow find it difficult to accept them." Socrates himself is king of truth. He stands as judge over all the gods. He determines what is possible and impossible. That is quite an assertion for someone claiming humility.

Sometimes Socrates leaves it open for both himself and Euthyphro to be judges. Other times, even Euthyphro takes a back seat to Socrates when Socrates takes on the seat of superior judge of Euthyphro's words: "An excellent answer, Euthyphro, and in just the form I wanted." Here the professedly humble Socrates already assumes he can judge excellence and proper form. That is another huge claim; it assumes Socrates already knows the ins-and-outs of all of reality. Where has his ignorance gone?

This all means that the largest part of Socrates' debate is over even before the *Euthyphro* gets going. That is quite a feat: the Trinity and the Christian faith (and any revelatory faith) have been excluded from the start, and Socrates has been enthroned as the almighty judge of truth, beauty and goodness.

If we want to understand this text from a Christian angle, then, we need to begin with a comparison between ultimate judges, between the God of the Christian faith and Socrates' solo human mind: Trinity vs. autonomy.

"Autonomy" means self-law, and it is a very important claim to understand. The meaning of the parts of the word tell us a lot about it. It comes from two Greek words, the first of which is *auto,* meaning "self." We see this meaning in words like *autograph* (self writing) or *automobile* (something that moves us around by itself). The second part of the word, *nomy,* comes from the Greek word *nomos,* meaning "law." We see this root in the name of the biblical book Deutero*nomy* (which means "Second Law" because the law was previously given to Moses in Exodus). So, *autonomy* means that someone is a "law unto themselves." An autonomous person gets to be the final authority on what is true and what is right. It is as if, during a game of chess, a pawn or a knight condemned the rules of the game and insisted that all the other pieces now play by checkers rules, no questions asked. It was the basic assumption of

Scenes of everyday life, like this student, were frequently depicted on Greek pottery. The very best pottery was made in Athens using the local, high quality, reddish brown clay.

Socrates and all of Greek philosophy, and it has come back with a more explicit vengeance since the 1700's and remains prominent in our day. Hopefully, you can see that this claim ("I can understand the world and know truth without the help of God, the gods or anything else!") is unbiblical. Yet few people who assume autonomy argue for it openly (probably because it would sound really arrogant). They just assume autonomy is the simple, natural, common response to life. In fact, though, it is the height of pridefulness.

Euthyphro, of course, cannot challenge Socrates on autonomy because Euthyphro shares the same faith. He, too, assumes his intellect is the highest court

of appeal. But imagine if a Trinitarian Christian could somehow converse with Socrates. We could ask simple, "emperor-has-no-clothes" sorts of questions: Why, Socrates, should I believe in your god? Why should I believe in your autonomy? Who made you King of Reality? Did you crown yourself? If not, who or what did? This is just a start. Socrates has no answer for these important questions.

### Socrates and Essences

The focus of the *Euthyphro's* debate is the nature of piety or goodness. Socrates challenges Euthyphro to give a "definition" of piety, and Euthyphro responds by giving several proposals, none of which live up to Socrates' demands.

The chief demand Socrates makes is that Euthyphro provide him with a *universal* definition applying to all times and places. Socrates wants him "not to tell me about one or two of these many pious actions, but to describe the actual feature that makes all pious actions pious." He wants a "single characteristic" that binds all pious actions together. Later Socrates describes this as wanting Euthyphro to "disclose its essence."

What does it mean to find the essence of something? As noted above, Socrates assumes a whole universe while pretending to be ignorant. Not every universe has these odd things called "essences" within them. Socrates' world does. Essences are pretty bizarre objects. They are required to do all sorts of miraculous things, like being in many different places at the same time. For Socrates, an essence is an object that somehow actually connects objects and actions of the same kind—"the actual feature that makes all pious actions pious." For example, all dogs have the same essence. The same essences bind everything of the same kind, whether oranges, shoes, trees or triangles. Essences are not like DNA strands; DNA strands are merely similar biological structures; Socrates and Plato insist on something stronger: the exact same essence must show up in each thing of a kind. The essence in this one dog here is exactly the same one that shows up in this other dog, even though the one essence exists in different places.

For Socrates, essences are also invisible "patterns" of some sort. Socrates says, "explain to me what this characteristic is in itself, so that by fixing my eyes upon it and using it as a pattern I may be able to describe any action, yours or anyone else's, as pious if it corresponds to the pattern." So an essence is not just an object that miraculously lives in each and every action of piety, it also can somehow be seen and serve as a rule, a pattern, a model for finding other acts of piety. If you can figure out the invisible pattern, the essence, of a triangle or orange or tree, then you can somehow "see" the same invisible pattern in other triangles and oranges and trees.

In the *Euthyphro,* Plato gives us only a hint of this elaborate and famous theory of essences or Forms, as they will later be called. Later, especially in Plato's *Republic,* we learn that Plato's world is divided into two dimensions, that of matter (flesh, dirt, metal, water, etc.) and that of essences or Forms (invisible, eternal, timeless, impersonal patterns) that magically bind all the material things together.

What is the motivation for thinking the world is made up of essences and matter? We get one hint in the *Euthyphro.* Socrates assumes that knowledge is always something universal. When Euthyphro defines piety as just "what I'm doing right now" that is too narrow because then no one else could be pious, no one else could stand in Euthyphro's sandals at that very moment. Goodness has to be more universal; it shows up many places. If goodness or piety cannot appear in many places, then there is no way to judge good and bad. It is all chaos. That is the word: *chaos.* For the Greek mind, chaos motivated just about everything. Greeks dreaded chaos, and so much of their philosophy was geared toward avoiding chaos in truth, goodness and beauty.

Christians are not motivated by a fear of chaos in the same way. Our world starts with the Trinity, a bond of three persons in one, who love and serve one another in harmony. The material world the Trinity creates follows the artistic design of Father, Son and Holy Spirit; it is not running wild or out of control. So Christians do not have the same motivation for a world of essences or Forms that Socrates and Plato (and Aristotle) do. Morality does not depend on us discerning some invisible, impersonal essences to hold everything together. We do not say, like Socrates and Plato, that by means of essences all things hang together; we say "in Him [Christ] all things consist" (Col. 1:17).

## Trinity and Polytheism

In the course of Socrates' search for the essence of piety, he sets up Euthyphro to lead him through various definitions. We hear Euthyphro start off by defining piety as "what I am doing now." But Socrates tells him he needs an essence, a general pattern. Euthyphro subsequently offers the following essences: "piety is that which is dear to the gods," "piety is that which all the gods love," "the godly and pious is that part of the just that is concerned with the care of the gods," and piety is "how to say and do what is pleasing to the gods at prayer and sacrifice." These are only four definitions. Some commentators find up to seven differing definitions, some find less.

Right at the center of these definitions, we find them grappling with the problems of Greek polytheism. This poses certain problems for both Socrates and Euthyphro, but it actually highlights much bigger problems in secular thinking in contrast with the Trinity.

The Trinity is not three gods; that would be polytheism or tritheism. Father, Son and Holy Spirit are three and one at the same time. The Trinity is one God in three persons. The Trinity's oneness and threeness are both equally important.

Every non-Christian culture is some sort of distortion of the Trinity. It is as if they try to break the Trinity apart. Some cultures (like Islamic cultures) break the Trinity in favor of Oneness. Conformity to that oneness becomes the overriding feature of those cultures. Other cultures distort the Trinity on the "manyness" side. They are polytheistic, believing in many gods, and difference and manyness often characterize those cultures, on the surface.

In ancient Greek polytheism we find this type of unifying force. The Greeks often appealed to Fate, another impersonal force that controls everything, including the gods. Other Greeks, especially the philosophers like Socrates, Plato and Aristotle, believed that Logic, another impersonal force, unified the world, locking essences together and ridding the world of chaos.

In the dialogue between Socrates and Euthyphro, we see the problems with polytheism coming to the surface. Early on, Euthyphro defines piety as "that which is dear to the gods." Socrates promptly points out that often "the gods are divided ... and feel enmity towards one another." Euthyphro then fixes that definition and suggests that "piety is that which all the gods love," thus making it explicit that, even though the gods sometimes disagree, that which they unanimously agree to would count as pious.

Socrates finds this definition unhelpful. Just as noted above, every culture is a distortion of the Trinity. Euthyphro naively ignores the problems of polytheism, but Socrates recognizes that "divided" gods destroy any universal absolutes. Unlike Euthyphro, Socrates understands the dangerous chaos of polytheism. But Socrates is no Trinitarian, so he cannot propose a genuine, personal oneness among the gods. He only knows the "many" gods (Zeus, Athena, Apollo, etc.). They are not one. Like the followers of Karma and Fate, Socrates opts for an impersonal force to save him from chaos. He places this force above the gods.

Socrates nudges Euthyphro toward adopting Socrates' faith in an impersonal goodness. We see this in his famous question (10a–11b): "Is what is pious loved by the gods because it is pious, or is it pious because it is loved?" What does this mean? It means that there is a standard above the gods (i.e., goodness) that rules over the gods. It has two parts: 1. "Is what is pious loved by the gods because it is pious?" 2. "Is it pious because it is loved by the gods?" Both parts are meant to demonstrate the problems with Euthyphro's reliance on the gods and move him toward faith in impersonal essences.

The type of argument that Socrates uses is called the dilemma. It happens when someone is faced with two choices, one of which must be chosen. These two

*School of Athens* by Raphael Sanzio (1483–1520)

choices are called the horns of the dilemma and the dilemma is often pictured as a bull. Socrates throws Euthyphro onto the horns of the bull.

How does it do this? Look at the second horn first. It asks "is an action pious because it is loved by the gods?" In other words, is something pious merely because all the gods love it? Socrates goes on to show a contradiction in Euthyphro's statements about being "god-beloved" and "piety." This part of the argument falls apart when we simply ask why the gods love something. If the gods do not love an action or a person because it is pious (remember that is the second part of the dilemma), then why do they love it? They must love it for no reason at all. In other words, is piety merely a personal whim of the gods? Is goodness arbitrary? Then the gods are irrelevant; humans, too, can arbitrarily love things. That option would take us back to chaos. It has to be rejected, and Euthyphro does.

But what of the first part of the dilemma: "is what is pious loved by the gods because it is pious?" Here we see Socrates driving a wedge between the gods and piety. He wants Euthyphro to see that there is a difference between the gods and piety. He is moving Euthyphro toward viewing goodness as an impersonal essence. This part of the dilemma means: do the gods love a pious action because they, too, see it as corresponding to a higher standard of piety (i.e., higher than the gods themselves). Are they looking up to the invisible pattern in the heaven of essences, too? Euthyphro agrees with this option: "it is loved because it is pious."

But where does that leave the gods? They become completely unnecessary; they are irrelevant to the question of goodness. If they love something because it exemplifies the eternal essence of piety, then they are just like us. Both gods and humans need to find essences together, since essences stand above both gods and humans.

Take a step back from the initial question. Now we can read it this way: is goodness independent of the gods or is goodness arbitrary? Independent or arbitrary? Choosing either option makes the gods irrelevant. Polytheism offers either personal but arbitrary gods (which are gods that you cannot count on—they are not the same every day but, to steal a biblical phrase, they are "new every morning") or the gods must resort to a oneness over and above themselves. That is a very typical dilemma for polytheistic cultures.

## Turning the Bull on Socrates

We could even use a form of Socrates' own famous question against him. "Socrates, is something true because you simply decree it so, or is it true because of some higher standard which your mind made up?" Either way, truth becomes random. Socrates and the whole autonomous tradition will want to insist that there is a higher, independent, non-random standard, namely, Reason. Reason is supposed to be this set of universal rules hanging in the air that everyone must obey; they have no personality but are more like laws of math for thought. But humans would have to be robots for this view of Reason to work; only robots follow rules precisely.

But similar challenges arise: Where did the god Reason come from? What are the laws of Reason made out of? Why should I believe in an invisible god? How do they differ from magic? Who decreed the laws of Reason? Why should I believe Socrates-Plato-Aristotle's claims about them? Why should I obey impersonal rules anyway? Did the Greek make them up? Why should ancient Greeks have authority over me?

Challenging Reason, of course, does not make us reject rationality; in other words, it does not make us reject orderliness, giving arguments, or refuting false claims. The Trinity is the Christian source of rationality, not Socrates. Scripture is the supreme standard. The Trinity is personal, not a set of mechanical rules. The Trinity lives and moves within history and peoples; Reason is frozen and faceless. The Trinity obligates us out of love and goodness, and we want to love in return. Reason cannot love and give grace. It operates only out of force (necessity), somehow magically pushing ideas around infallibly.

However we challenge Socrates, we should not be tricked into using his rules just on his say-so. His imagined world is hostile to God and Christianity, and his rules sometimes rule out our world from the start. Socrates needs to give an answer. He needs to defend his gods: Autonomy and Reason.

## Loving Death

"All those who hate me love death" (Prov. 8:36). Usually we think of this verse in terms of some bloody, ax-wielding criminal. Serial killers, we might say, hate God and love death. But we also find nicer, calmer sorts of people who love death. In the *Phaedo* we find nice, calm Socrates talking at great length about loving death.

Socrates tells us that death is "nothing more or less than" the "release of the soul from the body." He then urges the wise person to live a life in terms of this "release" by "separating the soul as much as possible from the body." By doing this, he says, the wise person can live "in a state as close as possible to death."

If Socrates loves death, then Proverbs leads us to think there must be some sense in which Socrates hates the God of the Bible. But how? Socrates seems rather innocuous; he is a little annoying and misled, we might say, but he is no serial killer or blasphemer. He is just a kind, noble pagan: "I have done my best in every way," he says. Surely, he cannot be said to hate the God of Scripture?

Scripture suggest something much deeper is going on. There is a very serious connection between loving death and hating the Trinity. The book of Romans provides some of the background. There we learn that we are not as innocent as we look on the surface. We all know the true God because God has made sure of that: "what may be known of God is manifest in them, for God has shown it to them" (Rom. 1:19). Paul tells us that even before Socrates' time, even "since the creation of the world His invisible attributes are clearly seen . . . so that they are without excuse" (Rom. 1:20).

Instead of rejoicing in God, they twisted things; they denied the easy truth: "although they knew God, they did not glorify Him as God, nor were thankful, but became futile in their thoughts, and their foolish hearts were darkened. Professing to be wise, they became fools" (Rom. 1:21, 22).

Socrates and Plato and all Greek philosophy, play a part in this ungrateful game. In some very important sense best known to God, Socrates truly knew the God of Scripture. But instead of being grateful, he insisted on his own way and became foolish. How might we see this in the *Phaedo?*

Another way of asking this question is: what drives Socrates to love death? What is it in his imagined world that makes death attractive? One important answer is: *perfectionism.* Socrates is in love with perfection. We know from the *Phaedo* and other places that he divides the whole cosmos into "two classes of things, one visible and the other invisible." Invisible things are essences or Forms or "absolute Realities" which "are always constant and invariable, never admitting any alteration in any respect or in any sense." Among these Forms he cites perfect or "absolute equality, beauty, goodness, rightness, holiness." These cannot be seen with the bodily eye, only the soul's eye, and they exist in some invisible dimension. But, and this is important, they are far more real than anything material. Everything material is somehow a lesser copy of them. Train tracks on earth appear parallel, but they are imperfect, mere copies of perfect Parallelism in the heavens; similarly, every beautiful woman or good action is a lesser copy of real beauty and real goodness which are invisible, unchanging, rules in the world of the Forms. This world is pure, uncontaminated, absolute and perfect. Socrates loves his imagined world of perfection more than anything else, even life.

In stark contrast, the God of Scripture loves all sorts of things Socrates would count as messy. "Can you send out lightnings, that they may go, and say to you, 'Here we are!'?" (Job 38:35). "Who can number the clouds by wisdom?" (38:37). "Can you hunt the prey for the lion, Or satisfy the appetite of the young lions" (38:39). "Does the eagle mount up at your command, and make its nest on high? Its young ones suck up blood" (38:27, 30).

Crooked lightning, serrated clouds, dying antelope, bloody baby eagles – the God of Scripture loves all these things. He boasts in them; they tell us about His style. Socrates turns up his nose at this sort of messiness: "the corporeal is heavy, oppressive, earthly, and visible." Yuck! Earthly rocks, he says, are "damaged by decay and corroded by salt water," causing "disfigurement and disease to stones and earth." Yick, earth!

Now we can see what Socrates' "noble" perfectionism leads him to. It leads him to despise creation. He loves perfection so much, nothing on earth matches up to it. He is ungrateful for creation, just as Romans 1 says. And instead of thanking God for all the wonderful messiness of the world, he resents it. He prefers another world, another creator free of messiness. He would prefer it if the Trinity were not the creator; he hates the God of crooked things. "Consider the work of God; For who can make straight what He has made crooked?" (Eccls. 7:13). Socrates prefers his own brand of absolute purity, but the God of Scripture says, "Where no oxen are, the trough is clean, but much increase comes by the strength of an ox" (Prov. 14:4). Ultimately, Socrates loves death so much he looks forward to his execution by poison in order to escape this world and enter his world of simplistic purity. To that we hear Scripture say, "Do not be overly righteous, nor be overly wise: Why should you destroy yourself?" (Eccls. 7:16).

This is one way, then, of understanding the Proverb "those who hate Me love death" within Socrates' life. Under his veneer of calmness and niceness, we find a deep resentment against God. The Trinity gives the gift of creation with a particular, twisted style, and Socrates rejects the gift. He can think up something better than God—a perfectionism that stands in judgment over the Trinity.

## Immortality and Life

The topics of death and body make up the first highlights of the *Phaedo,* and those lead into the topic which makes up the bulk of the dialogue: immortality of the soul, the view that the soul has life enough in itself to live on forever after death. The discussion about immortality is supposed to provide the basis for Socrates' calm confidence in the face of death: "I have a firm hope that there is something in store for those who have died, . . . and something much better for the good than for the wicked."

It is in this line of discussion that we find interesting contrasts between Trinitarian reality and Plato's views. Christians have long held that the dead in Christ live forever in fellowship with the Trinity, but that is not immortality. Immortality in Plato's sense does not need God or anything to sustain it. It goes by itself; it is rather automatic. It has a life of its own. Scripture says that God is immortal (1 Tim. 1:17), but it does not say that about created beings. We certainly do not have self-sustaining life in ourselves, and we certainly do not want to say that we are made out of unchanging, timeless stuff like Platonic souls. We live forever but always dependent upon the sustaining life of God, whether in blessing or cursing.

But look how narrow life has become on the Socratic vision. Socrates has thrown out the importance of the created order. Then he narrows life down to the intellect. Body is gone; no pleasure in feasts or marriage. Then we find that real life is not personal; it doesn't involve communication and friends. The good life for Socrates is being a Form. Life means turning into a pillar of timeless, invisible, changeless, loveless essence. Oddly, he is excited about this: "the Form of life . . . can never cease to exist."

In contrast, life in the Trinity is not some stiff, frozen rule. The Trinity is persons—Father, Son and Holy Spirit. Forever they have been communing, communicating and serving one another, all while mysteriously one God. Right at the heart of the Trinity is joy, the fellowship of friends, three and one. They have forever enjoyed one another's company, and at

*Death of Socrates* by Jacques-Louis David (1748–1825)

creation that love of life overflowed to us, calling us to join their dance. They sent the Son to take on our flesh, and as we join to Him in baptism and love, we are brought, forever, right into the very heart of the Trinity. Here is a company of friends and laughter that Socrates couldn't dream of. He was too angry at the gifts God was giving, and he convinced millions of others to love death rather than laughter.

So, Socrates' philosophy fails in the end to deliver to us a life worth living. His dilemmas fall back on their originator. Thankfully, we do not live in the world that Socrates describes, a world in which death is better than life. Instead, we live in a world brimming over with life pouring out of our God, the endless fountain of imagination which ceaselessly erupts with truth, beauty and goodness.

—*Doug Jones*

## For Further Reading

Spielvogel, Jackson. *Western Civilization.* Fifth Edition. Belmont, Calif.: Wadsworth/Thomson Learning, 2003. 74–76.

*Veritas Press History Cards: New Testament, Greece and Rome.* Lancaster, Pa.: Veritas Press. 15.

## Optional Activity

*Study the painting,* School of Athens, *which appears in the General Information above, then answer the following questions.*

1. How does the painting express some of the same interests as the *Euthyphro*?
2. Find Socrates, Plato and Aristotle (a later, equally famous, Greek philosopher) within the painting. (*Hint:* Socrates taught Plato and then Plato trained Aristotle. Aristotle rejected some of Plato's conclusions, setting up his own rival system of philosophy. Try to identify the two central characters and the young man four people to the right of the old man in the center.)
3. What does the fact that the Renaissance artist Raphael put Plato and Aristotle at the center of his work tell us about what he thought of their importance to philosophy?
4. Plato had a more spiritually directed philosophy, and Aristotle focused more on earthly questions. What about their figures in the painting lines up with this observation?

 READING ASSIGNMENT:
*Euthyphro,* Introduction–11a

## SESSION I: PRELUDE

### A Question to Consider

Is it always bad for people to argue? Why should we argue?

*From the General Information above answer the following questions:*

1. When did Plato live?
2. How do we characterize the Socratic style of dialogue?
3. Are the four dialogues wholly disconnected or do they capture a series of events in Socrates' life?
4. Why should these dialogues not be thought of as epic poems or great dramas?
5. What is the name of Socrates' wife and in which dialogue is she mentioned?
6. Why might Euthyphro think his plan at court is righteous and cutting-edge?

## SESSION II: DISCUSSION

*Euthyphro,* Introduction–11a

### A Question to Consider

What is goodness?

*Discuss or list short answers to the following questions:*

### Text Analysis

1. Socrates says he is looking for a pattern or model of piety on which he can meditate. What sort of pattern is he talking about? Give some characteristics that would please him.
2. What is Euthyphro's second definition of piety?
3. What does Socrates like about this second definition?
4. What does he dislike about this second definition?
5. What is Euthyphro's third definition of piety?
6. How does Socrates dismantle this definition?

## Cultural Analysis

1. What counts as piety in our contemporary secular society?
2. What counts as piety in Christian circles?
3. What part does television play in defining the good?
4. What part does the U.S. Supreme Court play in defining the good?
5. Almost every beginning university class in Ethics uses Socrates' challenge to Euthyphro as a challenge against the Christian faith. How would that challenge be attempted against a Christian view of goodness?

## Biblical Analysis

1. How does the Bible define moral goodness? (Ex. 20)
2. If this was the goodness that pleased, in light of Heb. 13:8, James 1:17 and Rom. 13:9; should we expect any change in these standards of goodness?
3. What are God's standards of goodness and moral holiness a reflection of? (Matt. 5:48)

### SUMMA

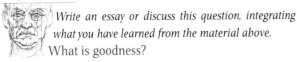
*Write an essay or discuss this question, integrating what you have learned from the material above.*
What is goodness?

## Optional Activity

Have a teacher or parent read over the *Euthyphro* and the worldview essay carefully. Now it is your turn to face the bull of Socrates' dilemma as a Christian. Have a discussion in which "Socrates" asks questions and see if you can pin the gadfly to the wall. After a short time, switch places and see if your parent or teacher can win the argument.

READING ASSIGNMENT:
*Euthyphro, 11b–16a*

# SESSION III: RECITATION
*Euthyphro*

## Comprehension Questions

*Answer these questions for factual recall.*

1. Why is Socrates going to court?
2. Why is Euthyphro going to court?
3. What are the details of the murder in question?
4. What sort of pollution is Euthyphro concerned about?
5. Why does Socrates want to become Euthyphro's student?
6. What is Euthyphro's first definition of piety?
7. Why does Socrates reject this first definition?
8. Why does Socrates say Euthyphro is like Daedalus?
9. What is the fourth definition of piety that Euthyphro gives?
10. How does Euthyphro end the discussion?
11. What does Socrates want to do?
12. How does Euthyphro's attitude change from the beginning to the end of the dialogue?

## Activity

Your reading assignment is the *Apology,* which is the trial of Socrates. To prepare for the Trial of Socrates activity in the next session, as you read this dialogue, consider the evidence—both for and against Socrates. The charges are two: atheism (meaning that Socrates denied the gods) and corrupting the youth (teaching them things that would harm both them and Athens). Compile a list of evidence for and against Socrates that you may refer to later.

READING ASSIGNMENT:
*Apology*

# SESSION IV: ACTIVITY
*Apology*

## The Trial of Socrates

The trial of Socrates was one of the most famous legal hearings in all of history. Plato sets before us a trial in which his mentor is found guilty of the charges against him (atheism and corrupting the youth). Plato, of course, is presenting the case against

Socrates in a way that will cause us to feel sympathy for his teacher. Today, we are going to revisit the trial, and you get to be the judge and jury.

To do this, follow these steps (*smaller groups or individuals may write a brief, which is a legal statement arguing the evidence*):

Elect a judge, two prosecutors (to set forth the case against Socrates—each of them will prosecute him on one of the charges) and two individuals to play Socrates.

Others will be the witnesses. Take out the lists that you created from yesterday's reading. The judge should write out the charges on the blackboard for all to see.

The first prosecutor is to be given ten minutes to make the case that Socrates is an atheist and the first Socrates is to be given ten minutes to defend himself. Other people from the jury can add evidence to either side by raising their hands and being called on to offer contributing statements.

The process is then repeated for the charge of corrupting the youth.

After both charges have been argued, there is to be a short time where jury members can ask questions of each other to clarify their decision.

Then all as jury are to consider whether Socrates is guilty or innocent. The majority of votes wins.

### READING ASSIGNMENT:
*Crito*

# SESSION V: DISCUSSION
*Crito*

## A Question to Consider

Is it wrong to avoid unjust punishment?
*Discuss or list short answers to the following questions:*

### Text Analysis

1. What are the arguments that Crito uses to attempt to convince Socrates to escape from prison?
2. Could Crito have worked out a way for Socrates to escape?

3. What harm does Socrates believe he will bring to himself if he consents and lets Crito spirit him away?
4. What does Socrates believe he would be wronging if he escaped?
5. How does Socrates claim that this wrong would be done? Why?
6. Why would Socrates say that his escape would prove that he was guilty?

### Cultural Analysis

1. What does our culture think that you should do to avoid unjust punishment?
2. Does our culture have any sense that breaking the law is wronging the law?
3. How could anyone corrupt the youth in our culture today?

### Biblical Analysis

1. What encouragement does 1 Pet. 4:15–17 give us concerning unjust suffering?
2. What does Christ in Matt. 10:22–24 say that His disciples should do when they are wrongly persecuted?
3. How is Paul and Silas's refusal to escape from the Philippian jail different from Socrates? (Acts 16:24–26)
4. How is Peter's escape from jail in Acts 12:5–10 justifiable?

### SUMMA

*Write an essay or discuss this question, integrating what you have learned from the material above.*
When is it right to seek to escape punishment?

### READING ASSIGNMENT:
*Phaedo*, Introduction–72e

# SESSION VI: DISCUSSION
*Phaedo*, Introduction–72e

## A Question to Consider

Why do people nearing death start talking about the big questions of life?

*Discuss or list short answers to the following questions:*

## Text Analysis

1. Does Socrates have a positive or negative view of the human body, and for what ills does he blame it?
2. How does he urge our intellects to live in light of the "prison" of the body?
3. What is the basic thrust of Socrates' Argument from Opposites (70a–72e)?
4. What sort of examples does Socrates give of opposites?

## Cultural Analysis

1. Has contemporary culture completely escaped Socrates' hatred of the body?
2. What is a secularist? Socrates was a secularist, but modern secularists do not talk about immortality the way he does. Why is that?

## Biblical Analysis

1. How does the creation account of Genesis 1 affirm that the material world and the body are not evil?
2. Look up the following passages in the book of Ecclesiastes: 2:24; 3:13; 5:18; 8:15; 9:7. Do they agree or disagree with Socrates' claims about life and the body?
3. How might Proverbs 14:4 be used against Socrates' notion of perfection (especially consider what Socrates would have thought about the kind of messes animals make)?
4. "All those who hate me love death" (Prov. 8:36). Make a short speech arguing that Socrates is a lover of death.

## SUMMA

*Write an essay or discuss this question, integrating what you have learned from the material above.*
Is the material world and body evil or good?

## Application

Plan a picnic. Find someplace beautiful in nature. Make up some tasty sandwiches. Take some fruit along as well. By using your outstretched arms and extended thumbs make a picture frame of nature and compete with your family members or classmates to see who can find the most glorious "picture." When God created the world, He said, "It is good!" Was He correct?

## Optional Activity

If you have the ability, go to a particularly beautiful place for your picnic. These places might include (but are certainly not limited to) the rolling hills of the Palouse in Northern Idaho, the rolling hills of Lancaster County, Pa., the Badlands in South Dakota, Napa Valley, the Rocky Mountains, the Grand Canyon or Longwood Gardens outside Philadelphia.

 READING ASSIGNMENT:
*Phaedo, 72e–89a*

# SESSION VII: ACTIVITY
*Phaedo, 72e–89a*

## Analyze the Art

*Study the painting,* Death of Socrates, *which appears in the General Information above, then answer the following questions.*

1. What differences can you see between the painting and the account in the *Phaedo?* (Hint: think about Socrates' posture when he drinks the hemlock.)
2. The painter of this work, David, was a supporter of the French Revolution. As we will discover in future years of study, the French Revolution returned to the Greek idea of radical autonomy that assumes "man is the measure of all things" and that Reason is the only sure way to discover truth. Before the Revolution, some radicals were oppressed and even killed for maintaining this belief. In light of this, why would someone sympathetic to the French Revolution pick this subject?
3. What might Socrates be saying just before he drinks the hemlock according to the *Phaedo?* (Hint: Look at the people around him for one possible answer and think about his most important ideas for another possible answer.)
4. In light of the fact that Plato believed that our world was only a shade of the world of Forms, why might a Socratic-Platonic sort of person object to the realistic style of the painting? What is most real in Plato's world?

# SESSION VIII: ACTIVITY

## *Death of Socrates*

Create your own artistic version of the *Death of Socrates*. This can be done in a number of different ways:

One way would be to draw a copy of David's *Death of Socrates* exactly as it is shown earlier in this chapter, or take the painting forward in time and show Socrates drinking the cup or lying dead in the same style as David.

Another option is to make a poster. Use an overhead projector and a transparency of the David piece to trace a copy of the work. Then paint it and put a title at the top of the poster. You might want to call it "Know Thyself"—this was Socrates' famous maxim. If you are feeling slightly more irreverent, you might want to try the title: "Know thy Drink!"

Or ignore the visual arts and write an ode to Socrates. An ode is a poem praising a person, place or thing. It might look like this first stanza from John Keats's *Ode to a Nightingale* (notice the allusion to Socrates):

> My heart aches, and a drowsy numbness pains
> My sense, as though of hemlock I had drunk,
> Or emptied some dull opiate to the drains
> One minute past, and Lethe-wards had sunk:
> 'Tis not through envy of thy happy lot,
> But being too happy in thine happiness,—
> That thou, light-winged Dryad of the trees,
>  In some melodious plot
> Of beechen green, and shadows numberless,
> Singest of summer in full-throated ease.

 READING ASSIGNMENT: *Phaedo*, 89b-118a

# SESSION IX: WRITING

*Phaedo*, 89b-118a

## Christ and Socrates

We continue practicing the *progymnasmata*, a series of exercises used for classical training in writing. You may remember that the *encomium* praises an individual. A companion exercise, called an *invective* or *vituperation,* condemns an individual, exactly the opposite of an encomium. Another exercise is called a *comparison*. A comparison takes the next step by weighing one individual against another and making a judgment about which one is the greatest. A comparison expounds the virtue of a specific person over and against another (e.g., Joe is a stronger warrior than Ted), but does not talk about virtue in a general sense (e.g., strength in war is admirable).

Although the encomium has six parts, the comparison has five. This is because the fifth part of the encomium (the Comparison) is incorporated into the other parts when writing a comparison. The *Prologue* comes first. It introduces the topic and, at the end of the paragraph, states or implies the opinion of the writer. The second part of this exercise is a paragraph called *Description of Heritage* comparing the persons in question. The writer looks for ways to praise or disparage the subjects on account of their family history. For instance, if a person comes from righteous parents, then highlight the fact that he learned his righteous habits at home and added to the glory of the family name. In a comparison, remember that the two people that you are considering must be viewed in relation to each other. So you might say, "Both Teddy Roosevelt and Franklin Roosevelt came from strong families that taught them tenacity, but Teddy Roosevelt's family did a better job of training him in righteousness. Next comes a paragraph called *Description of Upbringing*. The point is to show how the individuals profited from good education or overcame faulty education. Again, make sure that you compare the two people in this paragraph. You might say, "Both Washington and Franklin had educations that in many ways were lacking, but Franklin exceeded Washington in this area, because he worked so hard to train himself in the art of language that he became one the nation's most popular writers." The most powerful part of the comparison comes next: the *Description of Deeds*. In this section the writer discusses the excellencies or evils of the mind, body and fortune of the subjects. For example, the writer praises the practice of philosophical virtue, the way the person looked and his wealth, influence or social stature. Since Christianity has transformed our society it seems out of place to dwell on physical appearance or possessions, so instead the paragraph should concentrate on the actions and motives of the subject. This can be especially powerful if his life demonstrates a pattern. Again, comparing the two subjects is critical. In this section, you might say, "Although Grant conquered Lee on the battlefield, Lee's stellar Christian life has outshone all of Grants accomplishments." The final paragraph is an *Exhortation* or *Prayer* in which others are called on to imitate the best in the examples.

I. Prologue
- Introduce the topic
- State your opinion

II. Description of Heritage
- Praise or condemn them on account of their family histories

III. Description of Upbringing
- Show how the subjects profited from or were hindered by their education

IV. Description of Deeds
- Praise or disparage the excellencies or evils of their actions and motives

V. Exhortation or Prayer
- Call upon others to imitate one of the person's examples

# SESSION X: RECITATION

## Comprehension Questions

*Answer these questions for factual recall.*

1. What is the basic thrust of Socrates' Argument from Recollection (72e–76e)?

2. What is most real for Socrates?

3. How does the most real world of Forms differ from the material world?

4. What dangers might flow from treasuring an ideal, perfect world over this world?

5. Can you think of any counterexamples to Socrates'

## A JURY OF YOUR PEERS

In Socrates' day, jury service was voluntary but restricted to male citizens at least thirty years old. Each year, a jury panel of 6,000 was selected and sworn in. On any of the 150 to 200 days of the year that the courts were in session, anyone on the jury panel who wanted to serve (and collect jury pay) could report to the lawcourts.

The process of assigning jurors to cases differed in various periods. Each member of the jury panel was issued a wood or bronze allotment ticket (*pinakion*) that stated his name, deme and one of the ten letters from alpha to kappa. On each court day, the juror tickets were collected and used in conjunction with allotment stone machines (*kleroteria*) to select jurors at random.

The kleroteria had two sets of five, or one set of ten, vertical columns, each of which corresponded to one of the ten letters on the tickets. Tickets were placed in slots below the relevant letter such that the letter, but not the name, was visible. Several black and white balls were dropped into a container attached to a thin tube next to the horizontal rows of tickets. The rows next to black balls were rejected; those next to white balls were selected. The men whose tickets were in the selected rows would serve as jurors on that day.

Verdicts were determined by a simple majority vote. In the fifth century, jurors filed past two urns, one of which held votes for a conviction, the other those for acquittal. Each juror dropped a ballot pebble into one of the urns. In Aristotle's time, each juror was issued a set of two bronze discs with an axle running through the centers: the ballot for the defendant had a solid axle, for the plaintiff a hollow axle.

Speaking time in trials was divided evenly between the parties and measured by a *klepsydra*. A klepsydra was a water-clock consisting of a large ceramic vessel with a hole that drained into a second vessel set below it. The flow of water was stopped for the reading of evidence such as laws and witness testimony.

claims about opposites always creating opposites?

6. Why does the Argument for Recollection by itself not prove immortality?

7. What is the difference between immorality and immortality?

8. As the *Phaedo* begins, is Socrates dead or alive?

9. Why does Phaedo do most of the talking?

10. Where does the meeting with Socrates take place?

11. Why has the execution been so delayed?

12. Why are Simmias and Cebes a little upset with Socrates?

13. What does Socrates say he should have been working on instead of philosophy?

14. What does Socrates expect to see in the afterlife?

15. Are Simmias and Cebes convinced by Socrates' arguments?

16. What is a lyre? What is the objection that Simmias and Cebes make concerning the tuning of a lyre?

17. What is the objection that they make concerning the wearing out of cloaks?

18. Who gives Socrates the poison?

# OPTIONAL SESSION A

## Socrates in the Dock

Have three or four people act as friends of Socrates on his deathbed. Have the person playing Socrates explain one or both of the arguments for immortality and let the others discuss the arguments with him/her in casual style, not reading.

Next, add a twist. Have one or more of the friends become (act as) Christians. Let them pepper Socrates with questions. See if your Socrates can answer the questions of the Christians. If there are people watching the bedside conversation, have them help out both sides as the questions come up.

Change the argument and talk about the human body. Use the same arrangement and have "Socrates" run through his dislike of the human body and have other characters debate him about his negative views, with some defending the body from a biblical angle.

Make sure that you have a lot of tea to sip, but make sure that it is not hemlock!

# OPTIONAL SESSION B

## Evaluation

### Grammar

*All tests and quizzes are to be taken with an open Bible and open book. Write one or two sentences on each of the following questions. (2 points each)*

1. In the *Euthyphro,* as the argument proceeds, what does Socrates repeatedly press Euthyphro to give?

2. What is Socrates' famous challenge to Euthyphro's third definition (*Piety is that which all the gods love*)?

3. What are the two charges leveled against Socrates in the *Apology?*

4. What is the outcome of Socrates' Trial?

5. Why does Socrates refuse Crito's help to escape prison?

6. How does Socrates view the human body?

7. What is Socrates' first argument for immortality?

8. What is Socrates' second argument for immortality?

9. What sorts of objects make up Socrates' two classes of things? Give examples of each.

10. How does Socrates die in the end?

### Logic Questions

*Demonstrate your understanding of the themes of* The Last Days of Socrates *by answering two of the following four questions in complete sentences. Answers should be a paragraph or two. (10 points per answer)*

1. How does the Trinity differ from the world of the Forms?

2. How does a Christian view of creation conflict with a Platonic view of matter?

3. Why is the type of perfectionism practiced by Socrates in conflict with the Trinity?

4. Explain the Socratic–Platonic story about Forms. What are they? Why do they say we need them?

### Lateral Thinking

*Answer one of the following two questions. These questions will require more substantial answers than the prior essays. (12 points per answer)*

1. Compare and contrast Socrates and Christ.

2. Compare and contrast Socrates and King Solomon (Ecclesiastes) on the good life.

# THE EARLY HISTORY OF ROME

The study of history is the best medicine for a sick mind; for in history you have a record of the infinite variety of human experience plainly set out for all to see; and in that record you can find for yourself and your country both examples and warnings; fine things to take as models, base things, rotten through and through, to avoid.

*—Livy*

Some folks enjoy observing people. An airport is a particularly interesting place to do this. Think of the thousands of people passing through the terminals each day: where are they coming from? Where are they going? Why? Are they on their way home or heading out for a business conference? Who is that woman in green, and why does she look so sad? How many times have those guys over there backpacked around Europe? Will that couple running by make their connection? Where are those children's parents? Every person has a story, and for that one moment in the terminal or those few hours on a plane, hundreds of people with nothing else in common converge.

History is like an airport. In a battle, for one brief point in time, thousands of men clash together, each with his own childhood memories and reasons for fighting. In history, some people who are simply living out their lives are suddenly pulled together into the spotlight by converging circumstances; others strive to introduce themselves into that spotlight. Studying history, like trying to comprehend all of the threads of

In a painting from 1633, Romulus is seen raising his cloak to signal the Romans to attack and seize the Sabine women.

human existence streaming by your airport seat, would be overpowering without the comforting knowledge that there is indeed Someone who knows each of these people even better than they know themselves. God, the master Potter, has crafted people from clay and then brought them together in love, conflict, disease, business and death.

Yet certain people, and even some historians, do not see history as the movement of stories, but rather as lists of dates and battles, dry analyses of political cause and effect (frequently economic) or the conflict of ideas. Of course battles do happen, there are important dates to learn, and ideologies do drive men and movements. But we must never forget that behind all these things are real people, each with a distinctive laugh and a favorite food and a mother.

The Roman historian Livy is concerned with this very thing—portraying the lives and characters of those who formed the city and empire of Rome. Although he deals with political movements and wars, he always highlights the players involved by telling of their deeds or relating their delivery of a moving speech. These men and women sometimes alter the course of the Roman nation by their words and deeds; at other times they may be historically insignificant, but their lives serve as examples of courage, treachery or patriotism. Livy's first five books of *Ab Urbe Condita* ("From the Founding of the City") cover Rome's early history—from her beginnings in 753 B.C. to her first foreign occupation by the Gauls in 386 B.C.

# GENERAL INFORMATION
## Author and Context

During the reign of Emperor Augustus (27 B.C. to A.D. 14), Latin literature entered into its Golden Age. The poet Virgil was writing his epic poem, the *Aeneid* (you will have the pleasure of reading it in a few weeks), which traces the glory of Rome back to Aeneas, her ultimate founder. In the realm of prose, the historian Titus Livius (known to us as Livy) also chronicled the greatness of Rome. He lived from 59 B.C. to A.D. 17, and although not much is known about his personal life, certain things can be deduced from his works. He writes using very polished Latin, and

thus it is assumed that he was from an aristocratic or wealthy family which would have provided such an education for him. He also tends to show more sympathy to the senatorial party in his histories.[1] There is no record of him going into politics, however, and considering that he wrote 142 books on the history of Rome from 753 B.C. to 9 B.C., he probably did not have much time for anything else. Only 35 of those books have survived (this saddens some scholars, but relieves others). This chapter covers only the first five books.

## Significance

Livy fills his history of Rome with the people that lived in her, those who built up the monarchy and tore it down and those who pieced together the Republic (and eventually, of course, the Empire):

> Livy accepted a tradition going back to Aristotle (especially in the *Rhetoric*) and to Thucydides which explained historical events by the characters of the persons involved. As Aristotle said, "actions are signs of character." Because people are the sort of people that they are, they do the sort of things that they do, and the job of the historian is to relate what happens to the appropriate character.[2]

Livy delivers to us not only what happened, but he also shows us why these events happened, what motivates people to bravery or betrayal, why certain laws came about and so forth. This also gives us a perspective on Livy himself: What qualities did he (and no doubt others in his day) value? What wars would a first-century Roman deem honorable? Why does Livy call certain rulers good, while he openly condemns others?

Though they might pity or patronize him, modern historians do concede that Livy's historical work is important, not merely because of its sheer vastness, but because it was influential from the very first. The later historian Tacitus and the rhetorician Quintilian refer to it, and there is even a story that a man traveled from Spain just to look at Livy.[3] We may never know for sure how much of Livy's history actually happened and how much is mythical, but we do know that this is how a Roman mind perceived his own history, and that in itself can teach us many things.

## Main Characters

For Livy, a main character is not necessarily some political figure who conquered a tribe or formulated a new governmental policy. He loves to tell the stories of people who might be considered unimportant in the grand scheme of Roman history—their lives or actions may not have changed the course of a war, for example. But Livy brings out their heroism or villainy to show us how a true Roman should or should not behave. During the reign of King Tullus Hostilius (Book I, pp. 55-69), Livy does not write anything very interesting about the king himself, but rather tells the story of two sets of triplet brothers—the Horatii and the Curatii— who battle each other during the war with Alba. When the Tarquins and the men of Veii are waging war against Rome (Book II, pp. 108-26), we do learn about the leaders, but Livy also tells of Gaius Mucius, a brave young man whose assassination attempt on Porsena, king of Veii, leads to peace. There is also a slave girl named Cloelia, whose escape from the Veientes does not affect the outcome of the war, but whose bravery is admired by friend and foe alike. Many such tales are found throughout the other books as well. As you read through the books of Livy, pay attention to these brief narratives, which are sometimes no longer than a paragraph. While they may not be "important" in the sense that those involved did not significantly alter the course of Roman history, Livy includes them in his history for a reason.

In battles and senate meetings, the characters in Livy often give stirring or inflammatory speeches. When we read a newspaper today, we expect that the words within quotation marks are the very same words that the interviewed person said. However, in Livy's time, it was common practice for an author to put words into the mouths of historical figures. If he is a good author, he will endeavor to accurately reflect

the speaker's own views. Livy certainly endeavors to accomplish this goal. In the original Latin, he varies the style and vocabulary to portray the well-educated Ciceronian Latin of a senator, the rustic Latin of a slave, and so on.[4]

A final note on the characters has to do with their names. You may have noticed that many Romans have two or three names, and sometimes they have a nickname. Also, the name "Gaius" is the same as "Caius." At times it seems like everyone is named Appius Claudius.[5] I have tried to give the name that Livy uses the most or else the person's full name if there could be possible confusion.

## Summary and Setting

The first five books of Livy tell of the founding of Rome, the monarchy and the early Republic. Each book is summarized below, but there are a few terms that need to be defined first. For example, Livy did not need to explain what a *quaestor* was because his audience knew already (a quaestor was a Roman treasury official). However, a modern audience does need to understand those terms referring to the structure of Roman society in order to make sense of these histories.

In ancient Rome, the organization of the civil government reflects that of the family. In Book II Livy says that true patriotism "comes slowly and springs from the heart: it is founded upon respect for the family and love of the soil." The Roman family comprised the foundation of society, and, at its head, was the *paterfamilias*, the father of the family who could exercise unlimited authority over his household (including slaves). Individual families formed tribes (*gentes*). At the family level was also a system of patrons and clients, rather like the medieval practice of vassal and lord, where a client would render agricultural and military service, as well as his vote, in exchange for the patron's legal and physical protection. The patron-client relationship is not as significant in Livy as it is in other works, but he does refer to it now and then.

Roman society divided into two main classes, the ruling aristocrats and everyone else. The noblemen, called *patricians*, were usually wealthy and traced their family lineage back to the first senators under the reign of the kings. By Roman law, one had to be a patrician to hold the office of *consul* or senator. After the monarchy was done away with, the power (*imperium*) was given to two consuls, who were elected every year and who led the Roman armies into battle. Often a consul had already served as a *praetor* (an administrator and judge who also possessed the imperium), a *quaestor* (a treasury official) and/or a *censor* (an official responsible to take the census and also to assess property). In emergencies, the consuls resigned and a *dictator* was appointed to wield the *imperium* until he had dealt with the emergency situation (usually up to six months).

In addition to the patricians, there was the class of the common people or *plebians*, including not just the poor but even wealthy landowners or merchants who were not of patrician blood. Books II through V relate how this class struggled to gain a greater share in the Roman system of government. In 494 B.C., the plebians basically went on strike and moved out of the city of Rome. The patricians realized that they needed the plebians, who worked for them, fed them and fought for them, and thus to appease the people they created the office of *tribune*—two men (later five, and then ten) elected to represent the commoners. They were empowered to protect plebians (including themselves) from arrest and could veto laws, whether introduced by the Senate or the consuls.

Livy also refers to *lictors* and *equites*. A lictor was an attendant of a magistrate or consul, serving as his bodyguard and personal policeman. In other words, whenever a consul wanted to arrest somebody, he sent his lictors to arrest, summon to trial and even execute that person. The lictors also carried the rods (*fasces*), a bundle of sticks with an axe in the middle, which symbolized the magistrate's power (*imperium*). The equites were originally knights, men with horses

who served in the Roman military. They eventually form a third class, a sort of subset of the patricians, and were not required to be of noble birth (as long as they had enough money). The censor could determine if a patrician should be regarded as an *eques* or a *senator*.

Apart from all of these political offices, Livy mentions the *triumph* and the *thanksgiving* which followed military victories. A triumph was a procession by a victorious general through the city of Rome to the temple of Jupiter on the Capitoline hill. He was accompanied by the spoils of battle and captured slaves and was escorted by magistrates and senators. The Senate (and then later, the people) had to vote whether a general had the right to a triumph. A thanksgiving, also declared by the Senate, was a set time of just that—giving thanks to the gods (with ceremonies and sacrifices) for a victory.[6] Any other unfamiliar terms will hopefully be made intelligible by their context.

In these five books, Livy relates many events, mentions many people and includes many details. As you read each book, it may be helpful to have a broad overview of its content to refer to.

BOOK I: Livy describes the founding and expansion of Rome under the early kings, which included the famous hero Aeneas and the twins Romulus and Remus. After about two hundred years of monarchy, a powerful man named Tarquin ascended to the throne, whose arrogance earned him the nickname *Tarquinius Superbus*—Tarquin the Proud. His pride and the wickedness of his son Sextus resulted in a revolt, and a man called Brutus "the Liberator" drove out the Tarquins and, with them, the monarchy. Thereafter Rome, instead of being ruled by a king, was governed by two consuls who were elected each year. So began the Roman Republic.

BOOK II: This book, as well as Books III through V, is characterized by two things: internal strife between the common people (*plebs*) and the nobles (*patricians*) and external warfare with surrounding tribes. To handle some more serious military threats, the office of dictator was created, where one man was given supreme power for a short time (usually six months or less) to most effectively handle the military crisis. In 494 B.C., after the "Secession of the Plebs," the office of tribune—a representative of the common people—was created to satisfy plebian discontent. The common people gained another political victory when a proposal was set in motion that the plebian Tribal Assembly, and not the patricians, should elect plebian magistrates (especially tribunes).

BOOK III: The first part of this book is dominated by the strong but equitable Lucius Quinctius Cincinnatus, who served as consul and later as dictator. The tribunes began pushing heavily for a written law code in Rome, and thus, for a limited time, the form of government was changed to the *decemvirs*. This board of ten men was granted absolute power, but, as Livy admits, they were not all that effective, even though they did establish the Laws of the Twelve Tables. Then one of the decemvirs, Appius Claudius, overstepped his authority and was so wicked that a man named Verginius called for the replacement of the decemvirs by ten military tribunes.

BOOK IV: Conflicts between plebians and patricians continued, and the plebians succeeded in lifting the ban on intermarriage between the two classes. About this time the new office of censor was created. Outside the walls of Rome, the town of Veii in particular caused trouble, and it repeatedly joined with other tribes in an attempt to resist the power of Rome. More bickering continued within Rome, and thus, in order to pacify the plebians, the Senate decreed that soldiers would be paid out of public funds (406 B.C.).

BOOK V: War with Veii continued until dictator Marcus Furius Camillus obeyed a certain oracle, draining the Alban lake so that the Romans could at last sack this town. (You may remember Camillus from *Plutarch's Lives.*) From the north came the Gauls, who defeated the Romans soundly in the countryside and pursued them to Rome. The Romans retreated to the Citadel and managed to fend off the Gauls until Camillus, appointed dictator almost too late, returned and defeated the foreign invaders. Finally, in a rousing speech, Camillus urged the Romans to stay and rebuild their home, rather than migrating to Veii.

## Worldview

One night three students, Chris, Allie and Tom, went to a movie. Their favorite subject was history, and they all happened to have some extra cash, so they decided to go see the latest movie about the life of King Arthur—especially since the preview had said that this was the real, true story. After the movie, they took the opportunity talk it over—what parts they liked, what they would have done differently and that sort of thing. Allie and Tom were quite excited about the movie. Tom was saying things like, "Did you notice at the beginning, how they said it was based on new archeological evidence? And their weapons were very accurate, too." Allie, who wanted to be an archeologist someday, agreed: "And I really liked the way that the movie was

An eighteenth-century statue depicting the general Hannibal, the hero of the Carthaginians. In 217 B.C. he marched his war elephants from Carthage to the gates of Rome.

giving the historical picture of all the religions—the Druids, the early Christian church and the ancient Saxon beliefs."

Chris, however, was not so sure about the movie. He interrupted the others. "But it seemed to me that the movie wasn't about fact, but about what the writers wanted the facts to say."

Allie looked at him, confused. "What do you mean? Facts are facts," she said. "The movie was based on archeological evidence—stuff they dug up in England."

"Well, I don't think you can just have facts all by themselves. Everyone's got a way of looking at things, and that will change the way they see and tell about the 'facts,'" Chris said.

Tom, who wasn't sure yet which side to agree with, turned to Chris. "So how do you think the movie changed things? I mean, Allie's right. They were looking at actual, physical evidence, not at the myths and legends and stuff."

"All I'm saying is that the movie wasn't giving us this objective, unbiased picture of King Arthur. They weren't telling us what happened. They were preaching all kinds of values that our culture loves—everyone is born free, everyone has a free choice, we should always leave the natives of any country alone and that women make just as good warriors as men. It was total propaganda," Chris added, warming up to the debate. He could tell by Allie's face that she didn't agree. Tom still looked unsure.

The guys dropped Allie off first, and as she got out of the car she said in disgust, "Chris, you just always want to make everything religious." On the way back to Chris's house, Tom asked him more questions.

"So, Chris, are you saying that really there's no such thing as facts?"

"Not exactly. I mean, of course there are true things and there are events that people just made up. But what I'm saying is that when we think of 'history,' we wrongly think that it is something we study apart from any sort of religion. You can't be neutral in history—or in any subject, math and science, whatever. Just think if a Christian had done that King Arthur movie. It would be pretty different. I think Allie wants there to be a world where Facts rule. But that's not how it is. Remember how Jesus said that whoever wasn't with Him was against Him?"

"So you think that there really aren't archeologists,

but instead Christian archeologists and non-Christian archeologists."

Chris nodded. "The sad part is that even the Christian archeologists sometimes think like non-Christian ones. They go to church on Sundays, but at work they don't act like Jesus is Lord over the facts, Lord over history."

Tom didn't answer. He wanted to go home and do some serious thinking.

Many people today, like Allie, think that they can teach math or music or history from a so-called *neutral* perspective. They want to put religion in one box, math in another, music in another and so on. This is simply not possible—all of us, whether we admit it or not, have presuppositions, a religion if you will. Thus, we will teach math in either belief or unbelief; every movie, even the "historical" ones, will be either on God's side or not. When we read Livy (or any historian, for that matter), we should not be thinking, "Is his writing based on fact or legend?" Such a standard means that we are thinking like Allie—neutral "facts" are what matter to us, and we do not want anyone to be Lord of history—we just want there to be facts, whether or not God exists. Instead, we need to approach history in the same way that Chris went to the movie, asking questions like, "Is Christ the Lord of all things or not? Is He the Lord of history or not? What is this historian saying, and is it true, according to God's word? Does he think that Jesus is Lord of history or not?"

Livy is a historian, which means he is not writing about facts, but rather that he is interpreting the facts in a certain way and from a certain worldview. Even though his book is not a religious or theological or philosophical one, he cannot escape religion, theology and philosophy—none of us can. As he unfolds the story of Rome, he is also telling us what he thinks about the gods' involvement in that story. He also begins his work with a plain statement that he will be making moral judgments: there are "fine things to take as models, base things, rotten through and through, to avoid." He will tell us someone's story, presenting it in such a way that we will learn from it.

Just as the movie about King Arthur interpreted the facts (even though it pretended not to), many modern historians (like Allie) will present facts in a certain way, while at the same time saying that they are just reporting what happened. Livy, on the other hand, is a bit more honest than Allie and tells us that he is indeed interpreting the facts for us. He wants us to come to his history with some standard (whatever that may be) for what is good and right and apply it to the past.

As Christians, then, we need to ask "What is Livy's moral standard?" and "Is it a biblical one?" When Livy praises Servius Tullius as a good king, who reigned with "humanity and justice,"[7] this tells us that Livy must have some idea of what makes a good king versus a bad king and some way of distinguishing justice from injustice. As you read through Livy, look for these sorts of statements. Taken collectively, they reveal what sort of worldview Livy had: he was what could be described as "a moral pagan." He believed in the gods, and that belief affected his views on proper religion, morality among men and the greatness of Rome.

The Romans, like the Greeks, were polytheistic. They prayed to numerous gods, and even though Jupiter (also known as Jove and Zeus) is the head god, the other gods are powerful as well. Yet these deities are not like the God of the Bible, Who is fully omnipotent, omniscient and omnipresent; the Roman gods were thought to have limitations. This means that the gods are actually Really Powerful and more like Immortal Humans. They may be able to change people into animals and plants (as in Ovid's *Metamorphoses*), but they are not always able save their favorite city (as with Juno in the *Aeneid*). Because the gods are like us, only bigger and stronger, they have the same emotions we do—and this means that we have to keep them happy, because otherwise they will get angry and do terrible things to us. The gods can be appeased by proper ritual—by performing the right sacrifices at the right time, praying or promising the god a share in the spoils. In

A statue of the famous Apollo, by Vulcan, an Etruscan artist.

Livy's world we also have to pay attention to omens, strange events, plagues and natural disasters, because it was thought the gods are trying to tell us something through such things. If your average Appius does not understand what a certain sign means, he will seek out one of the many varieties of priest whose job it is to read entrails, count birds or consult religious scrolls.

Livy wrote his history in a world which believed in these many gods. However, he does not focus on the gods in the same way that Homer or Virgil does. In the *Iliad* or the *Aeneid*, the gods are major players in the action. If Juno gets offended, she will arrange for a storm to thrown Aeneas and his men off course. If Zeus is petitioned properly, he will turn the tide of the battle. Livy does not describe any such "behind the scenes" divine activity. Rather, what is more important to him is properly following religious ritual. Toward the end of Book V he tells the story of a young nobleman who, for the sake of performing a certain religious ceremony, left the Roman army holed up in the Citadel and walked right through the enemy army of the Gauls. The Gauls were so impressed that they let him carry out the ritual and then return in safety to the Citadel. A little later, when Camillus begged the Romans to stay and rebuild their city, he appealed to ritual, arguing that whenever they observed their religion properly, they fared well. But if they ever did not, the gods turned away.

A nation will become like what it worships. With these numerous and faulty gods heading up the heavenly realm, is it any wonder that there was so much strife in the Roman government? Why shouldn't the plebians and patricians have bickered

and fought continually, if they were just following the examples of the heavenly beings? The gods were often capricious, acting on whim, and they were even lustful—so what was to prevent a king or ruler from doing the exact same thing?

Yet it is at this very point that Livy shows us how inconsistent unbelief is. According to his worldview, there should be nothing wrong with Sextus's rape of Lucretia. The gods did the exact same thing, after all. But Livy still portrays Sextus in a negative light. He has a moral code, but it is neither unified nor consistent like God's laws are. We should not be surprised by Livy's inconsistencies, for he is just like the gods he worshiped.

Further examples will flesh out Livy's moral code a bit more. As mentioned previously, in his prologue he states that the purpose of history is to teach us what good things to imitate and what bad things to avoid. He has very pronounced opinions on what bravery is, how wrong deceit is and how much worse things are in his time than they were before. When recounting the reign of Tarquin the Proud, he says that, during a certain military campaign, the tyrant resorted to using "the un-Roman, and disgraceful, method of deceit and treachery."[8] In Book III Livy laments the loss of the good old days: "Fortunately, however, in those days authority, both religious and secular, was still a guide to conduct, and there was as yet no sign of our modern skepticism which interprets solemn compacts, such as are embodied in an oath or a law, to suit its own convenience."[9] At this point we Christians can certainly agree with Livy—deceit and treachery and oath-breaking are indeed sins. Just because Livy was an unbeliever does not mean that he will be wrong about sin at every point. God has given all men a certain measure of common grace,

The Romans borrowed religion from other people. For example, when they attacked the Etruscan city of Veii in 396 B.C., they begged Juno, the goddess of the enemy, to help them. Shown here is part of a household shrine typical of the day.

and it is by that means that Livy was able not only to write well, but also to get some moral things right.

However, there are instances where he prizes certain qualities which are not biblical virtues. During the reign of Servius Tullius, prophecies are made about a certain heifer—that whatever nation sacrifices her to Diana will possess the imperial power. Since a Sabine owns the heifer, a crafty Roman priest tricks the Sabine so that he, the Roman, can sacrifice the heifer himself and thus secure the imperial power for Rome. Although Livy does not openly approve of this action, he tells the story with a hint of admiration and concludes that all Rome, including the king, was delighted.[10] Biblically speaking, it is not generally considered loving to your neighbor to slaughter someone else's cow without their permission. In addition, Livy, as well as many generations of Romans, highly valued the virtue of Lucretia, who killed herself for the sake of her honor and chastity. Yet nowhere does the Bible demand such an extreme response to circumstances, and it certainly never condones suicide. This woman's example will be discussed in more depth later.

Livy's belief system, founded upon Roman morals and many gods, sharply contrasts with the Christian belief in the God Who is One and Three. The Triune God is indeed Many, but He is not many gods. He is also One, and Him only should we serve. Our God is also infinite and infinitely holy, wise, just and good. Thus we never need fear that He is out to get us because He got annoyed. Any judgments He gives are well-deserved, for He is the standard of good and evil. In Livy's world, there really cannot be a fixed standard of good and evil, because the gods can change their minds and then fire at will. God's laws flow from His character, and therefore they are consistent and righteous. Sometimes Livy's notion of good and evil agrees with the Christian view, and this is because of the common grace of God. Therefore, as Christians, we can still profit in many ways from reading Livy. Where his standards agree with ours, we may approve of or condemn those whom he does. Where Livy does not agree with the Bible, we should not agree with him.

If Livy were alive today, he would promote traditional values and good citizenship. If pressed, he would ultimately be unable to defend his standards, because they are based upon gods which are not infinite. In fact, he is very similar to many Americans who attempt to be good citizens and neighbors apart from the Word of God. Like Allie, they think that religion is in its own box and doesn't affect all areas of life. Like Livy, they may know that it is wrong to murder people, but they cannot truly defend their belief that it is wrong. They believe that America is a great nation, descended from great people. It is high time for us to learn from history, as Livy asserted by common grace, and repent and believe.

—*Natali H. Miller*

## For Further Reading

Spielvogel, Jackson. *Western Civilization.* Fifth Edition. Belmont, Calif.: Wadsworth/Thomson Learning, 2003, 103–112 and 137–138.

# Session I: Prelude

## Questions to Consider

Why should Christians study history? What does the Bible have to say about learning from or ignoring the past? Can forgetfulness be a sin?

*From the General Information above answer the following questions:*

1. What was Rome's first structure of government?
2. When and why was this replaced?
3. Match the following terms with their meanings:

| Censor | a. ten men granted absolute power to govern |
| Consul | b. administrator and judge, possessor of the imperium |
| Decemvirs | c. assessed property for taxes and took a census |
| Dictator | d. attendant of a magistrate or consul, serving as his bodyguard and personal policeman |
| Equites | e. common people |
| Fasces | f. elected to represent the commoners, initially two, then five, then ten |
| Gentes | g. father of the family, he could exercise unlimited power over his family and slaves |
| Imperium | h. individual families/tribes |

| | |
|---|---|
| Lector | i. allowed to rule temporarily for six months due to an emergency |
| Paterfamilias | j. Roman horsemen or knights that came to be a wealthy but not noble social class |
| Patricians | k. sticks with an axe in the middle, symbolizing the magistrate's power |
| Plebians | l. the first rulers following the rule of the kings |
| Praetor | m. the power or authority to rule |
| Quaestor | n. treasury official |
| Tribune | o. wealthy individuals who traced their lineage to the first senators under the reign of the kings |

4. Who were the patricians? Who were the plebians?
5. What is Livy's view of history (in other words, what are his goals in writing Rome's history)?

## Application

Have you ever forgotten to do something your parents told you to do? What was your initial reaction? What should it have been?

This is not a trite Sunday school application to history. We have trivialized forgetfulness, making it an excusable habit since we all do it. However, we would not apply such thinking to something like gossip: "We all do it, so, oh well." Hopefully, an example from daily life will show how important remembering commands is.

As you begin reading Livy's history, pay attention to the individual characters and their stories. Livy covers a good deal of material, and it is easy to be overwhelmed by the details. Keep in mind the broad scheme of the work, and observe how people's actions can alter the course of a nation.

**READING ASSIGNMENT:**
*Early History of Rome*, pp. 29–72

# SESSION II: DISCUSSION
*Early History of Rome*, pp. 29–72

## A Question to Consider

What is myth? What is legend? How do these relate to history?[11]

*Discuss or list short answers to the following questions:*

### Text Analysis

1. Where does Aeneas come from? Why did he leave there for Italy? What city did he found?
2. Who was Ascanius, and to where did he move the seat of government?
3. Who was Amulius?
4. How did Romulus become king?
5. Why did he arrange for the abduction of the Sabine women? How was it resolved?
6. How many of these stories about the founding of Rome are true? What is Livy's attitude toward sorting out myth and legend from "fact?" (pp. 29–30).

### Cultural Analysis

1. What is our culture's attitude toward myth, legend and anything that smacks of the supernatural?
2. Do the stories that our culture believes to be true (Darwin's view of the creation of man or the Big Bang) have any characteristics of mythology?

### Biblical Analysis

1. What characteristics of mythology does Christianity exhibit? (Gen. 1, Luke 2, 24)
2. Should this bother us?

## SUMMA

*Write an essay or discuss this question, integrating what you have learned from the material above.*
What should our attitude toward myth and legend be as Christians?

**READING ASSIGNMENT:**
*Early History of Rome*, pp. 72–104

# SESSION III: DISCUSSION
*Early History of Rome, pp. 72–104*

## A Question to Consider

Was the war against the Tarquins a just war?

*Discuss or list short answers to the following questions:*

### Text Analysis

1. Why was Tarquin assassinated, and was it justified?
2. Who was Lucretia?
3. Why did she kill herself, and was her suicide justified?
4. As a result, what happened to bring about the revolt against and the expulsion of the Tarquins?

### Cultural Analysis

The Romans upheld Lucretia as the model for womanly chastity and bravery. What qualities in women does our culture admire?

### Biblical Analysis

1. In light of what happened to Tarquin the Proud, what does the Bible say about monarchy (Rev. 19:16; 1 Sam. 8:5, 19–20)?
2. What scriptural examples are there of civil disobedience (Ex. 2, Josh. 2, Dan. 3, Acts 4)?
3. Is overthrowing a bad king always justifiable? What about Saul and David (1 Sam. 24 and 26)?

## SUMMA

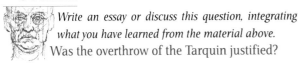
*Write an essay or discuss this question, integrating what you have learned from the material above.*
Was the overthrow of the Tarquin justified?

# SESSION IV: REPRIEVE

Admittedly, Livy has written material that is quite thick in his work, *The Early History of Rome.* Consequently, we recommend giving this day as a break for the student to simply read the next reading assignment during class.

READING ASSIGNMENT:
*Early History of Rome, pp. 105–128*

# SESSION V: DISCUSSION
*Early History of Rome, pp. 105–128*

## A Question to Consider

Can a country become an idol? Can a form of government become an idol?

*Discuss or list short answers to the following questions:*

### Text Analysis

1. How does Livy analyze Rome's monarchy?
2. Is his analysis correct? On what basis?
3. What was the office of consul, and why was it significant?
4. What happened to Brutus's sons?

### Cultural Analysis

1. What is the modern attitude toward democracy in the West?
2. What is our country's attitude toward monarchy?

### Biblical Analysis

1. What is the Bible's attitude toward monarchy? (1 Sam. 8)
2. What is the Bible's attitude toward democracy? (Judg. 17:5–6, 21:21–25)

## SUMMA

*Write an essay or discuss this question, integrating what you have learned from the material above.*
Do Americans idolize their government?

## Optional Activity: *Map Project*

Draw or trace a map of Italy or just the area surrounding Rome, preferably poster-sized. Using the maps on pages 438–440 of *Early History of Rome* or from other reference books or the internet,[14] begin keeping track of Rome and her neighbors. Include the significant places from Book I, such as Lavinium and Alba Longa. Your map should include both tribes (regions) and cities which have military, political or some other significance. Be creative—for example, you could use an old-fashioned style which has the towns represented by drawings of houses and a few sea monsters going about their business in the Mare Tyrrhenum. In the remaining sessions you will be asked occasionally to update your map. Also keep it handy while doing your Reading Assignments, so that you can better follow the action.

### READING ASSIGNMENT:
*Early History of Rome*, pp. 132–147

# SESSION VI: DISCUSSION

*Early History of Rome*, pp. 132–147

## A Question to Consider

Should America change to a two-consul government? What would be some advantages? Some disadvantages? What about a dictatorship?

*Discuss or list short answers to the following questions:*

### Text Analysis

1. Why did the Romans switch from a government run by two consuls and the Senate to one run by a dictator during a time of war?
2. What were the two main threats to peace in Rome that caused the people to consider appointing dictators?
3. Why was the dictator Manlius Valerius appointed dictator?
4. How were the tribunes different from the consuls and dictators? How was this office created?

### Cultural Analysis

1. What does our country think of divided authority?
2. Does our culture believe in divided authority in the family? Should it?

### Biblical Analysis

1. What is the biblical warrant for limited authority in the government? (1 Sam. 8)
2. What are the biblical warnings about kings? (Deut. 17:14–20)
3. The Bible sets forth three institutions to govern life: the family, the church and the state. Do any of these have divided authority like the consul system in Rome?

## SUMMA

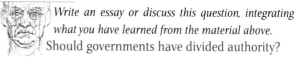

*Write an essay or discuss this question, integrating what you have learned from the material above.* Should governments have divided authority?

## Optional Activity

Classical training in rhetoric included preparatory writing exercises called the *progymnasmata*. These exercises in composition introduced the beginning student to basic forms and techniques that would then be used and combined when practicing more advanced exercises and speeches. One of these progymnasmata was called an *impersonation*. The impersonation seeks to imitate the style and characteristics of the person making the speech. To make an impersonation:

**DISCUSS** or think through the characteristics of the person whose speech you are emulating.
**READ** carefully through the speech that you are impersonating. In many cases you will write an impersonation of a speech that a person has not delivered, but this time you are simply asked to remake the speech that Servilius gave.
**WRITE** the speech yourself, without using the book.
**PRESENT** it to someone else.
**EXPLAIN** how different personal characteristics of this person come through in your impersonation.

One of the things to be careful about when you are writing the impersonation is that you must remember what has happened in the personal history of the character and also what will happen in the future. You have to remember to put them in the proper setting, however (i.e., you cannot make the young George Washington say, "I will be the first President under the new Constitution of the United States," because, when he was a boy, none of these existed).

If you wanted to write an impersonation of Romulus, for example, you would re-read the speech he gave to the Sabine women on pages 41–42. Then you would think about who Romulus was: a warrior, a man so proud he would kill his brother, and a king who wanted to firmly establish his city. Since you would be remaking his speech, you would write a speech using arguments similar to the ones Romulus used:

"Women of the Sabines, do not fear or worry about your future. It is not through any fault of yours that you now find yourselves in what seems a dangerous situation. Your parents are the ones who were too proud to even consider us as possible suitors, merely because we are citizens of a new city, and some of us may have had a dark past. Yet now we merely desire to build up our city, and we want you to be a part of that vision; as citizens of this city, you will share in her good fortunes, and you will also share with us our children, who will become the future leaders of our land. Besides, how can you blame us for looking on your beauty and wanting to have that beauty in our homes from this time forth? You are now our own beloved wives, and we will take good care of you, our children, and our homes."

*Write an impersonation of Servilius's speech on behalf of the common people (see the top of page 136).*

**READING ASSIGNMENT:**
*Early History of Rome,* pp. 147–189

# SESSION VII: RECITATION

*Early History of Rome,* pp. 147–189

## Comprehension Questions

*Answer these questions for factual recall.*

1. How did Coriolanus (Caius Marcius) rise to prominence?
2. Why did he join with the Volscians?
3. Who were the Fabii?
4. What did they volunteer to do, and what was the outcome of that?
5. Who was Publilius Volero and what did he propose?
6. In the war with the Volscians, how did Appius maintain discipline? Were such measures justifiable?
7. What was the Secession of the Plebs, and why was it significant?
8. Who was Gaius Mucius?
9. What was the difference between a tribune and a dictator?

The famous painting *Primavera* by the artist Sandro Botticelli shows Flora, the Roman goddess of spring and flowers.

Tarquin and Lucretia

# SESSION VIII: WRITING

## Progymnasmata

This writing assignment continues with the classical writing exercises called the *progymnasmata*. The *proverb* exercise takes a wise saying and demonstrates its wisdom. The proverb is a lot like a *chreia*, except that the person who utters the saying is often unknown.

The proverb exercise has eight parts. First, you should write a short paragraph praising the wisdom of the saying (this is like the *Panegyric* in the *chreia* in which you praise the wisdom of the speaker). Next, in a very short paragraph, you rephrase the statement. This paragraph is called the *Paraphrastic.* For instance, one might paraphrase the saying "Haste makes waste" this way: "if someone hurries, they often make mistakes." After that you write a paragraph called *From the Cause,* explaining the speaker's motivation for uttering the saying. Next, you write a paragraph called *From the Contrary.* This paragraph tells what would happen if the statement were not heeded. In the fifth paragraph, called the *Analogy,* you liken the saying to something else, usually something more concrete and easier to understand. An analogy points to a class of people or things as general truth (e.g., "the farmer knows the value of rising early"). The sixth paragraph is similar to the fifth. It is called the *Example,* and in it you show the wisdom of the saying by pointing your reader to a specific instance in which this wisdom was demonstrated (e.g., "Jesus woke early to pray"). The *Analogy* is different from the *Example* in that it is about a general practice, whereas the *Example* is about a specific person, place or thing. The difference might be best thought of in this way: if you were living on earth at the time of the example, you could point to it with your finger. "Farmer John Smith is waking early." You cannot point at an analogy, in this case a generalized "class of farmers." The next section of the proverb is called the *Testimony of the Ancients.* In it, you reference the testimony of a respected figure from the past who agrees with the saying (do not quote your father or mother, for obvious reasons). Finally, conclude the exercise with a short *Epilogue,* which summarizes your findings.

During one of the many times of civil unrest, one of the tribunes was assassinated. This action was defended by those who maintained that "the power of the tribunes being a bad thing must be put down by bad means" (p. 177).

*First, write a proverb amplifying the statement "The ends justify the means." Write this proverb from the perspective of one of the senators who was in favor of the death of this tribune. Second, write a short paragraph making a judgment about whether this proverb demonstrates true wisdom.*

Panegyric
  • Praise the wisdom of the proverb
Paraphrastic
  • Rephrase the proverb in your own words
From the Cause
  • Explain the motivation of the speaker
From the Contrary
  • Explain the consequences if the proverb is not heeded
Analogy
  • Liken the proverb to something else
Example
  • Point the reader to a specific instance in which the wisdom of the proverb was demonstrated
Testimony of the Ancients
  • Quote a sage person from the past who testifies to the truth of the saying
Epilogue
  • Summarize your previous paragraphs

Now, consider whether this proverb actually defends a righteous principle or whether it recommends sinfulness. Write a paragraph or two answering this question: Does the principle of *the ends justify the means* indicate that the murder of the tribune was, in fact, a righteous action?

READING ASSIGNMENT:
*Early History of Rome*, pp. 193–233

# SESSION IX: RECITATION
*Early History of Rome*, pp. 193–233

## Comprehension Questions

*Answer these questions for factual recall.*
1. How did the plague affect the war with the Aequians and Volscians?
2. What did the tribune Terentillus propose, and what was the response to his proposal?
3. Why was the revolt of Herdonius significant?
4. What sort of consul was Lucius Quinctius Cincinnatus (pp. 217–221)?
5. What sort of dictator was Lucius Quinctius Cincinnatus?
6. Why was the number of tribunes increased to ten?
7. Why was a commission sent to Athens? What were the results of their visit?

READING ASSIGNMENT:
*Early History of Rome*, pp. 233–259

# SESSION X: RECITATION
*Early History of Rome*, pp. 233–259

## Comprehension Questions

*Answer these questions for factual recall.*
1. Who were the *decemvirs?* What was their significance? What is Livy's analysis of their rule?
2. What were the Twelve Tables? Why were they important?
3. What sort of man was Appius Claudius?
4. When and why did the character of the decemviral government change?
5. What (in brief) were the two "revolting crimes" of the decemvirs?
6. How did Lucius Verginius "save" his daughter from Appius Claudius? Was his action justifiable?
7. What finally caused the decemvirs to resign?

READING ASSIGNMENT:
*Early History of Rome*, pp. 260–282

# SESSION XI: WORLDVIEW ANALYSIS
*Early History of Rome*, pp. 260–282

*You be the judge. Imagine that you are seeing the cases below and have to make judgment according to biblical law and according to the Twelve Tables. What would your decision be?*

**BIBLICAL LAW** Deut. 24:14 You shall not oppress a hired servant who is poor and needy, whether one of your brethren or one of the aliens who is in your land within your gates.
**TWELVE TABLES** 3.3. Against a foreigner the right in property shall be valid forever.

## CASE

Two men come before you with a property dispute. The first one is named Ram Patel. He is an Indian citizen living in America on visa. He owns a hotel. Edgar Smith is a "ne'er-do-well" descendant of Captain John Smith. He has claimed squatter's rights over portions of the hotel because, he says, the whole country belongs to Americans.

**BIBLICAL LAW** Gen. 9:6 Whoever sheds man's blood, by man his blood shall be shed; for in the image of God He made man.
**TWELVE TABLES** 4.1. A dreadfully deformed child shall be quickly killed.

## CASE

A young unwed couple comes before you. They have been charged with secretly killing their child that was born with Downs Syndrome. They claim that the child was deformed and could not have the quality of life that they wanted for him, and therefore, they killed him.

**BIBLICAL LAW** Deut. 19:17–19 . . . then both men in the controversy shall stand before the LORD, before the priests and the judges who serve in those days. And the judges shall make careful inquiry, and indeed, if the witness is a false witness, who has testified falsely against his brother, then you shall do to him as he thought to have done to his brother; so you shall put away the evil from among you.
**TWELVE TABLES** 8.23. A person who had been found guilty of giving false witness shall be hurled down from the Tarpeian Rock.

## CASE

You find out that a man testified falsely against his "friend" in a dispute about who was to take out the trash.

# SESSION XII: WRITING

## Progymnasmata

Classical training in rhetoric included preparatory writing exercises called the *progymnasmata*. These exercises in composition introduced the beginning student to basic forms and techniques that would then be used and combined when practicing more advanced exercises and speeches. One of these progymnasmata was called the *encomium*, a composition written to praise an individual. Its opposite exercise (which condemns an individual) is called a *vituperation* (or an *invective*). This writing exercise expounds the virtues or condemns the vices of a specific person (e.g., Joe is a strong warrior), but does not talk about virtue in a general sense (e.g., strength in war is admirable).

The encomium and the vituperation each have six parts. The *Prologue* comes first. It introduces the topic and, at the end of the paragraph, states or implies the opinion of the writer. The second part of this exercise is a paragraph called *Description of Heritage*. In this paragraph the writer looks for ways to praise or condemn the person on account of his family history. For instance, if a person comes from righteous parents, then highlight the fact that he learned his righteous habits at home and added to the glory of the family name. A vituperation would emphasize that he comes from a family or nation that taught him wrong beliefs or bad habits. Next comes a paragraph called *Description of Upbringing*. The point is to show how the person profited from a good education or overcame a bad one (this is for the encomium). For the vituperation you should attempt to show how he failed to profit from a good education or learned well the lessons of a bad education. The most powerful part of the encomium comes next: the *Description of Deeds*. In this section the writer praises the excellencies of the mind, body and fortune of the subject. For example, the writer praises the practice of philosophical virtue, the way the person looked and his wealth, influence or social stature. Since Christianity has transformed our society it seems out of place to dwell on physical appearance or possessions (i.e., he was evil because he was quite homely, or it is obvious that he was a good man because he was fabulously rich), so instead the paragraph should concentrate on the actions and motives of the subject. This can be especially powerful if his life demonstrates a pattern. Next is a *Comparison* of the subject to someone else to portray him in a favorable light (if it is an encomium). An unfavorable comparison is best for vituperation. The final paragraph is an *Exhortation or Prayer* in which others are called on to imitate this person's example or a proclamation to everyone telling them not to go down the wicked path that this person did.

*Write an encomium or vituperation on Cloelia (pp. 123–124).*
I. Prologue
   • Introduce the topic
   • State your opinion
II. Description of Heritage
   • Praise or condemn the person on account of his family history
III. Description of Upbringing
   • Show how the person profited or failed to profit from his education
IV. Description of Deeds
   • Praise or condemn the excellencies or deficiencies of his actions and motives
V. Comparison
   • Portray the person favorably or unfavorably in comparison to someone else
VI. Exhortation or Prayer
   • Call upon others to either imitate or shun this person's example

READING ASSIGNMENT:
*Early History of Rome*, pp. 287–330

# SESSION XIII: DISCUSSION
*Early History of Rome*, pp. 287–330

## A Question to Consider

Should common people be allowed to marry with the nobility?

*Discuss or list short answers to the following questions:*

### Text Analysis

1. What law did Canuleius propose?
2. What other policy was also put forward?

3. How did the consuls respond to Canuleius?
4. How did Canuleius defend his position?
5. What was the outcome of the debate?
6. How did the trouble in Ardea begin? How was it resolved?

### Cultural Analysis

1. What would happen if a legislator in our nation today proposed a law that would ban one class of people from marrying another?
2. How would you oppose this law if it were based on unbiblical grounds (such as a law banning interracial marriage)?

### Biblical Analysis

1. What two classes of people does the Bible say should never marry (1 Cor. 7)?
2. Why should these two "classes" avoid marriage?
3. If people from these two groups find themselves married, should they divorce?

## SUMMA

*Write an essay or discuss this question, integrating what you have learned from the material above.*
Should people from different races, social groups, economic backgrounds or religions marry?

## Optional Activity: *Debate*

If working in a group, divide into two teams, assigning one side to argue for and the other to argue against the proposed Canuleian Law. Students may draw arguments from the speeches on pages 288–290 and 290–294.

READING ASSIGNMENT:
*Early History of Rome*, pp. 330–363

# SESSION XIV: RECITATION
*Early History of Rome*, pp. 330–363

## Comprehension Questions

*Answer these questions for factual recall.*

1. What were military tribunes, and why was the office created?
2. What was a censor, and why was the office

created?

3. Who was Spurius Maelius?
4. How did the trouble in Fidenae start?
5. Who was Vettius Messius? What does Livy think of him?
6. What motivated the Volscians to prepare again to fight Rome (p. 332)?
7. What sort of general was Sempronius?
8. What sort of general was Marcus Postmius Regillensis? What happened to him?
9. What happened in the election of 409 B.C.?
10. What innovation did the Senate introduce with regard to soldiers? What was the response to it?

# SESSION XV

## Analyze the Art

*Look at the picture of the Roman patrician on this page and answer the following questions:*

1. Why is the patrician holding busts of his ancestors?
2. What can we learn about the Romans from this statue's expression and stance?
3. How do you think a statue of a commoner would differ from this statue?

## Possible Review Questions

*Answer each of the following questions in complete sentences. Most should be answered in a sentence or two.*

1. What was the Canuleian Law, and what was its significance?
2. What was a censor?
3. Who was Tempanius?
4. Who was Marcus Postumius Regillensis?

*Demonstrate your understanding of the Roman worldview as set forth in Books I–IV of Livy's history. Answer the following question in complete sentences; your answer should be a paragraph or so.*

1. The Struggle of the Orders continues through this book. In what issues do you agree with the patricians? The plebians?

 READING ASSIGNMENT:
*Early History of Rome,* pp. 367–397

# SESSION XVI: DISCUSSION
*Early History of Rome,* pp. 367–397

## A Question to Consider

Think of a time when you had a major disagreement with someone. What was it about? How did it get resolved?

A statue of an unknown Roman man from probably between 50–25 BC. We know he's a Roman because he wears a toga. Because he carries busts we know his father or grandfather served as one of Rome's top officials.

*Discuss or list short answers to the following questions:*

## Text Analysis

1. Who was Rome's great rival in the first half of this book?
2. Why did the Romans suffer initial defeat at Veii?
3. What omen occurred concerning Veii? How was this omen received in Rome?
4. How did the war with Veii end?

## Cultural Analysis

1. What does our culture think about political divisions in our own country? In the world?
2. What does our culture think about religious divisions?
3. What does our culture think about divisions within families?

## Biblical Analysis

1. Jesus says that a kingdom or house divided against itself cannot stand (Mark 3:24-25). How does this apply to the siege at Veii?
2. What does Scripture teach are effective means for resolving divisions and differences? (Matthew 5:38-48, 1 Corinthians 6:1-11)

## SUMMA

*Write an essay or discuss this question, integrating what you have learned from the material above.* How should we seek to heal divisions within our families, churches and society?

**READING ASSIGNMENT:**
*Early History of Rome,* pp. 397–408

# SESSION XVII: DISCUSSION
*Early History of Rome,* pp. 397–408

## A Question to Consider

What is loyalty? What loyalties should Christians have?

*Discuss or list short answers to the following questions:*

## Text Analysis

1. What happened at the siege at Falerii (see pages 400–402)?
2. How did Camillus handle the schoolmaster incident?
3. What did the Falerians and Romans think of Camillus's actions?

## Cultural Analysis

1. Are Americans patriotic?
2. Is our culture loyal to sports teams? Is this a healthy loyalty?

## Biblical Analysis

1. Jesus says, "He who loves father or mother more than Me is not worthy of Me. And he who loves son or daughter more than Me is not worthy of Me" (Matt. 10:37). Make a list of your loyalties and how you rank them. Do you think they are ranked biblically? How do your loyalties compare to those of your parents and friends? How are they similar, and how are they different?
2. How radical is our loyalty to God to be in light of Deuteronomy 13:6–11?

## SUMMA

*Write an essay or discuss this question, integrating what you have learned from the material above.* To be loyal to Christ should we stone unbelievers in light of Deuteronomy 13?

**READING ASSIGNMENT:**
*Early History of Rome,* pp. 408–435

# SESSION XVIII: RECITATION
*Early History of Rome,* pp. 408–435

## Comprehension Questions

*Answer these questions for factual recall.*

1. Why did the Senate re-institute the election of consuls?
2. How did Camillus alienate himself from the Roman people?
3. What brought about his exile?
4. Where did the Gauls settle, and why did they come?
5. What warning did the Romans receive concerning the Gauls?

6. What happened in the initial battles with the Gauls?
7. How did Camillus get involved?
8. Who was young Fabius, and why is his tale told?
9. Who was Pontius Cominus, and what role did he play in the war?
10. How did the sacred geese save Rome?
11. How did Camillus save Rome?
11. How did Camillus save Rome twice over?

## Map Project

Finish your map. You may want to add an inset sketch of Rome herself, showing the seven hills, the Citadel where the Romans made their last stand and other elements like the walls and the main thoroughfares out of the city.

# SESSION XIX: ACTIVITY

Remember that Livy's goal in writing his history is to set forth "both examples and warnings; fine things to take as models, base things, rotten through and through, to avoid." Go back through Books I–V and choose five characters whom Livy would consider good examples, and five characters to avoid. Determine what characteristics the good ones have in common, and what qualities the bad ones share. What sort of people were they? How did their deeds change Rome? Do you agree with Livy's assessment of these characters? Display your findings in a form like Chart 1, which suggests a few characters you might consider.

# SESSION XX: REVIEW

## Possible Review Questions

*Take some time to review all your foregoing notes and answers, but focus specifically on the following questions:*

1. What was Livy's great work, and when did he live?
2. What is Livy's view of history (in other words, what are his goals in writing Rome's history)?
3. What is the story of Romulus?
4. What is the story of the Sabine women?
5. What brought about the revolt against and the expulsion of the Tarquins?
6. How does Livy analyze Rome's monarchy?
7. What is the story of Horatius Cocles?
8. What is the story of Gaius Mucius?
9. What were the two main threats to peace in Rome?
10. What was the Secession of the Plebs, and why was it significant?
11. What is the story of Coriolanus?
12. What is the story of Cincinnatus?
13. What were the Twelve Tables? Why were they important?
14. What is the story of Verginia?
15. What was the Canuleian law?
16. What is the story of Spurius Maelius?
17. What is the story of Marcus Postumius Regillensis?
18. Why did the Romans suffer initial defeat at Veii, and how did they finally defeat the city?
19. What is the story of Camillus?
20. How did the sacred geese save Rome?
21. What is the story of young Fabius?
22. What is the story of Pontius Cominus?

---

*Chart 1:* **LIVY'S THE GOOD, THE BAD AND THE UGLY**

| PERSON | CHARACTERISTICS | HOW THEY CHANGED ROME |
|---|---|---|
| Romulus | | |
| Numa Pompilius | | |
| Tarquinius Superbus | | |
| Horatius Cocles | | |
| Appius Claudius | | |
| Falerian schoolmaster | | |
| Camillus | | |

# OPTIONAL SESSION A

## Evaluation

*All tests and quizzes are to be given with an open book and a Bible available.*

### Grammar

*Answer each of the following questions in complete sentences. Some answers may be longer than others. (2 points per answer)*

1. What is the story of Romulus?
2. What brought about the revolt against and the expulsion of the Tarquins?
3. What is the story of Gaius Mucius?
4. What were the two main threats to peace in Rome?
5. What was the Secession of the Plebs and why is it significant?
6. What is the story of Cincinnatus?
7. What are the Twelve Tables? Why are they important?
8. What is the story of Verginia?
9. What is the story of Pontius Cominus?

### Logic

*Demonstrate your understanding of the Roman worldview as set forth in Books I–V of Livy's history. Answer the following question in complete sentences; your answer should be a paragraph or so. Answer two of the four questions. (10 points per answer)*

1. What was the Roman view of monarchy?
2. What was the Roman view of suicide?
3. What was the Roman view of treason?
4. What was the Roman view of gods?

### Lateral Thinking

*Answer one of the following questions. These questions will require more substantial answers. (15 points per answer)*

Re-read Camillus's speech after the Gauls' occupation of Rome (pp. 429–434). How did Camillus argue for various Roman ideals? What can be learned about the Roman worldview?

# OPTIONAL SESSION B

## A Question to Consider

How should criminals be treated?

*Discuss or list short answers to the following questions:*

### Text Analysis

1. On page 65 Livy recounts the punishment of the oath breaker Mettius and calls it disgusting and inhumane. He then adds: "Save for that one instance we can fairly claim to have been content with more humane forms of punishment than any other nation." What is Livy's definition of "humane?"
2. Consider the story of Lucretia. Is it ever right to commit suicide?

### Cultural Analysis

1. What does our culture do to people who break their word? Can you think of any recent examples?
2. What does our culture do to people who break their wedding vows?

### Biblical Analysis

1. What is a biblical definition of "humane?" What does the Bible have to say about humane vs. inhumane forms of punishment? Look at Deut. 25:1–3, Ex. 21:24–25, and Deut. 19:19–21.
2. What does God say about victims of rape? What is true chastity? Look at Deut. 22:23–27, Titus 2:5, and 1 Pet. 3:2.

## SUMMA

*Write an essay or discuss this question, integrating what you have learned from the material above.*

Our laws forbid "cruel and unusual" punishments. Some say that this should keep us from ever putting anyone to death. Is capital punishment "cruel and unusual?"

# OPTIONAL SESSION C

## Progymnasmata

*Write an encomium or vituperation on Lucretia (pp. 100–103). For directions see Session XII.*

## ENDNOTES

1  Robert Ogilvie in the introduction to Aubrey de Sélincourt's translation of Livy, *The Early History of Rome*. London: Penguin Books, 2002, 2. (All page references throughout this chapter are to this edition.)

2  Ibid., 2–3.

3  Ogilvie in de Sélincourt, 6.

4  Ogilvie, 3–4.

5  Be glad this is not a Russian novel, where all the characters have at least twenty polysyllabic names and five or more nicknames.

6  This two-paragraph sketch on Roman society and government is based on Spielvogel, 108–9, and relevant entries in the *Oxford Classical Dictionary* (OCD). Oxford: Oxford University Press, 1996.

7  de Sélincourt, 89–90.

8  Ibid., 94.

9  Ibid., 219.

10  Ibid., 85.

11  Read especially the top of page 30 for Livy's view.

12  *This endnote appears only in the teacher's edition.*

13  *This endnote appears only in the teacher's edition.*

14  At the time of publication, the following sites had maps available: http://penelope.uchicago.edu/Thayer/E/Gazetteer/Maps/Periods/Roman/Places/Europe/Italia/Latium/1.html and http://www.princeton.edu/~humcomp/cla218/01.JPEG

15  *This endnote appears only in the teacher's edition.*

# LUKE AND ACTS

*That you may know the certainty of those things in which you were instructed.*

*—Luke 1:4*

Have you ever watched a video replay of a great game? Imagine that you missed out on a football game, let's say the Cotton Bowl. And it just happened that (in this imaginary world) Southern Mississippi played Alabama. And Southern won.[1] (As I said, this is imaginary). You are told that Southern won by a landslide! (Shouts and hog calls now erupt.) You are happy that Southern won, but you want to know the score. The score was 51-7. Now you want to know what happened. You want the blow-by-blow or play-by-play. So now you get to see the game on video. Even though you know exactly how it's going to turn out, even though you know the end—when you see the game on video you'll cheer at the scores and feel a little worry whenever your team (Southern) slips.

In a sense the whole Bible is that way for us. We may read the drama of the fall into sin. If we are really watching the game, we will feel worry. "Oh, no. What's God going to do now?" When we read of the enslavement of the Israelites and the cruelty of the pharaoh, we feel bad and then cheer for Moses. When we look at the Gospels, if we are fully engaged with the video replay, we feel the oppression of God's people. We cheer when the long-awaited Savior is born. We worry that Herod might kill him (even though we know the outcome). At the cross, we may have a taste of the despair that the disciples experienced (even though we know what the cross means). We need to hear the whole story, and we must rehearse that story.

In Luke and Acts, we have a central part of the story of the Bible. We have the peak of the mountain of God's revelation of His Son. We are told of His mother and Joseph, of his birth, of those waiting for him like Zacharias, Simeon and Anna, of his baptism, his temptation, his ministry, his death, resurrection and ascension. Then we see how He worked by the Spirit in the church and the gospel crossing all borders and barriers.

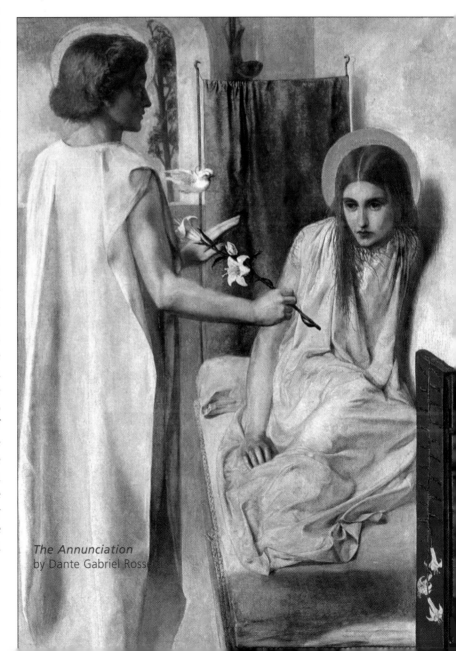

*The Annunciation*
by Dante Gabriel Rossetti

# GENERAL INFORMATION

## Author and Context

Luke wanted to give more than just the score; he told the whole story, play-by-play. His replay was so that the reader "may know the certainty of those things in which you were instructed." Luke addressed a Roman dignitary whose Christian name was "Theophilus" (Luke 1:3; Acts 1:1). Theophilus means "friend of God." The Greek word for "instructed" is *catecheo*. Theophilus had been "catechized" and brought into the Christian community. He knew the basic message of the gospel. Luke's purpose was that he be fully instructed in the Lord by knowing in detail "a narrative of those things which have been fulfilled among us." Under the inspiration of the Holy Spirit, Luke compiled this "orderly account" from "eyewitnesses."

Did Luke really write these books? Though there is no verse which tells us this, Luke has long been held to be the author of Luke and Acts. This traditional view is very solid. Early witnesses to Luke's authorship include the church fathers, Irenaeus and Tertullian. Even today no conservative scholar disputes his authorship.

The strongest basis for accepting Luke as the author is internal to the books. We have strong internal argument that Luke became a companion with Paul and wrote Acts as a participant in the story. We see this in the "we" passages in Acts (16:10ff; 20:5ff; 27:1ff). For example, "Therefore, sailing from Troas, we ran a straight course to Samothrace, and the next day came to Neapolis, and from there to Philippi, which is the foremost city of that part of Macedonia, a colony. And we were staying in that city for some days" (Acts 16:11–12).

From these texts we see that Luke traveled with the Apostle Paul. He was with Paul as Paul wrote Colossians. He is called a physician. And at the end of Paul's life, Luke was faithful to Paul, even though others had left him.

As shown in this drawing from the Book of Kells, Luke is frequently represented by the image of an ox. This iconography has its basis in early Christian traditions that thought of each of the four authors of the Gospels in terms of the figures mentioned in Ezekiel and Revelation— Matthew as the winged man, Mark as the Lion, John as the eagle and, since Luke begins and ends his Gospel at the Temple, he was associated with the ox, a common sacrificial animal.

## Significance

Luke diligently researched the things that he did not personally observe. God the Holy Spirit, in breathing out Holy Scripture (2 Tim. 3:16) uses the experience of the human author, whether of a weeping prophet or a careful scholar. Luke reports this as history, though it is not aimed at being a comprehensive history of the church. Still, it is a kind of literature which abundantly shows attention to detail, sequential actions, names of significant people, places and events relevant to the message of the book.

Together, Luke and Acts provide for "knowing the certainty" of the faith by explaining from the beginning the birth, temptation, baptism, earthly ministry, death, resurrection and ascension of Jesus. The continuation of this in Acts further explains how the risen and ascended Christ continued to act in the person of the Holy Spirit. It shows how the church spread the gospel from Jerusalem throughout the then-known world of the Roman Empire.

## Summary and Setting

There are good reasons to believe that Luke must have completed writing Acts around A.D. 62. First, the destruction of Jerusalem (A.D. 70), which would have been a huge event in relation to Luke and Acts, is mentioned as a prophecy (Luke 19:43, 21:6). With the strong themes of Jewish persecution of Christians and specifically of Paul, it is implausible to think that Luke completed Luke and Acts after the destruction of Jerusalem and its Temple, yet did not reference it. Thinking along these lines has led many scholars to conclude that all of the New Testament books were complete prior to A.D. 70, since there is no reference the destruction of the Temple. It would be like writing about Islamic terrorism in American and not referencing the terrorist actions of September 11, 2001. The silence is very loud.

Second, Acts ends with Paul in Rome under house arrest. It is believed that Paul was martyred under Nero in about A.D. 65. It is difficult to imagine why Luke would not have included Paul's death as a martyr if that took place prior to his completion of Acts.

Moreover, the date of Luke is important for an early dating of other books in the New Testament. Many scholars believe that Luke used the Gospel of Mark as a source. That places Mark prior to A.D. 62.

Most of the other New Testament texts, such as the Pauline epistles, fit within the travels of Paul as narrated by Luke.

Mary caring for God's son under the watchful gaze of angels and barnyard animals. This fresco is found in the lower church of St. Francis in Assisi—a building composed of two churches, one above the other. The upper church is bright and slender while the lower one is low and austere, containing many extraordinary allegorical frescoes.

## Worldview

We need stories. We need to hear the whole story rehearsed for us. The tension and the resolution of stories is built into the fabric of life. While this can be seen all through life, it can be most easily seen when you read a favorite story to a young child. Adults often read a book, and then set it aside to move on to other things. Not so for the two year old! Just as you finish the *The Very Hungry Caterpillar* or *Cat in the Hat,* what does the thrilled toddler often say? *"Read it again!"* You are ready for something new, but they take pleasure in hearing that same story over and over again. Hopefully, you have moved on in your literary tastes from Dr. Suess (if you have children, remember, *Green Eggs and Ham* will be at the top of your reading list again), but maybe you have a story or a movie that is like this. You can watch it many times without growing tired of it. As you watch it, you laugh more heartily as you understand the humor more deeply and your mind discovers the intricacies of the plot. If the story is really good, and if you have a community of friends that buys into it, you might even see many of the truths or humorous points of the movie being played out in real life. You might repeat lines of the story when your circumstances are like the ones in the movie. When something goes horribly wrong, and I am with friends, I might say, *"kickin' sitcheeayshun or paddlin' sitcheeayshun?"* or *"Where's the happy little tire swing?"* These are lines from a movie that we enjoy. Our lives have become ingrained in the story.

Thankfully, God has not left us with a blank screen or with antiseptic scientific terms and phrases. The Bible is not a book of equations. More than anything else it tells a story, a story grander than anything that has ever been heard. As Christians we know the basic events of the gospel. But just saying "Christ died for us" is not all there is to it. The story begins much earlier than this. We cannot understand Christ dying on the cross outside of understanding the earliest parts of the story. The first part of the story tells us that God created a wonderful, perfect world and placed our first father Adam in it. He gave Adam everything that he needed: a good job, a perfect working environment, good and diverse food and a perfect wife. More than this, God Himself was a friend to Adam. He talked with him and taught him. Adam, however, led our race in a rebellion against God by heeding the advice of God's enemy, the Devil. The

The *Presentation of Jesus in the Temple* by Rembrandt, completed 1627–1628. Here we see Simeon acknowledging his Savior, as God had promised him in Luke 2:21–38.

result of this rebellion, was exile, judgment and death. The story continues with Noah, Abraham, David and the prophets. At the gates of Eden, however, we get a preview of the end of the story. God could have abandoned the human race and left us all to serve Satan. That is what we had chosen. He, however, decides not to let us go, but instead to send the Seed of the Woman to crush the head of the Serpent. God punished the human race with death, but reveals that He intends to raise them to new life through the resurrection. In light of this, the cross makes sense and the love of God in the cross overwhelms us. This good news, this story of God's love, defines and creates reality and is the foundation of our lives. We live this story, and we need to rehearse the Fall and the patient hope of those in exile. Then there is great joy when we hear: "For there is born to you this day in the city of David a Savior, who is Christ the Lord" (Luke 2:11).

God has caused all of reality to teach us this story. Everywhere we look we can see the Fall and the gospel being played out before our very eyes. The seasons continually proclaim death and resurrection. Each meal sets forth the truth that our lives are sustained by the death of others before us. The story explains all of reality, so like little children, we need to learn to crave God's story and to enjoy seeing it played out before our eyes.

Jesus Christ is at the center of this story. We know of the birth, ministry, death and resurrection of Christ. No doubt, Theophilus knew this, too. Yet, as Luke provides a full narrative (replay) of Christ, we gain certainty and confidence. As a divinely inspired text, Luke and Acts add the central characters to the biblical portrait of the Triune God and His great salvation. In them we read directly of a humble King and Savior conceived by the Spirit of God in the womb of a virgin. Taken together, they are a magnificent contribution to the canon of the New Testament.

Beginning in the Gospel, we read of the familiar and unique narrative of the birth of Jesus Christ, and Acts ends with the gospel having been proclaimed to the entire, then-known world with Paul in Rome. While all of Scripture provides the truth of the work of God saving His people in history, the Gospel of Luke explains the central story of the incarnation of God's Son and His death and resurrection. Acts addresses the ongoing work of Christ through the church by the power of the Holy Spirit. It gives a narrative of the apostolic ministries of (primarily) Peter and Paul. Acts heralds the spread of the gospel from Jerusalem, to Judea and Samaria, to the "end" of the "earth" (Acts 1:8). This was preceded by the empowering of the apostolic messengers by the Spirit's coming at Pentecost.

What is history? How do we bring together all that has happened, and where will it end? Luke's sacred history centered on Christ. Acts, for example, according to John Calvin, is "the beginning of the reign of Christ, and, as it were, the renewal of the world is being depicted here. An account of the reign of Christ

In Rembrandt's *The Holy Family*, the artist creates a beautiful image of intimate, domestic happiness, Joseph gazing upon his Son as Mary plays with the toes of the Child.

beginning with his triumphant resurrection and exaltation, and continuing until his gospel has reached Rome itself, as Christ our king, puts all enemies under his feet." History is the unfolding of God's work. Luke makes it clear that the flow of time revolves around God's covenantal promise of redemption to the world. Beginning in Genesis 3:15, immediately after the Fall, there is a promise. The promise of Genesis 3:15 predicts a kingdom reign of a Messiah who will crush the head of the serpent. Throughout all of history this reality has been unfolding. The revelation of the Abrahamic covenant (Gen. 12:1–3) shows God's work to redeem the world by sending a promised Seed, Christ. Abraham would be the father of many nations.

The covenant is the key to history. Luke repeatedly draws attention to the Abrahamic promise as preached by the apostles. This is at the center of the song that Zacharias sings in Luke 1, called the Benedictus (Luke 1:70–73):

As He spoke by the mouth of His holy
    prophets,
Who have been since the world began,
That we should be saved from our enemies
And from the hand of all who hate us,
To perform the mercy promised to our fathers
And to remember His holy covenant,
The oath which He swore to our father
    Abraham.

This promise is on the lips of Peter in his first few sermons beginning at Pentecost (Acts 2:39):

For the promise is to you and to your children,
and to all who are afar off, as many as the Lord
our God will call.

This promise is proclaimed in Paul's first sermon (Acts 13:32–33):

And we declare to you glad tidings—that
promise which was made to the fathers. God
has fulfilled this for us their children, in that
He has raised up Jesus...

The covenant is a beautiful promise of redemption.

*The Descent of the Spirit by Doré.* This woodcut depicts the coming of the Holy Spirit at Pentecost found in Acts 2:4. Doré was a very prolific artist who illustrated many biblical stories in woodcarvings.

Yet, there are also covenant judgments for those who break covenant with God. The Gospel of Luke pays careful attention to the judgment of God, especially in relation to the Temple. It begins with the Temple priesthood (Zacharias) and ends with believers in the Temple. Then the center of Luke is Christ's journey toward the holy place. He "steadfastly set His face to go to Jerusalem" (9:51) which culminates in His symbolically destroying the Temple and its work (Luke 19:45). Jesus says the words of Jeremiah, who foretold the covenantal judgment of Judah (Jer. 26:6). Jesus foretells the covenantal judgment of A.D. 70 (Luke 19:43–47):

"For days will come upon you when your
enemies will build an embankment around
you, surround you and close you in on every
side, and level you, and your children within
you, to the ground; and they will not leave in
you one stone upon another, because you did
not know the time of your visitation." Then He
went into the temple and began to drive out
those who bought and sold in it, saying to
them, "It is written, 'My house is a house of
prayer,' but you have made it a 'den of thieves.'"

Luke (by quoting Christ) provides, not only the high water mark of history with the coming of Christ and His work on the cross—Luke gives us the principle of interpreting all of the Scriptures. Jesus says of the Scriptures, "all things must be fulfilled which were written in the Law of Moses and the Prophets and the Psalms concerning Me" (24:44) Therefore, the Word of God is rightly understood as Christocentric or Christ-centered. He explains that the central meaning of all the Scriptures (of the Old Testament) is that the Christ was "to suffer and to rise from the dead the third day, and that repentance and remission of sins should be preached in His name to all nations, beginning at Jerusalem" (24:46–47).

Therefore, Luke's worldview rests on a sovereign Ruler. God is Lord of history (Acts 2:23, 4:28). Luke has a linear view of history with the kingdom of God flowing like a river through the beautiful land of time. The kingdom is mentioned over forty times in Luke. Evil will not prevail, but Satan will be overcome, even as light overcomes darkness (Luke 11:20).

Luke shows us an incarnational world. In history Christ was not a mere idea, but was incarnate. He came into history, and his way was prepared by the ministry of John (Luke 16:16, Acts 13:32). Luke shows the details of the birth more than any other biblical writer. In Luke's worldview God became man in Jesus' conception (Luke 1:35). In history, while Quirinius was governor and Augustus reigned, the incarnation took place.

Christ is the center of reality. His story makes sense of all reality, and it is echoing before our eyes everyday. What has happened in the past centers on the coming of Christ in the fullness of time to be born of Mary in Bethlehem to live, die and rise again and to be ascended. From that time forward Christ will empower his people to "be witnesses to Me in Jerusalem, and in all Judea and Samaria, and to the end of the earth" (Acts 1:8).

While Matthew provides the Trinitarian formula of the name of the "Father, Son and Holy Spirit," Luke shows us the Trinity with an emphasis on the incarnate Son, the promise of the Father and the work of the Spirit. The Spirit is emphasized. This is seen in Jesus' and John's births (Luke 1:35, 1:15, 17). The work and role of the Holy Spirit is emphasized more than in the other Gospels.

Finally, in Luke's worldview, God redeems the lowly. The "last shall be first." Luke is the writer who gives us the parable of the Good Samaritan. His concern for the poor and outcasts, sinners, Samaritans, Gentiles and women is very clear. Restoration and salvation come to the humble.

Knowing us and our needs, God treats us like the little children that we are (or should endeavor to become). He gives us a story and then rehearses it before us again and again. God's story, however, is not like three minute tales that we adored while we were in diapers and demanded to hear time and time again. It has a richness and complexity that will always overwhelm and exhilarate us. Our lives are not a learning and fascination with this story and then a discarding of it to move on to more interesting things. As believers we do not learn the gospel and then go on to deeper truths. There could be no deeper truth. Our lives consist in going deeply into gospel. Each day we learn to lay down our lives and take up our cross and follow after Christ. Every time we approach the Lord's Table, He offers Himself to us as our great paradigm of sacrifice. As we watch winter give way to spring, we witness death and resurrection, and then finally in the summer we see God's blessing, as death leads to resurrection and as resurrection bursts forth into life and life leads to harvest and the rehearsal of the story begins again. Jesus Christ sits as King over this story and as the central point of the story. Luke and Acts provides us with a glorious picture of Christ's work of life and death and His continuing work as His Spirit guides His church and leads them more deeply into the story.

—*Gregg Strawbridge*

## For Further Reading

*Veritas Press Bible Cards: Gospels.* Lancaster, Pa.: Veritas Press. 97–128.

*Veritas Press Bible Cards: Acts through Revelation.* Lancaster, Pa.: Veritas Press. 129–135, 137, 140, 144, 145.

Josephus, *The Jewish Wars.* In *The New Complete Works of Josephus,* Whiston, William, trans. Grand Rapids, Mich.: Kregel Publications, 1999.

# Session I: Prelude

## A Question to Consider

The term epistemology is the term for *how we know what we know.* How do you know something? How do you know something for certain?

*From the General Information above answer the following questions:*

1. What evidence is there that Luke was the author of Luke and Acts? Who was Luke?
2. When were Luke and Acts written? What arguments could you provide for this view?
3. Some critics believe the Bible is largely a collection of stories with no basis in historical fact. How would you describe Luke's writing?
4. How is the gospel story placed before us everyday?
5. How does Luke focus on the Temple?
6. How does Luke show us an "incarnational world?"

READING ASSIGNMENT:
Luke 1–18

Rembrandt depicts the twelve-year-old Jesus in the Temple in this etching from 1654. Luke 2:46-47 describes the young Jesus sitting and talking to the religious leaders of his day. Note his weary father in the lower right, approaching to take his boy home.

## SESSION II: DISCUSSION
Luke 1–18

### A Question to Consider

How does the gospel fit with the religion of the Old Testament? Does it replace it? Does it leave it unchanged? Does it fulfill it?

*Discuss or list short answers to the following questions:*

### Text Analysis

1. After carefully reading Luke 1:67–80, Zacharias's song called the *Benedictus,* list some of the main themes. Which of these themes also appear as parts of the larger themes of the entire work of Luke and Acts?

2. What is in the center of the message of the *Benedictus?*

3. What does this show us concerning God's covenant with Abraham?

### Cultural Analysis

1. Where in the broader Chrstian community do you see the belief that Jesus came to replace the Old Testament?

2. Why is our culture so blind to promises that reach back into the ancient past?

3. Does our culture's lack of Old Testament covenantal sense affect our ability to keep promises?

### Biblical Analysis

1. How would you explain to someone unacquainted with the Bible the reason for Jesus' birth as it was?

2. Where is the first promise of Savior found in Scripture?

3. What do other prophecies foretell about Christ (Deut. 18:15–19, Ps. 110, Isa. 53)?

4. Would He be a king?

5. How did God prepare the world for the coming of Christ?

*Communion of
the Apostles
by Fra Angelico,
1451–1453*

## SUMMA

*Write an essay or discuss this question, integrating
what you have learned from the material above.*
What is Jesus' relationship to the promises
given to Adam, Abraham and David?

## Optional Activity

On poster size paper or a chalk board make two
rows of large circles with about ten circles in each. In
each circle in the top row write the name of an
important person, place or thing from your general
knowledge of the Old Testament (e.g., Adam,
Abraham, Isaac, Jacob, Moses, Egypt, the law,
tabernacle, sacrifices, prophets, temple, exile). Then in
the bottom row of circles fill in names of people,
places and things from the first chapter of Luke (e.g.,
Herod, Judea, Zacharias, Elijah, temple, priesthood,
angels, covenant, prophets). Draw lines to connect the
dots if any relationship between the two items can be
asserted, then discuss the relationships.

### READING ASSIGNMENT:
Luke 19–24, Acts 1–8

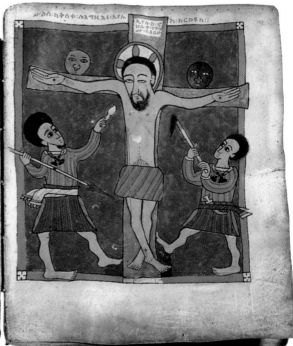

Two pages from a Gospel book tempera and ink on parchment (early- to mid-sixteenth-century Ethiopian). These manuscripts are very similiar to the Byzantine manuscripts that were made at the same time, hundreds of miles to the north.

# SESSION III: DISCUSSION
Luke 19–24, Acts 1–8

## A Question to Consider

What is the relationship of the gospel to civilization?

*Discuss or list short answers to the following questions:*

### Text Analysis

1. How is Rome related to the Gospel of Luke? (Luke 2; also think back to Livy's *Early History of Rome*)
2. How are Romans, soldiers and magistrates presented in Luke's writings? (Consider the following verses: Luke 7:6–9; 23:47; Acts 10:1–2; 27:1–3.)
3. What is the Apostle Paul's relation to Rome (Acts 19:21; 22:25–26; 23:11; 28:16)?

### Cultural Analysis

1. Does our culture recognize the importance of the gospel to civilization?
2. What is the gospel of our culture? On what principles are we trying to build an empire?
3. Is the "American Empire" Christian?

### Biblical Analysis

1. How are God's people related to the great world civilizations? Consider Ur (Mesopotamia) (Gen. 11:31), Egypt (Gen. 12:10, 50:7), Assyria (2 Kings 15:19), Babylon (1 Chron. 9:1), Persia (2 Chron. 36:20, Ezra 1:1), Greece (Dan. 8:21, 10:20) and Rome (Luke 2:1).
2. Will Christ's people ever be an Empire?

## SUMMA

*Write an essay or discuss this question, integrating what you have learned from the material above.*
Are Christians today part of an empire? Is America?

READING ASSIGNMENT:
Acts 9–19

# SESSION IV: DISCUSSION

Luke, Acts 1–19

## A Question to Consider

What is the gospel? Is it a message? Is it a power? Does it have a will of its own?

*Discuss or list short answers to the following questions:*

### Text Analysis

1. The "Great Commission" of Matthew 28:19–20 is well known. Is there a "Great Commission" in Luke? How is it similar to Matthew's? How is it different?
2. How is Luke 24:46–48 related to the larger themes of Luke?
3. Why is Acts 1:8 the key verse explaining the purpose of Acts? (Where is the "end" or the uttermost parts of the earth, if this is to be interpreted as the place into which the entire world flows?)
4. How does Acts 1:8 supply the outline for chapters 1 through 19 of the book of Acts?
5. Can you track the spread of the gospel by the baptismal examples in Acts? Fill in Chart 1, showing the movement of the gospel by the baptisms (the Great Commission says "baptizing them").

### Cultural Analysis

1. Does the church today still have a responsibility to be mission's minded?
2. What does the teaching and example of Acts mean for our vision of missions today?
3. Does your church support any missionaries? Where are they and what are they doing?

### Biblical Analysis

1. What is God's purpose regarding other nations in Genesis 12:3?
2. Does God care only about Israel in the Old Testament or are other nations his concern (Josh. 2, Jonah, Ruth, 2 Kings 5)?
3. How do the Psalms address other nations finding

---

> *Chart 1:* **THE SPREAD OF THE GOSPEL**
>
> | THE GOSPEL IN ACTS GOES TO . . . | WHO WAS BAPTIZED IN THESE PLACES |
> |---|---|
> | Jerusalem, Judea: (Acts 2) | |
> | Samaria: (Acts 8) | |
> | End of the Earth | |
> |    Transition: Apostle Paul (Acts 9) | |
> |    First Gentile: Cornelius (Acts 10) | |
> |    God-fearer: Lydia (Acts 16) | |
> |    New Convert Gentiles: The Jailer (Acts 16) | |
> |    Corinthians (Acts 18; 1 Cor. 1:14–16) | |
> |    Ephesus (Acts 19) | |

salvation (Ps. 2, 22 and 96)?

4. How does the concern for the Gentile nations arise in the ministry of Christ (Luke 4:25–26, Matt. 8:11)?

## SUMMA

*Write an essay or discuss this question, integrating what you have learned from the material above.* Where do you think the gospel is going today?

### READING ASSIGNMENT:

Acts 20–28

# SESSION V: RECITATION

Luke, Acts

## Comprehension Questions

*Answer the following questions for factual recall:*

1. For whom did Luke write his Gospel and Acts? (Luke 1:1–4)
2. Throughout the book of Luke, Christ's kingdom is announced in many ways. How is the kingdom announced at Christ's birth (Luke 1:31–34)?
3. How does the parable of the sower teach us about Christ's kingdom (Luke 8:4–15)?
4. How does the Lord's Supper show Jesus' disciples that they are participating in the kingdom (Luke 22:29–30)?
5. In what area is the gospel first proclaimed in Acts? (Acts 1:8–9)
6. What is the first border crossed as the kingdom message leaves Jerusalem and Judea?

*The Ascension* by Ford Madox Brown. Brown was born in France and was educated in various studios. Settling in England in 1846, he became a friend of the Pre-Raphaelites and was an influence on their work, though he was never a member of the Brotherhood.

7. How does the kingdom first come into contact with other nations (Rom. 9 and 10)?

8. How do Paul and Barnabas begin the missionary enterprise of the church (Acts 13:2)?

# OPTIONAL SESSION

## Draw a Chiasm

The Hebrews thought in parallels. This is seen in wisdom literature: Proverbs 1:2 says, "To know wisdom and instruction, to perceive the words of understanding." The second phrase is parallel with the first one and means the same thing using different words. A "chiasm" is a kind of parallel structure used frequently in the Bible. It is a literary tool used by biblical writers the way English poets use rhyme or meter. It has repetition of terms in a reverse pattern: A B C C B A. The name "chiasm" is from the Greek letter *chi* (X) which looks like an X. Most biblical chiasms emphasize the center of the *chi* (X marks the spot). What is really important is in the center. Here is an example of a simple chiasm (or you could come up with your own):

A The Crimson Tide deserve to lose.
    B The Eagles won by 40 points.
        C The Eagles rock.
        CC The Eagles rule.
    BB The Eagles won by a landslide.
AA The Tide is going down.

*Note:* Bible commentaries often mark the second series is this way A' B' C' (called "A prime," etc.).

Draw/write out the chiasm in the *Benedictus* of Luke 1:67–79.

Notice how the ideas relate to each other on each side of the chiasm. Why do you think the element at the center is being emphasized (Gen. 12, 15, 17; Rom. 4:13; Gal. 3:16)?

### ENDNOTES

1 This editor let such a wild dream remain in the text but wants the reader to know that even in a postmillennial society such dreams will not be realized. Southern Mississippi—you must be kidding!

2 *This endnote appears only in the teacher's edition.*

# AENEID

Which was more important; the Moon Landing or the Pilgrim Fathers landing at Plymouth Rock? Much can be said for the Moon Landing. It was the first time mankind landed on a natural object other than the earth. Neil Armstrong put it this way:

> One small step for man . . .
> one giant leap for mankind.

In a sense, he was right. He had gone where no man had ever gone, and his footsteps are still evident on the surface of the moon, as is the American flag.

Armstrong's trip to the moon is not like the landing of the Pilgrims, however, in one important way. No man is presently on the moon. Neil Armstrong was not coming to found a new civilization or establish a new country. He was just visiting (sort of like Columbus or Leif Erickson). A few other visitors followed. They drove around in a lunar rover. They even hit a few golf balls. The visit ended, and they left. It's been said that many technological advances that came out of the space program have benefited society, but nothing that Neil Armstrong did on the moon affected the cultural patterns of our lives.

On the other hand, the Pilgrims came to America to found a new civilization. This does not mean that they were rejecting everything from their mother culture, but even from the early days, they hoped that life in America would be different. We were to be a "city on a hill," a model country for others to pattern themselves after.

Thankfully, much that these early Puritans did became ingrained in the country that they helped found. Their religion became the religion of our country. Their work ethic seeped into the fiber of their posterity. Their

Photo of Edwin Aldrin, Lunar Module pilot— taken by Neil Armstrong

hearty piety became a model for their descendants.

Now, sadly, most of our country has rejected the beliefs of the Pilgrim Fathers, but still, their lives affect us greatly. We have greatly benefited from the lives that they lived and the expectations that they set.

What would you do, if you were called upon to found a new civilization? What sort of life would you lead if you knew that your life would be the model that an entire country would seek to emulate? What if that was your destiny?

In the *Aeneid* we meet the great Trojan hero Aeneas. He is reeling from the destruction of the city he loved, Troy. More importantly, however, he is going to found a "New Troy," and he is living a life (with the able aid of the poet Virgil) that will set a pattern for one of the greatest empires ever.

Pay careful attention to his life. You too might found an empire like Rome.

## Author and Context

In contrast to our lack of knowledge about that other great epic poet, Homer, we know quite a bit about Virgil. His full name was Publius Vergilius Maro, and he was born on the 15th of October in the year 70 B.C. He studied for the law but was turned aside into literary pursuits. He had gone to Rome to study law around 53 B.C., where he may have met Octavian, the future emperor Augustus. The future emperor was seven years Virgil's junior. In 47 B.C. Virgil moved to the Naples area to study philosophy under a teacher named Siro. There he joined a circle of Epicurean thinkers, and upon the death of his instructor, he inherited his

instructor's villa. Virgil made a name for himself as a poet with his *Eclogues* and *Georgics*, both of them being cycles of poems celebrating farming and the rustic life of the country. Virgil was a fastidious writer—he did not just dash off his work. He worked on the *Aeneid* from 30 B.C. to 19 B.C., which was the year he died. When he died, the poem was still in draft form (at least according to him), and so he ordered in his will that the manuscript be destroyed. That order was countermanded by Augustus, who commanded Varius Rufus and Plotius Tucca to edit the poem, but to make no additions of their own. Such are the turns of Providence, that here you are today, studying a two-thousand-year-old poem. The decision of an ancient Roman emperor has directly affected what you will be doing this week!

Venus, the Roman goddess of love, was married to the Roman god Vulcan but was the mother of Aeneas by a shepherd named Anchises. The most famous statue of this goddess is the *Venus de Milo*. In 1820 the sculpture was found on the Aegean island of Melos by a peasant named Yorgos. He hid it from the authorities but was later discovered by Turkish officials, who seized the sculpture. A French naval officer, Jules Dumont d'Urville, recognizing its importance, arranged for it to be purchase by the French ambassador to Turkey. After some repairing, the statue was presented to King Louis XVIII, who eventually presented it to the Louvre museum in Paris. The sculptor is unknown, and the date of origin is estimated to be the second century B.C. It is believed that originally one arm held a shield and the other a mirror. The drapery around her hips and legs, with its intricately carved folds, resemble the swirling garments worn by another famous Hellenistic statue—the glorious Nike of Samothrace.

## Significance

This epic poem may be considered as the central *aesthetic apologetic* (i.e., it is an attempted demonstration of Rome's beauty and goodness) for the Roman Empire. It is wonderfully done and has had an enormous impact over the course of the centuries. Virgil lived at precisely the time the Roman Republic was in fact becoming the Roman Empire, and as a friend of Augustus, he presented the case for the inevitability of Rome's greatness, and he did so very capably. Virgil lived through the assassination of Julius Caesar, he had to deal with the fact of Cicero's execution, and he was part of the turmoil in Rome that led to Augustus becoming the emperor. Julius had been an emperor in fact but not in name. Augustus was emperor in both fact and name, and he appears to have been a decent human being (as distinguished from some of his successors like Nero).

But at the same time, Christians need to take special care to think biblically on this subject. Augustus was the first to receive divine honors while he was alive, and the cult of emperor worship which he encouraged was particularly strong in Asia Minor, a region the apostle John had to address on the subject a short time later. John clearly identifies the Empire (which Virgil saw as glorious) as a Beast. How are we to reconcile all this? That will be a central part of our task in the worldview essay.

## Main Characters

Aeneas is a Trojan warrior and hero who survives the fall of Troy and whose destiny is to build a new Troy. His father is Anchises, and his son is named Ascanius (or Iulus). On the way to Italy, he stops in Carthage where he has a love affair with the queen, whose name is Dido. Latinus is the king of the Latins in Italy, and he is one who wants to welcome the Trojans. He is willing to give his daughter Lavinia to Aeneas in marriage. This arrangement is objected to by the queen, Amata, as well as by a local suitor for Lavinia's hand, the great warrior Turnus. Evander is a local king who comes to the aid of Aeneas, and his son Pallas is a significant figure in the subsequent conflict.

The gods are their usual capricious selves, and they include Jupiter, the king of the gods, Juno his wife (who is the patroness of Carthage and hostile to Aeneas), Venus (lover of Anchises and Aeneas's mother), Mercury, Minerva and Neptune. You are probably acquainted with all these gods and goddesses, but you will have to get used to their Roman names now that we are studying Latin poetry. Jupiter is Zeus (say "Zeus father" or "Zeus pater" three times really fast to see where the name Jupiter came from). Juno is Hera, Neptune is Poseidon, Minerva is Athena, Mercury is Hermes and Venus is Aphrodite.

## Summary and Setting

The setting of the poem is at the time of the Trojan War, which makes Aeneas a contemporary of Odysseus (or, to use his Roman name, Ulysses). They are both wandering the Mediterranean at the same time, which comes out when Aeneas encounters someone from Ulysses' crew. If we were to put them on a biblical timeline, they would be shortly before the reign of King David and belong to the same era. At the same time, there is a great difference between the works of Homer and this poem by Virgil. Homer wrote just a few centuries after the events he was describing, and in many ways he belonged to the same world. Virgil is describing them almost a thousand years later, and his poem is more about "modern" Rome than it is about ancient times.

Aeneas flees the destruction of Troy, and it quickly becomes apparent that his destiny is to found a new Troy. Different places for his band of refugees to settle do not work out, but the most promising of these is Carthage, where Aeneas becomes the queen's lover (or as *she* thinks of it, husband). But his destiny catches up with him, and he is forced to sail for Italy—leaving Dido in ruins and creating eternal enmity between Carthage and Rome. When he arrives there, war results from the rivalry of Aeneas and Turnus for the hand of Lavinia.

## Worldview

One of the most famous metaphors in the history of the world is the image that Jesus gave to Nicodemus in the third chapter of the Gospel of John. It is such a famous metaphor that people have stopped thinking about it. But what would it be like to really be born *again?*

The image certainly had Nicodemus scratching his head, wondering how it would be possible for a man to return to his mother's womb and be born over again. How could *that* work? But of course, as believing Christians know, Jesus was talking about the wonderful work of the Holy Spirit, who creates a new heart in an individual when he is converted. Unless that happens, Jesus said, a man will not see the kingdom of heaven. But less well-known is the fact that Jesus was also pointing to the rebirth of the whole nation of Israel, which happened at Pentecost shortly after this. Not only was Nicodemus born again (as an individual), so was all Israel reborn when she became the church.

Because of how God made the world, images of rebirth are inescapable, and it is not surprising that pagans and unbelievers resort to them as well. It is virtually impossible not to. For example, you have an image of death every night when you go to sleep and an image of rebirth every morning when you get up. And if you are particularly hard to get out of bed, your mother might even be persuaded that it is a *miraculous* rebirth!

We have the same pattern of death and resurrection in the seasons. Autumn is an obvious picture of aging and dying, winter pictures death, and spring is the time of rebirth. This obvious metaphor of rebirth is central in many pagan fertility religions, and it is present (although obviously in a different way) in the Scriptures as well.

So rebirth is a picture of new beginnings, and this image of a transforming new birth is absolutely essential for understanding the *Aeneid* properly. Furthermore, it is important to note that Virgil's use of this corresponds (in one sense) to how God made the world, and this accounts for part of the reason his poetry is so powerful. In another sense, Virgil is pointing to and honoring a "reborn Rome"—but the Rome he was honoring was godless. Within several generations, that same Rome became guilty of the blood of countless saints. In other words, the motif of a new birth (as Virgil rendered it) was not powerful enough to bring about a *true* transformation—there is only one Savior, only one way to bring about genuine transformation.

In order to understand how this attempt at describing a cultural rebirth failed, we have to recognize how Virgil made the statement in the first place.

The first and most obvious has to do with the transformation of Aeneas as an individual Trojan into a depersonalized symbol of Rome itself. The first half of the poem gives us a very three-dimensional figure. Aeneas laments the loss of his city and his wife, gets discouraged at the repeated failures of the refugees to find a place to live, falls in love with Dido, and so forth. Aeneas is a very human figure in the first half of the poem. But in the second half he "flattens out" considerably, to use the language of character development in literature, and this is not because Virgil was right in wanting the poem destroyed. This was not a flaw in the poem but is rather one of the great artistic features of the poem. This flattening is deliberate, as Aeneas is being transformed into the father of his country. He dies as an individual and is reborn as Rome itself.

To get an idea of the potency of "father of our nation" images, try to imagine George Washington brushing his teeth or trying to get mud off his shoes. In this poem, an individual is being transformed into a symbol of the great Roman Empire. Aeneas is being turned into that august picture of George Washington that used to look down upon us little schoolchildren in my elementary years.

We can see the beginning of this transformation by Book 5, when funeral games for Anchises are held in Sicily, *and Aeneas does not participate in them.* He is no longer an individual hero, competing with the others. In the next book, he descends into Hades, visits with the dead, and then returns to the land of the living. This descent to the Underworld clearly shows

This late-fifteenth-century dish depicts Aeneas arriving at Delos.

Virgil's intent. Aeneas comes back from the dead reborn. And when he does, it is with his chief characteristic (pietas or piety) reinforced and laid wholly at the feet of Rome. Aeneas is known as "pious Aeneas" from the beginning, but in the first half of the poem that pietas is constantly buffeted and tested. In the latter half of the poem, it does all the buffeting. Peter Leithart comments on this:

> Books 1–6 focus on Aeneas's conflict with his own *furor*—his passion for Dido, his despair and self-pity when things go wrong, his wish to return to Troy. If Aeneas is to achieve his destiny and face the dangers of founding the

Roman people, he must become wholly *pius*. Having gained control of his own passions, Aeneas is prepared for the external conflict that dominates Books 7–12, in which Aeneas battles not his own *furor* but the madness of Turnus.

One important qualification must be made here. By piety, it should not be understood in the modern sense that this word has taken on. In the ancient world, piety meant devotion to duty. Aeneas left Dido because of the demands of piety, that is, because of the demand of duty. He did not leave Dido with any particular sanctimonious expression on his face.

A second way to see what Virgil is up to is in his doctrine of reincarnation, which is, as doctrines go, *obviously* a doctrine of rebirth. And when Aeneas visits with Anchises in Hades, one of the things they do together is observe great spirits who have drunk from the river Lethe and then have forgotten their past. Having done so, they assume new identities in preparation for their new life in establishing the future Rome. Anchises points out the spirits who will eventually lead Rome to greatness, and so the hall of fame for all of Roman history is gathered there in Hades before it happens. Aeneas, still alive, is there, and of course he is the founder of it all. But also present are Romulus, Brutus, Cato, the Gracchi, Julius Caesar and, of course, Augustus. "The son of a god, Augustus Caesar, founder of a new age of gold, in lands where Saturn ruled long ago; he will extend his empire beyond the Indies."

The subtext is that if Rome is built by reborn spirits, Rome *is* a reborn spirit. When Aeneas arrives in Hades to see Anchises, he finds his father already contemplating the greatness of his descendants. "Deep in a valley of green, father Anchises was watching, with deep earnestness, the spirits whose destiny was light, and counting them over, all of his race to come, his dear descendants, their fates and fortunes and their works and ways ..."

Third, the occasion of the poem is also a testimony to this necessary theme of rebirth. In order to provide an effective apology for the Roman Empire, it was necessary to show that the glory that Rome was entering into was inevitable. But nothing is inevitable simply because a history is invented for it. For example, many of the participants in the funeral games of Anchises were ancestors of the great Roman houses of Virgil's day. A fictionalized past is an easy and cheap way to get current glory, and yet scrupulously honest genealogical research usually turns up as many horse thieves as it does Danish princes. While Virgil is flattering the aristocracy of his day, it is not *merely* flattery. He is not flattering aristocrats in a vacuum.

After a series of civil wars (in which he defeated Pompey), Julius Caesar assumed imperial authority without the dignity of the title *emperor*. Then Julius Caesar was assassinated in 44 B.C., and Rome was again thrown into a period of civil war. In 31 B.C. Octavian (Augustus) defeated Marc Anthony at the battle of Actium, and power was consolidated in his hands. But everyone knew (in principle, from weary experience) just how tenuous *that* kind of power could be. Virgil began work on the *Aeneid* the very next year, and it has to be recognized what a critically important work it was. A new regime is nothing without legitimacy, and conquerors are almost never content to have their legitimacy rest upon raw military power alone. No, it was necessary to authenticate the status quo through appeal to ancient realities. This was not being done for reasons of vanity, but rather as a means of governing—holding everything together. This is probably why (incidentally) Augustus permitted the abomination of Caesar worship. He was personally embarrassed by it, but went along with it for reasons of state. But the reason why this course of action (even with "good" motives) is so iniquitous can be seen in the horrible corruption of the subsequent emperors, some of whom were world-class dirt bags. And if there is one thing worse than a decent man who allows men to worship him as a god, it is a vile human being demanding to be worshiped as a god.

In short, when Virgil began this poem, Rome had just been reborn. But would the newborn baby survive? This rebirth had occurred on two levels. The first was that the ancient Roman republic had died, and it had to be shown that this republic was not being supplanted by a tyranny, but rather that the noble and great republic had died and had now been reborn in nobler and greater form. A doctrine of rebirth allows for an honoring of the past while simultaneously not following that past. The same kind of thing can be seen with the United States—our nation was established as a republic, but it has now become a democratic empire. As an empire, we still want to honor the Constitution and George Washington while simultaneously not paying any serious attention to them. The only way to do this (apart from schizophrenia) is through some sort of doctrine of death and rebirth.

For Virgil, this was the longer-term vision of death and rebirth for Rome. But there was a short-term vision of the same thing. Not only had the republic become the empire, but the chaos of recent civil wars had become the stability of Augustan peace. This element of rebirth was the one that Virgil himself had lived through. Remember the decade or more of turmoil between Julius Caesar's death and the ascension of Augustus to the imperial throne.

Fourth, we can see the distinction that Virgil makes between rebirth and reenactment. After the fall of Troy, the wife of Hector (Andromache) was taken as a war prize by the son of Achilleus, a man named Pyrrhus. Later, Andromache is taken by Helenus, a Trojan and another son of Priam. They build a city named Buthrotum, but it is a city based on nostalgia. It is not the future. In order to have a future, Troy must cease to be Troy and become Rome. Ironically, in order to live, Troy must die. This is why a concession made to Juno near the end of the poem is far more than a simple peace-keeping device. Juno acquiesces in the founding of Rome so long as it is not called Troy or Trojan. It *is* Trojan, and hence the glory, but it must not *be* Trojan—because death and rebirth are necessary. This is more than a simple trick by Virgil, telling a "just so" story, explaining why Rome is called Rome and not Troy.

Fifth, we should note Virgil's intent by comparing the shield of Aeneas with the shield of Achilleus. The notions of heroism are vastly different in Homer and in Virgil. In Homer, the glory of the individual warrior was crucial. Achilleus removed himself from the battle because his personal sense of glory was insulted, and things go badly for the Greeks as a result. Virgil has the same thing happen—Aeneas is removed from the battle—but it is because he is getting help and not because he is in a fit of pique. Aeneas has a far stronger sense of *pietas* (duty to his people) than does Achilleus. The *Iliad* begins with the rage of Achilleus and the *Aeneid* ends with the rage of Aeneas. But the occasions for the rage are extraordinarily different. Achilleus is enraged because Agamemnon insulted him by taking a woman from him. Aeneas is enraged because he sees the belt of Pallas, the son of an important ally, on Turnus, and Aeneas had vowed revenge for the death of Pallas. Aeneas at the end of the poem is Rome, administering justice.

This can be seen by comparing the shields of the two heroes. Both shields are given by divine mothers, both are crafted by gods and both reflect what the warriors carrying them are fighting for. The shield of Achilleus is filled with personal and individual scenes from everyday life. The individual note is struck. The shield of Aeneas is political and corporate. The social note is struck. To take modern examples, it is as though Achilleus's shield had the image of a farmer in Iowa, laboring with his corn, and the shield of Aeneas had an image of the inauguration of George Washington. All of this is to say that Homer was a blind bard who sang for marauding chieftains, and Virgil was a court poet, a friend of the most powerful man in the world. And it shows.

There is therefore no question but that Virgil is seeking to show us a Rome made new, a Rome reborn. He points to this in many ways, and while reading the poem, a fruitful exercise would be to look for other statements of this theme of rebirth in addition to those listed above. The general direction however is clear.

What is the Christian critique of this? It is, in summary, that all such attempts are satanic. But we need to qualify this in important biblical ways. When we think of things that are diabolical or satanic, we tend to think of troubled teenagers drawing pentagrams on the floor, along with a goat head or two. But this is a radical misunderstanding of what Satanism is. We must never forget that this is what our Lord Jesus was tempted to become. And part of this was the fact that He was shown the glory of all earthly empires. This surely included the glory of Rome, the empire that Jesus lived under. What does Scripture say?

> Again, the devil took Him up on an exceedingly high mountain, and showed Him all the kingdoms of the world *and their glory.* And he said to Him, "All these things I will give You if You will fall down and worship me." Then Jesus said to him, "Away with you, Satan! For it is written, 'You shall worship the LORD your God, and Him only you shall serve'" (Matt. 4:8–10, emphasis added).

The devil did not show Jesus some ugly old thing. He showed Him something *glorious,* something that had dazzled Virgil. Augustus had found Rome made of brick, and left it made of marble. But this glory did not dazzle the Lord Jesus, and He would not worship Satan in order to receive these kingdoms as a gift. And the devil who would receive such worship is not a demon in a red suit, with pitchfork and horns. He is an angel of light, the Apostle Paul tells us. "And no wonder! For Satan himself transforms himself into an angel of light. Therefore it is no great thing if his ministers also transform themselves into ministers of righteousness, whose end will be according to their works" (2 Cor. 11:14).

Virgil was not naïve about the costs of empire—as can be seen throughout this epic—and he was extremely sensitive to the suffering caused by the demands of pietas. It is pietas that demands that Aeneas leave Dido, and while Virgil clearly praises Aeneas for doing the right thing, he is also (equally clearly) sensitive to the human cost of this in the suffering of Dido. This is all the more striking because to make Dido a sympathetic character is counterintuitive to any apologist for Rome—she founded the city that was the archenemy of Rome, and it was her

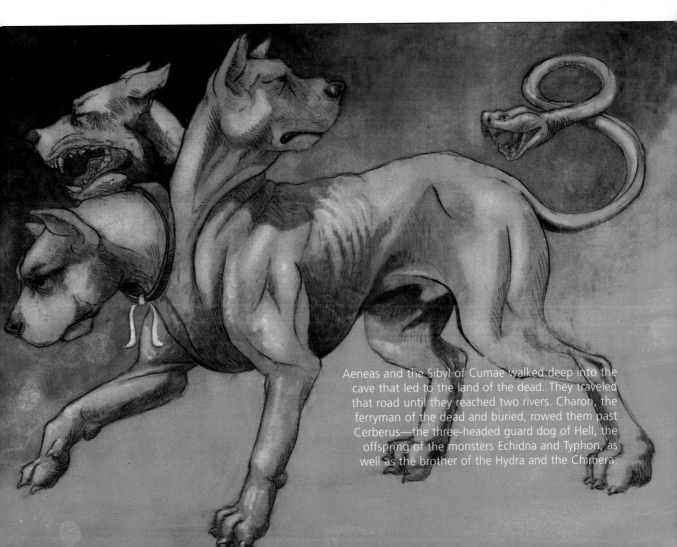

Aeneas and the Sibyl of Cumae walked deep into the cave that led to the land of the dead. They traveled that road until they reached two rivers. Charon, the ferryman of the dead and buried, rowed them past Cerberus—the three-headed guard dog of Hell, the offspring of the monsters Echidna and Typhon, as well as the brother of the Hydra and the Chimera.

As Dido's Carthage matured, elephants eventually became one of the main weapons of its armies. In one of the most storied attempts of Dido's Carthaginians to take revenge on Aeneas's Romans, Hannibal, the great Carthaginian general, crossed into Spain and led a herd of elephants through the Alps to attack Rome from the north. He used his elephants to charge into the Roman legion and break up their lines, with devastating effect.

words would seem to a Christian in the mid to late sixties, after the outbreak of the Neronian persecution. According to the Roman historian Tacitus, Nero had Christians trussed up and set on fire to provide light for a dinner party. The degradation that had come to Rome within such a short space of time was remarkable, and yet, to the faithful Christian, hardly surprising. How can *any* form of idolatry come to a good end?

Still, consider the words of Anchises. The beginning was promising. Roman law was famous, and the words "under law" were emphasized by them. In the same way, the *pax Romana* did bring in peace after a fashion, in that rough and ready way that empires have. But to battle the haughty and spare the meek it would be necessary to do something other than slaughter the meekest people who had ever lived and promote the bloodthirsty brutes who were particularly good at slaughtering the meek.

bitterness that brought about that enmity. But at the same time, Virgil also knew the costs of "no empire," and those costs would be even greater human suffering. So when I say that Virgil was "dazzled," I do not mean that he was swept off his feet. Rather, he knew that empire was necessary to hold everything together, and he also knew that empires are not established with so-so support. And so Virgil gave his considerable gifts to highlighting the glory that was Rome. And as we have seen, Scripture acknowledges the *fact* of that glory.

Like Virgil, the thinking Christian sees the Roman Empire as a mixed bag. But some of the things that were positive goods for Virgil were rejected by Christians as either evil or impotent. In Hades, Anchises says, "Remember, Roman, to rule the people under law, to establish the way of peace, to battle down the haughty, to spare the meek. Our fine arts, these, forever." It is hard for us to grasp how *ironic* these

This is why the New Testament writers, while encouraging Christians to honor the emperor and the established authorities (Rom. 13:1–7; 1 Pet. 2:17), are also under no illusions about the nature of the system they were up against. Paul knew that the Roman emperor would set himself up to be worshiped (2 Thess. 2:3), and the apostle John was even more specific. The beast in Revelation is Rome, indicating that John and Virgil had quite a different perspective. And Virgil's friend Augustus Caesar, the one whose decision preserved this poem for us, was the second head of that famous seven-headed beast.

Here is the mind which has wisdom: The seven heads are seven mountains on which the woman sits. There are also seven kings. Five have fallen, one is, and the other has not yet come. And when he comes, he must continue a short time. The beast that was, and

is not, is himself also the eighth, and is of the seven, and is going to perdition (Rev. 17:9–11).

Just as New York is the Big Apple, and New Orleans is the Big Easy, and Chicago is the Windy City, so Rome in the ancient world was the city of seven hills. And the seven heads of the beast represented this, and represented seven kings as well. And the second head of this beast, Caesar Augustus, the one in whose reign the Lord Jesus was born, was the patron of this great and glorious work of art.

Why should we study it then? It is a great and glorious work of literature, and we study it as Christians, understanding how it functioned in its time, and how it should function in ours. The Christian gospel has triumphed in the world, and we have brought back from our wars with the ancient gods and realms many trophies and souvenirs. This

poem is among them.

It is not likely that Luke, master of the deft understatement, was unaware of what he was doing in the ninth chapter of Acts, when he lampoons the impotence of Rome in creating a true human culture, a true human civilization. Just imagine a modern novel in which the village idiot was named Thomas Jefferson. Would that sort of thing happen by *accident?*

Now it came to pass, as Peter went through all parts of the country that he also came down to the saints who dwelt in Lydda. There he found a certain man named Aeneas, who had been bedridden eight years and was paralyzed. And Peter said to him, "Aeneas, Jesus the Christ heals you. Arise and make your bed." Then he arose immediately. So all who dwelt at Lydda

This wounded Amazon is part of a race of fierce warrior women of myth and legend. From birth they were brought up to be warriors. Their main weapons were the bow, the librys (a double edged axe), and a crescent shaped shield. The Amazons were said to be able to tame and ride horses long before the Greeks learned the skill. Some say there were two Amazon queens, one who ruled over domestic affairs and one who ruled over battle and warfare.

and Sharon saw him and turned to the Lord" (Acts 9:32–35).

Aeneas, the one who had carried his own father out of burning Troy, is here shown as paralyzed, incapable of carrying anyone. Moreover, this same Aeneas bore out of that destruction the gods of Troy. But the bearer of the ancient gods could do so no longer—he was paralyzed. Further than this, look at how Luke phrases the words of healing, with particular emphasis on the names. "Aeneas, Jesus the Christ heals you." Aeneas was healed by Peter, and as a result, all who dwelt in that region of the Roman Empire, celebrated with great honor by Virgil, looked at this healing of Aeneas and they turned to the Lord—or, more to the point, they turned to *another* lord, a Lord indeed.

Aeneas could no longer carry anyone. Aeneas needed to admit his need of a Savior, and needed to be carried himself by the healing power of the Lord Jesus.

—*Douglas Wilson*

## For Further Reading

Spielvogel, Jackson. *Western Civilization*. Fifth Edition. Belmont, Calif.: Wadsworth/Thomson Learning, 2003. 137–138.

*Veritas Press History Cards: New Testament, Greece and Rome.* Lancaster, Pa.: Veritas Press. 3, 4, 8.

# SESSION I: PRELUDE

## A Question to Consider

Does every person have a *destiny?*

*From the General Information above answer the following questions:*

1. What are some things we know about Virgil?
2. When was the *Aeneid* completed? What happened to the manuscript?
3. What is the primary purpose of the *Aeneid?*
4. Who is Aeneas, and when in history does he come onto the scene?
5. What exactly is he destined to do?
6. On his journey to Italy what enemy city of Rome does Aeneas visit? What happens there?
7. Who objects to Aeneas's marriage to Lavinia?
8. What significant gods and goddesses are involved in Aeneas's story? Give their Greek counterparts.
9. What is the difference between how Aeneas is portrayed in the first half of the book as opposed to how he is portrayed in the second half?
10. What key event in Book 6 marks his transformation?
11. What is *pietas?* What role does it play in this poem?
12. Who is in Hades along with Anchises?

 **READING ASSIGNMENT:** Book 1

# SESSION II: DISCUSSION

Book 1

## A Question to Consider

What is the most important thing that you can accomplish in life?

*Discuss or list short answers to the following questions:*

### Text Analysis

1. How does Virgil state that Aeneas came to Italy? Who worked against him in his mission? Why?
2. In Greek and Roman mythology, the goddess of strife, Eris, threw a golden apple before the goddesses of Mount Olympus, stating that it was a prize for the most beautiful one. The three goddesses who claimed it, Juno, Venus and Minerva, decided to have Paris, a Trojan and supposedly the most handsome of all mortal men, settle the matter. While each tried to bribe him, in the end he gave the apple to Venus because she offered him Helen, the most beautiful woman on earth. The fact that Helen was the wife of a Greek king only made matters worse. When Paris took Helen away, the Greeks gathered a great army and set sail for Troy, initiating the Trojan war. Are Juno's actions surprising in light of what you know about the gods?
3. What other factors are working against Aeneas? How does he respond?

### Cultural Analysis

1. How would our culture assess Aeneas and his mission?
2. What is the general view in our culture concerning Fate?
3. How much does our culture value doing one's duty?
4. What keeps people in our culture from doing their duty when they need to?

### Biblical Analysis

1. What does Scripture say is the most important thing we can accomplish in life?
2. How does this square with Aeneas's mission?

## SUMMA

 *Write an essay or discuss this question, integrating what you have learned from the material above.* Do we have a fate?

 **READING ASSIGNMENT:** Book 2

# SESSION III: WRITING

## Progymnasmata

This session introduces another of the writing exercises called the *progymnasmata.* Recall that these exercises in composition introduced the beginning student to basic forms and techniques that would then be used and combined when practicing more advanced exercises and speeches. One of these progymnasmata was called an *impersonation*. The impersonation seeks to imitate the style and characteristics of the person making the speech. To compose an impersonation:

- Discuss or think through the characteristics of the person whose speech you are emulating.
- Read carefully through the speech or event that you are impersonating (in many cases you will be asked to write an impersonation of a speech that a person has not given, but could have made at a certain time).
- Put the book away and write the speech yourself.
- Read it to someone else.
- After reading it, explain how different personal characteristics of this person come through in your impersonation.

Be careful to remember what has happened in the personal history of the character on which you are writing, and also remember what will happen in the future. You must to remember to keep everything in the proper setting (i.e., you can not make the young George Washington say, "I will be the first president under the new Constitution of the United States," because when he was a boy, of course, neither the Constitution nor the office existed, let alone the country itself).

In the times of Aeneas, people honored a relative who died by holding funeral games. Running was one of the popular events at these games. Aeneas held games to honor his father, Anchises.

*Aeneas had to tell a story of his great battle. Write an impersonation of Aeneas retelling his story. Incorporate at least two items: first, the emotion Aeneas was feeling as he recounted the past; and second, the sense of destiny Virgil meant to convey in this portion of the poem.*

READING ASSIGNMENT:
Book 3

# SESSION IV: RECITATION
Books 1–3

## Comprehension Questions

*Answer the following questions for factual recall:*

1. What are some words used to describe Aeneas in the opening lines?
2. What are some words used to describe Juno?
3. According to book 1, lines 40–41, why is Juno angry?
4. What adjectives are used to describe the founding of the Roman people?
5. After surviving the storm and landing on the coast of Libya, Aeneas receives a visit from his mother, Venus. What does she tell him?
6. How are Aeneas and his companions received by Dido?
7. What story does Aeneas tell in Book 2?
8. What emotions are evoked as Aeneas tells the story?
9. The portion of the story in Book 2 ends with what sad realization?
10. After Aeneas and his companions leave Troy they sail to Thrace where a funeral is held. Whose funeral is it? How did his death come about?
11. What did Apollo tell Aeneas about where to go? How was this interpreted?
12. What was wrong with his father's interpretation? How does this reinforce a key theme of the Aeneid?
13. Aeneas continues telling his story to Dido. While he includes many details in his story, he is stressing one primary theme. What is that important point that drives his understanding of their plight?

READING ASSIGNMENT:
Book 4

# SESSION V: DISCUSSION
Book 4

## A Question to Consider

What constitutes a marriage?

*Discuss or list short answers to the following questions:*

### Text Analysis

1. In the beginning of Book 4 what draws Dido to Aeneas?
2. What is the basis of the advice given by Dido's sister?
3. What effect does Dido's desire for Aeneas have on the fulfillment of her duties as queen?
4. When Juno sees what is happening, what does she want to do? Why? Are the gods consistent in their counsel concerning the relationship between Aeneas and Dido? Explain.
5. After Aeneas and Dido enter into a sexual relationship, Aeneas is reminded of his duty to go to Italy. How does Dido handle the "break up?"

### Cultural Analysis

1. How would Aeneas and Dido's relationship be viewed today?
2. What parallels can be drawn between what drew the two together and what generally draws people together in our culture?
3. How does our culture understand commitment, marriage and terminating relationships?

### Biblical Analysis

1. What insight does Scripture give concerning the nature of marriage?
2. How does Scripture address the popular view of marriage as a union with no real commitment?
3. Give a biblical critique of the "marriage" of Aeneas and Dido (Rom. 6:12–14, 2 Cor. 6:12–14).

## SUMMA

*Write an essay or discuss this question, integrating what you have learned from the material above.*
Are Dido and Aeneas ever married?

# SESSION VI: ACTIVITY

## Dido's Lament

The opera *Dido and Aeneas* was composed by Henry Purcell, an English composer of the seventeenth century. The opera was first performed in 1689 and is unique in that the heroes and heroines of pre-nineteenth-century operas almost never die. In this opera, of course, Dido commits suicide. The opera is divided into six sections:

SCENE ONE: Dido's Palace
SCENE TWO: Dido's Palace
SCENE THREE: The Witches' cave *(Cave Scene)*
SCENE FOUR: The Grove *(Grove Scene)*
SCENE FIVE: Harbour
SCENE SIX: Dido's death

Dido sings a very emotional song just before her self-inflicted death, known as "Dido's Lament." Here is the text:

**RECITATIVE:**

Thy hand, Belinda; darkness shades me:
On thy bosom let me rest:
More I would, but Death invades me:
Death is now a welcome guest.

**SONG:**

When I am laid in earth,
may my wrongs create
No trouble in thy breast;
Remember me, but ah! forget my fate.

*Listen to Dido's Lament. (This track is available online at www.veritaspress.com/store/SL_Resource_Download.asp.)*

*Consider these questions:*

1. What has death done to Dido?
2. What has death become to Dido?
3. What does Dido continually cry for in the lament?
4. What does she ask to be forgotten?
5. What emotional response does the music cause in you?
6. How does knowing the story help you to feel the music?
7. Should we pity Dido?

## Optional Activity A

Listen to the entire opera *Dido and Aeneas*. What is the main area in which the opera differs from the actual story in the *Aeneid?*

---

*Chart 1:* **PAGANISM AND CHRISTIANITY**

| **AENEAS** (Pious Paganism) | **DIDO** (Passionate Paganism) | **CHRISTIANITY** |
|---|---|---|
| God: | God: | God: |
| Man: | Man: | Man: |
| Sin: | Sin: | Sin: |
| Commitments: | Commitments: | Commitments: |

---

## Optional Activity B

Go and see a performance or rent a video of the entire opera of *Dido and Aeneas*.

**READING ASSIGNMENT:**
Book 5

## SESSION VII: ANALYSIS
Book 5

### Worldview Analysis

Compare and contrast the worldviews of Aeneas (pious paganism) and Dido (passionate paganism) with Christianity by completing Chart 1. Follow the models of the other two worldviews to construct your answers. For our purposes here, we are constructing a chart with four categories (God, man, sin, commitments). There could be other areas in which to compare their views.

### Optional Activity: *Funeral Games*

Set up some funeral games of your own and have a competition. While some events in the Aeneid might be difficult to repeat, many are quite easy. Here are some events to try:

**100 YARD DASH**
**1/2 MILE RACE**
**ARCHERY CONTEST**
**ARM-WRESTLING** (for the boys)
**GYMNASTICS** (for the girls)
**LONG JUMP**
**BADMINTON**

**READING ASSIGNMENT:**
Book 6

## SESSION VIII: DISCUSSION
Book 6

### A Question to Consider

What is life like after death?

*Discuss or list short answers to the following questions:*

### Text Analysis

1. How is Aeneas able to visit the underworld?
2. Who is his guide into Dis? Who is she? (*Hint: Check the glossary in the back of the book.*)
3. Why are some souls not permitted to cross the river Acheron?
4. What does Aeneas see individuals experiencing as he journeys through Dis? Who is the judge?
5. Who does Aeneas see amongst the suicides in Hades? How does she react to him?
6. What does Aeneas see in Elysium with Anchises?

### Cultural Analysis

1. How does this picture of the afterlife compare with popular views?
2. How likely would our culture accept the belief that there is a guide to the afterlife and that we can visit before we die?
3. How does the culture generally view the idea of a judge who determines our eternal fate?
4. According to our culture, who will go to heaven, and who will go to hell?

### Biblical Analysis

1. What does the Bible say about who may visit the afterlife before death (Heb. 9:27, 2 Cor. 5:8)?
2. What does Scripture state about where an individual will end up after death (Eph. 2:8, 9; Heb. 4)?

## Summa

*Write an essay or discuss this question, integrating what you have learned from the material above.*
How is the picture of Dis presented in the *Aeneid* consistent with hell? How is it different?

**READING ASSIGNMENT:**
Book 7

# Session IX: Recitation
Books 4–7

## Comprehension Questions

*Answer the following questions for factual recall:*

1. What is Dido thinking and feeling as Aeneas tells his story? What causes her to have hesitation? Who allays her concerns?
2. How does Juno get Venus to consent to the marriage between Aeneas and Dido?
3. What action does Jupiter then take?
4. Who tries to persuade Aeneas to stay? What is the result?
5. What does Dido finally do?
6. Where does the crew land after leaving Carthage?
7. What do they all do there?
8. What near-tragedy do they experience? Who saves them?
9. Where do they arrive at the beginning of Book 6?
10. Where does Aeneas visit in Book 6? Why?
11. When he visits Dis, who is Aeneas's guide? Who is the judge?
12. What do Aeneas and his father discuss?
13. Where does Aeneas arrive in Book 7? Who is there?
14. What does the voice from the Oracle of Faunus tell King Latinus?
15. What trouble does Juno stir up?

**READING ASSIGNMENT:**
Book 8

# Session X: Analysis

## Worldview Shields

Virgil's scenario of Aeneas receiving a richly decorated shield from the god Vulcan is drawn directly from Homer's *Iliad* (Vulcan's name is Hephaestus in the *Iliad*). Achilles is a warrior doomed to die in that epic poem, and his shield depicts scenes from Troy and a city in Greece. In the Greek city there are peaceful scenes of everyday life, while in Troy there is war and death. Depicted on the shield of Achilles:

1. Marriages are happening just like they always have.
2. Farming scenes, showing the normal change of the season and the harvest of crops.
3. War, with people being killed. This foreshadows the death of Achilles and demonstrates the fact that man is constantly at war.
4. Funeral with people being ushered into the Underworld. It is useless to try avoiding the Underworld and its hopelessness.
5. Fighting, illustrating the dissension among men.

Aeneas's shield in the *Aeneid*, on the other hand, reveals the glory of Rome in her victorious history. His shield foretells his wonderful destiny. Depicted on the shield of Aeneas:

1. The Roman Legion fighting victoriously. This points to the future Roman triumphs on the battlefield.
2. The Rape of the Sabines, referring to the founding of the city by force.
3. Romulus and Remus being fed by the she-wolf, the future glorious legend.
4. Senator Cicero arguing in the Forum, which illustrates the expansion and influence of Roman laws.
5. Great temples and theaters, depicting the glory of Rome's future.
6. Julius Caesar riding in triumph with many slaves in shackles. This foreshadows the riches and rule of Rome over the world.

*Complete Chart 2, comparing the two worldviews of Homer's Achilles and Virgil's Aeneas as depicted by the decorations on their shields.*

*Chart 2:* **WORLDVIEW SHIELDS**

|  | ROLE OF THE GODS | DESTINY | WHAT IT PICTURES | GENERAL TONE |
|---|---|---|---|---|
| Achilles' |  |  |  |  |
| Aeneas's |  |  |  |  |

## Optional Activity 1

Create your own artistic representation of either one or both of these shields.

## Optional Activity 2

Create an artistic representation of a Christian shield.

### READING ASSIGNMENT:

Book 9

# SESSION XI: DISCUSSION

Books 8 & 9

## A Question to Consider

Can someone escape fate?

*Discuss or list short answers to the following questions:*

### Text Analysis

1. In Book 8 how do Venus and Vulcan intervene on Aeneas's behalf?
2. What is depicted on the shield given to Aeneas?
3. In Book 9 what does Turnus attempt to do when he cannot find weaknesses in the defenses of the Trojans?
4. What is the result of Turnus's efforts?

### Cultural Analysis

1. How is this idea of escaping fate understood and interpreted in our culture today?
2. How does our culture use this language when it comes to destiny?

### Biblical Analysis

1. How does the Bible address the issue of escaping fate (Eph. 1:11)?
2. How do we respond then to the initial question, "Can we escape fate?" (Rom. 8:35–39)?

### SUMMA

*Write an essay or discuss this question, integrating what you have learned from the material above.* If the future is settled, why try?

### READING ASSIGNMENT:

Book 10

# SESSION XII: WRITING

## Progymnasmata

This writing assignment is one of the *progymnasmata,* called a *comparison.* You may remember doing your first comparison exercise while studying Plutarch's *Lives.* A comparison weighs one individual against another and makes a judgment about which one is the greatest. It expounds the virtue of a specific person over and against another (e.g., Joe is a stronger warrior than Ted), but does not talk about virtue in a general sense (e.g., strength in war is admirable).

Although the encomium has six parts, the comparison has five. This is because the fifth part of the encomium (the Comparison) is incorporated into the other parts when writing a comparison. The *Prologue* comes first. It introduces the topic and, at the end of the paragraph, states or implies the opinion of the writer. The second part of this exercise is a paragraph called *Description of Heritage* comparing the persons in question. The writer looks for ways to praise or disparage the subjects on account of their family history. For instance, if a person comes from righteous parents, then highlight the fact that he learned his righteous habits at home and added to the glory of the family name. In a comparison, remember that the two people that you are considering must be viewed in relation to each other. So you might say, "Both Teddy Roosevelt and Franklin Roosevelt came from strong families that taught them tenacity, but Teddy Roosevelt's family did a better job of training him in righteousness. Next comes a paragraph called *Description of Upbringing.* The point is to show how the individuals profited from good education or overcame faulty education. Again, make sure that you compare the two people in this paragraph. You might say, "Both Washington and Franklin had educations that in many ways were lacking, but Franklin exceeded Washington in this area, because he worked so hard to train himself in the art of language that he became one the nation's most popular writers." The most powerful part of the comparison comes next: the *Description of Deeds.* In this section the writer discusses the excellencies or evils of the mind, body and fortune of the subjects. For example, the writer praises the practice of philosophical virtue, the way the person looked and his wealth, influence or social stature. Since Christianity has transformed our society it seems out of place to dwell on physical appearance or possessions, so instead the paragraph should concentrate on the actions and motives of the subject. This can be especially powerful if his life demonstrates a pattern. Again, comparing the two subjects is critical. In this section, you might say, "Although Grant conquered Lee on the battlefield, Lee's stellar Christian life has outshone all of Grants accomplishments." The final paragraph is an *Exhortation or Prayer* in which others are called on to imitate the best in the examples.

*Write a comparison of Odysseus and Aeneas.*

I. Prologue
   • Introduce the topic

• State your opinion

II. Description of Heritage
   • Praise or condemn them on account of their family histories

III. Description of Upbringing
   • Show how the subjects profited from or were hindered by their education

IV. Description of Deeds
   • Praise or disparage the excellencies or evils of their actions and motives

V. Exhortation or Prayer
   • Call upon others to imitate one of the person's examples

READING ASSIGNMENT:
Book 11

Aeneas sets a standard of duty and devotion that results in the fierce fighting Roman Legions. In the underworld, he sees a vision of Rome's future armies marching out to conquest.

# SESSION XIII: DISCUSSION
Books 9–11

## A Question to Consider

Should the attitude toward war be "anything goes" and "win at all costs?"

*Discuss or list short answers to the following questions:*

### Text Analysis

1. In Book 9 what do Nisus and Euryalus do when they sneak out at night?
2. In Book 10, upon hearing of the death of Pallas, what does Aeneas do?

### Cultural Analysis

1. What is the popular idea concerning war in our culture?
2. Who is his guide into Dis? Who is she? (*Hint: Check the glossary in the back of the book.*)

### Biblical Analysis

1. What are some issues concerning war that are addressed in the Bible? See Numbers 1, 2 Chronicles 25 and Deuteronomy 20 & 23.
2. What specific principles can we draw from the Bible concerning the issue of what is appropriate during a war and what is not? Look up the following references:
   • 2 Samuel 9:1–8; Proverbs 25:21–22; Matthew 5:43–48
   • Romans 12:19–20
   • Proverbs 24:17–18
   • Psalm 2
   • Psalm 109
   • Matthew 5:43–45
   • Deuteronomy 20:10–12
3. What principles does Aeneas violate?

## SUMMA

*Write an essay or discuss this question, integrating what you have learned from the material above.* How should a Christian fight?

READING ASSIGNMENT:
Book 12

# SESSION XIV: RECITATION
Books 8–12

## Comprehension Questions

*Answer the follow questions for factual recall:*

1. How do Venus and Vulcan intervene on Aeneas's behalf?
2. Who is Pallas?
3. What is the significance of Aeneas's shield?
4. Who informs Turnus that Aeneas is away from the camp?
5. How is Turnus's plot foiled?
6. Who are Nisus and Euryalus? What do they do in Book 9?
7. How does Book 9 end?
8. What decree does Jupiter give early in Book 10?
9. Who kills Pallas? How does Aeneas respond?
10. Who is Camilla? What does she do?
11. How is the conflict finally resolved?
12. What happens to Queen Amata?
13. Why does Aeneas decide not to spare Turnus?

# SESSION XV: REVIEW

Grammar

1. When was the *Aeneid* written? What is the primary purpose of the poem?
2. Who is Aeneas, and when in history does he come onto the scene?
3. After surviving the storm and landing on the coast of Libya, Aeneas receives a visit from his mother, Venus. What does she tell him?
4. In Book 3 Aeneas continues telling his story to Dido. While he includes many details in his story, he is stressing one primary theme. What is that important point that drives his understanding of their plight?
5. What is Dido thinking and feeling as Aeneas tells his story? What causes her to have hesitation? Who allays her concerns?
6. Where does the crew land after leaving Carthage? What do they do there?
7. Where does Aeneas visit in Book 6? Why? What do Aeneas and his father discuss?
8. In Book 8 how do Venus and Vulcan intervene on Aeneas's behalf? What is the significance of

Aeneas's shield?

9. How did the following people die: Pallas, Amata, Turnus?

10. Why does Aeneas decide not to spare Turnus?

## Logic

1. Does Aeneas display *pietas* when he deserts Dido? Why? What is the other side to the argument?

2. What is the difference between how Aeneas is portrayed in the first half of the book as opposed to how he is portrayed in the second half? What event in Book 6 marks his transformation?

3. In light of Virgil's overall purpose in the *Aeneid*, what is the significance of the fact that Aeneas

does not spare Turnus?

4. Which gods or goddesses would have been content with the outcome of the story? Why?

## Lateral Thinking

1. Compare and contrast the *pietas* of Aeneas with that of Abraham in the Old Testament.

2. Discuss the significance of the visit to Dis. How do the following events enhance what Virgil is trying to accomplish in this section: going to Dis; visiting with his father; Palinurus; Dido; Romulus; and Caesar? Do you think Virgil is successful at what he is trying to do here? Why or why not?

*Aeneas' Flight from Troy* was painted by Frederico Barrocci in 1598 and depicts Aeneas, carrying his father Anchises, accompanied by his wife and son. This oil on canvas entered the collection of the Borghese family in Rome in the early seventeenth century. According to legend, Aeneas was the ancestor of Romulus, who founded Rome, and thus the painting confirmed the Borghese family's high status in the city.

While in Elysium with the spirit of his father, Anchises, Aeneas is shown the future glory of Rome. This sight of his destiny further fans the flames of his pious devotion to found the "Eternal City." As Aeneas saw the future city of Rome, we should expect that he looked upon structures like the Coliseum (pictured here) and marveled at how his descendants would outstrip even the glory of Troy.

# OPTIONAL SESSION A

## A Question to Consider

When should we show mercy in battle (especially concerning whether Aeneas should have shown mercy to Turnus)?

*Discuss or list short answers to the following questions:*

### Text Analysis

1. Give a brief summary of Book 12.
2. How does the duel unfold?
3. What does Turnus say when he realizes he is defeated?
4. What was Aeneas immediate reaction?
5. What finally causes Aeneas to kill him? What is going through his mind as he kills Turnus?

### Cultural Analysis

1. How would the culture interpret the actions of Aeneas?
2. Is acting out of revenge justified in our culture?

### Biblical Analysis

1. What does the Bible say about showing mercy to our enemies?
2. What does the Bible say about acting in anger and vengeance?
3. What does the Bible say about forgiving our enemies once they are defeated?
4. Based on this analysis of the biblical teaching on the matter, what should Aeneas have done?

## SUMMA

*Write an essay or discuss this question, integrating what you have learned from the material above.*
When should we kill our enemies in battle?

# OPTIONAL SESSION B

## Progymnasmata

Classical training in rhetoric included preparatory writing exercises called the *progymnasmata*. These exercises in composition introduced the beginning student to basic forms and techniques that would then be used and combined when practicing more advanced exercises and speeches. One of these progymnasmata was called the *encomium,* a composition written to praise an individual. Its opposite exercise (which condemns an individual) is called a *vituperation* (or an *invective*). This writing exercise expounds the virtues or condemns the vices of a specific person (e.g., Joe is a strong warrior), but does not talk about virtue in a general sense (e.g., strength in war is admirable).

The encomium and the vituperation each have six parts. The *Prologue* comes first. It introduces the topic and, at the end of the paragraph, states or implies the opinion of the writer. The second part of this exercise is a paragraph called *Description of Heritage*. In this paragraph the writer looks for ways to praise or condemn the person on account of his family history. For instance, if a person comes from righteous parents, then highlight the fact that he learned his righteous habits at home and added to the glory of the family name. A vituperation would emphasize that he comes from a family or nation that taught him wrong beliefs or bad habits. Next comes a paragraph called *Description of Upbringing*. The point is to show how the person profited from a good education or overcame a bad one (this is for the encomium). For the vituperation you should attempt to show how he failed to profit from a good education or learned well the lessons of a bad education. The most powerful part of the encomium comes next: the *Description of Deeds*. In this section the writer praises the excellencies of the mind, body and fortune of the subject. For example, the writer praises the practice of philosophical virtue, the way the person looked and his wealth, influence or social stature. Since Christianity has transformed our society it seems out of place to dwell on physical appearance or possessions (i.e., he was evil because he was quite homely, or it is obvious that he was a good man because he was fabulously rich), so instead the paragraph should concentrate on the actions and motives of the subject. This can be especially powerful if his life demonstrates a pattern. Next is a *Comparison* of the subject to someone else to portray him in a favorable light (if it is an encomium). An unfavorable comparison is best for vituperation. The final paragraph is an *Exhortation* or *Prayer* in which others are called on to imitate this person's example or a proclamation to everyone telling them not to go down the wicked path that this person did.

*Write an encomium on Aeneas.*

I.  Prologue
    - Introduce the topic
    - State your opinion
II. Description of Heritage
    - Praise the person on account of his family history
III. Description of Upbringing
    - Show how the person profited from his education
IV. Description of Deeds
    - Praise the excellencies of his actions and motives
V.  Comparison
    - Portray the person favorably in comparison to someone else
VI. Exhortation or Prayer
    - Call upon others to imitate this person's example

## ENDNOTES

1   *This endnote appears only in the teacher's edition.*

Imagine a time where
one city dominates the
world. In this world dominated
by this one single city, the power of
government makes a sudden shift, from the
rule of about four hundred men to a government
ruled by one man. Imagine all the possibilities that
could happen to the world based on what type of man
seized the reigns of office. What if he was a tried and
proven general? What if this leader was a teenager, a
mere boy? What if the leader was mean, selfish or
ruthless? What would people do if the leader was
really evil? What if the leader claimed to be a god or
even the "Lord, God Almighty?"

What or who would decide who the next king
would be? Would there be wars that divide the
allegiance of the nation to decide on subsequent
leadership, or would they find some peaceable
alternative for selecting the future king? It would be a
confusing world where each successive day reveals
new plots and plans, scheming and intrigue. This
would be a place where the world could be turned
upside down by an assassin's dagger. Imagine what it
would be like to be a mistreated slave whose sole job
is to bring pleasure to your evil master. Imagine what
it would be like to be in some other station of life—
maybe a famous athlete who all the boys want to
emulate. They will all come out to see you fight,
maybe to the death, in next week's bloody spectacle
that their culture calls games. What would it be like to
be a sailor, merchant, soldier, stone mason, architect
or some other occupation in a world where your
contribution is used simply as a tool for attempts at
grandeur by the whimsical leadership? This world
could change overnight with the death of the king
and would hang in the balance as rivals vied for the
vacant throne. Suppose that this city maintained itself

In this statue, Augustus wears a breastplate showing
heroes from Roman mythology. In Rome over eighty
statues were erected to honor Augustus. The small
statue at his leg is Cupid, signifying his divine ancestry
as a descendant of Venus, the mother of Cupid.

as a predator that fed on the neighboring countries, that it impoverished others for its own personal glory. Suppose this place is called Rome.

This world really did exist. When you imagined some aspects of this world, you were probably not far from the truth. Rome was in power in the first century B.C., and it was a time of turmoil for the whole world, as Rome, like a drunken sailor, attempted to stand upright and bully the world. And they had some success—for a time. Rome in 70 B.C. was struggling. In war after war, conspiracy after conspiracy, Rome was tired of its own family feud and wished to turn its brutish nature on the rest of the world. So they did, and the world reeled under their whip.

Thankfully, this world does not exist anymore. It has been destroyed and transformed by the gospel. As we read through *The Twelve Caesars* you will meet men of great courage and ingenuity, but you will also see men more like monsters than men. These Caesars were indisputably the most powerful men on earth, but they behaved in ways that are more gruesome, disgusting and vile than the most perverted criminal of our day, and they did so openly and pridefully. How can this be, you might ask? Where was the press to expose their wickedness? Where was the public outrage? The answer was: It was nowhere. The people of that day lived in darkness, without the light of the gospel, and so their rulers sinned with a fervor and vile imagination that is astounding. Thankfully, these rulers and their immorality have been pushed into the dark places of the earth and, if this sort of immorality occurs, it is done in the dark and people are embarrassed (and sometimes jailed) when it is exposed.

You also might ask, if they were so wicked as that, why read about them? We certainly do not read it to condone or even understand their deep immorality. What they did was awful, and we should learn to hate it and be sickened by it. We should also, however, be thankful that Christ's death destroyed this world. His gospel made this sort of behavior unacceptable (even to those who do not believe). He drove back the powers of darkness, and everyday we benefit from His conquest. Today, this wicked world of the Caesars might seem to us as if it were only fiction. We don't want to be corrupted by these stories, but neither are we allowed to forget what God has delivered our people from. It was a time when man had his plans and the God of heaven had His. It was a world that was about to undergo tremendous change, for in the days of Caesar Augustus, while Quirinius was governor of Syria in an obscure corner of the empire, a young virgin "brought forth her firstborn Son, and wrapped Him in swaddling cloths, and laid Him in a manger..." It is very important to understand the world into which Christ was born.

# GENERAL INFORMATION

## Author and Context

Gaius Suetonius Tranquillus was born in the hundredth year of Pax Romana ("peace of Rome"), A.D. 70, during the reign of the tenth Caesar, Vespasian. Suetonius enjoyed a public career and occupied numerous positions at

Augustus is portrayed as a very strong man in this statue. By the time of his death in 14 A.D., the Roman Empire had been consolidated.

the imperial court, including director of the imperial libraries. There he found the materials needed for his life's works. He was a man devoted to the more simple matters: those of learning, study, research and writing. His writings were extensive and centered predominately on biographies. The first of these biographies was *The Lives of Illustrious Men,* and next he wrote the better-known book, *The Twelve Caesars.* He is considered the first of the Latin biographers.

*The Twelve Caesars* chronicles the lives of the first emperors of Rome, beginning with Julius Caesar (49–44 B.C.) and concluding with Domitian (A.D. 81–96). These were the formative years of the empire that marked a period which began the Roman Golden Age and solidified a world that the gospel would enter with surprising success.

Suetonius is straightforward in his writing style and presents the lives of twelve important men with objectivity, frankness and clarity. He shows the Caesars for who they are, hiding none of their faults (of which there were many) and yet praising those qualities and achievements that were noteworthy. His subjects are some of the most influential men during this period which was so formative to Western Civilization. Suetonius gives us a picture that is not only graphic but reveals a culture wholly unfamiliar to the modern world. He is able to show in a short time the various aspects of a complex world that was changing rapidly.

## Significance

*The Twelve Caesars* covers a period important not only to our understanding of Rome and its culture but as the time when the New Covenant was inaugurated. Just as Alexander the Great "Hellenized" the world, spreading the Greek language and culture which underlay the foundation of the New Testament, the Roman world gave birth to tools through which the gospel would quickly be spread. As we seek to understand the teachings and context of the New Testament, we must understand the culture of Rome. Without a solid foundation in the Greek and Roman cultures, one is ill-prepared to understand the New Testament in all its fullness. Suetonius fills in important gaps and brings us face-to-face with Rome in all her struggles, glory and shame. His writing reveals her institutions and religions, her beauty and barbarity.

Suetonius also provides us with important references to the biblical timeline. We find the expulsion of the Jews from Rome under Claudius that forces Priscilla and Aquilla to take refuge in Corinth, where they meet Paul (Acts 18:1–3). We see the beginnings of great persecutions of the Christian "sect of the Jews." Astrologers during Nero's reign were pointing to Jerusalem as a place for a great universal king. We even see the state of mind of the emperor, Nero, whom Paul appeals to for a fair trial. *The Twelve Caesars* provides us with much valuable information, objectively assessing the times, events and men of the first century. With the loss of much literature from this era, it is hard to comprehend the value of an unbiased author whose works have been preserved. Suetonius is the first Roman author who does not eulogize the characters he is portraying but presents a matter-of-fact treatment of their lives. His work bears similarities to other ancient authors such as Livy, Thucydides and Plutarch. His research, however, shows surprising exactness and depth with unbiased frankness. His candor and focus on biography is unique to the ancient world and lands Suetonius among the elite class of Latin historians.

## Main Characters

Whenever the subject of writing is a famous or influential man, you have the grist for colorful action and intrigue. This is truly the case when we consider the Caesars of Rome. When one lays twelve successive rulers' lives next to each other in ancient Rome, material for a compelling story springs forth. Given the world they lived in and Suetonius's blunt style, *The Twelve Caesars* presents men of various abilities, temperaments, flaws, strengths and desires, each attempting to rule the largest empire on earth and each employing different methods, styles, strengths and liabilities to do so. The times were changing, and the moods of the masses were fickle. Suetonius presents the rise and fall, the glory and vice and the turbulent times of a fascinating world. Part of the intrigue comes from the fact that the majority of the Caesars selected successors ill-qualified for the task, whose self-centered worldview rendered them incapable of directing the empire toward good. The Romans had long since thrown off the ideals of the

Jesus Christ was born during the rule of Augustus Caesar.

Greeks and sought to run the empire as their whims dictated. Each Caesar was unique, yet each carried the baton passed to him by his predecessor. The Second Commandment, as given in Deuteronomy 5:8-10, pictures the cursing and blessing of God. There could be no clearer example of His punishment than the Caesars of Rome, where the sins of the father were visited on the third and fourth generations of those who hated God. Yet at the same time, in the back of your mind you must remember that in Palestine the work of the Holy Spirit was being poured out, enabling the reverse to be true. The promised blessing— "but showing mercy to thousands, to those who love Me and keep My commandments"—was in active fulfillment. The Caesars' lives are fascinating, and the times in which they lived pivotal, but we must not forget that this was a world that was about to go through the greatest transformation since the Flood.

## Summary and Setting

Rome in the first century A.D. was undergoing a shift from nearly five centuries of republican government (511-49 B.C.) to another five centuries of rule by emperors. What precipitated the change was one hundred years of convulsion, culminating in the awful Civil Wars, which fatigued the Roman spirit and removed hope from nearly all classes of the Roman populace. Without such struggles, the rule of an emperor was unthinkable. Yet, after various insurrections, revolts, coups and wars, Rome was ready for the unified, steady hand of a monarch. The initial Caesars strengthened Rome, revived hope, provided for the people and brought in the hundred-year era known as *Pax Romana*. Augustus Caesar, 31 B.C.–A.D. 14, was the second of these rulers and was proclaimed "Savior of the world," the one who inaugurated the Golden Age and the new world where Rome would be the city on the hill and the light of the world. It was declared that Rome would be a kingdom that would never be shaken, for it was the fated destiny of mankind.

The first few rulers of this new world were deified, and the rule of the Caesars became absolute. Daniel 2 describes the coming of the Empire of Rome. Daniel chronicles the successive kingdoms beginning with Babylon, moving through Persia and Greece and ending finally with Rome. Rome is exemplified as a kingdom of iron that smashes and conquers all the rest. Yet it is the empire that would be struck by Christ, Who would bring an end to the world as it was and establish the kingdom of God in the new world. Just at the time when the Romans were deifying Augustus, proclaiming him the "Savior of the world," Christ Jesus was born in Bethlehem. As Rome was attempting to extend its dominance, the Lord Jesus was ushering in the kingdom that would never be shaken and would fill the earth. This was more than the time when Rome would shift governmental styles; this was also the time marked out by the Father for the coming of the kingdom of God.

## Worldview

Rome was a rambunctious, growing empire that was expanding quickly. It was a place ill-equipped to handle the great levels of prosperity that conquest brought. Peoples and religions were assimilated into the growing polytheistic fabric of Rome. With all the prosperity and lack of guiding moral principles, the Roman citizens were exposed to, and willingly indulged in, every sort of luxury, entertainment, vice and debauchery. The achievements of Rome were impressive, and their military unmatched, but their culture as a whole was pervasively corrupt.

American culture today has many similar traits to that of Rome. Economically, socially, politically and religiously, we see America following in the footsteps of her distant forefathers. Of course there are signifi-

cant differences in many areas, since two thousand years separate the cultures, but the similarities are still remarkable. One must keep these eerie parallels in mind while reading Suetonius because they provide this generation with tremendous insights into the time we now live and allow us to be wise in the steps we take. Important inquiries about our own culture and future should result. Valuable lessons are available to us, indicating how we can be effective as Christians in a crooked and depraved generation that has rejected the wisdom of God.

The worldview of Rome was quite diverse, given the varied nature of the Roman population and the complexity of its culture. The Roman world was a unique blend of many different peoples spreading across three continents. Not only was it expansive, but with its myriad of beliefs and ideals, it was unique to the world stage. As you know, the foundation of Rome began with Romulus and Remus establishing a city to be a refuge and home to all the outcasts, slaves, criminals and destitute of the world. Rome, from its infancy, prospered by its might and will and was capable of conquering and expanding from early on. It did not take long for Rome to dominate the entire Italian peninsula after defeating the native Etruscans, Sabines and Samnites. As Rome continued to expand she competed for territorial rights to the western Mediterranean, leading Rome into the Punic Wars against the great maritime empire of Carthage. Rome was able to defeat Hannibal and Carthage. The result of this victory was Rome's expansion overseas, which brought further wealth and prosperity to the capital. Once expansion began, it was intoxicating to the new empire, and the thirst for more drove her to the furthest reaches of the Mediterranean Sea. Rome assimilated the places she conquered and used each victory to expand her economy and her control over the world. Like a beast, she consumed, exploited and moved into new territories. Her successful exploits led Rome to enshrine herself as a deity, demanding worship from all who came under, or were even exposed to, her control. The choice placed before the objects of her appetite was a simple one—acquiesce or be crushed.

The desire for survival and peace led most lands to succumb and seek refuge within the protection of the empire. Once conquered, inhabitants of the provinces made the best of their situation. Many sought citizenship within the empire, which guaranteed many benefits and privileges. Paul in his missionary journeys enjoyed a high degree of civility due to his citizenship (Acts 16:37; 22:26; 25:9, 10). The diversity of this collection of peoples and territories had its problems. How should they handle the varied belief systems that were now a part of the Roman world? They answered this in two ways. First, they used the resources of the empire to empower the military to rule with a heavy hand. This minimized insurrections and produced some stability. The second was to simply include each new god into the Roman pantheon. It was much easier for Rome to add a belief, new religion or new god than to attempt to eliminate it. The only requirement was that it not interfere with their chief deity—Rome. Much like twenty-first-century America, tolerance was one of the key, binding

This helmet, found in Pompeii, is typical of those worn by gladiators during the time of the Caesars.

elements that held this ancient Roman world together. Israel's King Solomon invited the same problem when he allowed his wives to worship all their foreign deities. Rome followed in these same footsteps and, even worse, enshrined herself as the central deity, the backbone of her national religion. This view of herself led Rome to view her subjects as servants and slaves who were to assist Rome in her glorification.

Human life in Rome was attributed little, if any, value. Life was certainly not sacred, and man was not understood as being created in the image of God. Man was there only to fulfill his function in the building, supporting and elevating of Rome. Most Romans fell into two classes of people: slaves and plebeians. The slaves were in destitute misery and seen as property with no rights. They were treated far worse as a whole than the slaves were in antebellum America. They

had no civil rights. The plebeians were citizens who possessed many rights yet, as far as the empire was concerned, they were at her service. The few in Rome who made up the upper class were called patricians. Although few in number, the patricians made up the majority of the ruling class in Rome. Their leaders ruled through the Senate. This was the republic of old. The times had changed, and Suetonius records the times when a new office-holder ruled—Caesar! The Caesars' power quickly increased. It wasn't long until each emperor, whether good or evil, held sway over the entire system. When the emperor sought economic changes, he would empower whomever he pleased to accomplish his goal. When the emperor wanted to provide shows and games, he could have anyone he pleased treated as his pawns for entertainment. Even senators might be forced to fight in the arena. Anyone called upon by Caesar to perform a duty, even if it meant death for entertainment's sake, was compelled to comply. Many during this time found it their job to die for the delight of Rome. The momentum and gravity of the empire during this time was effective in reducing people to objects in the hands of the emperor. Not only did he possess power, but he was also the final authority for right and wrong, truth and error. The emperor's beliefs became the enforced beliefs. If he was promiscuous or homosexual, then such was permitted. If he sought to curb immorality, laws would be enacted and enforced to assist that end. Nonetheless, the emperor himself was the measure and standard for truth, beauty and goodness. His rule was absolute, and he answered to no one. Some emperors proved good in the people's mind and had helped Rome. These were deified, as was the case with Julius, Augustus, Claudius, Vespasian and Titus.

However, it was not always quite so simple. The will of the people greatly affected all aspects of Rome's life. If they were oppressed and afflicted, there was unrest in the streets and insurrection on the horizon. Many of the emperors dealt with this problem in similar ways. They provided the people of Rome with two essentials—food and entertainment. As long as the people were well fed and pacified with games, they were content in their role as servants. The mood of the populace was something that emperors could not ignore without great peril to their throne. If an emperor lost the people's approval, he would be in dire straits and even in jeopardy of assassination. This counterbalance was a constant factor influencing the emperors. Suetonius shows this clearly. Many emperors met violent deaths when dissatisfaction was in the streets.

All the people of Rome were not enslaved in the traditional sense, but nearly all were enslaved in some ways. Many in the empire took advantage of the tremendous opportunities for trade and wealth which were opened to any free man. Rome's distraction from the true God was not just due to its polytheism. Rome was filled with every form of luxury and self-indulgence. Just as the emperor served his own purposes for aggrandizement, so did many of the citizens of Rome. Everywhere selfishness and individualism prevailed; these were foundational characteristics of the middle and upper classes in Rome. People were allowed to serve their own interests in every way possible as long as Rome was honored. This led Rome into just about every form of idolatry and debauchery imaginable. One of the chief sins

This mosaic shows the typical combat of gladiators. The term *gladiator* comes from the Latin word *gladius,* which means sword. People would fill the bleachers of the Coliseum and watch men fight to the death.

Shown on this relief are gladiators and beasts fighting. Think of this as a staged hunt. Animals were set loose in the arena while trained men hunted them down and killed them.

that can plague any society is self-indulgence. James states, "For where envy and self-seeking exist, confusion and every evil thing are there" (James 3:16). Rome allowed vices to reign and even encouraged them. They indulged themselves in what Galatians calls the works of the flesh: "Now the works of the flesh are evident, which are: adultery, fornication, uncleanness, lewdness, idolatry, sorcery, hatred, contentions, jealousies, outbursts of wrath, selfish ambitions, dissensions, heresies, envy, murders, drunkenness, revelries, and the like . . ." (Gal. 5:19–21). The Bible states that man left to himself falls to greater and greater levels of sin and depravity. According to Romans 1:18-31 such a downward spiral is itself a judgment from God—this was the case with Rome. Suetonius, although not a Christian, describes the enslaving effect of sin in detail in his work and shows how Rome offered every opportunity

to indulge the flesh. Their works were filled with cruelty, brutality, vulgarity, immorality, greed, debauchery, malice, slander and every form of impurity. Paul describes the world he lived in as "crooked and perverse," and he pleaded with the Christians in Philippi to flee. When sin is allowed to run rampant in an affluent culture, the results defy description.

Rome absorbed the achievements of the previous Mediterranean civilizations, especially those of the Greeks. Unfortunately, Greece's sense of virtue escaped the Roman mind (the Romans tended to pick up sinful practices from the Greeks, however). Rome idealized herself and marveled at her many achievements. Rome was seduced by a belief in her own invincibility, feeling that destiny was leading her to greatness as the new Tower of Babel or the ideal polis ("city"). All the successes and victories, omens and portents pointed to Rome as an empire that would rule over the entire world. The eclectic world of Roman peoples, cultures and beliefs led to a culture where all beliefs were allowed to coexist, so long as they did not claim preeminence. That was reserved for Rome herself, the chief deity.

The importance of the fertile ground of the Roman Empire in the plans of our Triune God cannot be overestimated. At the time the New Covenant was inaugurated, Rome was an empire like none other that came before. The advent, or coming, of Christ did nothing less than extend the kingdom of God to the world. It bridged the gap of the Greco/Roman world with that of the Hebrews. The New Testament was penned in the universal language of the day—Greek. The Greek language is filled with unique phrases and categories of thought. The New Testament utilizes these and presents the gospel in a beautiful tapestry, permanently filling the Greek world and language with the worldview of the Hebrews. This synthesis occurred during the period Suetonius writes, while the Roman Empire was seeking world dominance. Rome was not to be the enduring city it anticipated being. Instead, as St. Augustine puts it, it was revealed as just another installment in the temporary City of Man. Little did the Roman leaders know that in a remote outpost of the Roman Empire, alongside the animals at a manger, was born the King of Kings (and King of Caesars) Who would establish the City of God that was to be "built on the foundation of the Apostles and Prophets." The Roman Empire fostered despair in its inhabitants and a sense of hopelessness, making "the fields ripe for harvest" and at the same time providing the stability that was needed for the spread of the gospel.

The religious beliefs of Rome were numerous and diverse. Some turned to philosophy while others turned to the deities of their ancestors or some other object of veneration. This aspect of Rome's religion parallels the United States today, with its own national religion—*tolerance*—the key attribute in personal, private worship. In Rome could be found such philosophic groups as the Stoics, Cynics and Epicureans. The one characteristic that each of these groups shared was their belief that happiness and fulfillment are found within the heart of the individual and not in community. These are groups that quickly lost hope in the ideals of Rome and turned their hopes to themselves. The Bible in, of all places, the book of Romans, shows the futility of such an attempt: "There is none righteous, no not one; there is none who understands; there is none who seeks after God. They have all turned aside; they have together become corrupt; there is no one who does good, no, not one" (Rom. 3:10-12). We are all born sinful and lost. Any attempt to find something redeemable within ourselves is "vanity and chasing after the wind." Only a resurrected life in Christ has any good in it, and that is through the work of God in Christ. Paul says, "beware lest anyone cheat you through philosophy and empty deceit, according to the tradition of men, according to the basic principles of the world and not according to Christ. For in Him dwells all the fullness of the Godhead bodily; and you are complete when in Him, who is the head of all principality and power" (Col. 2:8-9). Therefore, the Roman who attempted to escape the depravity of this world by turning within found only a desperately wicked heart in which dwelt no good thing. Nonetheless, many educated Romans turned to these schools of thought for guidance.

Rome was also influenced by a myriad of interest groups and an elaborate array of social classes. These made up a diversified populace whose desires collectively shaped the culture. Each of these groups held different beliefs with regard to truth, fate, free will, society and government. It is difficult to categorize the Romans into any specific grouping apart from the following: they were forced to be devoted to the state and worship it appropriately—to support the state first and foremost. The people of Rome were obligated by their oaths and sense of duty to obey the state unconditionally. All mankind was called upon to bow down and serve the state of Rome. Rome had its military to enforce subservience and was willing to punish or destroy anyone who did not submit. Humanity was whipped, flogged, chained, beaten or killed in the most brutal and barbaric fashion. The apostle Paul, who was even a Roman citizen, routinely experienced Rome's brutality as she imposed her will. Paul was flogged with thirty-nine lashes five times, he was stoned, and he was beaten with rods three times . . . and all in a seven year period. These do not include Paul's later beatings, trials and eventual martyrdom. Rome's will was enforced with extraordinary viciousness.

Another aspect of Roman religion and beliefs that

was an integral part of the fabric of their culture is one that appears most central to Suetonius. This was the belief in omens, portents, signs, astrology and oracles. Although the beliefs of the Romans were diverse, nearly all looked to these for direction. They believed these assisted in the knowing of one's fate. Suetonius points to signs, wonders and omens continually in his work. We have seen this with the Greeks also, and this pagan approach to life continues with the Romans. Interestingly, many of the signs and wonders in Suetonius parallel biblical events and prophecies (Matt. 24; Luke 21) and should not be dismissed as mere superstition, for Suetonius was, in fact, quite objective. The Scriptures themselves are filled with these types of things. The important question to ask regarding these phenomena is to what do the Romans credit them. They denied the revelation of the Triune God and invented their own answers to these phenomena and then glorified them. The Scriptures always point to God as the author of all things, and truth is found nowhere else. God, the Father, Son and Holy Spirit, is the *Logos,* or reason, for all things visible and invisible. As Colossians 1:14–17 states, "Christ is the image of the invisible God, for by Him all things were created, things in Heaven and on earth, visible and invisible, whether thrones or dominions or principalities or powers. All things were created by Him and for Him. And He is before all things and in Him all things consist." In Rome they were darkened by sin and were left to their "vain imaginations." Little did they know that Rome was not the empire which was to be great forever but simply a pawn in the hand of Almighty God, readying the world for its coming Messiah.

The signs continued, and the explanations for these varied with each Roman. Some gave credit to Jupiter and Minerva, or to Nature and some to the work of God. They, nonetheless, were undeniable and everyone needed to account for them. The sovereignty of God is clear as you read Suetonius, just as it is when you read many of the ancient works. From the miracles that occurred during the Persian War to the Magi that came from the East following the star to the Christ, on to the amazing series of earthquakes, lightning, signs and wonders found in Suetonius, all contribute to magnify the most extraordinary event in history—the Incarnation. All the while, these arrogant people thought their "greatness" was of themselves.

The other culture that existed in the Mediterranean that is important to our worldview analysis is that of the Jews. They occupied the land bridge between Egypt, Mesopotamia and the Roman world. They were a peculiar people to the Romans, with their customs and strange worship. God had settled Israel in a strategic location that would allow them to be a light to the Gentiles. They were given the very words of God, the oracle of God and the prophets to direct them toward a life that would be blessed. Each family in Israel was given land by God to cultivate as an inheritance, and they enjoyed an agrarian life. Their hope was in the promise of glory. Life was sacred, morality central, and life revolved around feasts, festivals and the worship of Yahweh. This utopia was

Mark Antony set up the Second Triumvirate with Lepidus and Octavian. In Egypt he fell in love with Cleopatra. He committed suicide immediately after his defeat at the Battle of Actium.

interrupted through the loss of blessing because of unfaithfulness; they received the ruthless overlords of Rome. It was at this time that they received the Christ, Who would be the Savior of the world. The Jews rejected their Messiah, putting Him to death with the assistance of the Romans. They rejected Him because of the universal gospel He preached. They wanted the Messiah to elevate the nation of Israel and judge the pagan world. Instead, they judged the Author of Life and murdered Him with the consent of the Romans! To their surprise the Messiah rose from the dead and sent the gospel out through His saints to redeem the world. This must not be forgotten as you read Suetonius. The Roman world was in the process of changing. The Roman world was going through the great transformation. The world was becoming new, and the rulers of that age did not perceive it. The Roman world was becoming Christ's, Who was "given all authority in heaven and on earth."

As you read, know that Suetonius will present a world that is almost unimaginable today. So thoroughly has the gospel changed the world, that the world of Suetonius seems foreign, if not fictional. Praise God! Know, however that this was the age of transformation. As you read each page and marvel at how awful that world was, thank God for his grace that renews life and gives hope. And thank God for the tremendous blessing the gospel provides—even in the world.

—*Brent Harken*

## For Further Reading

Jones, Peter. *Capturing the Pagan Mind*. Nashville, Tenn.: Broadman and Holman Publishers, 2003.

Tacitus, Publius Cornelius. *The Annals of Imperial Rome*. New York: Penguin Publishers, 1996.

Spielvogel, Jackson. *Western Civilization*. Fifth Edition. Belmont, Calif.: Wadsworth/Thomson Learning, 2003. 112–131.

*Veritas Press History Cards: New Testament, Greece and Rome*. Lancaster, Pa.: Veritas Press. 12, 17, 19–22, 25–27.

# SESSION I: PRELUDE

## A Question to Consider

What influences have the greatest impact on the shaping of culture? Which one shapes culture most?

*From the General Information above answer the following questions:*

1. What was the time period for the Roman Republic?
2. What led to the fall of the Roman Republic?
3. What kind of government was the Roman Republic, and once the Roman Republic dissolved, what replaced it?
4. How was Rome able to hold its empire together when they appeared to be struggling significantly?
5. What parallels are there between Rome and America today?
6. What type of worship did Rome demand?
7. What class of people ruled Rome? Who were the other classes?

### READING ASSIGNMENT:
Chapter I. Julius Caesar

# SESSION II: DISCUSSION
Chapter I. Julius Caesar[1]

## A Question to Consider

Do motives drive actions? Are all motives conscious decisions, or are some unconscious?

*Discuss or list short answers to the following questions:*

### Text Analysis

1. What do you think Julius Caesar's political motives were? Did he achieve them in a morally sound and biblical way or not?
2. Why did Julius desire to be ruler of Rome? Was it for the good of Rome or for selfish reasons?
3. How did Julius Caesar achieve the approval from the Senate?
4. How did he get the approval of the people?
5. What did Caesar do to gain specific offices, such as Consul, Governor and Chief Priest, from the Senate?

Nero has gone down in history as one of the most outrageous haters of Christians. What started as a reign of moderation turned into an indulgence in every kind of excess. His life ended in suicide but not before using Christians as torches to light his garden where he entertained his guests.

6. What were Caesar's greatest gifts? Why were Caesar's troops so faithful to him? Did he use these effectively?

## Cultural Analysis

1. Would the tactics Julius used be good for today's politician?

2. Do American courts consider motives when trying a court case?

3. What would *most* people say is the most important quality for success in politics that a President must possess: honesty, purity, experience. a good record or sly rhetoric?

4. If Julius Caesar were alive today would he stand a chance of becoming President?

## Biblical Analysis

1. What qualifications does God require of leaders (Ex. 18:21; 1 Tim. 3:1–13; Phil. 2:3–8)?

2. Is it the will of man that brings him to power (1 Sam. 2:7; Ps 75:6–7; Dan. 4:34–37; Matt. 28:18; Rom 13:1–7)?

## SUMMA

*Write an essay or discuss this question, integrating what you have learned from the material above.*

Why did Caesar gain power?

## Optional Activity A

Create a public opinion poll that tracks Julius's popularity and the reasons for his popularity. First, create a timeline for every year of Julius's political life. Rate his popularity with the people and then rate his popularity with the Senate. Place the results side by side on the timeline. Leave a space to the right of each column where you can explain what increased or decreased his popularity. At each interval, discuss these changes and the methods he used to gain the people's support.

## Optional Activity B

During an election campaign, contact the headquarters of a political party and ask to interview one of the following: a candidate, a campaign chairman or someone in a similar position. Ask him the following questions: Why should someone vote for this candidate? Why is this candidate the best one for the job, and why is he better than his opponent? What will he do for me? What are his qualifications? Is this candidate morally sound? How do you know this about Him?

Compare the answers to the ones you gave in the Cultural Analysis section above. See if his answers reflect biblical standards.

READING ASSIGNMENT:
Chapter II. Augustus 1–65

# SESSION III: DISCUSSION
Chapter II. Augustus 1–65

## A Question to Consider

Are all men created equal?

*Discuss or list short answers to the following questions:*

### Text Analysis

1. What is meant that Augustus created a New Constitutional Order?
2. What power did the princeps possess? How did Augustus expand his control?
3. How did Rome select its next emperor?
4. How was the army important to Rome?
5. How did Augustus alter the army? Why would he do this?
6. How was Augustus able to bring frontier provinces under his control?
7. What was the Roman class system based on? Is this a good system? What led Rome to prosperity? How did she maintain it?

### Cultural Analysis

*(These questions are complex, and you may want to consult the sections on feudalism in the Spielvogel text. This system, with its distinct classes and contractual relationships between classes, is a good wall to bounce other systems off of and compare. Although they had their problems, medieval society had many beautiful elements and should be looked at in a favorable light.)*

1. How is the princep's rule of provinces similar to that found in medieval feudalism?
2. Is our system different from that of Rome or the time of Feudalism? How is it different?
3. Is ours a better system? Why or why not?
4. Do you think Rome and America see themselves as better than others? Why?

### Biblical Analysis

1. We should not lose hope. What did the world look like to the disciples just after Jesus was crucified?
2. King David and King Solomon created a new order in Israel. David's and Solomon's political lives are similar to Julius's and Augustus's. Identify what some of these similarities might be. (Pay special attention to which ones were conquerors, which ones governed in times of peace and who ruled during what could be called a "Golden Age.")
3. Under the Mosaic system, upon what were classes and leadership in Israel based (Ex. 18:13–27; Num. 2)?

## SUMMA

*Write an essay or discuss this question, integrating what you have learned from the material above.*

Why was Augustus successful as a political leader?

### Application

The people of Rome quickly lost hope in politics due to all the corruption that took place.

1. How should we as Christians view politics? Should we trust in political institutions for our hope, security, welfare and peace? Is the government the most essential institution on earth? We root for our school's and town's sports teams and America does the same in the Olympics. Should we do this? Should these be our chief allegiances?

2. How should we as Christians view culture?

**READING ASSIGNMENT:**
Chapter II. Augustus 66–101

## SESSION IV: RECITATION

Chapter II. Augustus 1–101

### Comprehension Questions

*Answer the following questions for factual recall:*

1. How many civil wars did Augustus fight?
2. What was the underlying motive behind each campaign?
3. Who joined Augustus in the second triumvirate?
4. How did Augustus dispose of Lepidus?
5. In what manner did Augustus break his friendship with Anthony?
6. What resulted from this?
7. What did Augustus do with Egypt?
8. Would you classify Augustus as ambitious for personal glory or for the glory of Rome?
9. What led to some of the people's hatred of Augustus?
10. How did he change their opinions?
11. What happened to unemployment in Rome?
12. What signs, portents and wonders pointed to Augustus's future greatness?
13. What signs, portents and wonders pointed to Augustus's death and deification?

This sardonyx cameo portrays Emperor Tiberius with his mother Livia and other members of the Julio-Claudius family.

### Optional Activity

*Write a short essay on the question below:*

Many leaders have attempted to reform a state and have failed. Why was Augustus successful?

## SESSION V: WRITING

### Progymnasmata

Classical training in rhetoric included preparatory writing exercises called the *progymnasmata.* These exercises in composition introduced the beginning student to basic forms and techniques that would then be used and combined when practicing more advanced exercises and speeches. One of these progymnasmata was called a *chreia,* or "saying exercise," and was simply a concise exposition of some memorable saying or deed.

A chreia has eight paragraphs. The first is the *Panegyric* which is a paragraph in which you praise the person who uttered the wise saying. The second is called the *Paraphrastic.* In this short paragraph you put the saying into your own words. This paragraph often begins with something like: "When Saint Augustine said that evil was the deprivation of good he meant that . . ." In the third paragraph, called *From the Cause,* you explain the motivation of the person. The fourth paragraph is called *From the Contrary,* and in it you explain what would have happened if the opposite of the saying or action had occurred. For example, "If Diogenes had not struck the inept teacher, bad education would have continued." In the fifth paragraph, called the *Analogy,* you liken the saying or action to something else, usually something more concrete and easier to

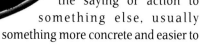

understand. The sixth paragraph is similar to the fifth. It is called *Example,* and in it you show the wisdom of the saying or deed by pointing your reader to a specific instance in which this wisdom was demonstrated. The *Analogy* is different from the *Example* in that it is about a general practice (e.g., "Education is like a harvest: you work hard and reap great reward.") whereas the *Example* is about a specific person, place or thing (e.g., "Erasmus studied many things and became a learned man."). The seventh paragraph is called the *Testimony of the Ancients.* Here you quote a sage person from the past who testifies to the truth of the saying. Finally, in the eighth paragraph, called the *Epilogue,* you sum up the chreia.

Write a chreia for the following statement: "Augustus was savior of Rome, and Jesus, the Son of God, is Savior of the world." This statement is based on two quotes, one by Publius Nigidius Figulus regarding Augustus, "The ruler of the world is now born," and the other by the apostle Mark, "The beginning of the gospel of Jesus Christ, the Son of God."

I. Panegyric
  • Praise the person(s) who uttered the wise saying(s)
II. Paraphrastic
  • Put the saying into your own words
III. From the Cause
  • Explain the motivation of the speaker
IV. From the Contrary
  • Explain the consequences if the opposite of the saying or action had occurred
V. Analogy
  • Liken the saying or action to something else
VI. Example
  • Point the reader to a specific instance in which the wisdom of the saying was demonstrated
VII. Testimony of the Ancients
  • Quote a sage person from the past who testifies to the truth of the saying
VIII. Epilogue
  • Summarize your previous paragraphs

**READING ASSIGNMENT:**
Chapter III. Tiberius

# SESSION VI: DISCUSSION
Chapter III. Tiberius

## A Question to Consider

Can a man suppress what is in his heart? Or put another way, if you have a particular private sin, will it come to the surface at some point?

*Discuss or list short answers to the following questions:*

### Text Analysis

1. Did Tiberius have any idea he might become emperor?
2. What relation was Tiberius to Augustus?
3. Give two reasons why Augustus selected Tiberius to be his successor?
4. Was Tiberius's selection for emperor uncontested, or did others have a claim to the throne?
5. When Tiberius ascended the throne, did he impose a heavy-handed rule?
6. How would you describe his style of rule? Did he attempt to rule well or was his rule selfish?
7. Once Tiberius left Rome for Carpeae, did his behavior as an emperor change? In what ways was it different?

### Cultural Analysis

1. How can rulers become so corrupt and perverse?
2. What is the eventual outcome of a life lived in secret sin.

### Biblical Analysis

1. Romans reveals the power of sin and its devastating effect (Rom. 1:18–2:16). How can we escape these awful consequences (Rom. 3:21–24, 8:9–17; 2 Pet 1:3–11, 2:20)?
2. Sin is in all of us, and if it is left there it will destroy us. Christ has made a provision that will cancel the power of sin. He has made atonement and redeemed us from the curse of sin. How? (Gal. 3:13, 2 Cor. 5:21, Rom. 7:7–25)

## SUMMA

*Write an essay or discuss this question, integrating what you have learned from the material above.*
Can sin be controlled?

## Application

Without this provision we would slide deeper and deeper into sin. Many disregard the Lord Jesus and decay, simply because they refuse to confess their sins, submit to God and be cleansed (1 John 1:9; James 4:7-10). Remember what Psalm 119:9–11 states, "How can a young man keep his way pure? By living according to Your word. I seek You with all my heart; do not let me stray from Your commands. I have hidden Your word in my heart that I might not sin against You."

 READING ASSIGNMENT:
Chapter IV. Gaius

# SESSION VII: WRITING
Chapter IV. Gaius

Before doing your writing assignment consider the questions below:

## A Question to Consider

What most influences the way a child turns out?

*Discuss or list short answers to the following questions:*

### Text Analysis

1. Who was Gaius's father? What was he like?
2. Suetonius sometimes compares people in his narratives. Why does he do this with Tiberius and Germanicus?
3. Was Gaius the first choice to succeed Tiberius? Why?
4. How long did Gaius rule, and what was he like?
5. Does Suetonius base the opinions he holds about Gaius on any identifiable worldview?

## Progymnasmata

The *proverb* has exactly the same parts as the *chreia* that you wrote in Session V. The only difference between a proverb and a chreia is that a proverb is usually a wise saying and is often anonymous.

Complete the Proverb below regarding Gaius for the following statement: "The sins of the fathers are visited on the third and fourth generations." You need write only the *From the Cause,* the *Analogy* and the

*Example* portions. The others have been completed for you. Be sure to include at least three causes for Gaius's behavior.

I.  Panegyric
   • Praise the wisdom of the proverb

"The sins of the fathers are visited on the third and fourth generations" is one of those statements that has been exhibited in every man from Adam to the present. It reveals the wisdom of God and tests the honesty of man. This statement opens the mind of man to his sinful state and his need for a redeemer who can form man in his own image. It comes directly from the law of God inscribed on the tablets at Sinai. Heeding it can lead us away from destruction and spare future generations an awful fate. Failing to heed this proverb can lead to horrifying results, as in the case of Caligula.

II.  Paraphrastic
   • Put the saying into your own words

Man inherently parrots his parents whether he desires to or not. This parroting and the effects of the patterns ingrained in the children by their parents leads to future imitation and additional blessing or, as in the case of Gaius, additional cursing.

III. From the Cause
   • Praising the motive or reason that caused the saying to be made

IV. From the Contrary
   • Explain what would happen if the statement were not heeded.

If this statement were not true, then there would be no justice in the world and people would become increasingly wicked with nothing to curb their hideous appetites. God brings judgment, however, destroying the seed of the wicked so that they will not prosper in and perfect their wickedness generation after generation. This, in a sense, is deliverance to the righteous people of the world. God will not let wickedness prosper.

V.  Analogy
   • An analogy points to a class of people or things as general truth

VI. Example
   • The example is a specific instance where the truth of the proverb is demonstrated

VII. Testimony of the Ancients
   • Reference the testimony of a respected figure from the past who agrees with the proverb

God over and over again in 1 and 2 Kings declares that a son repeats the evil of his father and at times even goes beyond his father in sin. This pattern takes its root particularly in Jeroboam, the son of Nebat. He leads the people away from the Davidic line of kings and forbids them to worship at the Temple in Jerusalem. Instead, he places idols in his land for the people to worship. The kings after him follow in this wicked pattern until the Northern Kingdom is wiped off the face of the earth.

VIII. Epilogue

• Summarize your findings

All creation is made after its kind. Trees, plants and animals reproduce in likeness. God has made man no different, and the duplication follows to the level of sin. We sin like our fathers, and the only solution is to be adopted into a new family other than that of Adam; we need the adoption into the household of God so we can bear His image instead.

## Optional Activities

Watch one of the movies listed below. The purpose for viewing these movies is to create a sobering, visual picture of how life in a cursed world apart from the grace of God is futile, sad, sinful and cruel. Due to the power of visual art, these should be viewed with extreme caution. Sections of these movies may need to be avoided, and skipping those sections will not cause the educational benefit to suffer. A follow up discussion of the material is recommended. *Note: there are other movies that can accomplish the same objectives.*

**DRIVING MISS DAISY:** A sad movie that shows the lost seeking to find meaning in life without God.
**ALL THE PRETTY HORSES:** A movie that shows many of the plot twists of life. It asks many important questions.
**SCHINDLER'S LIST:** This is a very dark movie that shows the reality of Nazi Germany's concentration camps and the depravity of man.

### READING ASSIGNMENT:
Chapter V. Claudius

Octavian was born in 63 B.C. He is depicted here as a very young man when, at the Battle of Actium, he led the forces that opposed Antony after Caesar's death.

# SESSION VIII: RECITATION
Chapter V. Claudius

## Comprehension Questions

*Answer the following questions for factual recall:*

1. What year was Claudius born?
2. What else significant happened to Augustus on that day?
3. Was Claudius esteemed as a youngster?
4. How old was he when he became emperor? What year was it?
5. How did he become emperor?
6. How did Claudius assure the loyalty of his troops? Did this really work?
7. When giving an oath, whose name would he invoke?

*Chart 1:* **CHART THE CAESARS**

| REIGN | | | | | | |
|---|---|---|---|---|---|---|
| **JULIUS CAESAR** 49–44 B.C. | **AUGUSTUS** | **TIBERIUS** | **GAIUS** | **CLAUDIUS** | **NERO** | **TIBERIUS** |
| LINEAGE | | | | | | |
| Lost in the original manuscript | | | | | | |
| GOOD QUALITIES | | | | | | |
| Great orator, compassionate, faithful husband, dedicated, courageous | | | | | | |
| BAD QUALITIES | | | | | | |
| Adultery, homosexual, cruel, incest, greedy | | | | | | |
| SECULAR EVENTS | | | | | | |
| Roman Civil Wars; Pompey clears Med. Of pirates; Gladiator Revolt under Spartacus; authors: Sallust, Caesar, Cicero | | | | | | |
| BIBLICAL EVENTS | | | | | | |
| None–Julius's life is between the testaments; (Note:Pompey brings Palestine under Roman rule.) | | | | | | |
| ACHIEVEMENTS | | | | | | |
| Bridged the Rhine, defeated the Gauls, conquered Britain, created the Roman Empire | | | | | | |
| EVIL ACTIONS | | | | | | |
| Bribes, unjust wars, murder, adultery, incest, pride | | | | | | |
| MILITARY EXPLOITS | | | | | | |
| Conquered Germania, Britain, won Civil War | | | | | | |

8. As a judge, was he good or bad?

9. What did he do to lawyers in Rome?

10. Why was it a good idea to stabilize grain supplies? What effect did this have on Roman society?

11. Were Claudius's public works necessary, beneficial or extravagant?

12. Why did Claudius expel the Jews from Rome?

13. Who was Chrestus?

14. Who did Claudius send to be governor of Judea?

15. How was Claudius's mind? What led Claudius to paranoia?

16. What was his relationship to Nero?

**READING ASSIGNMENT:**
Chapter VI. Nero 1–25

# SESSION IX: ACTIVITY

## Charting the Caesars

Create a chart that compares the Caesars. On the chart include as many of the list below as time permits. Put the Caesars across the top of the chart (Julius to Nero) and the other items down the left side. The amount of detail may vary from Caesar to Caesar. Working in a word processing program will make creating and working with a table much easier. Chart 1 depicts what we envision, with much of the material provided for Julius Caesar.

**READING ASSIGNMENT:**
Chapter VI. Nero 26–57

# SESSION X: ACTIVITY

*Continue to work on charting the Caesars.*

 **READING ASSIGNMENT:**
Chapters VII–IX. Galba, Otho, Vitellius

# SESSION XI: DISCUSSION

Chapter VI. Nero

## A Question to Consider

To what extent do our minds control us, and to what extent do our hearts?

*Discuss or list short answers to the following questions:*

### Text Analysis

1. What was Nero's father like? What did he say about the son born to him?
2. What role did Agrippina play in Nero's reign?
3. Nero's reign was quite different in the early years from the later years. Characterize the early years.
4. What were some of his praiseworthy accomplishments?
5. How did the Greeks view Nero compared to the Romans?
6. Nero persecuted Christians. How does Suetonius describe Christians? Why might he see them in this light?
7. What were some of the vices that characterized the second half of Nero's reign? What does Suetonius say caused this shift in Nero's behavior?

### Cultural Analysis

1. Nero's biological father understood how his influence would affect his son. Do you think parents have this much sway?
2. What about the gospel was such a threat to Rome during the time of Nero?

### Biblical Analysis

Our upbringing is very important, but more important is our relationship to God. How do we become related to Him (John 1:7, 3:16–17; Rom. 3:23, 4:11)?

## Application

Love God, obey God, walk in the light and serve Him faithfully. First John 2:15–17 states the following: "Do not love the world or the things in the world. If anyone loves the world, the love of the Father is not in him. For all that is in the world?the lust of the flesh, the lust of the eyes, and the pride of life?is not of the Father but is of the world. And the world is passing away, and the lust of it; but he who does the will of God abides forever." Live your life as a light that points to Christ always. In all facets of your life reflect the Lord's ways and standards, not just in the internals, but in the externals as well. Don't be surprised if this brings some hostility your way (Matt. 24:9; Mark 13:13).

## SUMMA

*Write an essay or discuss this question, integrating what you have learned from the material above.*

Should we expect Christian education to lead to persecution?

## Optional Activity

Rome was known as the Eternal City. At times in history its rule over most of the world was so thorough

---

**Chart 2: THE EVOLUTION OF ROMAN GOVERNMENT**

| GOVERNMENT | SOURCES | DATES | HOW IT STARTED | HOW IT ENDED |
|---|---|---|---|---|
| Monarchy | Plutarch's, *Lives*, Romulus and Livy, *The Early History of Rome*, 100–103. | | | |
| Republic | Livy, *The Early History of Rome*, book 2 | | | |
| Empire | Suetonius, starting with Augustus | | | |
| Christian Empire | Eusebius, *The Church History*, books 9 and 10 | | | |
| Fall | Augustine, *City of God*, book 1 | | | |

that people believed that God had destined Rome to rule the world forever. This belief came about for many reasons, but chief among them is that, from the founding of Rome by Romulus to the Fall of Rome to Alaric, there is a span of over one thousand years. That is five times longer than the United States has even been in existence. While this might seem like an almost miraculous state of stability, there were great changes in Roman government during that time. The chart you will create chronicles Rome's transformation from a monarchy, to a republic, to an empire and finally to a Christian empire and then to a fallen empire, although it could be argued that the Roman Empire continued to maintain rule in Constantinople until 1453.

READING ASSIGNMENT:
Chapters X. and XI. Vespasian and Titus

# SESSION XII: DISCUSSION
Chapters X. and XI. Vespasian and Titus

## A Question to Consider

Are signs, wonders and omens from God?

*Discuss or list short answers to the following questions:*

### Text Analysis

1. Where was Vespasian when Vitellius died? What was he doing there?
2. What signs and omens pointed to Vespasian becoming emperor?
3. Vespasian consulted the God of Carmel. Who was the God of Carmel?
4. Who affirmed the oracle and said Vespasian would be emperor?
5. Who completed the destruction of Jerusalem?
6. Was Titus a good emperor?

### Cultural Analysis

1. Part of Vespasian's career was in the holy land with Josephus. Do you think that he would have come in contact with Judaism or Christianity? As emperor, did he act like a Christian in any way?
2. Titus completed the conquest of the Holy Land and the destruction of Jerusalem. Do you know how many times Jerusalem was sacked in the past? Can you think of one time in the past that Jerusalem was sacked (2 Chron. 36:15–22)? Why was it sacked?

### Biblical Analysis

The destruction of Jerusalem is an event almost unfamiliar to the modern Christian. Should it be important to us? Consider this: The Jews flocked to Jerusalem in A.D. 70 to celebrate the Passover. Two million people were in Jerusalem when the Romans surrounded the city. Convinced that the Messiah (not Jesus, a different one) would come to deliver them, they stayed when the Romans offered them the option to leave in peace. When it was all said and done, the Romans had crucified more than 100,000 Jews. Plague, famine and murder within the walls claimed nearly one million lives before the Romans even entered the city! Three hundred thousand bodies were dumped over the south wall into the valley of Gehenna, where Israel had burned their

Cameos were made in the hope of immortalizing famous people. This cameo portrays Emperor Claudius with his wife.

sons to Molech centuries before. This was Israel's garbage dump and is the place Christ compared to hell. There were signs in the heavens as reported by Tacitus.[5] Soon after the Romans entered the city, the Temple was burned to the ground, and to retrieve the melted gold, the Romans dismantled every block, not leaving one stone on another. To this day the Temple has not been built again. The one million left alive in Jerusalem were sold into slavery and shipped to the ends of the earth.

> Jesus speaks of the end of an age in Matthew 24:1–31. Does it make sense to believe that He is speaking of the destruction of Jerusalem as described above?

## Application

Christ commanded us to disciple the nations, baptize them and teach them to obey the commands of Christ. If this is a parallel of Joshua, then we should see that we are in a battle and should expect good results. If we are in a battle, we need the armor of God (Eph. 6:10–18). If we have this armor then our duty is to demolish strongholds and anything that sets itself up against the knowledge of God (2 Cor. 10:3–6).

## SUMMA

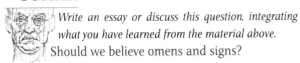 *Write an essay or discuss this question, integrating what you have learned from the material above.* Should we believe omens and signs?

 READING ASSIGNMENT
Chapter XII. Domitian

# SESSION XIII: WRITING

*Using the directions in Session V, write a chreia for the following statement: "God accomplished his will through Rome."*

# SESSION XIV: RESEARCH AND REVIEW

## Charting the Caesars

*Complete the chart previously started in Session IX by adding Galba through Domitian.*

# SESSION XV: RESEARCH AND REVIEW

## Charting the Caesars

*Continue to create the chart comparing the Caesars.*

# OPTIONAL SESSION A: RECITATION

## Comprehension Questions

*Answer the following questions for factual recall:*
1. List the good Caesars.
2. List the bad Caesars.
3. List the Caesars in order.
4. To which Caesar or during which Caesar's reign do the following correspond?
   a. Christ was born
   b. Christ died
   c. Considered stupid by the Romans when young
   d. Was a member of the second triumvirate
   e. Jews expelled from Rome
   f. Burned Rome
   g. Mt. Vesuvius erupted
   h. Tutored by Seneca
   i. He let the empire slide after he moved to Carpeae
   j. Shifted the Roman government from republic to empire
   k. Jerusalem destroyed
   l. Reigned while Paul was in Rome
   m. Four men who reigned during the same year

n. His reign began Pax Romana

o. Put Paul to death

p. First Caesar to proclaim himself God

q. Had the shortest reign of the good emperors

r. Was obsessed with performing and fame.

s. Is considered father of Rome

t. An acquaintance of Josephus

## ENDNOTES

1 Optional Reading Assignment: Spielvogel, pgs. 170–197. This reading from *Western Civilization* will augment your reading of Suetonius here.

2 *This endnote appears only in the teacher's edition.*

3 *This endnote appears only in the teacher's edition.*

4 *This endnote appears only in the teacher's edition.*

5 Tacitus, Publius Cornelius. *The Annals of Imperial Rome.* New York: Penguin Publishers, 1996. 5.10.

# JULIUS CAESAR

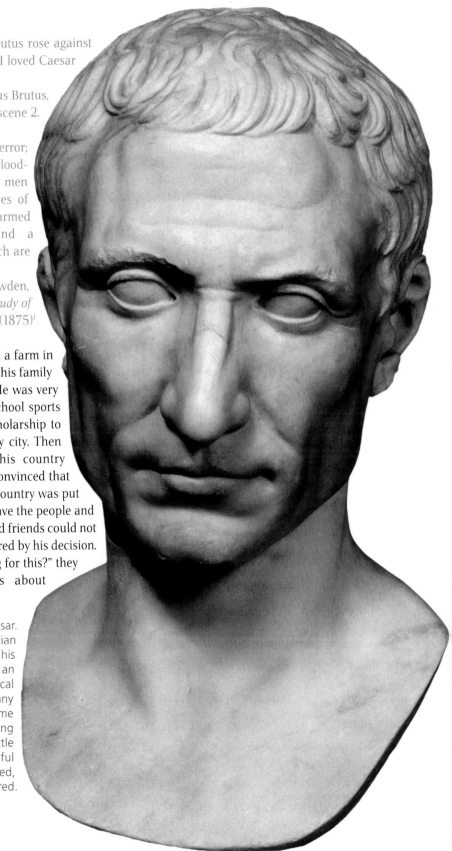

If then that friend demand why Brutus rose against Caesar, this is my answer: not that I loved Caesar less, but that I loved Rome more.

> —Marcus Brutus,
> *Julius Caesar*, Act 3, scene 2.

It is idealists who create political terror; they are free from all desire for bloodshedding; but to them the lives of men and women are accidents; the lives of ideas are the true realities; and, armed with an abstract principle and a suspicion, they perform deeds which are at once beautiful and hideous. . . ."

> —Edward Dowden,
> *Shakespeare: A Critical Study of His Mind and Art* (1875)[1]

Once there was a boy who lived on a farm in the middle of the country. He loved his family and friends, and they loved him. He was very smart and participated in many school sports and clubs and had just won a scholarship to study at the university in a nearby city. Then something horrible happened—his country decided to go to war. He became convinced that the best thing he could do for his country was put off college, join the military and leave the people and places he loved most. His family and friends could not believe it. They were hurt and angered by his decision. "How could you give up everything for this?" they asked. Some even had doubts about

A bust of Julius Caesar. He was born into an ancient Patrician family in 100 B.C. Before he met his untimely death, he embarked on an outstanding military and political career. Julius Caesar, more than any other person, transformed Rome from a republic to an empire, using the tools of charisma on the battlefield and with the people and careful rhetoric. For this, he was loved, hated, revered and murdered.

whether their country was right to go to war at all, and it seemed that they would never forgive him if he decided to go. The boy's mind was thrown into turmoil—would he have to choose between them and his country? Was his decision really the best thing for his country, his family and himself? It seemed so hard to know the right thing to do.

Could you ever love your country more than your closest friends? What would you do if you were forced to choose between them? Have you ever had to choose between hurting a friend and holding firm to what you believe? With *Julius Caesar,* Shakespeare invites us to think about this tough issue and many others like it, mostly through the character of Marcus Brutus, who comes to believe that his friendship with Caesar and his duty to his country are in a conflict that can never be resolved. Brutus must decide whether Caesar's ambition is dangerous enough to threaten the freedom of the Roman Republic. If so, he concludes that he must kill Caesar and accept whatever consequences follow. He determines he must eliminate this first of the Roman Caesars.

Does Caesar deserve it? Is Brutus an "honorable" man? Does the assassination solve the problem of tyranny and bring peace and liberty to Rome? This play asks all these questions— questions which require work, wisdom and maturity to fully answer. They lead us, moreover, to the larger questions of the nature and limits of authority and virtue, questions which no individual or society can leave unanswered.

William Shakespeare. His plays demonstrate a great depth of understanding concerning the human condition as presented in Christianity. He surpasses the Greeks in this way and shows himself to be the greatest play-wright of all time.

# GENERAL INFORMATION

## Author and Context

We know so little about the "real" William Shakespeare that it is not very useful to talk about his life in the hope of shedding additional light on his plays. In fact, several scholars over the centuries have argued that the true author of Shakespeare's works was a highly educated aristocrat, rather than a lowly actor who completed only grammar school. They think this is the only explanation for the huge vocabulary, thorough classical education and wide knowledge of history, poetry, science, medicine and foreign languages and litera- ture that are clearly displayed in his work. While the argument rages still, we shall assume Shake- speare's authorship, if only because of tradition and because no other specific candidate has been widely accepted. It is enough that Shakespeare has been one of the most influential writers of all time, and his work is usually regarded as the cornerstone of most subsequent Western literature. His plays are still performed and enjoyed, new film versions are periodically produced, and many of his plots and lines have become commonplace in Western culture, so much so that most people have forgotten their original source. (For example, watch out for the original joker who said "It was Greek to me" in Act 1, scene 2.) His works are famous for the richness and poetry of his language, his complex treatment of important themes and the depth and diversity of his characters. He was skilled at both humor and drama—writing very funny scenes in the middle of serious tragedies and often putting poignant elements into comedies.

Shakespeare lived during the Golden age of England under Queen Elizabeth I. Under Elizabeth's long reign, Protestantism finally gained a solid foothold in England, a government precedent was set as the monarchy cooperated more with Parliament and the Spanish Armada was destroyed, making the English navy a powerful force that helped to start a period of exploration and discovery. It was also a vibrant period in English literature that saw the publication of great works by Edmund Spenser, Christopher Marlowe and Ben Jonson. Perhaps most relevant to the study of *Julius Caesar* is the political climate at the time of its writing, since this play explores ideas of government, authority, rebellion, tyranny, anarchy and the value of the individual versus the state. Though the idea of the "divine right of kings" was still current in their thinking, and England was very much a monarchy under Elizabeth, she involved Parliament in her government more than her predecessors did. More importantly, by also supporting Protestantism in England, she made the later growth of representative government much easier. In Shakespeare's day, political ideas were starting to grow that would bring upheaval in the following century with Cromwell's revolution, "common law" theory and the work of John Locke, which placed political authority ultimately with the people and argued that revolutions could be justified. Much of this context will be better understood in the study of later times but merits mention here.

## Significance

*Julius Caesar* has significance both as a retelling of important historical events and as a literary re-interpretation that adds to and changes the meaning of those original events. Shakespeare chose Julius Caesar as a subject because of his huge shadow over European history—he is credited with making the key transition between the Roman Republic and the Roman Empire. Caesar remains an object of praise for his strong and charismatic leadership during a difficult time for Rome, but also an object of blame for his ambition and establishment of a dictatorship in place of a republic. He is like the "most popular" guy in school—adored by some and hated by others, but having the attention of everyone. Some people have such powerful personalities that it is hard to give a detached, objective judgment of their character. They also tend to become symbols or icons of what people love and hate, concrete targets that allow people to focus and embody abstract issues. Over the centuries, people have referred to the story of Caesar's assassination when discussing the nature of government, the corruption of ambition and power, the morality of rebellion and personal betrayal and the value of one man's life versus the common good.

The play itself has enriched our view of Caesar. Shakespeare treats the event and its characters, particularly Caesar and Brutus, with depth and fairness, refusing to take a strong, obvious stance for or against either one. We see Caesar's pride, but we still sympathize at his death. We may understand Brutus's patriotic and noble intentions but must admit that his actions do not solve Rome's problems. Like the historical events it portrays, the play has been used in the context of modern politics. For example, John Wilkes Booth, the actor who assassinated President Lincoln, revealed in his diary that he saw himself fulfilling the role of a noble Brutus striking a blow for liberty (Booth and his brothers performed *Julius Caesar* in November of 1864, just months before the assassination). In 1937, Orson Welles put on a modernized version of the play that compared Italian dictator Benito Mussolini to Caesar. The spirits of Caesar and the conspirators live on, adapting themselves to the times in which they live.

In addition, this play contains two of the most famous speeches in Shakespeare (and in the whole western literary canon): the pair of funeral orations by Brutus ("Not that I loved Caesar less, but that I loved Rome more") and Antony ("Friends, Romans, countrymen, lend me your ears"). Antony's speech in particular is an exceptionally well-crafted and powerful oration, admired for its skill and often held up as an example of the dangerous and manipulative power of a talented rhetorician who feels no constraint to live by God's law. Regardless, every student of debate and rhetoric can benefit from studying the art of persuasion in *Julius Caesar*.

Julius Caesar enriched Rome with his conquests and conquered Rome with his personality, setting the stage for the empire and the grandeur that can still be seen in these ruins.

## Main Characters

While reading *Julius Caesar,* you will probably be surprised to discover that Caesar does not seem to be the main character of the play. It certainly seems odd, too, that the title character can be killed off halfway through the play. Despite the rather sketchy portrayal of Caesar's character, however, the story of his fall is the core of the plot. All the other characters and their concerns center around his dominating figure, and the consequences of his ambition are profound and far-reaching.

Marcus Brutus is drawn with much more depth as a flawed but admirable character whose life is torn by an intense conflict between his love and respect for Caesar and his patriotism and love of freedom—he finds himself forced to choose between betraying his friend (and leader) and betraying his country. He develops and changes as his early suspicions grow to consume him, and he joins the conspiracy, finally obsessed with his ideals for Rome to such an extent that he is willing to violently murder Caesar. We see his human side as he interacts with his worried wife Portia and as he makes idealistic and naïve decisions which help to bring about his downfall.

Mark Antony and Cassius are the other primary players, but neither attains the depth of Brutus. In Mark Antony, Shakespeare provides an interesting, if shallow, portrait of a man who is good at manipulation, though he appears to have genuine love for Caesar as well. Cassius is even more clear-cut. If Brutus represents the "noble side" of the conspiracy, then Cassius represents the opposite. Obviously envious rather than idealistic, he deceives and flatters Brutus in order to secure his support and abuses the power he receives after Caesar's death.

## Setting and Summary

Caesar was active in politics from an early age and was part of the First Triumvirate with Pompey and Crassus. His alliance to Pompey was so close that his daughter was even married to him until she died in 54 B.C. Crassus was eventually killed in a battle, and Caesar's relationship with Pompey deteriorated as Pompey began to grow envious of Caesar's success. Eventually Pompey and the Roman Senate attempted to force Caesar to resign and disperse his army while he was on a campaign in Gaul, but Caesar marched into Italy and took command instead, finally defeating his rival in 48 B.C. and declaring himself dictator. Julius Caesar was a key figure in Roman history, usually seen as the leader who transitioned Rome from a republic to an empire. His reign and death were essential to pave the way for Augustus, under whose long and mostly peaceful reign Jesus was born.

For various details and characterizations, *Julius Caesar* depends heavily on Plutarch (remember him?), whose *Lives* were first translated into English in 1579, only about ten years before the start of Shakespeare's writing career. The play begins as Rome is celebrating Caesar's victory over Pompey's sons, which had occurred in 45 B.C. Cassius begins to criticize Caesar privately to Brutus while flattering him openly, though afterward they hear the report that Caesar refused a crown three times before a huge crowd. Cassius continues to coordinate the conspiracy, finally securing the support of Brutus the night before the planned murder. The next day, the ides of March, despite bad omens, Caesar appears at the Senate house and is assassinated. From there, Brutus and Cassius flee and the rest of the play surrounds the fallout of the murder, which brings destruction to many.

## Worldview

Despite Shakespeare's Christian context, the themes of *Julius Caesar* as revealed through its characters are basically Roman themes—ideas of honor, patriotism, friendship, authority and rebellion. Due to its pagan setting, it is not surprising that there is no reference to the Triune God, but there are also surprisingly few references even to the pagan gods,

except as general exclamations and oaths which have little real conviction ("O heavens!" "O ye gods!"). Though there are plenty of supernatural events in the play, such as the storm and other omens of Caesar's death, as well as the appearance of Caesar's ghost, they cannot be directly linked to the gods. The gods, in fact, have almost no role in the play. They are distant and detached from the affairs of men and governments. They are not active in rewarding the virtuous or punishing the guilty; they are not sources or inspirations for moral behavior; even their role in determining history is vague and ambiguous. They seem to live only in the speeches and imaginations of those who wish to believe in them.

Casca is perhaps the character with the most faith in the divine; but his belief in the gods consists in fearing their arguments among themselves and their stormy judgments on an imperfect world:

> Either there is civil strife in heaven,
> Or else the world too saucy with the gods
> Incenses them to send destruction....
> It is the part of men to fear and tremble
> When the most mighty gods by tokens send
> Such dreadful heralds to astonish us.

> (1.3.11–13, 54–56)[2]

Both Cicero and Cassius seem to mock his fearfulness. Cicero hints agnostically toward a natural explanation of the storm, while Cassius interprets it as a symbol of the destructive power of Caesar. Thus the storm, an "insurrection" of nature which seems to be a supernatural omen and a symbol of the traitorous disorder of Caesar's assassination, loses its force in the various interpretations of the characters. Caesar himself does acknowledge the gods. This is understandable, since he held the post of Pontifex Maximus (high priest) and helped to start the trend of regarding emperors as divine (he once had *deo invicto*—"undefeated god"—engraved below a statue of himself). In a moment of incredible pride just before his death, Shakespeare has him identify himself with the North Star and with Mount Olympus. This attitude bothers Cassius, as well it should, since he has seen Caesar's human weaknesses and so refuses to admit that Caesar is divine at all:

And this man
Is now become a god, and Cassius is
A wretched creature and must bend his body.

(1.2.115–117)

Caesar's strong belief in the gods and fate, however, ultimately contributes to his fall. When he goes to the Senate despite the pleas of his wife Calpurnia, he declares that he will do the courageous thing, because no matter what he does, fate cannot be avoided.

Among the other characters, though, the gods seem to matter little. Brutus, even at the most intense times, does not seek help from supernatural forces. He has one driving motive—his love for Rome and his duty to it—and he sees his own life's value totally in relation to Rome's welfare. In his most philosophical moment before the final battle, he can only hope to display patience in the face of "the providence of some high powers / that govern us below" (5.1.107). He does not pretend to know anything about these powers beyond the fact that he cannot resist them.

Cassius is not about to take things so submissively. He believes strongly in free will, the uncertainty of the "affairs of men" and the way his own actions determine his fate:

Men at some time are masters of their fates:
The fault, dear Brutus is not in our stars,
But in ourselves, that we are underlings.

(1.2.139–141)

Cassius is active in looking out for himself; he cannot depend on any gods to help him. At the end, reveals himself as a follower of Epicurus (5.1.70ff.), though at the same time he admits his faith is wavering.

How can we explain the differing views of Brutus and Cassius? While the popular religion of Rome served a large, complicated pantheon of gods and goddesses, in order to understand the real context of Brutus's patience and Cassius's willpower, we have to talk about the two main Roman philosophies, Stoicism and Epicureanism, which were more common among the upper classes. Both systems downplayed or changed the role and nature of their understanding of the gods dramatically, being more concerned with how people should act than with speculating about the nature of reality.
Stoics believed that reality is material, but that matter is divided into two types, the passive "stuff" of our

world and the unified principle or force that animates it. They called this cosmic force and order the *Logos,* which we could also think of as their version of God or Fate. The Stoic's goal was to live in harmony with this natural, universal order or reason by practicing wisdom, justice, courage and temperance. They thought that the most important thing was to know your duty and to do it well. Some forms of Stoicism emphasized the importance of submitting calmly to fate. This is why Brutus makes his final resolution to be patient beneath the acts of "providence," and why Cassius rebukes him with the words, "Of your philosophy you make no use, / If you give place to accidental evils" (4.3.145).

Epicureanism, on the other hand, denied that the gods had anything to do with our world. If they existed, they lived in an ideal realm of pleasure and could not be bothered with our small-time, mortal troubles, much like a man relaxing in a hammock and glancing occasionally at the activities of a nearby anthill. He might like to contemplate all the work the ants are doing, and he may even be impressed by some heroic act of ant bravery in a tiny, insignificant ant war, but he is definitely not involved in that world. This idea has important results. Because no gods or fate direct the world, the actions of our free will determine history. In addition, there is no afterlife and so we have nothing to fear from death. No god will judge us for our actions. Therefore, we should seek to live in serenity and pleasure—not a sensual and wild pleasure, but a moderate, aesthetic and intellectual one (Epicureans rightly realized that wild living leads to headaches, not happiness). This faith leads Cassius not so much to tranquility and pleasure, but more to trust in his own willpower, not to fear the supernatural storm and to dismiss any eternal consequences for his actions. His faith, though, falters near the end, as he begins to half-believe in omens and thus in the gods' involvement. Forgetting himself, he even wishes that the gods would be on their side in the coming battle.

It is easy to remember the difference between these two systems with a simple metaphor: Dogs are Stoics and cats are Epicureans. It does not take much imagination to think of a faithful dog following his master's every command, leaping through fields, streams, fences and shrubbery to bring back that ball or stick that was thrown for him. He knows his duty, and you can depend on him to do it, even if it kills him. Now picture a cat stretched out in a sunny spot beneath a window. He is friendly, but he basically looks out for number one. If he had his way, he would stay tranquil and calm all day long. He has his own free will, and he thinks he doesn't really need a master at all—he's certainly not afraid of his master. Even dog and cat names reinforce the comparison, if we want to take the simile further. The classic dog name is Fido—from the Latin for "faithful," and Stoics are defined by their faithfulness to the path of virtue. There really isn't a classic cat name, but some common ones are "Boots" (as in "Puss-in-Boots"), "Socks," or maybe "Mittens"— accessories meant to warm, protect and make you comfortable.

Let's look a bit more closely at these two philosophies. Though both of them strongly emphasize ethics—how we should behave—they do not adequately explain how we can discover true ethical rules. Is it wise, as the Stoics say, to live in accordance with the "natural reason" or "order" in the world? The world is not obviously a world of pure order. Galaxies collide, meteors pound the planets and stars collapse and explode. In the animal world, and in many human cultures, we see vicious competition for survival. Is this a good ethical textbook? By reasoning "naturally," Brutus justifies the killing of Caesar—at best a very questionable action. And what about an Epicurean quest for pleasure and serenity? Should we never stand up for a cause because it disturbs our calm? What if the pleasures of two persons are in conflict? Cassius's peace of mind and personal fulfillment are, to him, good reasons for the death of Caesar, and since there is no afterlife, he congratulates himself on saving Caesar twenty years of fearing death. It is clear that despite their attempt at providing fixed ethical values, Epicureanism and Stoicism cannot provide a sure guide to moral action for their followers.

The variety of views present in *Julius Caesar* keeps it from having a consistent worldview message on the nature of the gods or God, leaving the audience wandering between the opinions of each character, with little to guide them. We are left feeling alone in a complex and confusing world, where we do not know where to turn for wisdom, and even the most noble-seeming decisions lead to unforeseen snags. However righteous Brutus tries to be, he brings ruin on himself and his country, just like the corrupt, selfish Cassius. Epicureans and Stoics both end up defeated. The

"winner"—the only thing left—is the shrewd ambition and raw power of Antony and Octavius. The gods are simply too detached to figure in the final outcome. We may get dark, warning omens from them, but we cannot expect moral guidance, vindication or answered prayers. Power and ambition take all. The spirit of Caesar indeed lives on.

Like *Till We Have Faces*, we have in *Julius Caesar* a pagan story (with pagan characters and setting) being told by a Christian. The fact that the author is a Christian adds a layer of meaning on the pagan story, even if Christianity is never directly mentioned. We can begin to see how the characters' beliefs are being portrayed as wrong and unfulfilling. So when we see the play from a Christian point of view, its message becomes a critique of paganism that highlights the failures of its gods. Instead of a pantheon of gods that creates "civil strife in heaven," we acknowledge the unity, harmony and self-giving love within the Trinity. Instead of a detached, impersonal, universal life-force, we acknowledge the glorious diversity of the Persons in the Godhead and the true Logos who sustains all creation. Instead of faraway gods who are unknowable and unimportant to our personal and political affairs, we acknowledge the active, omnipresent God Who has promised that He shall be our God and we His people, that we may live "in" Him. God is our loving Father—we live near Him and he loves us, disciplines us, encourages us, provides for us and spends time with us. The Stoic god is like gravity or perhaps a *Star Wars* "force"—only not quite as neat (you can only use it as a motivation to do your chores, not to move things in the air). And the Epicurean gods (if they even exist) are like the rulers of a distant country that has nothing to do with you, and never will. The difference between our God's presence with us and the impersonal or distant pagan gods of Stoics and Epicureans is like light and dark. Shakespeare does not highlight this difference very much in the play—the closest he comes is forcing a comparison between the Christian and pagan ideas of destiny by having Brutus use the Christian word *providence* rather than the pagan word *fate*. As a Protestant, Shakespeare certainly would have held a strong view of providence, but he stops short of Christianizing the pagan idea—Brutus is clearly referring to distant, obscure "powers," not the involved, sustaining God of the Bible.

Of course, this view of divinity will define a view of humanity, both as individuals and societies. The world of Caesar, Antony, Brutus and Cassius has concepts of sin, salvation, judgment and progress that fit in with its theology. With Caesar's polytheism, sin can only be transgression of the gods' will (and Caesar himself is a god!). But since there is little harmony among the gods themselves, obeying one god may very well anger another, as is so clearly seen in Roman myths—Virgil's Aeneas is an example of piety, yet his piety does not help him against the vengeful anger of Juno. *Sin* and *obedience* are constantly shifting and eventually boil down to currying favor with the right gods at the right time, trying to stay out of the middle of their quarrels. The gods are not bound by a law outside or within themselves, so their judgments may be arbitrary and they may change their minds at any time. Like a double-agent spy, you cannot have fixed loyalties; you have to satisfy all sides and hope that no one finds out the game you are playing.

While Epicureanism and Stoicism seek to provide fixed ethical rules, the only consequences for virtue and vice are earthly ones, and the only motivation to be virtuous is to gain serenity or to live in harmony with the *Logos.* Epicurean gods make no law; in fact, one of Epicureanism's main goals is to eliminate fear of the gods, quite the opposite of the biblical fear of God. In the pantheism of the Stoics, each person is in fact a part of God, so the concepts of sin and obedience become meaningless. In the end, anyone may disagree that either of these systems is the true path to happiness; these philosophies become suggested guidelines rather than divine law. As in ancient polytheism, there is no "original sin," and so virtue, rather than grace, is the way of salvation. Even then, this earthly "salvation" of inner peace, pleasure and tranquility is not guaranteed; otherwise tragedy would not be possible. Sometimes the most moral people encounter defeat in this life, and if we believe Epicureans or Stoics, earthly defeat is total defeat. The only victory is in holding to one's principles even when they cannot save.

*"Et tu, Brute?" A first-century scabbard found in the Rhine.*

In this worldview, you have to follow uncertain guides to a doubtful destination, like a hiker who is forced to use a bad map, who could follow the trail exactly on paper and still end up lost or stranded on a dangerous cliff. You know that your precise map-reading skills—like Brutus's unswerving virtue—might destroy you; but like him, you resolve that whatever happens, the only certain victory will be in the final knowledge that you remained faithful to the map as he was true to his idea of virtue. Standing on the edge of the cliff as a storm rolls in, you hold up the map and shout, "At least I followed the trail!" In an uncertain world, you must set yourself up as the only certainty. The only solid faith is in oneself, and so the only sin is against oneself. Brutus's strong commitment to virtue shows the image of God in him, but it is fallen and misdirected.

Societies, too, struggle to find peace and harmony. If the community of gods is always fighting, how can we expect harmonious human communities? If it takes a Jupiter to smack down all competitors, like some cosmic professional wrestler, reigning by force over the gods, won't it take a Caesar to put all other Romans in submission to himself alone? Absolute rule becomes the only way to peace and order. If the gods do not matter, and only individual peace and tranquility, how can we maintain order in a fallen world? Epicureans often discouraged political involvement as too perturbing (Cassius is an exception), but this escapism does not work in societies of fallen people. Anarchy would reign. Peace requires active justice and fighting for the right, and this is often disturbing and unpleasant. Secluded, pleasure-loving Epicureans just do not have what it takes to stop crime and fight off invaders— imagine where we would be if our policemen, judges, soldiers and firemen were all art critics, bookworms or just plain couch potatoes—their skills would not be appropriate for their very necessary profession. Stoics, with all their preaching of duty and a "stiff upper lip," can do better, but it is still not enough. Though Stoics often anticipated Christianity by teaching that status, race and nationality are not ultimately important, their pantheism (the belief that everything is a piece of God) provides a bad model for human societies. It could be interpreted to support either totalitarianism (iron-fisted control of all of life, usually by government) or anarchy (no societal control at all). On the one hand, because each individual is really part of the one, divine *Logos*, it is this One that is really important—thus Brutus's concern for only the common good at the expense of Caesar's life. On the other hand, each individual is part of the divine, and there is no law above them—a potential recipe for anarchy. Imagine a sports coach who emphasizes "the good of the team" so much that he seems to forget that there are individual team members. He calls every play from the sidelines. No one can run, pass or score without specific instructions from him, and he doesn't allow any player to improvise during a game or become too much of a star. Another coach sits on the bench during practice and says, "Okay guys, just do whatever you feel like. Each of you is a Team of One." I don't think either coach would rack up many wins.

Because of all this, *progress*—the gradual salvation of the world as a whole—is absent from *Julius Caesar*. Instead, we find cycles between tyranny and anarchy. As the Roman Republic falls apart, Caesar rises to force it back together. After his death, anarchy reigns again until Octavius and Antony again keep it together under a shared rule. Remembering our Roman history, we know what happens after that—further conflict between Octavius and Antony, resulting in the absolute rule of Octavius as Augustus Caesar. The stability at the end of the play that follows the victory of Octavius and Antony is an illusion. The cycles of tyranny and anarchy remain in the background, haunting the play just like the ghost of Caesar.

—Jared Miller

## For Further Reading

Spielvogel, Jackson. *Western Civilization*. Fifth Edition. Belmont, Calif.: Wadsworth/Thomson Learning, 2003. 98–99, 122–131, 363–366, 434–435.

*Veritas Press History Cards: New Testament, Greece and Rome*. Lancaster, Pa.: Veritas Press. 19, 20.

Leithart, Peter. *Brightest Heaven of Invention: A Christian Guide to Six Shakespeare Plays*. Moscow, Idaho: Canon Press, 1996. 73–110.

# Session I: Prelude

## A Question to Consider

How would you define *ambition*? Is it a virtue or a vice, and why?

*From the General Information above discuss or list short answers to the following questions:*

1. What is the historical importance of Julius Caesar?
2. What was the Golden Age of England under Elizabeth I?
3. What are some distinctive aspects of Shakespeare's work? Why is he so respected and admired?
4. Why do some doubt that the historical William Shakespeare actually penned the plays that we read?
5. How is *Julius Caesar* like C.S. Lewis's *Till We Have Faces*?
6. Who was Pompey?
7. What did Epicureans and Stoics believe, and how can comparing them to cats and dogs help us remember the difference?
8. Compare the philosophy driving Brutus with that of Cassius.
9. What is most striking about the gods in this play?
10. What are the circumstances of Julius Caesar's death?
11. What two great speeches take place after the murder of Caesar?

## Optional Activity 1: Reading Aloud

Read aloud part of Act 1. If working in a group setting, assign students to read the different characters. Get into it. Encourage as much "acting" as possible. You might especially enjoy the opening scene with the punning, "saucy" cobbler.

## Optional Activity 2: Music

You may find it interesting to listen to G.F. Handel's opera *Giulio Cesare*, which was first produced in 1724. It is set in Egypt before the events in Shakespeare's play and tells of the relationships between Pompey, Julius and Cleopatra. Discuss the themes at work in the libretto as well as the music.

## Optional Activity 3: Outline

Outline the play by act and scene as you read it, which will help you to pay attention to Shakespeare's sometimes difficult language. The outline will serve as a ready resource for discussion. For each scene, you should record a brief summary of the plot. For most scenes, you should be able to list any themes as well as brief notes on the major characters involved. Key passages, whether for plot points, themes or characters, should be recorded with act, scene and line number. You may also wish to note favorite or memorable passages.

**READING ASSIGNMENT:**
*Julius Caesar*, Acts 1 and 2

# SESSION II: RECITATION

*Julius Caesar*, Acts 1 and 2

## Comprehension Questions

*Answer the following questions for factual recall:*

### ACT I

1. How does Shakespeare, through the tribunes' speeches, depict the "mob" of common people in Act 1, scene 1 (1.1)? What fault do the tribunes find in them? How does the mention of Pompey foreshadow Caesar's fate (Hint: look ahead to 3.1.128–130)?
2. What does Brutus's response to the shouting (1.2.86–87, 140–42) reveal about the reason he is "at war" with himself (1.2.43–54)?
3. What is Cassius's evaluation of Caesar? Of Brutus? Does he believe in fate (1.2.62–169, 274–288)?
4. How is the mob depicted when Caesar refuses the crown?
5. Where do the conspirators agree to meet near the end of the act? Why do you think they choose that place?
6. Why do the conspirators want Brutus on their side? How does Cassius plan to win him over? How do these things reflect on the rightness of the conspirators' cause?

7. What kind of man is Cassius? Why is his "lean and hungry look" (1.2.204) appropriate to his character?
8. Why do you think Shakespeare chose to have Caesar's refusal of the crown occur off-stage? (Hint: What spin does Casca give when he retells the story, and what is Brutus's reaction to seeing Caesar afterward?)
9. How do Casca, Cicero and Cassius interpret the storm and the other unnatural events? What does Cassius's attitude toward Casca's fear show about his character?

### ACT II

1. Summarize Brutus's reasons for joining the conspiracy against Caesar.
2. How does Caesar respond to the storm and omens? What does Nature mimic? Why does he follow Decius's interpretation of Calpurnia's bloody dream?
3. How might Caesar's acceptance of Decius's argument in 2.2.102–114 be used to show that he is indeed ambitious?
4. Why does Brutus argue to spare Antony in scene 1?
5. While Brutus is planning insurrection, how is insurrection already at work in his own life? (Hints: What is going on in his thoughts? How is his relationship with Portia?)
6. What do his opinions in his speech arguing to preserve Antony's life show about his character and motives (2.1.177–198)?
7. Brutus is, above all, against the "spirit of Caesar." What does he mean? Is it possible to separate a person from his goals, ideals and actions (2.1.184–186)?
8. Caesar decides to go to the Forum in spite of the omens, and he uses the idea of fate to justify his decision, arguing that whether he goes or not, the gods' will shall be done (2.2.31–34). Critique this reasoning.

**READING ASSIGNMENT:**
*Julius Caesar*, Act 3

# SESSION III: DISCUSSION

*Julius Caesar*, Act 3

## A Question to Consider

How would you define *tyranny* and *anarchy?* What makes a leader a tyrant?

*Discuss or list short answers to the following questions:*

### Text Analysis

1. How does the play explore tyranny and anarchy? Who represents tyranny? Anarchy?
2. How do the storm and omens on the night before Caesar's death relate to the theme of anarchy?

### Cultural Analysis

1. Where do you see elements of tyranny in our own culture? What about elements of anarchy? If there is tyranny in our government, how is it fundamentally different from ancient tyranny?
2. How is the U.S. Constitution our nation's attempt to solve these problems?

### Biblical Analysis

1. How was Israel governed before the era of kings (Ex. 18:14–26; Num. 15:32–36, 35:34; Deut. 17:8–9, 19:12; Judg. 17:6, 21:25). "Every man did what was right in his own eyes"—was that a good thing or bad thing?
2. What was God's view of putting a king over Israel? Are kings necessarily tyrants (Deut. 17:14ff, 1 Sam. 10:17–19)?
3. There is authority even in the Trinity. Jesus obeys the Father and is sent by Him, and they both send the Spirit (John 14:16, 26; 15:26). At the same time, the Persons are not in a state of anarchy, each doing whatever he wishes. There is authority and equality, unity and diversity. How might the relationship of the Trinity give us clues about balancing liberty, authority and equality?

## SUMMA

*Write an essay or discuss this question, integrating what you have learned from the material above.*
Jesus declared himself a king (see John 19:12). How did His authority challenge worldly leaders like Augustus Caesar?

## Application

1. How do these same issues play out in families?
2. Based on this discussion, what changes would you recommend to our current government?

# SESSION IV: DISCUSSION

## A Question to Consider

Today, America's official policy is that our government will not assassinate foreign leaders. Is this policy correct? Is it ever right to kill the leader of another country? Of our own country?

*Discuss or list short answers to the following questions:*

### Text Analysis

1. Who is in the right, Brutus or Caesar? Is Caesar's authority legitimate? Is the assassination justifiable?
2. Assume Brutus is right that Caesar is dangerous and ambitious. Should he have participated in the plot?
3. Why does Brutus finally give in and participate in the conspiracy?

### Cultural Analysis

1. Is one individual's life worth sacrificing, through a murder, for the good of the country?
2. What stance does our culture take on rebellion in the context of home, society and government?
3. Is it possible to value rebellion in our individual lives while valuing good citizenship in our public lives?

### Biblical Analysis

1. Examine Romans 13. What conclusions about assassination could we draw from this passage alone?
2. David had the chance to assassinate Saul (1 Sam. 24:4–6; 26:9), but he refused to do so. Ehud, however, freed Israel by assassinating King Eglon (Judg. 3:14–22). Why are these two events not contradictory?

## SUMMA

*Write an essay or discuss this question, integrating what you have learned from the material above.*
What is the difference between assassination and murder?

# SESSION V: RECITATION

## Comprehension Questions

*Answer the following questions for factual recall:*

1. How does Artemidorus try to warn Caesar? Why is Caesar's response significant, especially coming right before he is assassinated for his personal ambition?

2. In Caesar's speech to Cimber (3.1.43–55), he condemns flattery. How did Decius evaluate Caesar's resistance to flattery in 2.1.220–229?

3. Summarize Caesar's final speech about constancy (3.1.66–81). What does he mean by "wilt thou lift up Olympus?" (3.1. 83)? Why would Shakespeare place such a proud, lofty speech just before the assassination?

4. What is the tone of Brutus's first response to Antony after the murder (3.1.183–195)?

5. How does Antony balance the delicate situation immediately after the murder in his dealings with the conspirators (3.1.167–252)? How does he save his own skin while still remaining pro-Caesar (neither a "coward or a flatterer")?

6. Why does Brutus, despite Cassius's better judgment, allow Antony to speak a funeral oration?

7. Antony calls on "the spirit of Caesar" to get revenge (3.1.295). Compare this to Brutus's meaning of the "spirit of Caesar" earlier in 2.1.182–186. Do you think Shakespeare meant the phrase to have a double meaning? (Hint: Look ahead to 4.3.320 and 5.3.105–107.)

8. Summarize Brutus's funeral oration (3.2.16ff.). What is its tone? Is the crowd convinced by him?

9. Summarize Antony's oration (3.2.52ff. Identify his main arguments as well as his emotional appeals. Which of his techniques do you think are the most effective?

10. Of Brutus's and Antony's speeches, which one is prose? Which one is poetry? Why?

11. What happens to the crowd under Antony's rhetorical power?

12. What is the significance of the mob scene with Cinna the poet immediately following the assassination (3.3)? Consider also the play's former references to "the multitude" or "the common people."

# SESSION VI: DISCUSSION

In a group setting, choose two volunteers to read Brutus's and Antony's speeches aloud (others may read the parts of the citizens scattered throughout Antony's). Select readers the day before so that they can practice their parts several times. *Consider a small reward (announced ahead of time) for the most moving speaker.* If not in a group setting, individuals can read the same material aloud, practicing a different style for each of the two main characters.

## A Question to Consider

What is rhetoric? Is it a good thing, a bad thing or just a neutral tool? How should we use it, if at all?

*Discuss or list short answers to the following questions:*

### Text Analysis

1. Who do you think demonstrates more integrity in his speech, Brutus or Antony?

2. The "multitude" in *Julius Caesar* becomes a frighteningly powerful and irrational force, as we clearly see in the case of Cinna the Poet (3.3). What role did rhetoric play?

3. Can we blame the multitude for their actions, or were they in some way forced or manipulated by rhetoric? Who is guilty for the riots, the crowd or Antony?

### Cultural Analysis

1. Define *rhetoric*.

2. Which of these things contribute to the morality of a speech?
   a. Sincerity
   b. Character of the speaker
   c. Goal of speech
   d. Techniques used by speech
   e. Arguments used

3. Give examples of rhetoric that you encounter every day.

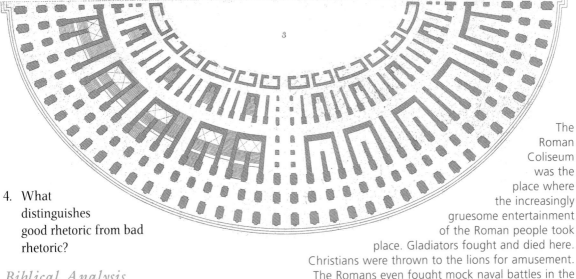

4. What distinguishes good rhetoric from bad rhetoric?

### Biblical Analysis

1. Look at Genesis 3 as an example of bad rhetoric. What makes the rhetoric wicked?
2. Look in the Bible for examples of godly uses of rhetoric to persuade other people or God Himself. Does God use it when talking to His people? Some examples are Exodus 32:11–14; Job (the entire book, but especially chapters 4 and 9–40); Psalm 30; Matthew 21:33–45.
3. The Bible states that teachers have a serious responsibility toward those under them (see Hebrews 13:17, James 3:1). What aspect of rhetoric is being addressed here?

### SUMMA

*Write an essay or discuss this question, integrating what you have learned from the material above.*
Which speech, Brutus's or Antony's, is more effective and why? You may know that you will be learning Rhetoric in your schooling in the future. What does this imply about this future study?

The Roman Coliseum was the place where the increasingly gruesome entertainment of the Roman people took place. Gladiators fought and died here. Christians were thrown to the lions for amusement. The Romans even fought mock naval battles in the Coliseum by filling up its lower level with water.

### Application

Why not just use purely logical arguments? Does rhetoric really matter?

## SESSION VII: WRITING

### Progymnasmata

In this session we return again to the writing excercises called the *progymnasmata*, in particular the excercise called an *impersonation*. The impersonation seeks to imitate the style and characteristics of the person making the speech. To compose an impersonation:

- Discuss or think through the characteristics of the person whose speech you are emulating.
- Read carefully through the speech or event that you are impersonating (in many cases you will be asked to write an impersonation of a speech

that a person has not given, but could have made at a certain time).

- Put the book away and write the speech yourself.
- Read it to someone else.
- After reading it, explain how different personal characteristics of this person come through in your impersonation.

Be careful to remember what has happened in the personal history of the character on which you are writing, and also remember what will happen in the future. You must to remember to keep everything in the proper setting (i.e., you can not make the young George Washington say, "I will be the first president under the new Constitution of the United States,"

Portrait of a Roman man that dates from the third century A.D. Portraits of this artistic quality were common throughout the Roman Empire.

because when he was a boy, of course, neither the Constitution nor the office existed, let alone the country itself).

*Write an impersonation of Antony's funeral speech. Rewrite it with a more calm and rational tone or write it with a more angry, emotional tone. After choosing either of these, consider what affect your speech would have had on the audience. When you are done with your writing, reread Antony's speech and see how much more effective it is than yours (Shakespeare was a master of rhetoric, wasn't he?).*

### READING ASSIGNMENT:
*Julius Caesar*, Acts 4 and 5

# SESSION VIII: RECITATION
*Julius Caesar*, Acts 4 and 5

## Comprehension Questions

*Answer the following questions for factual recall:*

### ACT IV

1. Summarize the meeting between Antony, Octavius and Lepidus. What do they discuss together? What discussion do Antony and Octavius have after Lepidus leaves (4.1)?
2. Describe the discussion Cassius and Brutus have (4.3.1–144). How is the argument resolved?
3. What has happened to Portia? How does Brutus handle it?
4. Why does Brutus decide to march to Philippi?
5. What omen does Brutus see?
6. What does the first meeting reveal about the motives and character of Octavius and Antony (4.1)?
7. Compare the meeting scenes between Antony, Octavius and Lepidus on one side and Brutus and Cassius on the other. Why do you think Shakespeare placed the two scenes next to each other? How is the presence of strife within each side significant?
8. What is the significance of Portia's death?
9. How is the visit of Caesar's ghost symbolic?

10. How does Brutus and Cassius' meeting further define their characters and reveal their original motives? What kind of leader does Cassius turn out to be? Brutus?

## Act V

1. In what philosophy does Cassius believe? Why is his faith in it shaken?
2. What is Brutus's "philosophy" of action if they lose the battle? Why is he against suicide? Why does he refer to Cato (5.1.112–130)?
3. Briefly summarize the battle.
4. What is Antony and Octavius's final opinion of Brutus (5.5.76–89)? Compare it to their words against Brutus in 5.1.32–75.
5. Cite several differences between Shakespeare's and Plutarch's stories of the assassination and aftermath. Why might Shakespeare make the changes he did?

# Session IX: Discussion

## A Question to Consider

What is tragedy?

*Discuss or list short answers to the following questions:*

### Text Analysis

1. Does Caesar fit the model of a tragic hero? Why or why not?
2. Could Brutus be considered the tragic hero of this play?
3. Could Cassius be considered a tragic hero? Rome itself? Why or why not?

### Cultural Analysis

1. How do we use the word *tragic* in everyday life? How is that different from tragedy in literature?
2. Is the modern, scientific, atheist/agnostic world-view essentially tragic?
3. How does this worldview affect the creation of tragedy in literature?

### Biblical Analysis

1. Consider the stories of Adam and Eve (Gen. 3) and Jesus (e.g., Matt. 27–28). Are these stories tragic? Explain.

2. In what senses might the biblical worldview be considered tragic? How is it not tragic (Gen. 3, Rev. 21–22)?

## Application

The biblical worldview is not fundamentally tragic. It is one of victory and blessing for God's people. This should make us rejoice every day. "All things work together for good . . ." (Rom. 8:28). There is never a final defeat for those faithful to God. This should encourage us through tough times and spur us on to good works when things appear to be going well.

## Summa

*Write an essay or discuss this question, integrating what you have learned from the material above.* Much tragedy involves cause and effect between faults and punishments. How can this inform our own lives? How do tragedies teach us?

## Optional Activity: Writing

Write an essay about the theme of "honor" and "nobility" in *Julius Caesar.* Note where and how Shakespeare uses the words. How does this relate to the major themes of the play?

# Session X: Evaluation

## Comprehension Questions

Grammar

*Briefly identify the following characters, things or people with one or two sentences. (2 points each)*

1. Briefly describe the different ways in which insurrection/rebellion manifests itself in *Julius Caesar.*
2. Summarize Brutus's reasons for joining the conspiracy against Caesar.
3. Why does Brutus spare Antony?
4. What grievances do Brutus and Cassius bring against one another in the aftermath of the assassination?
5. What are the two main meanings of the phrase "the spirit of Caesar?"
6. What is a "tragic hero?" Who are the candidates for the tragic hero of the play? What are their tragic faults?

## Logic

*Questions should be answered with a paragraph or two. (10 points each)*

1. What role does rhetoric play in the world of *Julius Caesar?* How should rhetoric be defined and used from a Christian perspective?

2. There are numerous morals taught in the play *Julius Caesar?* Describe the one you think most important. Support your arguments by referring to specifics of the play.

## Lateral Thinking

*This essay challenges you to take concepts and ideas learned in* Julius Caesar *and see the connections that these ideas have in other works that we have read this year. Write up to a 1,000 word essay on one of the three questions. (15 points)*

1. Classic tragic heroes are noble (even admirable) yet often flawed. Compare the nobility and flaws of Caesar, Brutus, Oedipus and Antigone.

2. Compare the falls of Caesar, Brutus and Cassius to the fall of Oedipus. Do they each have a "moment of truth" or moment of knowledge, particularly self-knowledge, caused by their falls?

3. Trace the themes of insurrection, betrayal, violence and justice in the plays of Aeschylus and Sophocles. Compare to *Julius Caesar.* How do these themes relate to tragedy?

# OPTIONAL SESSION A: WRITING

## Progymnasmata

Classical training in rhetoric included preparatory writing exercises called the *progymnasmata.* These exercises in composition introduced the beginning student to basic forms and techniques that would then be used and combined when practicing more

This coin bears the imprint of Julius Caesar. The emperors that followed issued coinage with their own images on them as well. It was, no doubt, a coin like this one bearing the image of Emperor Tiberius that Christ said to "Render therefore to Caesar . . ." in Matthew 22:21.

advanced exercises and speeches. One of these progymnasmata was called the *encomium,* a composition written to praise an individual. Its opposite exercise (which condemns an individual) is called a *vituperation* (or an *invective*). This writing exercise expounds the virtues or condemns the vices of a specific person (e.g., Joe is a strong warrior), but does not talk about virtue in a general sense (e.g., strength in war is admirable).

The encomium and the vituperation each have six parts. The *Prologue* comes first. It introduces the topic and, at the end of the paragraph, states or implies the opinion of the writer. The second part of this exercise is a paragraph called *Description of Heritage.* In this paragraph the writer looks for ways to praise or condemn the person on account of his family history. For instance, if a person comes from righteous parents, then highlight the fact that he learned his righteous habits at home and added to the glory of the family name. A vituperation would emphasize that he comes from a family or nation that taught him wrong beliefs or bad habits. Next comes a paragraph called *Description of Upbringing.* The point is to show how the person profited from a good education or overcame a bad one (this is for the encomium). For the vituperation you should attempt to show how he failed to profit from a good education or learned well the lessons of a bad education. The most powerful part of the encomium comes next: the *Description of Deeds.* In this section the writer praises the excellencies of the mind, body and fortune of the subject. For example, the writer praises the practice of philosophical virtue, the way the person looked and his wealth, influence or social stature. Since Christianity has transformed our society it seems out of place to dwell on physical appearance or possessions (i.e., he was evil because he was quite homely, or it is obvious that he was a good man because he was fabulously rich), so instead the paragraph should concentrate on the actions and motives of the subject. This can be especially powerful if his life demonstrates a pattern. Next is a *Comparison* of the subject to someone else to portray him in a favorable light (if it is an encomium). An unfavorable comparison is best for vituperation. The final paragraph is an *Exhortation or Prayer* in which others are called on to imitate this person's example or a proclamation to everyone telling them not to go down the wicked path that this person did.

*Write an encomium or vituperation on your choice of Caesar, Brutus, Antony or Cassius; or write a comparison of Brutus and Cassius. Try to stick to source material from the play (cite particular passages), though Plutarch may be helpful for some material on the characters' background. Note that if the book tells little information you may omit a section. Try, however, to use what you do know to create a section of the encomium. For instance, we do not know much about Marcus Brutus' education, but we do know that he came from a Senatorial and Patrician family and thus we can reason out many things (e.g., he was taught to love freedom).*

I.  Prologue
    - Introduce the topic
    - State your opinion
II. Description of Heritage
    - Praise the person on account of his family history
III. Description of Upbringing
    - Show how the person profited from his education
IV. Description of Deeds
    - Praise the excellencies of his actions and motives
V.  Comparison
    - Portray the person favorably to someone else
VI. Exhortation or Prayer
    - Call upon others to imitate this person's example

# OPTIONAL SESSION B: ACTIVITY

## Debate

An age-appropriate activity, drawing on students' developing argumentative skills, is a class debate on the following question: "Was Brutus justified in helping to assassinate Julius Caesar?" (If a debate is not possible due to having only one student, have the student prepare two short speeches to present orally in front of the teacher, arguing for both sides of the question as equally as possible, with an additional, briefer speech telling which side he or she agrees with and why. Do *not* let the student simply read a written speech.) Allow students to appeal only to the play for source material. This will help them realize that a work of historical fiction is an independent literary work and should be judged on its own merits and not simply on its historical accuracy. It is also a good jumping-off point for discussing the blurry lines between biography, story and history. Leave time for discussion at the end to review the debate went.

Before starting, review the structure of a formal debate (opening arguments, rebuttals, cross-examinations, closing arguments) and choose who will have the burden of proof. Have students divide the labor on each team and prepare their arguments for homework. Not all students need speak, but all should be involved in collecting material for the arguments, anticipating objections and arguments from the other side, writing prepared opening arguments, taking notes as the other side speaks, etc. Ideally, schedule a complete class period for the debate and include a panel of faculty or parents to judge the winners and provide prizes—competition helps to spur achievement.

# OPTIONAL SESSION C: PERFORMANCE

Put on a production of a long scene, an act, or the entirety of *Julius Caesar*, creating costumes and sets and choosing music to accompany it. Perform it live in class or make your own film version.

Alternatively, attend a live production of the play if one is showing in your area sometime during the year. *Julius Caesar* is not one of the most commonly-performed Shakespeare plays, so this may prove difficult. Several film versions exist, however:

1950, directed by David Bradley, starring Harold Tasker (Caesar), Charlton Heston (Antony) and David Bradley (Brutus).

1953, directed by Joseph L. Mankiewicz, starring Marlon Brando (Antony), Louis Calhern (Caesar) and James Mason (Brutus).

1960, modernized and retitled An Honorable Murder, directed by Godfrey Grayson, starring John Longden (Caesar), Norman Wooland (Brutus) and Philip Saville (Antony).

1970, directed by Stuart Burge, starring Charlton Heston (Antony), Jason Robards (Brutus) and John Gielgud (Caesar).

1979 (BBC TV version), directed by Herbert Wise, starring Richard Pasco (Brutus), Charles Gray (Caesar) and Keith Mitchell (Antony).

1979 (U.S. TV version) directed by Michael Langham. Watch for Morgan Freeman as Casca.

Teachers are cautioned to view any film before presenting it in class or recommending it. Be sure to discuss the live production or film in its own right, in addition to using it to discuss Shakespeare's text. Explore what a production of a play can add to the text and how a production can alter its interpretation and message. The teacher could even collect scenes from various versions onto a single tape or DVD and compare them with the class, discussing why various actors and directors chose to interpret the play as they did.

## ENDNOTES

1   Quoted in *Shakespeare: Julius Caesar,* Peter Ure, ed. Casebook Series. London: Macmillan, 1969.

2   For this and subsequent references to the play find three numbers separated by periods to identify act, scene, and line. Thus "2.1" refers to the entire scene 1 of Act 2, and "3.2.75" refers to Act 3, scene 2, line 75. Exact line numbers may vary depending on your edition.

# REVELATION

Imagine that the President of the United States wrote you a personalized, handwritten letter. You look at the return address and see the very signature of the President of the United States on the envelope. Can you imagine going home and saying, "Oh well, maybe I'll get to this next week. I don't have time for that guy. Who is he? And why would he be writing me?" Of course you would not do that. In fact, you probably would not get very far from the mailbox before ripping open that envelope and finding out "what does he have to say to me?" And what if, when you opened the letter from the President, you found it saying something like this:

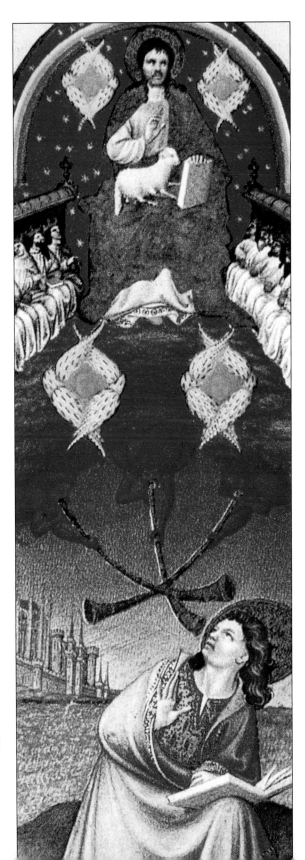

Dear Friend,

  Recently, I learned of a dangerous thief loose in the town in which you live. I need help in apprehending this dodgy criminal. My detectives have learned that in the near future he is going to attempt to come and rob your home and harm you and your family.

  Do not, however, be afraid. I have my agents watching your house, and they will nab the thief and protect your family. One of them will work from your basement so that he will be ready to catch the robber at a moment's notice. He will come dressed as a plumber with a large toolbox. Please let him in. The tools in his box are the surveillance equipment and weapons that he needs to protect your family and to apprehend this dangerous menace.

  Thank you for your help.

  Sincerely,

*John Q. Washington*
PRESIDENT OF THE UNITED STATES

Pictured from a Book of Hours is a depiction of John, the author of Revelation, experiencing his vision of heaven. Note the many details gleaned from Revelation, including the elders surrounding God's throne.

"Wow!" you think, "this sounds important."

Now, imagine that the person who received this letter made some mistakes interpreting it as they read. First, they thought that it was a form letter written to everyone in the community or maybe even everyone in the country. They also read the phrase "near future" and imagined this to mean "in the next couple years." A person making these sorts of mistakes would prepare very differently from the person who read the letter correctly. One can even image the person who read the letter wrongly greeting the FBI agent disguised as a plumber at the door and saying, "Plumber? We don't need a plumber; we have no leaky pipes." He would begin to shut the door.

"But I am *the* plumber," the agent might say, "the one in the letter, the one who is here to protect you."

"I hardly think we need protection from leaky pipes. I can fix most of them myself," the homeowner might say. "Have a nice day." He shuts the door and leaves the agent outside.

This story might seem far-fetched but it does highlight the importance of interpreting material correctly. Well, God has written us a letter and has certified its contents, and He says, "I want you to be blessed and to know how to live your life. Here are my instructions." The book of Revelation is an exciting and mysterious book for many. It is full of images like seven-headed dragons, flying horses and swarms of locusts. At first glance it seems like a science fiction novel, full of odd and fantastic images. Yet it is important to remember that the book of Revelation is part of the Bible. Since it is God's Word to His people, then it is important that we not only read, understand and believe it, but that we also do the things it instructs us to do.

# GENERAL INFORMATION

## Author and Context

In the opening of this particular book of the Bible we have a lengthy chain of communication described for us, as to how the apostle John came to receive this book:

> The Revelation of Jesus Christ, which God gave Him to show His servants—things which must shortly take place. And He sent and signified it by His angel to His servant John, who bore witness to the word of God, and to the testimony of Jesus Christ, to all things that he saw. Blessed is he who reads and those who hear the words of this prophecy, and keep those things which are written in it; for the time is near. (vs. 1–3)

Notice the chain of command. God the Father has given a revelation to His Son, Jesus Christ, for the sake of His servants. Christ has given this to the angel who brings it to John, who turns and delivers it to us. This is a very important thing. This kind of elaboration of the chain of communication is not given in any other book of the Bible. This is a book that was delivered by angels to an apostle from the very Son of God, Who Himself received it from His Father. This is the revelation of Jesus Christ received from God the Father. The apostle John, John the son of Zebedee, wrote down what the angel revealed to him. John was a sort of secretary or reporter who took notes about the things Jesus showed him and told him.

The Greek word for *revelation* is a word that means an "unveiling." It is what you do to a statue. A sculptor carves out a statue, and then he puts a drape over it and puts it out in the public square. Then the day comes for its unveiling, when everyone will be able to see it. The cover is removed, and now the truth is in front of everyone. So too, God tells us by the very name of this book that He wants to show us something. He wants to tell us the truth about history. Here is the unveiling of it all for you. This is one of many proofs that God does not intend the book of Revelation to stay a secret or hidden message that no one can understand. God expects us to understand it, and that is why the book is called the *Revelation*.

## Significance

Like the Old Testament prophets, John makes it clear that his word has a specific, divine origin. John does not have a message of his own. John is only bearing something in his hands to us.

The book of Revelation is highly figurative literature. There are visions and symbols and images. What often happens is that many Christians go to the book of Revelation as though it were a newspaper account written ahead of time. But is the book of Revelation written like a newspaper? No. The book of Revelation is prophetic literature. The book of Revelation is full of figures of speech or images that have to be interpreted. For example, chapter thirteen contains the description of the beast. The beast has seven heads and ten horns and comes up out of the Mediterranean Sea. While this could be literal, no one in the Christian church interprets it as an actual monster God has created for the occasion.

So, how can we understand these things? Remember the angel? God is going to tell us what these things mean. We all have an ability to take a piece of literature, at least if it is clearly written as this book is, and to make sense out of it even though it is highly figurative. It is not really all that difficult. After we have interpreted all of these figures, and we have gone through the outline, what does God want us to know from the book of Revelation? Very simply, *God wants us to know that His kingdom, the kingdom of His Son Jesus Christ, is going to triumph over all opposition.* We're going to win.

In the very first verse we read: "The Revelation of

The woman clothed with the sun gives birth to a son who will rule all the nations with an iron scepter and is called Faithful and True, the Word of God and wears the name King of Kings and Lord of Lords. The twelve stars she wears symbolize the twelve tribes of the Old Testament and the twelve apostles of the New Testament. The dragon is not able to attack the woman because she is protected by God, but her offspring, the individuals within the church, can be attacked. The woman is safe for 1,260 days but there is no mention of the fate of the woman after that time.

Jesus Christ, which God gave Him to show His servants—things which must shortly take place." Notice these events must *shortly* come to pass. That is worth emphasizing. What is being referred to in this book is not optional. It is not just possible or even probable. It must happen and quickly. God has promised that certain things would take place in history, and therefore they must take place. In verse 2 John validates that this book does not contain hearsay, but what he himself saw or experienced. God miraculously gave John a vision of things that were going to take place and John related this to the church. There is wonderful visual imagery here: revelation, showing, signifying, seeing. The emphasis then is that John is going to lay out before us in a beautiful color panorama the course of history as God has decreed it.

John expected his book to be read aloud in the churches. The key to understanding the book of Revelation, which most people do not appreciate, is that the book of Revelation is written against the backdrop of Old Testament imagery and illusions. It has been estimated that of the 404 verses that are found in the book of Revelation, 278 of them contain allusions of some kind to an Old Testament passage or particular verse. Therefore, is it essential that people understand the Old Testament to be able to understand the book of Revelation. The Christians who first received this book of the Bible, unlike many modern Christians, were steeped in the imagery of the Old Testament. They had listened and imagined the Word of God as the Old Testament was read to them, week after week in the synagogues.

## Summary and Setting

Christians welcomed this book because of their precarious situation. They were being written to a people being persecuted under the Roman emperor Nero just prior to A.D. 64. John identified himself with them when he wrote: "I, John, both your brother and companion in the tribulation and kingdom and patience of Jesus Christ, was on the island that is called Patmos for the word of God and for the testimony of Jesus Christ" (1:9). John had been banished to an island for preaching the Word of God, as he writes to Christians who are undergoing persecution and a tough time. We sometimes think we have it tough today. Imagine what it was like in the

early days of the church when the church was a far smaller minority in that culture. And not only small, but hated, slandered and persecuted. From previous chapters, you will remember that Nero even took Christians and impaled them on stakes, covered them with tar and lit them aflame to light his parties. In that day you can be sure that Christians would have rejoiced to hear things from the Old Testament; how God delivered His people, how God made promises, how there were prophecies that were going to yet be fulfilled, that God will conquer, God will vindicate, God will assert His dominion and rule.

The apostle John wrote to these persecuted Christians so that they would understand, rejoice, take comfort and be blessed in hearing his words. This is why verse 3 of chapter 1 pronounces a blessing upon the reading and hearing of Revelation: "Blessed is he who reads and those who hear the words of this prophecy, and keep those things which are written in it . . ." The blessing is not simply upon hearing the book—it is a blessing upon keeping the book. This is why Revelation 22:7 says, "Blessed is he who keeps the words of the prophecy of this book." We must obey the book of Revelation.

## Worldview

What if the book of Revelation was a letter that came in your mailbox one day? It might seem longer than the letters that we normally write today (could you imagine an email this long?). Length, however, would not be the only aspect of the letter that was odd. Its subject matter is not what we normally expect to receive in the mail. When is the last time you wrote to someone concerning the Pale Riders, Scorpions with heads like men and swords coming out of people's mouths? Imagine as well, however, that you received the letter from someone you trusted more than anyone in the world. To make matters even more frightening, this man that you would trust with your life says of all of this destruction: "It will shortly come to pass." You might be tempted to board up the windows, store up some canned goods and head out into a rural area. There would be only one part of the letter that would comfort you: you are promised that you will overcome in the end, even though you might be persecuted in the meantime.

At first this might sound strange, but that is exactly

what it was like for first century Christians. Revelation came to them as a letter, arriving one day in their pastor's mailbox. He, no doubt, had an interesting afternoon read. This letter came from the apostle John, the Beloved Apostle (who was called this by Christ Himself). He was likely the most revered and respected man living on earth for Christians at that time. As your pastor read the letter to you in church, I am sure that it would have been frightening at some points, especially when it says, "and this will happen soon."

As we consider this book, we must understand the world in which it was first read.

In the early days of the Roman Empire, there was the development in Asia of what came to be known as the emperor cult—the worship of the emperor as God himself. This eventually spread throughout the entire Roman Empire, but especially in Asia minor, where the churches of Jesus Christ are identified: the seven churches of Asia minor. On that very soil persecution came to those who would not put incense on the bust of the emperor and say, "Caesar is lord." When Christians said, "No, Jesus is Lord, we will not give that title to Caesar," they were killed. Often they were thrown to the lions or put into the stadium for people to look upon as they were savagely murdered. The Romans were entertained by watching Christians die horrible deaths.

There was great hatred of the Christian church. Furthermore, the early days of the church were made worse because those who should have been the closest to

"Blessed is the one who reads the words of this prophesy, and blessed are those who hear it and take to heart what is written in it, because the time is near." Revelation was written by John for the edification of the church. John begins by defining the purpose of the book. It is the revelation of Jesus Christ, which God gave him to show his servants what must soon take place. John warns that the events described in the book will occur soon. He was writing to the people of his generation. They had every reason to believe that *soon* meant soon to *them*.

The terms *angel* and *angels* appear eighty-four times in Revelation, though it does not always denote what we commonly think of as angels. In ancient Greek, the word *angel* can refer to a heavenly *or earthly* messenger. Heavenly angels are divided into different types in Scripture, including archangels, cherubim and seraphim. Seraphim are a special class of heavenly attendants stationed on each side of the throne of God in a double choir. Many scholars believe that their title is derived from the Hebrew noun *saraph*, "a fiery and flying serpent," as is spoken of in Numbers 21:6 ("So the LORD sent fiery serpents among the people, and they bit the people; and many of the people of Israel died."), and the brazen image of which stood in the Temple in Isaiah's time. This seraph is from a detail in a medieval illumination of a vision.

Christians and understanding the fulfillment of Old Testament prophecy, those who had traditionally and historically been identified as the people of God, unbelieving Jews persecuted the Christians. As we read the book of Acts, the Jews stirred up trouble for Christians. Over and over and over again, Luke points out to us how it is that the Jews who had rejected the Messiah created difficulty for those who had come to see Jesus as the Messiah.

We have here a collision of worldviews. On the one hand, you have Jews persecuting the church and stirring up trouble for it, and on the other hand the Roman world, in Asia Minor and in the very heart of the Empire, is also persecuting Christians. It is in the midst of all this persecution that John writes from his exile and says, "I have good news for you. Jesus is going to triumph over all opposition." The Christian worldview will prevail in history. *That is the theme of the book of Revelation.*

The book of Revelation has its own outline. As the old saying goes, when all else fails, read the instructions. The book of Revelation has its own interpretive guide built right into it. We see it in chapter 1 verse 19. What has led up to verse 19 is that John has been given a vision of the glorified Christ, and he describes this glorious vision of Christ for us in the middle section of chapter 1. When he is finished seeing and describing this, John is taken back by it. Verse 19 gives his commission. We read, *"Therefore write the things which you have seen, and the things which are, and the things which will take place after these things."* That is it, very simply. John, write about what you have seen already, write about the things that are currently the case, and those things that will shortly come to pass hereafter.

In Revelation 4:1, we have language that also helps us if we are trying to be good interpreters of Scripture and good detectives: "After these things I looked, and behold, a door standing open in heaven. And the first voice which I heard was like a trumpet speaking with me, saying, "Come up here, and I will show you things which must take place after this."" So, chapter 1 verse 19 tells us that we have three sections in this book: (1) what John has already seen, (2) what is now the case, and (3) what will be hereafter. Chapter 4 verse 1 says now I am going to show you the things hereafter. So we know where we can find the breaks.

What has John seen previously? We find this in chapter 1—the vision of the glorified Savior in the midst of the seven candle stands. The candle stands are the churches. And Jesus says, "I am with the church. I walk in the midst of the church as a glorified, sovereign Savior." Does this sound like anything else we hear in the New Testament? What does Jesus say right before He is ascends to the right hand of God? *"All authority has been given to Me in heaven and on earth. . . .and lo, I am with you always, even to the end of the age"* (Matt. 28:18, 20). Central to the Christian worldview is the fact that we worship and serve a living, sovereign Lord Who has all authority in heaven and on earth. This is God's glorious, symbolic, figurative repeating of that promise. Jesus said, "I am with My church, and I am the glorified Savior. I am the sovereign. I govern and judge over all. John, write what you have seen." So, we are given in the first section of the book of Revelation the first thing we need to know about this book. It assures us that in the midst of great persecution, in the midst of terrible times for God's people, Christ is with His church, and He is the sovereign One.

Next, John is told to *"write the things which are"* (1:19). Looking at chapters 2 and 3, we can do this by subtraction. We know chapter 4 begins *"hereafter,"* and we know that chapter 1 dealt with the things that he has seen previously. That leaves chapters 2 and 3. When we look at chapters 2 and 3, we see the letters to the seven churches in Asia Minor. What persistent theme do we find in these letters to the seven churches? The general pattern we find in all seven of these letters is that, first of all, we have an address to the angel—the word "angel" was used to describe the minister of the church—the one who is the messenger of God to the church. (The Greek word *angelos* has a broader meaning than just the spiritual beings that do God's bidding; it simply means "messenger." Angels are God's messengers. So, if you are using Greek, you could rightly greet the postman by saying, "You're an angel.") There is a commendation of the church, a rebuke of the church, an exhortation, then the formula: *"He who has an ear, let him hear what the Spirit says to the churches,"* and then a promise is made. In every case the promise has to do with overcoming and triumphing. He who overcomes, he who perseveres in victory, will follow the promises given to him. The Christian worldview is one of

A panoramic view of Jerusalem today shows no sign of the impending disaster written about by John. The gold-domed Dome of the Rock is an Islamic mosque that sits on the very same site as the Jewish Temple that was destroyed in A.D. 70, as was predicted in Revelation.

victory! Remember, we're gonna win.

In terms of what God wanted John to give us, we now understand two thirds of the outline. The first thing we need to know is that Christ the sovereign, glorified Savior is in the midst of His church. Secondly, He speaks directly to His church. He says to repent of the things that are wrong. Be encouraged by My presence, and know that I will give a reward to those who overcome, those who are victorious in My name. Then we come to chapter 4, and we now begin the third section of the outline: things which shall happen hereafter for John.

How far hereafter are we talking about? For the most part we are talking about the generations of the early church, because the beginning and end of the book have already told us

In many ways the first-century events told of by John represent the end of the time that looked forward to the coming of Christ, overseen by Jewish priests as pictured on the left, and the beginning of the covenant, as pictured by the minister of the gospel on the right.

these are things that are shortly to come to pass. This does not prevent John from eventually looking ahead to the second coming of Jesus Christ and the new heavens and the new earth, but that is the postscript at the end of the book. The main body of the prophecy of the things to take place hereafter—chapter 4 to the middle of chapter 20—have to do with two particular dramas that John is going to play out for us.

How do we know that this section is to be broken down into two particular sections? There is a little-known clue here that we have to pick up on. It is not difficult. It is unfortunate that so many people have suppressed it and not paid attention to it, but you will notice that in chapters 4 and 5 a seven-sealed scroll is introduced to John. This scroll, which is rolled up, has seals along the edge—seven of them. In order to get into the contents of the scroll, John has to break the seals. At the breaking of each one of these seals, he gets a preview of what is to come. Why do I say this? John has not entered the document yet; he has not broken all of the seals. Let's think of it with a rough analogy: It is kind of like when we buy a book; we can see on the dust cover a description of what is going to be inside the book. Likewise, John gets these previews of the important elements of what is going to take place once the scroll is opened up.

So, we have the seven-sealed scroll, but then later in the book, John is given another book and is told he is to prophesy again. Look at Revelation 10:7–11:

> but in the days of the sounding of the seventh angel, when he is about to sound, the mystery of God would be finished, as He declared to His servants the prophets. Then the voice which I heard from heaven spoke to me again and said, "Go, take the little book which is open in the hand of the angel who stands on the sea and on the earth." So I went to the angel and said to him, "Give me the little book." And he said to me, "Take and eat it; and it will make your stomach bitter, but it will be as sweet as honey in your mouth." Then I took the little book out of the angel's hand and ate it, and it was as sweet as honey in my mouth. But when I had eaten it, my stomach became bitter. And he said to me, "You must prophesy again about many peoples, nations, tongues, and kings."

At the beginning of the *"things which will take*

*place after this"* section (1:19), John is given a scroll. He is shown a scroll that has seven seals, and when that is opened and God has finally explained to him what that is all about, then John encounters another book—a small book—which is in the hand of this angel who stands upon the sea. Near the end of this section, John is told to take that book and eat it, because he is going to prophesy again.

This is not hard to figure out. John has one prophecy—the seven sealed scroll—and now he is going to prophesy again—now the little book. This time he is told he is going to prophesy over many people, tongues and nations. Previously he has prophesied about only one; now he is going to prophesy about many. To put it very simply, *there are two prophecies here.* We have a prophecy about a particular people, a nation—the seven-sealed scroll—and then John is going to prophesy again—internationally—over many peoples. Then, at the end of the book of Revelation, we will see a reference to what God is going to do at the end of history.

The important thing for the church living in persecution in John's day, is to see that Christ was going to defeat all of their enemies. They were going to see the victory of Christ's kingdom. There was going to be a judgment prophecy against a particular nation—that nation was Israel. God was going to finally be done, covenantally, with those unbelieving people who crucified the Messiah and continued to reject Him even after He was raised from the dead. Believing Jews like the apostles and the many that believed at Pentecost were going to be incorporated into a new, believing body with Gentiles who had come to trust in the Messiah. John saw a prophecy where Israel was going to be destroyed by God. And then there is going to be an explanation in chapter 12 of how that victory was possible, and the explanation always has to do with things that are behind the scenes.

The Christians of John's day, as well as all Christians throughout history, are given faith, hope and courage in the face of difficulty and persecution, since our worldview enables us to see beyond the moment. We know how the story ends. Jesus destroys all His and our enemies, and we overcome the world! We can see the flow of the book of Revelation. Jesus begins by saying He wants us to know that He is the glorified, sovereign Savior and that He is with us. He wants us to know that even though we are having a tough time, victory awaits us.

Jesus assured the Christians in John's day that, even though the Jews hate you and the Romans are persecuting you, nevertheless, I am with you. And I have all power and authority in heaven and earth. Therefore you are going to accomplish what I commissioned you to do. You are going to disciple the nations. In chapters 2 and 3 Jesus writes to the seven churches and says, "Listen, I have things that I want to command you, and I have things that I want to rebuke in you. Repent. He who has an ear to hear let him hear what the Spirit says to the churches. He who overcomes will have the following promise given to him. I expect you to be a victorious church, an overcoming church. I want you to surmount this opposition. My kingdom is going to prevail. So let Me tell you what is going to happen hereafter. In the first place, I am going to judge those wicked Jews who are persecuting you and creating trouble for you. They have now filled up their wickedness to the uttermost and God in history is going to repay them." Thus we see the judgment on the Jewish people. Note that in A.D. 70, about six years after the apostle John wrote the prophecy of Revelation, God used the Roman Empire to destroy Jerusalem.

We then find out that this is because Satan has been cast down to earth. God's people are going to see the victory even over the Jews because Satan is being controlled and being dominated by God Himself. Satan is not satisfied. He is going to go out and persecute the church in the Roman Empire as well. You are going to see the Roman Empire now arise against the church, but I will destroy it as well. The vision of God destroying the Roman Empire reaches its climax in Revelation 19 with the vision of Jesus Himself, riding forth on a white horse, going out to conquer all opposition.

Now when we read that story, because He is slaughtering everybody who is in His path, we might think this must be a vision of judgment. Look at all of that blood. Look at all of that gore. This is terrible stuff. We must remember, however, that this is figurative language—symbolic language—and John clearly tells us in Revelation 19 that Jesus rides upon this white horse, and *"out of His mouth goes a sharp sword"* It is not that Jesus is taking a literal sword and

Detail from a woodcut by Albrecht Dürer depicting the Beast out of the Sea found in Revelation 13:1–10.

From a Book of Hours. The triumphant Christ enthroned with kings worshiping Him. He is King of kings and Lord of lords.

hacking His enemies to death. He is talking about the sword that comes out of Jesus' mouth. This is common biblical imagery. We all know that the sword of the Spirit is the Word of God. Jesus, now proclaiming the word of God upon a white, victorious horse, goes out and defeats all opposition. *This is the Great Commission being fulfilled.* This is why it is so important for Christians to understand that the entire Bible—the word of God—forms the very foundation of our view of the world.

We must ask ourselves the question: if God is going to destroy the Jewish persecutors, and if He is going to destroy the other persecutors, then His kingdom is going to be the one that conquers the nations—how is that possible? This is where we get the millennial explanation that John gives in Revelation 20. Since God is restraining Satan, he will deceive the nations no more—*the word of God is going to conquer the nations, not Satan.* He may be active in the world, but with respect to deceiving the nations he is restrained—he is on a chain. Then, at the very end of history, we will see that, even though there is a final apostasy, Jesus will return in judgment and introduce a new heavens and a new earth wherein righteousness dwells. At that time, God will wipe every tear from our eyes.

This must have been a great encouragement to John as he sat in prison at Patmos. It makes no difference what the Jews say against me, or what the Romans want to do to me. *Jesus is going to have the final word—He is going to have the final word in history—His kingdom is going to be victorious* over the nations—*He is going to have the final word in eternity, and in eternity He will comfort me.* All of what I have gone through, all of this tribulation, will have been worthwhile. This was an encouragement to the apostle John, to the first century Christians and to all Christians throughout history.

The book of Revelation is not given merely for an academic collation of prophetic tid-bits. Revelation has been given as marching orders. Revelation has been given as a new way of seeing things. It is a matter of pulling back the draperies so that we can understand what history is all about and respond accordingly. It commands a certain form of life from us and profoundly affects our behavior in the world. It does not just affect the way we think about the world to come, it affects what we do in the world that is here and now. And so the words of this book should mold and shape our lives.

In John 14:23 and 24, Jesus makes it a mark of discipleship that we keep His words. "He who does not love Me does not keep My words," Jesus says. And now Jesus comes and lays before us a view of history that He wants us to have and wants us to obey. Are we His followers? Is He really the King? Is He our Lord and Master? To suggest God gave us a book that was going to trip us up rather than to enable us to obey and please Him and bring glory to His Name is an intolerable conclusion.

The book of Revelation is a blessing to us. The book of Revelation is a gift from God so that we might be thoroughly equipped to every good work. This is consistent with Matthew 28:18. Jesus says, "And Jesus came and spoke to them, saying, "All authority has been given to Me in heaven and on earth." If He is the King, then get to work. If He is the King, go into the world. If He is the King, make all the nations my servants. The book of Revelation has been given to inspire us, not just in the midst of persecution, but also through persecution to victory. Every Christian should study the book of Revelation.

—*Randy Booth*

## For Further Reading

*Veritas Press Bible Cards: Acts through Revelation.* Lancaster, Pa.: Veritas Press. 32.

*Veritas Press History Cards: New Testament, Greece and Rome.* Lancaster, Pa.: Veritas Press. 26, 27.

DeMar, Gary. *Last Days Madness.* Atlanta, Ga.: American Vision, 2001.

Holford, George Peter. *The Destruction of Jerusalem: An Absolute and Irresistible Proof of the Divine Origin of Christianity.* Nacogdoches, Tex.: Covenant Media Foundation, 2001 [1814].

# SESSION I: PRELUDE

## A Question to Consider

What is the purpose of the gospel? Will it be successful?

*Discuss or list short answers to the following questions:*
1. What was the cult of emperor worship?
2. By whom were the early Christians persecuted? Why?
3. What do the candle stands symbolize?
4. What earthshaking event happened in A.D. 70?
5. Who are the angels mentioned Revelation 2 and 3? Why is this interpretation legitimate?
6. What is the message of the book of Revelation?
7. Why does the gospel make its way throughout the world? (What is Christ doing that will cause this? What has happened to Satan that will allow it?)

READING ASSIGNMENT:
Revelation 1–9

# SESSION II: DISCUSSION
Revelation 1–9

## A Question to Consider

When was Revelation written? To what events is it referring?

*Discuss or list short answers to the following questions:*

## Text Analysis

1. From the first chapter, does it seem that the coming of Christ being mentioned in the text is near or far in the future?
2. When does it seem that Christ is coming to judge the churches (2:16, 3:11)?
3. When the souls of the martyrs cry out for justice, does it seem that the judgment is far in the future or near the present (6:9–11)?

## Cultural Analysis

1. Does our culture have a sense that sin leads to judgment?
2. Does the church today teach that sin leads to judgment?
3. Does our culture (and especially the majority of the church) believe that the events referred to in Revelation are going to happen in the future or that they happened in the past? How do you know?

## Biblical Analysis

1. How can those who believe in dating Revelation after A.D. 70 explain the time passages that seem to point to the fact that the events of this book are going to happen "soon" (2 Pet. 3:8)?
2. How does Rev. 22:6–20 bolster the case of those trying to establish the early date?
3. How could Matthew 24 also strengthen the early date case?
4. What does the order given to John in Revelation 11:1, imply about the Temple?

## SUMMA

*Write an essay or discuss this question, integrating what you have learned from the material above.*
When was Revelation written, and what is it talking about?

### READING ASSIGNMENT:
Revelation 10–22

# SESSION III: WRITING

## Progymnasmata

Classical training in rhetoric included preparatory writing exercises called the *progymnasmata*. These exercises in composition introduced the beginning student to basic forms and techniques that would then be used and combined when practicing more advanced exercises and speeches. One of these progymnasmata was called the *Confirmation*. It is paired with a counterpart called the *Refutation*. These exercises confirm or refute a statement. The first section of the confirmation/refutation is called *From the Reputation of the Proponents*. In this section, the person writing a confirmation seeks to praise the reputation of the person who made the statement. Conversely, the person writing the refutation seeks to accentuate the worst aspects of the reputation of the person who made the statement. (If the statement is not attributed to a particular person, this section may be replaced by a short *Prologue* which introduces the subject.

The second part of this exercise is a paragraph called *Exposition*. In this part of the confirmation or refutation, the writer explains the issue and relates background material that will enable someone to understand why the statement was made. In the *Exposition* the writer tells the reader his own opinion, so the thesis must be made clear in this section (e.g., While Homer says that Achilles was a hero, I will show that he was really just a mindless warrior.) The final part of the exercise is where the writer tries to prove or disprove the statement. The writer may choose from several proofs to accomplish this. Not every one of these ways of arguing for the statement need be used in a single exercise. *From the obvious* seeks to show that the truth of the statement is clear. *From the convincing* seeks to set forth the facts that show how persuasive the statement is. *From the possible* attempts to show that the statement is, in fact, possible. This section is particularly important if the statement seems fantastic on the surface, (i.e., say you were confirming that an axe head can float; see 2 Kings 6:6). *From the consistent* argues that the statement being confirmed is both acceptable and reasonable. *From the proper* argues that the statement affirms what is proper. Finally, *From the rational* states that what is being argued for makes rational sense. If someone were writing a refutation instead of a confirmation, the parts would be just the opposite. This means that they would be: *From the obscure,* which seeks to show that the truth of the statement relies on things doubtful or vague. *From the unconvincing* seeks to set forth facts that show how unpersuasive the statement is. *From the impossible* attempts to show that the statement could not happen. *From the inconsistent* argues that the statement being refuted does not agree with itself or reality. *From the improper* argues that the statement affirms what is inappropriate. Finally, *From the irrational* states that what is being argued for makes no rational sense. The final section of the confirmation or refutation is called the *Epilogue.* In it, the writer sums up his arguments and gets one last chance to prove his point.

*Confirm or refute the following statement: Most of the events in Revelation refer to the destruction of Jerusalem.*

statement is unknown)

II. Exposition
   • tell the reader your own opinion
III. From the obvious
   • show that the truth of the statement is clear
IV. From the convincing
   • set forth the facts that show how persuasive the statement is
V. From the possible
   • show that the statement is, in fact, possible
VI. From the consistent
   • argue that the statement is both acceptable and reasonable
VII. From the proper
   • argue that the statement affirms what is proper
VIII. From the rational
   • show that the statement makes rational sense
IX. Epilogue
   • sum up your arguments

## CONFIRMATION

Most of the events in Revelation refer to the destruction of Jerusalem.

I. From the good reputation of the proponents (in this case use a Prologue because the proponent is unknown)
   • praise the reputation of the person who made the statement
      • introduce the subject (if writing a Prologue because the one who made the

## REFUTATION

Most of the events in Revelation do not refer to the destruction of Jerusalem.

I. From the evil reputation of the proponents (in this case use a Prologue because the proponent is unknown)
   • accentuate the worst aspects of the reputation of the person who made the statement
   • introduce the subject (if writing a Prologue because the one who made the statement is unknown)
II. Exposition
   • tell the reader your own opinion
III. From the obscure
   • show that the truth of the statement relies on things doubtful or vague
IV. From the unconvincing
   • forth facts that show how unpersuasive the statement is
V. From the impossible
   • show that the statement could not happen
VI. From the inconsistent
   • argue that the statement being refuted does not

Seen here is a detail from Dürer's woodcut, *St. John's Vision of Christ and the Seven Candlesticks,* which was originally published in Germany in 1498.

agree with itself or reality

VII. From the improper
- argue that the statement affirms what is inappropriate

VIII. From the irrational
- argue that the statement makes no rational sense

IX. Epilogue
- sum up your arguments

In typical symbolism Dürer depicts the Lamb of God, Jesus Christ, who shed His blood for the sins of His people.

# SESSION IV: RECITATION

## Comprehension Questions

*Answer the following questions for factual recall:*

1. What is John's description of the resurrected Christ like in chapter 1?
2. What is the condemnation from Christ for the church in Ephesus (2:1–7)?
3. How does Christ describe the Jews who are persecuting the church (2:8–11)?
4. To which of the seven churches does Christ seem to give the worst report?
5. What are the four living creatures of Revelation 4 like?
6. Why was Christ found to be worthy to open the scroll and break its seals?
7. In light of other biblical passages, to what do the upheavals in heaven probably refer (Rev. 6:12–17, see also Isaiah 14:12, Num. 24:17, Matt. 2:2)?
8. How would the "sealing of 12,000 from each tribe" be explained by those who think that the events described refer to the destruction of Jerusalem?
9. What does the angel instruct John to do with the book (10:8–11)?
10. Why is the dragon trying to devour the child? How is the child saved (Rev. 12)?
11. What is the number of the beast in Revelation 13?

12. When God treads out the wrath of His wine press, what happens in "the city" in Revelation 14:17–20? (Optional research: In light of what Josephus says in *Jewish Wars* 3.10.9, how does this strike you?[4])
13. Who is the whore (17:9, 18)?
14. Why does the gospel make headway in the world (Rev. 19, 20)?
15. How does God describe the new heavens and new earth? What is it a return to (Rev. 21:1–22:5)?
16. When does Christ claim that these things will come about (Rev. 22)?

# SESSION V: ANALYSIS

## The Millennial Positions

*Review the following summaries of the millennial positions and then complete Chart 1:*

*Premillennial[5] Position:* The premillennial view asserts that God will continue to gather Gentiles into the church and that the world will become increasingly corrupt. As the end of the world nears, there will be a seven-year period of tribulation. Christ will return and rapture His church away (1 Thess. 4). This means that believers at that point will be removed from earth and up to heaven to be with Christ.[6] After the church is removed, the power of the Antichrist will be unleashed and God's saving work will focus on a reconstituted Israel (which will again perform sacrifices in a Temple). These believing Jews will be persecuted and killed by the Antichrist, who will then institute a one-world government and make everyone bear his mark in order to purchase goods. This evil creature will finally be destroyed at the climactic Battle of Armageddon, in which the forces of evil will be destroyed and the Final Judgment be commenced.

*Amillennial Position:* The prefix *a-* means "without," and true to its name the amillennial position is that the millennium mentioned in Revelation 20 is not a literal one, but is figurative. Amillennialists believe that the millennium is happening right now and that Christ is reigning right now. The world will continue to polarize between good and evil, with the good becoming more holy and the wicked becoming more sinful. Finally, Christ will return and do away with the wicked in the Final Judgment.

*Postmillennial Position:* This position says that Christ's reign on earth will begin after a long period in which the gospel has conquered the world, which is living in general trust in God and faith in Christ. While this position has much in common with the amillennial position, its outlook on the future is significantly different. Postmillennialists see the spread of the gospel through the world as a sign that Christ is accomplishing this world conquest and have great hope as they look toward the future, believing that Christ will conquer the world and wipe out His and our enemies.

# OPTIONAL SESSION: ACTIVITY

## Debate

Now that you have some understanding of the different millennial positions, it is time to try to convince others. In a group setting, students should choose the millennial position they wish to defend and take ten minutes to convince their audience. Then, the student should take questions from the audience to see if his argument can stand up to examination. If you have enough students, have one representative from each position lay out their cases first. After that, allow the students who are presenting the cases to question one other and then open it up to questions from the audience.

**CHART 1: MILLENNIAL DISTINCTIVES**

|  | PREMILLENNIAL | AMILLENNIAL | POSTMILLENNIAL |
|---|---|---|---|
| Is the millennium a literal reality? |  |  |  |
| When will the millennium occur? |  |  |  |
| Why does Revelation speak so much of Israel? |  |  |  |
| To what does the binding of Satan refer? |  |  |  |
| What does the future look like? |  |  |  |

# ENDNOTES

1   *This endnote appears only in the teacher's edition.*

2   *This endnote appears only in the teacher's edition.*

3   *This endnote appears only in the teacher's edition.*

4   Josephus. *The Jewish Wars.* 3.10.9. Here he gives a description of the destruction of Jerusalem that mirrors the destruction John describes.

5   There are different types of premillennialism, and this definition fits only the major elements of the Dispensational Premillennial position. This is by far the most commonly held view in Christendom, and since there is limited space, we will deal with this premillennial variation exclusively. Pardon is asked of George Eldon Ladd and other Historic Premillennialists.

6   Again, there are different views among premillennialists concerning the time of the rapture of the church. Some believe that this "snatching away" will occur before the seven years of trials, others think that it will not happen until after all of the hardships. Still others think that it will happen at the mid-point of the trials. Finally, at least one preacher believes that it will happen sporadically throughout the seven years. We could perhaps call this position a "pan-tribulational" Rapture.

# SECONDARY BOOKS

First Semester

# CHOSEN BY GOD

James pulled up a chair at the coffee shop and looked at his friend about to sit down with a latte. "Did you see the news yet?"

"No," said John.

"Earlier today some terrorist bombed the Liberty Bell in Philadelphia."

"Oh, man. Was anyone hurt?" asked John.

"Yeah, about 10 people were killed, and about 20 were hurt."

John looked shocked, "What happened?"

"Well, some woman got into the area using a stroller with a fake baby. You know, like a realistic looking doll or something. She took out the baby and got past the guards and then blew it up, committing suicide in the process."

"That's unbelievable. Don't they have some way to know about bombs with all the security stuff?"

"I guess it was something they didn't figure out until it was too late. It's insane."

John looked down and thought of a friend he'd known whose dad died in Iraq. "Boy, imagine all those people and their families. Sometimes you just don't know why these things happen."

With disgust James said, "It's just another stupid attack. It's all pointless."

"Well, I guess they made their point! They are trying to scare us and it's working."

"But I mean the bigger point. This kind of thing doesn't have any point in the big picture. It just happens."

John looked up with surprise, "I think they have a purpose. They . . ."

"What are you saying? That these accidents mean something?"

"I think the terrorists meant something by it. I'm sure they chose the Liberty Bell as a symbol, and if we find out who's behind it all, they'll probably say that they're crushing the fake liberty of America, the great Satan. And you know, it's strange, but it will probably mean

*The Crucifixion —a fresco by Giotto. Millions of people across the world agree that Jesus was crucified as payment for sins— but for the sins of whom?*

that a lot of people will lose some liberty. They'll probably be under surveillance and all that, with a lot more security all over the place," said John.

"Yeah, I know all that. That's not what I'm saying. I mean in the big picture. I don't think it happened for a reason," James said.

"But don't you believe in God?" John asked.

"Yeah, but God didn't cause these people to be blown up. That evil woman did that and whoever else was backing her. God didn't do it. He didn't have anything to do with it."

Feeling a little more heat in the conversation, John said, "Maybe some of our problems seem random. It's hard to understand in the middle of it all. And maybe we don't always know..."

"You're not going to tell me you think God made this happen. No way!" James said, interrupting.

"If God is God and could stop anything, then, in a manner of speaking, He had to be in control of this too."

"What kind of God are you talking about. My God is a God Who loves, and this couldn't be His will," said James.

From our vantage point a lot of horrible things happen. We naturally ask whether James or John is right. Is it all meaningless or is God working out His purposes through it? *Chosen by God* by R.C. Sproul is a great book to help us deal with such complex ideas.

The conversation of James and John continues migrating from disasters, such as the bomb-inflicted kind, to even more serious ones—the kind that have eternal consequences. James and John move their debate to the discussion of who is in control of salvation.

"Wait a minute. If God is in control of people's choices, then God chooses who's going to be saved. I just can't believe that," said James.

"Don't you see, James? If God knows all and is all-powerful, then God can make all His purposes happen."

"But what about free will? I don't believe we're all robots. We choose our own destiny."

"I think the only way we can be sure of these kinds of things is to see what the Bible teaches."

Sproul's book will shed biblical light on these kinds of conversations. It will help us examine what the Bible teaches about God's character, role and control in salvation. It will discuss the meaning of free will and how our sinfulness affects our will.

# GENERAL INFORMATION

## Author and Context

If you were to scan through the radio, chances are you would hear Dr. R.C. Sproul. His radio program, "Renewing Your Mind," can currently be heard in over 50 countries. If you were to browse titles at your local bookstore, chances are you would see several of the many books he has written. If you were to look for Christian books on ethics, prayer, marriage, suffering, and the glory of God or biblical studies, chances are you would see Dr. Sproul's books. What's more, if you were to look at liner notes of the rock music recording, "Van Halen III" (1998), you would also see Dr. Sproul being "thanked." (He has also been known to play golf with "acid" rock star, Alice Cooper.)

He is a kind of statesman of the Reformed faith in our day. Currently, he is the chairman and president of Ligonier Ministries and Senior Minister of Preaching at Saint Andrews Chapel in Sanford, Florida. He has taught at a whole host of seminaries and colleges. With all of this, what is he trying to do? His vision is in his own words, "I dream of a new reformation, a reformation that is not simply a renewal of life but a new vision of life: a vision that yields new forms and structures in society and culture. As long as Christians restrict their Christianity to a religion, a faith that is compartmentalized and isolated from life, they can have revival but never, ever reformation. We need to hear and do the Word of God in all of our lives."

## Significance

Is God in control? Does God save us by His own doing or do we help save ourselves? What part do we play in our salvation? To answer these questions one must grapple with the classic doctrine of predestination.

According to Sproul, "Predestination means in its most elementary form, that our final destination, heaven or hell, is decided by God not only before we get there, but before we are even born. It teaches that our ultimate destiny is in the hands of God. Another way of saying this is: From all eternity, before we ever lived, God decided to save some members of the human race and to let the rest of the human race perish. God made a choice—he chose some individuals to be saved unto everlasting blessedness in heaven and others he chose to pass over, to allow them to follow the consequences into eternal torment in hell."

Predestination, when rightly understood, helps us see the grace of God. We will not think He's a mean wizard, manipulating the world in a spiteful way. This biblical doctrine shows the glories of a loving God who saves sinful people. Through understanding this, we see a loving God with gracious purposes and how sinfulness prevents people from choosing God on their own. God must change people's hearts. God saves sinners. Sinners do not save themselves, either wholly or partially.

The word *predestination* is scary to some people. One person once said upon hearing it, "That word's not in the Bible!" But of course it is in the Bible. What does it mean? When we do understand it, we will find comfort in the teaching of God's grace. It gives us a sure hope of heaven because it bases salvation on God's power, not ours. It is not by our own strength, but because of God's grace that preserves us to the very end. We love Him because He first loved us.

Whether we believe in predestination or not will affect how we live, how we worship, how we view our neighbor and, of course, how we understand who God is. The importance of grappling with this idea biblically is hard to overestimate.

## Summary and Setting

Many of you have previously studied the Reformation. Remember when Martin Luther nailed the 95 Thesis to the Wittenberg Door and the fireworks that resulted? John Calvin was also an important person during the Reformation. The "Reformation" teaching about God's grace, regarding the sinfulness of man and salvation was clearly taught by John Calvin (1509–1564), a great Protestant Reformer. Remember also when, in 1621, Plymouth was established as a colony by setters from Europe? Many of these adventurous pilgrims were seeking a land where they would have the religious freedom to live and worship according to biblical teaching. At the heart of all they believed was clear commitment to the understanding of predestination.

Of course, this belief didn't end there. Into the

1700's we see great men of God like George Whitefield and Jonathan Edwards preaching and teaching the biblical view of predestination. Unfortunately, not all popular preachers held to this biblical view. In the 1830's an influential preacher named Charles Finney led many to reject this teaching. Other great men followed Charles Finney's teaching against predestination. These men even include Billy Graham. In fact, during most of the twentieth century most Christians did not believe in predestination.

Sproul teaches the same view of predestination that Calvin and

Charles Finney declared that the right revival techniques could produce new Christians. Though an ordained Presbyterian, he preached freedom of the will, salvation, personal holiness, and the perfection of society.

these other great men taught—that salvation is by God's grace and is not earned or merited by the sinner. Most of the Protestant church held this view too, all the way through the early 1900's. In the past one hundred years many people have denied these views of salvation. Around the 1920's even those churches that were "Reformed," found themselves fighting over the authority of Scripture and whether the Bible was really true in all that it said. Under attack were many teachings like the virgin birth of Christ, the deity of Christ, salvation by Christ alone through faith, and the truth of the Word of God. In those days, some people in the church started denying Scripture and other major doctrines of the faith (for example, they did not believe that Jesus was God). The response to this from Bible-believing Christians often involved the formation of new denominations and institutions (seminaries and

Bible colleges) committed to historic Christian views and especially a high view of the Bible.

In this context, in America there has been a growing conservative Bible-believing evangelical Church. But this evangelical movement has largely been fueled by the "Arminian" conception of salvation, from James Arminius (1560–1609). Arminius taught that salvation is dependent on the free will of man. Each person determines his or her own destiny by the choices they make. God's salvation is possible for every person but it is up to the individual. As one preacher put it, God casts a vote for you; the devil casts his vote against you; and you cast the deciding vote. James Arminius's views of the gospel are everywhere on TV and in tent revivals, much as they were in the days of Charles Finney. Along with those views comes the practice of trying to make all the circumstances right to help someone "decide for Christ." Music, exciting testimonies, and altar calls are used.

It is in this context that the work of men like Dr. Sproul is so helpful. He has made the Reformational views clear and understandable to a wide audience. He has taught that salvation is by the grace of God alone, and it is not dependent upon the free will of men. *Chosen by God* is a very clear and sympathetic discussion of the main issues on God's control in salvation. It is a great introduction to the basic Christian doctrine of predestination.

## Worldview

As you read Chosen by God you will encounter a very descriptive example of what many today believe regarding how a person becomes a Christian. Imagine that you have fallen into the ocean off a large ship. You are exhausted and drowning as you have tread water for more than an hour. After much looking, the captain of the ship has finally found you and steered the ship toward you. As it approaches, you see a life preserver with a line attached to the ship thrown toward you, landing within your reach. All you must do to be saved from drowning is grab hold, and the crew will pull you back into the boat. This is a very popular view of how God saves us. But is it biblical?

Remember James and John at the coffee shop? Imagine them to be a modern day version of James Arminius and John Calvin. Joining them for a cup of coffee and lively discussion might put us into the thick of a very real and ongoing debate that affects far more than we might realize. Even what we conclude from a simple reading of the newspaper or watching the 6:00 news will be affected by our views of God. Our view of God's power and control in and of the world will be different whether we believe that God is in control and predestines or whether he is not in complete control. We mentioned the fictitious example of the bomb in the baby carriage earlier that killed 10 and injured 20. Was God in control of such an evil act? Did God have control of the world when the vast atrocities of the twentieth century occurred? Did things like the Holocaust or the Killing Fields of Cambodia go unnoticed by God? Maybe he was unable to do anything to stop such carnage. Maybe he could have stopped madmen like Pol Pot or Hitler but chose not to. Could these events even be part of a broader plan that was ordained from the foundation of the world to bring glory to Him? Our worldview matters when we begin to talk about what is happening in the world.

To some, events like terrorist actions and wars and everything else is a random occurrence of events with no meaning or connection at all. Some people believe nature, as if it has a mind of its own, demonstrates control on events and circumstances. Some believe life itself is just going to end with no ultimate meaning—evolution caused our existence, and evolution, being what it is, means there is no ultimate meaning, and

John Calvin was born in France on July 10, 1509. He was a brilliant scholar and studied law until, at the age of 23, he experienced a conversion and from then on was a fervent Christian and scholar of the Scriptures. In 1536 he published his famous *Institutes of the Christian Religion*.

there is no God. Life is for today but nothing more and signifies nothing. To others, like those who embrace certain Eastern religions, life is all a dream. What we think is real is not—it is an illusion. Some of this gets a little too deep into other areas of study, and we will not pursue them further here. But we must be careful to not simply say, "God did not allow that evil event to occur. He would never do that." When we say this, we are left with the only possible conclusion that God is not in control.[1] We must not be illogical. We must think clearly with the mind God has given us.

So let us start with what we do know. The God of the Bible is Lord and Creator of all. There is nothing over God and nothing outside of His control. It is His personal will which governs all, not an impersonal set of natural causes or chance. He brings about all of His holy will.

The God of the Bible is a living God, and His work is accomplished by, through and with the natural forces and choices of people. History is His story. God is in control. The Bible even records supernatural and unexpected changes in the way God normally sustains the universe. Jesus frequently miraculously healed many people. The Red Sea was parted by God to allow the Israelites to escape from the Egyptians. Nature is within God's control. The scriptural doctrine of God's complete control extends to every detail of the universe (even the number of hairs on our heads are known and controlled by God).

When we discuss events in the world, we find that many Christians look at the world as out of control—that God is not really in charge, or at least not in complete control. Such thinking tends to be a part of what some Christians believe about salvation. They imagine their hope of salvation resting on the choices of individual people or on how the message is

This painting of the *Adoration of the Magi* underscores the fact that God's chosen people come from the far reaches of the world.

presented. Have you ever heard someone say "If only I had used different words or examples, they would have responded and they would have become a Christian?" As if they were to blame for the failure (or to praise for the success). To be sure, God uses people and circumstances. However, these individuals

cannot take comfort in knowing that God's purposes are being worked out in the world for His glory and for the edification of His people. As biblical Christians we are to look at the world through the lens of Scripture. What we see is a creation that is fallen because of sin. We see men made in the image and likeness of God, but they are now corrupt. Scripture says that we are dead in our sin. We see how God has worked in history to save His people. At the center of history stands the cross of Christ. Across the centuries, we see the advance of the gospel and the transformation of the world by the kingdom of God. And, undergirding all of this, we know that there is a God who is the sovereign maker and ruler of heaven and earth.

When we look at the flow of historical events through the lens of Scripture, we see the plan and purposes of God being carried out. He has been in control of all of history. Without this central commitment, the events of history are meaningless. With this knowledge we can take true comfort with believers through the ages. "And we know that all things work together for good to those who love God, to those who are the called according to His purpose" (Rom. 8:28).

As Dr. Sproul says, we should take great comfort in the fact that there is not one "maverick" molecule in the entire universe that is not entirely and completely under God's control. Scripture teaches us God's complete sovereignty. If we are thinking biblically, then we know that every atom of every molecule of every single thing was not only created by God, but is continually sustained and directed by Him! God is in control to the minutest degree. We may strain to comprehend how a holy and righteous God could so intricately control the workings of a fallen and wicked world (without contaminating Himself with our sin), but we need not ask whether He controls it. He does.

This view is a striking contrast with what the unbeliever sees in the world. He views everything as a cosmic accident that has been evolving for millions of years without meaning or purpose. God's Word, however, clearly denies this, saying, "I stretched out the heavens with My hands, And I ordained all their host" (Isaiah 45:12). The value of seeing this is illustrated in the precarious and delicate position we rest in and take for granted. With 100 billion stars like our sun, it is a powerful tribute to assert that the whole host of all these flaming masses is "the work of Thy fingers" (Ps. 8:3). The Lord "counts the number of the stars; He gives names to all of them" (Ps. 147:4). The wonder in God's creation with the variations and incredible attention to detail is remarkable to consider. Consider the stars as an example. Every photon of light from our sun travels 93 million miles to the earth. Amazingly, if it produced only one percent more heat, or if our atmosphere were different, or even if our clouds did not do their job in releasing heat back into space, the earth would literally wither, and we would die. If the sun produced one percent less heat, the earth would soon be unbearably cold. In fact, while earth's temperature is very constant, the moon's surface temperature varies 850 degrees each lunar day. Is it not God who sets the thermostat? His sovereign control shines by day and twinkles by night. Yet, we rest and take as the norm that our world is secure from frost or fire. Have you ever met any sane person who lived with the fear that they would wake up and find the temperature to be 200 degrees below zero?

God's sovereignty can be shown by specific biblical statements dealing with different kinds of events. He controls "nature." "He did good and gave you rains from heaven and fruitful seasons . . ." (Acts 14:17). He controls nations. Daniel 2:21 says, "He removes kings and establishes kings . . ." Even calamity and evil are "caused" by Him. He is "the One forming light and creating darkness, causing well-being and creating calamity . . ." (Isa. 45:7). Even in the crucifixion of Christ the sinful actions of men are not outside His power. Acts 2:23 refers to Christ as "delivered up by the predetermined plan and foreknowledge of God. (He was) nailed to a cross by the hands of godless men . . ." The very smallest details of life are under His meticulous care. "Not one [sparrow] will fall to the ground apart from your Father" (Matt. 10:29-30). Judgment is predetermined, says Jude 1:4. "Those who were long beforehand marked out for this condemnation . . ." And of course then, salvation is in His hand. Romans 8:30 tells of the golden chain of predestination. "Whom He predestined, these He also called; and whom He called, these He also justified; and whom He justified, these He also glorified."

Whether we are "James" or "John" in the coffee shop conversation, we know the Bible must be our standard. As Christians we must conform our thinking to God's Word. When we look at Scripture we see repeated statements of His complete sovereignty and rule. In the broadest possible terms—God is in complete control. The domain of His rule is, quite simply, including everything. The Lord has decreed whatever happens. From the beginning to the end, from the creation to the consummation, from the heavens to the earth, from the sky to the sea, from conception to death—the sovereign Lord is the One in complete control. "His sovereignty rules over all" (Ps. 103:19). Who is in control? Or who is Lord? This is perhaps the most central question we will ever face.

—*Gregg Strawbridge*

# SESSION I: PRELUDE
## Questions to Consider

*Contemplate or discuss the sovereignty and will of God in the following questions:*

### Part A

1. Was the birth of Christ God's will?
2. Was the crucifixion God's will?
3. Was the creation of man God's will?
4. Was the fall of man God's will?
5. Jenny was a sixteen-year-old girl who got pregnant. Was that God's will?
6. Jenny had an abortion. Was that God's will?
7. Was the parting of the Red Sea, which allowed all of Israel to escape the Egyptians, God's will?
8. Was the drowning of the Egyptians afterwards in the Red Sea God's will?
9. Was the slaughter of millions of innocent people

slaughtered by political tyrants (e.g., Hitler, Stalin, Pol Pot) in the twentieth century God's will?

## Part B

1. What are the most fun or most enjoyable things we do, and why do we do them?
2. What are some things you least enjoy?

*Read the following passage:*

"God, who made the world and everything in it, since He is Lord of heaven and earth, does not dwell in temples made with hands. Nor is He worshiped with men's hands, as though He needed anything, since He gives to all life, breath, and all things. And He has made from one blood every nation of men to dwell on all the face of the earth, and has determined their preappointed times and the boundaries of their dwellings, so that they should seek the Lord, in the hope that they might grope for Him and find Him, though He is not far from each one of us; for in Him we live and move and have our being." (Acts 17:24–28)

3. If God is your Creator and He controls when and where we live, how is God related to what we enjoy? Have the students explain orally or in writing with short explanations of how God controls our likes and dislikes.

## READING ASSIGNMENT:

Chapters 1–3

*Watch a television preacher for several minutes in preparation for a discussion at the next class. The program should be preaching and not a healing service.*

# SESSION II: DISCUSSION

Chapters 1–3

*The following quotes are from well-known Christian leaders from the past. Discuss which men believe in the sovereignty of God and predestination and which ones do not.*

Billy Sunday (1862–1935) was an evangelist born in Iowa. A professional baseball player in the National League, he was saved in 1886, and travelled as an evangelist from 1896 to 1935.

"Every heart that has been subdued by sovereign grace takes Jesus Christ to be the chief object of its love." —*Charles Spurgeon*

"All over the world I have been privileged to see people respond in faith to the simple—yet profound—message of God's love in Jesus Christ. They have come from every conceivable social, racial, political, and ideological background, for Christ transcends the boundaries that divide us. And in Christ they have found the answer to their deepest spiritual longings. They have discovered the truth I discovered as a teenager, a truth affirmed by all who truly commit their lives to Christ and seek to follow Him: Jesus Christ will change our lives if we will let Him." —*Billy Graham*

"Watching a condemned criminal being led to the execution chamber: There but for the grace of God go I." —*George Whitefield*

"The first thing for a Christian to do is to look for means to do something for God." —*Billy Sunday*

"After we are renewed, yet we are renewed but in part, indwelling sin continues in us, there is a mixture of corruption in every one of our duties; so that after we are converted, were Jesus Christ only to accept us according to our works, our works would damn us, for we cannot put up a prayer but it is far from that perfection which the moral Law requireth. I do not know what you may think, but I can say that I cannot pray but I sin—cannot preach to you or others but I sin—I can do nothing without sin; and, as one expresseth it, my repentance wants to be repented of, and my tears to be washed in the precious blood of my dear Redeemer." —*George Whitefield*

"There is a sense in which conversion is the work of God. There is a sense in which it is the effect of truth. There is a sense in which the preacher does it. And it is also the appropriate work of the sinner himself." —*Charles Finney*

"When God calls a man, He does not repent of it. God does not, as many friends do, love one day, and hate another; or as princes, who make their subjects favourites, and afterwards throw them into prison. This is the blessedness of a saint; his condition admits of no alteration. God's call is founded on His decree, and His decree is immutable. Acts of grace cannot be reversed. God blots out his people's sins, but not their names." —*Thomas Watson*

"Remember, there is nothing that happens in your daily life, but what was first of all devised in eternity, and counseled by Jesus Christ for your good and in your behalf, that all things might work together for your lasting benefit and profit." —*Charles Spurgeon*

"All things whatever arise from, and depend on, the divine appointment; whereby it was foreordained who should receive the word of life, and who should disbelieve it; who should be delivered from their sins, and who should be hardened in them; and who should be justified and who should be condemned." —*Martin Luther*

"The Christian, therefore, is justified no longer than he obeys, and must be condemned when he disobeys or Antinomianism is true . . . In these respects, then, the sinning Christian and the unconverted sinner are upon precisely the same ground." —*Charles Finney*

"When we attribute foreknowledge to God, we mean that all things always were, and perpetually remain, under his eyes, so that to his knowledge there is nothing future or past, but all things are present. And they are present in such a way that he not only conceives them through ideas, as we have before us those things which our minds remember, but he truly looks upon them and discerns them as things placed before him. And this foreknowledge is extended throughout the universe to every creature. We call predestination God's eternal decree, by which he determined with himself what he willed to become of each man. For all are not created in equal condition; rather, eternal life is foreordained for some, eternal damnation for others. Therefore, as any man has been created to one or the other of these ends, we speak of him as predestined to life or death." —*John Calvin*

1. List the men above and tell which of them believe in the sovereignty of God and predestination and which of them do not?
2. How do you think their beliefs affected their ministries?

## Cultural Analysis

*Answer these questions:*
1. Whom did you observe on television?
2. Did the TV preacher promote God's sovereignty? Why or why not?
3. Does Christian TV and radio teach that man can save himself by his free will at any time? How?
4. Why do religious programs which do not reflect the sovereignty of God get air time?
5. What are some examples in our broader Christian culture which show a high view of our independence and a low view of God's sovereignty?

 READING ASSIGNMENT:
Chapters 4, 5

# SESSION III: HYMN STUDY

## A Question to Consider

Name a song you have sung recently. Did you consider the meaning of the words as you sang it?

*If possible sing this hymn together with the class or read the words aloud:*

### I Know Whom I Have Believed

I know not why God's wondrous grace
To me He hath made known,
Nor why, unworthy, Christ in love
Redeemed me for His own.

*Refrain:*
*But I know Whom I have believed.*
*And am persuaded that He is able*
*To keep that which I've committed*
*Unto Him against that day.*

I know not how this saving faith
To me He did impart,
Nor how believing in His Word
Wrought peace within my heart.
*Refrain*

I know not how the Spirit moves,
Convincing us of sin,
Revealing Jesus through the Word,
Creating faith in Him.
*Refrain*

I know not what of good or ill
May be reserved for me,
Of weary ways or golden days,
Before His face I see.
*Refrain*

I know not when my Lord may come,
At night or noonday fair,
Nor if I walk the vale with Him,
Or meet Him in the air.
*Refrain*

## Hymn Background and Author[2]

Daniel Webster Whittle's hymn, "I Know Whom I Have Believed," first published in *Gospel Hymns No. 4,* 1883, was set to music by James McGranahan. Whittle was born on November 22, 1840, in Chicopee Falls, Massachusetts and died at the turn of the century, March 4, 1901, in Northfield, Massachusetts.

Whittle was an American evangelist, Bible teacher and hymn writer. Through the influence of D.L. Moody, he entered full-time evangelism and worked with P.P. Bliss and James McGranahan. He wrote (mostly under the pseudonym El Nathan) the words for about two hundred hymns. Moody once said, "I think Major Whittle has written some of the best hymns of this century."

He served as a major in the War Between the States, and so he became known as "Major" Whittle. He was with General Sherman on his march to the sea and was later wounded at the battle of Vicksburg. He tragically lost his right arm, and ended up in a prisoner-of-war camp. Recovering from his wounds in the hospital, he began to read the New Testament. He felt some conviction, but he was still not ready to become a Christian. Shortly after his reading, a hospital orderly woke him and said a dying prisoner wanted someone to pray with him. Whittle did not want to do it, but the orderly said, "But I thought you were a Christian; I have seen you reading your Bible." Whittle then agreed to go. This is what he recorded at the bed side:

"I dropped on my knees and held the boy's hand in mine. In a few broken words I confessed my sins and asked Christ to forgive me. I believed right there that He did forgive me. I then prayed earnestly for the boy. He became quiet and pressed my hand as I prayed and pleaded God's promises. When I arose from my knees, he was dead. A look of peace had come over his troubled face, and I cannot but believe that God, who used him to bring me to the Savior, used me to lead him to trust Christ's precious blood and find pardon. I hope to meet him in heaven."

After the war, Whittle became treasurer of the Elgin Watch Company in Chicago, Illinois. In less than 10 years, though, he entered into an evangelistic ministry.

*After reading the above information, discuss or write answers to these questions:*
1.  How is sovereignty and predestination expressed in this hymn?
2.  Do you think Daniel W. Whittle was intentionally

reformed in his thinking and musical expression?

3. What can we learn about people who do not believe in God's sovereignty and predestination from this hymn?

### READING ASSIGNMENT:
Chapters 6, 7

## SESSION IV: DISCUSSION
Chapters 6, 7

### A Question to Consider:

Have you ever wished you knew the future? What would you do with a knowledge of the future? Would it change you or your plans?

*Discuss or list short answers to the following questions:*

### Text Analysis

1. Does God only know the future or does He determine it? How do you know?
2. What is wrong with the view that God merely has information of the future but no control?
3. What is the "foreknowledge view" of predestination? Why is it wrong?
4. What are some logical problems in denying God's control over the future?

### Cultural Analysis

1. What are some examples within non-Christian culture that show an interest in knowledge of the future?
2. Why do people desire this kind of foreknowledge?
3. Is God's sovereignty accepted by our culture as even a possibility? Give an example.

### Biblical Analysis

1. In what ways is the idea of foreknowledge used, and in what ways is it not used? (Feel free to review these texts: Acts 2:23, Rom. 8:29, Rom. 11:2, 1 Pet. 1:2, 1 Pet. 1:20.)
2. What do the Scriptures teach about foreknowledge?
3. How does Romans 8:29–30 support Sproul's explanation of predestination?

4. What biblical texts seem to support Arminian thinking or free will? How are they understood by Reformed thinkers?

### READING ASSIGNMENT:
Chapters 8, 9

## SESSION V: WRITING
Chapters 8, 9

### A Question to Consider

It would seem that if some are predestined to be saved that some are also predestined to be damned. Is this true? Why or why not?

### Writing Exercise

You now should have a reasonable understanding of predestination. We know that some Christians do not believe that predestination is biblical.

*Read the story of Lydia's conversion in Acts 16:6–15 and write a short story detailing her conversion in your own words. You may write it from either perspective; someone who believes in predestination or someone who does not. If time permits alter the story to represent the opposite belief.*

## SESSION VI: RECITATION
Chapters 8, 9

*The following questions are excellent for classroom discussion or can be answered as a writing exercise:*

1. What is fatalism?
2. What is wrong with fatalism?
3. What is the difference between predestination and fatalism?
4. Did Jesus die for everyone?
5. In what way is the Calvinistic belief called *Limited Atonement* limited?
6. In what way is the Arminian view of the atonement limited?
7. How do we evangelize if we believe predestination is true?
8. Why should the doctrine of predestination never be used as an excuse not to evangelize?
9. Do you believe Sproul teaches accurately about predestination? Why or why not?

# OPTIONAL SESSION: ACTIVITY

*You have just read the chapters dealing with Adam's Fall and the chapter that deals with the acrostic TULIP. Below you will find instructions for playing TULIP Trivia to see if you have fully understood what you have read.*

## TULIP Trivia

### TULIP TRIVIA DIRECTIONS:

Divide the class into three teams. Each team goes in turn and asks for a question from the five categories. If the person answering the question fails to do so correctly, the question is offered to the other teams.

### TULIP CARD GAME DIRECTIONS:

A card game alternative to the TULIP Trivia game to accomplish the same learning is provided as an option. Make cards that have the questions from the classroom game on one side and the answer on the other side. Shuffle the cards, then answer the question on the front. If you answer correctly, add 10 points to your score. You may pass on up to three cards in each game. After answering ten cards, add up your score. Next time you play, compare your score to see if you have improved.

## ENDNOTES

1 This is the conclusion of Rabbi Harold Kushner in his best selling work: *When Bad Things, Happen to Good People.* New York: HarperCollins, ed. 20, 1982. While the conclusion that God wanted to help but couldn't, might absolve God of responsibility for evil, the god whose people say, "Though I walk though the Valley of the Shadow of Death, I am comforted because *thou would really like to be with me but can't,"* is a god that gives people no comfort.

2 At the time of this publication, www.cyberhymnal.org provides music and lyrics, as well as biographical information on Whittle. There is also an alternative (contemporary) tune to the lyrics recorded and published through Christ Community Church (PCA), Franklin, TN www.christcommunity.org.

# TILL WE HAVE FACES

*How can they meet us face to face till we have faces?*

What would you do if you heard the voice of God?

What would you say to God if you had a chance to ask Him questions? You might ask Him about suffering in the world. You might ask him about some sort of deep personal pain that you have felt. "Why is my life going the way it is?" "Why did my life turn out the way it did?" Would you even know what to say?

In this story we meet a person who got the chance to question the gods. She wanted to question them more than anything else in the world because she thought, she knew, that they had ruined her life and took from her all that she had loved. Will the gods have an answer to her question? Will she even know what to say? Read on and discover.

## GENERAL INFORMATION

### Author and Context

The author of this work is the well-known Christian apologist C.S. Lewis. He was born in Northern Ireland and grew up in a home full of books. He fought and was

Eros (Cupid) is the son of Aphrodite and is famous for shooting his arrows at humans and gods to make them fall in love. In this version of his myth, he is called Ungit's son—or the god of the Mountain.

wounded in the First World War. Eventually, he became a Fellow of Language and Literature at Oxford and then a professor of Medieval and Renaissance Literature at Cambridge. Although in his early years he was an atheist, he converted to Christianity and used his massive literary talents to defend and propagate the faith.

His writings have been extremely influential. He wrote in a number of different areas. His most famous works were imaginative works of fiction, the most famous being *The Chronicles of Narnia* (studied later this year). He also wrote the *Space Trilogy*, but this book, *Till We Have Faces*, was his personal favorite (and justifiably so). He also wrote books concerning his field of academic study like *Studies in Medieval and Renaissance Literature*. In these works he tried to reintroduce to a growingly secular and agnostic literary culture the authors that they had dismissed. Milton and

Clive Staples Lewis was born on November 29, 1898 in Belfast, Ireland. *Till We Have Faces: A Myth Retold* was first published fifty-eight years later, in the same year he was married to Joy Davidman—to whom the book is dedicated.

Dante would certainly fall into this category. Finally, he wrote theological works like *Mere Christianity* and the *Problem of Pain*. Many of these books resulted from the activity of a group of writers called The Inklings. This group included J. R. R. Tolkein and Dorothy Sayers.

*Till We Have Faces* was a complex idea that Lewis worked on throughout his life. It is a retelling of the Myth of Cupid and Psyche, which was written down in the ancient world by a poet named Apuleius. Lewis' story, however, attempts something extraordinary. It uses a pagan myth to criticize two pagan worldviews, rationalism (represented by the Greek Fox and his teaching) and ritualistic mysticism (represented by the priests of Ungit). These two worldviews were evident in Lewis's day and in ours. He also tries to demonstrate truths about the Christian Worldview without removing the characters from their pagan world.

## Significance

In the scope of Lewis' writing, this book has had little influence and is not widely read. In Lewis's opinion, however, this was his greatest and most important piece of imaginative literature. After he published it critics, either through appalling blockheadedness or misreading the book, panned the book, giving it awful reviews. It fell into obscurity and was read by a very happy few. In many of the lists of Lewis's writing, it is not even mentioned. Lewis, however, was right about this book. It is his best.

In recent years *Till We Have Faces* has been receiving increasing interest and a wider reading and is increasingly being recognized as extraordinary work.

## Main Characters

There are two contrasting main characters in this book. One of them is Orual (pronounced "ORE-oo-al"), princess and later queen of Glome, a small kingdom near to but not part of the Greek world. Orual is a dutiful, homely child who grows up in the castle going unnoticed by most. Her half-sister Psyche is the other main character. Psyche is opposite Orual in almost every way. Orual's ugliness is contrasted to Psyche's goddess-like beauty. Orual and almost everyone else in Glome comes to love and almost worship Psyche, who begins to display miraculous powers of healing as a plague and famine sweep through Glome. Orual's mother-like and possessive love for Psyche and Psyche's "abduction" by the gods causes Orual to write the first part of her book (which is the book that you are reading).

The other sizeable character in the book is the Fox. He is a Greek slave who has been spared hard labor, because as a Greek he is assumed to be a suitable tutor for the girls of the royal house. He loves the girls, especially Orual and Psyche. He represents Greek philosophy and its wisdom in this story.

There are other characters that are important in parts of the story. The priest is the counterpoint to

Fox's Greek philosophy, advocating a mysterious religion of ritual and sacrifice devoted to the mystifying Ungit. The god of the Mountain, although hidden, plays an important role by calling Psyche to himself. Bardia, a soldier and eventual captain of the army play a growing role in the story. Redival, Orual's pretty and shallow sister, is also important at points.

## Summary and Setting

The book, set in a fictional pre-Christian kingdom somewhere on the outskirts of Greek influence, comes to us in two parts. The first part is Orual's charge of guilt against the gods. The second part of the book reveals how Orual's opinion of the events described in the first part of the book have been radically altered by some extraordinary occurrences which radically change her perspective.

The first part of the book is full of tragedy. Orual's mother has died and Psyche's mother dies giving birth to her. Orual is considered ugly and is despised by her sister Redival. The kingdom of Glome is ruled over by King Trom who above all desires, but can not produce, a male heir. Marginalized because her father wants a son, Orual and her sisters live relatively carefree lives. Orual finds her joy in two people: Fox, a Greek slave that has been appointed her tutor; and Psyche, her godlike half-sister who eventually becomes the center of Orual's life. Conflict arises when Psyche is taken from Orual. As Orual grows older she eventually becomes the Queen of Glome and rules wisely. Once when she is traveling abroad she finds a temple dedicated to the goddess Istra. Talking to the priest she is shocked to hear a recounting of the story of her sister, Psyche. Orual's role in the story, however, has been altered (at least in her opinion) and blame for Psyche's trouble is laid as a charge against her jealous sister. Ingeniously, Lewis has the priest recount Apuleius' original story at this point. This "slight" causes Orual to return to Glome and begin her accusation against the gods which ends the first part of this book. The rest of the book describes the life-altering changes that occur when the gods actually find a way to answer Orual's charges.

## Worldview

Those who love cakes particularly appreciate the layered ones. The layers usually consist of cake interspersed with icing, but some cakes are even more complex, having different types of cakes, different icings and new and unusual, sweet-tasting sauces and jellies on certain layers. The more layers a cake has the more delicious complexity and goodness it can exhibit. C.S. Lewis's *Till We Have Faces* is like an incredibly delightful, many-layered cake.

To bake a cake you need only a few things: eggs, flour, sugar, milk and oil. If you want a great cake, however, you need many other ingredients. To make a superb cake, however, you need one more thing . . . a great cook. Great cooks can create cakes that are works of art, full of layers of so many different tastes and flavors. Some of these layers might be made up of flavors that on their own would taste awful. Under the care of a great cook these flavors, which on their own might be sickening, are transformed into a mouth-watering delight.

Thankfully, this book is the product of one of the greatest cooks, C.S. Lewis. He takes the many worldviews represented in this work (some of them wonderful, others repulsive) and skillfully works all of them together to bring about a final product that makes his point masterfully.

The first layer of the cake is the worldview represented by the narrator in the first part of the book. This can be seen in Orual's understanding of God and the gods, her view of man and her understanding of salvation. Prepare your palate, because this first layer is bitter, representing the outlook of a bitter woman.

Orual is in a setting where she knows little of the true God and what she thinks she knows about the gods she despises. She knows nothing of the Trinity and even imagines that there are many gods. She knows of the hidden and horrible goddess Ungit, whose religion is the official one of Glome, who demands strange ritual, sacrifice and prostitution. There is also the "god of the Mountain," who calls for sacrifice and both "marries" and "devours" his victims.

This multiplicity of god leads Orual to reject any divine ethics and to define ethics on her own. As she deals with the loss of her beloved Psyche and is undone by hearing the priest blame her for Psyche's fate, she seeks to justify her actions by writing her angry diatribe or outburst against the gods. The gods, both Ungit and the god of the Mountain, are condemned for their selfishness and for daring to

**ODE TO PSYCHE** by John Keats

O Goddess! hear these tuneless numbers, wrung
　　By sweet enforcement and remembrance dear,
And pardon that thy secrets should be sung
　　Even unto thine own soft-conched ear:
Surely I dreamt to-day, or did I see
　　The winged Psyche with awaken'd eyes?
I wander'd in a forest thoughtlessly,
　　And, on the sudden, fainting with surprise,
Saw two fair creatures, couched side by side
　　In deepest grass, beneath the whisp'ring roof
　　Of leaves and trembled blossoms, where there ran
　　　A brooklet, scarce espied:
'Mid hush'd cool-rooted flowers, fragrant-eyed,
　　Blue, silver-white, and budded Tyrian,
They lay calm-breathing on the bedded grass;
　　Their arms embraced, and their pinions too;
　　Their lips touch'd not, but had not bade adieu,
As if disjoined by soft-handed slumber,
And ready still past kisses to outnumber
　　At tender eye-dawn of aurorean love:
　　　The winged boy I knew;
　　But who wast thou, O happy, happy dove?
　　　His Psyche true!

O latest born and loveliest vision far
　　Of all Olympus' faded hierarchy!
Fairer than Phoebe's sapphire-region'd star,
　　Or Vesper, amorous glow-worm of the sky;
Fairer than these, though temple thou hast none,
　　Nor altar heap'd with flowers;
Nor virgin-choir to make delicious moan
　　Upon the midnight hours;
No voice, no lute, no pipe, no incense sweet
　　From chain-swung censer teeming;
No shrine, no globe, no oracle, no heat
　　Of pale-mouthed prophet dreaming.

O brightest! though too late for antique vows,
　　Too, too late for the fond believing lyte,
When holy were the haunted forest boughs,
　　Holy the air, the water, and the fire;
Yet even in these days so far retir'd
　　From happy pieties, thy lucent fans,
　　Fluttering among the faint Olympians,
I see, and sing, by my own eyes inspired.

offend Orual's sense of morality.

The goddess of Glome and the god of the Mountain are pictured as uniformly wicked by Orual. The main characteristic for which they are blamed is their self-centeredness. Ungit takes from the people of Glome and, according to Orual, gives nothing back. Young women become "crones" in her temple. The god of the Mountain unleashes plagues and demands sacrifices. What is even worse is that both of these deities seem intent on taking the best of Glome. The sacrifice that is chosen is Psyche, the most perfect and beautiful woman in Glome. Even worse than this, the gods seem to make those that they "steal" willing and even desirous to go. This power infuriates Orual, who feels that Psyche has been stolen from her. But this is only the first bitter layer of the cake.

This view is complicated, however, by the fact that communion and communication with the gods is uncertain. The people of Glome have no scripture and although they worship and placate the gods, they do not know them. This is true both of Ungit, who is worshipped through a huge amorphous, shapeless rock, and the god of the Mountain, who both eats and loves his sacrifices. The gods, however, do seem to be communicating in a couple of ways. First, the Priest seems to have some way of communication with the gods. He knows that the god of the Mountain is demanding a sacrifice and that Psyche is it. How he has discerned this, however, is unclear. Second, the gods are calling some people to them. This is seen in Psyche's willingness and desire to go be sacrificed to the god of the Mountain. She has felt this internal call all of her life beckoning her to the mountain.

The ethics and morality of this book are complicated as well. The great moral quandary of this book occurs when Orual and Psyche meet each other on the Mountain after the sacrifice. As they speak, both realize that they are living in different worlds. Psyche believes that she is living in a castle and has become the wife of a god. Orual sees no castle and, although she is at a loss to understand how Psyche could be so healthy and even more beautiful while living alone in the wilderness, surmises that Psyche has lost her mind and has been abducted by some rogue living in the mountains. The disagreement reaches its zenith or height when Orual stabs herself and threatens even more harm to herself if Psyche will not lay aside her trust in her husband and light a lamp at night to discover her husband's identity. That night, Orual, staring over in the direction of Psyche's "palace" catches a glimpse of the otherworldly home. Orual, however, refuses to trust the god of the Mountain, leading to Psyche's exile from her garden paradise. Orual blames the gods for this because they did not give her enough clear evidence.

In this the master chef, Lewis, demonstrates his ability. Through this dilemma he is demonstrating antithesis. The way of life is to trust the god of the Mountain. Psyche, out of love for Orual, disobeys her husband, the god, and finds herself sent away from the palace. Righteousness results from faith

## ODE TO PSYCHE *continued*

So let me be thy choir, and make a moan
    Upon the midnight hours;
Thy voice, thy lute, thy pipe, thy incense sweet
    From swinged censer teeming;
Thy shrine, thy grove, thy oracle, thy heat
    Of pale-mouth'd prophet dreaming.
Yes, I will be thy priest, and build a fane
    In some untrodden region of my mind,
Where branched thoughts,
    new grown with pleasant pain,
    Instead of pines shall murmur in the wind:
Far, far around shall those dark-cluster'd trees
    Fledge the wild-ridged mountains steep by steep;
And there by zephyrs, streams, and birds, and bees,
    The moss-lain Dryads shall be lull'd to sleep;
And in the midst of this wide quietness
A rosy sanctuary will I dress
With the wreath'd trellis of a working brain,
    With buds, and bells, and stars without a name,
With all the gardener Fancy e'er could feign,
    Who breeding glowers, will never breed the same:
And there shall be for thee all soft delight
    That shadowy thought can win,
A bright torch, and a casement ope at night,
    To let the warm
      Love in!

*Ode to Psyche* was written by Keats in 1819 and was inspired by the Roman author Lucius Apuleius's second-century work, *The Golden Ass.*

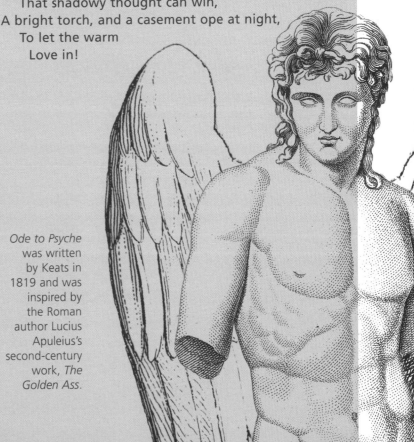

which causes obedience. Sin is a self-centered distrust of the gods and rejection of their grace.

In the second part of the book (or layer of the cake), however, the bitterness of Orual's early view of the gods is transformed because she gains a clearer view of herself and her love. Observing Orual's view of herself helps us to understand her view of man in general. At first, she sees herself and her Psyche (and by extension all men) as mistreated slaves of the gods. People strive and try, but the gods visit wrath. People love, but the gods feel that they may snatch whatever they want from people. She sees people as good and the gods as wicked.

The transformation of Orual's understanding turns wisdom into folly. During the first part of the book, Orual seems to be pursuing the path of wisdom. She makes mistakes, but ones that seem justifiable. She intensely loves those around her, Psyche and Fox. She rules wisely and demonstrates courage in the duel with King Argan. All of this is turned on its head in the second part of book. In it, she is unmasked. Her love of Psyche is shown to be selfishness. Her love of Bardia is seen to be devouring. Her hatred of the gods is shown to be the cries of the egotistical child demanding that all in this world and the next bow to her will. Finally, standing naked in the courtroom of the dead, she realizes what a fool she has been and repents of her folly.

As Orual ages she begins to see herself as she really is. She sees that her original worldview was actually made of sawdust and library paste. She realizes that she has become the devouring goddess Ungit and that all of the evil that she heaped upon the gods is really a picture of what she is like. Ironically, she even takes on the physical characteristics of Ungit, being veiled all the time. Her love hurt Redival, destroyed Bardia and caused Psyche to distrust her husband the god of the Mountain. The final recogni-

"I think what frightened me . . . was the holiness of the smell that hung about him— a temple-smell of blood . . . and burnt fat and singed hair and wine and stale incense. It is the Ungit

tion of her wickedness comes in a vision in which she reads her accusations against the gods in a giant courtroom. These accusations are not the well-written first part of our book, but are instead the heart of her accusation, which in the vision she repeats over and over, which is that the gods were unjust in taking Psyche because Psyche belonged to Orual. But this is just the second layer of the cake. In it, the gods are justified in their actions, and the pride of selfish humanity is humbled.

These layers, however, await a final consummation which is realized at the end of the book. In this layer the chef sets himself apart from other, lesser cooks. In her final vision, Orual sees the great tasks that Psyche completed after Orual convinced her to distrust the god of the Mountain. She sees in Psyche a redeemed humanity whose love is a giving of oneself to another rather than a self-centered taking. Finally, Orual is transformed into a woman like Psyche, and both of them are ready to meet god. But this is just another layer.

In this, Lewis both affirms the *imago Dei* and pictures its transformation. While there is no clear picture of the incarnation in *Till We Have Faces*,[1] the god of the Mountain does seem to have some human form. There is a clear picture of what restored humanity looks like. Lewis pictures the holiness and righteousness that God works in us as something that makes us more substantial physically. Closeness to God is reflected in humans becoming "more human." When Orual sees Psyche's image reflected in the water as God nears them (there are two women), she realizes, "I had never seen a real woman before." The presence of the *imago Dei* assumes the true God, who is revealed at the end of the book. If a god like Ungit were to create people, they would not be well fitted for this type of restoration. The layers of the cake, both the bitter and the sublime, now make Lewis' case so clear. His story both confronts you, intrigues you and delights you.

Lewis also uses this final transformation of worldview to critique the worldview of rationalism (which is the belief that human reason is to be judge over all reality). At the beginning of the book, rationalism is presented in a favorable light because of the goodness of its main proponent, the Fox. Fox teaches Orual and Psyche Greek philosophy, which Lewis summed up in an essay as a "clear and thin"[2]

religion based on platitudes and maxims. This religion rejects the necessity of sacrifice and generally trusts in the goodness of man. It is this religion that Orual clings to throughout her life. This religion was represented in Lewis's experience by the secular schools of thought spawned by the Enlightenment. In the courtroom vision, however, this worldview is shown to be inadequate. Its flavor is weak and paltry, but this is only seen in contrast to the beautiful fullness of those who find peace with God. Lewis has the Fox himself repent of it before the court saying, "I didn't know; but I never told her I didn't know. I don't know now. Only that the way to the true gods is more like the house of Ungit . . . oh, it's unlike too, more unlike than we yet dream, but that's the easy knowledge, the first lesson; only a fool would stay there, posturing and repeating it. The Priest knew at least that there must be sacrifices. They will have sacrifices—will have man."

By this Lewis critiques the Greek worldview and its more recent descendants. Lewis, also, however, rejects the unknowing mysticism of the Ungit religion, which he called "dark and thick."[3] This religion overflows with ceremony and sacrifice, dark mystery and opaque or unclear ritual. This religion is shown to be wrongheaded, but it remains closer to the truth than the Greek secular religion. (One can only imagine in the world of the book that the religion of Ungit is an ancient echo of the true religion passed down from the children of Noah after the Flood, but which has become confused and had many accretions and additions to it.[4]) Somehow, by the initiative of the gods, Psyche and Orual both gain a glimpse into the true religion and see behind the shadow of confused Ungit worship. Now, the reader has reached the tastiest part of this "dessert" that both amazes the reader and always leaves them awestruck.

So, in a story about ancient paganism, we have stumbled into the true religion, or have we? Lewis lays before us a case in which real salvation seems to be taking place without the name of Christ ever being uttered or any sort of conception of the church (except perhaps the Courtroom of the Dead).

Can there be salvation outside of the church and outside of Christ? To answer this, initially one must recognize that Lewis is telling a story about the ancient pre-Christian past. During this time it is clear through examples like Jethro and Melchizedek that remembrances of the gospel did at times resound in ancient cultures. Finally, it must be recognized that Lewis, in this case, is not contemplating salvation outside of Christ,[5] but that the true God chose, in this story, to reveal himself to these two sisters who lived far for the sound of His promises.

Lewis, of course, has been accused (and justifiably so) of opening the door of salvation wider than the gospel allows. In *The Last Battle*, Lewis shows a sincere worshipper of the false god Tash being accepted by Aslan on account of his sincerity.[6] From this Lewis has been charged with Universalism, a dangerous heresy which denies that any will eventually be damned, but that God will have mercy on all. In *Till We Have Faces*, Lewis might be criticized concerning his view of the afterlife, because he lets Fox into the Courtroom of the Dead instead of sending him to Hell (Tartarus for the Greeks).[7] It is unclear, however, what this courtroom represents (it might be a place of lesser punishment in Hell). In the case of Psyche and Orual, the true God has chosen to reveal himself to these two and has in the end redeemed them and made them ready for heaven. Orual's description of this is, of course, not done in theologically astute language (it would be out of place if it did). Her descriptions do, however, give us a clear picture of repentance, salvation and a stunning picture of the beatific vision in which humans get a "face to face" view of divine glory.

No matter how skilled our cook is, we must judge whether Lewis is justified in presenting a picture of the gospel in pagan garb. To make a judgment about this, one needs to understand both Lewis' purpose, the structure of the book and his cunning. In the first part of the book, Orual's complaint against the gods, Lewis effectively gets his reader to see the world through the lens of Orual's worldview. The reader learns to hate the gods and see Orual as a wronged party. By the end of the second part of the book, however, the opinion of the reader is likely to have shifted 180 degrees. This shift is likely to give his readers a sense of imbalance, because they will have thought that they understood the compelling story during the first half of the book, but in the second part of the book they, along with Orual, find that they did not understand anything. This bit of literary craftiness can cause people to re-examine what they think about themselves and about God. So, Lewis crawls into pagan skin and tells a pagan story full of pagan religions which in the end demonstrates the utter inadequacy of paganism and sets forth the fact of salvation and an intriguing picture of deliverance.

This probably does not answer all of your questions, but hopefully it will whet your appetite. The cake is set before you. Let's eat!

—*G. Tyler Fischer*

"She has only just begun to be a goddess. For you must know that, like many other gods, she began by being mortal."

READING ASSIGNMENT: Chapters 1–5

# Session I: Prelude
Chapters 1–5

## A Question to Consider

If you could ask God one question, what would it be? Why?

*Discuss or list short answers to the following questions:*

### Discussion

1. Imagine you are Abraham being commanded to sacrifice Isaac? What would you ask God?
2. What if you were Job in the midst of his trials? What would you ask and why?
3. Have you ever been falsely accused? How did you respond?

In this book we are going to witness someone laying the charge of unfairness at the feet of the gods. (This story takes place in a land far from the gospel.) The first part of the story might seem just like a story, but it is not. It is an argument for a court. As you read through the story, see if you can discern what the gods have done to Orual, the narrator of the book, that would make her wish to take them to court. Right now, take out a paper and put at the top of it: *Orual's Case Against the Gods.* Fold it a couple of times and use it as a bookmark. As you are reading the book and come to a place where the gods seem to have done something unfair, unfold the paper and write the reason down. It does not matter if the paper gets a little tattered. Also, for this one assignment (if it is acceptable to your teacher), you need not use your best handwriting. (There is a reason the writing should be of the sloppier sort that you will learn later.) But make sure that you can read the reasons that you write. Fill out your sheet with things that you might have already noticed in your reading.

Also take some time to discuss this question: What kind of occurrences or events cause people to accuse God of being unfair?

## Comprehension Questions

1. Who are the two main characters of the book and what are they like?
2. Who was C.S. Lewis and what were some of the books that he wrote?

3. What difficult task does Lewis attempt in this book concerning the presentation of Christian and non-Christian worldviews?
4. Who was Apuleius, and what part does he play in this story?
5. Why is the book divided into two parts, and what are the two parts of the book?
6. Why is this book likened to a many-layered cake?

 **Reading Assignment:**
Chapters 6–8

# Session II: Discussion
Chapters 6–8

*Compare your* Case Against the Gods *sheet to the following list:*

- Psyche's longing for the Mountains and her castle there.
- The gods caused Psyche's good actions to bring about her destruction.
- her "healing" of Fox
- her willingness to touch the sick people
- her commitment to try to save her nurse maid
- The gods (the priest and the people … and the lot) have demanded that Psyche be sacrificed to save Glome from the curse.
- The gods have been wooing Psyche all of her life, making her want to be sacrificed on the mountain.
- The gods ruined Orual's last sight of Psyche by having her painted up like one of the women from the house of Ungit.
- The gods make nature beautiful and cause people to hope before they visit some even greater disaster on them.

## A Question to Consider

What is love?

*Discuss or list short answers to the following questions:*

### Text Analysis

*The case for Orual's love for Psyche:*

1. How did Orual care for Psyche when she was young?
2. How did Orual react when Redival accused Psyche of acting like a goddess?

A detail of *Psyche Receiving the First Kiss of Love* by François Gérard, 1798.

3. How did Orual react when the King "gave way" and gave Psyche up to be sacrificed?
4. What was Orual willing to do after Psyche was sacrificed to honor Psyche's remains?

*The case against Orual's love for Psyche:*

1  Does Orual comfort Psyche in her last hours?
2. What is the concern of the first words that Orual says to Psyche?
3. When Psyche talks of having no one to love but her and the Fox, Orual admits to not even wanting him mentioned. Why does Orual think this?
4. When Psyche lets Orual know that she has always had a secret longing for the Mountains, what does

Orual believe that this implies about her relationship with Psyche?

5. Orual admits that bitterness was mixed with her love. Why was it there?
6. What is the last thing that Orual says to Psyche? Why does she say this?

*Biblical Analysis*

1. In John 3:16, what defines God's love for the world?
2. In John 15:13 what does Christ say defines someone's love for his brother?
3. Which love does biblical love fit, Orual's for Psyche or Psyche's for Orual?

## SUMMA

*Write an essay or discuss this question, integrating what you have learned from the material above.*

How does the Bible define love, and does Orual's love for Psyche fit within this definition?

READING ASSIGNMENT:
Chapters 9, 10

# SESSION III: RECITATION

Chapters 9, 10

*What does your* Case Against the Gods *sheet look like now? Here is an additional charge for the list of charges that Orual laid against the gods to this point in the story:*

- The gods made Psyche and Orual see two different worlds in the Valley of the Gods.

## Recitation

*Answer the following questions for factual recall:*

### Chapters 1–10

1. What did Fox think of the gods?
2. Who is Ungit?
3. What role does Orual take in Psyche's life?
4. What is Psyche like?
5. Did Psyche's touch make the people well? What was Psyche's touch accused of doing?
6. What does the Priest say that love is?
7. Why is the King relieved when he finds out that Psyche is the Accursed?
8. Who comforts whom when Orual meets Psyche? Why is this ironic?
9. What grieves Orual most concerning Psyche's sacrifice?
10. Whom does Orual find on the Mountain?

READING ASSIGNMENT:
Chapters 11–13

# SESSION IV: WRITING

Chapters 11–13

*What does your* Case Against the Gods *sheet look like now? Here are additional charges for the list of charges that Orual laid against the gods to this point in the story:*

- The gods caused the rain, which made Orual completely reject Psyche's version of the truth.
- The gods caused Orual to see the castle for a minute in the morning mists, but it was not enough evidence to convince her.

## Writing Assignment

Is the castle that Orual saw in the mists real?
*Directions: Make sure that you have a thesis and a well-reasoned response. You should at least have three reasons why the castle is real, or is not. You should also have a couple of reasons why you know that the other side (or sides) of the argument is wrong. Defend your position well. You will not be judged on whether you are right or wrong about the castle (only the rest of the story will reveal that fact) but whether you defend your position logically.*

READING ASSIGNMENT:
Chapters 14–16

# SESSION V: WORLDVIEW

Chapters 14–16

*What does your* Case Against the Gods *sheet look like now? Here is an additional charge for the list of charges that Orual laid against the gods to this point in the story:*

- The gods changed the past and made it appear (even to Orual) that she had always known that Psyche's lover was a god.

## Worldview Analysis

*Fill in Chart 1. Reason through what the different characters think concerning these questions. For some you might not have enough information to give an answer. When the book has not given us enough information just write a question mark.*

READING ASSIGNMENT:
Chapters 17–19

| Chart 1: **CHARACTER WORLDVIEWS** | | | | | |
| --- | --- | --- | --- | --- | --- |
| | PSYCHE | FOX | ORUAL (before meeting the god) | ORUAL (after meeting the god) | PRIEST |
| What do they think about the gods? | | | | | |
| What do they think about man? | | | | | |
| What is sin (how is it defined)? | | | | | |
| How can man find salvation? | | | | | |
| How will the world end? | | | | | |

# SESSION VI: DISCUSSION

Chapters 17–19

## A Question to Consider

Is Christianity at its root mystical or rational?

*Discuss or list short answers to the following questions:*

### Text Analysis

The story describes the *mystical* religion of Ungit and the god of the Mountain:
1. List several similarities to Christianity.
2. List several differences from Christianity.

The story describes the *rational* teaching of the Fox:
3. List several similarities to Christianity.
4. List several differences from Christianity.

### Cultural Analysis

1. Where do we see rationalism today?
2. Where do we see mysticism?

## SUMMA

*Write an essay or discuss this question, integrating what you have learned from the questions above.* Which one of these two (mysticism or rationalism) is biblical Christianity most like?

READING ASSIGNMENT:
Chapters 20, 21

# SESSION VII: ACTIVITY

Chapters 20, 21

## The Trial of the Gods

*Today we are going to serve as judge and jury as we consider the case that Orual has laid out against the gods. To do this, follow these steps:*

- Elect a judge, a prosecutor (to set forth Orual's case) and a defense attorney (for the gods). For time sake these are to be the people whose last names start with or come nearest after the letters "C," "S," and "L," respectively.

- All of you will be the witnesses. Take out your book marks and read the charges that you have written against the gods. The judge should write out the charges on the blackboard for all to see. The prosecuting and defense attorney should write the charges on notebook paper. (People need not repeat the charge if someone has already read it.)

- The prosecutor is to read Orual's own summation beginning with the paragraph that starts with the second to last paragraph in Chapter 21 ("Yet at last after infinite hindrances…") reading to the end of the chapter.

- Finally, have someone read the original story of the myth written by Apuleius which Lewis recapitulates at the end of the book (you may skip the first paragraph and the last two paragraphs).

*The defense attorney should then set forth (with the help of the jury) any defense that the gods have concerning the charges.*

*Then all as jury are to consider whether Orual is justified in her charges against the gods. Majority vote wins.*

*Please save the official list of the charges because we will examine them later.*

### READING ASSIGNMENT:
Part II, Chapters 1, 2

# SESSION VIII: DISCUSSION
Part II, Chapters 1, 2

## A Question to Reconsider

What is love?

*Review the answer that we found last time, especially keeping in mind how the Scripture corrected and shaped our view.*

*Discuss or list short answers to the following questions:*

### Text Analysis

1. Consider Orual's love for Bardia as revealed in her conversation with Ansit. What are Ansit's charges against Orual.
2. Consider what it means for Orual to be Ungit. What characteristics do Ungit and Orual share?

### Biblical Analysis

*Read 1 Corinthians 13, the famous "Love Chapter."*

### SUMMA

*In light of Ansit's charges and 1 Corinthians 13, write an essay or discuss whether Orual's love for Bardia matches with or differs from the biblical characteristics of true love.*

Did Orual love Bardia?

### READING ASSIGNMENT:
Part II, Chapters 3, 4

# SESSION IX: DISCUSSION
Part II, Chapters 3, 4

## A Question to Consider

Can someone be saved without hearing the gospel?

*Discuss or list short answers to the following questions:*

### Discussion

1. Did Orual and Psyche know anything of the gospel?
2. What aspects of the religion of Glome taught Orual and Psyche truth about true religion? (See the first statements of Fox in the last chapter.)
3. If faith (in the real God) and repentance (from sin as the real God defines it), are saving graces, can Psyche and Orual actually have been saved?
4. Can God, the real God of the Bible, reveal Himself to people outside of the normal means of having the gospel preached to them by a minister?
5. Is Lewis giving us a picture of Christian conversion? How do you know?
6. Are all people redeemed at the end of this story? Is Fox?

### Cultural Analysis

1. What does our culture think will happen to people who do not believe the gospel?
2. What would our culture say about a God that sends people to Hell eternally, if they never hear or have a chance to hear the gospel?
3. What is wrong with our culture's thinking?

### Biblical Analysis

1. What does Paul say in Romans 10:14?
2. Does this mean that Orual and Psyche's salvation cannot be real?

### Application

1. The reaction of some has been to say that we need not work hard as missionaries because, if God wanted to save the lost, He could do it without our help. What is wrong with this?
2. Some groups have focused all efforts on reaching the lost and no time on building Christian culture in the places where the gospel has already

Orual sees across a river a herd of rams of the gods and thinks, "If I can steal but one golden flock off their sides, I shall have beauty." Orual is trampled in her effort, enabling another woman to harvest the golden wool without effort.

reached. What is wrong with this?

3. Why do we evangelize the heathen nations? What is to be our motivation?

4. What should this lead us to do concerning the lost?

## SUMMA

*Write an essay or discuss this question, integrating what you have learned from the material above.* Can someone be saved without hearing the Gospel?

## Optional Activity

1. Write a short essay on whether Lewis is guilty of presenting an improper view of salvation, answering the question: "Has Lewis opened the door of heaven too wide in order to let Psyche and Orual in?"

2. Read James Henley Thornwell's wonderful essay on "The Sacrifice of Christ, the Type and Model of Missionary Effort."[8]

# OPTIONAL SESSION A

## The Trial of Orual

*Today we are going to reopen the case concerning Orual and the gods (see Session VII). Follow these steps:*

1. Let the three people whose birthdays are closest to New Year's Eve serve as the judge, defense attorney and prosecutor.

2. Get out the official record of the charges and the

*Chart 2:* **WORLDVIEW ANALYSIS**

|  | ORUAL WHEN PSYCHE WAS BEING TAKEN TO THE SACRIFICE | ORUAL JUST AS SHE FINISHES WRITING PART ONE OF HER BOOK | ORUAL AT THE END OF THE BOOK AFTER HER LAST VISION |
|---|---|---|---|
| What are the gods like? |  |  |  |
| What is man? |  |  |  |
| What defines sin? |  |  |  |
| What is salvation? |  |  |  |

sentence of the jury.

3. Re-examine the charges and discover what Orual would think of them now.

4. The defense attorney should read aloud what Orual read from the book near the end of Part II, Chapter III to the end of the chapter.

5. How was she answered by the gods when no one said anything?

6. Does this clear the gods of all charges? Let the jury consider and decide. Majority vote wins.

7. Next, turn the tables and consider if Orual is guilty of slandering the gods.

# Optional Session B

## Quiz

### Grammar (2 points each)

1. Who is Ungit?

2. What does Fox teach Orual and Psyche concerning the gods?

3. In their first meeting in the Valley of the Gods, about what do Psyche and Orual disagree?

4. What does Orual hear at the Temple of Istra?

5. Name three of Orual's charges against the gods.

6. What does Orual do in the courtroom of the dead?

7. What is reflected in the pool at the end of the book?

### Logic (3 points per blank)

*Fill in Chart 2 to describe how Orual's worldview is changed and transformed through her experiences.*

### Lateral Thinking

(14 points each)

Answer the following in light of this quote from the first paragraph of the introduction to C.S. Lewis's book *The Four Loves,*

". . . The first distinction I made [concerning love] was therefore between what I called Gift-love and Need-love. The typical example of gift love would be that love which moves a man to work and plan and save for the future well being of his family which he will die without sharing or seeing; of the second, that which sends a lonely or frightened child to its mother's arms."

1. How does God's love for Abraham in Genesis and for Israel in Exodus differ from Orual's love for Psyche in Part I of *Till We Have Faces?*

2. Is the calling that Psyche felt toward going to the Mountain a good example of the doctrine of Predestination as explained in *Chosen by God?*

3. What are the similarities in the actions of Orual leading up to her manipulating Psyche into disobeying her husband and in Satan's actions leading to Adam's fall in the garden?

## Endnotes

1  In a sense, Psyche is sort of a Christ character. She connects the world of the gods to the world of human beings. She, however, fails like Adam and breaks covenant with her husband, the god of the Mountain. The god of the Mountain is also Christlike in some ways. He takes a human bride as Christ takes the Church.

2  Hooper, Walter. *C.S. Lewis. A Companion and Guide.* London: Harper Collins, 1996. 253.

3  Ibid.

4  This is seen many times in tribal settings, where the people have been unaffected by modern, rationalistic culture. Their stories sometimes echo the fact that long ago their ancestors knew the real God, but that now they are trapped worshipping the unpredictable and vicious lower gods. Paul calls this the worship of demons (1 Cor. 10:20).

5  "They will have man" sets the stage for the coming sacrifice of Christ.

6  This can be seen at the end of the series in *The Last Battle.*

7  The ancient world had a conception of hell that was made up of Hades and Tartarus. While some cultures had no positive vision of the afterlife (In the *Odyssey* Achilles says that he would rather be a slave in the world of men than a king in the Underworld, and Gilgamesh seems to view the afterlife as being eaten by worms and eating dirt). The Romans did have a concept of Elysium, a place in the afterlife where the righteous enjoy eternity (for Virgil the righteous were the builders and supporters of the empire). Tartarus was a place in Hell where the wicked received punishment. Strikingly, the New Testament writers use the words Hades and Tartarus to communicate concerning hell (Matt. 16:18 and 1 Cor. 15:55 use the word Hades while 2 Pet. 2:4 uses the word Tartarus.

8  At the time of publication a pithy portion can be found at www.chattablogs.com/okcalvin/archives/008662.html

Orual becomes, as in the myth, "a little ant, and the seeds were as big as millstones; and labouring with all my might, till my six legs cracked, I carried them to their places."

# THE MAGICIAN'S NEPHEW

What if a fairy tale came true and suddenly you became one of the characters in the story?

Out of the blue one morning you woke up and stumbled into a world of talking animals, witches and magical enchantments. In *The Chronicles of Narnia*, C.S. Lewis presents us with just such a tale. This tale begins with a young boy, Digory, and his faithful friend, Polly. At first, their adventures seem fairly run-of the-mill, but through trickery and magic they stumble into Narnia, a land full of amazing creatures and wonderful adventures. If this marks the beginning of your reading in the *Chronicles*, I hope that you enjoy these stories as much as others have down through the years.

## GENERAL INFORMATION

### Author and Context

C.S. Lewis hardly needs any introduction. An Oxford don (or tutor) who specialized in medieval and renaissance literature, he was also well-known for his popular apologetic defenses of the Christian faith, as well as his works of fiction. His fiction for adults is represented by *Till We Have Faces*, and his well-known "Space Trilogy." *The Magician's Nephew* is the first of seven in *The Chronicles of Narnia*, a series of books written for children and (very importantly) written from a child's point of view. In calling *The Magician's Nephew* the first, we are following the chronological order of Narnian time, the order Lewis preferred, rather than the order in which Lewis actually wrote the books.

C.S. Lewis was born in 1898 and died in 1963. *The Chronicles of Narnia* were written in the early fifties, when Lewis was in his fifties, and the memories of the Second World War were still fresh.

Uncle Andrew Ketterley —a wicked, cruel magician like the ones in all the old fairy tales.

*The Chronicles of Narnia* are what Lewis called a great "supposal." *Suppose* there was another world with all these creatures in it, what might the true faith look like in that different world? The books are not strictly speaking allegorical in the sense that *Pilgrim's Progress* is allegorical. An allegory is a story in which people, things and events have a symbolic meaning which is often instructive. Although we can say that Aslan is Christ in Narnia, this is not because he represents Christ in our world, but rather because he would be Christ, if such a world as Narnia existed.

## Significance

In the clothing of C.S. Lewis's "supposals," we find all the great themes and doctrines of the Christian faith. In *The Magician's Nephew*, Lewis shows us the important doctrines of Creation and Fall. After Digory and Polly view the desolate Charn, a world that has almost died, they are then privileged to witness the creation of Narnia. But not only do they witness it, so does the Witch, and Uncle Andrew, and the cabby and his horse. The fact of the Witch's presence is presentation of the Fall. She is there because Digory pretended to have been enchanted in Charn, overpowered Polly and rang a bell that awakened Jadis, the last queen of Charn. Because of this sin, the Witch is present at the creation. When Aslan's song brings the good world of Narnia into existence, it immediately has to deal with the presence of evil.

Aslan sings the world into existence, and this is a glorious retelling of the creation of the world found in Genesis. The embodiment of evil is found in the world shortly thereafter in the person of Jadis, the former queen of Charn. But she has been brought there by the folly and sin of Digory in the first place and then secondarily by Digory's attempt to fix everything himself. As he tried to get her back into her own world, he unwittingly brought her into the new world of Narnia. And thus we have the elements of Creation and Fall.

This Fall is similar to and, simultaneously, unlike Adam's Fall. The similarities are obvious (Digory falling into sin by the trickery of Jadis), but the differences are also striking. The chief difference is that Digory, unlike Adam in the Garden, is already a fallen being. He is a sinner when he rings the bell and when he witnesses the creation of Narnia.

## Main Characters

The two human children who have this adventure are Digory Kirke and Polly Plummer, next door neighbors and playmates in late nineteenth-century London. Jadis is the last queen of Charn, an evil and despotic empire found in another world. She is brought into Narnia on the day of its creation, and assumes her role there as the "devil" of that world. Uncle Andrew Ketterly is Digory's uncle, and he fancies himself a very important magician, although it becomes apparent that he is only a dabbler in spells. The cabby is not a central figure in the story, although he is important to the history of Narnia, in that he becomes Narnia's first king, King Frank, and his wife becomes Queen Helen. Strawberry, the cabby's horse, becomes Fledge, the first of Narnia's flying horses.

And of course, Aslan is the central character in this book because he is the central character in all the books of the *Chronicles*—whether he is present or not.

## Summary and Setting

Digory Kirke is a boy from the country who has had to move to London because his father is away in India and his mother has become very ill. They move to live with Digory's (mad) Uncle Andrew and his sister. Digory is miserable because of his mother's illness, and in this condition he makes friends with Polly. While they are exploring in the attic, they stumble into Uncle Andrew's study. He tricks Polly into touching a magic ring, and she is transported out of our world. Digory has to follow her in order to bring her back. The two children find themselves in a "Wood between the Worlds," with small ponds leading into many different worlds. They decide to go exploring and find themselves in Charn. Digory awakens Jadis, the last queen of Charn, by striking a little golden bell. When they escape back to the Wood between the Worlds, Jadis is dragged along, and then she is brought back to London the same way. She goes off to conquer our world, and with great difficulty, the children manage to transport her back to the "in between place," the Wood between the Worlds, this time dragging Uncle Andrew, a cabby and his horse with them. Thinking they are taking her back to Charn, they jump into another pool, only to find themselves in Narnia at the moment Aslan creates

I'm tall, fat, rather bald, red-faced, double-chinned, black-haired, have a deep voice, and wear glasses for reading. The only way for us to get to Aslan's country is through death, as far as I know: perhaps some very good people get just a tiny glimpse before then. Best love to you all. When you say your prayers sometimes ask God to bless me,

Yours ever,
C.S. Lewis
*—from a letter written, near his death, to a group of fifth graders*

Used by permission of The Marion E. Wade Center, Wheaton College, Wheaton, IL.

that world. Aslan sets Digory to the task of obtaining an apple that will grow a tree to protect Narnia from the evil that was introduced on the day of her creation. Digory and Polly come back to our world with an apple from that tree of protection, an apple which is then used by Aslan to heal Digory's mother.

## Worldview

Have you ever wanted to do something very much? And at the same time, you knew that you must not do that very thing? Sometimes wanting to do the wrong thing can be very powerful, and if this kind of temptation had hands it would seize you by the throat.

*The Magician's Nephew* is a striking book about this sort of temptation. The main character is Digory Kirke, an important figure in the other books of the Chronicles, even when he is not immediately present.

He is a kindly but crusty old professor in *The Lion, the Witch, and the Wardrobe,* a book in this series to be read later, and in him we are probably meant to see Lewis's old tutor, Kirkpatrick, a figure who also shows up as McPhee in *That Hideous Strength,* another of Lewis's famous works.

The story is book-ended with the accounts of two temptations. Digory fails the first test in the hall of royal images in Charn. A great line of kings and queens fill that hall, as though it were a gigantic waxworks. In the middle of the hall is a stand with a little golden bell and hammer, and an inscription that the children can mysteriously read. The inscription invites whoever reads it to go mad wondering what would have happened had he only struck the bell. Polly wants nothing to do with it, but Digory pretends to himself that he was enchanted, twists Polly's arm, and taps the bell, which is, of course, the disastrous action which brings Jadis back to life. This is also the ultimate reason why evil makes its way into Narnia. In a subsequent book, we discover that this is the reason why Aslan has to die at the hands of the White Witch (who is Jadis in a later form).

But near the end of *The Magician's Nephew*, Digory is tempted by Jadis again (for it was clearly she who placed the bell and inscription as a means to bring her back). This time the temptation occurs in another enclosed area, but in this case the enclosure is a garden. Again, Digory is faced with an inscription which he can mysteriously read, and again he does what the inscription says, but this time it is in line with the directions given to him by Aslan. In the meantime, Jadis has made her way to the same garden and has taken fruit from the tree in the center of the garden. She tempts Digory to disregard the instruction of Aslan and to partake with her of the forbidden fruit. This time, Digory refuses. He does so partially on the basis of his knowledge of Aslan (he also sees the wickedness of Jadis when she suggests leaving Polly behind), and although he occasionally doubts his obedience, he reassures himself on the way back that he did the right thing by thinking of Aslan's compassion for him.

At this point, it is important to understand the difference between testing and temptation. In the New Testament, the word for *test* and the word for

*temptation* are the same word. This creates something of a problem. How can we be told that God never tempts anyone (James 1:13), and yet Jesus teaches us to pray to God the Father that we not be led into temptation (Matt. 6:13)? Although the word is the same, there are two very different concepts here, and the two inscriptions of *The Magician's Nephew* provide us with a perfect example of the difference between them.

Although Digory is tested twice, an important difference should be noted between the two temptations. The inscription in Charn is *designed* to get the one who reads it to do the wrong thing. The intent of the person who placed the bell and hammer there was to awaken unlawful curiosity and to get the person to sin, to do evil. But the inscription in the garden of the west invites the person who reads it to do the *right* thing. But, of course, any such invitation can be turned around—which is precisely what Jadis does, and she invites Digory to do the same. In a world where right and wrong exist, a test from the right can readily be turned into a temptation from the wrong. An invitation to come through the gate can be twisted into the disobedience of climbing over the wall.

Now the reason Digory fails the first test, and the reason he is lured and enticed by the second lies in his similarity to his Uncle Andrew. But unlike his uncle, he eventually follows Aslan's lead, and his curiosity is clearly redeemed and translated into the wisdom he shows in subsequent books.

Throughout the *Chronicles*, how a person treats animals is often a measure of how good or evil he is. Uncle Andrew shows his true colors right from the start in his regard for guinea pigs. Here we see one of the unwitting assistants in Ketterley's quest for magical knowlege. Yellow rings are for entering into the Wood between the Worlds, and green rings are for exiting.

But when he is struggling against temptation in this book, he is motivated by some of the same things that motivate his uncle—curiosity and a desire to *know*. When Uncle Andrew begins to explain about the dust from another world, even though he has just caused Polly to disappear, Digory is interested in spite of himself. Using remarkable reasoning ability, he figures out that the Wood between the Worlds is kind of like a cosmic attic, an in-between place, through which you can get into various worlds, just like he and Polly got into Uncle Andrew's study. In his curiosity, Digory wants to go off exploring in other worlds. And of course, he is the one who strikes the bell to see what happens.

This family resemblance between Digory and Uncle Andrew is something that Lewis very much wanted us to see and recognize. First, they are members of the same family; Digory is his nephew. Secondly, they are both very curious. Third, Polly points it out: "'You looked exactly like your Uncle when you said that,' said Polly. 'Why can't you keep to the point?' said Digory." Fourth, Digory is oblivious to his own wrong-doing just as Uncle Andrew was (although in Digory's case, he did acknowledge it when Polly confronted him). And fifth, Digory had a tendency to rationalize what he wanted to do in the same way his Uncle Andrew did, as shown above when he said that Polly was getting off the point.

This is related to another issue that Lewis brings in throughout these books. Lewis makes a definite point of inculcating the need for honest confession of sin. It is not an instance of morbid introspection—far from it. The reader is simply taught the virtue of straightforward honesty in confession. Digory apologizes to Polly (after a fashion) when she demands it, but he confesses honestly and completely in the presence of Aslan.

But he is only a boy, and he has had a good upbringing. He has not been hardened by years of this folly as his uncle had been. In addition, although the curiosity is definitely there, Digory is motivated by more than *just* curiosity. Digory's other great motivation is his desire to see his mother well again. When Digory raises that possibility to his Uncle Andrew, his uncle just brushes it off because he does not care. He wants to grow battleships in the fertile Narnian ground, but dismisses the possibility that anything in Narnia might make Digory's mother well again. Uncle Andrew thinks only of himself, but Digory is very concerned for the health of his mother.

Jadis even takes Digory's love for his mother as a basis for one of her appeals to him. He can use this forbidden knowledge (that he *does* have a real desire for) in such a way as to see his mother healed. The temptation strikes with double force—he can satisfy his curiosity, *and* see his mother well. Uncle Andrew doesn't care for others, but Digory still does and wants desperately to see his mother healed. This is one of the most powerful themes in this book, and probably arises from Lewis's empathy for Digory in his terrible situation. C.S. Lewis's mother died of cancer when he was just ten years old, so he knew just what this was like.

We therefore are invited to see the end result of forbidden knowledge in Jadis, the intermediate result of it in Uncle Andrew, and the first stirrings of it in Digory. According to Lewis, one of the characteristics of all magicians was their vanity. This is something that Jadis and Uncle Andrew have in common. Even though Lewis makes it clear that Jadis has a lot to be vain about (she is strikingly beautiful and extremely powerful and competent), at the same time she is capable of being silly because of vanity. Lewis gives us just a touch of this so that we might know that it is there. But in Uncle Andrew, who has a lot less to be vain about, his vanity stands out in high relief. Jadis terrifies him, but as soon as she is out of sight, he begins imagining that she might fall in love with him.

Another important characteristic of magicians, and this provides the structure for another important theme in this book, is the fact that they believe themselves to be above ordinary morality. Both Uncle Andrew and Jadis affirm that there are two standards of morality, one for "ordinary people" and the other for the elite, among whom these magicians consider themselves. By pointing to this, Lewis is following one of his masters, G.K. Chesterton, who spent a great deal of time pointing out the splendor and glory of the ordinary.

One of the things that distinguishes *The Chronicles of Narnia* from other literary works of fantasy is that these books are intended to drive us back to ordinary life with a deeper appreciation for what we find there. Although C.S. Lewis takes a dim view of English clothes (particularly starched collars), in many ways these stories are designed to make children love and appreciate English history and culture, not to mention eggs and sausages for breakfast. A love for ordinary people, living ordinary

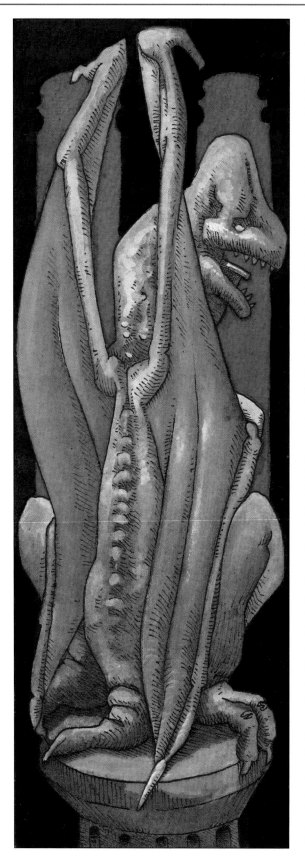

lives, pervades all these books. But in order to make us appreciate an ordinary Englishman, living an ordinary life, Lewis does an extraordinary thing—he shows us Trufflehunter the badger. And by this means, we come to love the ordinary because we have seen just how extraordinary it actually is.

The same thing goes for ordinary morality. This "ordinary morality" is the moral sense that we learn from the stories passed down through the experiences and cultural tales of the past. These tales tell us that dragons and serpents are evil and that witches are wicked. It helps us to fit our lives into the stories that our culture tells. In this case, Digory comes to realize that magicians really exist, just like they do in the stories. But when Digory realizes that the stories are true, he accepts them across the board—if there are really magicians, just like in the stories, then there must be *evil* magicians, just like in the stories. And if that is the case, then this story will end as all good stories do, with the evil magician getting his just deserts. This rattles Uncle Andrew (temporarily), but he quickly returns to his folly. By the end of the book Uncle Andrew is a buffoon, and is perfectly harmless. But when the book begins he is quite a scary figure.

It is important to note that when Digory resists the second temptation, the basic reason he does so is because of the ordinary morality instilled in him by his mother. He appeals to this himself, and Lewis makes a point of noting it after the fact. Things like "do not steal" were pounded into boys' heads a lot more thoroughly than they are today, Lewis says. The point is crucial. Digory knows what to do in a strange garden, tempted by a witch, in a world that his mother never heard of, and he is equipped to do the right thing because of an ordinary rule that she taught him. Saying that it is "not that simple" and that rulers and extraordinary people must be allowed to do as they please, is seen by Digory for what it is—a desire for clever people to be as selfish as they please, and with disastrous results for those around them.

We have noted that Digory learned about magicians from "the stories." This is an important point on two levels. We will have occasion to note this

In one of the courtyards in Charn they found a fountain with a great stone monster in the center. The winged sculpture had its mouth open and you could still see a bit of piping at the back of its mouth, out of which the water used to pour.

in our discussion of the other books of the *Chronicles* because it is something that Lewis points to again and again. C.S. Lewis believed that a diet of the right kind of story was absolutely essential to a child's mental and spiritual health. In *The Chronicles of Narnia,* the children are constantly guided by what they learned in the books they had read. If they were steeped in the right kind of book, they knew what to do and they knew whom to trust. If they were deficient in their reading, then they were helpless to understand what was happening to them. Digory had not believed in the stories he had read, but he had read them. And when he found himself in the middle of a fairy tale, he knew what to do. He knew what kind of character he was supposed to be. He was oriented.

This also provides us with a clue to understanding *The Chronicles of Narnia* themselves. Lewis wanted children to read his books and to come away from them with the same store of common knowledge that the children in his stories had. In other words, he is doing the same thing in his books that was done by the books he talks about. He is handing down a tradition—robins are to be trusted, and dragons are not to be trusted. Witches are bad, tyrants are bad, and kings are good.

This is no minor point, and, incidentally, it is one that is regularly challenged today through a process we might call metaphor-morphing, or *metamorphing* for short. Symbols are important, and this includes the symbolism of witches, orgres, dragons, tyrants, children in the woods, birds and so on. But in recent years, there has been a great push to make dragons and ogres the sympathetic figures in stories, and to make princes and knights into scoundrels. In Lewis's work, and in *The Magician's Nephew,* the symbolism of right and wrong is entirely intact and right side up.

One last point should be made about this book, and it is also one which appears in a number of the other stories in the *Chronicles.* Aslan's voice divides those who hear it. Digory and Polly, Frank the cabby and Strawberry his horse, and Jadis and Uncle Andrew tumbled into Narnia just moments before Aslan begins his creation of that world. He sings the stars into existence, as well as the sun, the trees, the grass, and all the animals. In response to his voice, the earth begins boiling, and animals come bursting out. Aslan gives the gift of speech to some, and the others go off to the life that has been given to them.

But when Aslan begins singing, his voice is entirely one of grace, love and goodness. The only already-created audience is that small band of six— two children, two magicians, and a man with his horse. Four of the two instantly love the voice, and the other two instantly hate it. Jadis hates it, but understands it well. Uncle Andrew hates it, and retreats into a foolish belief that the lion *can't* be singing—it must be simply roaring. But the point is this: everything comes down to love. At the moment Narnia is created, the question is, "How will you respond to Aslan?" At the moment Narnia dies, and all created things stream up to the door where Aslan is standing, the question is the same. "How will you respond to Aslan?"

Further, Lewis does not leave the option of a neutral third way open. One *must* hear Aslan, and having heard him, one must either approach or recoil. There are only two fellowships in that world (just as there are only two fellowships in ours), and they are the fellowship of love and the fellowship of the grievance. One is characterized by liberty and freedom, and the other by resentments, whether great or small. All creation is personal, and every creature must love or hate the Person who sang it into existence.

—*Douglas Wilson*

## For Further Reading

Ford, Paul F. *Companion to Narnia.* New York, N.Y.: HarperCollins, 1980.

# SESSION I: PRELUDE

## A Question to Consider

If you were going to write a fictional account about the creation of a world, what are some questions you think would be important to answer in your fictional account?

*Discuss or list short answers to the following questions:*

1. From what you have read in the Worldview section, what similarities and differences can be seen between the Fall of Adam and Digory's ringing of the Bell in Charn?

2. In the New Testament, why can the difference between temptation and testing become confusing?

3. What is the difference between temptation and testing?

4. How is the temptation of Jadis different from the test of Aslan?

5. In what ways is Digory similar to his Uncle Andrew?

6. What two motivations guide Digory's actions in Narnia? Are these good or evil?

7. What are some of the characteristics of magicians that Lewis brings out in this book?

8. What is "ordinary morality"? Why did C.S. Lewis think this was so important?

9. In our culture (think especially of children's literature, TV and cinema), where do we see examples of a perversion of "ordinary morality" or *metamorphing*?

10. Does Lewis leave a possibility of neutral response to Aslan? What are the possible ways to react to Aslan?

## Optional Activity

*Using the* Companion to Narnia *as a resource, read through the following entries that have to do with* The Magician's Nephew.

ASLAN

CHARN

CREATION

CURIOSITY

DIGORY

JADIS

KETTERLEY, ANDREW

MAGIC

POLLY

RINGS

WOOD BETWEEN THE WORLDS

READING ASSIGNMENT:
Chapters 1–3

# SESSION II: DISCUSSION
Chapters 1–3

## A Question to Consider

Is curiosity a good thing?

*Discuss or list short answers to the following questions:*

### Text Analysis

1. Each of these characters has/had an 'ordinary' life at one point. That is, a life which did not go beyond the common, everyday life lived by most people around them. What do you think Polly and Digory's ordinary life was like before they met each other?

2. Do you think Uncle Andrew has ever led an ordinary life?

3. Each of these characters takes steps to try to go beyond their ordinary life. How have they done this and why?

4. How does the concept of "curiosity" tie into any of the above factors?

### Cultural Analysis

1. What good events, discoveries and/or inventions has curiosity brought us?

2. In contrast, what potentially harmful events, discoveries or inventions have come from curiosity as well?

3. Do you think people are encouraged or discouraged to be curious today?

4. What limitations are placed on curiosity in our culture?

### Biblical Analysis

1. There are many instances in the Bible where people have followed their curiosity with disastrous results. Look at the following two passages: Genesis 3:6 and 1 Samuel 6:19. What serious consequences came from following their curiosity? Should they have known better?

2. Clearly we should not allow our curiosity to lead us into sin; it certainly does not excuse sin. Yet, there are still many areas where it may not be immediately clear whether we should follow our curiosity or not. What do you think the following verses teach us about whether or not we should follow our curiosity? 1 John 2:16, Proverbs 1:5-7; 1:8-9; 14:15.

## *Application*

How can we know when to pursue our curiosity and when not to?

### SUMMA

*Write an essay or discuss this question, integrating what you have learned from the material above.* Is curiosity a good thing or a bad thing?

READING ASSIGNMENT:
Chapters 4-6

## SESSION III: RECITATION

Chapters 1-6

### Comprehension Questions

*Answer these questions for factual recall.*

1. How is the attic like the Wood between the Worlds?
2. Does Uncle Andrew believe himself to be bound by moral obligations? Why or why not?
3. Why does Uncle Andrew believe he has the right to do whatever he wants?
4. How is the Wood like the attic?
5. What were Polly and Digory's first reactions to Charn? Were they similar or different?
6. Did they change their minds the longer they were there?
7. What were their reactions to the first rulers of Charn? Did they feel the same way about the later rulers?
8. How does Queen Jadis describe Charn? Is she proud or ashamed of its character?
9. How was Charn destroyed? Do you think C.S. Lewis intended any parallel for today's world?
10. What comparisons do you see between Uncle Andrew and Queen Jadis?
11. How and why is Jadis different in Charn, London, and in the Wood between the Worlds?
12. How does C.S. Lewis compare Uncle Andrew to Jadis?

READING ASSIGNMENT:
Chapters 7-10

## SESSION IV: ACTIVITY

Chapters 7-10

### Creation Comparisons

*Groups may want to use the following activity as a contest. Students could be divided into teams or act as individuals.*

There are clear comparisons between the Creation of Narnia in these chapters, and the Creation/Fall of our world as described in Genesis 1-3. First make a list of all the similarities and differences you can think of from memory. Draw a line across your paper. Now go back and re-read the Narnian and Genesis accounts to see what you missed and complete your lists below the line.

READING ASSIGNMENT:
Chapters 11-12

"Eliminate all other factors, and the one which remains must be the truth" declared Sir Arthur Conan Doyle's Sherlock Holmes. Holmes and Doctor Watson lived at 221b Baker Street between 1881-1904. Lewis uses the famous detective to set the time period for this first account of magical travels in *The Chronicles of Narnia*. He also uses the Bastables from E. Nesbit's book *The Bastable Children* to help set the stage chronologically, as well as lifting the idea of children magically bringing a queen back to London from Nesbit's *The Story of the Amulet*.

## SESSION V: ACTIVITY
Chapters 8–12

Throughout *The Magician's Nephew* you have seen some characters that are retreating from their own ordinary world and escaping into one they deem better, more interesting or perhaps more exciting. Sometimes this escape is through imaginary play, sometimes it is with delusions of grandeur and at other times it is a true escape right out of their world.

If you were able to make a retreat, to design one from your imagination, what would it look like? Where would it be, and who would share it with you. What sorts of things would you take with you, what would it have in it, etc.?

*Construct your own imaginary retreat by either creating a diorama (a three-dimensional scene using images, pictures, and objects setup in front of a painted background), or by drawing a nice, detailed picture. Then write 2 or 3 paragraphs explaining why you have chosen the elements that you have.*

### Directions

1. Decide on a scale. This is important, because you want your diorama to represent something real. It will not look real if your pieces are all out of proportion to one another. If you have something in mind that you absolutely want to be part of your diorama, use that scale.
2. Collect your materials. Some things you may find helpful to build with: cotton balls, clay, playdough, sand, sugar cubes, pipe cleaners, yarn, scraps of material, toothpicks, old magazines, and small plastic figures. To add definition and color you may want paint, pencils, crayons and/or markers.
3. Decide on a background. You can paint or draw your own, use wrapping paper, wallpaper, postcards or anything else you can find. Just remember that whatever you use should be consistent with the scale you have chosen.
4. Choose a container to build your diorama in. May projects use smaller cardboard boxes or shoeboxes, but you can use anything, so long as it sturdy enough to hold all your items and light enough to move around easily.
5. Build your diorama from the back to the front. Start with the background, and don't forget the sky/ceiling and the ground/floor. Place larger items in the back, with smaller objects toward the front. Secure all your items with either putty or glue.

### Optional Activities

The journey of Digory, Polly and Fledge out of Narnia and toward the hill of the garden is written about with clear description of the landscape and geography.

*Paint a picture of a segment of the land they are flying over.*

If you would rather write than paint, consider the following. While they rest for the night, a very interesting tree grows, from which they are able to get their next morning's breakfast. Imagine the tree that would grow from a piece of your favorite snack food.

*Write a detailed paragraph on what your tree would look like and what the fruit would look and taste like. Your paragraph should include not only the physical description of its trunk, bark and leaves, but could also include the kind of climate it grows best in, what kind of soil it prefers, how it is affected by wind or other types of weather, etc. Think how different a palm tree is from a weeping willow or a cactus.*

 **READING ASSIGNMENT:** Chapters 13–15

## SESSION VI: DISCUSSION
Chapters 13–15

### A Question to Consider

You've been saving up since your last birthday to buy a newly released program or game for your computer. It comes with a mail-in rebate for $5. You decide that getting $5 back is worth the effort so you send the rebate in. When the check arrives, you discover that there was a mistake, and the check is written out for $50. What do you do? What if the check is for $10?

You've been invited to sleep over at a friend's house. Not only is this one of your best friends but your parents are really good friends with their parents as well. They ask to watch a movie which has just come out for rental and following your parents rule you give them a call to ask them if it's okay for you to watch the film. (Your family rule is that until your parents have previewed a film and given you their okay you're not allowed to watch a film—they have not yet seen this film.) The phone rings and rings—they're not home. What do you do?

*Discuss or list short answers to the following questions:*

## Text Analysis

1. Why does Digory approach the gates to the garden by himself?
2. What is the essential command in the poem, and who is issuing the command?
3. What happened to Digory because he looked at the apple and smelled it before putting it away?
4. Did Digory notice a difference in the Witch when he saw her in the garden?
5. Aslan has placed a test in front of Digory. He has told him to pluck an apple from the tree in the garden and to bring it back to him. Aslan has also given further instruction through the poem outside the garden. We have already seen how Digory fell into one temptation by not staying as far away as he could from disobeying these commands. Now he has further temptations placed before him by the Witch. How does she tempt him?
6. Though Digory starts to stumble in his steadfastness towards Aslan, how is he able to remain firm to his intent and pass the test?

## Cultural Analysis

1. Which of the following are temptations? If it is a temptation, what is the good rule/command/law that is being twisted or warped? What justifications might people give to excuse their giving in to the temptation?
   - To exceed the speed limit
   - Getting a tattoo
   - Drinking alcohol without parental permission
   - Getting your ears pierced (one time or multiple times)
   - Buying the $150 pair of shoes vs. the Wal-Mart specials for $25.
2. Does our culture encourage resisting temptations?

*"Narnia, Narnia, Narnia, awake. Love. Think. Speak. Be walking trees. Be talking beasts. Be divine waters."* And so Aslan not only created Narnia and its animals, but also brought forth personifications of nature: dryads, hamadryads, the River god, satyrs, and naiads—that is, water nymphs, as seen above in this detail of an archaic relief.

## Biblical Analysis

1. Read Genesis 22:1–19. What are the basic elements of this test?
2. What are the basic similarities and differences between Abraham's test and Digory's test?

## Application

How can we recognize a temptation? When we know we are being tempted, what should we do about it?

## Summa

*Write an essay or discuss this question, integrating what you have learned from the material above.*
If there is a difference between being tested and being tempted, what is the difference?

## Optional Session: Recitation

Chapters 8–15

## Comprehension Questions

*Answer these questions for factual recall.*

1. By what criteria does the Cabby judge whether or not one should be afraid of death?
2. Uncle Andrew, the Witch and the Cabby all hear Aslan's song. In what ways is their experience of hearing his voice similar and/or different?
3. One gets the idea that back in England the Cabby would have liked to stay in the country with his wife and Strawberry. Why did he then leave and move to London?
4. What did Lewis mean by the following quote: "For what you see and hear depends a good deal on where you are standing: it also depends on what sort of person you are." How does this apply to the Cabby and Uncle Andrew?
5. How does Aslan help Digory to confess his sin honestly?
6. Do you think the Cabby was a Christian man in England?
7. How does Aslan show surprising sympathy for Digory and Digory's mother?
8. Does the new King of Narnia treat Digory and differently from Polly when they are leaving to go on their quest? What do you think Lewis was trying to demonstrate by this incident?
9. What does Fledge teach the children about prayer?
10. What do the children do to make sure that they will not forget how to find the garden? What parallel for your life do you think Lewis would like you to make?
11. Why can the tree protect Narnia?
12. What is the Witch's destiny?
13. How does Aslan warn Digory and Polly about the twentieth century?
14. Where did the famous wardrobe come from?

## Endnotes

1   *This endnote appears only in the teacher's edition.*

# THE LION, THE WITCH
# AND THE WARDROBE

Vain the stone, the watch,
the seal, Allelujah,
Christ has burst the gates of hell,
Allelujah,
Death in vain forbids Him rise,
Allelujah,
Christ has opened paradise,
Allelujah.

Nothing stirs the soul like the proclamation of the gospel on Easter morning. "He is risen!" announces the minister. "He is risen, indeed!" proclaim the congregation. Often, churches even celebrate Easter by recapitulating that blessed morning by having services as the sun rises. Joy fills every heart. This joy is particularly deep if in the minds of the people they remember the service held two nights before on Good Friday. Good Friday is a time filled with joy, but this joy is rightly mingled with sorrow. Christians rejoice that Christ goes to the cross to save them. They grieve at the horror of their sin which Christ paid for on the cross. On Easter morning, however, grief is overwhelmed by joy. The truth is too good to be true. Christ has put away our sins. He died for them, but now the tomb is empty. He is alive! Death is destroyed. The minds of the faithful reel as the old world is undone and a new world is born as Christ emerges from the tomb.

In every age the world is captivated by Christ. The Middle Ages had their Passion Plays. The modern world has its motion

Used by permission of The Marion E. Wade Center, Wheaton College, Wheaton, IL.

This oak wardrobe was handcarved and built by C.S. Lewis's grandfather. It originally stood in Lewis's boyhood home in Belfast. Later it was moved to his home near Oxford, England. According to his brother, Warren, it was the inspiration for this first Narnia story.

pictures. This retelling always says too much or too little because the story of the actual death, burial and resurrection is settled. Any addition can be dangerous conjecture; any omission can round the edges off a Christ that is beyond our imaginings. Even our digitally enhanced stereo quality images and sounds fall short.

In this book, however, we come face to face with Christ. In this children's tale, we witness the center of history replayed in ways that enlighten us, distress us and finally overwhelm us.

# GENERAL INFORMATION

## Significance

Just as *The Magician's Nephew* gave us a story that carried the doctrines of Creation and Fall, so *The Lion, the Witch and the Wardrobe* tells the story of redemption and salvation. In this book, Edmund betrays his brother and two sisters and, through his treachery, becomes the lawful property of the White Witch, and she demands what is rightly hers. In response to this, Aslan makes an arrangement with the Witch and gives himself to her in exchange for Edmund's life. He meets her at the Stone Table, and there he is bound, insulted and slain. The Witch was appealing to Deep Magic (the demands of justice or the law), but did not understand that there was a Deeper Magic (the power of grace). Aslan comes back to life again, and defeats the Witch. Through this story, children can clearly see the nature and power of a substitutionary atonement. Although Aslan dies in exchange for Edmund, Lewis clearly means for us to extend his death more broadly. In *The Last Battle*, the last king of Narnia, Tirian, says that it was through the blood of Aslan that all Narnia was saved.

After Aslan comes back to life, he goes to the Witch's castle where she has many Narnians kept, having turned them all to stone. In a wonderful image of the gift of the Holy Spirit, Aslan brings them back to life by breathing on them.

## Main Characters

In this book, we are introduced to the four Pevensie children, Peter, Susan, Edmund, and Lucy. On her first visit into Narnia, Lucy meets Mr. Tumnus the faun, and later when all the children are there in Narnia, they all meet Mr. and Mrs. Beaver. Jadis the evil queen of Charn has become the White Witch, who rules Narnia and holds it under her wintry spell. Despite his brief appearance, Father Christmas is an important character as well, providing an important counterpart to the Witch.

And of course, Aslan is the central character in this book, just as he is in the other books.

## Summary and Setting

The Pevensie children are taken out of the German blitz on London during the Second World War, and so the book is placed in 1940. They go to an old house owned by Digory Kirke (whom we met as a young boy in *The Magician's Nephew*). Professor Kirke was born in 1889, so he is fifty-two now. He had brought back an apple from Narnia which had healed his mother, and afterwards he planted the core. It grew into a semi-Narnian tree, but blew down in a storm. Unable to bear the thought of disposing of it, he had the wood made into a wardrobe and placed in his house.

Lucy stumbles into Narnia through the wardrobe, and there she meets Mr. Tumnus, who tells her about the White Witch and how Narnia is always winter and never Christmas. When she gets back to

"I myself do not enjoy the society of small children . . . I recognize this as a defect in myself," Lewis once wrote. Then he sent the four Pevensie children during the air raids at the beginning of *The Lion, the Witch and the Wardrobe* to live in the country with someone just as unsuited to care for children as himself—the Professor Digory Kirke.

England, the others do not believe her story. Then she and Edmund make it through, and Edmund encounters the Witch, but he is won over to her side through some enchanted dessert called Turkish Delight. When they get back to England, Edmund betrays Lucy by denying he had been there. But finally, all four make it into Narnia.

They discover that Mr. Tumnus has been taken by the Witch, and Mr. and Mrs. Beaver meet them. Edmund deserts them in order to betray them to the Witch. As the Witch is pursuing them, Aslan arrives in Narnia, and the deep winter turns to the spring of May in just a matter of hours. Edmund is rescued, but the Witch demands him back on the basis of ancient law. Aslan gives himself instead and is cruelly treated and killed on the Stone Table. But because of Deeper Magic, he comes back to life, kills the Witch and restores Narnia. The four children rule Narnia for fifteen years during Narnia's Golden Age and almost forget England. But then their adventure concludes with them tumbling back through the wardrobe door, with almost no time elapsed in England.

## Worldview

If you found yourself transported in time to the foot of the Cross, what would you do? You would be surrounded by a crowd, many of whom were mocking and reviling the Lord. Off to your right, the soldiers would be getting out their dice as they examined Jesus' seamless cloak. Women would be weeping, and there you would stand: the only one except Christ who knew the whole story. Eventually, the sky would go dark, and, after the wrath of God was finished with Him, Christ would cry out, "It is finished." The Greek word would actually be better translated, "Paid in full." I am sure that many on that day would have been puzzled by this word. There is no evidence that even the most faithful of the disciples knew anything but grief as Christ was laid in the tomb. If you were there, however, you would know the whole story. Would your reaction be any different from theirs?

As we begin this tale about the center of Narnian History many of you will be familiar with this book. That's wonderful! Some of you might be coming to the book for the first time. That's wonderful too! What an adventure awaits you! The story, or should I say *The Story*, has seldom been better retold.

With this second book, we have to spend a little time on chronology and time—what is called in the books "the usual muddle about times"—because English time and Narnian time do not run on parallel tracks. Indeed, there does not seem to be *any* rule to it, other than that they both run in the same direction.

Digory and Polly find their way into Narnia in the year 1900, and since they were present at the creation of Narnia, that would be the year 1. That story is told in *The Magician's Nephew*. The next visit to Narnia (by Peter, Susan, Edmund, and Lucy in *The Lion, the Witch, and the Wardrobe*) is in 1940, but 1,000 years of Narnian time have gone by. During the rule of these four, the adventure of Shasta and Aravis occurs, as told in *The Horse and His Boy*. But then, in the Narnian year 1015, the four children go back to England, but virtually no time has elapsed there. They then make it into Narnia again in 1941 a year later (in *Prince Caspian*) only to discover that it is the Narnian year 2303. When they return to England after this adventure, Peter and Susan are told they will not be coming back to Narnia again. But Edmund and Lucy do come back, bringing Eustace Clarence Scrubb with them, for *The Voyage of the* Dawn Treader. This is in the summer of 1942 in England and the year 2306-7 in Narnia. Then, a few months later, in the autumn of 1942, Eustace comes back to Narnia with Jill Pole, and they rescue Prince Rilian in the Narnian year 2356. That story is told in *The Silver Chair*. In 1949, Eustace and Jill are called back to Narnia again for *The Last Battle*. It is now 2555 in Narnia, and that world ends, and everyone is summoned "further up and further in." Because of the differences in times, Digory could see that world created when he was twelve years old, and see it end over twenty five hundred years later when he was sixty-one.

The action of *The Lion, the Witch and the Wardrobe* occurs in the middle of Narnian history. The tree of protection planted by Digory has somehow been circumvented—the White Witch has been ruling in Narnia for 100 years and has made it so that it is always winter and never Christmas. This mention of *Christmas* as a *Narnian* holiday is an interesting interruption in the great "supposal" that Lewis has undertaken. Normally, he makes it clear that Christ is known by this name in our world, but known as Aslan in that world. Since this was the first of the Narnia Chronicles to be written, it is reasonable to suppose that C.S. Lewis was still working some of the details out. We may reckon it as an inconsistency, but even so, it is a glorious inconsistency. Father Christmas somehow fits.

There are just a few other things like this—details that fit in *The Lion, the Witch and the Wardrobe* just fine (because we are used to them there), but which we would be surprised to find in one of the later books, after Lewis had hit his stride. For example, the image of Mrs. Beaver using a sewing machine is extremely *odd* in this very medieval (or what was to become medieval) world. She appears here not so much a talking beaver, but rather a humanized (and industrialized) beaver. And one of the illustrations by Pauline Baynes reflects this "humans in animal skins" understanding, where she has Aslan walking on his hind legs alongside the Witch, with two paws behind his back. When C.S. Lewis was a boy, he wrote a story about talking animals called *Boxen,* and in that story the animals were simply people who looked like animals. These odd details in this book simply appear to be a vestige of that approach, but by the time Narnia matures as a world in Lewis's mind, they disappear.

The center of this book is profound. Lewis understands the nature of sin, as well as the provocations to it, and yet he does not use those provocations in order to explain away personal responsibility for sin. As the book begins, Peter is thirteen, Susan is twelve, Edmund is ten and Lucy is eight. Edmund has been in a bad situation at school and has taken to

"Tell you?" said the Witch, her voice growing suddenly shriller. "Tell you what is written on that very Table of Stone that stands beside us? Tell you what is written in letters as deep as a spear is long on the fire-stones on the Secret Hill?"

bullying those younger than he is. Among the four, he is next to last, and the only one he can really lord it over is Lucy. And so he does. Not only do the Pevensie children have their petty squabbles, but this shows there are also some fundamental issues present that could cause great problems for them as adults. Later in the *Dawn Treader,* Lucy is tempted to say a spell that would make her beautiful beyond all mortal reckoning. She is tempted to do so, in part because of how she has been compared to Susan. It is similar here. Edmund is the younger brother who chafes under the leadership of Peter, and that chafing ends in his treachery. Peter, for his part, does something that makes the situation worse. When they are explaining Edmund's betrayal of them to Aslan, Peter takes responsibility for the part his earlier anger with Edmund may have played in pushing Edmund toward the Witch. Even though Peter's anger was a response to a petty treachery on Edmund's part, Aslan does not contradict Peter.

Lucy makes it into Narnia on her own, but because her absence took no time at all in England, and because the back of the wardrobe is solid when they all go check, she is not believed. Peter and Susan are concerned for Lucy and go talk to Digory Kirke about her. He astonishes them with his response, and that response is fundamental to Lewis's defense of the Christian faith, or his apologetic approach. He uses the same argument in *Mere Christianity.* There are only three possible responses to Lucy's story about Narnia. Either she is out of her mind, or she is lying or she is telling the truth. The professor says that she is clearly *not* out of her mind, and Peter and Susan

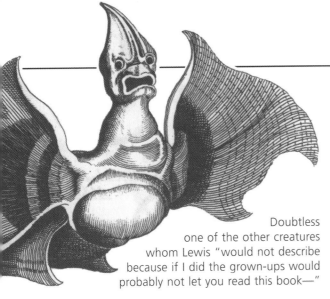

Doubtless one of the other creatures whom Lewis "would not describe because if I did the grown-ups would probably not let you read this book—"

testify that she is far less likely than Edmund to be telling lies. And that leaves the only remaining option, which is that she is telling the truth. "Bless me, what *do* they teach them in these schools?"

The argument applies to Jesus Christ in a very straightforward way. Jesus claimed to be the Son of God, which is the kind of thing that honest men in their right minds don't do. It is the same as claiming that you are the queen of the fairies, or, to use Lewis's example, that you are a poached egg. This means that Jesus, if He is *not* the Son of God, is a liar or a lunatic. But the penetrating nature of His moral teaching and example excludes both those options. And that means He was telling the truth.

Epistemology is the branch of philosophy that concerns "how we know what we know." For most philosophers this is a matter for argument, discussion and debate, but Lewis addresses this profound question in a faithful Christian fashion. There are two aspects to this, and they are the issues of *loyalty* and *story*, respectively.

Edmund has already become something of a bully in England. He teases Lucy over the Narnia adventure she claims to have had, and then when he finds himself in Narnia, he realizes that he was wrong. He cannot find Lucy and shouts out an apology (because he has to) to the surrounding woods. Then, when she does not answer (because she is not there), Edmund blames *her* for not accepting his apology. This clearly shows that no heart issues have been dealt with at all. In this condition he meets the Witch, she gives him enchanted Turkish Delight and makes him promise to bring his brother and two sisters to her. She is concerned because there are four empty thrones at Cair Paravel and a prophecy that four sons and daughters of Adam and Eve will fill them.

When Edmund and Lucy make their way back into England, Edmund lets Lucy down by denying having been there with her. Peter is angry with Edmund for stringing her along like this, and the problem between Edmund and Peter grows deeper. When the four of them get back into Narnia, Edmund unwittingly reveals that he has been there before, and Peter gets furious with him. Nothing is clearer than the fact that Edmund has a fundamental and basic problem. His heart is not in the right place at all.

With this basic problem driving him, Edmund is the one who raises all the basic epistemological questions. How do we know, Edmund asks, if the robin is really a good kind of bird, one to be trusted? How do we know that the Witch is wicked and that the fauns are good? Maybe it is the other way around. Maybe the Witch has been slandered, and she is a very nice lady indeed. How do we know that Mr. Tumnus really saved Lucy? Edmund's responses show that he is devoid of the common morality that we mentioned in *The Magician's Nephew*. He can not see what should be obvious from the stories that he has heard, or should have heard. Witches are evil. In other words, the one whose heart is filled with treachery is very concerned with the issues of treachery. His loyalty, which ought to be to his brother and sisters, has been twisted, and he goes over to the Witch. He does this, claiming that he does not know that the Witch is wicked at all—this is just a story he has heard. But he *does* know that Peter, Susan and Lucy are his brother and sisters, and he *does* know that he owes them his love and allegiance. He departs from this, telling himself a very complicated story in order to justify it in his own mind, when all the time, the truth is as easy as any decent nursery rhyme. He betrays his family members (that he knows very well to be decent people) for the sake of a very dubious Witch.

Because the others are not in this poor spiritual condition, they are able to rely on those things that they are supposed to rely on. Their stock responses are good, and Peter says they know to follow the robin because robins are good birds in all the stories. These stock responses could easily be dismissed as literary clichés, but that is not how Lewis treats them at all. Stories are repositories of cultural wisdom, and in them we learn that witches and ogres are bad and that robins and beavers are good.

Many Christians today do not know how they are supposed to behave because they have not read the right stories, or they have not read enough of them. This means that they cannot see the story they are currently in, and this means they do not know what to do. If we were to write a story in which a little boy is transported to a cloud palace, and he is told that he might live there forever in bliss if only he does not go into the room in the northwest tower, we know two things immediately—provided we have read the right kind of stories. We know that the boy will in fact go into that room, and that there will be some kind of redemption—a way of putting right the mess that he caused by this disobedience. This is nothing less than the story the Bible tells us about our first parents in the Garden. They were told not to eat from one tree, but then they did. And then God put everything right again through Jesus Christ.

The serpent in the temptation raised all the same questions that Edmund did. The devil and those in sin always gravitate to such deep questions of philosophy. How do we *know* if we will die if we eat from this tree? How do we know that the Witch is evil and bad? Scripture teaches us that the process of intellectual unbelief arises from heart problems. In the first chapter of Romans, the apostle Paul reasons this way. Because men would not honor God as God, and because they would not give Him thanks, God gave them over to an intellectual futility. Their minds were darkened because their hearts were rebellious. The response to this is to love and honor God, and this means that we should love and honor His kind of story. And bringing us back to our point under discussion, *The Lion, the Witch and the Wardrobe* is His kind of story.

Because Lewis is writing a "supposal" and not a strict allegory, we should not look for a one-to-one correspondence for every point of Christian doctrine. Although Aslan gives up His life in exchange for Edmund in this story, we do not have a parallel to the Christian doctrine of the Incarnation. Aslan did not *become* a lion in these stories, he always appears as a lion. He is a lion before his death on the Stone Table, and he is a lion afterwards. In this, we have a departure from the gospel story as it actually happened in our world. The second person of the Trinity *became* a child in the womb of Mary, and He was *born* in Bethlehem. This becoming a man is very important in understanding the gospel properly.

But that is not how it happens in Narnia. Aslan is

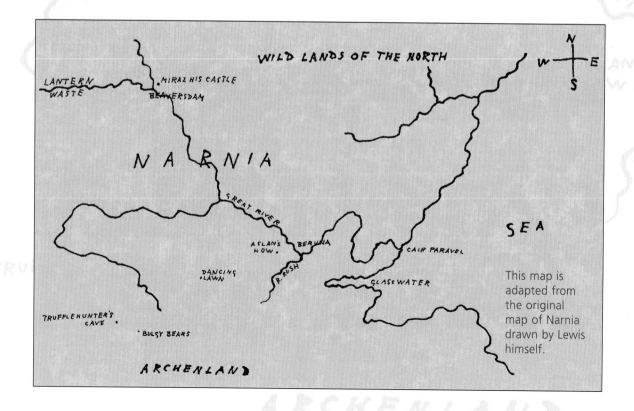

This map is adapted from the original map of Narnia drawn by Lewis himself.

a lion at the moment of creation, and he is a lion in *The Last Battle*, as the characters from all the stories crowd into the real Narnia. C.S. Lewis is not advancing a novel heresy through this—he affirmed and taught the doctrine of the Incarnation. In fact, he once wrote an introduction to Athanasius's book *On the Incarnation*. We should account for this simply by saying that these are seven stories for children, and we cannot expect Lewis to get every detail of biblical theology into these books. That is pressing them beyond the clear intent of the author. What is astonishing is that he got as much into the books as he did, and it would be ingratitude to complain that Aslan doesn't have twelve disciples, or a mother named Mary.

After Aslan has died and come back to life, Lucy and Susan, who were the two witnesses of his death, have a discussion about whether or not Edmund should be told about what Aslan did for him. Susan thinks not, but Lucy believes that somehow Edmund ought to know. Lewis never tells us directly what happened, but the indicators are that Edmund found out. It was not done in a corner, and Edmund's subsequent behavior indicates he knew. By the time of Tirian, all Narnia knew and reckoned it to have been done for all of them. And, of course, the child reading these books is invited to know, really know, that we serve a God who gave Himself for us.

—*Douglas Wilson*

## For Further Reading

Ford, Paul F. *Companion to Narnia*. New York, N.Y.: HarperCollins, 1980.

# Session I: Prelude

## A Question to Consider

We have all experienced a wrong or injury to ourselves. It may be that something was stolen from you, that there was damage to your reputation, or one of many other possibilities. In some of those circumstances, how have you experienced justice or satisfaction that amends were made or compensation was given?

*Discuss or list short answers to the following questions:*

1. Look up *atonement* in the dictionary. What do you think substitutionary atonement means?
2. What does substitutionary atonement mean for the Christian?
3. How is substitutionary atonement relevant to *The Lion, the Witch and the Wardrobe?*
4. What is one of the major differences between the substitution Jesus made and the one Aslan made?
5. What were the relationships like among the four siblings at the opening of the book?
6. Who is the White Witch?
7. How does Edmund come to be under the power of the White Witch?
8. What is the nature of the curse on Narnia?
9. What are the parallels between the cursed worlds of Narnia and Earth?

## Optional Activity 1

*Draw a map of Narnia on poster board. You may use the map shown as your model or choose your own from another source. Sketch in the details and then color with paint or watercolor pencil. Make it large enough that you can embellish it with additional drawings and detail as you read through the rest of the Narnia series. This map will serve you well not only with this book, but also with the next five books in the Narnia series to track adventures and keep your bearings.*

## Optional Activity 2

*If you have already read* The Lion, the Witch and the Wardrobe, *use the* Companion to Narnia *as a resource and read through the following entries:*

> **WARDROBE**
> **PETER PEVENSIE**
> **SUSAN PEVENSIE**
> **EDMUND PEVENSIE**
> **LUCY PEVENSIE**
> **TUMNUS**
> **WHITE WITCH**
> **MR. AND MRS. BEAVER**
> **FATHER CHRISTMAS**

 **Reading Assignment:**
Chapters 1–4

# SESSION II: DISCUSSION
Chapters 1–4

## A Question to Consider

Have you ever built a long, complex domino chain? Often you've worked for quite some time to get your intricate pattern just right. Then something happens—maybe the dog is let into where you are playing. The dog goes bounding across the dining room floor starting what feels to you like a shock wave. The wave travels through the floor and up the legs of the table. You know what's going to happen and are powerless to stop it. You look frantically to see just which domino is going to be shaken enough to fall over—you sight it, but it's too late; you cannot catch it. As you watch helplessly, your whole domino chain goes down.

Our words can be like the first domino in a whole domino chain—they set off a series of events that we wish we could stop.

What are some types of things people say or do that they often wish they could undo? What effects can it cause?

What can cause people to say those sorts of things?

*Discuss or list short answers to the following questions:*

### Text Analysis

1. How is Lucy's reaction to what she finds in the wardrobe similar to her reaction when she first sees Mr. Tumnus? What might this show about her character?
2. How does Mr. Tumnus react at first to Lucy? How is his reaction similar to Lucy's first reaction to him?
3. How is their treatment of one another different from Uncle Andrew's treatment of the creatures he meets when he came to Narnia in *The Magician's Nephew*?
4. Does Lucy trust Mr. Tumnus? Why? How does she feel in his company? Was this trust deserved?
5. Edmund has his own visit with someone from Narnia. How is his interaction with the Witch

"Further in, come further in. Right in here. We're not safe in the open!" Mr. Beaver is the first talking animal the children meet in Narnia. He is an industrious and loyal beast who puts his life on the line to safely lead the Pevensies to the Stone Table.

different? Are her goals similar to those that Mr. Tumnus originally had?
6. What are some of the differences between Mr. Tumnus and the White Witch? Should Lucy and Edmund be excused for trusting themselves to Mr. Tumnus and the White Witch, respectively?
7. Mr. Tumnus speaks like a friend to Lucy and encourages her. Do her own brothers and sister make her feel the same way when she tells them of her experiences in Narnia?

### Cultural Analysis

1. Often as nations approach elections, politicians begin to mudsling and call each other names (a practice hardly consistent with the dignity required for the office they seek). What drives them to do this?
2. What effect can *public servants* have on our culture?

### Biblical Analysis

1. In James 3:2–12 there are six different analogies given for the tongue. They can be paired into groups of two. What are these three different groups, and what do they tell us about our speech?
2. James tells us the power our tongues can have. What does Psalm 141 tell us about how we can keep our tongues from evil?

### Application

The only sure way to keep our tongues from evil is to do as David did—keep our eyes on God and pray that the Lord would put a guard over our mouths. When we are focusing on ourselves, our own wishes, our own desires and acting out of pride, we are sure to say things which will be destructive.

## SUMMA

*Write an essay or discuss this question, integrating what you have learned from the material above.*
Do we really believe that what we say matters?

## Optional Activity

Mr. Tumnus plays some lively dance songs on an instrument bearing some resemblance to a recorder. As Narnia bears many features resembling the Middle Ages, Lewis may have imagined this music as medieval as well. Locate some medieval recorder music. Is it what you imagine Mr. Tumnus may have listened to? If you are able, get some sheet music and some friends and play some medieval recorder music together.

**READING ASSIGNMENT:**
Chapters 5–8

# SESSION III: RECITATION
Chapters 1–8

## Comprehension Questions

*Answer these questions for factual recall.*

1. Why do the four Pevensie children come to the house in the country?
2. What was Narnia like before the reign of the White Witch?
3. What is the prophetic hope for all Narnians?
4. When Lucy returns from her second trip into Narnia, Peter and Susan decide something should be done. What do they decide to do? Why do they think something must be done?
5. What does the Professor ask them with regard to Lucy?
6. What do Peter and Susan tell him about Lucy's truthfulness?
7. What warning does the Professor give them with regard to accusations of lying?
8. What logical alternatives does the Professor give Peter and Susan? What does he rule out and why?
9. What is another reason the Professor gives for believing Lucy?
10. What course of action does the Professor suggest?
11. When Peter finds himself in Narnia what is his first reaction?
12. How is Peter's conduct different from Edmund's when Edmund finds himself in a similar situation?
13. What are the children's reactions when they all get to the deserted cave of Mr. Tumnus?
14. What evidence is given that the Witch rules through fear?
15. How many times does Edmund state, "How do we know?"
16. How do the children respond to the name of "Aslan" being spoken?

## Optional Activity

Food is an integral part of each book in *The Chronicles of Narnia*. What three major mentions of food have there been so far? How does the food chosen reflect the nature of the people offering food?
*Pick one of the meals and have your own Narnian meal.*

**READING ASSIGNMENT:**
Chapters 9–11

# SESSION IV: ACTIVITY
Chapters 9–11

## A Narnian Whodunit

*Please note that due to the amount of text required, all materials for this activity are in the teacher's edition.*

During this lesson, you and your classmates or family are going to play the part of six fictional Narnian characters. One of you has committed the shameful act of passing information on to the Witch. Which one of you? You need to ask questions and use your accumulated knowledge of Narnia to find out.

### RULES

The game is played in three rounds. During each round, you will be given an information card. This card will give you facts about yourself—some facts you want to reveal (as others interact with you and ask you questions) and other facts you will try to conceal. During Round One, you introduce yourself to your fellow characters. During Rounds Two and Three you ask questions of one another, trying to find out information that the character may be concealing. On your information card you may be given information with regard to another character that you may want to publicly accuse them of. You may also be given a suggested question to ask another character. You *must* tell the truth to any question asked of you. Your teacher will announce the end of Round One (Introductions), and the end of Rounds Two and Three. At the end of the third round, you will all state your theory as to who is the so-called spy (even if you think it is yourself), and your reasons for your theory. Then the true motives will be fully revealed to all—including those of the "spy."

## PREPARATION

You may use your maps (if you made them in Session I) and may want to develop a timetable of events from the time the four Pevensie children came through the wardrobe, making note of any special circumstances which you think may help you unravel the mystery. You should also have paper and pencil available to keep a record of what you learn about your fellow Narnians.

## TIMETABLE

*Not all the following facts are relevant.*

DAY ONE: Sometime after Lunch the Pevensie children arrive in Narnia. They meet Mr. Beaver and travel from Mr. Tumnus's cave to the Beavers' house. There they eat dinner. Before it gets dark, Edmund leaves to go the Witch's castle. When the Beavers realize that Edmund has gone, they quickly pack and leave the house, traveling south on the western bank of the river. It snows to cover their tracks, and there is a full moon. That night they sleep in the beaver safe-house. Meanwhile, Edmund has arrived at the Witch's castle. When she learns his siblings are in Narnia, she heads to the Stone Table. However, she must travel many miles to the west in order to find a suitable place to take her sleigh across the frozen river before she is able to head back east to the Beavers' dam and then head south along the river. She travels all night long by moonlight.

DAY TWO: The Pevensie children awake to presents from Father Christmas. While they continue their walk south, it becomes plainly obvious that spring has broken into Narnia, it is not just a thaw. The Witch comes across a group of revelers enjoying a meal that Father Christmas has left for them. She continues southward, knowing that she is still far behind the children.

Let's begin.

 **READING ASSIGNMENT:**
Chapters 12–14

"When Adam's flesh and Adam's bone
Sits at Cair Paravel in throne,
The evil time will be over and done."
In Narnia, Cair Paravel is a castle that sits on the pennisula at the mouth of the Great River, its west door hung with peacock feathers and its east door open to the Sea and Aslan's country.

# SESSION V: RECITATION
Chapters 9-14

## Comprehension Questions

*Answer these questions for factual recall.*

1. What does Edmund imagine during the conversation at the Beavers' house?

2. What finally makes Edmund leave the Beavers' house?

3. Is Edmund completely rebellious?

4. Who do the children and the Beavers meet after they leave the Beavers' house?

5. What presents does Father Christmas give to them? How are they appropriate to the person?

6. What does Father Christmas think about women in combat?

7. What does the White Witch think about the Christmas banquet she comes across?

8. What is the turning point for Edmund?

9. How does the Witch react when her dwarf mentions the name of Aslan? Is her reaction any different from what it was in *The Magician's Nephew?*

10. What is Aslan like?

11. Is Peter brave?

12. What does Aslan do with Edmund after he is rescued from the White Witch?

13. How does the Witch respond to Aslan at their initial meeting?

14. What does Edmund say during the exchange between Aslan and the Witch?

15. When Aslan comes to the Stone Table, how does the Witch's treatment of him change?

READING ASSIGNMENT:
Chapters 15-17

The impressive crowd of creatures constituting Aslan's court at the Stone Table included dryads, naiads, centaurs, a unicorn, leopards, an eagle and a huge dog. But also included in that company was a seemingly unimpressive bird—a pelican. It may seem peculiar to the reader, but since Aslan is Christ in this story, the inclusion of the pelican fits. In heraldry and church art, the "Pelican-in-her-piety" is a symbol for the Savior because it was believed that the pelican would tear open her breast in order to feed her young with her blood. So in this story the pelican foreshadows Aslan's own self-sacrifice.

A lit lamp-post in the middle of a wood is the first magical sight the children have as they enter Narnia and the last thing they see before they leave. Unintentionally planted by the White Witch over a thousand years before, the tree of iron "with a lantern set on the top" marked Lantern Waste—the westernmost region of Narnia.

## SESSION VI: ACTIVITY
Chapters 15–17

Write a description of a well-known person using the following rules. You may not use names or any specific information which would give away the person's identity too easily. When you have finished writing, find someone to read the paragraph to and see if they can guess who you have described.

As you will see (or have seen), it is very difficult to accurately describe someone. What is important or obvious to you, may not be that important or that obvious to someone else and vice versa. We all tend to describe people based on our own experiences or our own beliefs.

# OPTIONAL SESSION A: WRITING

Saint Augustine takes on a very difficult task when he attempts to describe God in *The Confessions.*

> What, therefore, is my God? What, I ask, but the Lord God? "For who is Lord but the Lord himself, or who is God besides our God?" Most high, most excellent, most potent, most omnipotent; most merciful and most just; most secret and most truly present; most beautiful and most strong; stable, yet not supported; unchangeable, yet changing all things; never new, never old; making all things new, yet bringing old age upon the proud, and they know it not; always working, ever at rest; gathering, yet needing nothing; sustaining, pervading, and protecting; creating, nourishing, and developing; seeking, and yet possessing all things. Thou dost love, but without passion; art jealous, yet free from care; dost repent without remorse; art angry, yet remainest serene. Thou changest thy ways, leaving thy plans unchanged; thou recoverest what thou hast never really lost. Thou art never in need but still thou dost rejoice at thy gains; art never greedy, yet demandest dividends.[2]

Is that how you imagine Aslan? It is how Lewis thought about Christ, and therefore the way he tried to write of Christ himself in the *Chronicles.* The biggest difference is that Lewis does not try to describe Aslan outright; he uses allegory (symbolic representation).

Make a list of the categories Augustine uses above (notice they are divided by semicolons) and write or discuss how Lewis uses allegory or imagery in *The Lion, the Witch and the Wardrobe* to convey some of the same ideas. Hint: you will probably find chapters 8, 10 and 12–17 to be the most helpful.

# OPTIONAL SESSION B: WRITING

"A great part of art consists in imitation. For the whole conduct of life is based on this: That what we admire in others we want to do ourselves." —Quintilian

"What has been is what will be, and what has been done is what will be done, and there is nothing new under the sun." —Solomon (in *Ecclesiastes*)

C.S. Lewis devoured fairy tales as a youth. He said that he read them in secret when he was young and openly when he was an adult. One of his favorite authors of that genre was Edith Nesbit. While Lewis enjoyed all her stories, there is one in particular which seems to have had a greater effect on his imagination, *The Aunt and Amabel,* which was first published in 1908.

A copy of this short story is included in the Additional Resources of the teacher's edition. It has also been republished in a collection of Edith Nesbit stories called *The Magic World.*

1. What are some elements common to both *The Aunt and Amabel* and *The Lion, the Witch and the Wardrobe?*

2. While both these stories share some common elements, they are obviously quite different from one another as well. If you were to imagine a world you could get to through a wardrobe door, what would it look like? Who would you meet there? For what purpose would you be allowed into that world? Write your own short story or adventure including the common elements which you listed above.

## ENDNOTES
1   At the time of publication, the following sites had very good maps available.
    http://www.lindentree.org/vmap2.html
    http://cslewis.drzeus.net/pictures/narniamap.html
2   The Confessions I. iv.
3   *This endnote appears only in the teacher's edition.*

# THE HORSE AND HIS BOY

What if you had been born in Saudi Arabia? What would your life be like?

Is life everywhere basically the same? ("We go to church on Sunday; they go to Mosque on Friday.") Or is it radically different? ("I would like to be a pastor when I grow up." "I am training to be a suicide bomber.") At some points in history, these questions come to the forefront of Christian thinking. The future will be greatly affected depending on how we answer these questions. What will our answer be?

Sadly, misguided Christians seem to be in the business of downplaying the differences between their religion and others. Sometimes this practice goes so far that people begin to imply and even openly state that different religions are basically the same. This practice of mixing religions is called *syncretism*, and it is dangerous. When syncretism occurs, many conservative, Bible-believing pastors and theologians begin to write thick books on the vast differences between the true religion, Christianity, and false religions like Islam or Hinduism. Often, however, these weighty volumes of theology have little effect on the onslaught of syncretism because the average church member has trouble understanding some of the arguments or how the arguments relate to the practical aspects of living our lives. Often, stories are able to communicate such differences much more effectively. In *The Horse and His Boy*, Lewis makes an insightful and convincing argument against any syncretism between the religion of Narnia and the faith of Calormen. He does this not by listing all of the theological arguments, but simply by talking about the life of the people and displaying how a relation-ship with the true God forms at the center of a joyous and adventurous life and a beautiful society, while the worship of false deities leads to a pale, ugly and dull existence. May the reading of this book inoculate you against the foolishness of any syncretism and open your eyes to the beauty and joy that can come only from knowing the true God.

## GENERAL INFORMATION

### Significance

In *The Magician's Nephew*, we have the doctrines of Creation and Fall. In *The Lion, the Witch and the Wardrobe*, we have the doctrine of the Substitutionary Atonement, the idea that Christ took our sins upon Himself—as our substitute. In this book, *The Horse and His Boy*, we find a strong treatment of the doctrine of Providence. In speaking of these "doctrines" it is important to emphasize, yet again, that Lewis's point was not to sugarcoat a series of doctrines taken out of a systematic theology with a thin coating of story. The doctrines, or dogmas or truths are found here just as we find them in Scripture—incarnate *in* the story. And according to Lewis, nothing was more exciting than dogma—provided it was contained in its natural habitat. In this book, Aslan is behind all events, and he draws everything together. We see the authority of oracles and the power of Aslan as he operates to see that the oracles are completely fulfilled.

### Main Characters

The main characters are the Talking Horses, Bree and Hwin, and the children who ride them, Shasta and Aravis. Shasta was brought up by a poor fisherman named Arsheesh, in the land of Calormen, but has always felt a longing for the North. Aravis is the daughter of a Calormene noble, but decides to flee from a forced marriage to an obnoxious man. Bree and Hwin are Talking Horses from Narnia, who were captured when they were foals and put to use as dumb beasts in Calormen. The Hermit of the Southern March plays a key role in welcoming the refugees to the northern lands, directing Shasta in his further duty and helping the other three as they adjust to freedom, the North and Aslan. Prince Rabadash of Calormen has been courting Queen Susan, and his temper turns foul when he begins to suspect he will be rejected.

The Horse in this story is named Breehy-hinny-brinny-hoohy-hah. He was captured as a foal and grew to be an adult in the service of the Calormenes. Though proud and a bit of a doubting Thomas, the strong, dappled horse is used in the providence of Aslan to steal a young boy and ultimately save both Archenland and Narnia.

## Summary and Setting

*The Horse and His Boy* provides us with a good opportunity to discuss the "layout" of the world of Narnia. In many ways it is a small world, and it is located on a circular disk. It is not round like a ball, as ours is. This world contains only three countries to speak of, with some wilderness areas outside those countries. Narnia is the farthest north, and just south of that is Archenland, a country very much like Narnia. South of Archenland is a desert, and south of that is the cruel and powerful empire of Calormen. Far to the west is the land of Telmar, but this land doesn't really show up on the maps.

Narnia is very clearly English in a medieval kind of way, and Calormen is a southern empire with swarthy inhabitants, and answers roughly to some kind of Islamic power—but at the height of its power and glory. Think of an empire like that held by the Ottoman Turks in the late medieval and early modern period. Not only does this book present the reality of providence, it also presents a contrast between two very different kinds of civilization.

Aravis would have enjoyed her first meal in the beautiful, pillared room of Lasaraleen's palacial home, if her childhood friend's spoiled pet monkey hadn't been climbing about it all the time.

## Worldview

C.S. Lewis is drawing on an ancient literary plot device in this book. When King Lune of Archenland has twin sons, an oracle is pronounced over the two of them, and it is said that Cor will one day save Archenland from the greatest danger which ever threatened her. The former Lord Chancellor of Archenland, a traitor named Bar, kidnaps Cor in order to keep this from happening. But what he does to *prevent* the prophecy from happening is precisely what Aslan uses to *cause* the prophecy to be fulfilled. This is the same kind of thing that can be seen in the Oedipus story by Sophocles, which will be read later this year: a prophecy is told at birth of this prince of Thebes, and all the attempts of everyone to avoid the fulfillment of that prophecy are actually the instruments for fulfilling it. In the story of Oedipus this is the result of fate. But in Narnia, as in the Christian doctrine of Providence, that which brings all things together in fulfillment is a person, in this case Aslan.

Bar's ship is pursued as he is fleeing to Calormen, and he is defeated in a battle at sea. Before that defeat, Cor is put in a small boat with someone to attend him, and that person sacrifices his life to save the baby. The boat "happens" to land where Arsheesh is, and Arsheesh "happens" to be sleepless that night, and so Shasta is brought up in Calormen. Later in the book, the Hermit of the Southern March sums up a central theme of this book, when he says he has "never met any such thing as Luck."

Shasta genuinely learns this lesson. His initial response is to attribute his successful arrival in Narnia to luck. But he catches himself and says, "at least it wasn't luck at all really, it was *Him.*" C.S. Lewis emphatically denied anything like luck or chance. He taught that all things are governed by a wise Providence, and this is just what Scripture teaches. As Cor put it, somehow Aslan "seems to be at the back of all the stories."

Providence refers to the oversight of all things that God provides, and this happens on a scale so large that it is impossible for a human mind to get around it. Not only is the scale of organization too large for us to understand, we are also confronted with the mystery of free will in this world where all things are ordained by a wise Providence.

This is really one of the great questions, and *The Horse and His Boy* provides a wonderful setting for a discussion of it. When the oracle (or prophecy) is given at the beginning of Cor's life, it is necessary for that oracle to be fulfilled. And yet, the characters in the book do not suddenly become puppets as they act out that fulfillment. The history that Aslan is in back of is truly a free history, and yet this free history has Aslan at the back of it, in all things great and small.

When Aslan intervenes directly, this is of course the action of Aslan. But the book makes clear that the action of Aslan lies in back of everything else as well. The direct actions of Aslan in the story include pushing the boat with Cor in ashore, making sure that Arsheesh was awake, making Hwin and Aravis team up with Bree and Shasta, protecting Shasta from the jackals, pursuing them to the Hermit so that they would run faster, walking alongside Shasta in the fog and so on. In all these instances, Aslan is a character in the story—but he is also, in another sense, the author of the *entire* story. He is not just steering things "generally," because the doctrine of Providence extends down into the little things as well. As Jesus put it, the hairs of our head are all numbered, and not a sparrow falls to the ground apart from the will of the Father (Luke 12:6–8).

Aslan's presence is assumed throughout the story. His periodic appearances are not intended to tell us that he is absent the rest of the time. Rather, his appearances are to remind us that he is always present and guiding—it is just that we sometimes are privileged to *see* it. Aslan is always present, but periodically visible. And this is why the Hermit can say there is no such thing as luck.

But how is this consistent with free will? For no

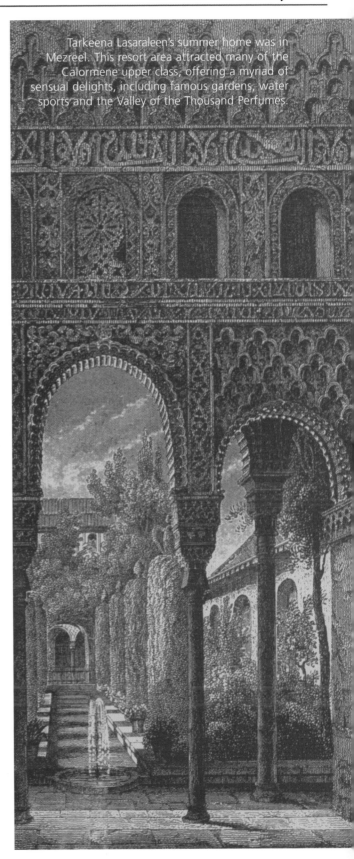

Tarkeena Lasaraleen's summer home was in Mezreel. This resort area attracted many of the Calormene upper class, offering a myriad of sensual delights, including famous gardens, water sports and the Valley of the Thousand Perfumes.

one taught more clearly than C.S. Lewis that we are free and responsible creatures. In various places, Lewis made clear that he did not oppose divine sovereignty and creaturely free will. For example, in one passage in *Perelandra,* another of his fictional works, he makes plain that at the ultimate level, Freedom and Necessity are really the same thing. As the famous British preacher, C.H. Spurgeon, once put it, he never tried to reconcile divine sovereignty and human responsibility because he never reconciled friends.

Free will and divine sovereignty are not inconsistent with one another, but they are a mystery. We are not capable of "doing the math" in such a way as to show how they are harmonious. But they are in fact harmonious, and the best way to make this plain is always through telling a story. Reading through *The Horse and His Boy,* we have no sense at all that Shasta is a puppet, or a robot, and yet everything he does and feels fits in with the fulfillment of the oracle and contributes toward it. He yearns for the north before he knows why. The solution to this problem is not to be found in logical proofs, but rather in story. And this is why those who deny either human freedom or divine sovereignty in order to make them "consistent" (with some denying one and the rest denying the other) actually have the same problem. Their problem is that they do not understand story.

The writing of C.S. Lewis is so compelling that a generation after his death, his books remain bestsellers. And this means that some people who want to like Lewis, but who have been influenced by some of the changing cultural fads and fashions, have to deal with some things that Lewis wrote that are most definitely *not* "politically correct." Lewis's treatment of Calormen is one of those areas. In the Narnia stories, and particularly in *The Horse and His Boy,* we have a contrast between two different kinds of cultures, two different kinds of civilizations.

Several examples of this stumbling can be found in

> The Great Lion permeates this tale in a way that is quite different from the other *Chronicles.* Aslan does not whisk children from our world to intervene in Narnian history but instead weaves many seemingly insignificant and unrelated elements into a beautiful tapestry depicting his sovereignty.

*Companion to Narnia* by Paul F. Ford. In most respects this is really an outstanding and helpful book. But there are several places where the entries say some atrocious things, and it is because Lewis was not politically correct. One example of this is the entry under sexism, which is filled with a bunch of contemporary hooey on that subject and apologizes for Lewis's historic Christian understanding of the relationship of men and women, boys and girls, and which tries to pretend that Lewis was "growing" in this area. Ford's book is like a splendid Persian rug, gloriously woven, which someone cut in two for some reason, and then sewed in a six-inch swath of bright orange shag carpeting.

The other example is a passing comment on Calormen in a footnote. Ford says, "Like many Englishmen of his era, Lewis was unconsciously unsympathetic to things and people Middle-Eastern. That Lewis opts into this cultural blindness is regrettable" (p. 95).

This is said because Calormen is very clearly a Middle-Eastern civilization, and C.S. Lewis is very clearly unsympathetic to it. But there was nothing *un*conscious about it; Lewis knew exactly what he was doing.

All cultures are inherently religious. The tyrannical and despotic nature of Calormen was a necessary function of their worship of a demon-god, the "inexorable Tash." It is too weak to say that cultures are the residue of fundamental religious commitments. Culture *is* a religious commitment. Lewis saw this very clearly, and he set it forth in this book deliberately. But he is not a mindless propagandist either. He acknowledges that Calormen boasts many impressive achievements. He knows that nobility is not unknown among them (which can be seen through the character Emeth in *The Last Battle*). In this book, Aravis is a native of Calormen, and she is a young noblewoman—truly noble—who becomes a queen in Archenland. But at the same time, Narnian and Archenlander culture is self-consciously asserted as being *superior* to the culture of Calormen.

But the Calormenes are not treated as though they were orcs, entirely evil. They are a fallen culture, and they worship a false god. Therefore, given the premises of their worship, there is no real salvation. Of course their culture will be characterized by cruelty, sensuality, luxury and despotism. There are

Calormene individuals who escape this—but they escape it through coming to Aslan. The fundamental issue is always one of religious worship. Narnians are sinners just as the Calormenes are, but because they worship that which is true, salvation is possible. Tyranny is possible in Narnia (think of the White Witch in the past, or Miraz in the future), but because Aslan is there, salvation is possible.

Lewis greatly prefers Narnian (and English) butter to Calormene (and Turkish) oil. He greatly prefers the English breakfast. But credit is given where credit is due, and Lewis also says that he greatly prefers the Calormene art of story-telling to the clunky English way of essay-writing. In all this, it is clear that Lewis is writing as a Christian, which means that he believes that Christian cultural expressions are right, and, on the contrary, that demonic cultural expressions are wrong. But also, because he is a Christian, he is fair-minded about it.

The worship of a false god will necessarily result in slavery under despotism. And the worship of the true god will necessarily result in liberty under authority. In Calormen, the despotism is so thorough that Ahoshta, the Grand Vizier, has to grovel before the Tisroc. And in Narnia, the lowliest badger is free. This is not a regrettable instance of Lewis showing us his blind spot. This is one of his central points; it is one of the reasons he was writing.

But in the grip of modern "multicultural" assumptions, some of Lewis's fans have to explain this unfortunate "lapse" away. It is important that the students who are working through this book be taught the importance of this. Cultures that have been shaped by the worship of the true God are *superior* to cultures that have not been. This is all of grace—no one deserved or earned any of it. There is nothing to boast of; in fact, recognition of this need for humility is one of the features of cultures that have been shaped by true worship.

This is why the Narnian royalty walk down the streets of Tashbaan, with their arms swinging free, and they are chatting happily. They are not being carried about in litters, with deference to them being enforced with a club. They are not pretentious; the men go bareheaded. Shasta looked at that humility and was delighted by its loveliness. When Aravis meets King Lune, he is in his grubby clothes, having just come from the royal kennels. But he is the model of a righteous king—his royalty is carried on his shoulders *humbly*. Lewis is making the point that these things do not happen by accident. They are a function of whether Tash is served or Aslan.

In our world, one of the civilizations that Lewis was using for his narrative model was the monarchies of Christendom, particularly the English monarchy of the medieval period. That is held up as something noble and admirable. The principles of chivalry pervade these books, and it is very clear that Lewis rejected modernity as a worldview (which is not the same thing as rejecting indoor plumbing), and sought to instill an appreciation for that world through these books. At the same time, the greatest historical threat to Christendom down through the centuries has been Islam. The perennial presence on Europe's southern borders has been an Islamic presence, and more than once it was believed that Europe was lost. Looking at the current situation, some believe the same thing *now*. Calormen is a thin disguise for this state of affairs, and Lewis's point should be taken seriously. Multiculturalism is a lie, and the Narnia books are a good way to get that lie out of the system.

One other incident in this book should be highlighted, and that is the revelation of Aslan to Shasta as he walked in the fog toward Narnia. As Shasta was walking, he became aware of a presence beside him which terrified him. Finally, Shasta speaks, and the presence says that he has waited long for Shasta to speak. When Shasta finally asks, "Who *are* you?" the answer that comes is threefold. This threefold answer is a wonderful exhibition of the Trinity. Aslan says, three times, "Myself." The first *myself* is the Emperor-Beyond-the-Sea, and is an immense voice, low, and it shakes the earth. The second is Aslan. The third *myself* is a revelation of the Holy Spirit, being nearly inaudible and yet coming from everywhere, pervading everything.

When the fog lifts, Shasta finds a footprint of the lion in which a spring begins to flow. Shasta is refreshed by drinking from it, and it is after this encounter with the triune *myself* that Shasta acknowledges that it was not luck that preserved him (a Calormene concept, take it away!), but rather, it was *Him*.

—*Douglas Wilson*

## SESSION I: PRELUDE

### A Question to Consider

When I was younger, I could not understand why airplanes didn't fall out of the sky. I knew that they were big and heavy. Rocks are big and heavy. When rocks got thrown up, they came down very quickly; when airplanes went up in the air, they should come down very quickly. I could see, of course, that they did not. Several times, some well intentioned adult tried to explain all the physics of the situation to me in language that they thought I should be able to understand, to no avail. Did that stop me from ever flying? No, it did not. Even though I did not understand it, I believed that the plane I was flying on would somehow stay up in the air–and it always did.

Now that I am older, I still do not understand how they stay up in the air, but it is because I can't be bothered to understand it, not because I am too young to understand.

Do you have any similar experiences–times when though you don't understand the way something works, you accept it by faith because you observe it as true and an older wiser person affirms it is true?

*From the General Information above answer the following questions:*

1. What device does Lewis use in *The Horse and His Boy* which is similar to that used in *Oedipus?*
2. Why must the prophecy be fulfilled?
3. Does Aslan cause the prophecy to be fulfilled by his "direct" intervention only, that is, actions we actually see or hear about him doing?
4. What does *providence* mean?
5. Why is providence difficult for us to understand?
6. Why is it easier to see these two concepts co-exist in a story?

### Optional Activities

If you made a map of Narnia for *The Lion, the Witch and the Wardrobe,* add to it while you read through *The Horse and His Boy.* Keep in mind the difference in *scale.* In *The Lion, the Witch and the Wardrobe,* it takes the children only two days to walk from Lantern Waste to Cair Paravel. In *The Horse and*

*His Boy,* Shasta and Bree are riding for weeks to reach Tashbaan.

If you have already read *The Horse and His Boy,* use the *Companion to Narnia* as a resource and read through the following entries:

> **SHASTA**
> **ARAVIS**
> **BREE**
> **HWIN**
> **RABADASH**
> **LASARALEEN**
> **AHOSHTA**
> **CALORMEN**

**READING ASSIGNMENT:**
Chapters 1–3

## SESSION II: DISCUSSION
Chapters 1–3

### A Question to Consider

If someone asked you to describe French, German, Arabic, Japanese and American culture, how would you describe them?

How would you define *culture?*

*Discuss or list short answers to the following questions:*

### *Text Analysis*

1. How would you describe the culture of Narnia using examples from *The Magician's Nephew* and *The Lion, the Witch and the Wardrobe?*
2. How would you describe the culture of Calormen with what you have observed so far in *The Horse and His Boy?*
3. How have Aravis and Shasta been influenced by growing up in Calormen?
4. How have Bree and Hwin been influenced by being born in and having at least their early youth in Narnia?
5. Does the story indicate that one culture is superior to the other? How so?

## Cultural Analysis

1. Multiculturalism is the view that all cultures, from that of a spirit-worshiping tribe to that of the most advanced industrial civilization, are of equal value. There is often an assumption that truth is culturally based, and therefore, since there are multiple descriptions of reality, no one description can be true in any ultimate sense. Certain groups in America strongly promote this belief in multiculturalism. In what ways have you seen language change to become more "culturally inclusive?"

2. How have you seen books, especially textbooks, become more "inclusive" in their information?

## Biblical Analysis

1. Read James 4:4. Why does James call the people adulterous?
2. What does James 4:4 mean when it says "friends with the world?"
3. If we keep our focus on the Lord, and act in such a way that He is pleased, rather than the way our culture may dictate, what should we expect? (See John 15:18–19.)

## Application

We no longer are part of a culture that has Christian values and truth as its acknowledged foundation. We must therefore be careful not to become a part of the world around us, but to question our cultural norms, and, where we find them lacking, stand instead on the truth of God's word—even if it brings hatred and persecution upon us.

## SUMMA

*Write an essay or discuss this question, integrating what you have learned from the material above.* Can one culture be superior to another?

## Optional Activity

Horseback riding would be a great activity at this point. Try to find a place where

The Hermit of the Southern March is a 109-year-old man who lives along the southern edge of Archenland. He lives in an old, stone house with a thatched roof and keeps goats. Lewis has the Hermit call the horses and his goats "cousins," conjuring a character that feels like a magical and mystical Saint Francis of Assisi.

> "The giants were ordered to the right, and before going they all took off something they had been carrying on their backs and sat down for a moment. Then Shasta saw that what they had been carrying and were now putting on were pairs of boots: horrid, heavy, spiked boots which came up to their knees."

they will let you ride hours on end so that you get a real taste of what it is like to wake up the next morning as Shasta felt. You may want to have other family members ready with the hot water bottles upon your return! Don't forget to pack the appropriate food: meat pasties, figs and some nice green cheese!

### RECIPE FOR MEAT PASTIES
*The Dough:*
Soften together 1 1/2 tsp yeast and 1 Tbs sugar in 1 cup of lukewarm water. Add 1 1/2 tsp salt and 2 1/2–3 cups flour (mixed whole wheat and white).

Knead 10 minutes. Cover and set in a warm place to rise until doubled in bulk, about one hour. (Prepare filling while dough rises.)

Punch dough down. Divide into six sections and roll each out into a circle, approximately 1/4" thick. Fill with 1/2–3/4 cup filling, placing the filling on one half of the circle, leaving a 1/2" rim. Moisten the rim with water, fold the empty side over and crimp the edge with a fork. Bake on a buttered tray at 450° F for 15–20 minutes or until crisp and lightly-browned. Brush each pasty with a little butter as it comes out of the oven.

*The filling:*
1 lb. fresh spinach
1/2 cup minced onion
2 cloves crushed garlic
2 Tbs butter
1 lb bulk Italian sausage
1 lb ricotta cheese
2 cups mozzarella
1/2 cup parmesan
salt, pepper
dash of nutmeg

1. Wash, stem and finely-chop spinach. Steam it quickly, on medium-high heat, adding no additional water. When wilted and deep green, it is done and should be removed to mixing bowl using a slotted spoon.
2. Sauté onion and garlic in butter until translucent and soft.
3. Cook sausage, breaking into small pieces, until no longer pink.
4. Combine all ingredients, mix well, salt and pepper to taste.

READING ASSIGNMENT:
Chapters 4–6

# SESSION III: RECITATION

Chapters 4–6

## Comprehension Questions

*Answer these questions for factual recall.*

1. What does Shasta seem to think of Aravis?
2. Describe Arsheesh and Kidrash Tarkaan.
3. What are the traffic regulations in Tashbaan?
4. Do the Narnians treat one another in a way familiar to Shasta?
5. Do the Narnians appear to have a different attitude about their women than the Calormenes?
6. What is Shasta's view of grown-ups, and how do you think he came to have this view?
7. How does this view of authority affect his thoughts about the Narnians?
8. On what terms do Shasta and Prince Corin part from one another?
9. At what moment does Shasta start to become afraid at the tombs?
10. What comforts him in his fear?

READING ASSIGNMENT:
Chapters 7–9

# SESSION IV: ACTIVITY

## Calormene Storytelling

In this session we will seek to develop the art of storytelling.

"For in Calormen, storytelling (whether the stories are true or made up) is a thing you're taught, just as English boys and girls are taught essay writing. The difference is that people want to hear the stories, whereas I never heard of anyone who wanted to read the essays" (chap. 2).

There have been several examples in the book so far of the Calormene storytelling art. Which ones can you remember?

Make a list of the rules/techniques that you imagine could have been used to teach the Calormene art of storytelling.

Now that you have thought of the elements to Calormene storytelling, plan your own story. Your story should be told in the first person and should abide by all the rules for Calormene storytelling. Before telling your story to your class or family, you may want to write an outline and practice some of your Calormene-style language.

READING ASSIGNMENT:
Chapters 10–12

# SESSION V: RECITATION

Chapters 7–12

## Comprehension Questions

*Answer these questions for factual recall.*

1. What are some of Lasaraleen's interests? What are some of Aravis's interests?
2. What does Lasaraleen think makes a man a desirable husband?
3. What critical thought does Aravis have of the Tisroc (may he live for ever)?
4. What is Prince Rabadash determined to get?
5. Why does he want this so badly?
6. What does the Tisroc (may he live for ever) think of freedom?
7. What are the Tisroc's (may he live for ever) reasons for allowing the Prince to go?
8. Do Shasta and company take the shorter route?
9. What brave deed does Shasta do, and what is his reward?
10. What is Shasta's first impression of King Lune?
11. How does Shasta come to realize that something is by his side in the dark?
12. What sorts of fears does Shasta have as to the identity of the unknown thing by his side? How is

13. When Shasta asks directly, "Who are you?" what answer is he given?

14. When Shasta was able to see who had been walking and talking beside him, what was his reaction?

**READING ASSIGNMENT:**
Chapters 13–15

# SESSION VI: ACTIVITY
Chapters 13–15

## A Question to Consider

Imagine yourself in the following settings. How do you conduct yourself?

At a dinner with your family at a fancy restaurant?

At the dinner of a family reunion or of a holiday dinner with your extended family?

At a fast food restaurant with some of your friends?

What are some of the reasons our behavior changes from one setting to the next?

*Discuss or list answers to the following questions:*

## Character Analysis

*For the following list of characters, answer the questions below, substantiating your viewpoint from the text.*

> HWIN
>
> SHASTA
>
> ARAVIS
>
> BREE

1. Describe their behaviors and characteristics?
2. Is their behavior consistent throughout the book?
3. If there is some change to their character in the book–what is the major change and what brings it about?
4. By the end of the book, what characteristic(s) have they all come to hold in common?

## Optional Session: Activity

Making a game from material you have read is a great way to reinforce the story. Pick an episode from *The Horse and His Boy* to make your own game, perhaps basing it on a board game you already own. Alternatively, play *Escape from Tashbaan.*

### Escape from Tashbaan

**OBJECT OF THE GAME**

To travel through Tashbaan and be the first to exit either via the Tisroc's Palace or the Bridge to the Tombs of the Ancient Kings.

**MATERIALS**

Gameboard *(available in the Additional Resources in the teacher's edition*
Die
Playing Pieces *(flat marbles, stones, dried corn, figures from another board game, etc.)*

**RULES FOR THE GAME**
**TO START**

You must roll either a 1 or a 3 to get onto "Start." Once you get onto Start, you must wait until your next turn to roll again. Multiple players may occupy the same space at the same time, including the Start space.

**TO MOVE THROUGH TASHBAAN**

Upon your turn, roll the die and move forward the corresponding number of spaces. If you land on a cobblestone space, your turn is over. If you land on a circular Rollspot, roll the die again. The board is divided into the different-colored sections of Tashbaan. Match this roll of your die to the number corresponding to your current colored section. Follow the instructions for that number.

If the consequence of a Rollspot places you on another Rollspot, treat it as a non-Rollspot.

When you arrive at the cobblestone between the houses of the Narnians and Lasaraleen you will need to make a choice which way to go. Once you have made your choice of direction, you must stop on that space even if you rolled a higher number. Play passes to the next player.

**TO FINISH**

To finish the game, you do not need an exact role of the die. The first player to leave Tashbaan is the winner.

The prince of Calormen was a proud and rash man, who, when offered mercy, arrogantly declined and was punished by Aslan. But justice was mixed with mercy—"You shall not always be an Ass," declared Aslan. Then the Lion instructed him how he could break the spell. The prince was freed from his animal form at the great Autumn Feast in the temple in Tashbaan.

# PRINCE CASPIAN: THE RETURN TO NARNIA

Every day our loyalties are tested, but in the great moments of history loyalty is tested in extraordinary ways. One of our great advent hymns resounds

> Let all mortal flesh keep silence
> And with fear and trembling stand
> Ponder nothing earthly minded
> For with blessing in His hand,
> Christ, the Lord, to earth descendeth,
> Our full homage to demand.[1]

Often our Christmas cards proclaim: "Peace on Earth!" A cursory reading of the story of the Nativity of our Lord, however, shows that this phrase is mistaken (if taken out of context—which it constantly is). Christ's birth does herald blessing, but He, as the hymn says, "demands homage." Christ's entire life is a loyalty test, and people and rulers crumble in the face of it. Herod faces a challenge to bow the knee to the rightful king; he chooses to murder all the infants in Bethlehem in order to seek to protect his faltering rule. Peter is in his fishing boat, but when Christ calls him to be loyal, he abandons his career to follow his King. The rich young ruler faces a test of loyalty— "Your savior or your wealth;" he goes back to his gold with downcast face.

At times, during Christ's ministry we see loyalties vacillating and changing. Judas presents the most striking example. He, for the entire ministry of Christ, pretends loyalty, only to betray his Lord in the end. Paul provides the counterpoint to Judas. He opposes Christ violently, but when the Lord knocks him to the ground, Paul's loyalty is given to Jesus personally, and permanently.

Today, each of us faces issues of loyalty. Will you be obedient to your parents? Will you hide your faith? Will you crumble and betray Christ or His people? Will you, like Paul, hold your loyalty come what may? As we consider *Prince Caspian,* may the story help us to understand and pursue loyalty to our King.

## GENERAL INFORMATION

### Significance

Thus far in *The Chronicles of Narnia,* we have seen a treatment of Creation and Fall, Atonement and Providence. In this book, we see the central theme

The magic horn of Queen Susan the Gentle which is used to summon the Pevensies back into Narnia.

of Government. The questions that derive from authority, loyalty, submission, legitimacy and succession are pervasive throughout the book. Lewis saw that it is not possible to act as though the only ultimate questions were "theological" and limited to the confines of one's brain. Rather, what we believe about ultimate realities will have practical and institutional ramifications, such as how we obey or disobey the institution of government. How loyalty makes this application is the theme of this book.

## Main Characters

The main characters are (again) the four Pevensie children, Peter, Susan, Edmund and Lucy. They have returned to Narnia to place Prince Caspian on the throne instead of his uncle, the usurper Miraz. Trufflehunter is the faithful badger who typifies all the Talking Beasts of Narnia, and Trumpkin is the faithful dwarf, who at the same time does not believe in Aslan. Doctor Cornelius is Caspian's tutor in the court of Miraz, and he turns out to be part dwarf and part human. Nikabrik is a pragmatic black dwarf on Caspian's side who has been soured by bitterness. Aslan is present throughout this story, but his visible presence is more limited than in some of the other books.

## Summary and Setting

Remember that Narnian time and English time run on different schedules. In the years since the Pevensies were in Narnia, about thirteen hundred Narnian years have passed. Some humans who stumbled into the land of Telmar have since invaded Narnia and conquered it. They have suppressed the "Old Narnians," the Talking Beasts and so on, and, because of their fear of the sea, they have allowed a great wood to grow up along the sea. Narnia has been conquered by Caspian the Conqueror, also known as Caspian the First.

By the time our book opens, Caspian the Tenth is growing up in the court of his Uncle Miraz, a man who murdered Caspian's father, the rightful king, Caspian the Ninth. When the wife of Miraz, Prunaprismia, has a baby boy, Caspian's tutor tells him to flee in the middle of the night because his life will certainly be taken.

The rest of the book is taken up with the fight between Caspian and Miraz for control in Narnia.

## Worldview

Where are we to place our loyalty? Where should our allegiance be? For Lewis, the complexity of this question is acknowledged, but the solution is nevertheless simple. We place our loyalty in accordance with our duty to *persons,* and we do not make decisions in order to line up with *abstractions.* The modern state is dedicated to propositions and abstractions (e.g., We hold these truths to be self evident that all men are created equal); the medieval feudal state (which is very much the model for Narnia) was founded on loyalty to persons (e.g., I, Baron Marcus de Ford, owe my fealty and allegiance to my dread Sovereign, King George of Westphilia). The law was not personal, but it always concerned persons. The modern law is impersonal (as all law is), but it tries (with varying degrees of success) to avoid personal application and loyalties.

Succession, the idea of who will be the next leader, and legitimacy, the right that a leader has to be the leader, are very practical questions, and in the medieval, feudal setting, they are *personal* questions. Government is a family affair.

At the very beginning of Narnia, Frank and Helen are placed on the throne by Aslan himself. They and their descendants rule with integrity for a long time. But after about nine hundred years, the White Witch has managed to conquer Narnia. After the long winter, she is overthrown by Aslan, and he places a second dynasty on the throne. Peter, Susan, Edmund and Lucy are not descended from Frank and Helen. But they *are* descended from Adam and Eve, which is what gives them their legitimacy. Lewis does not tell us who reigns over Narnia in their stead after they go back to England, but whoever it is, they are not descended from the Pevensies. Nevertheless, Narnia remains peaceful until the invasion of the Telmarines in the Narnian year 1998—over nine hundred years after the Golden Age of Peter, Susan, Edmund and Lucy.

The Telmarines are an aggressive, practical lot, and they conquer Narnia for their own purposes, subduing the Old Narnians. They are descended from pirates in our world, who stumbled into the world of Narnia through a cave on an island in the South Sea. Their ancestry, in other words, is not a distinguished one. Yet, they too are descended from Adam and Eve, which means that legitimacy is possible. Caspian the

First conquered Narnia, and, by the time of Caspian the Ninth, a kind of genuine nobility had developed among the Telmarines. By the time of Prince Caspian, the Telmarines have been ruling Narnia for three hundred years, and they have genuine legitimacy. Even though the Old Narnians are suppressed, the murder of Caspian the Ninth by Miraz is treated as an act of genuine treachery, and Caspian the Ninth had some genuinely noble friends who had to be murdered or exiled in some way.

Prince Caspian, because he is a son of Adam, is acknowledged by the Old Narnians as their rightful king. And Miraz is seen as a usurper and tyrant. After his murder of Caspian the Ninth, Miraz begins calling himself "Lord Protector" instead of "King" (which is what Oliver Cromwell called himself when he replaced Charles I). After Caspian, Rilian rules, and the Telmarine line continues down to the end of Narnia, where Tirian, the last king of Narnia, faithfully serves Aslan to the last.

Thus we have three basic dynasties. The first is that of Frank and Helen and their descendents. The second is that of the Pevensies (and whoever followed them). The third is that of the Telmarines. Now all this is *very much* like the tangled real history of the kings of England. England became an identifiable nation under Alfred. But several centuries later, the last Anglo-Saxon king Harold was defeated by Caspian the First . . . I mean *William!* And the House of Windsor that sits on the throne of England today is a very different line than that of the Stuarts that preceded it. For Lewis, different dynasties did not affect legitimacy. What mattered to him most was whether the king was one who intended to rule by law. Legitimacy is therefore a matter of law and not simply a matter of descent. And the law was something that the king was to submit to, and not something that he controlled according to his whims. Moreover, the law as an institution took history into account. This is how the Telmarine line could become legitimate over time. Because Caspian was a son of Adam, and because he intended to follow the law in his rule of Narnia, he was the heir apparent.

This may seem very complicated, but it was very simple to Trumpkin and Trufflehunter. Trufflehunter was a simple beast, and he knew that Narnia needed to be ruled by a son of Adam. Beasts don't forget, as he put it. When a son of Adam appeared in their midst, and he had a clear and obvious claim on the throne, Trufflehunter immediately swore fealty (faithfulness to a leader, particularly a feudal lord) to him, and that was that.

This same kind of dogged and simple loyalty is also seen in Trumpkin. He knew what his immediate duties were, even though he did not believe in Aslan (as he ought to have done) at the ultimate level. He has taken sides with Caspian as well, and when Doctor Cornelius gives Caspian Queen Susan's Magic Horn, he does not believe in its power. He does not want word of the Horn to get out among their troops, because he does not want any false hopes aroused. When Doctor Cornelius says that the Horn is likely to summon help to one of three places—the Stone Table (where they were), Lantern Waste or Cair Paravel, Trumpkin grumps that belief in the Horn looks to have the immediate result of losing them two fighters instead of gaining them extra help.

The ruins of Cair Paravel are found in this story on an island at the mouth of the Great River instead of on a peninsula. The apple orchard, planted by Lilygloves the chief mole outside the north gate, had grown up to the walls and all was in complete disarray.

But when Caspian is challenged by Nikabrik, Trumpkin gets angry and volunteers to be one of the messengers who goes to meet the help (that he does not believe is coming). This astonishes everyone, and it results in one of the great lines (and great principles) found in the Narnia stories. Trumpkin is asked about it—*we* thought you didn't believe in the Horn. "No more I do, your majesty. But I know the difference between giving advice and taking orders. You've had my advice, and now's the time for orders."

In this, Lewis is striking a blow against one of the great plagues of the modern church—the problem of *individualism*. In the grip of individualism, we tend to believe that each person is a prophet, priest and king unto himself, and he does not have to do anything required of him by an authority if he does not feel like it. In other words the individual thinks he is entirely independent—of his teachers, parents, church leaders, etc. And, of course, this means that authority is not really authority. The ultimate court of appeals is in the heart of each individual.

Of course, each individual decision is made in individual hearts. But having the decisions made *in* each individual heart is very different from having the standard for the decision *be* the individual heart. When Trumpkin does this, he is the one deciding (how else could it work?), but he is making the decision to submit himself to another. It is a decision to submit, despite Trumpkin's self-conscious disagreement with what is being done. Trumpkin is a true individual, but he is also a loyal subject. He thinks for himself (in this case, wrongly), but his poor thinking does not lead him astray, because he submits himself when he knows that he must.

Lewis gives us an amazing array of characters who display different relationships to these central thematic questions of loyalty and legitimacy. We have Caspian, who is of the line of the hated Telmarines. But he is the lawful heir, and his uncle is the tyrant. We have Nikabrik, who is opposed to Miraz, just as he ought to be, but this is not borne of any true love for Aslan. He will team up with anyone or anything in order to fight his enemies. His only real loyalty appears to be to the dwarfs, and everything else is just a tool toward that end. We have Doctor Cornelius, who is a half-breed, working in the court of

Trumpkin went down the steps of the ruined Cair Paravel into the dark coldness and dusty splendour of the treasure house. The Dwarf's eyes glistened as it saw the wealth that lay on the shelves. There was a kind of path up the middle (as it might be in a greenhouse), and along each side at intervals stood rich suits of armour, like knights guarding the treasures. In between the suits of armour, on each side of the path, were shelves covered with precious things—necklaces and arm-rings and finger rings and golden bowls and dishes and long tusks of ivory, brooches and coronets and chains of gold, and heaps of unset stones lying in piles any how as if they were marbles or potatoes—diamonds, rubies, carbuncles, emeralds, topazes and amethysts. "It would never do to let Nikabrik see this; never," Trumpkin muttered to himself.

Miraz. He and his kind are held in contempt by many Old Narnians, and yet he is one of the best friends that Narnia ever had. We have Trufflehunter, who is on the right side, and he is on the right side in the right way. We have Trumpkin, whose immediate loyalties are sound, but who does not believe in Aslan. He is on the right side for the wrong reason, but his wrong reason is very different from Nikabrik's wrong reason. When someone says that if they call on the evil powers to help them against Miraz, that means they will forfeit the help of Aslan. Trumpkin cheerfully says that what is *more* important is the fact that they would forfeit the help of Trumpkin. We have a Telmarine soldier who fought in the battle against Aslan, and yet Aslan breathes on him and bequeaths to him a great blessing back in our world. It is all very messy.

At the same time, it is all very simple. But it is only simple in the context of *story*, because story is capable of showing us the *people*. Loyalties are personal, and yet moderns have been trained to think of such personal loyalties as somehow suspect. Whenever we hear about a man who hires someone else because he knows him from the club they both belong to, we suspect foul play. When we hear that a father hired his son, we think of it as a form of corruption; it even has a name: *nepotism*. We want all hiring to be "objective" and "fair," and what we mean by this is that we want it to go through an impersonal process. We want decisions like this to be made in a machine-like fashion so that it will be "fair."

Another illustration of this is the modern military, in contrast to the older manner of fighting that characterized Christendom. In the old days, when men went to war, they would join up with men from their own village, town or region. This is why there would be a regiment from Virginia or from Maryland. But today, recruits are (deliberately) processed in such a way as to prevent any such geographic concentrations. And our fighting units are now something like the 101st Airborne.

The reason our creaturely loyalties are personal is because we worship the triune God, who is personal. Three Persons within the Godhead share infinite and eternal personal fellowship with one another. Because this is true, and because we imitate the God we worship, our creaturely loyalties are personal. This is what the Bible plainly teaches: "If we walk in the light as He is in the light, we have fellowship with one another…" (1 John 1:7). In Narnia, it is just the same way. Everyone who loves Aslan has a natural affinity for everyone else who loves Aslan. And everyone who does not love Aslan recoils from those who do. This is how personal friendships are made and developed. Further, this is how stable Christian societies and cultures develop.

We are tempted to misrepresent this by saying that this is how bad leaders take over and rule as if they have absolute power. This is what is called *tyranny* and *despotism*. But let us return to the example of Trumpkin. He swears an oath of personal fealty to Caspian, and is prepared to follow him to the death. He is prepared to follow him to the death in the execution of a mission he personally thinks is foolish. And this is in fact how we meet him. While he is on his way to Cair Paravel, he is captured by the Telmarines, and they are taking him to be executed when the Pevensies rescue him. In short, he is fully prepared to lay down his life in the pursuit of what he thinks is a wild goose chase, and he is prepared to do this because his personal loyalty to Caspian demands it. Now, does this mean that Trumpkin has surrendered all personal and individual responsibility? Not at all.

As mentioned above, Nikabrik wants to bring in the ogres and werewolves, and perhaps the White Witch, to aid them in their fight with Miraz. Trumpkin makes it very clear that, if the ogres and other nasty creatures are brought in as their allies, he, Trumpkin, will be gone.

This brings us to two principles that we must learn here in Narnia. First, under Aslan, all authority is personal. Second, short of Aslan, no authority is absolute. Trumpkin is not going to give over to Caspian unquestioned allegiance regardless. He is willing to submit on a host of lesser things, even where he disagrees. And he will submit his life on those things, because Caspian is the king, and Trumpkin knows the difference between giving advice and taking orders. But at the same time, Trumpkin knows the difference between wickedness and righteousness, and he will not be allied with wickedness. If Caspian would tell him to

attack on the right flank, and he believes an attack on the left flank is wiser, he would obey and attack on the right. But if Caspian would tell him that he has to work together with the ogres, Trumpkin would have been down the road. This is not inconsistent with his oath of fealty, because, in the medieval world, no feudal oath was absolute.

In the medieval world (and remember, Narnia is part of that world), when an oath of fealty was taken, this meant that there were obligations on both sides. A vassal owed allegiance to the feudal lord, and the feudal lord owed protection in accordance with the law to the vassal. When a lord did not protect his people, he forfeited their covenanted fealty. This was part of the constitution of feudal Europe, and vestiges of this system can be found as late as the American War for Independence. King George III was the feudal lord of the American colonies, and because he refused to protect them from the attacks of Parliament, the colonies (legally) renounced their feudal loyalty to him.

People tend to think that, in the medieval world, unquestioning obedience was required and that we in the modern world are free. But this is actually the reverse of the truth. The modern state makes absolute demands and requires total and complete submission, with no corresponding demands made upon the rulers. The regimes of Nazi Germany, the Stalinist Soviet Union and Mao's China are all modern states, and in many ways their murderousness is *unique* to modernity.

In free Narnia, a hedgehog could live his entire life in complete freedom. Because he owed allegiance to the king, if an invader came, the king had the authority to call upon the hedgehog and all the other Talking Beasts to come and fight under the king's banner. And after the war, the creatures would all return to their homes and the freedom of their personal lives. A creature might be called upon to die for the king. But no one was ever required to live for the king, because living for the king—paying taxes to keep him in opulence, being constantly fearful about his anger—has a name, and that name is slavery.

—*Douglas Wilson*

## For Further Reading

Ford, Paul F. *Companion to Narnia*. New York, N.Y.: HarperCollins, 1980.

# SESSION I: PRELUDE

## A Question to Consider

To what are you loyal?

*From the General Information above answer the following questions:*

1. What does loyalty mean?
2. In the Narnian government, do we see people giving their loyalty to ideas/abstractions or to persons?
3. What were the two requirements for rulers in Narnia?
4. Who ruled over Narnia during the three different dynasties?
5. What is the parallel between the Narnian dynasties and those of English history?
6. How do Trufflehunter and Trumpkin exemplify the right kind of loyalty given to a ruler?
7. How does Nikabrik's loyalty differ from Trufflehunter's and Trumpkin's loyalty?
8. What is the problem with individualism?
9. Is the authority of Narnian rulers absolute? Why or why not?
10. Are Narnian creatures expected to live for their king?

## Optional Activity 1

If you made a map of Narnia for *The Lion, the Witch and the Wardrobe*, add the appropriate elements and countries as you read through *Prince Caspian.*

## Optional Activity 2

If you have already read *Prince Caspian,* use the *Companion to Narnia* as a resource and read through the following entries.

TELMAR
MIRAZ
CASPIAN X
NURSE
DOCTOR CORNELIUS
TRUFFLEHUNTER
TRUMPKIN
NIKABRIK
GLENSTORM

READING ASSIGNMENT:
Chapters 1–4

# SESSION II: DISCUSSION
Chapters 1–4

## A Question to Consider

We all have favorite stories from when we were young. Some of the stories are ones we read ourselves, others were read to us, perhaps by a parent. We probably read our favorite stories (or asked to have them read) over and over again. We might even read them today and still remember many of the little details. What are some of your favorite stories? What do you love about them? What do your favorite stories have in common?

*Discuss or list short answers to the following questions:*

### Text Analysis

1. Have the stories that the Pevensie children heard had any effect on them? (Examples from *The Lion the Witch and the Wardrobe* will also prove helpful.)
2. What seems to affect Susan so far in *Prince Caspian?* Is it "story" or something else?
3. Prince Caspian is tremendously affected by "story." What kinds of stories is he told and by whom?
4. How do other Telmarines respond to the old stories? Does their reaction have any effect on Caspian?
5. Prince Caspian has heard the same stories as other Telmarines—why is his reaction different?

### Cultural Analysis

1. Our culture seems to be divided into two camps with regard to "story." One camp says, "Believe what you want, as long as you recognize that it is only an inspirational story for you and may not be

In *Prince Caspian* Susan discovers an ancient chesspiece made of gold with tiny rubies set in the horse's head (only one had been knocked out). The drawing of the knight piece shown here is based on a chesspiece from the Isle of Lewis Chess Set. This famous set was found in 1831 on a beach near Ardroil in Uig, Lewis, by a farmer in pursuit of a cow. The seventy-eight chessmen carved from walrus ivory were discovered in a small stone-built chamber. Believed to be carved between A.D. 1150–1170—and possibly Norse in origin—they are the most complete collection of ancient chessmen in existence today.

applicable at all to anyone else." This camp will encourage you to read "story" from many different cultures to draw whatever you want to from them and learn in the process that there is no universal truth. The other camp says that we should not be encouraged to read fantasy stories that encourage us to believe in anything that is beyond the concrete "truth" of science or any story that may encourage a behavior that is no longer fashionable. What is society's current response to the stories of Creation, the Flood, the Virgin Birth and the Resurrection?

2. What is society's current response to stories such as "Sleeping Beauty" and even the *Little House* books?

## Biblical Analysis

1. The Lord could have recorded the history of the world as a boring history lesson using a list of events, dates and thou shall and shall not laws, but obviously He did not, and the history of this world from Creation through Revelation is presented in story. The Lord created us in such a way that we orient our beliefs within a story, *His* story. Jesus himself does most of his teaching with parables. Read Luke 8:5–8. What are some of the points that Jesus is teaching?

2. In this parable, how does the story format make His instruction more powerful?

3. Will truth presented in story always be understood? Why or why not? (Cross-reference with Isaiah 6:9–10.)

## SUMMA

*Write an essay or discuss this question, integrating what you have learned from the material above.*

Is the reading of stories important?

## Optional Activity 1

Prince Caspian and Doctor Cornelius spend many an hour on the great central tower looking at the stars. Miles away, the centaur Glenstorm looks at the same stars and reads there of forthcoming events. Spend some time star-gazing yourself. This can be done through a trip to a local planetarium. You can also do some stargazing from your own neighborhood, with or without a telescope.[2]

## Optional Activity 2

As there are names for different historical periods, there are also names for different musical periods as well. During the Romantic and Impressionistic Periods, there was a new style of composition called the "tone poem." This is a piece of music which does not follow structural rules, but rather tells a story. Some of the more famous tone poems are *Night on Bald Mountain* by Moussorgsky, *Die Moldau* by Smetana, and *Till Eulenspiegel* by Strauss. (These pieces should all be available at your local library.)

Listen to one (or all) of these pieces and hear the stories they tell.

READING ASSIGNMENT:

Chapters 5–7

"Apples, heigh-ho," said Trumpkin with a rueful grin. "I must say you ancient kings and queens don't overfeed your courtiers!" The Red Dwarf quickly becomes a "dear little friend" to the Pevensie children. He is brave and loyal, but not a believer in Aslan—even after meeting the High King drawn back out of the far past.

# SESSION III: RECITATION
Chapters 4–7

## Comprehension Questions

*Answer the following questions for factual recall:*

1. Why have Telmarines come to fear the sea?
2. Prince Caspian has been raised on the stories of Old Narnia. Does he also share the Telmarines' fear of the woods?
3. When Prince Caspian observes the country of Narnia, does he see a happy country?
4. Doctor Cornelius had taught Prince Caspian a great deal of history. Yet Doctor Cornelius appears to despair that his teaching has not had any effect on Prince Caspian. Why?
5. What is the relationship supposed to be between men and beasts in Narnia?
6. Of the four in the cave (Caspian, Trufflehunter, Nikabrik and Trumpkin), who believes in the old stories?
7. One of the five Black Dwarfs suggests going further up to the crags to introduce more creatures to Caspian. Who is it they suggest Caspian meet?
8. How do Caspian, Trufflehunter, Trumpkin and Nikabrik respond to this suggested meeting?
9. How does Glenstorm know that Caspian is going to visit him?
10. What does Glenstorm know that Caspian has not yet realized?
11. Trufflehunter wishes they could get another group of Narnians on their side, and at the suggestion Trumpkin, accuses him of having a great imagination. What is this group? Does Trumpkin resemble today's scientists?
12. Why does Glenstorm need to remind Nikabrik to "Do as you are told?"
13. As full Dwarfs, how do Nikabrik's and Trumpkin's responses to Doctor Cornelius differ?
14. How does Trumpkin show his true loyalty to Caspian?
15. Are the countries of Archenland and Calormene still in existence after the passage of over a thousand years? How do we know?

READING ASSIGNMENT:
Chapters 8–9

# SESSION IV: ACTIVITY
Chapters 8–9

## Essay

*In* The Chronicles of Narnia *books read to date, you have read of many kings and queens in the lands of Narnia, some good, some bad. Write an essay on two good rulers, the Pevensie children and Caspian the Tenth, and two evil rulers, the White Witch and Miraz, to answer the following question:*

What are the main differences between these two groups of rulers?

## Optional Activity

*Continue the writing assignment and consider other rulers and the subjects who served them:*

**THE RULERS**
King Frank and Queen Helen
King Lune
The Tisroc and Rabadash

**THE FOLLOWERS**
The Loyal Followers of the Good Rulers
The "Loyal" Followers of the Evil Rulers

READING ASSIGNMENT:
Chapters 10–12

# SESSION V: RECITATION
Chapters 10–12

## Comprehension Questions

*Answer the following questions for factual recall:*

1. Who does Lucy initially think is waking her in the forest?
2. How does Lucy react when she finally sees Aslan?
3. Has Aslan actually grown?
4. How does Aslan handle Lucy's complaints?
5. Does Lucy discover what would have happened if she had followed him?
6. Aslan extends a second chance to Lucy to follow him. Is it easier for her to follow him now?
7. How do the others react when Lucy tells them yet again (but this time in the dead of night) that Aslan wants them to follow him—even though

they cannot see him?

8. How does Lucy handle Susan's disbelief and anger?

9. How does Susan eventually apologize to Lucy?

10. How do the others greet Aslan once they can all see him?

11. How do the badgers greet Peter and Edmund at Aslan's How?

12. What grudge does Nikabrik bear with regard to the blowing of the horn?

13. How does Nikabrik view the oath he made to support Caspian as King of Narnia?

14. Ultimately, who does Nikabrik want to help them?

 READING ASSIGNMENT:
Chapters 13–15

# SESSION VI: DISCUSSION
Chapters 13–15

## A Question to Consider

You are going to plan the ultimate birthday celebration for your best friend. What will it be like?

*Discuss or list short answers to the following questions:*

### Text Analysis

1. In this last section of the book, Lewis includes some unusual figures in the revels. Who are they? Why might some consider their placement in the world of Narnia "strange?"

2. Do these characters do whatever they want during the revels?

3. Lewis once wrote, "Sometimes I can almost think that I was sent back to the false gods there to acquire some capacity for worship against the day when the true God should recall me to Himself."[3] Do you

In Roman mythology Bacchus—as depicted by Caravaggio in this late sixteenth century oil painting—was the son of Jupiter and Semele. As an infant Bacchus was placed in the care of nymphs, who, for their care, were rewarded by being placed among the stars as the Hyades. When Bacchus grew up, he discovered how to make wine but was struck with madness by Juno and wandered through various parts of the earth. The goddess Rhea eventually cured him, and he set out to teach people how to cultivate the vine. Henry Wadsworth Longfellow in his *Drinking Song* writes of Bacchus:

*Fauns with youthful Bacchus follow;*
*Ivy crowns that brow, supernal*
*As the forehead of Apollo,*
*And possessing youth eternal.*

*Round about him fair Bacchantes,*
*Bearing cymbals, flutes and thyrses,*
*Wild from Naxian groves or Zante's*
*Vineyards, sing delirious verses.*

think this quote gives any clue as to why Lewis may have used these pagan gods in his story?

4. Is this a celebration that the creatures initiate themselves, or something they are invited to?

5. In what ways do they celebrate? Do we know what they are celebrating?

6. There seems to be a clear choice put before men and creatures—join the celebration or run away from it. What types join and what types run away? (Earlier in the book there was someone who refused to join a celebration—do you remember who?)

### Cultural Analysis

1. Too often in our culture, people do not see the gifts of God and the freedom of God, much less understand that this is why we celebrate anything. What are the usual reasons people have celebrations now?

2. Does our culture produce celebrations that we should value?

3. Do the celebrations of Christians in our culture generally show the joy and wonder of the blessings of a life of covenant faithfulness and the joy of living under the rule of Christ?

### Biblical Analysis

1. In 2 Samuel 6:12b–19 there is a celebration going on. What is the cause of this celebration?

2. What role does Christ have at the wedding feast at Cana? (John 2:1–10)

3. In Luke 7:33–35, Jesus reminds us of insults with which He and John the Baptist have been castigated. Why was Christ called a "glutton and a winebibber (drunk)"?

4. Are there any similarities between the celebration of David and the wedding feast at Cana and the one we have looked at in *Prince Caspian*?

5. Does everyone join into these celebrations? Do we?

### Application

Lewis knows that celebration is an important activity for humans. Celebration is part of every culture and every religion. However, celebrating can be a dangerous activity because of its wild abandon, if it is not a response to God's goodness and is not under His Lordship. Jesus celebrated at weddings, at the biblically mandated feasts and in non-biblically mandated holidays like the Festival of Lights or Hanukkah.[6] Celebration should be an important aspect of our lives. With your parents, consider the passages mentioned in this session and carefully plan out an upcoming holiday celebration. This might mean a special meal with special drink, inviting friends and special activities like dancing or singing. Let your goal be to have a celebration that reflects the goodness and joy that you have in Christ.

### SUMMA

*Write an essay or discuss this question, integrating what you have learned from the material above.*

What are the best celebrations, and what should they be like?

## Optional Session A

Prince Caspian was trained in all the arts as a young knight and future king. One of these arts was, of course, sword fighting. In *Prince Caspian* we see two important sword fights, one in which King Edmund takes part, the other, King Peter. Acting out sword fights can be a fun way of re-telling part of the story.

To act out a sword fight, of course, one needs swords. The inexpensive plastic or metal kind will be useless if you have any intent of actually having the swords hit one another, since they will break easily. A better alternative is to make a simple sword from wood.

Your scripted fight will take place between High King Peter and King Miraz. It is a combination of offensive and defensive moves. See the charts on the next two pages for instructions for this battle. Please remember to practice these moves carefully and slowly before you speed up your routine to try to make it look realistic. Sword fighting is like a dance; start slowly and learn your moves until you do not have to think so hard about them, and then very gradually speed them up. You may want to have them add in some ducking, rolling and other moves as well.

# Sword Fighting: *Offensive and Defensive Moves*

## BASIC OFFENSIVE MOVES (OM)

1. To attack with the basic vertical cut, raise the sword above your head and strike downward onto your opponent's head.

2. Swing your sword parallel to the ground from right to left, making a horizontal cut aimed at the opponent's left shoulder.

3. Swing your sword parallel to the ground from left to right, making a horizontal cut aimed at the opponent's right shoulder.

4. Swing with a downward cut to your opponent's left leg, guiding your sword at a 45-degree angle.

5. Swing with a downward cut to your opponent's right leg, guiding your sword at a 45-degree angle.

## BASIC DEFENSIVE MOVES (DM)

1. Raise the sword above your head, keeping it parallel to the ground. You may want to point the sword slightly toward the ground so the blow is directed to the side. Be certain the blade of your sword is high enough above your head to keep from being hit.

2. Holding your sword vertically with the point up, move your sword to the left side of your body to fend off the strike.

3. Holding your sword vertically with the point up, move your sword to the right side of your body to fend off the strike.

4. Parry an attack to your left leg by swinging the sword down to your left side at a 45-degree angle. Be sure to point your blade toward the ground.

5. Parry an attack to your right leg by swinging the sword down to your right side at a 45-degree angle. Be sure to point your blade toward the ground.

| KING PETER | KING MIRAZ |
|---|---|
| (OM) 2, 3, 4 and 5 | (DM) 2, 3, 4 and 5 |
|  | (OM) 3 (slow swipe to the side of the head) |
| (DM) Duck under the swipe | (OM) 1 ,1 and 1 |
| (DM) 1, 1 then run to the side of the last strike, with both fighters quickly turning to face each other |  |
| (OM) Charge in, 2 and spin | (DM) 2 |
|  | (OM) 5 cut while Peter spins then fake kick to the back of Peter's knees. After he falls, make a fake kick to his stomach, rolling him onto his back. |
| (DM) 5 then fall face down, dropping sword. Get up on all fours. When Miraz kicks your stomach, roll onto your back. Reach for your sword while still on your back. |  |
|  | (OM) 1 to the ground where Peter is reaching. |
| (OM) Reach sword in time, and while still down deliver a 4 cut | (DM) block 4 |
|  | (OM) deliver 1, 1 to Peter, who is still down |
| (DM) Block the first 1, roll out of the way of the second 1 and get onto your feet. |  |
| (OM) Attack with 2, 2 and 3 | (DM) Block 2, 2, 3 |
|  | (OM) Attack with a 1 |
| (DM) Defend with a 1 |  |
| (OM) Lunge forward with 1, 2, 3, 4 and 5 | (DM) Defend 1, 2, 3, 4 and 5 |
| (OM) Continue attack with 3, 4, 5 and 1 | (DM) Block 3, 4, 5 and 1 |
| (OM) From the last 1 spin into a 3, wounding Miraz, who falls onto the ground, senseless | (DM) Get your sword into positionjust too late to fend off Peter's 3 so it looks like he hits you on the side of the chest, wounding you severely |

## ENDNOTES

1   "Let All Mortal Flesh Keep Silence," from the Liturgy of St. James. Arranged by Gerard Moultrie, 1864; tune Picardy arranged by Ralph Vaughan Williams, 1906. This song can be found in many hymnals or, at the time of the publication of this material, on the Internet at http://www.cyberhymnal.org/htm/l/e/letallmf.htm.

2   At the time of publication the site http://www.SkyAnd Telescope.com is available as an excellent resource. Go to their link for "Sky Charts," and you can get a customized sky chart based on your zip code, or city and country. It will show you the whole night sky based on the location, date and time you enter.

3   Lewis, C.S. *Surprised by Joy.* New York: Harvest, 1955. 77.

4   *This endnote appears only in the teacher's edition.*

5   *This endnote appears only in the teacher's edition.*

6   Carson, D.A. *The Gospel According to John.* Grand Rapids, Mich.: Eerdmans, 1991. 391.

# THE VOYAGE OF THE DAWN TREADER

Today journeys often seem safe. From wherever you read these words, you could be on the other side of the world tomorrow if you had the money to purchase the airfare. Odds are, you would arrive safely. Even more amazing, you could be back the day after tomorrow. In the ancient world, travel was more frightening and full of adventure. Today, trips can be enjoyable and exciting, but they almost never have the sense of exploration that the treks of Odysseus or Aeneas did. We risk so much less in our travel. Not long ago, however, travel, especially by sea, was treacherous. One hymn says it this way:

> Eternal Father, strong to save,
> Whose arm hath bound the restless wave,
> Who biddest the mighty ocean deep
> Its own appointed limits keep;
> Oh, hear us when we cry to Thee,
> For those in peril on the sea!

This great hymn is the U.S. Navy Hymn and reportedly was sung during the last worship service held on the HMS Titanic.

While journeys are quite different today than they have been in the past, one aspect remains the same. All voyages have a destination. Most times the destination is known. Odysseus wanted to reach Ithaka. Christ set His face like flint to journey to Jerusalem and the cross. You go to your grandma's house on Thanksgiving or Christmas. Some have no certain geographic destination, but they do have a goal, like the quest for the Holy Grail. When we travel, we do so with an objective.

In many ways the Christian life is like a journey. God's word even calls us strangers and sojourners in this world. For God's people, even those living under David's righteous rule and in Medieval Christendom, we are never quite at home in this world. We are always longing for something more. While this world and God's blessings in it are not to be made light of or disparaged, we long for God's presence and to live with him in the New Jerusalem where we will see Christ face to face.

Christian literature has always proclaimed this longing. Hebrews tells us that Abraham was longing for this eternal city. Paul tells us that we are all citizens of the Free Jerusalem that will come down from heaven. Augustine speaks of the City of God. Dante ventures into Paradise. Bunyan's quest was for the Celestial City. Here, in *The Voyage of the Dawn Treader*, Lewis teaches us about this longing and about the adventure that lies before every believer as we set our sights "further up and further in."

## GENERAL INFORMATION

### Significance

*The Magician's Nephew* is about Creation and the Fall. *The Lion, the Witch and the Wardrobe* is about Substitutionary Atonement. *The Horse and His Boy* is about Providence. *Prince Caspian* is about Personal Government.

*The Voyage of the Dawn Treader* is about Regeneration. In this book we meet one of the most developed characters in the *Narnia* stories, that of Eustace Clarence Scrubb. He is introduced to us as a pro-foundly self-centered individual. How he was transformed into a very different kind of boy is a significant part of this story. An additional theme is the destiny of all those who love and serve Aslan (those who are regenerated as Eustace was), and this is shown to us in the life and translation of Reepicheep.

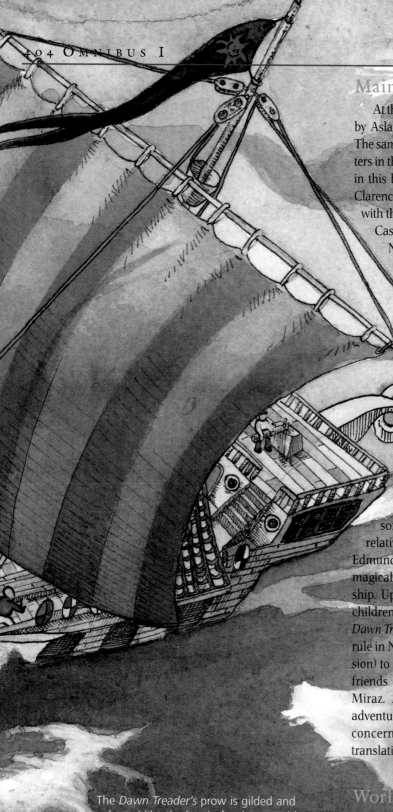

## Main Characters

At the end of *Prince Caspian*, Peter and Susan are told by Aslan that they will not be coming back to Narnia. The same, however, is not said of two of the main characters in this book, Edmund and Lucy, and they come back in this book for their last visit. Their cousin is Eustace Clarence Scrubb, and he is dragged along into Narnia with them. In Narnian time, it is about three years after Caspian has defeated Miraz and become king of all Narnia. Reepicheep is one of C.S. Lewis's most memorable creations, and in this book his nobility really shines forth. Drinian is captain of the *Dawn Treader* and is an important secondary character. Aslan does not occupy a large portion of this book, but again, his presence is assumed and important everywhere.

## Summary and Setting

Peter is studying for an important exam with Digory Kirke. Susan has gone to America with her parents. And so this means that Edmund and Lucy must spend some time in Cambridge with the Scrubbs, relatives who are equally progressive and tiresome. Edmund, Lucy and Eustace (their cousin) are drawn magically into Narnia through a painting of a Narnian ship. Upon being rescued from the ocean, the three children discover that they are on a Narnian ship, the *Dawn Treader*, and Caspian, who has consolidated his rule in Narnia, has taken an oath (with Aslan's permission) to sail to the far east to try to find seven nobles, friends of his father, who had been sent away by Miraz. As they travel east, they meet with many adventures, but the two most important adventures concern the transformation of Eustace and the translation of Reepicheep into Aslan's country.

The *Dawn Treader's* prow is gilded and shaped like the head of a dragon with a wide open mouth. She has only one mast and one large, square sail, which is a rich purple. Where the golden dragon wings end, the ship is green, and springing from the stern is a carved dragon's tail. She has a long hatch fore of the mast and one aft, with benches below for rowing.

## Worldview

The structure of this book is the time-honored and simple one of a journey, with adventures along the way. Three English children are pulled into Narnia and find themselves on a Narnian ship after that ship is already underway on a voyage to the eastern end of that world. As they travel with the ship's crew, they encounter a number of amazing sights and challenging obstacles. But the center of the book concerns the transformation of Eustace. Eustace Clarence Scrubb (a name he *almost* deserved) is an insufferable little boy. He is about nine years old when this adventure happens to him, and it is hard to believe that a boy that age can be quite as intolerable as he is. But he is able to do this through the help of his parents, who were quite as insufferable as he, and through his description of Eustace's parents, Lewis makes clear his distaste for progressive, health-faddist moderns who love everything new-fangled, rational and artificial but despise anything that is organic and came about before the creation of automobiles. He could not abide such people. We can only imagine what his reaction would be to the version of these people that we have around today.

One of their many failings was that they provided Eustace with a very sorry, modern form of education. We have seen in previous *Narnia* stories how training in the right kind of story equipped children to face the adventures that came to them in Narnia. And although Eustace is what modern educators would call a good student, he was trained to read all the wrong kinds of books. They had pictures in them of grain elevators, and fat foreign children doing exercises in model schools (a clear allusion to communist propaganda). These books addressed imports, exports and drains, but they were weak on dragons, and this is why Eustace comes into Narnia in a high state of ill-preparedness. This setting is the reverse of Mark Twain's *Connecticut Yankee,* where a modern makes his way back to medieval times, the better to show off his superiority to the poor dummies who lived back then. But Lewis reverses this point. The modern who finds himself inhabiting a medieval world is clearly the inferior.

Not only was Eustace's education poor, but because it was grounded on silly, secularist principles that contend that the world works fine without God being involved, Eustace's natural selfishness was reinforced. In his education there was no gospel to address the problem of sin. The end result is that Eustace Clarence Scrubb is a real piece of work.

And Lewis draws this out in loving detail. In part he does this by means of including excerpts from Eustace's journal, which is a striking change of voice for these books. It is the only use of an extended first-person singular voice anywhere in the *Chronicles,* and the effect is quite vivid. We have a direct glimpse into Eustace's mind, and what a bent and self-important mind it is, too! But this also enables us to get to know Eustace in more detail than the other characters. In many ways, Eustace is the best-developed character (Aslan excepted) in all the Narnian stories, and this makes his transformation even more vivid and interesting.

The *Dawn Treader* is buffeted by a heavy storm, and the afflictions that this storm brings about only reinforce Eustace's selfishness. When they finally make it through the storm, they have to find land where they may work on refurbishing the ship. When they get there, Eustace, in his typical self-centered way, slips off somewhere in order to avoid some work. He gets lost and stumbles his way into a dragon's valley. Shortly after his arrival there, he notices the dragon and freezes in place, hoping that he will not be seen. But the dragon is an ancient one, decrepit, and it is crawling out of its cave in order to drink from a pond, and when it finally gets there, it dies. Eustace finally reassures himself that the dragon is dead, and then, because of a sudden rainstorm, he takes refuge in the dragon's cave. There he finds the dragon's treasure and foolishly puts a bracelet on his arm. If he had been prepared by the right kind of stories, he would not have done so, but we have already seen that Eustace is weak on dragons.

When he awakens, he slowly discovers, to his great horror, that he has turned into a dragon. He makes his way back to the crew of the *Dawn Treader,* and begins to realize that he (in his true, dragonish nature) is a genuine burden to the others and that he is a real outsider. When Eustace had been a boy, he had *looked* like the others, but had been an outsider in fact. Now, as a dragon, he looks nothing like them, but is longing to be rejoined to them. But this longing cannot accomplish that desire. Eustace is now *objectively* outside. As the others cannot really figure out a way to "undragon" him, he begins to realize what a hopeless position both he and they are in. He cannot really come with them, and they cannot really leave him. Eustace begins to realize (for the first time in his life) what a selfish boy he has been.

It is very important to emphasize that both Eustace and the crew of the *Dawn Treader* cannot accomplish what absolutely needs to be accomplished. Eustace represents the sinner who needs to be converted, the one who needs to be undragoned. The crew of the *Dawn Treader* represent the "church," the group of people into which a conversion would place Eustace. But neither is capable of accomplishing the great miracle of undragoning the poor boy.

When Eustace shows up as a boy again, he meets with Edmund first, and tells him the story in detail. This enables Lewis, just as he did with the earlier journal entries, to tell this part of the story in the first-person singular again (using "I" instead of the usual third person "he, she, they"), and again in Eustace's voice. And what Eustace describes is a glorious picture of the absolute hopelessness of "self-conversion" and the absolute necessity of having Aslan do it all.

According to Aslan, Eustace has to bathe himself in a fountain—which is a clear picture of baptism. But this "baptism" is not something he can manipulate to his own ends because Aslan tells him he must get "undressed" before he bathes. Eustace figures out that this must mean that he has to shed his dragon skin in order to come to the water. This shedding of the dragon skin is representative of repentance—repent and be baptized. And so Eustace scrapes himself free of his skin, starts to go to the water and realizes that he is just as scaly, knobby and dragonish as ever. His self-efforts at repentance do not "get to the root of the matter." His repentance, in other words, is superficial. It is well-intentioned (as far as that sort of thing goes), but it is utterly inadequate. So Eustace tries again, with the same ineffectual results. Lewis is making it abundantly plain

that men cannot convert themselves, and they cannot prepare themselves (by themselves) for conversion.

All autonomous efforts at repentance, conversion and faith, done only with our own human strength, will necessarily be failures. In his insistence on this point, Lewis stands in the great orthodox tradition that denies that regeneration is a cooperative affair between God and man. There is a subtle distinction here that many miss, but it is plain enough when it comes to us in the form of a story. Of course, Eustace "does things" in this account. He is told to come to the water, he is told to shed the dragon skin, which he tries to do, and he is told to let Aslan do it, which he rolls over and does. But in all this, Eustace *contributes nothing* to the essential repentance, which is the taking away of the dragon skin and the dragon nature. Lewis is pointing to the *monergistic* nature of regeneration, which means that God is the only one who does the work. Being born again is not a cooperative effort between God and man (the word for that would be *synergistic*) but is entirely the work of God alone.

The other great theme of this book is the noble desire for heaven. Eschatology is the study of the "last things," but it can refer to two different kinds of last things. One is the sort of thing we will see in *The Last Battle,* where we are talking about the end of history, and which we will discuss there. The other is what might be called personal and individual eschatology, issues of heaven or hell—or, in Narnian terms, the individual going to Aslan's country. To illustrate this, Lewis shows that Reepicheep has lived his entire life with a desire weighing heavily upon him—the desire to sail to the utter east and make his way somehow to Aslan's country.

The reader has to recall that Narnia is a flat world, not a

The Narnian flag is a rampant lion on a green field.

globe like ours. Surrounding the world of this flat disk is a ring of enormous mountains, and these mountains are not part of that world—they are outside that world entirely, and are Aslan's country. When Reepicheep was born, a prophecy was spoken over him, clearly indicating that he would sail to the easternmost part of that world and somehow make his way to Aslan's country. In this, he is like Enoch or Elijah in our world—men who were translated into the presence of God without going through the normal process of dying. In our next book, *The Silver Chair*, we will see that when someone who loves Aslan dies, he is taken to Aslan's country and is there restored to everlasting life. But Reepicheep, a mouse beloved of Aslan, makes his way there directly.

Reepicheep is the soul of honor, courage, and glory. He is the epitome of the cavalier warrior, and though Aslan at one point wonders if he and the other mice do not make a bit too much of honor, their love still conquers him. In *Prince Caspian,* Reepicheep is sorely wounded in battle, and although Lucy's cordial heals him, it does not restore his tail that has been cut off in the battle. When Aslan is deciding whether to restore his tail, all the other mice take out their swords to cut off their own tails if the request is denied. This love for Reepicheep mirrors the love the mice have for Aslan back at the beginning, when they chew the cords loose that bind Aslan to the Stone Table in *The Lion, the Witch and the Wardrobe*. It is then that they first become Talking Mice, a response of Aslan to their love. This love continues throughout the books, and it becomes clear in this book that the love of honor was a product of love, not vanity. Reepicheep uses his sword as a means to an end, and when he finally puts out toward the final east in his coracle, he throws his sword away, knowing that he will not have any further need of it. He used the sword to defend honor and not honor to defend his sword.

It is indicated in our book that Reepicheep probably made it safely to Aslan's country. In the *The Last Battle* he is shown to us there, and he is the last one in that book to issue the glorious welcome, "Further up, and further in."

One other section of this book is worth commenting on. When the adventurers of the *Dawn Treader* come to the island of the Dufflepuds, they are at first alarmed because the Dufflepuds are invisible, and it is easy to imagine them being a lot more ferocious than they actually turn out to be. But, as events would have it, they are all quite harmless and more than a little stupid. They are ruled with a kindly but firm hand in the person of Coriakin, a star who had erred in some fashion and was given the rule of these very thick creatures as a form of discipline. He longs for the day when he will be able to rule them through wisdom, instead of through the rough handling he must give them (a handling that was the only thing their stupidity could understand).

But the Dufflepuds exhibit a peculiar kind of folly. They are not simple, understanding themselves to be simple. Rather, they think they are wise. Their Chief is one they look up to (heartily), and they are in the grip of an adversarial relationship with Coriakin. When he tries to get them to change something (for their own good), they stubbornly insist on doing what seems wise to them. They plant boiled potatoes to save the cooking later. They wash dishes before dinner to save time later. In all this, Lewis intends for us to see a small model of humanity. The Dufflepuds are mankind, and Lewis looked forward to the time when we will be governed by wisdom instead of rough justice.

But until we learn the lessons contained in this book, not to mention the others, we will continue to see the public affairs of our culture governed by men who think that water is certainly "powerful wet."

—*Douglas Wilson*

## For Further Reading

Ford, Paul F. *Companion to Narnia*. New York, N.Y.: HarperCollins, 1980.

# Session I: Prelude

## A Question to Consider

Have you ever been at the seaside to watch a sunrise or a sunset over the water? (If you have never had the pleasure of seeing one in person, imagine a painting or a photograph of such a scene.) How did you feel when you looked at that site?

*Discuss or list short answers to the following questions:*

In *Prince Caspian*, we explored the importance of "story." However, we did not touch specifically upon the fantastic element of story, what some would call "faerie." Why is it so important to have dryads, naiads, river gods and all these other elements in a story which are not "real?" After all, a dragon might be excused as just a rather fantastic dinosaur, but not a river-god. Nevertheless, Lewis has stated that when we threw out the dryads, we threw out ourselves. What did he mean by this? Let's see.[1]

1. When Lewis looked around his world, he saw a world packed with will, intelligence, life and other positive qualities. After he became a Christian, he knew that what he had perceived before was the image of God in nature, "For his invisible attributes, namely, his eternal power and divine nature, have been clearly perceived, ever since the creation of the world, in the things that have been made. So they are without excuse" (Romans 1:20). This will, this intelligent life, is represented by mythic creatures—a dryad is not a tree, but rather a representation of what we know about trees. In the Narnia books you have read so far, how have you seen Lewis represent nature?

2. With the advance of scientific thought and the Age of Reason, a dryad was now said to be something of our own imagination, rather than something that belonged with the tree. A dryad was our own subjective thought, our own emotions projected onto that tree. The tree itself was nothing more than wood, leaves, moisture, etc. How have you seen this idea spread in our culture?

3. Eventually, men took the final leap. If a dryad was just a projection of our own emotions onto a tree, then the idea of a soul for our own selves is just as much a matter of projected emotions and wishful thinking. Have you ever met anyone who thought that they were no different from a tree?

Therefore, for Lewis, myth (especially the romantic view of nature) leads to an acceptance of the supernatural and a healthy speculation and wonder as to how that supernatural may express itself in other realities.

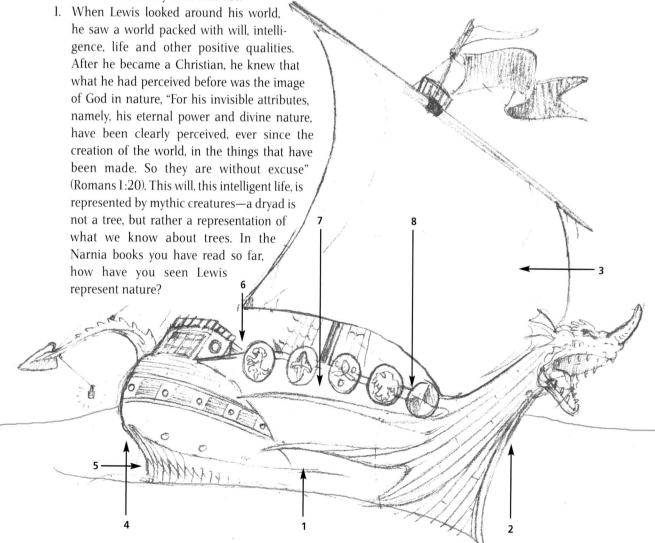

*Read the following poem and answer the questions below.*

## THE WORLD IS TOO MUCH WITH US
by William Wordsworth[2]

> The world is too much with us; late and soon,
> Getting and spending, we lay waste our powers;
> Little we see in Nature that is ours;
> We have given our hearts away, a sordid boon!
> This Sea that bares her bosom to the moon,
> The winds that will be howling at all hours,
> And are up-gathered now like sleeping flowers,
> For this, for everything, we are out of tune;
> It moves us not.—Great God! I'd rather be
> A Pagan suckled in a creed outworn;
> So might I, standing on this pleasant lea,
> Have glimpses that would make me less forlorn;
> Have sight of Proteus rising from the sea;
> Or hear old Triton blow his wreathed horn.

4. Does Wordsworth think that people wonder and delight in Nature?
5. What do you think Wordsworth means when he writes, "We are out of tune?"
6. If being a "Pagan suckled in a creed outworn" is one choice—what is the other choice?

As you read through *Voyage of the Dawn Treader* you will notice that Eustace represents men who see nothing in life but fact, practicality and a utilitarian use for things. The Narnians, of course, do not see life this way at all. The contrast between these two life views is stark. Also take note of all the many ways Nature is brought to life to have a wonder and majesty all its own, not one given to it by the imagination of a man.

## Optional Activity 1

As you know, this is a book where much of the action takes place on board a sailing vessel. If you are not familiar with the terminology, you could miss out on some of the nuances of the action. Look up the following terms and label the ship diagram on the previous page.

STERN
BOW
PORT
STARBOARD
HULL
RUDDER
TILLER
MAINSAIL

## Optional Activity 2

If you have previously read *The Voyage of the Dawn Treader,* use the *Companion to Narnia* as a resource and read through the following entries.

CASPIAN X
DRINIAN
REEPICHEEP
EUSTACE CLARENCE SCRUBB
LONE ISLANDS
CORIAKIN
RAMANDU
*DAWN TREADER*

## Optional Activity 3

If you made a map of Narnia for *The Lion, the Witch and the Wardrobe,* it will do you absolutely no good for this book. The Narnians themselves have no maps to guide them, since they are voyaging into parts unknown. However, in the middle of their journey, they are provided with a map of their travels thus far, a map drawn in amazing detail. Draw your own map of the Eastern seas, and next to each island, draw a scene from an event associated with that island. There are many maps of Narnia available as a basis for a drawing. Many publishers include a map of Narnia on the inside front or back covers of the book. In addition, the *Companion to Narnia* has several maps of Narnia and the surrounding areas. Finally, there are many sites on the internet which post Narnia maps with different styles of art.[3]

 **READING ASSIGNMENT:** Chapters 1–3

# SESSION II: ANALYSIS
Chapters 1–3

## A Question to Consider

What sort of artwork do you like? Why do you like it? As Lucy, Edmund and Eustace look at the painting, they have this discussion:

## LOST IN PRONUNCIATION

Eustace's rhyme: "Some kids who played games about Narnia/Got gradually balmier and balmier" is not a close rhyme in the United States; it sounds much better in England. There, the words *balmier* and *Narnia* rhyme more closely. There also the words *balmier* and *barmier* sound alike, so much so that they are used interchangeably. *Barmy* and *barmier* are real words; they mean "frothy"—from *barm,* which is brewer's yeast formed on ale while it is fermenting. (A British phrase for mentally unbalanced is "barmy in the crumpet.") The British used to say *barmy* to mean "bubble-brained." In the United States *balmy* only means "fair weather."[4]

"Do you like that picture?" [Eustace] asked.

"For heaven's sake don't get him started about Art and all that," said Edmund hurriedly, but Lucy, who was very truthful, had already said, "Yes, I do. I like it very much."

"It's a rotten picture," said Eustace.

"You won't see it if you step outside," said Edmund.

"Why do you like it?" said Eustace to Lucy.

"Well, for one thing," said Lucy, "I like it because the ship looks as if it was really moving. And the water looks as if it was really wet. And the waves look as if they were really going up and down."

Of course Eustace knew lots of answers to this, but he didn't say anything. The reason was that at that very moment he looked at the waves and saw that they did look very much indeed as if they were going up and down. He had only once been in a ship (and then only as far as the Isle of Wight) and had been horribly seasick. The look of the waves in the picture made him feel sick again. He turned rather green and tried another look.

On the following page are two pictures of similar ships; one is *Ships in Distress off a Rocky Coast* that was painted by Ludulf Bakhuizen and the other is by an anonymous illustrator.

There are many questions that can be asked when looking at and comparing pictures such as these. Try some of the following:

1. What makes either of these works good? Is it the believability of the image; do you "buy it?" Is it the use of color and value (shading)? Is it the artist's draftsmanship skills?

2. Which of these two pieces is more accurate in its depiction of a ship? Which of them would Lucy like better? Which one would Eustace prefer? Why?

3. Do either of these pictures elicit an emotional response from the viewer?

4. Is there a story (narrative) being told in either of these pictures? If so, what is happening? Would Eustace prefer the diagram or the story? What about Lucy?

5. Do *you* like either of these pictures?

## Optional Activity

Take a trip to a local art museum. Apply the questions asked of the two paintings you critiqued above to the art work you see there.

READING ASSIGNMENT:
Chapters 4–6

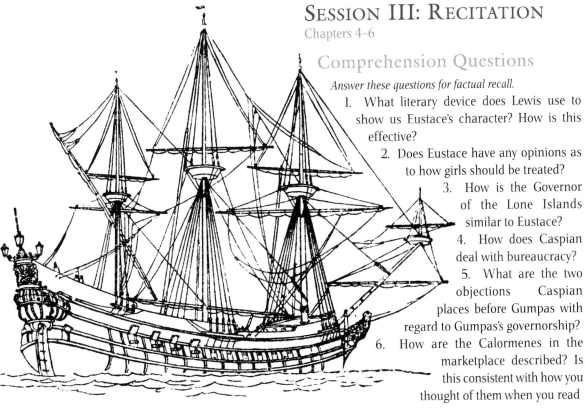

# SESSION III: RECITATION
Chapters 4–6

## Comprehension Questions

*Answer these questions for factual recall.*

1. What literary device does Lewis use to show us Eustace's character? How is this effective?

2. Does Eustace have any opinions as to how girls should be treated?

3. How is the Governor of the Lone Islands similar to Eustace?

4. How does Caspian deal with bureaucracy?

5. What are the two objections Caspian places before Gumpas with regard to Gumpas's governorship?

6. How are the Calormenes in the marketplace described? Is this consistent with how you thought of them when you read

*The Horse and His Boy?*

7. Most of us would be thrilled to not be sold as a slave. Is Eustace relieved that he is not sold?

8. As you read through Eustace's diary entries, what sort of a person does Eustace think he is?

9. Why does Eustace not know what "get two dozen" means? How does this deficiency also gets him into trouble later on?

10. What country does Eustace think he might like to live in?

11. At the moment Eustace realizes that as a dragon he can do anything he wants to the others, what great thing happens?

**READING ASSIGNMENT:**
Chapters 7–9

# SESSION IV: DISCUSSION
Chapters 7–9

## A Question to Consider

What is a habit? How did the habits that you have come about? How do bad habits develop?

*Discuss or list short answers to the following questions:*

### Text Analysis

1. How does Eustace's dragon "outside" resemble his dragon "inside?"

2. Why does Eustace come to regret his "dragon" nature? After all, it has not been troubling him at all for the first part of the voyage or, for that matter, for his whole life up to this point.

3. Before Eustace was a dragon, he looked like other members of the crew of the *Dawn Treader* but did not want to be with them and was, in fact, an outsider. Now that he wants to be with them, can he?

4. Is there any good that comes from Eustace peeling off his dragon skin?

5. Why does Eustace allow Aslan to tear at him with his claw, exposing himself in the most vulnerable of ways?

6. What are the differences between what Eustace is able to do for himself and what Aslan is able to do?

### Cultural Analysis

1. Do you think our culture encourages us to try to change for the better?

2. How does our culture suggest we are to accomplish these changes?

### Biblical Analysis

1. Read John 3:1–21. What do we know about who Nicodemus is?

2. In John 3, what does Nicodemus say he knows about Jesus?

3. Assuming Nicodemus had an earnest desire to be closer to God somehow through Jesus' teachings (after all he did sneak out to see him in the night) why was he having difficulty hearing what Jesus was saying to him?

4. How do we know from this passage (John 3) that there is absolutely nothing we can do to be saved, and that it is faith in the work of Jesus alone that will reconcile us to God?

## SUMMA

 *Write an essay or discuss this question, integrating what you have learned from the material above.*
Can we change ourselves?

**READING ASSIGNMENT:**
Chapters 10–13

# SESSION V: DISCUSSION
Chapters 10–13

## A Question to Consider

What is the difference between a dream and a nightmare?

*Discuss or list short answers to the following questions:*

### Text Analysis

1. Is there any source of light when the *Dawn Treader* sails into the blackness?

2. What sensations do they have as they sail into the darkness?

3. Why are the sailors tempted to go onto the island?

4. Are they in any actual danger?

5. C.S. Lewis wrote that in stories there were two ways that children were frightened. The first was a kind of fright, or phobia, against which ordinary courage was helpless. The second was a kind of fright from the realities of life against which a child should be taught courage. The first had no place in their stories, the second was necessary and helpful.

"Let there be wicked kings and beheadings, battles and dungeons, giants and dragons, and let villains be soundly killed at the end of each book .... It would be nice if no little boy in bed, hearing, or thinking he hears, a sound, were ever at all frightened. But if he is going to be frightened, I think it better that he should think of giants and dragons than merely of burglars. And I think St. George, or any bright champion in armour, is a better comfort than the idea of the police."[5]

How is this quote relevant to the events on the Dark Island?

6. How are these fears felt on Dark Island different from the many other dangerous and fearful episodes the humans have faced?

### *Cultural Analysis*

1. Lewis writes of two different types of fear presented in story. Do you think our culture supports this separation? That is, do you think our culture tries to eliminate presenting a source of fear against which ordinary courage is helpless, while promoting a healthy fear of the realities in life against which courage can prevail?

2. How do many people in our culture deal with their fears?

### *Biblical Analysis*

1. Read Psalm 27. What does David write of in this Psalm that could cause him to fear?

2. What are the different ways David combats his fear?

3. How are Lucy's actions near the Dark Island similar to David's actions?

### *Application*

Help those younger than you to have courage. Find a group of youngsters (at school or church or a younger sibling) and read some good stories to them (with their parents' permission, of course). Any story about St. George and the Dragon would be good for the boys. If you have the right sort of boys, they will really enjoy hearing about the slaying of the dragon and in no time will be making their own armor and searching for dragons behind every bush. For young ladies, a different type of story might be necessary. The *Little House on the Prairie* series can be super examples of young ladies showing courage (especially note the way they are taught to control their emotions—even when faced with hardship they are not to let their emotions overcome them or give in to despair).

### SUMMA

*Write an essay or discuss this question, integrating what you have learned from the material above.*
Is it wrong to be afraid?

READING ASSIGNMENT:
Chapters 14–16

# SESSION VI: RECITATION
Chapters 1–16

## Narnian Quiz Show

This game can be played by any number of players, though the traditional number is 3–4. It can also be played in teams. The object of the game is to correctly answer as many questions as possible. Questions are in five categories with five levels to each category (within each category the questions increase in difficulty as you move down through the five levels).

**RULES FOR THE GAME**

A die shall be rolled by each player/team to determine who will go first.

The player who goes first shall pick a category and

Coriakin had many strange, polished instruments in his home, including an astrolabe, orrery, chronoscope, poesimeter, choriambus and a theodolite.

The Stone Knife is enshrined on Aslan's Table on World's End island, where each morning the sun's first rays sparkle along its cruel edge. Like the cross of Christ, this instrument of death has been transformed into a symbol of grace.

level to be given a question from. The question shall be read, and the first player to "ring in" is given the first opportunity to answer the question. "Ringing in" can be done by raising a hand or ringing a bell.

If the question is answered correctly, the player chooses the next question.

If the question is not answered correctly, the other players may ring in for a chance to answer.

This process continues until all questions have been selected.

The player to accumulate the most points at the end is the winner.

The questions and answers are listed in the teacher's edition. Here are the categories:

**LORDS & LADIES**
**TIME & TRADEWINDS**
**MYTH & MAGIC**
**SITES & STORY**
**NAME & NUISANCE**

# OPTIONAL SESSION A

Time to go sailing! There are many different ways to get a feel for what it is like to be out on the open water.

Arrange for some sailing lessons. This may be able to be done through a local boating or yacht club, or a public marina.

Go on a sailing trip. This can be as simple as a trip out onto the water and back, to a several day sailing trip out onto the open waters of an ocean.

In the area where you live, you may have access to one of the "tall ships." Go for a tour, or better yet, get a trip out on one of them. Several of the tall ships will do two- or three-day voyages.

If you cannot sail in a boat, just sail a boat. Make your own model boats with materials you find around the house and have sailing competitions.

## ENDNOTES

1    These ideas are laid out in Lewis's introduction to D.E. Harding's *The Hierarchy of Heaven and Earth.* New York: Harper, 1952.
2    If you enjoyed this poem, you may want to take some time to read additional works by William Wordsworth or Percy Shelley.
3    *This endnote appears only in the teacher's edition.*
4    This information taken from Kathryn Lindskoog's *Journey into Narnia.* Pasadena: Hope Publishing, 1998.
5    Lewis, C.S. *On Stories and Other Essays on Literature.* New York: Harvest, 1982. 39–40.

# ISAIAH

*Look to me, and be saved, all you ends of the earth: for I am God, and there is no other. —Isaiah 45:22*

There was once a baseball team called the Knickerbockers. The team had about fifteen players in all and a wise, experienced coach who instructed the boys how to play well and hard, so well in fact, that they were in first place half way through the season. Unfortunately, though the coach taught them how to play fair and compete like men, the captain was a boy who always looked for a way to twist the rules or finagle a call. He was often mischievous, and this is how he was chosen to be captain in the first place. He spread rumors about other players who would have been chosen by the team and set friends against friends so that just the few votes of the more cowardly boys would elect him.

Like any team, some players were better than others, but overall, when the Knickerbockers came out to play hard and fair they won. But tragically, and despite the coaches repeated warnings, the influence of the team captain ultimately prevailed, and few of the Knickerbockers resisted whining at the umpire's calls, bad-mouthing the other team and generally playing sloppy ball. For a time the team could play like this and still win, but soon the attitude and antics took their toll and many losses followed.

One of the players who respected the coach confronted the captain. "You have taught us all to whine and play dirty," he said, "and now we play like sissies and can't win a game." Of course, the captain denied the accusations and blamed their losing streak on the umpires, other boys on the team and even the coach. He told the boys they needed to figure out new strategies to work around the rules, and he said that anyone opposed to the idea didn't love the

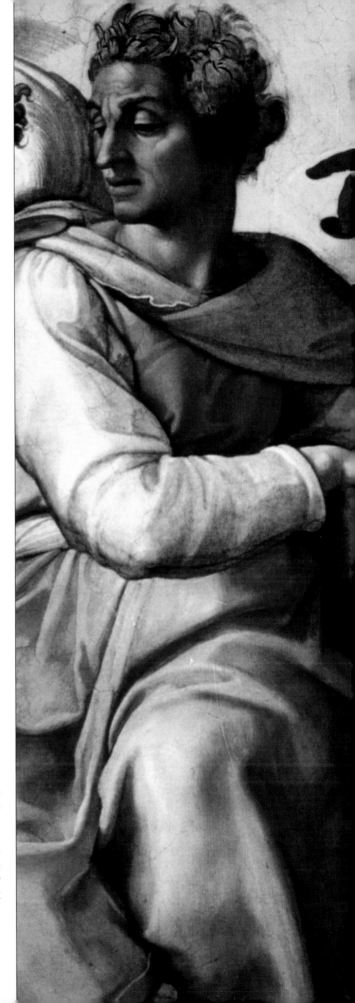

Michelangelo's impact on painting, sculpture and architecture was gigantic in his day, and it continues even up to today. Even Raphael referred to the Sistine Chapel sibyls in his fresco of Isaiah in Sant'Agostino. Isaiah is shown here in a detail from the Sistine Chapel. On the chapel five prophets alternate with five sibyls, with Isaiah sitting opposite the Erythraean Sibyl. This alludes both to the universality of the message of Redemption and to the concept of a harmony of the pagan world to the scriptures.

team. But the boy who had confronted the captain truly loved the team and would have rather seen the Knickerbockers play clean and lose than play dirty and win. After one particularly devastating loss, the coach huddled the boys in the outfield and asked them if they had anything to say for themselves. "We have lost eight straight games and are well out of first place," the boy who had confronted the captain said. "If we knock off our bad attitudes and get the chips off our shoulders we might be able to come back and make the playoffs. But it doesn't look good."

Have you ever been part of a group that decided to do the wrong thing? How did you respond? The prophet Isaiah lived through the reigns of at least four different kings of Judah, and he saw the people turn from God to worship pagan idols. He witnessed the conquest of the kingdom of Israel just to the north by the Assyrians, their people taken captive and their cities destroyed, and he knew that Judah awaited the same fate if she persisted in idolatry. What would it be like to live in a nation you knew could not last for much longer if it continued to refuse to worship the Lord with a true heart? Have you ever thought of God as a judge of particular nations in real history? And is it possible that the same thing still happens today?

No country today stands in the same place as Israel did in the Old Testament. As a nation they were God's Chosen People. But many of the issues Isaiah faced in his day confront us as well. Like those against whom Isaiah prophesied, we also call evil good and good evil, and expect God not to notice. Isaiah shows us what God expects and how to confront sin. He also sees the coming of Jesus who would ultimately die for the sins of the world and usher in a kingdom unlike any other—one that would bring peace to all nations.

# GENERAL INFORMATION

## Author and Context

Uzziah, Jotham, Ahaz and Hezekiah ruled successively as kings over Judah during the prophecies of Isaiah (1:1). He was the son of Amoz, who was perhaps the brother of Azariah, the king of Judah.[1] Isaiah lived in the eighth century, probably from 763-690 B.C., born 13 years after the first Greek Olympic games and ten years before the traditional date of the founding of Rome. He married a prophetess and bore two sons, Shearjashub (meaning "the remnant will return) and Mahershalalhashbaz ("Hastening to the spoil, speeding to the prey"), both who had really long names of prophetic significance for the kingdom of Judah. Living in Jerusalem, the capital of the southern kingdom of Judah, Isaiah prophesied for many decades. In the year that King Uzziah died he sees the Lord, high and lifted on His throne, surrounded by six winged creatures called seraphim who cry "Holy, holy, holy is the Lord of hosts: the whole earth is full of His glory" (6:3). Unlike Jonah who bolted in a boat when God commanded him to preach to Nineveh, Isaiah willingly responds to God's call: "Here am I; send me" (6:8). And unlike Nineveh where 300,000 repented in one day, God sends Isaiah to a stiff-necked people with blind eyes, deaf ears, and unrepentant hearts (6:9-10).

Church tradition has it that Isaiah was sawn in half, as alluded to in the Epistle to the Hebrews (11:37), during the persecution of King Manasseh, when he filled Jerusalem like a bath with innocent blood (2 Kings 21:16). The name "Isaiah" is a combination of two Hebrew words meaning "Yahweh will save" or "Yahweh is salvation." Isaiah has been named the "Evangelical Prophet" because he preached so bluntly against the compromised kings and religious leaders and because he saw Jesus the Messiah, Who would ultimately come and redeem Israel from exile and sin.

## Significance

Standing at the head of the prophets, the book of Isaiah contains such a variety of literary forms and broad range of themes that reading it can be like watching a movie where scenes switch from the gore of a combat field to the leisure and laughter of a banquet. The prophet accomplishes what has been called the duty of a preacher, to comfort the afflicted and afflict the comfortable.

Though God brought up Israel as His children, they did not know Him (1:4). Israel deserted and ignored God like a rebellious teenager. How could a holy God stand for injustice and evil among His own people? "How the faithful city has become a harlot! It was full of justice; righteousness lodged in it; but now murderers" (1:21). And yet how could God wipe out

His chosen nation Israel who possessed the promises of Abraham, Isaac, Jacob and David, and through whom the Messiah would ultimately come? This profound tension even carries into the New Testament when God would again have to deal with the Jews, who had turned away from him. Suppose a great king had promised his kingdom to his only son if he would be faithful, and yet the son took his inheritance and squandered it hunting and gambling. How could the king continue to be just and still give the kingdom to his son? And yet, if he disinherited his son from the throne, how could he fulfill his obligation to his people to provide an heir to rule over them justly and wisely?

God chose Israel as His special people, and he promised Abraham that through his seed all the families of the earth would be blessed. If God wiped out Israel, then Abraham's people would be finished, and the seed of David extinguished. The Messiah cannot come from Israel if there is no Israel. But every Israelite knew that God is holy and cannot stand for sin to run unchecked. Isaiah relieves this tension with his explanation of the *remnant;* though the people would be judged and conquered, God would preserve a faithful remnant of Israel that would once again return and flourish as a nation.

The apostle Paul picks this up in his explanation of election and God's relationship to the Jews, His chosen people, in Romans 9–11. The Jews were not entitled to salvation simply because they were circumcised in the flesh. They are not all Israel who are of Israel, Paul would say. Being religious on the outside does not necessarily mean love for God from the heart. Isaiah attacks hypocrisy and presumption.

He also prophesies the coming of the Gentile nations to Yahweh, a

This mosaic is found in Saint Mark's, Venice, a Byzantine-styled church that was built around 1050.

hope that was fulfilled in the cross of Christ and the birth of the New Testament church at Pentecost. The apostle John says explicitly that Jesus fulfilled the prophecies of Isaiah and that the prophet "saw His glory and spoke of Him" (John 12:41). In fact, of the 66 chapters of Isaiah, 47 are directly quoted or alluded to in the New Testament multiple times, making the book one of the most quoted—if not the favorite—of Jesus and the New Testament writers.

## Setting

Like wolves lurking around a flock of sheep, hostile pagan nations surrounded Israel during Isaiah's life: Syria, Moab, Edom, Philistia and the two superpowers of Egypt in the south and Assyria in the east. Twenty-five hundred years later, hostilities have not changed much in the Middle East. Palestine sat between these two empires, causing Israel and Judah to ally with one against the other, and tempting them to trust in horses (i.e., military and political power) instead of Yahweh.

In the days of king Ahaz, Pekah the king of Israel allied with Rezin of Syria to conquer Judah. The rising threat of Assyria under Tiglath-pileser III forced the weaker powers to unite willingly or by force. Through Isaiah, God warned Ahaz that the alliance would be futile; Judah, the house of David, would prevail and the Assyrians would crush the alliance. We learn in 2 Chronicles 28 that Ahaz defied the warning of the Lord, paid Assyria for protection and even instituted idolatrous sacrifices to the Assyrian gods in God's temple. After Tiglath's death, Shalmaneser and Sargon conquered Israel, the northern kingdom, and deported the population in 722 B.C. Judah still stood but on wobbly legs. The next king of Assyria, Sennacherib, sent his massive armies against Hezekiah. Under pressure to look to Egypt for aid and living in the

This terra-cotta relief is said to be one of the idol-gods of the Assyrians named Ishtar. "They shall be turned back, They shall be greatly ashamed, Who trust in carved images, Who say to the molded images, 'You are our gods.'" (Isaiah 42:17)

shadow of his father's cowardice and idolatry, Hezekiah beseeched the Lord for deliverance, and God answered him, miraculously slaying 185,000 Assyrians.

Sadly, in Hezekiah's later years he would compromise with Babylon and bring judgment upon Judah. The idolatry of the next king, Manasseh, involved human sacrifice, a common feature of pagan religion that devours its own. Isaiah witnessed and prophesied the rise and fall of these nations. He foresaw the captivity of Judah and destruction of the Temple at the hands of the Babylonians in 586 B.C., and also the return of the remnant that would rebuild and prepare the way for the Messiah, Who would draw all men to Himself.

It is interesting to note that the events recorded in Isaiah are happening in the same place and with the same nations but mostly at an earlier time than are recorded in the works of the secular historian Herodotus. He wrote about the Persians (aka Assyrians) focusing mostly on the time period shortly after the Temple was destroyed in 586 B.C.

## Worldview

How would you react if all of your teammates had bad attitudes and decided to cheat and play dirty? And what would be the most effective means of persuading them away from compromise? Anyone who has been in a situation where everyone is doing the wrong thing and there is pressure to conform knows the difficulty of resisting. Facing the captain of the Knickerbockers is exciting and admirable in retrospect as we read about it, but doing it at the time would have put knots in your stomach.

Now up the stakes. Not your baseball team, but your church, neighbors, civil leaders and nation. What would you do if God told you to go naked and barefoot for three years as a sign that he would destroy the United States? Why would He ask you to do such a thing? Old Testament prophets often led bizarre and exciting lives, doing and saying things that confused and angered their audience—and us who read them thousands of years later. Prophets came from all walks of life: priests (Ezekiel), kings (David), judges (Deborah), shepherds (Amos), and while some appeared briefly and remain obscure, others, like Isaiah, interacted with kings and proclaimed the fate of nations.

Sometimes the prophets appeared shocking and dramatic. By going naked and barefoot, Isaiah reveals the shame, poverty and weakness that will overcome Egypt and Ethiopia when the Assyrians conquers them. God tells a story with the actions of the prophet, and often, by his offensive words and deeds, he reveals the *truly* offensive—the sins of the people. Robbing the poor, ripping off widows, lusting after money, perverting justice in the courts—sins against a holy God, and not the nakedness of Isaiah, are the real outrage.

Over 25 times in the book, Isaiah refers to God as "the Holy One of Israel," a phrase that occurs only six other times in the Old Testament. Isaiah's call to prophesy sets this tone for his career. He sees the Lord enthroned, high and exalted surrounded by seraphim:

> And one cried to another and said: "Holy, holy, holy is the Lord of hosts; the whole earth is full of His glory!" And the posts of the door were shaken by the voice of him who cried out, and the house was filled with smoke. So I said: "Woe is me, for I am undone! Because I am a man of unclean lips, and I dwell in the midst of a people of unclean lips; for my eyes have seen the King, the Lord of hosts." Then one of the seraphim flew to me, having in his hand a live coal which he had taken with the tongs from the altar. And he touched my mouth with it, and said: "Behold, this has touched your lips; your iniquity is taken away, and your sin purged." (6:3-7)

Even more overwhelming than standing at the bottom of Niagara Falls with millions of gallons of water thundering down, the glory of God undoes Isaiah. The seraphim cry "holy" three times, emphasizing the complete Trinitarian holiness of God. In Hebrew the letters *im* function like the letter *s* does with English nouns. Adding *s* makes a noun plural. So one of the names for God, *Elohim*, gives us a hint that God is Triune. *Elohim* is plural just like *seraphim* (more than one angel) is the plural of seraph. Of course God is only One God, but He is three persons: Father, Son and Holy Spirit, and this Trinity is reflected in "Holy, holy, holy," which the burning angels chant eternally before God. We see perfect holiness in God Himself, an eternal society in which Father, Son and Holy Spirit love each other eternally. You might say we see the personality of holiness and our example for loving God and one another. The question "How should we honor our parents?" can be answered by asking how the Spirit honors the Son. Sin complicates our world, but we can look to the three persons in the one godhead for guidance. What happens when a sinful person comes into the presence of such wild, loving holiness? Sin has to be punished or cleansed, and so Isaiah is purged by a fiery coal.

Just as God is holy, so he commands Israel to be holy: "For I am the Lord your God. You shall therefore consecrate yourselves, and you shall be holy; for I am holy" (Lev. 11:44). Being holy for an Israelite, as for us, does not mean one could not sin—or else God would have commanded in vain! But God wants His fallen people to come back to holiness. This means sins committed must be confessed and repented, turned away from. Forsaking unholiness by faith brings a person and a nation back into fellowship with God, back into His holiness. When men are reconciled to God, the *imago Dei* is restored. But instead of forsaking sin, Judah forsakes God and provokes Him to anger (1:4). The people are like a broken pot that refuses to let God put it back together again. And it only gets uglier when they try to make themselves better by their own efforts and ideas. It is like putting the pot back together with Elmer's Glue. Here Isaiah describes Israel's desperate situation:

You are indeed angry, for we have sinned—in these ways we continue; and we need to be saved. But we are all like an unclean thing. And all of our righteousnesses are like filthy rags. (64:5-6)

How many times have you heard someone say that people are basically good? Or that you must believe in yourself? Isaiah describes the nature of man very differently. He compares our good deeds, or at least what we would call our good deeds, to filthy rags. These filthy rags refer to clothing stained with blood that made someone ritually unclean, an uncleanness that would forbid someone from worshiping God until they were ritually cleansed. You could not go to church if you had spent Sunday morning diving through mud puddles. Not only is a bloody garment gross and dirty in a sanitary sense, but it represents moral defilement. Israel's *good* deeds, presented as worthy in themselves, make them repugnant, dirty things in God's sight. They could not go to church trusting in their own goodness. Isaiah might say that the last thing to believe in is yourself. On your own, you cannot approach God.

Once someone has stopped looking to God for salvation and righteousness, it becomes easy to change the standard for that righteousness. We see this on every level of our lives. When our parents, teacher, coach or anyone tells us to do something and we do not do it, what do we say? "I thought you meant this other thing" or "I had to do something else first." In other words, we make excuses for not doing it or change the thing that was to be done. Our own former president Bill Clinton debated and split hairs over whether he really broke his word and the law when he committed adultery in the Oval Office. We are not much different as a nation from the Israel that Isaiah prophesied against.

> Woe to those who call evil good, and good evil; Who put darkness for light and light for Darkness; Who put bitter for sweet, and sweet for bitter! Woe to those who are wise in their own eyes, and prudent in their own sight! (5:20-21)

When the Israelites failed to live up to God's law, they changed the standard so they could feel good about themselves and justify their evil. Very few people who are in the grip of sin will ever admit that what they are doing is in fact sin. The captain of the Knickerbockers blamed others for the losing streak and insisted that more cheating would enable the team to win. When God asked Adam if he had eaten from the tree, he blamed the woman and God: "The *woman* whom *You* gave to be with me, she gave me of the tree, and I ate" (Gen. 3:12). Men want to pass the buck. This is part of the fallen *imago Dei*. But men also want to be righteous, and if they will not submit to God's way—death to self and resurrection—they will make their own, calling evil good and good evil. How do abortionists rationalize their actions? Do they call their position "pro-murder?" Of course not. The right to kill kids is slanted as a "pro-choice" position. If you disagree with that, they say, you are against freedom, against giving women a choice. And we all know that the United States was founded on freedom, right?

Even though Israel was the chosen nation of Yahweh, they broke their special relationship to Yahweh which is described as a covenant.

> Now therefore, if you will indeed obey My voice and keep My covenant, then you shall be a special treasure to Me above all people; for all the earth is Mine. And you shall be to Me a kingdom of priests and a holy nation. (Exodus 19:5-6)

But the covenant, though designed to bless and prosper Israel as God's "peculiar treasure," would bring curses upon the nation if they rejected it and shirked their responsibilities. God will not have drunken, greedy and unjust people for His priests. If someone gave you ten million dollars, you would have an opportunity to be faithful and generous, blessing your family, church and the poor. But you could also be selfish and foolish, squandering it all on Twinkies for yourself. The covenant is a great gift to those who are faithful, but a terrible curse on those who reject God. Isaiah offers to the people the mercy of the Lord and restoration to holiness, but he also prophesies doom to the hard hearted.

> "Come now, and let us reason together," says the Lord, "Though your sins are like scarlet, they shall be as white as snow; though they are red like crimson, and they shall be as wool. If you are willing and obedient, you shall

eat the good of the land: But if you refuse and rebel, you shall be devoured by the sword;" for the mouth of the Lord has spoken it. (1:18–20)

God chose the Israelites as His covenant people, but in order to thrive in this close relationship, the people had to *act* like the chosen, that is, to love God and their neighbor. In the same way, Paul asks the rhetorical question to the Christians in Rome, "Shall we continue in sin that grace may abound? Certainly not!" (Rom. 6:1–2). God wanted to wash the scarlet sins of Israel, but hypocrites do not want to be clean. We still see this hypocrisy in the church today. We bear the name "Christian," and yet our divorce rates, business practices and lust for material things hardly differs from that of the world. Isaiah confronts the Israelites who are part of the elect nation of God, who worship in the synagogues and temple, but persist in their sins.

At the same time that Isaiah faces the sins of the rulers, priests and citizens of Judah, he also recognizes his connection to them. "So I said, "Woe is me, for I am undone! Because I am a man of unclean lips, and I dwell in the midst of a people of unclean lips" (6:5). Not all of the boys on the Knickerbockers succumbed to cheating and bad attitudes. But they still lost with the team and no doubt shared their bad reputation. Although we never witness the prophet participating in the idolatry, lust and evil of the people, he still confesses that he dwells with them and is part of them. God covenants with individuals as we see in Abraham and his descendants, but He also covenants with groups of people: families, churches, nations. This is a tough

concept for us because we are used to thinking of ourselves solely as individuals. Isaiah's own righteousness, as seen in his confession of sin, does not separate him from the consequences God brings on the nation. Nor does he try to remove himself from his backslidden countrymen, but instead rebukes, teaches, preaches and challenges them out of love. The boy who confronted the captain and tried to change him loved the team the most, and he did not pretend they were playing well or fair. Loyalty does not mean whitewashing over faults. It says in Proverbs that faithful are the wounds of a friend. Isaiah was a true friend to his nation. In the same way, Jesus, the greater Isaiah, weeps over Jerusalem even as he predicts its destruction within one generation.

"O Jerusalem, Jerusalem, the one who kills the

**DEFEAT OF SENNACHERIB**
Peter Paul Rubens, one of the foremost painters in Western art history, painted this battle scene of King Hezekiah defeating the Assyrians.

prophets and stones those who are sent to her! How often I wanted to gather your children together, as a hen gathers her chicks under her wings, but you were not willing!" (Matt. 23:37)

As a true patriot, Christ loves the nation with a love that causes Him to preach against her sins.

Isaiah also addresses pagan nations who have rebelled against God. The very instrument that God will use to judge Judah will also undergo judgment. Apocalyptic language, sounding a lot like the end of the world, describes the fall of Babylon: "For the stars of heaven and their constellations will not give their light; the sun will be darkened in its going forth, and the moon will not cause its light to shine" (13:10). This cosmic imagery is symbolic, meaning that the nation will be wiped out, as it is later by Cyrus of Persia (45:1). Jesus uses the same "sky falling" language when He predicts the destruction of Jerusalem; the sun would be darkened, the moon would stop shining, the stars fall from heaven and powers of the heavens be shaken (Matt. 24:29). Many Christians today mistake the language of Matthew 24 as meaning that the world would come to an end. But Jesus simply uses the same figures of speech as Isaiah. We still use symbols such as stars on our flags to indicate countries or states like the fifty stars on our spangled banner. And we use similar symbolic language to mean violent defeat such as "I'm going to punch your lights out!" Of course, we are not speaking of literal light bulbs. With language about the darkening of the heavens, Isaiah was prophesying the destruction of Babylon just as Christ speaks of the destruction of Jerusalem.

Though Isaiah preaches judgment, he also promises salvation. The last third of the book describes the reign of the Messiah, Who will bring peace to Israel and draw all nations to Himself. God will send out His Elect One who with the Spirit will bring forth justice to the Gentiles (42:1, cf. Matt. 12:18). We read in chapters 52 and 53 of the Suffering Servant who would endure horrific punishment and grief for our transgressions. The Messianic reign and restoration of the *imago Dei* comes only through the atoning death of the Messiah. This unthinkable self-sacrifice results in the redemption of the world:

"Sing, O barren, you who have not borne! Break forth into singing, and cry aloud, You who have not labored with child! For more are the children of the desolate than the children of the married woman," says the Lord. (54:1)

Jerusalem is like a barren woman until the Messiah comes and redeems her. The Apostle Paul quotes this passage, referring to the Jerusalem which is free and the mother of us all—Jews and Gentiles live in the new Jerusalem (Gal. 4:27). "For behold, I create new heavens and a new earth; and the former shall not be remembered, or come to mind.... I create Jerusalem as a rejoicing, and her people a joy" (65:17–18). Through Christ we live in the new heavens and new earth, and like Israel we build houses and inhabit them, plant vineyards and eat the fruit of them (65:21). The Messiah has come and the increase of His government and peace will have no end.

The Knickerbockers finished their season badly, but they would be back for another year. The coach and the few players who wanted to play straight would be joined by many new teammates, and the team would get a new captain who would lead them to victory. Just when it looked like Israel would be completely destroyed, a faithful remnant would survive and become a new Israel that would include the Gentiles. God remains just and the justifier. Unfaithful Israelites are cut out and true Israel remains. Isaiah's words are fulfilled in the last days and continue to be fulfilled as all nations flow to the house of the Lord: "And many people shall come and say, 'Come, and let us go up to the mountain of the Lord, to the house of the God of Jacob; He will teach us His ways, and we shall walk in His paths'" (2:3).

—*Jerrold W. Owen*

## For Further Reading

Spielvogel, Jackson. *Western Civilization*. Fifth Edition. Belmont, Calif.: Wadsworth/Thomson Learning, 2003. 33–49.

*Veritas Press Bible Cards: Chronicles through Malachi and Job*. Lancaster, Pa.: Veritas Press. 75.

2 Kings 16

READING ASSIGNMENT: Isaiah 1–22

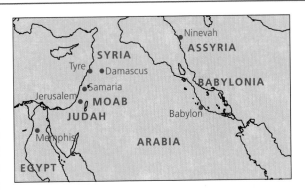

# SESSION I: PRELUDE

## Questions to Consider

Can you think of any prophets in our culture today? What or who do they prophesy against? Have you ever tried to confront someone when you thought they were doing something wrong? How did he respond? Imagine how hard it would be to confront the president of the United States when you knew he would be furious and could punish you however he wanted.

*From the General Information above answer the following questions:*

1. Who was Isaiah?
2. Did he live in the northern kingdom of Israel or the southern kingdom of Judah?
3. What kings ruled during his time as a prophet?
4. Why did God send him?
5. What does Isaiah's name mean?
6. Which nation did Ahaz compromise with, following after their gods?

 READING ASSIGNMENT: Isaiah 23–46

# SESSION II: DISCUSSION

Isaiah 1–34

## A Question to Consider

Are all of us responsible for the sins America has committed?

*Discuss or list answers to the following questions:*

## Text Analysis

1. What kind of relationship did Israel have with God?
2. What were some of the particular sins Israel had committed that God was judging?
3. Did Isaiah commit these same sins?
4. Did Isaiah see himself as sharing the guilt of these sins?
5. Why did Isaiah identify himself with Israel?

## Cultural Analysis

1. What are some of the corporate (national) sins that are common in our world today?
2. Do we as a culture ever cry out to God? What do we ask him to do?
3. Do we as a nation call evil good and good evil? How so?
4. Think about the "pro-choice" abortion movement. Who do the pro-choice supporters think is affected by their choice?

## Biblical Analysis

1. What does the Bible teach about the effect of the sins of individuals upon others?
2. Read 2 Samuel 24. David disobeys God and takes a census, which God had forbidden him to do. Who suffers for David's sin?
3. In the Bible, God deals with people individually, but also corporately as nations. Read part of Solomon's prayer of dedication in 1 Kings 8:33–36. Who has sinned? What must happen for the people to be forgiven?

## SUMMA

*Write an essay or discuss this question, integrating what you have learned from the material above.*
Are we each responsible for the sins that our nation has committed? What should our response be?

 READING ASSIGNMENT: Isaiah 47–66

A The people that walked in darkness
B have seen a great light;
A They that dwell in the shadow of death,
B upon them hath the light shined.

*Find more examples of parallelism in this passage.*

Now take some time to write a passage of *parallelism* as a class. Just to get the feel for it write one about your pet, or the pet of a friend. Write it in the ABAB format listed above. After the completion of this challenge, try your hand at a "chiasm" or ABBA form.[2] Write this one in praise of your earthly father. Now, finally, after our practice we can write one concerning our heavenly Father. Choose either form, and, if you are in a group, give some special praise to the one who writes the best one.

## Optional Activity

Handel's *Messiah* sets many texts from Isaiah to glorious music, the "Hallelujah Chorus" most famously. Listen to a recording of the "Hallelujah Chorus." You might want to stand as so many audiences do at Christmas performances! As time allows, find other passages from Isaiah that Handel "quotes."

This bronze head of a horned snake-dragon was a symbol for the Babylonian god Marduk. Marduk defeated a gigantic dragon and, following the battle, cut the beast in two. With half of the creature he made the sky, and with the other half he made the earth. Then he created the Tigris and Euphrates rivers from her eyes and made mountains from her udders.

# SESSION III: ACTIVITY

Isaiah is filled with Hebrew poetry. Read Isaiah 9:1–7 out loud. What pictures does Isaiah use to describe the coming of the Messiah? One device of Hebraic poetry is *parallelism* where an idea is repeated a second time in different language. Verse two is a parallelism:

# OPTIONAL SESSION A: RECITATION

## Comprehension Questions

*Answer these questions for factual recall.*

1. What cleanses Isaiah when he appears before God's throne (chap. 6)?
2. What kind of woman does Isaiah prophesy will bear the Messiah, and what will she call Him (chap. 7)?
3. Who is Hezekiah (chap. 36)?
4. How does he defeat Sennacherib (chap. 37)?
5. How does Hezekiah respond when Isaiah tells him he will soon die (chap. 38)?
6. How does God respond to Hezekiah?
7. To whom does Hezekiah show his wealth (chap. 39)?

8. What are the consequences?
9. Who will eventually lead Israel out of captivity (chap. 45)?
10. How will the Messiah save His people (chap. 53)?
11. What people does Isaiah say will be redeemed along with the remnant (chap. 60)?

## OPTIONAL SESSION B: LATERAL THINKING

*Discuss the following questions or answer in a short essay.*

1. Where do we see the Trinity appear in Isaiah? How is holiness manifested in the Trinity? Would you describe the law of God as personal or impersonal?
2. Isaiah praises one kind of beauty and despises another kind. Read Isaiah 3:16-24 and 4:2-6 and describe these opposing beauties. What sort of beauty does our culture honor in television, magazines and movies? How would Isaiah confront this idea or caricature of true beauty?

## OPTIONAL SESSION C: ART APPRECIATION

1. Read pages 70-72 in Janson's *History of Art for Young People* about the art of Babylon. Look at the picture of the Ishtar gate which was completed about

In Isaiah 36 and 37 Hezekiah pleaded with the Lord to save him and his people from Sennacherib and his Assyrian army. God answered by slaying 185,000 men of the Assyrian army. Sennacherib ran but was slain shortly after by his own sons. Here King Sennacherib is depicted on his throne. Notice his facial features are defaced—perhaps after his murder.

the time of Isaiah. Read what Isaiah says about Babylon's idols in Isaiah 46. How are the gods of Babylon described, and how is the living God contrasted with them? Do we make and worship any idols today?

2. Plan a trip to a museum that has a collection of ancient artifacts, including objects worshiped or thought sacred by pagan cultures. Continue the discussion in the question above.

## ENDNOTES

1 Israel was split into two kingdoms soon after the death of Solomon. The northern kingdom retained the name Israel, while the southern kingdom was called Judah. Isaiah prophesied to Judah though at times addressed both kingdoms as Israel.

2 This style should not be mistaken for the Hebrew word for Daddy, *Abba*. Nor does it have any connection to an 80's rock group from Scandinavia.

# JEREMIAH

In the few weeks of summer before going into the first grade, my big brother and his friends were playing "rocket launch." They had trouble finding a suitable rocket. The dog, Sandy, would not cooperate. My older sister refused the job outright. Being the little brother, well—I was the rocket. We had a nice grassy hill beside our house, just perfect for the launching pad. Phillip, my big brother, would launch me. I would sit on his feet and he would kick me up into the air about twenty feet. His friends were like the splash-down at the bottom of the hill. They would catch the human rocket. We had several successful launches and splash-downs. Then my mom saw what we were doing. She looked out the back door and shouted, "You boys stop that! Someone's going to get hurt." "Alright," everyone shouted. The rocket launch went into repair mode for a while, and then, as though she had never said anything, we were back at it. Blast off! My mom warned us, but we did not listen.

My first few months in the first grade were kind of miserable. We had to write constantly, and it is hard to write with your arm in a cast. I had a cast that went all the way to my wrist. I could not hold a pencil very well. My mom warned against the rocket-launching fun, but I crashed and burned. I remember looking at my arm after the crash. It looked like a stair-step.

We hear many warnings that we do not listen to. My mom did not say, "I told you so." At the time she was heart-broken and upset, trying to get me to the emergency room. She was sad and upset that I had been hurt. She was also a little mad at my brother.

We have all been in situations where we could say, "I told you so." The prophet we are studying, Jeremiah, could have said, "I told you so," over and over again. He warned the people of Judah, but they did not listen. In the end, he saw all the worst things imaginable happen just as he had predicted. He did not sit back and say, "I told you so." He suffered through them all, and, while telling people the truth of what was going to happen, he was rejected and assaulted many times.

*Jeremiah Laments the Devastation of Jerusalem*
This is a detail from one of Rembrandt's first masterpieces. It was painted in 1630.

# GENERAL INFORMATION

## Author and Context

Jeremiah prophesied from c. 626 to 586 B.C. He authored both Jeremiah and Lamentations. Jeremiah had Baruch as a devoted friend (Jer. 32:12). He worked with Jeremiah as a secretary and faithful attendant (36:4–32). Baruch probably wrote down many of the prophecies Jeremiah gave. The first verse in the book tells us that Jeremiah's father was Hilkiah (1:1). Jeremiah's name probably means "the Lord establishes." Jeremiah began his ministry at about age twenty in the thirteenth year of Josiah (626 B.C.). He lived during the reforms of Josiah as a youth and most of his prophecies were given during the reigns of Jehoiakim and Zedekiah. The story line of the book stretches from about 627 to 562 B.C. The book of Jeremiah picks up about sixty years after the close of the book of Isaiah and deals with the last forty years of Judah's decline to their final fall.

One problem in studying Jeremiah is sorting out the chronological order of the prophecies. The book does not follow the order in which things happened. There is a mixing of early and later messages which makes it difficult to know the order. For example, chapters 1–6 and 11–12 are set in the time of King Josiah's reforms, while chapters 7–10, 14–20 and 22:1–19 and chapter 26, seem to refer to the later time when Nebuchadnezzar came to power. If the messages are not chronological, what is the basis of the arrangement? The arrangement of the book places the promised grace of the new covenant (Jeremiah 31) as central to the book. It is thematically arranged. Jeremiah's book is like a beautiful rose in the center of thorns. The judgment of God and the misery of sin are all around. But what is at the center is God's promise of salvation. The new covenant is a wonderful promise that God will be merciful to His disobedient people and forgive their sins. This is fulfilled in the work of Jesus Christ.

## Significance

Just as the bright pedals and perfect arrangement of the rose stand out amidst the thorns, so God's great mercy is at the very center of these prophecies of

Gustave Doré illustrates Jeremiah dictating to Baruch, his scribe, in this wood cut.

judgment and impending doom. Jeremiah is an island of gospel promises in the stormy sea of judgment on the people of God. In Jeremiah's time many prophets and priests were disobeying the Lord. Jeremiah 8:11 says of those prophets and priests, "They dress the wound of my people as though it were not serious. 'Peace, peace,' they say, when there is no peace." While false comforts were given, Jeremiah was called by God to give a message which no one wanted to hear. Rejected and often despairing, the weeping and lamenting voice of one man still echoes over 2,600 years later.

The land of Judah was all that was left after the Assyrians devastated the kingdom of Israel and carried off its inhabitants in 722 B.C. Babylon threatened the people and called for Judah's allegiance. Would God save them from the Babylonians in spite of the wickedness of the people? Jeremiah's voice made it clear: No! Repent or perish. Yet, at the time, many false prophets gave soothing words of "peace, peace." They falsely promised deliverance from Babylon. But God was using Babylon to judge and correct His people.

Today we can easily slide down the same slope. We can use religious truths that act as lying words, "The temple of the Lord, the temple of the Lord, the temple of the Lord" (7:4). We can hide behind our religious affiliations, churches and doctrinal correctness. But just like the words, "The temple of the Lord," godly organizations, churches and doctrines can be "lying words" when used as a replacement for true worship and doing the will of God.

## Setting

Jeremiah lived in a tragic time. He warned of God's judgment, but was rejected. To grasp all that the book means, one must understand the time and setting. His ministry overlaps the reign of several important Biblical kings: Josiah, Jehoiakim and Zedekiah. He also overlaps several of the other prophets. He begins his ministry at the time of Nahum, Zephaniah and Habakkuk and ends at the time of Daniel and Ezekiel. Remember that the northern kingdom (usually called Israel) had been captured and scattered by Assyria by 721–722 B.C. The prophet Hosea spoke of this (e.g., Hos. 8:9–10). The remaining part of God's people were in the south, called Judah. Great crises were growing there. All kinds of moral and religious wickedness-were caused by Manasseh, Judah's most evil king (686–643 B.C.). King Josiah made great reforms (641–609 B.C.) with the rediscovery of a scroll of the Law (perhaps Deuteronomy) (2 Kings 22–23). Still, the reforms lasted only a short time and were somewhat external. Then Jehoiakim (609–597 B.C.), Josiah's son, returned to idolatry and even practiced child sacrifice. Jehoiakim disregarded the warnings of the Lord spoken by Jeremiah (Jer. 36). He even burned the written prophecies of Jeremiah. Then Jehoiachin, son of Jehoiakim, acted wickedly, too. When Nebuchadnezzar attacked Jerusalem in 597, Jehoiachin was taken captive along with the nobility of Jerusalem, as the city was largely plundered (2 Kings 24:1–17). In 2 Kings 24:17, the text says, "Then the king of Babylon made Mattaniah, Jehoiachin's uncle, king in his place, and changed his name to Zedekiah." Despite Jeremiah's warnings, Zedekiah rebelled against Nebuchadnezzar in 589 B.C. because he listened to false prophets promising deliverance. He heard the message that he wanted to hear. "Peace, peace." Then Nebuchadnezzar attacked Jerusalem, and after eighteen months of breaking into the walls, destroyed it, along with the palace and the Temple. Most of the people of Judah were taken into captivity in Babylon (586 B.C.). This background of the "exile" to Babylon and the return to the land of Israel became the setting for much of the New Testament's teaching. There is also a sad end to Zedekiah. "Then they killed the sons of Zedekiah before his eyes, put out the eyes of Zedekiah, bound him with bronze fetters, and took him to Babylon" (2 Kings 25:7).

## Worldview Essay

We often hear only what we want to hear. Our parents may give us warnings that we do not want to heed. We may choose to ignore something because we do not like it. In Jeremiah, the people, and often the leaders of the people, rejected Jeremiah's warnings. They heard what they wanted to hear. That is why they listened to false prophets. Without a clear commitment to hear all of God's Word, we will only hear the "truth" that we want to hear. Partial truths often turn out to be wholly false. In our worldview, the one whose voice is always heard is our ultimate authority. Whether it is a person's own desires (their god is their belly) or reason (Rationalism) or a false

religious authority (like Mormonism), God intends for us to listen to Him. Christians should know God's voice is plainly heard in Scripture.

One's view of who is in authority is like the foundation of a great skyscraper. The strength and stability of the building rests on the depth of the foundation. Is God deep enough to be trusted as the foundation? We must know God more to truly trust Him. The Scriptures help us to know Him by telling us about who He is and what He does. We can trust the voice of God because of His character.

Jeremiah shows us the character of the God of Scripture. We learn more of the solidness of His righteous character and the depth of His mercy. The book shows the righteousness and grace of the Triune God, as well as the heart-wrenching story of the sinfulness of people and deserved judgment. Yet we see an undeserved redemption and promised salvation. The essential meaning of Jeremiah is punishment and consequences for sin. Still, the Lord will provide a future deliverance for His people and judge the other nations for their evil. All of this sets the stage in history for the coming of Christ.

Because the Lord is the Triune God of Scripture, the book of Jeremiah provides a strong example of how He reveals Himself. He speaks authoritatively. Over fifty times we find the phrase, "the Word of the Lord" in Jeremiah. God speaks and His Word is true. Jeremiah 1:9–10 records the very mission of Jeremiah:

> Then the LORD put forth His hand and
> touched my mouth, and the LORD said to me:
> "Behold, I have put My words in your mouth.
> See, I have this day set you over the nations
> and over the kingdoms,
> To root out and to pull down,
> To destroy and to throw down,
> To build and to plant."

God's Word is voiced through His chosen man. "Before I formed you in the womb I knew you; Before you were born I sanctified you; I ordained you a prophet to the nations" (1:5). Jeremiah's call as a prophet to the nations shows the way the God of Scripture reveals Himself and how He speaks authoritatively. Prophecy in Scripture was a message to a historical people in an ongoing relationship. The prophet unveils God's plan and intentions for judgment and deliverance. We see in the prophets, especially Jeremiah, that there are consequences for not listening to the warnings of God's coming judgment. So, we should not think of the prophetic Word as mere future information. Prophecy is not a bare foretelling of events to come (e.g., "Here's the winning lottery number."). Not at all. Its purpose is warning, comforting and exhorting God's people to action. The Word comes as a word of promised judgment or promised blessing.

> Therefore thus says the LORD God of hosts:
> "Because you speak this word,
> Behold, I will make My words in
> your mouth fire,
> And this people wood,
> And it shall devour them.
> Behold, I will bring a nation
> against you from afar,
> O house of Israel . . ." (5:14–15).

In Jeremiah we also see another reason for trusting the voice of the Lord. We see the characteristic of God's sovereignty. In Jeremiah 18:1–12 we have the image of a potter which is often alluded to in Scripture. In ancient times, pottery not only served as dishes and pots and pans do today. It also was used for containers of all kinds: grain storage, wine and water storage and as chamber pots (which were the ancient equivalent of the restroom). Which kind of pot is being shaped by the potter? God has the power and the right to shape, reshape or throw away the clay as He wishes. God is completely sovereign over all. Paul uses the image of the potter and the clay found in Jeremiah in Romans 9:20–23,

> Does not the potter have power over the clay, from the same lump to make one vessel for honor and another for dishonor? What if God, wanting to show His wrath and to make His power known, endured with much longsuffering the vessels of wrath prepared for destruction, and that He might make known the riches of His glory on the vessels of mercy, which He had prepared beforehand for glory,

The announcement of the potter's power is also a message that should be heeded. God can pronounce destruction. But if the people repent, He can reshape the pot. God is so sovereign that He takes into account what the message of God's sovereignty will affect.

The prophet, Jeremiah, preaches of the need for Judah to repent in Dore's wood cut.

The Lord's character in Jeremiah is not like ugly concrete—strong but rough. God's character shines like beautiful, polished granite. He is judge, and He is compassionate. Jeremiah 3:12 speaks both of God's anger toward backsliding Israel and of His mercy, "I will not cause My anger to fall on you. For I am merciful." God's compassion is illustrated with the promised return from exile (12:15, 30:18, 31:20, 33:26). Those who return will worship God, knowing more completely His mercy. ". . . 'Praise the LORD of hosts, For the LORD is good, For His mercy endures forever' . . . For I will cause the captives of the land to return as at the first" (33:11).

Jeremiah provides a very direct picture of man in Adam, the human condition. In the very well-known words of Jeremiah 17:9, "The heart is deceitful above all things, And desperately wicked; Who can know it?" Not only do we have the capacity to deceive others, people have a great capacity to completely deceive themselves. Our hearts are a spring. They may get polluted from outside, but the most important pollution is in the very source. Jesus would say it this way in Mark 7:20-23,

> "What comes out of a man, that defiles a man. For from within, out of the heart of men, proceed evil thoughts, adulteries, fornications, murders, thefts, covetousness, wickedness, deceit, lewdness, an evil eye, blasphemy, pride, foolish-

ness. All these evil things come from within and defile a man."

For example, Jeremiah condemns many sins of idolatry, including the sacrifice of children to the honor of Baal-Molech (7:31; 19:5; 32:35) and the worship of "the queen of heaven" (7:18; 44:19). Jeremiah denounces sins of immorality, such as dishonesty, injustice, oppression of the helpless and slander. These violations of God's law become a covenant lawsuit against the representatives of the people, the priests and prophets.

Thankfully, Jeremiah shows us the Savior of such sinful people. In many cases Jeremiah parallels the actions of Jesus Christ in His earthly ministry. Words from Jeremiah (chapter 7) are spoken by Christ in the "cleansing of the temple" when He attacked the money-changers. When Jesus attacked false religious practices in Jerusalem, He was saying what Jeremiah had said: this place will be destroyed. This is what had already happened in Jeremiah's day (to Shiloh, 7:12). Christ's words parallel this with the promised judgment of the destruction of Jerusalem.

> Assuredly, I say to you, all these things will come upon this generation. O Jerusalem, Jerusalem, the one who kills the prophets and stones those who are sent to her! How often I wanted to gather your children together, as a hen gathers her chicks under her wings, but you were not willing! See! Your house is left to you desolate. (Matthew 23:36-38)

Just as Jeremiah was rejected, so Christ was rejected. The Scriptures say of our Lord, "He came to His own, and His own did not receive Him" (John 1:11). Jesus gave the same message and acted like Jeremiah warning that Jerusalem would be destroyed. In the center of Jeremiah's book of warnings and weeping, he links the covenant-breaking people of Judah with the promised hope of a new covenant. This new covenant is central for the people of God today, since Christ is the mediator of the new covenant (Heb. 8:6). The very name of the second portion of the Scriptures proclaiming Christ's actions is the New Testament (an older term sometimes used for "covenant").

When our mom gives us a warning, we ought to listen. If we do not, we may find that we will be wearing a cast. We also know that our mother's love does not stop, even in the middle of breaking our arms and legs. The voice of God, our final authority, warns and tells of judgment—many broken bones. Yet God never stopped loving His covenant people. He promises salvation for those who turn to the Lord. This voice sounds from the very center of Jeremiah. In the midst of sin, misery and judgment, he writes of a new covenant of forgiveness through the final sacrifice of Jesus. The work of Christ on Calvary and the Lord's Supper, which celebrates His sacrifice, fulfill the new covenant. Christ's death is the basis of forgiveness, and the Supper is the rehearsal dinner of His victory. Christ stated and promised, "For this is My blood of the new covenant, which is shed for many for the remission of sins. But I say to you, I will not drink of this fruit of the vine from now on until that day when I drink it new with you in My Father's kingdom" (Matt. 26:28-29).

—*Gregg Strawbridge*

## For Further Reading

*Veritas Press Bible Cards: Chronicles through Malachi and Job.* Lancaster, Pa.: Veritas Press. 75, 76, 79-81.

# READING ASSIGNMENT:
Jeremiah 1–15

# SESSION I: PRELUDE
Jeremiah 1–15

## A Question to Consider

Have you ever said, "I told you so?" Have you ever refused to listen to a warning?

*Discuss or list short answers to the following questions:*

1. Who was Jeremiah, and why is he called the "weeping prophet?"
2. When did he live? What happened before he lived and just after he lived?
3. How do we know that Jeremiah was able to give God's Word?
4. How was God dealing with His people in Jeremiah's day?
5. What wicked king led Judah into backsliding just

before the ministry of Jeremiah?

6. What king's reforms occurred during the ministry of Jeremiah?
7. What happened in Judah after the reign of Josiah?
6. How old was Gregg when he broke his arm?

### READING ASSIGNMENT:
Jeremiah 16–33

# SESSION II: DISCUSSION
Jeremiah 1–33

## A Question to Consider

Are there consequences for doing wrong actions? What are some examples from past readings this year?

*Discuss or list short answers to the following questions:*

### Text Analysis

1. According to Jeremiah 3, what are Israel's sins like?
2. What has been the result of this sin? (3:3)
3. To what does Israel's hard-hearted rejection of God's warnings lead? (4:5–31)
4. In chapter 5, what sins does God accuse Israel of committing?
5. What is to come upon the people because of these sins? (5:14–31)
6. What sinful practices are the people of Judah using in worship according to Jer. 7?
7. What will be the consequences of this perverted worship?

### Cultural Analysis

1. Which nations are at war in the world today?
2. Are there any actions of the nations at war which are clearly sinful?
3. Is it possible that God is using any of these wars to bring about His judgments?
4. If God uses a nation in His judgment for the stopping of evil, does that mean that He approves of that nation and that no judgment will come to them?

### Biblical Analysis

Read Psalm 2 and Psalm 67. Will God judge nations other than Israel (and Judah)?

## SUMMA

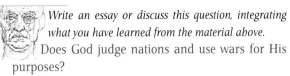

*Write an essay or discuss this question, integrating what you have learned from the material above.*
Does God judge nations and use wars for His purposes?

### Optional Activity

List the events of Jeremiah's day as presented in 2 Kings 23–25.

## Time Line Activity

Create a time line of major events during Jeremiah's life. Use the information below or supplement this with resources that you may have (such as a Bible dictionary).

**640/39 B.C.**
Josiah's reign begins—He is eight years old—Reigns 31 years—Zephaniah begins prophetic ministry throughout Josiah's reign
**631 B.C.**
Josiah begins to seek God—He is sixteen years old in the eight year of his reign.
**627 B.C.**
Josiah begins his reforms—He is twenty years old in the twelfth year of his reign.—Jeremiah's call to prophetic ministry—First ten chapters of Jeremiah cover period of Josiah's reign.
**621 B.C.**
Josiah orders Temple repairs—He is 26 years old in the eighteenth year of his reign—the Law is rediscovered—the Temple and the land are cleansed of idolatry—the covenant is restored (see Jeremiah 11:1ff) and the Passover is celebrated.
**612 B.C.**
Babylon defeats Assyria—City of Nineveh falls
**609 B.C.**
Josiah Is killed at Megiddo—Josiah's son Jehoahaz reigns threee months—Egypt installs Jehoiakim as king—He reigns eleven years
**609–597 B.C.**
Habakkuk's prophetic ministry begins
Jeremiah's "Temple Address" (see Jeremiah 7:1–8:12)
**605 B.C.**
Nebuchadnezzar defeats Egypt at Battle of Carchemesh (Jer. 46:2)

This illuminated manuscript from France, circa 1410, shows the destruction of the Temple in Jerusalem and the deportation of the Jews to Babylon. The piece was executed by an artist dubbed "Master of the Breviary of Jean sans Peur." The illumination displays a thorough familiarity with the work of the de Limbourg brothers—famous for the illuminated manuscript called Très Riches Heures.

**604 B.C.**
Ashkelon falls to Nebuchadnezzar (Jer. 47:5ff; Zeph. 2:4ff)

**601 B.C.**
Daniel and friends taken to Babylon as royal hostages

**599 B.C.**
Nebuchadnezzar besieges Jerusalem

**598 B.C.**
King Jehoiakim dies—His son Jehoiachin ("Jeconiah" in 1 Chron. 3:16 and "Coniah" in Jer. 22:24) takes the throne

**597 B.C.**
The first fall of Jerusalem—Jehoiachin surrenders to Nebuchadnezzar—The first deportation (around 10,000 Jews) to Babylon—Jehoiachin's uncle Mattaniah (renamed Zedekiah) reigns as vassal king—He reigns eleven years.

**593 B.C.**
Ezekiel begins prophetic ministry (for twenty years)

**589 B.C.**
Pharaoh Hophra rules Egypt—Zedekiah conspires with Hophra and rebels against Babylon

**587 B.C.**
The second fall of Jerusalem—The second deportation

READING ASSIGNMENT:
Jeremiah 34–52

# SESSION III: RECITATION
Jeremiah 1–52

## Comprehension Questions

*Answer these questions for factual recall.*

1. What was the purpose of Jeremiah's prophetic work? What biblical text addresses this?
2. What does Jeremiah say would happen to Judah?
3. What sins of Judah are mentioned in Jeremiah?
4. How did the people of Anathoth respond to Jeremiah's proclamations? What did they do to him?
5. How are the people likened to water cisterns (wells for storing water) in Jeremiah 2?
6. Give one example of the kind of rejection faced by Jeremiah.
7. What does Jeremiah 31 teach?

# OPTIONAL SESSION: ACTIVITY

## Seeing the New Testament in Jeremiah

The importance of Jeremiah's teaching to the New Testament cannot be overestimated. The list below includes a reference from Jeremiah and a New Testament reference. In each instance, write a brief explanation of how the New Testament passages use Jeremiah's prophecy to explain what has happened during, and as a result of, the ministry and sacrifice of Christ. Notes in some Bibles may prove helpful for this exercise.

1. Jeremiah 31:31–34 / Hebrews 8:6–13 and Hebrews 10:16
2. Jeremiah 31:15 / Matthew 2:16–18
3. Jeremiah 7:11 / Matthew 21:12–13; Mark 11:17; Luke 19:46
4. Jeremiah 32:6–9 / Matthew 27:9–10
5. Jeremiah 18:6 / Romans 9:21
6. Jeremiah 9:24 / 1 Corinthians 1:31
7. Jeremiah 32:38 / 2 Corinthians 6:16b

## Advanced Questions

1. How is Jesus Christ related to the prophecy of Jeremiah 23 and 33?
2. Are children of believers included in the new covenant?
3. What Church practices are affected by one's view of the new covenant?

## ENDNOTES

1  *This endnote appears only in the teacher's edition.*

# MINOR PROPHETS

What if churches all over your hometown began bursting into flames and Christians began to disappear in droves? Certainly, two things would happen. First, other Christians would begin to pray about it, hoping that God would help the police to find and stop whoever was doing it. Second, a lot of investigating would begin in hopes of nabbing the arsonists and kidnappers. So, the praying and investigation begins, but it is fruitless. Still, every night or two another church is burnt and a bunch of Christians disappear. You start worrying. What if your church is next? What if you or your family is taken? One night you are unable to sleep, so you are sitting in your bed, looking out your window at 2:00 A.M. You can see the First Christian Church up the hill near to your house about five blocks away. Suddenly, you see a flash of light. Someone is trying to burn the church. Without thinking—who can think straight this early in the morning?—you dash to the garage and hop on your bike. Peddling as fast as you can, the glow of the now-blazing building illuminates the road before you. You can hear the sounds of hooting and hollering and the loud rumble of motorcycle engines. "Back to McMurry's Cave!" you hear one of the hooligans shout, as the assortment of Harley's and Yamaha's rip through the night.

OK, this is the part of the story where you are really not thinking

straight—remember, it is 2:15 A.M. You know McMurry's Cave (you used to play there as a child) and you decide that you will track them down and find out why this band of ruffians is so intent on destroying the church. Curiosity has got the better of you. So, peddling with fury, you quickly arrive at the cave. As you race to the cave, you imagine what these criminals will be like. They have eluded law enforcement so deftly that you imagine that they are probably

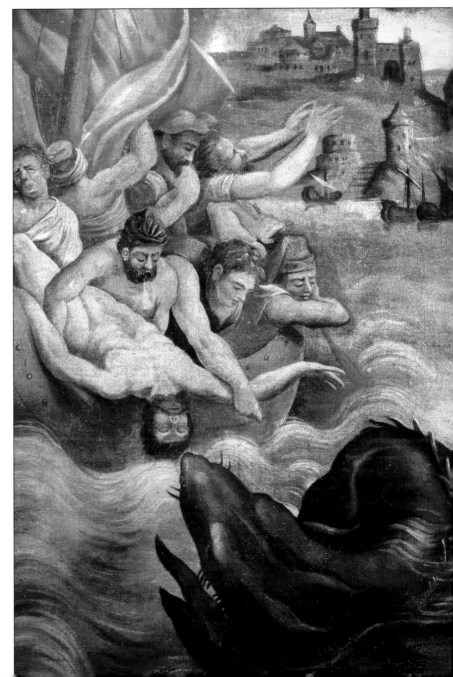

This depiction of Jonah being thrown into the sea was done by an unknown artist in 1606. Notice the great fish that served as Jonah's living quarters for three days waits in the foreground.

an extremely intelligent, disgruntled group of committed atheists who had gained a hatred of Christianity from bad experiences in Sunday School. (Remember you are not thinking straight!)

Arriving at the cave and finding a nook where you can see and hear, but not be seen or heard, you find that you could not have been more wrong. You thought that you would find criminal masterminds reading Bertrand Russell and listening to Schopenhauer, but what you find is a rowdy biker gang engaged in a wild party. The name of the gang is the Brothers of Screwtape and their leader, Urich, does not remind you of Moriarty. His only talent seems to be that he can drink three beers at once and belch to the accompaniment of music that sounds something like animals being tortured. In fact, the whole gang is a bunch of misfits, and they are engaged in every sin imaginable . . . with gusto.

Suddenly, your mind starts to kick into gear, and you realize what sort of danger you are in. Some people at your church have disappeared never to be heard from again. You might be next. Thankfully, many of the gang members have fallen asleep in a drunken stupor. You decide that you need to go home and call the police. Before you move from your safe hiding place, you pray (quietly). As you pray, you find yourself asking God to bring justice to these vagabonds. You even ask God why He has allowed these wretched sinners to persecute His people.

As you whisper, "Amen," and open your eyes you are aghast at what you see. God gives you a glimpse into the world of the spirits. All around the camp of the biker gang you see angels (not demons) who are planning out the next church that will be destroyed. You gasp . . . God, it seems, is on *their* side! Why is God helping these mad men persecute His people?

As you peddle back home, you think about the Christians in your community. You realize that the lives of many are full of sin. Some complain about what God

requires, like resting on the Sabbath (what a miserly God! He makes us rest).[1] They would rather work seven days than six, for they love money. Others cheat their neighbors in the marketplace. They love themselves more than others. Maybe this is why God is using the gang to persecute His people?

If you had lived during the time of the minor prophets (850–450 B.C.), you would have encountered such a situation. What would you do in such a time? Whom do you think God would send to make things right? What would God do to His beloved people? Questions like these would have been on your heart if you sought to serve God during this time.

# GENERAL INFORMATION

## Author and Context

The minor prophets of the Old Testament include the last twelve books in our English Bibles: Hosea, Joel, Amos, Obadiah, Jonah, Micah, Nahum, Habakkuk, Zephaniah, Haggai, Zechariah and Malachi. Each book is named for the prophet who spoke the prophecies in the book so named. We call them "minor" simply because their writings are shorter than other prophets like Isaiah, Jeremiah and Ezekiel.

Who are the prophets themselves, though? While we have some information about the prophets, we actually know very little about them. Usually each prophetic book tells us what town the prophet came from and under which kings he served. This is not universal, however, as some of the books give us even less personal information. In the end, the prophets present themselves as relatively unimportant messengers of God's important Word. So, our eyes and ears should be fixed on the message in order to understand the messengers.

## Significance

We can see the broad significance of the minor prophets in the storyline behind them. During the time of the minor prophets, Israel and Judah neglect the covenant God made with them on Mt. Sinai. They fail to remember their deliverance from Egyptian bondage, they forget the Lord's covenant mercies and twist God's law to serve their own unjust ends. God's people are not a light among the surrounding nations, and instead they add to the sinful darkness of the heathen. Mere men mock Yahweh's holy name, and so the Almighty raises up His prophets. Through the prophets, God calls His people to repentance and pronounces fierce woes on the wicked; He utterly destroys rival cities, nations, kings and cultures with the horrors of His holiness. God vows to lead His covenant people away into captivity by the wicked Assyrians and Babylonians.

And yet God's coming in judgment also contains the promise of a return from exile under the Persians and a coming salvation of the world. The Jewish return to the Promised Land occurs around 459 B.C. under Ezra and 444 B.C. under Nehemiah, during the same period of time in which Herodotus is writing his *Histories* far away in Halicarnassus. Through the Messiah, God's judgment will turn to mercy. God will remember the covenant He has made with His people. All the nations will one day come to worship the one true God—the God of Abraham, Isaac and Jacob. Through this storyline we see how our Triune God destroys wickedness to establish righteousness; how He brings low before raising up; how the pattern of death and resurrection is built into His story of His creation. Lastly, the New Testament picks up on many of the images and metaphors used by the minor prophets (e.g., stars falling, mountains leveled, etc.) to describe the fulfillment of these prophecies in the first century A.D.

## Setting

Under Jeroboam II's reign in Israel (793–753 B.C.), the people of Israel grew in wealth, pride and oppression of the poor. At the same time, the nation of Assyria experienced internal turmoil under the weak rule of Adad-nirari III (810–783 B.C.). By 745 B.C., however, Assyria's Tiglath-pilesar III (also called Pul in the Old Testament) came to power and greatly strengthened the nation. After Tiglath-pilesar III, his son Shalmaneser V ruled Assyria (727–722 B.C.) and took the northern tribes of Israel captive in 722 B.C.

As Israel was taken captive, it looked as though the Assyrians would take Judah as well. But we read in 2 Kings 18 how good King Hezekiah sought the Lord, and the Lord slaughtered 185,000 Assyrians in a single night. Over one hundred years later Nabopolassar, king of Babylon, fought the Assyrians the entire duration of his reign (626–605 B.C.), finally toppling the Assyrians in the last year of his reign. During the same time, Josiah, the last good king of Judah (640–609 B.C.) instituted a number of short lived reforms among God's people. But Nabopolassar's son, Nebuchadnezzar II, became king (605–562 B.C.) after his father's death, and it is under him that Judah was led into captivity through three deportations to Babylon (605, 597 and 586 B.C.). In the last Babylonian deportation, Jerusalem was razed to the ground. Within fifty years of the destruction of Jerusalem, however, a Persian king named Cyrus II seized control of Babylon (539 B.C.) and then later decreed that the Jews were permitted to return to the Promised

Mosaics depicting Hosea and Micah from the Basilica of Saint Mark the Evangelist, the cathedral church of the city and seat of the Patriarch of Venice since 1807. The relics of Saint Mark were brought here in 828 from Alexandria. It was said that Mark had evangelized the people of the Veneto, becoming their patron saint.

The prophet Amos depicted by Gustave Doré.

Land. At about this same time, the Persians and the Medes were waging war against the Scythians (*Histories* 4.83–144). After this decree of Cyrus, Nehemiah and Ezra returned to Judah to rebuild the walls of Jerusalem and the Temple. This was also the period in which the last of the minor prophets ministered to God's people. By 475 B.C., the Jews finished rebuilding the Temple in Jerusalem, and some time in the following decades the last prophet of the Old Testament, Malachi, prophesied. His book is the last in the Bible before the coming of Jesus Christ.

## Summary and Setting

In reading the minor prophets, there are many challenging images, metaphors and historical situations. If we understand the main thrust of each book, however, we have a roadmap for navigating difficult passages and seeing the overall worldview and message. So, let us chronologically consider brief summaries of each book to help us through the minor prophets.

OBADIAH (c. 845 B.C.). Probably around the same time as Joel and Elisha's ministry, Obadiah presents a very clear prophetic message: God will come in judgment against Edom because Edom did not come to the military aid of Judah when Judah needed it. The brotherly ties between Jacob (father of the nations of Israel and Judah) and Esau (father of the nation of Edom) bound Edom to assist Judah in God's eyes, despite the centuries that had passed since the days of Jacob and Esau.

JOEL (c. 835 B.C.). Joel pronounces that the day of the Lord is coming and urges God's people to repent. He promises the Lord will again look favorably upon His people when they repent and that He will restore Israel before the coming of Jesus (2:18–27), bring another day of the Lord after the coming of Jesus (2:28–3:8) and bring yet one more day of the Lord upon the Gentiles (3:9–17). In the end, the result of God's judgment is to destroy sin and establish peace, cleansing and righteousness (3:18–21).

JONAH (c. 800 B.C.). Jonah lived around the same time as Amos, and his prophecy to Ninevah probably occurs no later than 773 B.C. Knowing that God is gracious, Jonah rejects God's command to preach repentance to Ninevah and heads out to sea in the opposite direction. Jonah subsequently finds himself in the belly of a great fish and then pleads with God to have mercy upon him. After God graciously resurrects Jonah from the belly of the fish, God sends him to Ninevah to preach. The inhabitants of the city repent of their sins in light of God's message, yet the book ends with Jonah not being pleased at God's work of redemption.

AMOS (c. 760 B.C.). Amos had two callings: he was a shepherd in Judah and a prophet to Israel during the reign of Jeroboam II. In his prophecy, Amos lashes out at the social injustices of Israel: they neglect the poor, cheat each other and do not love righteousness. God speaks through Amos that His justice will be like a hunting lion after Israel, if they do not repent. The ultimate point of God speaking in this way to Israel, however, is revealed in Amos 5:15. God sends Amos not only to pronounce judgment against Israel, but also to persuade His people to repent in light of the fierceness of His holiness.

HOSEA (c. 760-720 B.C.). Hosea ministered as prophet through the reigns of the Judean kings Uzziah, Jotham, Ahaz and Hezekiah. While Amos prophecies concerning the injustices of Israel, Hosea prophecies against the idolatry of Judah and the resultant injustices. In chapters 1-3, the Lord commands Hosea to marry a prostitute (Gomer) and to redeem her from her infidelities and covenant breaking. Following these events, God then uses Hosea's relationship with Gomer to illustrate His relationship with Judah (chapters 4-14). Though Judah commits adultery with false gods by not worshiping the Lord as He has commanded, God brings judgment against His wife and promises to redeem her.

MICAH (c. 737-690 B.C.). Micah of Moresheth brought God's covenant lawsuit against Samaria and Jerusalem during the reigns of Jotham, Ahaz and Hezekiah. According to Micah, God will tread down the high places, the workers of iniquity and all that exalt themselves without walking humbly before God—including those in foreign nations. Micah denounces princes, leaders and all those that do not

love God's mercy and live in righteousness. Yet God continues to maintain a remnant of His forgiven followers, and He will bless this remnant to conquer the whole earth with God's righteousness.

NAHUM (c. 650 B.C.). Like Obadiah, Nahum centered his sights on a people other than Israel or Judah: the inhabitants of Ninevah (between 664 and 612 B.C.). In the prior century, Ninevah had repented of its sins under the prophecy of Jonah. Yet now, Ninevah dares to set itself up against the holy God (cf. 1:2-8). God thus taunts and mocks this city and makes it very clear that no hope or mercy will be shown to Ninevah. God's anger is stirred, and nothing can turn away His wrath. Nahum, in other words, is one of the most frightful war poems ever written. As foresworn, God brings judgment upon Ninevah when Nabopolassar, king of the Babylonians (also called Chaldeans), seizes control of the city in 612 B.C. The root lesson here is that God loves to be merciful but brings vengeance against those who act treacherously toward His kindness.

ZEPHANIAH (c. 640 B.C.). In similar fashion as Joel, Zephaniah promises that the day of the Lord will soon arrive and that the wicked will not stand. Zephaniah claims Ninevah and Assyria will fall, and he even speaks woe to the city of Jerusalem—which he likens to a filthy, polluted, unclean city. Through the coming judgment, God pledges to keep a remnant and vows to grant the remnant forgiveness and cause their salvation to be a blessing to all the nations.

HABAKKUK (c. 609 B.C.). Habakkuk's prophecy appeared before the conquering of Judah by Babylon, taking the form of a dialogue between the prophet and God. Initially, Habakkuk questions how long God's law will be neglected. From this, the Lord promises to raise up the wicked Babylonians to destroy the wicked who live in Judah. Habakkuk responds with amazement that God would use an even more wicked nation to punish Judah. But God teaches Habakkuk the ways of His wisdom and that these ways can be grasped only by faith. Though wickedness seems to cover the whole earth in Habakkuk's view, God promises to eventually cover the earth with His righteousness, just as the seas are covered with water.

Haggai (c. 520 B.C.). In the decades prior, the Babylonians had destroyed Jerusalem and the Temple, yet God provided for the remnant and allowed them to return and rebuild under the Persians. Under Darius, king of Persia, God raised up the prophet Haggai to motivate His people to finish reconstructing the Temple. Once they finish building the Temple, God's Spirit does not return to the Temple, though He assures His people that He still is with them. By not sending His Spirit to fill the Temple, God points forward to the future return of God's glory. At this future time, God will begin to bring the nations to the true Temple. In the meantime, God's people should remember that their sin makes them unclean and that the lessons learned in their prior captivity must not be forgotten.

Zechariah (c. 520 B.C.). Like Haggai, Zechariah prophesied to motivate the people to finish reconstructing the Temple. Though they sin and have not learned to hate sin and love righteousness, God still considers His people as the apple of His eye. And whereas Haggai points toward Jesus Christ in a shadowy way, Zechariah points forward to Jesus Christ explicitly, through his complex dreams and visions. Though we cannot here unpack all of the features of Zechariah's prophecy, we see very clearly that God Himself will be pierced for the sins of His people in 12:10. When this happens, God will gloriously pour out His Spirit upon the nations and ultimately bring them all to salvation.

Malachi (c. 444 B.C.). Malachi is the last book of the Old Testament and the last minor prophet. And here we find that God's people are still unwilling to forsake their sins. They wrongly complain about God's failure to love them and the weariness of doing what God commands, and so God threatens to come again to judge their sins. In other words, God's people have not yet truly returned from exile, for they still seek other gods and refuse to follow Yahweh. The glory of God's people fades more and more in the centuries that follow, until Jesus Christ leads His people out of the captivity of their sins.

Gustave Doré's illustration of the people mourning over the ruins or Jerusalem, as described in Joel and Malachi.

## Worldview

Throughout our lives, we often experience the betrayal of a friend or even a family member. Small scale betrayals might include a cruel story told behind our back, while large scale betrayals usually include something more diabolical. Yet, regardless of its final size, all betrayal is alike. It starts when someone unexpectedly acts towards another according to a lie rather than the truth. Betrayal can start out small, but over time it grows into something hurtful, ugly and irrational. Betrayal, like other sins, works like leaven: just a little bit is enough to affect the whole loaf.

All of creation bears a relationship to God and one another and we often call this relationship a *covenant*. Certain obligations, promises and punishments for disobedience are attached to covenants, and God tells us in the Bible what these terms are. For instance, all of creation is required to lovingly serve the Triune God and each other, whether they want to or not. Or to pick another example, the relationship of Esau to Jacob should have been enough for Edom to come to Judah's aid (see Obadiah). Even though Jacob and Esau had been dead for centuries, and even though they were placed into the same family simply because that is the way God wanted it, they still under the covenant obligations of family. Refusal to act according to the covenant relationship is an act of betrayal and brings God's wrath. For Judah and Israel in the Old Testament, God required them to act according to the special covenants established with them as God's chosen people. Judah and Israel had been given countless blessings through history—the chief of these being a special covenant relationship with God.

Like traitors who give their nation up to the enemy, or like unfaithful spouses who forget their wedding vows, God's people rebelled against God and betray the kind covenant relationship God established. During the early years of the ministry of the minor prophets, God warns His people about harboring sin and allowing it to grow in their lives. God's covenant people should not be participating in sin, and God reminds His people of the curses that are a part of their covenant relationship with Him. Those refusing to repent of their sins are ultimately betraying the very God Who gave them life, a nation, the privilege of serving God and every other blessing..

But in time all sin must be dealt with, and it can be dealt with in two ways. God either destroys the sin and the sinner; or the sinner finds forgiveness for his sin through God's lovingkindness. Those finding forgiveness are declared righteous by God. Those refusing to repent are damned. So, regardless of how it is dealt with, the fact is that God will most certainly deal with sin. Sinners might deny they are covenantally accountable to God, but God still holds them accountable.

God's certain dealing with sin, however, looks strange at first glance. For example, God makes it clear that He preserves a remnant of faithful, repentant people within Israel and Judah. Though God grants the faithful forgiveness for their individual sins, God's faithful still pass through some of God's judgments alongside the wicked. Why would God do such a thing? The righteous should be spared and only the wicked suffer, right? To be specific, could you be a forgiven Israelite and still have the Assyrians take away all of your land? The answer is, obviously, Yes.

In the minor prophets, we see this strange picture over and over again. The wicked prosper for a time at the expense of the weak and the righteous. When God's judgment falls upon the wicked, the weak and the righteous suffer alongside of the wicked. But in due time, God brings utter destruction to the wicked and raises up His righteous remnant to better things than they once had. In the midst of judgment and difficulties, God's righteous cling to God's promises and trust in Him as He brings them through hardship. The wicked, on the other hand, know no comfort and hope. And through the sufferings, God is ultimately being kind to His righteous people but ultimately destroying those betraying Him. Thus, the wicked suffer unto despair, while the righteous suffer unto glory. In other words, there can be no glorious resurrection without a death. Humility precedes exaltation—the meek inherit the earth. The last end up first. God works according to this pattern throughout the Scriptures, and God's people find great comfort as they apply it to their own lives.

Just as a little sin leavens the whole loaf, so too does a little faith in God's promises leaven the whole loaf. As God promises judgment upon sin and wickedness, God promises mercy and blessing to those repenting and trusting in Him. The righteous, who God leads into captivity and suffering, also receive God's promises of a coming righteous Messiah (King). This Messiah will suffer in place of the righteous, and the Messiah will lead His people in glory. Though God's people live in exile from the Promised Land, God will grant an even greater land (the whole earth) when the Messiah comes to lead His people out of captivity. Though God's people witness the destruction of their Temple, the Messiah will establish a Temple (His Church) greater than that of Solomon's.

When we look at the large, strange picture of how God conducts history, we might be tempted to think betrayals are the most prominent feature. After all, history is *filled* with the wickedness of man. While we must affirm that man's sin is a major feature of history, we must not lose the bigger picture of God's justice and lovingkindness. God judges sin and destroys it, *so that* His righteousness, peace and rest come into focus. At the end of history, the minor prophets tell us that the earth will be filled with God's glory—not man's sinful betrayals. While not at all losing sight of the wickedness of sin, we must see the larger picture of how God is covering the earth with His righteousness: "For the earth shall be filled with the knowledge of the glory of the LORD, as the waters cover the sea" (Hab. 2:14).

In other words, things are often not what they seem in our wisdom. With God's wisdom as revealed by the minor prophets, we see that the rise of the wicked and the rise of the righteous both serve God's ends. All things work according to God's timing and His counsel—Romans 8:28 makes this clear. This gives God's faithful people a sure hope and comfort in times of trouble. In the ups and downs of the centuries, God is bringing His creation into His rest and righteousness through Jesus Christ. Against this backdrop we see how "the just shall live by faith" (Hab. 2:4). This faith is not blind trust. It is a faith that believes God is perfect and good in how He conducts history. It is a faith not easily shaken when difficult times come. It is a faith that trusts in the covenant promises revealed by the minor prophets that find fulfillment in Jesus Christ.

—*J.C. Evans*

## For Further Reading

Spielvogel, Jackson. *Western Civilization.* Fifth Edition. Belmont, Calif.: Wadsworth/Thomson

Learning, 2003. 30-49[2]

*Veritas Press Bible Cards: Chronicles through Malachi and Job.* Lancaster, Pa.: Veritas Press. 69, 72, 75 and 95.

Leithart, Peter. *A House for My Name.* Moscow, Idaho: Canon Press, 2000. 161–239.

 **READING ASSIGNMENT:**
Obadiah, Joel, Amos, Jonah

# SESSION I: PRELUDE

Obadiah, Joel, Amos, Jonah

## A Question to Consider

Why can it be said that our parents punish us when we do wrong because they love us?

*From the General Information above answer the following questions:*

1. Who were some of the minor prophets in the Old Testament, and what did these prophets do?
2. When God brings judgment upon someone or something, is this a merciful act, an act of wrath or both?
3. Why do we call the minor prophets *minor*?
4. What nations (other than Israel and Judah) do the minor prophets talk about?
5. What is the storyline of the minor prophets?
6. When did the minor prophets minister to God's people?
7. How many minor prophets are there?

 **READING ASSIGNMENT:**
Hosea, Micah and Nahum

# SESSION II: DISCUSSION

Hosea, Micah and Nahum

## A Question to Consider

Does the commission of a sin open the door to more and greater sins? If so, is there often a progression from bad to worse?

*Discuss or list short answers to the following questions:*

### Text Analysis

1. What particular sins does God condemn in Jonah and Hosea?
2. What are some of the promises God speaks through the prophets Jonah and Hosea? How are these promises comforting?
3. In what year and by whom is Israel taken captive? Judah? What might explain the differences in years and captors?

### Cultural Analysis

1. Even though we do not live in the Old Testament kingdoms of Judah or Israel, does the Old Testament message of faithfulness to the God of the Bible have relevance? How about for unbelievers?
2. Can God bring destruction on us as a nation and still make good on His promises to bless?
3. How are our sins today similar to those addressed by the minor prophets? Name one clear and significant way our sins are different from those found in the minor prophets?

## SUMMA

 *Write an essay or discuss this question, integrating what you have learned from the material above.*
What does conscious toleration of sin lead to?

 **READING ASSIGNMENT:**
Zephaniah, Habakkuk, Haggai, Zechariah, Malachi

## SESSION III: RECITATION

Zephaniah, Habakkuk, Haggai, Zechariah, Malachi

### Comprehension Questions

*Answer these questions for factual recall.*

1. What sin did the nation of Edom commit that caused their condemnation as recorded in Obadiah?
2. How is God's judgment pictured in the book of Joel? Why?
3. Why is Jonah headed to Tarshish?
4. What happens at the end of the book of Jonah that discourages the prophet? What lesson is God trying to teach Jonah?
5. Whom does God command the prophet Hosea to marry? What is she like?
6. Of what is Hosea's marriage symbolic?
7. How do God's actions toward Ninevah change from the book of Jonah to the book of Nahum?
8. How is the city of Jerusalem described in the book of Zephaniah?
9. What is Habakkuk's objection to God's announcement of judgment?

Micah was a prophet of great moral strength and wisdom. This portrayal of him was started by Hubert van Eyck and completed by his brother Jan in 1432. It is painted on the back of the doors of the polyptych of the Mystical Lamb.

10. What is Haggai commanding the people to do?
11. What warnings and promises does God give His people in Malachi?

## OPTIONAL SESSION: DISCUSSION

*Discuss the following questions or answer in a short essay.*

1. Now that Jesus Christ has come, how does this make our situation different from that of the minor prophets?
2. Are we morally different from God's people in the Old Testament? What should we learn from them?
3. Having read the minor prophets, do you think Christians should have a pessimistic or optimistic

outlook on the future? In other words, what has God promised in our age?

4. What are some rival notions of what the future holds for Christians?

5. Throughout the minor prophets, we see the use of catastrophic imagery (for example, stars falling and mountains melting). Do we find this imagery elsewhere in the Bible, and is it being used in a similar situation?

6. What are the major concerns of the minor prophets as they tell the story of history?

7. Where is God directing all of history, and what are some of the means by which God directs history?

### Endnotes

1   Sadly, with the rest that some Christians have practiced over the ages (i.e., sort of a holy "Time Out"), we see that we can turn the most gracious gifts into joyless burdens.

2   Spielvogel's section "The Hebrews: 'The Children of Israel'" in chapter 2 is factually wrong. We know the Old Testament to be a reliable account of history and God's providential work. It is not in conflict with archeology, and it is increasingly relied upon by secular scholars to understand ancient history.

# SECONDARY BOOKS
Second Semester

# THE SILVER CHAIR

"Let go and let God." How many times have we heard that statement in our day? It is certainly true, but only in one sense. We have seen and will see how God regenerates sinners. Dragons cannot "undragon" themselves—no matter how hard they scrape. A scale or two might come off, but the dragon remains a dragon. He needs to stop trying and submit to the Lion of Judah, Who has the ability to change a "heart of stone into a heart of flesh." Sinners must "let go and let God" make their dry bones live.

"Let go and let God," however, can be misleading when we consider how we grow in the Christian life (growing in the Christian life is a process called *sanctification¹*). Becoming more holy, however, is not just a work that God does to us. It is work that God does with us. We can not do it without Him. The hymn writer Robert Robinson says

> Come, Thou Fount of every blessing,
> Tune my heart to sing Thy grace;
> Streams of mercy, never ceasing,
> Call for songs of loudest praise.
> Teach me some melodious sonnet,
> Sung by flaming tongues above.
> Praise the mount! I'm fixed upon it,
> Mount of Thy redeeming love.

Robinson recognized that our serving God was based on God's work in us. That is why he calls on God to *"tune"* his heart. We also have to recognize, however, that even when we are believers. The battle against sin is not over . . . it is only beginning. God graciously gives us His word to sanctify us. It tells us, in God's law, how He would have us live to please Him. At times as believers, we even find ourselves fighting against God's grace. In the same hymn Robinson wisely recognizes this truth, saying

> O to grace how great a debtor
> Daily I'm constrained to be!
> Let Thy goodness, like a fetter,
> Bind my wandering heart to Thee.
> Prone to wander, Lord, I feel it,
> Prone to leave the God I love;
> Here's my heart, O take and seal it,
> Seal it for Thy courts above.

In this book of *The Chronicles of Narnia*, we will see how God uses His word to *sanctify* us, and we will learn that He even uses our own failures to bring us along and to bring us to His purposes.

Throughout the *Chronicles* Lewis borrows creatures from classical mythology, but in this book he invents one. The glum and practical marsh-wiggles were inspired by the author's pessimistic gardener, Fred Paxford.

# GENERAL INFORMATION

## Significance

The central theme of this book is the importance of the Spiritual Disciplines. *The Magician's Nephew* gives us Creation and Fall. *The Lion, the Witch and the Wardrobe* gives us the Substitutionary Atonement. *The Horse and His Boy* is a wonderful treatment of Providence. *Prince Caspian* is about Loyalty and Government. *The Voyage of the Dawn Treader* is about Regeneration. In this book, *The Silver Chair*, Eustace (now reformed) Scrubb and Jill Pole are summoned into Narnia, and given a mission by Aslan. *The Silver Chair* is about the fulfillment of that mission and how Aslan gave certain "signs" to follow in order to accomplish that mission. The book is about the importance of (the discipline of) following these signs. It also teaches that sanctification is by grace, just as salvation is, because the company muffs the first three of the four signs given—and yet Aslan is kind to them, and they accomplish their purpose despite this failure.

## Main Characters

We have already met Eustace Scrubb. The Pevensies can no longer come back into Narnia, and Eustace is now the main character. He brings Jill Pole with him to Narnia, and they are given a mission by Aslan. That mission is to find and bring back Prince

Glimfeather is the first Narnian Jill meets. He is a white owl about four feet tall who cleverly saves the children from Trumpkin, putting them under lock and key. Then later, at a more "sensible" hour, he carries Jill to the meeting of the Parliament of Owls.

Rilian, the son of Caspian the Tenth, and his queen, the daughter of Ramandu, whom he met in *The Voyage of the Dawn Treader*. Glimfeather is an owl who meets them as they arrive in Narnia and brings them to Puddleglum the Marsh-wiggle, one of Lewis's more memorable creations. Puddleglum agrees to go with them to the north to search for the lost prince. On their mission they encounter the Lady of the Green Kirtle, who is in the same family of northern witches as the White Witch was. And of course, Aslan is a character throughout the book, although he is present only at the beginning and the end.

## Summary and Setting

Caspian and his queen have a son, Rilian. When he is about twenty, his mother is killed by a green serpent when they are all out on a Maying expedition, which is a ritual celebrating springtime. Rilian goes out seeking revenge upon the serpent, but meets with a Green Lady instead, with whom he falls in love. Because she is a witch, she enchants him, and he disappears from Narnia. Aslan summons Eustace and Jill into Narnia in order for them to find the lost prince. The adventure ensues in which they are faced with many challenges and find themselves failing at many points. Aslan, however, is working out his will even through their mistakes.

## Worldview

Before we get to the gift of the signs to Jill (and their importance in the story), we have to discuss for a few moments how she comes to the position of being able to receive them. Eustace and Jill are both students at Experiment House, the kind of modern school that C.S. Lewis loathed. The school is completely secular and is a place where ordinary kids are bullied because the Head (we would say Headmaster in America) thinks that bullies are interesting psychological subjects. Eustace (prior to his transformation in *The Voyage of the Dawn Treader*) used to fit right in. But now that he has changed, he has found himself standing up to the bullies that run the school. In this new circumstance, he comes upon Jill who is crying behind the gym because of the treatment she had been getting. As they talk, he tells her a little about Narnia, and explains the reason he is now so different. They both call out to Aslan but are interrupted by the bullies. In order to escape, they try a door in the wall of the school grounds, and both find themselves in Aslan's country.

As they are walking along there, they come to the edge of a precipice, and because Jill despises Eustace in his fear of heights, she shows off by standing a little bit too close to the edge. She loses her head, and Eustace, trying to stop her from falling, falls himself. Aslan rushes to the edge of the cliff, and blows him to Narnia. All of this is in order to provide Jill with the same kind of necessary spiritual experience that Eustace has in the previous book. As you should recall, Eustace goes through the experience of regeneration in which he is "undragoned." This is not something he could do by himself at all. And Jill, even though she

is not as insufferable as Eustace was, is still in need of the same transformation. The sin that she commits in Aslan's country sets the stage for this.

After she has had a good cry, she discovers that she is terribly thirsty—in other words, she comes to an awareness of her need for grace. She goes looking for water, and she finally finds a stream. But between her and the stream is the lion. She feels as though she will die if she does not get to the water, but she would much rather have the water without the lion. In talking to him, she quickly discovers that he is the kind of lion who makes no deals when it comes to this kind of thing. He tells her there is no other stream, and she will die if she does not come to drink from this one. He refuses to move for her sake, and he makes no promises. When asked if he eats little girls, he replies that he has devoured kings and empires, and that would include little girls. In short, all of this is to make the emphatic point that Aslan cuts no deals and that the repentant sinner who comes to him must do so without any conditions at all.

When Puddleglum and the children first meet the black knight, he is silent and in the company of the Lady of the Green Kirtle. The knight has no device on his shield, so they are unable to identify him. His lack of discourse with the travellers inspires the marsh-wiggle to muse with ghastly cheerfulness that he might be just a skeleton or someone invisible.

After she has come to the water (in a wonderful picture of conversion), she says to Aslan that she and Eustace had called out to someone named Aslan. Aslan reveals himself to her by name, but also lets her know that she would not have called out to him at all unless he had first been calling her. Just as the Bible says, we love Him because He first loved us. When we come to Christ, it is only possible because Christ has summoned us first.

Now, it is in this setting, with Jill well-converted, that Aslan gives her the signs to follow. The language that Aslan uses in teaching her these signs has definite echoes of Deuteronomy 6:4-9. The signs are the law of Aslan, they are his commandments. He tells Jill to memorize them, internalize them, get the signs down into her bones, so that when the time comes, the appropriate sign will be seen as fulfilled, and complications will be avoided. This is Lewis's doctrine of sanctification—how a Christian makes progress in the Christian life.

Of course, all the Christian life is to be lived out by grace. But the reason for taking the signs in this way is that it gives grace raw material to work on, and that raw material must also be understood as grace. When we see God's Word with the eye of faith, we do not set grace and law against one another, as though they were enemies. Elsewhere, Lewis compares this to learning how to dance. When someone is first learning to dance, they are not really dancing. It would be more accurate to say that they were counting. "*One,* two, three! *One,* two, three!" But once the dance has been mastered (and mastered by some form of rote learning), it is possible for the dancer to stop counting and to start thinking about the one he is dancing with. It is the same here. If Jill had done what Aslan told her to, which was to say the signs every night, and again every morning, the signs would have become second nature to her, and she would have been free to think about Aslan and his guidance, and he would have had signs in her mind that were clearly already there, and which he could bring to her mind quickly. But as it was, Jill started neglected her spiritual disciplines, and pretty soon the signs got muddled in her mind, and then they were distracted by the Lady of the Green Kirtle who told them that the giants of Harfang would take them in out of the cold. Soon she and Eustace could think of nothing but getting warm, which is not what they were told to think about.

This is not to say that the law and gospel cannot be contrasted, but it demonstrates that our attitude toward both of them is determined by our spiritual state. In one sense, the law and the gospel can be contrasted in the same way that a carrot and a stick can be contrasted in their power to motivate a mule. The *stick* of God's law threatens the unbeliever as he approaches a holy God, condemning him and driving him to find Christ. God motivates not only with the *stick,* however, but also with the *carrot* of the gospel. He offers Christ to the sinner and, with Christ, full and free forgiveness. The law condemns the unbeliever (driving him to Christ) and the gospel appeals to the unbeliever (attracting him to Christ). God both pushes and pulls us into His kingdom. In this way the law and the gospel can be contrasted.

The reaction of believers and unbelievers to both the law and the gospel is not a story in contrast but one that shows the great divide between these groups. Those who reject Christ hate the law of God because it condemns them. They also hate the gospel. Paul points out this reaction in 2 Corinthians 2:16 when he says that the smell of Christ that pagans sense among believers is the "aroma of death" to them. For those who trust in Christ, however, the gospel is the "aroma of life" and law, instead of being only a *stick* threatening Hell, becomes a blessed pathway along which believers strive to walk, because they long to please God with all that they do, say and think. In this way, Christians, striving to keep the law by loving God and their neighbors (although imperfectly), find the law to be a wonderful expression of God's grace, because He does not leave us in the dark, but tells us how to live a life pleasing to Him.

In later years of study, we will see this contrast between believers and unbelievers played out in many venues, perhaps most strikingly in Dante's *Divine Comedy.* The *Comedy* chronicles Dante's visits to Hell, Purgatory and Heaven. The unbelievers that Dante meets in Hell are suffering awful punishments, and while they suffer they are railing against God, themselves and others. These damned souls hate both the law and gospel because they hate the God that made both of them. The souls in Purgatory are being cleansed of their sins. In order to be cleansed they are suffering punishments very similar to the ones being suffered in Hell. The reaction of these believers, however, is strikingly different. They see these punishments as both just and good. They love both the law and the gospel because both come from the God Whom they love.

Puddleglum remains conscious of the signs, and when they are unwittingly crossing the ruined city of the giants, he is almost on the verge of figuring it all out. But even though he suspects they are passing right by two of the signs, he allows Eustace and Jill to pressure him into abandoning his questions, and to come with them. Later they all recognized this, and Puddleglum (typically) says that he did not do well enough—he says that he should have insisted on working through the signs.

This relates to another issue. In several places in this book, we see Lewis's resistance to a philosophy that is commonly called *reductionism*. Another simple name for reductionism could be called "nothing-buttery." For example, when someone says that something is "nothing but" the matter that makes it up, he is being a reductionist. If someone were to point to this sentence (the one you are reading right now), and say that it is "nothing but" ink on a page, this simplistic error could be refuted very quickly. It is *possibly* true that the sentence in question is nothing but ink and paper *physically* (although we do not even know that), but the reductionist approach to the sentence is obviously false. The *meaning* of the sentence is not made out of paper and ink.

The reductionist himself knows this, because he expects people to take *his* words seriously. Lewis placed a high priority on countering reductionism wherever he could. In *The Voyage of the Dawn Treader*, Eustace is corrected when he says that in his world a star is a flaming ball of gas. The response is that even in our world that is not what a star is, but only what it is made of. Pointing to what a thing is *"made of"* and reducing it to only that is an extremely dangerous mistake. A person who is created in the image of God is "nothing but" a certain number of chemicals that can be purchased with relative ease, and which do not even cost that much. And yet a human being is much more than the chemicals that make up his body.

Golg, like his fellow Earthmen is a native of Bism. It is an inhabitant of Underland—or the Shallow Lands, as they call it—against its will. This situation makes the normally fun-loving, jig-dancing creatures very sad and somber when the children first encounter them.

In *The Silver Chair,* Lewis attacks reductionism in several places. The first place is where he simply illustrates the error. One of the signs was that they were to follow certain instructions they met when they came to the ruined city of the giants. They took this as following the words "under me" which they had come across in snow without recognizing. When they saw the words from Harfang, it was obvious that they had to get under the ruined city. But when the enchanted Rilian hears this, he dismisses it as laughable. The words were all that remained of an ancient and larger inscription. It was all "nothing but" a coincidence.

After Puddleglum ruined the Witch's attempts at reenchanting them by filling the room with the smell of burnt Marsh-wiggle, he then answered her attempts to enchant them with her reductionism. Lewis is showing clearly his view that this materialistic philosophy is little better than witchcraft. She was saying that Aslan was "nothing but" a cat, made bigger by the imagination. She said that the sun was "nothing but" a lamp, made bigger in the imagination.

Puddleglum defies her by saying that it is not true—but that, even if it were true, he would not submit to her. If the world was nothing but what she pointed to, then the world was a pitiful place, and if the only place to get away from that world was through the imagination, then so be it. He was going to be a Narnian even if there were no Narnia. And he would serve Aslan, even if she was right and Aslan did not exist. It is important to distinguish Puddleglum's wonderful statement of dogged loyalty here with the common device found among liberal theologians, when they say that what matters is not that Jesus rose from the dead, but rather that we believe He did. This is not an answer to the thrumming of the witch; it *is* the thrumming of the witch.

"... the Dwarfs had already got all the snow and all the sods off a large strip of the hillside round the original hole, and the pickaxes and spades were now going ... a dozen or so Moles, newly waked and still very sleepy, and not best pleased, had arrived. But as soon as they understood what it was all about, they joined in with a will."

And this brings us back to the matter of the signs. Because Puddleglum was a native Narnian, the things of Aslan were settled in his bones. This fundamental act of faithfulness in defying the witch was one which arose from long force of habit. But the time of testing, the time when you are being enchanted, is not the time to develop a habit. The habit is either already developed, and can be drawn upon, or it is not, and cannot be.

This is why Aslan gave them a long journey, with testing on the way. That testing was so that they could instill certain habits so that when the ultimate test came, they would have reserves to draw upon. Aslan blew them from his country into Narnia. But he could just as easily have

blown them to the ruined city of the giants and saved everyone a lot of walking. But his point was not to save on the walking, but rather to build a certain kind of character in Eustace and Jill—the kind of character that would rise to the occasion when necessary. So he gave them the journey, along with something that would cultivate that kind of character during the course of the journey. That was the point of the signs.

The signs were not absolutely necessary to the finding of Rilian. Aslan knew where Rilian was the whole time, and if he wanted to use Eustace and Jill in the rescue, he could have made it easy for them. But "easy" establishes no character, and it makes for dull reading indeed.

When God gives us His law, and instructs us to meditate on it day and night, and to teach our children when we walk along the road, and when we rise up, and when we lie down, He is not taking the short cut. We too readily think that God is interested in the "rules" for their own sake, rather than seeing that He is interested in growing a certain kind of creature. The kind of creature He wants to grow is the one who can think of doing *this* when it seems that everything in his mind and body wants to do *that*.

Once out of Aslan's country, the air is thicker, and the distractions are great and many. In such a place, signs are a great help and encouragement in accomplishing what God wants us to accomplish. And because we live in a world very like Narnia in this regard, it would be safe to say that C.S. Lewis wanted children to learn to say their prayers daily, to read their Bibles, and to go to church. Otherwise they will never find and defeat the witch.

—*Douglas Wilson*

## For Further Reading

Ford, Paul F. *Companion to Narnia.* New York, N.Y.: HarperCollins, 1980.

# SESSION I: PRELUDE

> The rain it raineth all around
> Upon the just and unjust fella;
> But chiefly on the just because
> The unjust stole the just's umbrella.
> —Anonymous

## A Question to Consider

Your fairy godmother floats down to you some evening and says you have two choices, and only two. You may choose either a life free of trouble or one where trouble vexes you at every turn. I hope it would be safe to say that all of us would count this question as a "no-brainer" and would thank God for the opportunity to spend the rest of our days on this planet trouble-free. However, on this side of heaven none of us will experience a trouble-free life.

What sort of trouble can we find ourselves in due to circumstances entirely beyond our control? What sort of trouble can we find ourselves in that is our own fault?

*From the General Information above answer the following questions:*

In *The Silver Chair* many of the main characters are on a quest. In the course of their journey they have to face many troubles, problems and difficulties. Sometimes outside circumstances make the journey difficult, and sometimes action (or lack of action) on the part of the characters makes it more difficult.

1. Describe Experiment House.
2. What is the most significant theme of *The Silver Chair?*
3. How is Jill converted?
4. What is *reductionism?*
5. Why do they fail to heed Aslan's signs?
6. How should the law and the gospel be contrasted?
7. How do the attitudes of believers and unbelievers determine their view of both the law and the gospel?

## Optional Activity 1

If you made a map of Narnia for *The Lion, the Witch and the Wardrobe,* add the appropriate elements and countries as you read through *The Silver Chair.*

New items to add to the map will include the Marshlands of the north, the River Shribble, Ettinsmoor, the Ruined City and Harfang. You may also want to draw a map of what you imagine the underworld looks like to the travelers journeying from under the Ruined City through the Deep Realm, over the Sunless Sea to the city of the Dark Castle and then back up to Narnia.

## Optional Activity 2

If you have already read *The Silver Chair,* use the *Companion to Narnia* as a resource and read through the following entries.

**JILL POLE**
**RILIAN**
**GLIMFEATHER**
**PUDDLEGLUM**
**QUEEN OF UNDERLAND**
**UNDERLAND**

READING ASSIGNMENT:
Chapters 1–4

# SESSION II: DISCUSSION
Chapters 1–4

## A Question to Consider

List some emotions. Of what use are your emotions?

*Discuss or list short answers to the following questions:*

### Text Analysis

1. In these opening chapters, the emotions of the main characters are deeply involved with some pivotal decisions they make or acts they commit. How do emotions control the events that occur behind the gym at Experiment House?
2. How do Jill's feelings get Eustace into trouble on the cliff?
3. Do you think Rilian's emotions had any significant part in his being brought under the control of the Lady in Green? (Contrast Rilian's behavior with his father's at the time of his mother's death and afterwards.)

### Cultural Analysis

Let's consider how one particular emotion is viewed in our culture, the feeling called *love*. Imagine you are doing a poll of Americans. According to their understanding, some of their definitions of love are
 a. When we work to not harm others, when we act in such a way that is non-violent and seeks to free others from their suffering
 b. A nice, warm, fuzzy feeling, typified by the emotions felt in this month's Hollywood teenage chick-flick
 c. All of the above
 d. Other
1. What would the average American answer be?
2. In what ways do you see option A in our culture?
3. In what ways do you see option B in our culture?

### Biblical Analysis

1. God defines himself as "love"—not just that He loves, but that He is love (1 John 4:8). Does this mean that God is only interested in helping all of us to be free from "bad" feelings and that He just wants us to be happy (cf. Heb. 12:5–6, Hosea 11:4)?
2. Is the love of God a warm, fuzzy, emotional feeling He has towards us (cf. Zeph. 3:17, Rom. 5:7–8, 8:38–39)?
3. What does it mean that "God is love?" (Think especially of why it might be important for God to be a Trinity for Him to be love. That is, what were the persons of the Trinity doing before the world began?).

### Application

Our emotions wrap together the complexity of "us," our feelings, our thoughts, our beliefs—and spur them to some action. Without emotion, we become a flat, black and white machine that has given up the created *imago Dei*. Yet we also need to recognize (as did Caspian) that our emotions can be used for good or evil.

### SUMMA

 *Write an essay or discuss this question, integrating what you have learned from the material above.* Is acting on our emotions a good thing?

**READING ASSIGNMENT:**
Chapters 5–6

# SESSION III: RECITATION
Chapters 5–6

## Comprehension Questions

*Answer these questions for factual recall.*

1. Why do you think the green serpent killed Rilian's mother?
2. There are two reasons Eustace is suspicious that the Parliament of Owls is up to no good. What are they?
3. What is the lion's invitation, and how does Jill respond to it? What does her response result in?
4. Why has Jill called to Aslan in the first place?
5. How will Aslan guide her while she is down in Narnia?
6. What is the first thing to go wrong in Narnia? Whose fault is it?
7. Puddleglum's thinking will be of great benefit to the children later on. What early display of his logic do we see here?

8. What view of their trip does Puddleglum have? Why does he volunteer to go?

9. What did Jill think of giants, and why?

10. Was living on the creatures they were able to shoot as pleasant for Jill as she was expecting?

11. What could the children see from the top of the bridge?

12. What does Lewis say would be the response to anyone seeing the horse the Green Lady was riding? Does the Lady's loveliness compare to that of the horse?

13. What does the Green Lady tell the children and Puddleglum about the road they had seen? How does this change their thinking?

14. What is the cause of the first serious argument among the travelers? Does this argument remind you of any other argument you have read in the Narnia chronicles?

15. In what two ways do their travels become more difficult after they meet the Lady?

**READING ASSIGNMENT:**
Chapters 7–9

# SESSION IV: DISCUSSION
Chapters 4–9

## A Question to Consider

Describe what characterizes a "spoiled-rotten" child. What makes them this way?

*Discuss or list short answers to the following questions:*

### Text Analysis

1. What is the consequence of missing the first sign?

2. Do the consequences of missing the first sign help the children to keep their focus on the remaining signs?

3. What are the children spending their time thinking of as they travel?

4. What criteria does Jill use to judge whether or not she likes the King and Queen?

5. How does Aslan put the children and Puddleglum back onto the right path?

6. Have they done anything to deserve that knowledge?

### Cultural Analysis

1. How is our culture harmed by not obeying the First Commandment: You shall have no other gods before me?

2. What harm has come about from disobeying the Fifth Commandment: Honor your father and your mother, that your days may be long in the land that the Lord your God is giving you?

3. What harm has come from disobeying the command to not covet?

### Biblical Analysis

1. What is grace (Rom. 3:19–31)?

2. Does following Christ mean that we do not need to follow God's law (Rom. 8:31)?

## SUMMA

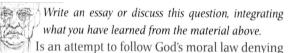

*Write an essay or discuss this question, integrating what you have learned from the material above.*

Is an attempt to follow God's moral law denying God's grace?

**READING ASSIGNMENT:**
Chapters 10–13

# SESSION V: RECITATION
Chapters 10–13

## Comprehension Questions

*Answer these questions for factual recall.*

1. What is a common refrain in Underland?

2. Whom do they see down there?

3. What is the one bright spot they consider as they are on their long journey through Underland?

4. How does the Black Knight explain the engraved "under me?"

5. What does Jill think of the young man?

6. What does the Knight say while in the chair?

7. What do the children and Puddleglum decide to do?

8. What are the different responses to the Knight when he is freed from the chair?

9. What are the two things Rilian says to the Queen now that he is himself?

10. What does the powder on the fire do?

11. What replaces the enchanting smell?

12. What is Puddleglum's great statement to the Queen after he puts out her fire?

13. Why is Rilian happy that the Witch turned into a serpent?

 READING ASSIGNMENT:
Chapters 14–16

# SESSION VI: WRITING
Chapters 14–16

A few books previously in *The Horse and His Boy,* the idea of "providence" was introduced as a theme in *The Chronicles of Narnia.* God's providence is certainly a great theme throughout *The Silver Chair.* Write a brief essay (a page or so) comparing and contrasting (showing the similarities and the differences between) how the idea of providence is displayed through both these two books.

# OPTIONAL SESSION

## Activity 1: Spelunking

You may live in a place where cave exploration is possible. Arrange for a tour, a lantern tour if you can manage it. Some caves even have special "grubby" tours where you have to crawl through tight places and climb over rock piles to complete your tour— with only the light available from the lamp on your hardhat! If you want to empathize with Jill, this would be an excellent activity to pursue. The internet is a great source to locate options. At the time of publication the following sites had general cave information available: *cavern.com* and *www.caves.org.*

A virtual tour can be experienced at *www.goodearthgraphics.com/virtcave.html.*

The following site has general information about caves available without having to filter out the "millions and millions of years" language that supports belief in evolution: *www.answersingenesis.org* then enter "caves" in their general search field.

## Activity 2: Cave Dwellers

When C.S. Lewis imagined the country of Bism, he created the "Earthmen" as its inhabitants. As you think about underground caves, deep places in the earth or what the bottom of a volcano might be like, what sort of creature do you imagine? Draw a picture of this creature and write a description of how it lives.

### ENDNOTES

1  The setting apart of the Christian for the glory of God. Sanctification takes place *positionally* at conversion, *progressively* through life, and *ultimately* in glory.

On the shield, redder than blood or cherries, was the figure of the Lion. "This signifies that Aslan will be our good lord, whether he means us to live or die. And all's one, for that."

# THE LAST BATTLE

The old man reclined on his bed, hardly a man worth fearing, but he had nevertheless been feared. Living many months in exile apart from his congregation had made him ready for this last and final exile.

They say that in his last days he began to gain glimpses of a new and beautiful land. He began to speak of it, and these words became the inspiration for the hymn *The Sands of Time are Sinking*, which says,

> The sands of time are sinking, the dawn of Heaven breaks; The summer morn I've sighed for—the fair, sweet morn awakes: Dark, dark hath been the midnight, but dayspring is at hand, And glory, glory dwelleth in Immanuel's land.

This old frail man had faced down kings. Once when James VI of Scotland had said that the king was the law (or *Rex Lex*), Samuel Rutherford answered with his earthshaking writing *Lex Rex* (or "the law is king"). Foes of tyranny (like the founding fathers of America) would cling to this book, almost burning it into their memory. Rutherford had suffered so much for his congregation, for his country and for his faith, but now all of that was fading away:

> ". . . [R]emember that all worlds draw to an end and that noble death is a treasure which no one is too poor to buy."

I shall sleep sound in Jesus, filled with His likeness rise, To love and to adore Him, to see Him with these eyes: 'Tween me and resurrection but Paradise doth stand; Then—then for glory dwelling in Immanuel's land.

And so like the great Rutherford, Lewis contemplates the end of the world in *The Last Battle*. In this final installment of the *The Chronicles of Narnia* the world and all in it face their end. Like Rutherford, however, they reach the same conclusion:

> And glory—glory dwelleth in Immanuel's land.

# GENERAL INFORMATION

## Significance

*The Last Battle* outlines both C.S. Lewis's eschatology and his peculiar form of Christian Platonism. The word eschatology means the study of the "last things," and in this book Lewis describes the end of Narnia, and indeed, the end of that entire world. With this, Lewis brings his Narnia set full circle. He begins with Creation in *The Magician's Nephew,* and ends with the Last Judgment in *The Last Battle.* In between, he has addressed all the great themes of the Christian faith—sin, salvation, revelation and the nature of faithfully living before God. He has done this by means of story, and in this book he brings the whole matter to a genuinely satisfying conclusion. While we will have finished the series with the reading of this work, we are never really done with these books. We can always go further up and further in.

"You've *got* to do it now, Puzzle. . . . You know you don't understand these things. What could a donkey know about signs?"

## Main Characters

King Tirian is the last king of Narnia, and he is a central figure in this book. His dearest friend is the unicorn Jewel. The human children who are summoned from our world to help him are Eustace and Jill, now a few years older than they were in *The Silver Chair.* The evil ape Shift is responsible for the great deception, in which he passes off Puzzle the donkey as the return of Aslan. Rishda Tarkaan is a Calormene warrior who helps to arrange the betrayal of Narnia. Poggin the dwarf is the only dwarf who remains loyal to Aslan and Tirian, and the other dwarfs (not all named individually) are still a significant "character" in the book. Emeth is a Calormene warrior who has been accepted by Aslan. In the great reunion in the true Narnia, many of the characters from the previous books appear. Of course, as usual, Aslan is the central figure, whether he is physically present or not.

## Summary and Setting

The book begins with Shift the ape and Puzzle the donkey. They find a lion skin and Shift devises the trick of making an Aslan costume for Puzzle. A little after, we meet King Tirian and Jewel at a hunting lodge in the north, away from Cair Paravel. Word comes to the king that trees are being chopped down and that an angry Aslan has returned to Narnia. Tirian and Jewel go to investigate, and when they discover that Talking Horses have been enslaved, in anger they attack and kill the Calormene slave drivers without warning (thus dishonoring themselves by failing to give their enemies a chance to defend themselves). When Tirian realizes he has dishonored himself by doing this, he surrenders to the Calormenes. They bind him, and in his imprisonment he cries out for help from Aslan and the Friends of Narnia. Eustace and Jill arrive and liberate the king, and they begin figuring out a way to resist the evil deceptions that are being imposed on Narnia. They confront the forces of evil at the Stable, and so begins the Last Battle of Narnia. It ends by the good Narnians being "defeated," and thrown into the Stable as a sacrifice to Tash, but the Stable door is actually the entry into Aslan's country. Immediately afterwards, Aslan calls an end to Narnia, and all the creatures in the world stream to the Stable door, meet Aslan, and either veer off into the darkness, or enter into joy. The book ends with all the characters being summoned "further up and further in," and they discover that heaven is always bigger on the inside than it is on the outside.

## Worldview

There are three important issues to address as this book is read, enjoyed and studied. In many ways, it needs to be read as the capstone of the all the other books and enjoyed in that context.

The first issue is Eschatology, or Lewis's doctrine of the end of history. In order to talk about this we have to note a few common eschatological assumptions that many contemporary Christians have concerning our world. Although Christians differ about many things, there are generally not various schools of thought concerning *Narnian* eschatology. But what we assume about the end of *our* world will obviously show up in Narnia, and this was true for Lewis the author as well as for us as his readers.

One of the most popular current notions is called *premillennialism,* and is characterized by belief in a secret rapture of all Christians, a seven year tribulation and the literal return of Christ prior to His reign in Jerusalem for one thousand years. The position is so named because Christ returns before (*pre*) the one thousand years (*millennium*). Premillennialism is so common today that it scarcely needs explanation. Much of popular Christian fiction has focused on this teaching. The reason it is mentioned here is because it is so common that many might be tempted to find traces of it in Narnia. It should be noted that there is really no indication that this particular eschatology played any role in Lewis's description of the end of Narnia. There is no real Narnian equivalent of the *Left Behind* approach to the end of history.

Another millennial position among Christians is called *postmillennialism.* This is the belief that the gospel will conquer all the nations of men, and that the world will come to general faith in Christ before the end of history. Because (for example) Calormen does not come to faith in Aslan before the end, this is not really Lewis's position either.

That leaves *amillennialism,* which is the view that Christians rule with Christ in a *spiritual* sense throughout the course of the church age, but this spiritual rule is not necessarily translated into any historical rule of the faithful. In some versions of this, history goes from bad to worse and ends in a dark pessimistic cataclysm (very similar to premillennialsim). In other versions, history goes on pretty much as it always has, with both good guys and bad guys on either side, with each becoming more self-aware of their goodness and badness. The conflict therefore intensifies, but is not really resolved until the end of history. This appears to be the view Lewis takes, and we might call it optimistic amillennialism (or postmillennialism lite).

We should identify it as some form of amillennialism because that entire world is not brought to faith in Aslan. But there are several reasons for calling it an optimistic view. First, although the faithful Narnians lose the Last Battle, Aslan ends the world almost immediately afterwards. In other words, Cair Paravel is conquered by a sneak attack from Calormen, but how long do the Calormenes get to enjoy the fruit of their victory? It is taken away from them by Aslan almost right away. The intervention is so quick that it is almost erroneous to say that the faithful Narnians lost the battle.

The second reason is more telling. The history of Narnia runs for 2,555 years. Frank and Helen are established as king and queen in the year 1, and Tirian is king in the year Narnia falls. That history is punctuated with two difficult periods. The White Witch rules Narnia under her tyranny from the year 900 to the year 1000. Then in 1998, Telmarines invade Narnia, and although their rule is not as bad as that of the White Witch, it is still despotic and is rough on the Old Narnians. This line of rulers, beginning with Caspian I and ending with the usurper Miraz, lasts for 305 years. These are the two bad patches of road, lasting for a total of 405 years. What is Narnia like in the intervening 2,150 years? Fortunately, Jewel tells us.

But the Unicorn explained to [Jill] that she was quite mistaken. He said that the Sons and Daughters of Adam and Eve were brought out of their own strange world into Narnia only at times when Narnia was stirred and upset, but she mustn't think it was always like that. In between their visits there were hundreds and thousands of years when peaceful King followed peaceful King till you could hardly remember their names or count their numbers, and there was really hardly anything to put into the History Books. And he went on to talk ... of whole centuries in which all Narnia was so happy that notable dances and feasts, or at most tournaments, were the only things that could be remembered, and every day and week had been better than the last. And as he went on, the picture of all those happy years, all the thousands of them, piled up in Jill's mind till it was rather like looking down from a high hill onto a rich, lovely plain full of woods and waters and cornfields, which spread away and away till it got thin and misty from distance (chap. 8).

This is *hardly* a pessimistic view of history. And it is extremely significant that the two times Narnia falls under wicked or despotic rule are in the *middle* of her history, with glorious centuries of peace on either side. The last king of Narnia is a faithful king, who fights a difficult battle well and who serves Aslan as a true prince should. When Tirian finally meets Aslan in his country, the account is that "Tirian came near, trembling, and flung himself at the Lion's feet, and the Lion kissed him and said, 'Well done, last of the Kings of Narnia who stood firm at the darkest hour'" (chap. 13). Tirian is highly commended, which means that Narnians as a people (and probably Archenlanders) were faithful to the end.

If Miraz had been the king at the end, with a number of despots before him, that would have reflected a pessimistic amillennial view. Or if Narnia had gone the route of Charn, where all the good kings and queens were early in their history and the wicked ones came later, then we could say the same. But that is not the case at all.

The second issue we must address involves some philosophy. After the Friends of Narnia are inside the Stable Door, they spend some time trying to figure out where they are. After they do, the Lord Digory says, "You need not mourn over Narnia, Lucy. All of the old Narnia that mattered, all the dear creatures, have been drawn into the real Narnia through the Door . . . It's all in Plato, all in Plato: bless me, what *do* they teach them at these schools!"

And since this Omnibus project constitutes a significant part of your schooling, we do not want to fall under the Lord Digory's reproach—and that means that we have to talk about Plato for a bit. There are many aspects of Plato's thought and methods that show up in the Narnia Chronicles, but we only have space to discuss the most significant of them, along with Lewis's modification of Plato. It is quite possible that you have studied Plato or are currently studying his work. If so, you will find it helpful in understanding Lewis here.

Plato wanted to know what made a chair a chair, or an apple an apple. Philosophers like to think about such things, and the answer he came up with was that every chair in the world partakes of an ultimate "Chairness" somehow. The same goes for "Appleness" and so on. Chairness, Appleness, Bookness, all inhabit the realm of the *Forms*, which was the ultimate Spiritual Place. In the realm of the Forms, you would encounter the Ultimate Chair, and every chair that you ever saw on earth was what it was simply because it was participating somehow in that Chair.

You should be able to see at once how this relates to Aslan's country. The Narnia they had all known and loved was not the real Narnia, not the ultimate Narnia. The Narnia outside the Stable door was in the Shadowlands, the Narnia inside was the real Narnia. Further, the Narnia they had fought and died for was only what it was because of its participation in the Narnia of Aslan's country. So far, this appears to be a fairly straightforward application of Plato. But Lewis gives us several significant adaptations.

First, in Lewis the process does not appear to stop. Aslan keeps growing bigger as those who serve him grow, and they keep growing forever. This is typified by the fact that the "further up and further in" motif never really stops. When they get to the center of the true Narnia and enter the garden there, they discover that that garden is bigger on the inside than it was on the outside. In Lewis's application of this, we do not have an "upper story" world with all the Forms in it, and then a "lower story" world with all the Shadows. Rather, we are peeling an infinite onion with us discovering that each ring, when we get to it, is bigger and more real than the previous one. One realm of Forms replaces another and each realm of the Forms that we pass out of falls behind us into the Shadowlands. There is nothing *wrong* with the Shadowlands; it is just that more Reality is always in front of us. This is a glorious and mystical vision, although admittedly hard to sketch on the blackboard.

Another distinctive contribution that Lewis makes to this vision is found in his very Christian view of matter. The Greek or Hellenistic tendency (which Plato certainly represents) was to view ultimate things rationalistically, understood only by the mind, and only the realm of mind or spirit represented that which was truly Real. The realm of tangible matter was viewed with suspicion or contempt. Put another way, in Plato's realm of the Forms, it is hard to imagine discovering that the Ultimate Chair was any good for sitting in.

But in Lewis, the further in you go, the more *solid* everything gets. This same perspective is clear in his book *The Great Divorce,* where heaven is inhabited by the Solid People and hell is inhabited by the ghost-like wraiths. Lewis, as a thoroughgoing Christian, is not embarrassed by matter at all. This is only right, because all Christians are what they are because of the Incarnation of Jesus Christ—the Lord Jesus took on a material body, and this is a body which He still has. Lewis points to this by making Aslan a "true beast," meaning that he has whiskers, a point that Bree found disrespectful until he met the real Aslan.

In making these points, it is important to note that Lewis did not believe himself to be drawing us an actual map of the afterlife. Rather, it would be more helpful to think of him as pointing in a general direction. Whatever we think of the afterlife, we must think of it being more Real than what we experience now, not *less* Real. Whatever we love here on earth

(assuming it is something that is proper to love) will find its counterpart in the resurrection. This is just another way of saying that good things are (in a certain sense) indestructible. Nothing of value is ever ultimately lost. This is a wonderful Christian doctrine, and the Lord Jesus tells us that the Last Judgment will include, among other things, a reckoning up of the glasses of water that were given for Christ's sake. In Lewis's view, there is a godly Calormen in the Real World, indicating that there was some kind of good reality in the earthly Calormen that was not visible to Shasta.

And this relates to our last point, one which has troubled more than one evangelical reader of *The Last Battle* and has to do with the lot of the "righteous heathen." Emeth is a noble Calormene warrior who has served Tash with true devotion all his days. He has hated the name of Aslan, but believes that the plot to overthrow Narnia is dishonest and wicked, and he challenges Rishda Tarkaan to let him go into the Stable to "see Tash." This is reluctantly granted, and Emeth goes in and fights one of the assassins who is stationed inside the door. Having killed him, he finds himself in Aslan's country, and eventually the Lion comes to meet him. Upon seeing him, Emeth instantly submits to him. "Surely this is the hour of death, for the Lion (who is worthy of all honor) will know that I have served Tash all my days and not him. Nevertheless, it is better to see the Lion and die than to be the Tisroc of the world and live and not to have seen him" (chap. 15).

Aslan shows his anger at the "Tashlan" lie and rejects it utterly. The reason he receives Emeth is *not* because Aslan and Tash are one, but rather because they are opposites. Aslan can receive no treacherous service, and Tash can receive no honorable service. Aslan says that though Emeth did not know he was serving Aslan, he was in fact serving Aslan. Emeth did not know Aslan, but what mattered is that Aslan knew him.

This must not be confused with universalism (the view that everyone is ultimately saved). Lewis rejected that view forcefully, and early in *The Last Battle,* he had Tash carry Rishda Tarkaan off to his own place, presumably hell. And there was a great stream of creatures who came up to the Stable Door at the end of the world and who veered off into the darkness. Lewis is clearly not teaching that everyone is saved.

Nor should it be confused with a second chance after death, where a creature enters heaven rebellious

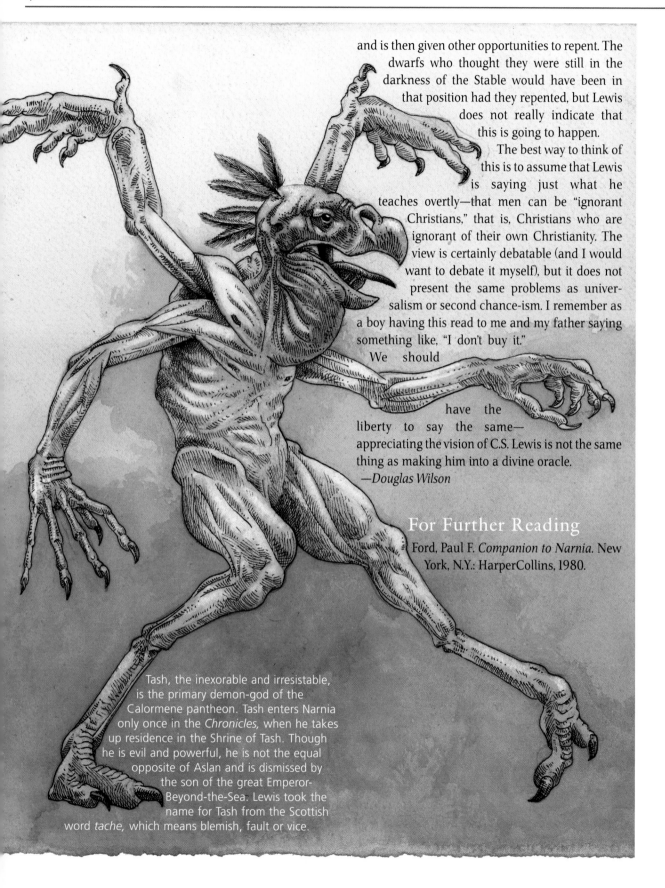

and is then given other opportunities to repent. The dwarfs who thought they were still in the darkness of the Stable would have been in that position had they repented, but Lewis does not really indicate that this is going to happen.

The best way to think of this is to assume that Lewis is saying just what he teaches overtly—that men can be "ignorant Christians," that is, Christians who are ignorant of their own Christianity. The view is certainly debatable (and I would want to debate it myself), but it does not present the same problems as universalism or second chance-ism. I remember as a boy having this read to me and my father saying something like, "I don't buy it." We should have the liberty to say the same—appreciating the vision of C.S. Lewis is not the same thing as making him into a divine oracle.

—*Douglas Wilson*

## For Further Reading

Ford, Paul F. *Companion to Narnia.* New York, N.Y.: HarperCollins, 1980.

Tash, the inexorable and irresistable, is the primary demon-god of the Calormene pantheon. Tash enters Narnia only once in the *Chronicles,* when he takes up residence in the Shrine of Tash. Though he is evil and powerful, he is not the equal opposite of Aslan and is dismissed by the son of the great Emperor-Beyond-the-Sea. Lewis took the name for Tash from the Scottish word *tache,* which means blemish, fault or vice.

# SESSION I: PRELUDE

## A Question to Consider

Imagine your parents tell you that the family will be going on a fabulous vacation at some point in the future. They do not tell you exactly where, and they do not tell you when—just that it will be fabulous. What sorts of things would you guess about this trip, what would you talk about with your friends and family members? What might you argue with your siblings about with regard to this vacation? How would it affect how you lived life from one day to the next?

*From the General Information above answer the following questions:*

1. What is the millennium (Rev. 20:2–5)?
2. Complete the small chart below to show the sequence in which the three views arrange end times events. For our current age use the initial **C**, an **M** for the millennium, an **X** for Christ's return and finally an **N** for the new heaven and the new earth.

> **PREMILLENNIALISM:**
> **POSTMILLENNIALISM:**
> **AMILLENNIALISM:**

3. You have read how one particular point of view, amillennialism, shows itself in *The Last Battle*. How might someone's belief in premillennialism show itself? Postmillennialism?

## Optional Activity 1

Family interview. If you do not know what your family and church eschatological views are, ask your father. Use this opportunity to find out why those views are held, and ask if these beliefs impact their actions.

## Optional Activity 2

If you made a map of Narnia for *The Lion, the Witch and the Wardrobe*, add the appropriate landmarks as you read through *The Last Battle*. New items to add to the map will include Cauldron Pool and the Great Waterfall.

## Optional Activity 3

If you have already read *The Last Battle*, use the *Companion to Narnia* as a resource and read through the following entries.

> **TIRIAN**
> **JEWEL**
> **SHIFT**
> **PUZZLE**
> **RISHDA TARKAAN**
> **POGGIN**
> **GRIFFLE**
> **EMETH**
> **PLATO**

 **READING ASSIGNMENT:** Chapters 1–4

# SESSION II: DISCUSSION

Chapters 1–4

## A Question to Consider

One day at lunchtime, an acquaintance of yours lets you know that they forgot their lunch and were wondering if you could share some of yours with them. You are happy to share. A few days later, the same thing happens again, and a few days later yet again. A pattern has soon started, and you seriously consider packing more food on a permanent basis. What circumstances would lead you to continue sharing your lunch, what circumstances would lead you to decide to no longer share your lunch?

*Discuss or list short answers to the following questions:*

### Text Analysis

1. What is the nature of the relationship between Puzzle and Shift?
2. Read again through the sections of chapter one where Shift persuades Puzzle to do various things. If possible, have one student read the part of Shift and another the part of Puzzle. Each time Shift makes a request, what qualities are revealed about his character? Each time Puzzle agrees to do what Shift asks, why does he agree? In Chart 1, fill in what each action says about the quality of their character.

**Chart 1: SHIFT VS. PUZZLE**

| ACTION | SHIFT | PUZZLE |
|---|---|---|
| Nicest foods eaten by Shift | | |
| Animal skin from Caldron Pool | | |
| Wearing the lion skin | | |
| Fetching food from Chippingford | | |
| Wearing the lion skin | | |

3. Should Puzzle have known that Shift was using him?
4. If Puzzle had realized that Shift was using him, do you think he would have behaved differently?

## Cultural Analysis

1. On what basis are people encouraged to form friendships?
2. If people in our culture had to make a choice, do you think they would say they respected Puzzle or Shift more? How would people acting like Puzzle be judged by our culture?

## Biblical Analysis

1. What should describe our actions towards others (1 Cor. 13:4–7)?
2. Are we to be friends with just anyone (2 Tim. 3:1–7)?
3. Are these two passages in opposition to one another?

## SUMMA

*Write an essay or discuss this question, integrating what you have learned from the material above.*

Should we continue to love others, even though we may know or suspect that they are using or taking advantage of us? Should we be friends with non-Christians?

"But courage, child: we are all between the paws of the true Aslan."

## Application

To who we show compassion is a different choice than with whom we form friendships. Showing the love of God to others is something we are commanded to do, even to our enemies (Luke 6:27). Friendships should be formed with care, for in this case we are making ourselves vulnerable to not only show love and affect others, but to be affected by them.

READING ASSIGNMENT: Chapters 5–8

# SESSION III: WRITING
Chapters 5–8

As *The Chronicles of Narnia* draw toward their conclusion, you have become very familiar with the types of creatures you find in Narnia, as well as many of the surrounding countries. You may wish for more stories and wish this were not the last, or express as Jill does, "Oh, this *is* nice! Just walking along like this. I wish there could be more of *this* sort of adventure. It's a pity there's always so much happening in Narnia." Jewel corrects her and explains that she is quite mistaken. "In between [the Sons and Daughters of Adam and Eve] visits there were hundreds and thousands of years when peaceful King followed peaceful King . . ." (chap. 8)

Jewel tells her of many of the kings and queens, heroes and legendary creatures of old, but these stories are not shared with the reader, and so you may create your own. As individuals or teams, brainstorm what these stories may have been. Decide who your audience will be, then you draft your tale in outline form before developing it into full story format.

You may want to have your story typed out in book format, leaving empty spaces to add illustrations. Many word processors will print in book format so that when you fold the printed sheets together, it is as if the book is bound. By putting cardstock on the outside before you staple the sheets down the middle, you will have something resembling a paperback book pamphlet.

**READING ASSIGNMENT:**
Chapters 9–12

# SESSION IV: RECITATION
Chapters 1–12

## Comprehension Questions

*Answer the following questions for factual recall:*

1. How is Narnia deceived into thinking Aslan has returned? What kinds of things is "Aslan" asking of the Narnians which throws them into confusion?
2. How do Tirian and Jewel initially feel about the news that Aslan has returned? What changes this reaction?
3. Why is Tirian captured?
4. Do Rishda Tarkaan and Ginger the Cat at first believe in Aslan or Tash?
5. How does Tirian recognize Tash? Where did Tash go?
6. Why are there so few Narnians present at the last battle?
7. During the hard times in Narnia on her first visit, Jill often wished for creature comforts. Does she react the same way during this visit?
8. What hope does Poggin have to eventually win back Narnia? Why doesn't Tirian share his optimism?
9. There are only around thirty Calormene soldiers and many Narnian creatures. What fear keeps the Narnians from attacking and overwhelming the Calormenes?
10. What happens to most of the animals once the battle starts?
11. What evil thing do the Dwarfs do, and how does Tirian instruct Eustace?
12. How does Rishda want to atone for his earlier unbelief in Tash?
13. What is the difference between the worshipers of Tash and Aslan as they approach the one they worship?

14. Why is Susan not with the others when Tirian greets them? Does this mean Susan is lost forever (cf. John 6:37–40)?

## Optional Activity

As taught elsewhere in this guide, the world of Narnia is very much a medieval world, filled with knights, castles, battles, dragons and chivalry. One of the ways the medieval world recorded noble deeds was through tapestries. A tapestry recording the history of Narnia would begin with its Creation and end with the door through which all life streamed and was judged. You can make your "tapestry" small with pencil, ink and watercolor or large on poster sheets to cover the side of a room or hallway. It is also possible to use tempera paint directly on cotton sheeting to create a tapestry affect. In this case, it is easiest to sketch your idea first, and then use an overhead projector to project the image onto the cloth. Use a pencil to sketch the outline and then paint.

**READING ASSIGNMENT:**
Chapters 13–16

# SESSION V: DISCUSSION
Chapters 13–16

## A Question to Consider

Can someone be saved without actually knowing of Christ or hearing the gospel?

*Discuss or list short answers to the following questions:*

### Text Analysis

1. In what Narnia books have you read about Tash, and what is told about him?
2. What have the Calormenes been taught about Aslan?
3. How do Rabadash and Emeth differ in their reaction to Aslan once they see him?
4. Why is Emeth "claimed" by Aslan?

### Cultural Analysis

1. What does our culture thinks of Jesus?
2. Many people in our culture believe in some sort of life after death. How do many people view this life after death, and how do they think they can attain it?

## Biblical Analysis

1. Is Naaman biblical evidence that people can be saved without trusting in the true God (2 Kings 5)?
2. What will happen to people who do not hear the gospel (Rom. 10:14)?
3. How much does someone have to know to be saved (Luke 1:41)?

## SUMMA

 Write an essay or discuss this question, integrating what you have learned from the material above.

Can those who do not hear the gospel be saved?

## Application

Preach the gospel to the nations. We can argue over the merits or demerits of Emeth, but in the end, God has clearly called us to serve Him by taking the gospel out to the nations. Do not let Lewis's debatable supposition at this point keep you from obeying God's clear command.

# SESSION VI: ANALYSIS
## Chapters 13–16

*Some of the books you have read this year convey their author's belief of what life after death will be like. Their visions are quite different, though there may be more similarities between works such as* Gilgamesh *and the* Odyssey. *However, for each question in this exercise, you are to compare the vision of the afterlife conveyed in the* Odyssey *(Book 11) vs.* The Last Battle.

1. Is the afterlife more real or less real than life on earth?
2. Can you get to the afterlife without dying?
3. Is there anything strange about the size of the world that we see in the afterlife?
4. Is the world a real world with living things?
5. Is the afterlife a place the characters yearn to get to? Why or why not?
6. Does everyone who has died go to the same place?
7. Once there, is the afterlife what the characters expected? Do they long to return to life? Are they happy to be in the afterlife?
8. Are the characters transformed in any way by going from one world into the next?
9. What quotes about the two different worlds stand against one another and summarize many of these questions?

One mysterious character that appears twice in the *Chronicles* is the mythological phoenix. Herodotus records that the phoenix came from Arabia every 500 years carrying his father's body embalmed in an egg of myrrh. He wrote, "I have not seen a phoenix myself, except in paintings, for it is very rare and only visits the country . . ." This Arabian bird was said to resemble an eagle with brilliant gold and red plumage. Before the phoenix died it built a nest of incense twigs and laid down in it and died. The ancient Egyptians linked the myth of the phoenix with their civilization's longings for immortality, and in Chinese mythology, it symbolized virtue and grace. At the end of the first century Clement of Rome became the first to reinterpret the myth of the phoenix as an allegory of the resurrection and of life after death.

# OPTIONAL SESSION

C.S. Lewis filled the Narnia books with celebrations. Every single book has a grand, joy-filled party in it somewhere. What better way to honor the books than by throwing your own celebration? As a class or as a family, plan your celebration by brainstorming. First, what will your party be like? Will it be in a hall resembling Cair Paravel, or will it be in a field around a huge bonfire. Remember some of the celebratory scenes from the books, and take your pick. Next you will need to decide on the foods to have. List all the different foods and feasting you can think of from the different books, and then again, take your pick and plan. Then you should recall different events or favorite selections and think of games. Some of the more obvious games will be sack races (Dufflepuds), boat races (*The Voyage of the Dawn Treader*) or crawling on your belly through an obstacle course (*The Silver Chair*).

Feasts were also attended by song and dance. Find some appropriate period music and perhaps even practice some Elizabethan dances for court or some wild Dryad and Fawn dances for around the bonfire.

# THE BEST THINGS IN LIFE

Praise the Lord!
Oh, give thanks to the Lord, for He is good!
For His mercy endures forever.
*Psalm 106:1*

And we know that all things work together for good to those who love God, to those who are the called according to His purpose.
*Romans 8:28*

Have you ever experienced something in your life that you knew deep down inside was really *good?* Maybe it was a heart-to-heart conversation or an unusual shared experience with a friend in which you were drawn closer together and experienced true friendship. Or the love your parents showed you through a real sacrifice on their part. Or maybe the first time you visited the ocean or mountains and experienced the majestic beauty of God's creation.

I still have vivid memories of goodness from the time my dad took me to see my first major league baseball game at old Connie Mack Stadium in Philadelphia. I was eight years old and loved playing baseball and following the Phillies baseball team. I will never forget when I first caught sight of the field as we walked down to our seats along the third base line. It was the most perfect baseball field I had ever seen, a shining emerald green sea of perfectly cut grass glistening in the sunlight, exquisitely offset by the taupe brown geometry of the diamond and bounded by the straightest, brilliantly white foul lines and batter's box in the universe. Out on the field and milling around the third base dugout were players in bright, white and red pinstripe uniforms with the bright, red Phillies logo across their chests. Across the way were the opposing players from Los Angeles

wearing their classic Dodger blue and gray uniforms. This Eden-like field of color was surrounded by what, to my young eyes, were large yet cozy double-decked stands on three sides. Hovering over right field was a monstrous steel wall over three stories tall, and in right centerfield was the largest scoreboard in the world (at least it seemed that way to me).

As my dad and I took our seats, the crowd was buzzing and the smell of fresh mown grass mixed delightfully with the aroma from the carnival boardwalk fare of hotdogs, popcorn and cotton candy. I was so excited, I felt like my heart was going to thump out of my chest. The whole magnificent scene was covered by a cloudless, perfectly blue summer sky. To me, this was like paradise and the Garden of Eden all rolled up into one. It was *GOOD.* Though of course there was much that day that was far from perfect as I know now (some of the stands were very old and practically collapsing, the players were not perfect, but very much sinners like you and I, the management was greedy and inept and no doubt many of the fans in the stands had plenty of problems of their own). God had graciously kept those things from my sight in order to grant me a true taste of the good and a small foretaste of His overflowing goodness that awaits all His faithful servants when He completes the redemption of this world in the fullness of time.

Socrates dialogues with several characters affiliated with Desperate State University.

This modern depiction of Socrates shows the philosopher in deep thought. He actually never wrote down his ideas. They were reported by his pupils—most notably Plato.

*The Best Things in Life* is a modern, fictional "Socratic" dialogue about good things. More specifically, it addresses the basic question *What is the good life?* In a series of instructive, interesting and sometimes amusing dialogues, a come-back-to-life Socrates engages several characters affiliated with the fictional Desperate State University, including Peter Pragma and Felicia Flake, in discussions about the modern understanding of the good life and the role that money, power, pleasure, success and truth play in achieving it. Along the way Socrates addresses real life questions about the purpose and goal of education, choosing a career, knowing ourselves and God, the meaning of success and doing good, and the relationship of drugs, sex and music to power, pleasure and truth. In the final chapter, Socrates conducts an "Oxford tutorial" in which he refutes Felicia Flake's argument that all values are subjective, and he defends the existence and necessity of objective values.

## GENERAL INFORMATION

### Author and Context

The author of *The Best Things in Life* is philosophy professor Peter Kreeft, a prolific writer of popular apologetics books from a Christian *natural law[1]* point of view, including *The Best Things in Life, The Unaborted Socrates* and *How to Win the Culture War: A Christian Battle Plan for a Society in Crisis.* The natural law approach assumes that, by using their natural, God-given reasoning skills, all people, whether or not they submit to God, will agree on what is right and wrong in life. (We will see later why this approach poses biblical problems.) Kreeft's alter ego in the dialogues is the famous Greek philosopher Socrates, whom the author brings back to life in an effort to straighten out some fuzzy-thinking, modern college characters. The real Socrates, you will remember, was an Athenian gadfly/philosopher who got himself in trouble with the city's leaders by being a general busybody and hanging out with notorious anti-democrats (including relatives of his famous student, Plato). Constantly questioning and revealing the logical flaws in the views of the city leaders, as well as other philosophers, eventually led to charges of impiety (failing to honor the traditional Greek gods) and corruption of the youth (teaching them his philosophy). The charges stuck, and he was eventually condemned to death. Refusing to accept exile, he committed suicide by drinking poison. Plato idealized his life, trial and death in the *Apology, Crito* and *Phaedo*. Socrates is best known for his moral philosophy and the doctrine expressed in his famous Socratic paradox "No one does wrong voluntarily." In other words, Socrates believed that wrongdoing was due to a lack of knowledge, rather than sin, a notion we Christians know to be wrong.

## Significance

*The Best Things in Life* is an entertaining example of analyzing modern moral and "lifestyle" issues in the classic form of a Socratic dialogue. Socratic dialogues were first made famous by Plato's writings that claimed to document some of Socrates' actual dialogues as well as his trial. Socratic dialogues use a question and answer format to explore and logically evaluate many types of issues. In education the "Socratic method" has been used for generations, and for many years it was virtually the exclusive form of instruction in American law schools. In essence, the Socratic method is a form of cross-examination in which basic assumptions and positions on issues are probed and challenged by logical and leading questions. This technique is very effective in finding inconsistencies, contradictions or arbitrariness in the way we think about issues and problems. It is much less effective in positively demonstrating a coherent worldview.

*The Best Things in Life* also reveals the strengths and weaknesses of what is known as the "natural law" approach to ethics and apologetics championed by, among others, Plato, Aristotle and Thomas Aquinas. Natural law assumes that there is a universal agreement about basic morality that all people, regardless of faith or culture, can know through natural human reason. As we shall see, this view conflicts with certain key biblical truths about the nature of man and his reasoning capabilities.

The strength of Kreeft's approach is his use of logic to question the assumptions of modern thinking about important ethical issues such as money, power and pleasure. Requesting his dialogue partners to give coherent reasons for their particular views exposes the faulty assumptions behind those views, forcing the partners either to find alternative reasons or abandon their views altogether. Unfortunately, Kreeft's method is undermined by the book's *man*-centered (rather than *God*-centered) approach to ethics that inadvertently reinforces the *unbiblical* notion that we can find the truth about right and wrong by our own human reasoning apart from God. The Bible tells us this is impossible because all sinners "suppress the truth in unrighteousness," which makes their thinking about things like ethics distorted and ultimately futile (Rom. 1). God has so wonderfully made us for Himself that we *cannot* even *think* rightly about ourselves, about God or about His world without being in relationship with Him. As a result "the fear of the Lord is the *beginning* of knowledge" (Prov. 1:7) not the end goal of our reasoning process. Only with renewed minds transformed by God can we know truly what is good (Rom. 12:2). *The Best Things in Life* never reveals this truth, but instead implies that we can come to know the truth about these important issues through our own reasoning without a mind renewed by God.

## Main Characters

The main character is, of course, the back-from-the-dead Socrates, who claims to be just a seeker of "knowledge for knowledge's sake" and generally represents the view of the author in the book's dialogues. Socrates is intent on helping people find truth through sound and logical reasoning. He clearly believes, correctly, that much modern thinking about truth and morality is neither sound nor logical. Peter Pragma is the first of Socrates' two main dialogue partners. He is a typical modern American college student trying to figure out what course of study he should choose as a major. He has not thought deeply about any of the issues Socrates brings up and is mainly concerned about getting a job in which he can earn a lot of money to attain his vision of the good life—material comfort. Felicia Flake is a student who seeks immediate happiness and fulfillment through experiences with drugs, sex, music and political causes. She believes that whatever makes you feel happy at the moment must be good and that there are no objective values that are true for everyone.

## Summary and Setting

*The Best Things in Life* is divided into a series of three dialogues. In the first series (chaps. 1–6) Socrates meets Peter Pragma, who is studying for an exam on the campus of Desperate State. Socrates engages Peter in a conversation, in which Peter is gradually and reluctantly drawn into examining his goals and motives for going to school, choosing a career and considering what "the good life" really is.

The second series of dialogues (chaps. 7–11) stars Socrates and Felicia Flake, who discuss the use of drugs, rock music, sex and love, feminism and the ethics of communism and capitalism.

The final dialogue (the Interlude and chap. 12) is an "Oxford tutorial," in which Socrates helps Felicia understand the reality and necessity of objective values, values which underlie the specific ethical issues addressed in the previous dialogues.

## Worldview

I'll never forget one eventful day in my high school biology lab. I came into class, and there, lying on top of the stone cold laboratory table was the stiff, chilled carcass of a black and tan cat, lying on its back, legs sticking up in the air, head slightly turned, bulging black eyes starring me right in the face. I shuddered as my lab partner let out a muted

Peter Pragma, the befuddled college student bent on the most pragmatic path to wealth and "happiness."

screech. Our biology teacher promptly informed us that we were about to dissect the dead animal (that's right—cut it open and take it apart!) so that we could learn all about cats. We proceeded s q u e a m i s h l y, contorted faces and weird noises accompanying our every move. Gradually, we became less uncomfortable with our job (I cannot honestly say we were ever *comfortable* with it) and we began finding various "parts" of the cat, like its heart (smaller than I imagined), lungs, stomach and intestines (*yyyuuck!*). In the process we learned how the cat's blood circulated, how he breathed and how his bones and muscles were put together. For the next week or so, discussion around the school revolved around how weird it felt to do the dissection—and who loved it, who hated it and who got sick doing it!

Believing I now knew a lot about cats, I did not give the matter further thought until a few years later when we got our first pet cat. (My only previous pet was a dog.) As I watched the cat over time, I was amazed at how different she was from the dogs I knew. I noticed how graceful all her movements were, how quickly her moods seemed to change, how *many* moods she had, how she seemed to disappear then, suddenly and without warning, reappear, how quick she was, and how she could turn so . . . I don't know, *mysterious*, I guess. Whatever else you could say about that cat, she had *personality*—and she was no dog. This got me thinking that maybe I had not *really* learned about cats in my biology lab after all. Oh sure, I learned something about the physical *parts* of cats and the physical structure and design of their skeletal, circulatory and other "systems" (as the biologists like to call them), but it taught me little about what real live cats were like. I also learned that dogs and other animals had physical and biological "systems" very similar to cats, yet they were definitely *not* like cats. Creatures are creatures, *not* primarily because of their physical designs, but in the *life* that God gives them and the way they live in relation to their environment, other creatures and the Lord God. Wondrously designed as they are, their physical systems and parts are nevertheless useless without the sustaining *life* provided by God.

Moral life is like the cat. *The Best Things in Life* discusses, debates and "dissects" the ethical life to learn about its design and parts, what's right and wrong, good and bad and how we should live. And with respect to many of the *parts*, it comes to biblical conclusions. Yet the book's worldview is not biblical, because it views morality as something separate and *apart* from, or as something leading *to* religion. Trying to *be* moral without acknowledging and trusting in the moral source, the Triune God of Scripture, is like trying to make the cat live by putting its parts back together again. It is not possible. Apart from God, ethical laws are as dead as the dissected cat. Just as we do not have the power to turn dead body parts into a living cat, so we do not have the power to turn moral laws or ethics into a moral *life*. Only through the power of the Lord Jesus Christ can we truly *live* "the good life."

We need to stop for a moment and consider why *The Best Things in Life*, and so many people, Christians and non-Christians alike, mistakenly assume that our moral actions can be separated from our personal relationship with God. (Why do they believe it can be dissected like the cat parts?) To reapply an observation by the Romantic poet, Wordsworth, "we murder to dissect." There are many reasons dissection does not work, not the least of which are unbiblical views of God, the nature of man and how and why we are saved. But one big reason is the myth of the "virtuous pagan." (No, this is not the title of a major motion picture, coming soon to a theatre near you.) People see unbelievers doing external (outward, visible) good works—for example, giving to the needy or helping a neighbor in distress. They reason that if unbelievers and believers both do good (and bad) works, then being moral must not be directly connected to their relationship with God. In theological discussions, this has traditionally been called the "problem of the virtuous pagan." In other words, if morality cannot be separated from our faith and worldview, how do we explain the obvious fact that unbelievers sometimes do external good works—for example being a "big brother" to a fatherless child or helping a sick neighbor? The Bible tells us the answer: there is more to good works than the visible and external part. Out of the heart come the issues of life. Every visible or external act we do is connected to our invisible, internal attitudes. Truly good works, those that God thinks are good, must be good inside us, as well as externally good.

The Bible tells us that such good works must meet at least three biblical criteria: the right *standard*, the right *goal* and the right *motive*. The right standard is obedience to God's laws (1 John 3:4 tells us that "sin is lawlessness"). The right ultimate goal of moral action is the Glory of God. (In Matthew 6:33 Jesus tells us to seek first the Kingdom of God; 1 Corinthians 10:31 says ". . . whatever you do, do all to the glory of God"; and Colossians 3:23 commands us "And whatever you do, do it heartily, as to the Lord and not to men"). Finally, the right motive must be faith in Christ informed by the love of God. (Romans 14:23 says ". . . whatever is not from faith is sin." See also 1 Corinthians 13.) These three components must be combined to make a work truly good.

Given these biblical parameters, let us revisit the situation of the virtuous pagan. Suppose the unbeliever's virtuous act is to give generously to the needy. He meets the criteria of right standard by following God's law with respect to the external helping of those in need and less fortunate than ourselves. However, he does not have either the right ultimate goal or motive, because in giving, he neither seeks the glory of God nor is motivated by faith in the love of Christ. He might have selfish goals and motives (for example, a motive to appear good to others in order to gain election to a political office), or he may have what appear to be good motives and goals (for example, a motive of eliminating suffering in the world with the goal of seeking the happiness of all people). In neither situation does he meet the biblical requirements for good works. In the latter situation this may seem harsh to us, until we remember that the "virtuous" unbeliever is in rebellion against God and therefore seeks man's happiness *apart* from God (the only Person who can actually give us happiness). This is in reality an unspeakable evil, as well as a flat out impossibility. Yet God, in His wisdom, uses these unbelieving works which are not truly good to accomplish real good, including, in this case, materially providing for the needy.

Let us investigate further how, in *The Best Things in Life,* Socrates "tries to make the cat live again" in his approach to ethics. Socrates sometimes hints at, often skirts around, but never acknowledges or addresses, the heart of "the good life"—loving the Lord God with all our heart, soul and mind. He often speaks as if we can naturally find the right way to live if we but commit ourselves to sound reasoning and seek "knowledge for knowledge's sake." Socrates is wrong, because the truth *cannot* be found apart from life in Jesus Christ (Who is the Way, the Truth and the Life). Romans 1 tells us that unbelievers know the true God but in rebellion naturally "suppress the truth in unrighteousness." The result is futile thinking, foolish hearts and debased minds. "Professing to be wise, they became fools." The unbeliever is not a neutral "seeker after truth." He is consciously or unconsciously rebelling against God and, for his own good, needs to be lovingly confronted with this truth. Thus, to tell an unbeliever to follow his reason wherever it leads, rather than submit to Christ, Who alone can renew our minds, is to condemn him to an endless and fruitless search for the good life. Likewise, to lead him logically to certain moral truths *without* showing him that they *must* be connected to the lifeline of the Triune God is unbiblical. Socrates apparently *thinks* he knows cats, when in fact he has only dissected them. He can accurately point out various designs and parts of the good life but does not know the source of the good life.

As with all of life, God requires us to follow His word in defending the faith and leading unbelievers to the truth. Only God can actually open the eyes and hearts of unbelievers to see the truth, but he requires us to be *faithful* witnesses and apologists. God tells us in 2 Corinthians 10:4–5 that the weapons of our spiritual warfare are "mighty in God for pulling down strongholds, casting down arguments and every high thing that exalts itself against the knowledge of God, bringing every thought into captivity to the obedience of Christ." Notice the two step process. First, we are to storm the citadel of unbelieving thought—that is, undermine the worldview, idols and arguments of the unbeliever. After this demolition job, we are to show the unbeliever how to see the world as it really is— that is, build up a biblical understanding of the world. In *The Best Things in Life* Socrates does a fairly good job of demolishing some modern worldviews, but instead of pointing to the biblical God as the only way to truth, he offers up only pagan platitudes about following "our common master," or "the authority of the argument" or "the light of reason." His inability to lead his dialogue partners to the source of truth is due to his unbiblical view of God and man.

Although the new-and-improved Socrates in *The Best Things in Life* shows obvious Christian influences, He still evidences a profoundly unbiblical understanding of God and man's condition. With respect to God, Socrates is very coy, mysteriously suggesting that a god or gods may be behind the good life he is discussing, but never disclosing anything about this god. Sometimes his remarks suggest that, if we follow the common master and the light within, we may find this god. Sometimes his god seems to be a vague force in nature. At other times Socrates' god is the "first cause" that we need to start reasoning about things. Socrates' god ends up being an empty concept that can be filled with anything the reader conceives of as god. Because Socrates' god is unknowable and impersonal, it is impossible to follow or be obedient to his will. In contrast to Socrates' god, the God of Abraham, Isaac and Jacob has disclosed Himself and His deeds publicly, in history, and tells us about ourselves, our problem, the way to salvation and the good life and His ongoing redemption of the world. Jesus followed His Father's will perfectly, and through a personal relationship with Jesus and His Spirit we are given the ability to follow His will also. Following the will of God is the *only* true good life.

Socrates' unbiblical concept of God leads him to an unbiblical view of man and salvation. Although Socrates challenges the flawed thinking of the other characters, he cannot see how to challenge the root cause of their futile thinking, nor his own—a rebellious heart toward the Creator. Socrates still believes that man's problem is ignorance rather than sin, and that removal of ignorance through right reasoning will lead him to the truth. He has no logical basis for this belief, so he never actually tries to prove it. In fact he cannot prove by his reason that reason will lead to the truth. In other words, he has no logical support for his logic. If he submitted to the Lord God, he would then know both the foundation of logic, as well as its limits.

Alas, Socrates unreasonably sees no limits to his logic and so treats it as his god and his authority. For example, when Socrates tries to open Peter Pragma's mind to consider alternatives to a Science or Business major at Desperate State (the majors that Peter calculates are the most likely to bring him wealth and, therefore, happiness) he suggests liberal arts because they "seek knowledge for its own sake." Socrates goes on to suggest that such knowledge will enable Peter to know and improve himself and liberate him from the "cave of ignorance." Socrates says he has devoted his whole life to knowing himself. (He gives us no report about whether he has succeeded.) Later in the book Socrates tells Felicia Flake that "my authority is . . . the authority of the argument . . . . we shall examine [your position] by the light of reason." Without any biblical qualification, these statements can only convey the idea that reason is our authority and that our salvation will come through acquiring knowledge, rather than through a right relationship with Jesus Christ. The Bible tells us not only that knowledge and reason are *not* our salvation, but that true knowledge, of ourselves, God and how we fit in His world, is impossible apart from the Lord. Remember, Proverbs tells us that the fear of the Lord is the *beginning* (not the end) of knowledge. To understand how everything else fits in His world, we *first* have to fear (that is, know personally and revere) the God Who created us and made us for Himself.

At another point Felicia asks Socrates "What is happiness?" Socrates responds that happiness is "knowledge of truth." So far so good. If Socrates had gone on to say that Jesus is the Truth, he would have spoken truth. But alas, he does not. He lamely explains (essentially begging the question) that truth is "saying what is real, saying of what-is that it is." Socrates should have followed his own advice by going on to *say* Jesus is the Truth!

Socrates' entire method of defending "the good life" is flawed because he wrongly assumes that unbelievers are genuine, neutral truth-seekers. In order to lead someone from one place to another, we first must identify where they are coming from. The Bible explicitly states that all unbelievers suppress the truth about God in active rebellion. As we noted above, unbelievers know God (there are no *real* atheists), but because they are in rebellion against him, they neither glorify Him nor give Him thanks but instead "suppress the truth in unrighteousness." The result is inevitable: futile thinking, foolish desires and minds set against God. Nevertheless, the worship of God is built in to our very being—when we rebel against God, we cannot avoid worshiping *something*, whether it be money, power, pleasure, career, our brains, another person, even ourselves.

Felicia Flake, poster child for the slogan, "If it feels good, do it."

When unbelievers thus exchange the truth of God for a lie and worship created things rather than the Creator, God gives them up to "vile passions," to which they become enslaved. But for the grace and mercy of our Lord all of us would be in this perilous situation with no way out.

Given this biblical truth, leading the unbeliever to think that his problem is one of ignorance, and if he just thinks better he can reason his way to truth, is like telling someone whose car needs a new engine that all he needs to do is read the Driver's Manual and he'll be back on the road in no time. Like Adam and Eve in the Garden, we are self-deceived when we think we can see and judge the truth about ourselves and our relationship with God, the world and others, *apart from* a fear of the Lord.. A defense of the good life based on a *biblical* understanding of man will *not* reinforce this self-deception on the part of unbelievers.

*The Best Things in Life* focuses extensively on the questions of "the good life" and objective truth. In addressing these questions, however, the book utilizes a "bottom-up" approach, attempting to reason up from man's experiences or desires to attain certain truths. This man-centered ("anthropocentric") approach is the opposite of the Bible's approach. The Bible defines goodness and truth by looking at God and His works and then reasons *down* to man and creation by analogy. The Bible talks about goodness a lot. In fact, it mentions the word over six hundred times. And acknowledging that God is good is foundational to biblical thinking about moral goodness. Fundamentally, *good* means "what God is and does." "For the Lord is good," says Psalm 100:5. Good is defined in terms of God (including His character, His actions and what He creates), not in terms of an ideal standard floating around in space—or in our minds! Good is not the abstract quality or ideal conjured up by the philosophers.

In order to put things in proper perspective, we need to look at what the Bible says about some important concepts that are related to that which is good: prosperity, blessings, pleasure and success. Prosperity denotes an abundance of material or spiritual blessings and is one of God's gifts we noted above. God gives temporal (limited in time and place) prosperity to many people. It is yet another sign of God's goodness. But true prosperity that has eternal value is totally dependent on the blessings of covenantal obedience before God. And this obedience is possible only through the power of the Holy Spirit in our lives. Christ gives us His Spirit when we enter into the new covenant of His blood that was shed for us for the remission of our sins. Psalm 1:3 says that the godly person prospers in all he does, and it gives us the image of a well-watered tree that produces its fruit in its season. This shows that prosperity is a process in which we fulfill the purpose for which God created us through responding in love and obedience to Him.

Blessing is related to prosperity and assumes that someone has given you the benefit or prosperity by which you are blessed. That someone, of course, is God, for all blessing is ultimately from God and is solely a result of His love. The abundance we have all around us in the world is a divine and universal blessing, not limited to believers and not deserved in any way. God "makes his sun rise on the evil and on the good, and sends rain on the just and on the unjust" (Matt. 5:45). But the permanent blessings of life are directly connected to God's covenant with His people, first introduced

Fudge Factor, president of Desperate State. Socrates implies that Factor is computer-like in his thinking, that he responds only to those problems for which he has been "programmed."

when God called Abraham: "I will make you a great nation; I will bless you and make your name great; And you shall be a blessing. I will bless those who bless you, and I will curse him who curses you; and in you all the families of the earth shall be blessed" (Genesis 12:2–3). The opposite of blessing and obedience is curse and disobedience. They are two sides of the same coin, and there is no "middle" or "neutral" ground. True blessing does *not* always include *material* blessing of prosperity during our time in this sinful world. During the ongoing spiritual warfare in which all believers participate, many, like Jesus Himself, will be called to suffer in His name. Yet this suffering, too, will be a blessing and ultimately result in the great and awesome *spiritual and material* blessings of the New Heavens and New Earth when Christ's redemption of His world is complete (see Revelation 21).

In our world where the process of redemption is still ongoing, *material* prosperity (having a lot of *things*) is *not* always connected to righteous behavior. The wicked often prosper for a time. In our day obvious examples include the people making lots and lots of easy money selling pornography (see Psalms 10, 12, 37 and 73). However, this material prosperity of the wicked is rarely, if ever, accompanied by any spiritual or psychological prosperity and comes to a crashing end for the wicked, often in this world, but *always* at death. God judges the wicked, and their prosperity will be no more (Ps. 73). This should help us remember that we cannot judge the spiritual state of a person one way or the other by his material possessions alone.

Although *The Best Things in Life* looks at "happiness" as an end goal in life, the Bible talks about a related, but more fundamental and deeper, concept called "joy." Joy is far deeper than emotional happiness and sometimes may not be accompanied by happiness at all. C.S. Lewis, in his book *Surprised by Joy*, defines joy as an "unsatisfied desire, which is itself more desirable than any other satisfaction," and should be "sharply distinguished both from happiness and from pleasure." Lewis was drawn to God by his desire for joy and found it only by submitting to God, Who is the source of all joy.

—*William S. Dawson*

# Session I: Prelude

## A Question to Consider

A genie named Arthur (not all genies are men from Arab countries, you know) pops out of the bottle when you pick it up. She says, "If you will describe your idea of *the good life,* I will grant it for you." How do you answer her?

What do you think is the most important thing necessary for a good life?

What do you think truth has to do with the good life?

*From the General Information above answer the following questions:*

1. What does "Natural Law" assume?
2. What happened to Socrates?
3. Why can morality not be established by reason alone?
4. What is good? How do we know what good is?
5. What is truth? How do we know what truth is?
6. Can morality be separated from our relationship with God?
7. What is the problem of the "virtuous pagan?"
8. What is the answer to the problem of the "virtuous pagan?"
9. Can our method of defending the faith be separated from our relationship with and understanding of God?
10. Can we ignore what the Bible says about unbelievers when we try to convince them of the truth of God's existence?
11. How should we go about confronting the unbeliever?

## Optional Activities

These dialogues may come alive more if they are read out loud (even acting out the characters), especially if there are different readers for each character. As you read the dialogues out loud, stop where appropriate to talk about the arguments of the characters. (This could be a multi-day expansion.)

 Reading Assignment:
Forward and Chapters 1–5

## Session II: Recitation
Forward and Chapters 1–5

## Comprehension Questions

*Answer the following questions for factual recall:*

1. What is the first way that Socrates claims that something can be good?
2. What is the other way that Socrates says that things can be considered good?
3. What does Socrates say is the way we can liberate ourselves from the "cave of ignorance?"
4. Science technician Marigold Measurer proudly tells Socrates that the ancients feared and worshiped nature, but we (moderns) conquer nature (p. 40). How does Socrates respond?
5. What does Socrates say is the key difference between humans and computers?
6. Why can computers never become like humans?

**Reading Assignment:**
Chapters 5–6

## Session III: Discussion
Chapters 5–6

## A Question to Consider

What is success? (How would you define it? What would you consider examples of success?)

*Discuss or list short answers to the following questions:*

### Text Analysis

1. How do Peter Pragma and Socrates define "success" in Pragma's discussion with Socrates?
2. What is the difficulty in defining success?
3. What is the good life?
4. What is the problem with Socrates' approach to finding the good life?

### Cultural Analysis

1. What does our culture generally believe about the greatest good?
2. What does our culture think is the role of education? Why is it impossible to seek means to the biblical end of God's glory in government schools?

3. What evidence in the culture around us points to its worship of money, pleasure, fame and power as the greatest goods in life?
4. Over the past several years, many studies have shown that the current behavior of evangelical Christians in ethics and morality is no different from the behavior of unbelievers. If the studies are accurate, what does this tell us about what evangelical Christians think about the connection between their relationship with God and ethics or morality?
5. In what ways does our culture seek to suppress the glorification of God in our lives? In what ways does the contemporary church, inadvertently or otherwise, acquiesce (give in) to this suppression?

### Biblical Analysis

1. What does the Bible say is the nature of the good (Ps. 100:5; Mark 10:18; Luke 18:19)?
2. What do the following biblical passages say about the separation of morality and ethics from a relationship with the Lord: Luke 18:19; Psalm 16:2; Romans 1?
3. What does the Bible say about what our end goal and means should be for our education? For our "careers" (Rom. 1:21; 1 Pet. 4:16; 1 Cor. 6:20)?

### Summa

*Write an essay or discuss this question, integrating what you have learned from the material above.*

How should the Bible's true revelation about the nature of the good apply to our own lives, including our educational and career goals?

**Reading Assignment:**
Chapters 7–9

## Session IV: Recitation
Chapters 5–9

## Comprehension Questions

*Answer the following questions for factual recall:*

1. How does Socrates show that only God could prove that there is no Santa Claus?
2. What are universal negative statements?
3. In what sense can we never prove them?

According to Socrates in *The Best Things in Life*, the reindeer employed by jolly ol' Saint Nick fly by magic. But this is not neccesarily the case. And thankfully, the sciences come to our aid in explaining this great mystery.

Larry Silverberg at North Carolina State University asserts that reindeer fly due to centuries of selective breeding and (more recently) bioengineering. They become buoyant when their lungs are filled with an appropriate mixture of helium, oxygen and nitrogen. And Professor Ian Stewart of Warwick University says that, "Reindeer have a curious arrangement of gadgetry on top of their heads which we call *antlers* and naively assume exist for the males to do battle and to win females. This is absolute nonsense. The antlers are actually fractal vortex-shedding devices. We are talking not aerodynamics here, but *antl*aerodynamics . . . .. These spin off a whole system of vortices, carefully tailored to generate the right amount of lift for such high speeds. So the reindeer hang from their antlers as they fly—which is why the antlers are on top and at the front. This phenomenon is exploited by the supersonic Concorde jet, but it is only apparent on antlers at very high velocity.

There are approximately 2.1 billion children under the age of 18 in the world, and assuming that there are 2.5 children per house, Santa Claus has to make 842 million stops on Christmas Eve. If Santa travels against the direction in which the Earth rotates, he has 172,800 seconds to make these deliveries, or about two ten-thousandths of a second per household. So, in order to deliver all the presents, the reindeer have to fly at speeds of 6,000 times the speed of sound.

4. In what sense can we prove them?
5. Why does Socrates say we should not seek money, power or honor as ends to the good life?
6. What is Socrates' argument against seeking bodily pleasures as the greatest good?
7. Why does Socrates argue for censorship of music in Chapter 8?
8. Can you identify the weak link (undercutting the whole argument) in Socrates' case for censorship of music?
9. In Chapter 9 Socrates says arguments from authority are the "weakest of all arguments" (p. 113). Is this always true?
10. When would it not be true?

READING ASSIGNMENT: Chapters 10–12

# Session V: Discussion
Chapters 10–12

## A Question to Consider

Do you think pleasure is good, bad or neither? Why?

*Discuss or list short answers to the following questions:*

### Text Analysis

1. What do the characters in *The Best Things in Life* think about pleasure?
2. Why does Socrates think that the pleasure of music is so dangerous?
3. What is the main problem with living the good life through the pursuit of pleasure, according to Socrates?
4. Why is truth better than pleasurable illusion, according to Socrates?

### Cultural Analysis

1. Does our culture say pleasure is good, bad or neutral?
2. How does our youth culture treat music?
3. What does our culture believe about truth and knowledge?

### Biblical Analysis

1. What does the Bible tell us about the nature of pleasure (Eccl. 2:24; Ps. 35:27; 1 Tim. 6:17; Rev. 21:4,6; 22:2)?
2. What is wrong with Socrates' analysis of pleasure (Eccl. 2:24; Ps. 35:27; John 14:6; 1 Tim. 6:17; Rev. 21:4,6; 22:2)?
3. What is the Bible's view of music compared to Socrates' view?
4. What is the connection between pleasure and joy in the Bible?

## Summa

*Write an essay or discuss this question, integrating what you have learned from the material above.*
Why does Socrates' approach to ethics in *The Best Things in Life* ultimately fall short in seeking to convey true morality?

# Session VI: Writing

## Progymnasmata

One of the classic "Rhetorical Figures" that were used to develop good rhetorical communication is called *exergasia*. This Latin word literally means "working out." In exergasia, the writer repeats the same idea one or more times, each time changing the words used, the style or the general treatment of the idea. This is a standard method for explaining, amplifying, varying and emphasizing an idea. For this assignment, read Romans 1:18–32 and notice how the Apostle Paul masterfully uses exergasia to drive home his main point that all men in sin suppress the obvious knowledge of God and as a result God gives them over to futile thinking and a debased mind. Now reread the first part of this passage, Romans 1:18-23, and rewrite it in your own words using exergasia.

# Optional Session

## Philosopher Boot Camp

*In this class we will attempt to actually do some of what the fictional Socrates did in this book.*

### OPTION 1: GO TO COLLEGE

*Reread the first dialogues with Peter Pragma.*

Arrange a meeting with a college student or an older person (preferably one who is currently trying to decide on a career path).

In order to do this, and do it well, involve a teacher, parents or maybe your pastor or a college minister to help you find someone to interview. The person who you are going to interview needs to have some sort of answer to the question "What are you going to do with your life?" This does not mean that he has to have a completely thought-out answer, but that he should not (or will not) say: "I don't know." Prepare several types of interview questions in case some of them are ineffective.

When you meet with the person, give him an explanation of what you are doing:

I am (your name), and I am seeking to practice philosophy as an amateur. The great task of the philosopher is to find wisdom, and I have come to learn it from you. I want to ask you a few questions about life, attempting to discover what you are planning for your life and why you are planning it. I will be asking a lot of questions, trying to discover your motivation. This might be a little awkward (I am only an amateur in training), but bear with me.

Ask the interviewee what he is planning to do and then (like the gadfly of Athens) question him about why he is going to do it.

Carefully record a summary of the answers.

Write a short report on your findings and deliver it to others:

Make sure that, unlike Socrates, you are careful to make sure that you act Christianly. Do not berate or publicly embarrass your interviewee. (He is probably bigger than you anyway and might make you drink hemlock or even Pepsi).

Make sure to thank him and give him a candy bar or some small token of your gratitude when finished with the interview. (College students will treat you well if you give them free food).

**OPTION 2** (especially good in groups):

*Follow the basic pattern above but go to the local mall or shopping center and set up a booth or a sign that invites people to come and answer some questions about life. The sign might read:*

Help this amateur philosopher better understand life. (If you don't, I will have to write a long boring report . . . Please, help!)

Depending on the rules of your local mall, you might have to get permission to do this, so make sure you call ahead.

If you wish to apply a bit of style and panache, make up a T-shirt that says *A m a t e u r Philosopher* in big letters on the front.

Report to your class, other classes or parents your most interesting findings.

"Pop" Syke, psychologist and passing "guru" of Felicia Flake. Syke is an aging, Epicurean hippie.

**OPTION 3** (if social interaction outside the family is not available)

Carefully interview an older sibling or a parent. Treat them with added kindness and respect (or avoid the tea for the next two weeks).

## ENDNOTES

1   In its strictly ethical application, natural law is the rule of conduct which is prescribed to us by the Creator in the constitution of the nature with which He has endowed us. According to Thomas Aquinas, the natural law is "nothing else than the rational creature's participation in the eternal law."

2   *This endnote appears only in the teacher's edition.*

3   *This endnote appears only in the teacher's edition.*

# THE UNABORTED SOCRATES

"Why sow where the ground makes it its care to destroy the fruit? Where there are many efforts at *abortion?* Where there is *murder before the birth?* For even the prostitute you do not let continue a mere prostitute, but make her a murderer also . . . or rather *something even worse than murder. For I have no name to give it, since it does not destroy the thing born, but prevents it being born.* Why then do you abuse the gift of God, and fight with His laws, and follow after what is a curse as if a blessing, and make the chamber of procreation a chamber for murder, and arm the woman that was given for childbearing unto slaughter?"

—John Chrysostom
(ca. A.D. 347–407, *Homily 24* on Romans)

See if you can remember the name of this story. There's a famine in the land, and a family living at the edge of the forest is starving. With but half a loaf of bread left—not even enough to feed the whole family—the mother convinces the reluctant father to abandon their son and daughter deep in the forest to fend for themselves. They take the children into the recesses of the forest to chop wood. After falling asleep next to the blazing campfire, the children awake to find their parents have disappeared. They walk all night long and the next day unsuccessfully try to find their way home. With only a few berries scattered on the ground to eat, they are very hungry. After falling asleep under a tree, they awake on the third day and keep walking, only to find themselves deeper in the woods and hopelessly lost. If help does not come soon they will surely die. Then they see an attractive bird perched on a tree above them. After listening to the bird's lovely song, they follow its flight toward a little house where it perches on the roof. Coming closer to the house, they see that it is made of

Just as the author brings Socrates into our modern world, the artist here depicts Socrates in modern clothes, yet in the style and colors reminiscent of an ancient Greek vase. Socrates thought that people would behave well if only they knew the truth. Hmm…

bread with a cake roof and sugar windows! Starving, the boy ravenously eats a roof shingle while the girl gnaws on a sugary window.

The children ignore a gentle voice inquiring from inside the house, continuing to consume pieces of the house without distraction. The door opens abruptly, and out hobbles a woman "as old as the hills," leaning on a crutch. She inquires where the children came from and then invites them in, bidding them take shelter from the woods. The old woman makes them a fine meal of pancakes and fruit and provides clean cozy beds. The children think they are in heaven.

Getting up early, the old woman gazes at the two children sleeping peacefully. Suddenly she grabs the boy with her bony arms, drags him to the backyard and, before he knows what's happening, locks him in a little shed-styled jail with a barred door. Going back into the house, the old woman yells at the girl to get up and fix her imprisoned brother something to eat to fatten him up. "When he's nice and fat I'll eat him up," she exclaims in triumph. The girl wails loudly but to no avail. She has no choice but to do as she is told. Each morning the old woman goes out to the shed and orders the boy to stick out his finger so she can feel how fat he is getting. Each day the boy sticks an old bone through the bars, and the old woman with her poor eyesight thinks it is his finger. After four weeks, though his finger feels as scrawny as ever, the old woman loses patience. She shouts to the boy's sister to prepare the kitchen, for tomorrow she will butcher the boy and then cook him. Sobbing with grief the little girl cries out to God for help.

The next morning the grief-stricken girl fills up the kettle with water and lights the fire. "First we'll do some baking," says the old woman. "I've already heated up the oven and kneaded the dough." Pushing the little girl over to the flaming oven, she orders her to crawl in and see if it is hot enough to bake the

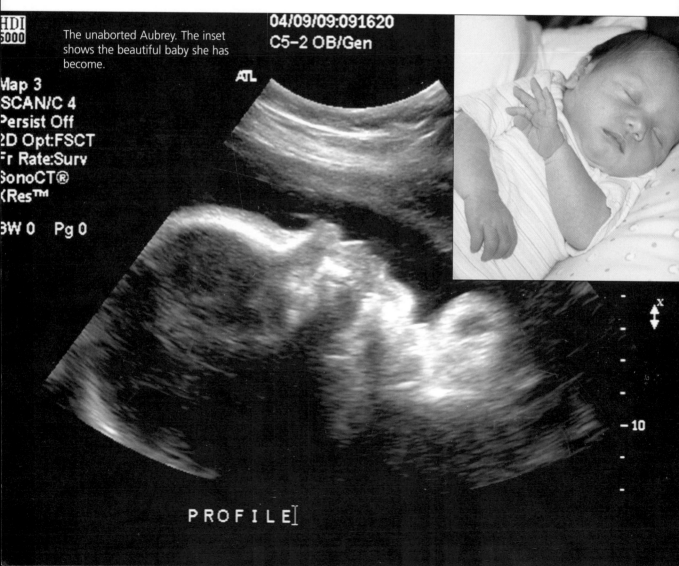

The unaborted Aubrey. The inset shows the beautiful baby she has become.

PROFILE

bread. The old woman is planning to push her in and bake her, but the suspicious girl dallies around, complaining that she does not know how to get in to check the fire. The impatient old woman scolds the girl and hurries over to the oven, sticking her head in and saying "Just look, even I can get in." Just at that moment, the little girl gives the old woman one big shove into the oven, shuts the iron door and bolts it. The old woman begins screeching frightfully, then horribly burns to death as the girl runs off to save her brother. The thrilled and relieved children hug, kiss and jump up and down for joy.

After loading their pockets with goodies and treasure from the old woman's house they head out to find their way home. With the help of the forest creatures they do, in fact, find their way home. Running into their house they emotionally embrace their father. Tears of joy stream down their father's face, for not only has his wife died but he has not had one happy moment since the day he abandoned his children in the forest. As the children empty their pockets of treasure, their worries are over and they live happily ever after.

Of course, the story is *Hansel and Gretel*. The universal fear of children being rejected by their parents is what makes this classic fairy tale so compelling. Ultimate rejection in real life is abandoning in the woods, so to speak, helpless babies who have no chance to fend for themselves. When parents do this to babies outside the womb, it is called *infanticide* ("killing of infants," from the Latin *infanticida*). When it is done to babies inside the mother's womb, it is called abortion ("premature delivery destroying the life of the unborn," from the Latin *abortionem*). As the great saint and church father John Chrysostom noted in the quote above, it is particularly heinous when a mother's womb, made by God to protect and nurture life, is turned into a den of destruction and death.

Abortion and infanticide are ancient pagan practices that were outlawed with the coming of Christianity to the West, until the latter part of the twentieth century, when Western society's apostasy (turning from the faith) and disobedience reached the point of legalizing abortion. The book you are about to read, *The Unaborted Socrates*, is an attack on current pro-abortion and pro-choice thinking, based on a "natural law" approach to the issue. As in your previous book by the same author, *The Best Things in Life*, it is

written in the form of Socratic dialogues between a modern Socrates and various characters who defend the practice of abortion. Although the book is on the "right" side of the abortion issue, it has the same weaknesses and deficiencies as *The Best Things in Life*.

# GENERAL INFORMATION

## Author and Context

Philosophy professor Peter Kreeft is a prolific writer of popular apologetics books from a "traditional" or "conservative" point of view, including *The Unaborted Socrates, The Best Things in Life,* and *How To Win The Culture War: A Christian Battle Plan For a Society In Crisis.* Kreeft wrote *The Unaborted Socrates* to "strip away the emotional issues and get to the heart of the rational objections to abortion," as the back cover of the book notes. Abortion has been a major ethical issue in the United States since the American church began to wake up from its slumbers several years *after* the famous *Roe v. Wade* Supreme Court Decision of 1973 that first legalized abortion in the United States. Kreeft uses the literary form of Socratic dialogues to explore and undermine modern arguments in support of abortion.

It is important to put the abortion problem in historical perspective. Violence and disrespect for human life was a common part of the ancient pagan cultures of death. Power and violence, rather than love and service, ruled these pagan societies that oppressed slaves, the poor and children as a matter of course. The Greco-Roman world, for instance, displayed its disdain for life in its numerous wars, crucifixions, tortures, infanticides and abortions. The ancient pagan worlds sometimes sacrificed children for cultic religious purposes (to manipulate or "pay-off" the gods). Baby killing for personal or social purposes was also rampant. What we would call "lifestyle" abortions were common among the rich who did not want to share their wealth with many children, and also among the poor who thought that they could not support many children.

In ancient Greece and especially in Rome, abortion and infanticide were common practices at every level of society. One of the widespread methods of infanticide in ancient Greece and Rome was called "exposure." Exposure simply meant leaving the baby somewhere out in the elements, like *Hansel and Gretel,* to die.

As one modern scholar noted, the "Greeks enjoy the dubious distinction of being the first [in the West] positively to advise and even demand abortion in certain cases." In his utopian *Republic,* Plato requires abortion for all women who conceive after forty years of age. Despite believing that the unborn child was a living being, Plato considered the state's ideals and "needs" more important than the life of the unborn child. In support of his call for an early form of eugenics, Aristotle also requires abortion or exposure in certain circumstances. Aristotle argues in his *Politics* that the state must regulate marriage, limit the number of children and destroy weaker and deformed children. Pregnancies surpassing the limit must be aborted, and "no deformed child shall be raised." Both Greek philosophers believed that children existed only for the sake of the state and had no "right to life" otherwise.

Rome fared no better than the Greeks as a protector of the unborn. In Rome abortion and infanticide increased over the centuries and by the first century B.C. was widespread. The earliest Roman law code, the Twelve Tables (ca. 450 B.C.), permitted fathers to expose any female or deformed babies. Although Cicero formally criticized the practice of abortion in the Roman republic, both pagan and later Christian writers tell us that abortion occurred regularly among rich and poor, free and slave, young and old, for the duration of the empire. When Augustus became Caesar during the time of Christ, he realized the need to build a strong state and thought strengthening the family and promoting rather than discouraging children would help him solidify the empire. His reforms, however, never prohibited abortion, and the practice flourished, especially since it was less visible than

Professor Atilla Tarian, ethicist, abortion apologist and speaker at the I.C.I.C.L.E. convention.

infanticide. Abortion was common at the highest levels of the empire. After an affair with his niece Julia, the emperor Domitian (51-96 A.D.), a fierce persecutor of Christians, forced her to undergo an abortion, from which she died.

Only through the growth and influence of Christianity in the empire did Rome eventually outlaw abortion. During the first three centuries of the church, the Christian witness against abortion was strong and virtually unanimous. That witness concentrated on three important themes: the unborn in the womb (fetus) is the creation of God; abortion is murder; and God's judgment is on those guilty of abortion. The earliest Christian writings after the New Testament (such as the *Didache, Epistle of Barnabas,* and *Apocalypse of Peter*) uniformly prohibit and condemn abortion and infanticide. The *Apocalypse of Peter* provides for the damnation of both husbands and wives guilty of abortion and for the salvation of aborted infants, painting a graphic picture of Hell's population, including the following scene:

> And near that place I saw another gorge in which the discharge and excrement of the tortured ran down and became like a lake. And there sat women, and the discharge came up to their throats; and opposite of them sat many children, who were born prematurely, weeping. And from them went forth rays of fire and smote the women on the eyes. And these were those who produced children outside marriage and who procured abortions.

The *Apocalypse* understood abortion as the culpable murder of a human being.

The first church body to enact punishment for abortion was the

Council of Elvira in A.D. 305. Nineteen bishops from all over Spain met to decide several important issues, including punishments for abortion. A larger Council of Ancrya met in 314 A.D. in Asia Minor and similarly enacted punishments for abortion. During the fourth and fifth centuries, five major church fathers—Basil, Jerome, Ambrose, Augustine and Chrysostom—condemned abortion, and the church's position against abortion was settled for the next fifteen hundred years. All of Christendom condemned abortion and infanticide until very recently. On the heels of succumbing to the Darwinian evolution myth, much of Europe, in an advanced stage of apostasy, first legalized abortion in the latter half of the twentieth century. America soon followed, succumbing in 1973 with the legalization of abortion by the Supreme Court. The church was so weak and indifferent that, to its everlasting shame, *not one* major evangelical church, institution or spokesman publicly opposed or condemned the Supreme Court's decision at the time. It took many years for a small minority in the church to begin serious opposition to the now-entrenched abortion industry.

## Significance

*The Unaborted Socrates* is a challenging and entertaining example of analyzing the modern abortion issue in the classic form of a Socratic dialogue.

Socratic dialogues were first made famous by Plato's writings claiming to document some of Socrates' actual dialogues, as well as his trial. In education the "Socratic method" has been used for generations, and for many years was virtually the exclusive form of instruction in American law schools. In essence, the Socratic method is a form of cross-examination in which basic assumptions and positions on issues are probed and challenged by logical questioning. This technique is very effective in finding inconsistencies, contradictions or arbitrariness in the way we think about issues and problems. It is much *less* effective in positively demonstrating a coherent worldview.

*The Unaborted Socrates* also reveals the strengths and weaknesses of a rationalist and "natural law" apologetic applied to a specific ethical issue. Natural law assumes that there is a universal agreement about basic morality that *all* people can know, regard-

less of faith or culture, through natural human reason. This view of morality conflicts with what the Bible reveals to us about man's nature and his reasoning ability.

The strength of Kreeft's approach is his use of logic to undermine the assumptions of modern, unbiblical arguments in support of abortion. *The Unaborted Socrates* erroneously implies that we determine the right and wrong of abortion through our own reasoning abilities independent of God. Only if we submit to God as our authority can *we* determine and know that abortion is wrong and why it is wrong. Because Kreeft does not acknowledge God or His word as his ultimate authority in the Socratic dialogues in *The Unaborted Socrates*, he is unable to clearly establish or prove that the fetus is a person and that abortion is therefore murder.

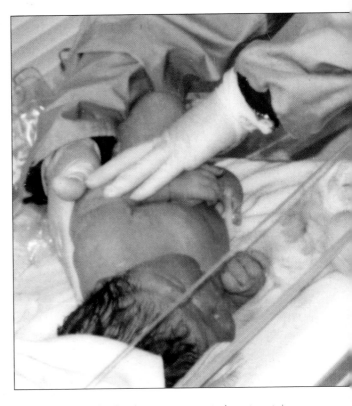

Premature births that once meant almost certain death are now handled so well medically that a child born weighing one pound can survive. This advancement comes from the medical community—the same community that aborts the unborn. What a tragic irony.

## Main Characters

The come-back-to-life Socrates, ancient Greek philosopher and gadfly (last seen in *The Best Things in Life*) returns to stimulate, irritate and otherwise prod his dialogue partners to cogitate on (think about) their pro-abortion views. The new and much improved Socrates takes on a doctor who runs an abortion clinic, Dr. Rex Herrod, philosophy professor Attila Tarian, who specializes in ethical issues, and that wacky psychologist "Pop" Syke returning from *The Best Things in Life* for more logical pummeling. Notice the humorous allusions (referring to things indirectly) in the characters' names. "Herrod" the abortionist reminds us of King Herod, the ultimate baby killer, who attempted to kill the baby Jesus in Bethlehem, slaughtering all the boys younger than two years of age. "Attila Tarian" evokes both Attila the Hun (the terrible barbarian invader and destroyer) and the word "utilitarian," implying the terrible, destructive nature of supposedly humane utilitarian ethics that promote women's "right" to abortion as useful to society. Of course, "Pop" Syke alludes to the popular yet shallow and irrational nature of modern psychology.

## Summary and Setting

*The Unaborted Socrates* is divided into a series of three dialogues. In the first, Socrates engages Dr. Herrod in a discussion at his abortion clinic in Athens, Greece about whether abortion is a good or bad thing. Dr. Herrod boldly states: "Let my opponents tell me why it is *not* good, if you please. The onus of proof is on them, not on me." He goes on to explain that his opponents, the anti-abortionists, have only a weak, "emotional" response when they call abortion "murder." Dr. Herrod acknowledges that the issue of whether the fetus is a person is "the crux of the argument." In Dialogue Two, Socrates, Dr. Herrod and his philosopher friend, Attila Tarian evaluate the latter's five reasons "for more liberal abortion laws." The reasons are that 1) most opposition to abortion is from the church, 2) you can't legislate morality, 3) restrictive abortion laws are unenforceable, 4) every child should be a wanted child and 5) liberal abortion laws are compassionate. In the third and final dialogue, Socrates says "it is argument that enables me to find the truth" and asks Pop Syke to help him by arguing with Socrates about the abortion issue. Socrates says that there are five alternatives with respect to a woman's "reproductive freedom," chastity, contraception, abortion, adoption and motherhood. Abortion is evil, and one of the four other alternatives is always preferable to it even if difficult, because it is better to suffer evil than commit it. Socrates ends his arguments by acknowledging that the abortion issue logically always goes back to the issue of whether the fetus is a person. Socrates argues the affirmative, but in the end cannot logically "prove" this fact.

## Worldview

As a mother gently lays her infant son down to nap, she is startled by a piercing rapping sound at her front door. "Just a minute," she yells as she tucks her son in. Suddenly there is a loud bang, followed by a tremendous crashing sound as the front door is trampled by Roman soldiers. The mother screams as an officer orders the soldiers to search the house for any male children two years or younger. One of the soldiers grabs the baby boy from his crib, breaks his neck and then stabs him through the heart with one swift stroke of his short sword. As the mother sobs uncontrollably the first soldier announces that by decree of King Herod all baby boys in Bethlehem two years and younger are to be destroyed. The emotionless soldiers proceed to leave the house quickly as the mother wildly throws household items at them and wails hysterically.

There are very few people in our society today who would condone King Herod's ghastly action in Bethlehem. Yet *many, many* more babies are being killed each month in the United States, *with our government's approval,* simply because they are inside the womb rather than outside. Why is this so, and how did our society come to routinely accept such terrible behavior? And why does *The Unaborted Socrates* not make a more powerful positive case that abortion is wrong? There are many factors influencing why we have become an "abortion culture," but these factors all have in common a more aggressive rejection of the gospel by many outside the church and a failure of obedience and faith inside the church. The weakness of *The Unaborted Socrates'* case against abortion results from its reliance on "natural law" arguments rather than the power of biblically-based arguments.

Socrates vaguely hints at, but never actually acknowledges or addresses, the heart of the abortion problem—a failure to acknowledge the Lord God as our ultimate authority in life and ethics. Socrates assumes we can naturally find the right way to live by simply focusing on sound reasoning, failing to recognize that as sinners we are not neutral "seekers after truth." In fact, unbelievers consciously or unconsciously are rebelling against God and, for their own good, need to be lovingly confronted with this truth. To tell an unbeliever to follow *his* own reason wherever it leads (as Socrates does) rather than submit his reasoning to Christ, who alone can renew his mind and save him from futile thinking, only reinforces the unbeliever's chief delusion—that *he* is ultimately the determiner of right and wrong about moral issues like abortion. God requires believers to be obedient to Him not only in following the truth but also in *how we argue for the truth.* Fighting abortion is part of our spiritual warfare. God instructs us to wage that warfare using the mighty weapons God has given us to pull down strongholds and cast down pro-abortion arguments that exalt man's authority over God's authority. First we undermine the pro-abortionist's position by showing him why his pro-abortion worldview is arbitrary and self-defeating. Then we confront him with the necessary and inevitable authority of God's word for all of life and what God says about abortion.. The Unaborted Socrates does a fairly good job of showing the arbitrary and contradictory thinking of the pro-abortionist but fails to show its root cause—the failure to submit to God's authority in determining the truth about abortion. Socrates' inability to lead his dialogue partners to

the source of truth is a consequence of his unbiblical view of God and man.

Since *The Unaborted Socrates* addresses a very important moral issue, we need to step back for a moment and remember what God has told us about the connection between morality and our relationship with Him. Morality *cannot* be separated from God and our relationship with Him. True moral goodness is a personal act or attitude, in response to the Lord's kindness, which receives God's blessing. And the Triune God of the Bible is the *only* ultimate authority in ethics, as in all other areas of life. Unfortunately, many Christians over the years have not understood this basic truth. For too long American Christians have falsely assumed that what Christians believe about right and wrong is what any "right-thinking person," Christian or not, also believes. Because we live in a sinful world where unbelievers sometimes appear to do good, they assume that morality is somehow separate and apart from salvation or "religion." Appearances, however, can be deceiving. Morality and our relationship with God are insepa-rable. Because God made us whole people, our lives cannot be chopped up into separate categories that do not affect each other. Right outward moral action requires a corresponding right intent and attitude from our hearts inside us. Although unbelievers, thanks to God's grace in restraining sin, do sometimes conform outwardly to God's law, their actions still fall short of true morality because they do not have the right motive and goal for those actions. Christians who, in sin, fail to have right motives and goals also fall short of God's moral requirements.

When Christians unbiblically separate ethics from their faith, one of

"Pop" Syke, psychologist and all-around "touchy feely" guy.

two things happens. They either do not apply the right (biblical) standard, or in arguing with unbelievers, they defend the right standard in the wrong (unbiblical) way. That is, they base their argument *for* the right standard on some authority *other than* God's word that they think the unbeliever will submit to (such as reason, science or tradition). In so doing, they unwittingly mislead the unbeliever by reinforcing his *false* view that the Triune God of the Bible is *not* the authority for all ethics.

This is the situation we find in *The Unaborted Socrates*, an apologetic work meant to persuade unbelievers that abortion is wrong. The author, a Christian, argues for the right standard in calling abortion evil, but never points to God or His word as the ultimate *authority* for the standard, instead arguing that "our common master . . . the light of reason" leads us to the right conclusion. Either he really believes that reason, rather than God's word, is the ultimate authority over ethics, *or* he thinks something like this: "Unbelievers will not listen to the Bible, so I will convince them that abortion is wrong based on reason or science, which they are more likely to accept as authorities. Either way, the unbeliever is misled, and the author exposes his arguments to attack since in reality God is the only authority for prohibiting abortion. As a result of this major strategic mistake, the worldview of *The Unaborted Socrates* is, on the whole, not biblical, even though there are aspects of the book (most obviously its anti-abortion stance) which clearly agree with and are dependent on God's word.

A person's beliefs about God affect his thinking about and acting in the world. Another way of saying this is that our understanding about any matter in life is directly dependent on our theology (how we understand the nature and character of God). This is so for at least two reasons. First the Trinitarian God of the Bible is the creator, sustainer and controller of all reality—it's His world and nothing we do or think can change this fact. Second, a person's view of God must influence the way he sees and understands God's world. A faithful Christian will understand that true knowledge *begins* with the fear of the Lord and, therefore, *sees* the world in faith *as it really is.* Even an unfaithful person, because he is living in God's world, is forced to acknowledge many things about the world that are biblical and therefore true, yet because of his

rebellion against God, he will distort or suppress truths that would force him to do certain things he does not want to do, such as acknowledging the true God and His demands for a righteous life.

Socrates' view of God in *The Unaborted Socrates* is what makes his worldview problematic. Socrates' god seems to be a vague and mysterious being neither he nor anyone else knows much about (or Socrates won't tell us about him). At one point in his dialogue with Dr. Herrod, he briefly discusses the difference between faith and reason. Socrates asserts that whereas reason is common, "like the light of day," faith is not. "Whether true or false, beliefs about the gods are neither plain nor common." Socrates goes on to say that belief in the gods are mysteries, varying from place to place and person to person and are thus obscure. Finally, he betrays a complete lack of understanding of reality when he says "I do not see why [the abortion issue] is theological at all. Why must we speak of the gods in order to speak of the fetus?" The answer, of course, is that the way we perceive the fetus will be determined by our beliefs about God, His creation of the fetus and His purpose in so doing. Even if we do not talk explicitly about God when discussing the fetus, what we assume about God will determine our position on issues with respect to the fetus.

Since Socrates' ultimate authority, and therefore his main god, is his own reason, he convinces Dr. Herrod to join him in "serving the common master," which he seeks to "follow wherever it leads." It's as if Socrates thought "the gods are a mystery we can't figure out, so let's forget about them and rely instead on our own logic and reasoning ability, which everyone can agree on." Socrates appears to be oblivious to the fact that in real life this "common" reasoning has produced nothing but disagreements about all kinds of things, including moral issues like abortion. Reasoning is anything but common and is hardly a "master." Socrates' assumption that all decent, right-thinking people, whether believers or unbelievers, will come to the same conclusion if they simply apply their reason to the issue is simply wrong. Socrates' mistake is to personify and make a god of the very reasoning ability that *should* lead him to acknowledge and worship his creator God. Marred by sin, when our reason is not submissive to God's truth, it leads to the very futility in our thinking that Socrates is trying to avoid! In short, Socrates' god, whether reason or some mystical divine within us, is not the Triune God who has revealed himself to us in Jesus Christ and the Scriptures.

Nevertheless, because the author has been deeply influenced by Christianity, many of his views about man and ethics are biblical. Ironically, these views are only truly defensible in a world governed by the Triune God of the Bible. Socrates' mystical or rational god cannot sustain Socrates' own arguments. For example, Socrates argues that right and wrong are not subjective (just personal opinions) but objective (right or wrong for everybody). This is true *only* because God, through his character and laws is the determiner of right and wrong for everybody. If we supposed the Triune God did not exist (which is impossible) then there would be nothing to prevent each of us from deciding right and wrong for ourselves. This impossibility was the great temptation of the Serpent that duped Adam and Eve in the Garden. But because of his unbiblical theology, Socrates does not make this clear to his dialogue partners, instead arguing about who is imposing values on whom and demonstrating that it is a self-contradiction to say (objectively) that there is no objectivity. While the latter point is certainly true, this does not *prove* Socrates' case for objective truth. Only recognition of the Triune God of Scripture as the author of all truth solves the issue of objectivity and allows us to see reality as it really is. With respect to our main issue, abortion, Socrates upholds the biblical truth that the fetus is a person, that life is sacred and that abortion is a moral evil. His reasoned "proof" depends on the argument that abortion is murder, which in turn depends on the argument that the fetus is a human being. The latter can only be *proved* if grounded on God's revelation about the unborn to us in His word.

Having noted some biblical aspects of *The Unaborted Socrates,* we must point out some clearly unbiblical things about the book. Aside from failing to arguing his case biblically, the most serious error of Socrates is his unbiblical belief that "all evil doing is rooted in false ideas, in ignorance of the truth." No assertion of Socrates could be further from the truth. This false idea about man's problem (that ignorance rather than sin is our problem) has been a staple of pagan suppression of the truth since ancient times. The Greeks were a major peddler of this convenient but

hopeless attempt at guilt reduction ("I did not know!") which directly contradicts God's word (Rom. 1:18–32). Plato, among many others, was a famous promoter of the view that our problem is not sin but ignorance. This view has also been a staple of the American heresy that "neutral" government schools will provide the education we need to overcome our ignorance, and thus, all our problems.

—*William S. Dawson*

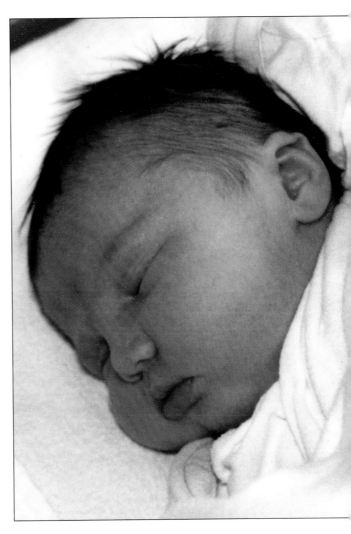

## For Further Reading

Beckwith, Francis. *Politically Correct Death.* Grand Rapids, Mich.: Baker Books, 1993.

Brown, Harold O. J. *Death Before Birth.* Nashville, Tenn.: Thomas Nelson, 1977.

Gentry, Kenneth L. *The Christian Case Against Abortion.* Memphis, Tenn.: Footstool Publications, 1989.

# SESSION I: PRELUDE

## A Question to Consider

Is a fetus a human being? How do you know?

*From the General Information above answer the following questions:*

1. What is abortion? How is it different from infanticide?
2. Why did the ancient pagans permit or encourage abortions?
3. Can our method or way of defending the faith and its position on abortion be separated from our theology or our relationship with God? (Can we ignore what the Bible says about unbelievers when we try to convince them that abortion is wrong?)
4. Why is this "natural law" approach used by our author and by other Christians?
5. Why does the "natural law" argument against abortion fail to prove that the fetus is a human being?

## Optional Activity

These dialogues may come alive more if they are read out loud (even acting out the characters), especially if there are different readers for each character. As you read the dialogues out loud, stop where appropriate to talk about the arguments of the characters. (This could be a multi-day expansion.)

READING ASSIGNMENT:
Pages 11–40²

Socrates holds two pictures depicting the slaughter of the innocents ordered by King Herod in Matthew 2:16–18. The smaller picture is a miniature painted on vellum for a book of hours by an unknown French artist (c.1490–1500); the larger is a painting done by Valerio Castello in 1658. Both pieces are entitled *Massacre of the Innocents*.

# SESSION II: RECITATION
Pages 11–40

## Comprehension Questions

*Answer the following questions for factual recall:*

1. At the bottom of page 15 Herrod argues that his work as an abortionist should be "presumed good or at least neutral, until proved evil." What does he mean by the "onus" or burden of proof?
2. Why does Socrates say that if Herrod has this presumption, Herrod is in the stronger position to begin the argument?
3. On whom would the Bible place the burden of proof?
4. What do Herrod and Socrates agree are the three elements that establish murder?
5. Which of the elements does Herrod argue is not applicable in abortions?
6. How does Socrates define killing?
7. Socrates tells Herrod that unless they "follow our common master" their argument will just be a contest of wills, like two kids playing king of the mountain. What is the "common master," and how does Socrates say we should follow it?
8. Dr. Herrod argues that human beings are essentially animals with computer-like thinking skills. What is Socrates' response?
9. How biblical is that response?
10. Who are the "new gods," and where did Socrates meet them?

 READING ASSIGNMENT:
Pages 41–75

# SESSION III: DISCUSSION
Pages 41–75

## A Question to Consider

What do you think religion or theology (knowledge of God and His world) has to do with the issue of abortion?

*Discuss or list short answers to the following questions:*

### Text Analysis

1. What does Herrod think about the key question of whether the fetus is a person?
2. What does Socrates think of the relationship of theology to the abortion issue?
3. Why does Socrates think he can come to the truth about abortion by ignoring God and simply following "the common master" of his own reasoning?
4. What is the problem with Socrates' approach to abortion through human reason rather than through God's word?

### Cultural Analysis

1. What does our culture generally believe about abortion?
2. What does our culture believe about God and abortion?
3. How and why have people justified "safe and legal" abortion in our culture?

### Biblical Analysis

1. Why should those who trust in Christ believe that they can find out the truth about abortion (Col. 2:2–4)?
2. What do the Scriptures tell us about the "person-hood" of the fetus (Ps. 139)?
3. What is the relationship of God's law to abortion (Ex. 21: 22–23)?

## SUMMA

*Write an essay or discuss this question, integrating what you have learned from the material above.*
How should the Bible's true revelation about abortion apply to our own lives and the life of the church?

 READING ASSIGNMENT:
Pages 75–118

# SESSION IV: RECITATION

Pages 75–118

## Comprehension Questions

*Answer the following questions for factual recall:*

1. What is Socrates' response to Attila Tarian's first argument in support of more liberal abortion laws: that historically most of the opposition to abortion has come from religious organizations such as the Catholic church?

2. What is wrong with Socrates making the statement that his arguments are not "based on religion?"

3. What does Socrates say about the Catholic church's position?

4. How does Socrates' defense of the Catholic position reveal his religious thinking?

5. What is Socrates' response to Attila Tarian's second argument in support of more liberal abortion laws: that tolerance requires us not to "legislate morality?"

6. What is Socrates' argument in response to Attila Tarian's third argument in support of more liberal abortion laws: that unenforceable laws like anti-abortion laws should not exist?

7. What is Socrates' argument in response to Attila Tarian's fourth argument in support of more liberal abortion laws: that every child should be a wanted child?

8. What is Socrates' argument in response to Attila Tarian's

Doctor Rex Herrod, abortionist

fifth argument in support of more liberal abortion laws: that compassion for the poor and victims of rape require liberal abortion laws?

9. How does Socrates respond to Attila Tarian's argument that right and wrong are relative concepts rather than absolute concepts?

10. What is the foundation for absolutes according to Socrates?

READING ASSIGNMENT:
119–155

# SESSION V: DISCUSSION

Pages 119–155

## A Question to Consider

If the world were a perfect place would everyone be equal in every way? Do all attempts to make situations righteous and just end up making all results equal?

*Discuss or list short answers to the following questions:*

### Text Analysis

1. Pop Syke argues in Dialogue III that prohibiting abortion is unjust to women. He asserts that "justice demands equality." How does Socrates define justice in relation to equality?

2. How does Socrates demonstrate the confusion of justice with equality?

3. What does Socrates say results from this confusion of justice and equality?

### Cultural Analysis

1. How does our culture confuse justice with equality?

2. Where do you see our culture's mass confusion regarding justice and equality?

## Biblical Analysis

1. What does the Bible say about equality (Rom. 3:23, Gal. 3:28, Eph. 5:21 ff.)?
2. What is the biblical view of justice (Ps. 119:121, 1 Cor. 1:30)?

## SUMMA

*Write an essay or discuss this question, integrating what you have learned from the material above.* How does the Bible relate justice and equality?

# SESSION VI: DISCUSSION

## A Question to Consider

Should Christian kill abortionists?

*Discuss or list short answers to the following questions:*

## Text Analysis

1. According to Socrates is abortion murder?
2. What does Socrates say about the difference between doing wrong and having wrong done to you?

## Cultural Analysis

1. What does our culture think about people like Paul Hill and Eric Rudolph?
2. Why is our culture inconsistent in their assessment of people like this?
3. How does the church react to people that murder abortion doctors or that blow up abortion clinics in this manner?

## Biblical Analysis

1. What is the punishment for murder (Gen. 9:5–6)?
2. To whom has God given the task of executing murderers (Rom. 13:1–4)?

3. What should be the punishment for people who murder abortion doctors (Gen. 9)?

## SUMMA

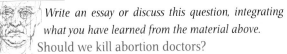

*Write an essay or discuss this question, integrating what you have learned from the material above.* Should we kill abortion doctors?

## Application

Write a letter to your Congressman or Senator to explain to them what you would have them do concerning abortion.

## Optional Session

*All tests and quizzes are to be given as open book and Bible. Answer each of the following questions in complete sentences. Most can and should be answered in a sentence or two. If you are simply reviewing, answer the questions below in written form or orally (2 points per answer).*

1. What do Herrod and Socrates agree are the three

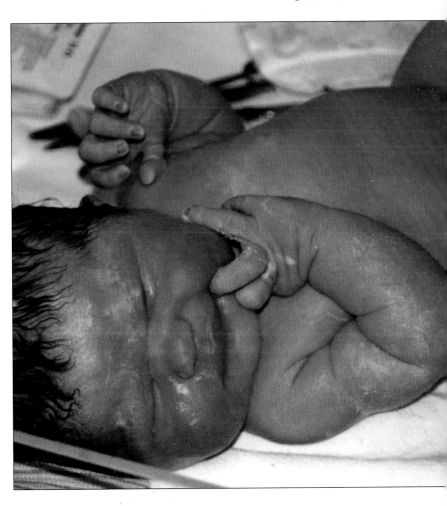

elements that establish murder? Which of the elements does Herrod argue is not applicable in abortions?

2. Socrates tells Herrod that unless they "follow our common master" their argument will just be a contest of wills, like two kids playing king of the mountain. What is the "common master" and how does Socrates say we should follow it?

3. Who are the "new gods," and where did Socrates meet them?

4. What is Socrates' response to Attila Tarian's first argument in support of more liberal abortion laws: that historically most of the opposition to abortion has come from religious organizations such as the Catholic Church?

5. What is wrong with Socrates making the statement that his arguments are not "based on religion?"

6. How does Socrates' defense of the Catholic position reveal his religious thinking?

7. What is Socrates' response to Attila Tarian's second argument in support of more liberal abortion laws: that tolerance requires us not to "legislate morality?"

8. What is Socrates' argument in response to Attila Tarian's fourth argument in support of more liberal abortion laws: that every child should be a wanted child?

9. What is Socrates' argument in response to Attila Tarian's fifth argument in support of more liberal abortion laws: that compassion for the poor and victims of rape require liberal abortion laws?

10. How does Socrates respond to Attila Tarian's argument that right and wrong are relative concepts rather than absolute concepts?

## Logic

*Demonstrate your understanding of the worldview set forth in* The Unaborted Socrates *by answering the one of the following questions in complete sentences. Answers should be a paragraph or two.*

1. How should the Bible's true revelation about abortion apply to our own lives and the life of the church?

2. Should we kill abortion doctors?

## ENDNOTES

1 *This endnote appears only in the teachers edition.*

2 All page references are to Kreeft, Peter. *The Unaborted Socrates.* Downers Grove, Ill.: InterVarsity Press. 1983.

3 *This endnote appears only in the teachers edition.*

# GALATIANS

What would happen if you woke up one morning and there was an angel in your room telling you that you could only be saved by eating a quart of peanut butter each day? For many in our culture today, this would be a signal for them to get out the spoon, a tall glass of milk and get to work. For others it would probably signal the beginning of a new denomination, a new diet craze or at least a decent infomercial. A snappy jingle would signal the coming of salvation as it almost always does in our society.

Our society fruitlessly craves another gospel; any other gospel will do, except the real one. We will drink ten glasses of water an hour, meditate while water cascades down the plastic waterfall beside our pet rock. We will hum a mantra. We will invest money in businesses in parallel universes. We will make pilgrimages to Tibetan villages. Anything, except submit.

In this little book of Galatians, however, the danger in our present attitude becomes clear. We crave novelty because we hate truth and the demands that it makes on us. We long for easy fixes because we would rather drink ten glasses of water an hour than face the horrible fact that we cannot do anything to save ourselves. We are afraid to tell that lying angel to leave because we neither know nor have confidence in the real gospel.

Liberty is a precious thing, and one of the things that history has taught us is that liberty undefended is very soon not liberty at all. The cost of liberty is always a battle of some sort. Because Galatians is so concerned with the theme of liberty, it is not surprising to find that it was written in the midst of theological battle. And as we study the book, we will also discover that battles often contain other elements besides the obvious element of overt fighting. A modern sailor on a submarine might find himself fighting by sitting in the dark control room, doing math problems. As an extension of life, battles often encompass everything, and any of the details of life might find themselves included.

Caravaggio depicts the conversion of Paul on the road to Damascus.

# GENERAL INFORMATION

## Author and Context

The book of Galatians was written by the apostle Paul, who wrote the majority of the books in the New Testament. The letter was probably written from Antioch, and it was not *just* from Paul. Salutations at the ends of letters are simply greetings, but people named at the beginning are those who are helping to speak authoritatively, and this letter is also from "all the brethren." Paul is writing from the Galatians' mother church, the church at Antioch in Syria, and there were many brothers there who were "with Paul" on this issue. The letter is addressed to multiple churches throughout the region of Galatia.

## Significance

Galatians is the great charter of Christian freedom. All Christians at all times need to stand fast in the liberty that Christ has bought for us, and brought to us, and we must always refuse every form of sinful bondage. This short epistle teaches us how to do this.

We are accustomed in Christian circles to speak of God's amazing grace. But something *else* that is amazing is how quickly Christians can be tempted to drift away from this amazing grace. And Paul marvels at it—how readily the Galatians were unsettled! How quickly they were removed from the Father, the one who had called them into the grace of Christ (1:6). And when they began to be removed from the true gospel, they went to the only alternative, which was necessarily a false gospel.

Of course, another gospel cannot really be another gospel—there cannot be more than one of them (1:7). And this means that this "new and improved" gospel is actually a turning aside from the gospel; it is perversion. Moreover, such perversions are no accident. Whenever there is perversion, there is a pervert. "Someone" was troubling the Galatians and trying to lure them away from the gospel of free grace.

## Main Characters

The main characters in this short letter are the apostle Paul himself, his adversaries, who are commonly called the Judaizers, and the Galatians, who were wavering between these two positions.

Other persons of importance are Peter, Barnabas and James. These three men occupy an interesting position in the book because doctrinally they all agreed with Paul, but their emphases differed, depending on their circumstances. James had a problem with men who claimed to be representing him, but who then went off and insisted that Gentiles must be circumcised to be saved (which James did *not* agree with). And Peter and Barnabas were guilty of hypocrisy in that they agreed with Paul but adapted their behavior in order to not provoke the Judaizers.

## Summary and Setting

The letter to the Galatians was written to a collection of churches in the Roman province of Galatia—churches such as Lystra, Iconium and Derbe. These cities were located in what is now modern day Turkey. Paul had gone through this area on his first missionary journey, but no sooner had he gotten back to Antioch than he discovered that false teachers were following in his wake and disrupting the churches he had founded. Not only this, but the apostle Peter had capitulated to the same error at the mother church in Syrian Antioch, causing a crisis there. All this occurred just before the Jerusalem council (which is described in Acts 15), placing the writing of Galatians in the mid to late 40's. This is significant because it makes this classic Pauline statement of the gospel one of the *earliest* books of the New Testament.

The view that Galatians was written to *ethnic* Galatia cannot really be sustained. This view is called the *North Galatian* theory, and the one outlined above is called the *South Galatian* theory. North Galatia is north toward the Black Sea, and was an area settled some time before by migrating Gauls (hence the name *Galatia*). The Roman province of Galatia was toward the south, and it contained a number of churches that Paul is recorded as having founded in the book of Acts.

Battles can be very exciting, but they may also include some very mundane details. The book of Galatians reflects this kind of thing. Some of the most important issues that confront the human race are treated in this book—but so are some minor details of the apostle Paul's travel arrangements. These details become important because of their context, and that is why we will have to pay close attention to them.

The book of Galatians teaches extensively on the relationship between law and grace. Two of Doré's famous woodcuts illustrate this relationship.

## Worldview

So, have you ever thought about what it would be like to be in a battle? In doing this, it is always very easy to imagine the excitement and dread before the battle or the glory afterwards. Parades and drums, uniforms and training lend themselves to a curious kind of anticipation, but it is all very orderly, and the awarding of medals and honors after the war is the same way, very orderly. But the reason why the military needs to be so disciplined and ordered before and after battles is that in the *midst* of battle, all appears to be chaos and confusion. It is no different with the great doctrinal battles of the church, and the book of Galatians contains an important account of one of the earliest of those battles. But because it was written in the middle of the fight, we have to be careful in order to make good sense of it.

As we consider Paul's argument throughout this white hot little book, we see him answering objections to his position that had been raised by his adversaries. He even answers one of those objections in his first breath. His apostleship was either denied by his adversaries, or it was claimed that his apostleship was of a secondary kind. He was called a "second-generation" apostle, and he meets this head-on in the first verse—he begins fighting the battle in the first verse. He was an apostle in

the strongest sense of that word—not by men, not by a man, but by Jesus Christ and God the Father. Paul was an apostle of resurrection power, an apostle of the liberty that new life gives. He was therefore not going to submit to a *compromise* between life and death.

According to Paul, the benchmark against which everything else was to be measured was the gospel that had been preached to the Galatians at the first. Paul says this two ways—""what we have preached to you" (1:8) and "what you have received" (1:9). This primitive gospel outranks everyone, whether the emissary is apostolic or angelic. It *certainly* outranked the false brothers who were troubling the Galatians.

These false teachers were doubly damned. The word Paul uses in the first chapter (*anathema*) means cursed or damned, and so adamant is Paul about this that he repeats his grave *anathema* twice, and he does it deliberately for emphasis. The gospel is not something that men have the authority to alter or improve, or adjust to fit with the times. Anyone who attempts this falls under the divine curse. Paul makes it very plain that if he wanted to be a man-pleaser, he made the wrong choice in becoming a servant of Christ (1:10).

Paul says he did not receive this gospel from man. He did not learn it in the classroom of a seminary somewhere. Rather, he received it by the revelation of Jesus Christ. The word here is *apocalypse,* or unveiling (it is the same word that names the *Apocalypse,* the book of *Revelation*). How did Paul come to possess this gospel? He received it in a revelation of Jesus Christ. Paul talks about this revelation in another place, when he is giving his testimony before King Agrippa. "[A]t midday, O king, along the road I saw a light from heaven, brighter than the sun, shining around me and those who journeyed with me" (Acts 26:13). He was in no way disobedient to this heavenly vision (Acts 26:19). Jesus

Paul indicates that, when we seek to live "under the law," we are not sons of Sarah by Abraham but, like Ishmael, slaves and sons of Hagar.

Christ *appeared* to him and ordained him as a minister and as a witness (Acts 26:15–18). This is why it was so important for Paul to fight this particular battle, and the New Testament shows us that he was a faithful warrior to the end of his life.

We have all heard about the conversion of Saul on the road to Damascus. But what exactly was he converted *from?* The answer to this question is highly significant, and we need to get it right if we are to understand the rest of this epistle. That is why this essay is going to concentrate on this and some related questions—when this context is understood properly, the rest of the book will fall into place verse by verse.

When Paul had first preached to the Galatians, he also had told them about his previous life before he

had encountered Christ. He refers to that important fact here again. Paul mentions "Judaism" twice in these two verses (1:13–14). He refers to it as an objective set of beliefs, as a religion distinct from the church of God and as one with an identifiable body of belief, which he here identifies as the tradition of his fathers. This Judaism is *not* to be understood as the faith of those Jews in the old covenant who looked forward to the coming of Messiah in true and genuine faith. Mary and Joseph, Anna, Simeon, John the Baptist, *et al.* were *not* advocates of this Judaism. A few chapters later, Paul makes this point as bluntly as such a point can be made (4:21–26). Those who desired to be "under the law" were in effect *Ishmaelites.* Proud of their descent from the free woman Sarah, they were actually sons of Hagar, sons of a slave, and not true sons of Abraham. But Paul wants us to remember that it was the kind of mistake that is easy *for a certain kind of heart* to make. After all, both women lived in the household of Abraham.

Those born "after the flesh" will always persecute the sons of the free woman (4:29). Just as Ishmael taunted Isaac, so a deep antipathy continues down to the present. This is what accounts for Paul's savagery against the church of God before his conversion. He says this strongly in two ways. First, he not only persecuted the church of God, but he did so "beyond measure" (1:13). The word here is *hyperbolen,* which could be rendered by our idiom "over the top." His persecution was precisely not measured, but rather blind and irrational. He says this in another way when he says the result of his attacks was that the church was *destroyed* or *wasted.* The only other time this word is used, besides in this chapter (1:13, 23), is in Acts 9:21, when people are talking about Saul's assault on the church. And remember the word Luke used to describe how Paul *savaged* or *mauled* the church (Acts 8:3; 9:1). This was no ecclesiastical misunderstanding. Paul was an evil, wicked and unconverted man. He was an insolent, blaspheming man (1 Tim. 1:13). Paul was in the battle after his conversion, as we can see in Galatians. But he was also in the battle before his conversion—on the other side. And the deep antipathy that exists between those born of the flesh and those born of the Spirit shows us, yet again, why this is a battle and not just an interesting philosophical discussion.

But it is not enough just to be "against" something.

This painting by Fra Angelico shows Jesus washing the disciple's feet. Paul was not one of the original twelve disciples, yet his apostleship is clear.

Before his conversion, Paul was certainly that, but men are created in such a way as to *need* a god in their system, and their god cannot be silent. It is not enough to be against the true God. An idol is logically necessary. And the idol must speak and direct those who worship him. In this case, the god was Judaism, and this god spoke through the tradition of the fathers. These traditions had the effect of supplanting the Word of God (and this is precisely the effect they were *intended* to have). Idols are never shy about expressing their will and desire.

This is important because some scholars today want to represent the pre-Christian Saul as a *faithful* representative of Old Testament religion. The reasons for this vary, but the results of thinking this way are consistently destructive. Saul's conversion was *not* simply a matter of coming to understand the transition to a new economy of salvation. Scripture teaches

that Saul was not like the Bereans at all (Acts 17:11).

Early in the book, Paul takes a curious turn—he starts talking about his travels and journeys and timetables. Remember what we said about battles getting confusing. It is strange that in the middle of a doctrinal dispute Paul pulls out his ticket stubs and boarding passes to prove when he had traveled where. But he does this to show that he did not "get his gospel" at secondhand from men. He gives a detailed account of his trips to Jerusalem. While this was not an important fact in itself, it had become important because of the false accusations that had been leveled at him. This is what was meant earlier about how battles make details important. The North and the

South fought at Gettysburg, and the details of that terrain were important. But the fighting was not *over* that particular acreage. Larger issues always make details important.

The false teacher(s) at Galatia were saying that Saul was instructed in the rudiments of the Christian faith by the apostles, which would make him (at best) a second-tier apostle. His adversaries could then claim that as a pupil, he was not a very good one. *They,* in fact, had gotten their lessons right. This is why Paul had to emphasize that he had *not* conferred with flesh and blood (1:16). Not only that, but he did not even *go* to Jerusalem until three years *later* (1:17–18). When he finally got around to going to Jerusalem, he was there for the very short space of fifteen days—hardly time to get even a *deficient* seminary education (v. 18).

The only other person ranked among the apostles that he saw there was James, the brother of the Lord. This is interesting because James was not numbered among the Twelve and was apparently not even a believer in Jesus until after the resurrection (John 7:5; 1 Cor. 15:7; Acts 1:14). But he soon assumed a position of authority in the Jerusalem church (Acts 12:17). Paul acknowledges him as a pillar (2:9) and one of some repute (2:6), and here in this place he seems to number him among the apostles. But his acquaintance with James was first made during that short two-week visit.

So Paul was in Damascus, then Arabia and then back to Damascus for three years (Acts 9:19ff; 2 Cor. 11:32–33). He then came to Jerusalem for just over two weeks, and the visit was cut short by an attempt on his life (Acts 9:29). He then went to Tarsus (in the province of Cilicia) for ten years, when Barnabas brought him down to Antioch (in Syria) for a year. So then, fourteen years after his conversion, he went to Jerusalem for the second time (Gal. 2:1).

Now let us go back to Gal. 1:20, a place where Paul swears an oath before God. He says that this account of his trips to Jerusalem was *absolutely* accurate—so help him God. Given this vow, it is nothing short of astounding that there are conservative Bible scholars who identify the Jerusalem visit discussed in Galatians 2 with the Jerusalem council visit of Acts 15. This skips over the famine relief visit (Acts 11:27–30), and makes Paul's vow false.

Paul has been emphatic about how many times he has been to Jerusalem (1:20). This visit to Jerusalem described in the second chapter of Galatians must therefore be the famine relief visit described in Acts 11. Let us consider how they line up. First, Paul identifies the two visits as the same. Second, both visits were in response to a revelation (Gal. 2:2; Acts 11:28). Third, both visits were for the sake of the poor (Acts 11:29; Gal. 2:10). Fourth, Paul took Barnabas on both trips (Acts 11:30; Gal. 2:1). Fifth, Paul does not mention the decision of the Jerusalem council in the book of Galatians, which would be really strange if the council had already decided in his favor.

Paul tells us something additional about the Acts 11 visit that we do not learn from Acts, which is that Paul met with the leaders (those who were "of reputation") in the Jerusalem church (privately) in order to set out his gospel before them, the gospel he was preaching to the Gentiles. Titus was a Greek and, therefore, had not been circumcised. He accompanied Paul and Barnabas on this trip, and he was received as a brother (just the way he was) by the Jerusalem leaders. And this was not because they did not notice he was Greek. Certain men had demanded that Titus be compelled to accept circumcision. Paul's party refused to accommodate them, even for a minute, *and the Jerusalem leaders had sided with Paul.*

Paul now recounts a problem he had with Peter at Antioch, and this happened because Peter was to be blamed (2:11). Peter had been eating together with Gentiles, but when men from James came to Antioch, he withdrew from the Gentiles because he was afraid of "the circumcision" (i.e., the Jews who came from James—2:12). This caused other Jews to stumble into *hypocrisy,* even including Barnabas (2:13). When Paul saw they were not walking in accordance with gospel, he asked an unanswerable question. If Jews do not have to live like Jews, then why should Gentiles have to live like Jews? (2:14).

We must pay close attention. What should we call it when a sect refuses to share communion with other Christian churches? Paul calls it hypocrisy and a functional denial of justification by faith alone. The irony is that many sects refuse to share communion because of how tightly they say they *hold* to justification by faith alone. This simply gives us a double layer of hypocrisy and a remarkable denial of justification through their restrictions on table fellowship.

Those Galatians who desired to be under the law had this problem—they were refusing to listen to the law (4:21). Abraham had two sons. Ishmael was born of the concubine, Hagar, and Isaac was born of the free wife, Sarah (4:22). The son of the slave woman was after the flesh, but the son of Sarah was the fulfillment of promise (4:23). Now, Paul says, messing with our modern view of theology in which all "real" theology is writing in systematic and technical language, this is an allegory. Mt. Sinai (where the Ten Commandments were given) corresponds to Hagar, which corresponds to Jerusalem below, all of which tend to spiritual bondage over generations (4:24-25). But the heavenly Jerusalem is free and is our spiritual mother (4:26). Paul quotes Isaiah 54 here. The barren woman is now more fruitful than the other woman (4:27). We Christians, Paul says, are like Isaac—children of promise (4:28). The analogy is a far-reaching one. There is always antipathy between the two children (4:29)—remember our illustration of the battle! The children of the flesh are to be disinherited; they cannot be joint heirs (4:30). Christians are the children of Sarah, not Hagar (4:31).

So Sarah was a type of the Christian church. Her long years of barrenness correspond to her time in the Old Covenant. She was the wife of Abraham, but she was barren. Paul argues that the Jerusalem above is a woman who used to be barren and who now has a multitude of children. She is the free woman—but there was a time when the free woman appeared to be fruitless and the slave woman appeared to be fruitful. The church above is our mother. The heavenly Jerusalem is not built on a mountain that can be touched by human hands (Heb. 12:18ff). Come, the angel said, I will show you the bride, the wife of the Lamb. And John was shown the new Jerusalem, descending from heaven (Rev. 21:9-10). This is the church, this is our mother.

This transition from the Old Covenant to the New is the point where Sarah has borne her freeborn son, and the slave woman is divorced and put away. Now are there no more temptations or

Sixth-century mosaics of Peter (left) and Paul, found in Ravenna, Italy.

pitfalls? Of course not. Until the world ends, there will always be those who live carnally in unbelief and those who live in faith, by faith and unto faith. Over time, the ratios between these two groups change, but we are always dealing with them, even within the Christian church. We are promised that the children of the free woman will overrun the earth. Abraham was promised the world (Rom. 4:13), and his (free) children *will* possess it. And five years before the Last Trump, there will be some poor foolish church member clutching at his unbelief, wanting to be known as a son of Sarah, but actually being Hagar's son. This wonderful letter summons us and commands us to be *unlike that man*. The just shall live by faith, and the meek will inherit the earth. This is basic to all spiritual wisdom. Among the children of Sarah, there will always be children of Hagar, and may we never be found in that number.

In summary, if we understand the kind of Jew that Paul was before his conversion, we will also understand the kind of Jews against whom he was contending, and how dangerous they were. Paul understood their mindset because he used to share it fully. He knew the battle from both sides, having fought on both sides. And what seems like confusion to us was not to him—he was a very wise general. And if we understand how Paul received his gospel, and how he was transformed by it, we will understand how important it is that this gospel not be compromised. But in order to understand this, Paul makes it clear that we have to see and understand the timetable of his visits to Jerusalem. This is why learning the missionary journeys of Paul is so important. And when these basic issues are understood, a verse by verse handling of the book should fall into place more readily. We are not studying obscure facts; we are studying the map of a battlefield.

—Douglas Wilson

## For Further Reading

Calvin, John. *John Calvin's Sermons on Galatians.* Carlisle, Pa.: The Banner of Truth Trust, 1997.

# SESSION I: PRELUDE

## A Question to Consider

What makes a true Christian?

*After reading the background material above, answer the following questions:*

1. Who was the apostle Paul?
2. When did he live, and what is he known for?
3. What is the argument in the book of Galatians all about?
4. How is it possible for a son of Sarah to be a son of Hagar?
5. Why is the ability to understand this important to spiritual wisdom?
6. What is the difference between the North Galatian theory and the South Galatian theory?
7. Why did the apostle Paul believe that the number of times he had been to Jerusalem was so important?
8. Who were the Judaizers? How were they different from the Jews?
9. In Galatians 2 why must Paul be referring to the famine relief visit of Acts 11?

## Optional Activities

On a large white sheet of construction paper, construct an unmarked map of the eastern end of the Mediterranean Sea. Then, using a Bible dictionary, the internet or another resource, include all the cities that Paul visited during his missionary journeys and, with different colored markers, trace out his three missionary journeys. When this is done, draw in the province of Galatia and then shade in ethnic Galatia.

### READING ASSIGNMENT:
Galatians

# SESSION II: DISCUSSION
Galatians

## A Question to Consider

What does it mean to be a true Christian?

*Discuss or list short answers to the following questions:*

### Text Analysis

1. Was Paul being prideful in saying that he did not learn the gospel from the other apostles?
2. Do angels and apostles have the authority to change or alter the gospel? Why or why not?
3. Paul confronted Peter publicly at Antioch. Why did he feel this was necessary?
4. Is it possible to start the Christian life by our own effort? Can we continue it by our own effort?
5. What does Paul's illustration of Israel as a child and Israel as a grown-up mean?
6. Besides the obvious content of the lists, what is the difference between the works of the flesh and the fruit of the Spirit?
7. What does the category "false brethren" mean?

### Cultural Analysis

1. How would a Judaizer look dressed up in modern Christian clothing?
2. What is "legalism?" What forms can it take?
3. Can the gospel be protected in any era without a fight?

## SUMMA

*Write an essay or discuss this question, integrating what you have learned from the material above.*
What is the difference between the law and grace? Does grace set us free and law enslave us? Can both do the opposite? Can our lives be bound by grace and liberated by law?

# SESSION III: RECITATION

## Comprehension Questions

Answer the following questions for factual recall:

1. Does Paul bless the Galatians, despite his distress over the direction they are going (1:3–5)?
2. When did God decide to save Paul (1:11–17)?
3. Had the churches in Judea heard of Paul (1:18–24)?
4. Who were the false brethren (2:1–10)?
5. Did Paul have a problem with the authority of the Jerusalem apostles (2:1–16)?
6. Does justification by faith alone mean that sinning is all right (2:15–21)?
7. Paul says that Peter and Barnabas fell into hypocrisy. What kind of hypocrisy (2:11–16)?
8. How does Paul rebuke the Galatians (3:1–9)?
9. If the Galatians were true Christians, why did Paul have to warn them?
10. What does baptism do to various social relations (3:15–29)?
11. When did Israel grow up into adulthood (4:1–7)?
12. Israel in its youth was under the training of the law. What were the Gentiles under (4:8–20)?
13. Can sons of Sarah become sons of Hagar (4:31–5:10)?
14. Why is false religion the foundation of false living (5:1–26)?
15. Name and define five works of the flesh (5:19–21).
16. What are the fruit of the Spirit (5:22–23)? Define each one.
17. What is the alternative to biting and devouring (the besetting sin of the religiously scrupulous) (6:1–10)?

. . . if you are led by the Spirit, you are not under the law. Now the works of the flesh are evident . . . But the fruit of the Spirit is love, joy, peace, longsuffering, kindness, goodness, faithfulness, gentleness, self-control. Against such there is no law. And those who are Christ's have crucified the flesh with its passions and desires. If we live in the Spirit, let us also walk in the Spirit.

# OPTIONAL SESSION

*The Counterfeit Gospels* Game

Today we are confronted with false gospels on all sides. In Chart 1 you will find a synopsis of a number of false gospels. In a couple of sentences isolate the problem with each of these "gospels." If you can find the problem, you get one point. If you can identify the group who is preaching this gospel, you can earn another point. The one with the most points at the end wins. The losers have to eat peanut butter. Note however, that one of the explanations is the real gospel. If you can identify it and not claim that it is heretical, you earn an additional five points (and if you believe it, eternal life).

*Chart 1:* **THE COUNTERFEIT GOSPELS GAME**

| THE GOSPEL IS: | PROBLEM WITH THIS GOSPEL: | GROUP PREACHING THIS GOSPEL: |
|---|---|---|
| You must first become a Jew, be circumcised and then you can become a Christian. | It makes salvation contingent on your action of circumcision. | The Judaizers in Galatians (you should have gotten this one) |

You are saved by baptism and kept in saving grace by the grace of God which comes through the seven sacraments of the church. So, you are saved by a mixture of God's grace and your own works done in love.

The Father is the true God who is called Jehovah. Jesus was a created being who was originally called the Archangel Michael. Jesus rose spiritually, not bodily from the dead, and will save 144,000 people who will go to live with God in Heaven.

God is a great and pure mind. All matter is only imaginary, and so is death and pain. Jesus did not live physically (how could He, since matter does not exist?) but only appeared to. We must liberate ourselves by rejecting matter.

God the Father begat Jesus and Lucifer and many others. Jesus became God, and we can be saved by Christ's atonement and good works. When we are resurrected we are placed in one of three realms, and if we live a good enough life, we can become gods.

There is only one God, and His name is Jesus. You must be saved by speaking in tongues, being baptized in the name of Jesus only (remember He is the only God) and keeping certain rules.

Jesus came, lived a perfect life and died as a perfect sacrifice to turn away God's wrath from His people. People are saved by the regenerating work of the Holy Spirit which results in trust in Christ's finished work. This faith necessarily results in good works which are the result, not the cause, of salvation.

Jesus was a great moral teacher, but was not God. We are not really certain that there is a God, but if there is, He would tell you that you should really try to be nice to other people because that is at the core of the teaching of the historical Jesus.

Jesus provided a spiritual salvation, but His work needs to be perfected by the coming of the "Lord of the Second Advent."

Man is born without a fallen nature and must earn his salvation by working hard to turn away from sin (which he can do if he tries hard enough).

# ROMANS

For the invisible things of him from the creation of the world are clearly seen, being understood by the things that are made, even his eternal power and Godhead; so that they are without excuse: Because that, when they knew God, they glorified him not as God, neither were thankful; but became vain in their imaginations, and their foolish heart was darkened. Professing themselves to be wise, they became fools, And changed the glory of the uncorruptible God into an image made like to corruptible man, and to birds, and fourfooted beasts, and creeping things. Wherefore God also gave them up to uncleanness through the lusts of their own hearts, to dishonour their own bodies between themselves: Who changed the truth of God into a lie, and worshipped and served the creature more than the Creator, who is blessed for ever. Amen.

Little Coyotito was dying. Without medical attention the scorpion bite would surely result in death. His parents Kino and Juana rush him to the doctor in town. To their dismay, however, they are turned away because they are poor natives who cannot pay for treatment. In an act of desperation Kino heads for the sea to dive for pearls. Their prayers are answered when he surfaces with the largest pearl he has ever seen! Could Coyotito now live? Will Kino's precious son now receive the treatment he needs? Kino has surely hoped so, but the outcome is not as he expects.

Jesus spoke of a pearl of great value, that if found would lead the one seeking it to sell all of his possessions just to buy that pearl. This pearl, however, was very different from the one found by Kino in Steinbeck's novel, *The Pearl*. And the result of possessing the pearl Jesus spoke of would be radically different. What was this pearl of great price Jesus described in Matthew 13:46? It was the kingdom of God, the gospel.

What exactly is the gospel? In a nutshell, how do you define it? For whom is it? Is it for everyone or only a select few?

A college professor once told his class of New Testament students that regardless of their performance on quizzes and tests and other assignments for the course, if they memorized the book of Romans, they would automatically receive an "A" in the class. But why would he make such a concession? Or was it a concession? What did he know that they might not have known?

Romans presents the most valuable jewel of all time, the gospel. But what is the gospel? Romans is the most thorough and precise explanation of the gospel in the New Testament. For whom is it? Paul does not skirt the issue! He tackles the much-debated topic of election head on in his letter to the Romans. How can a holy God have anything to do with sinful man, and how can man have any connection to the living God? Romans has the answer. How about the complicated issue of the

We see here remains of the Dioscuri Temple in Rome. When we study the book of Romans, we should not forget that the matters Paul addressed were to real people in a real place.

inclusion of the Gentiles? You guessed it, Romans gives insight into this issue as well. How is man to respond to the gospel? Practical application is not missing from this deeply theological treatise!

Romans is the heart of the New Testament. If you were stranded on a deserted island, what would you have if you had *only* the book of Romans? You would have the very core of what God wants you to know. You would have the very heart of what God's message to mankind is. And if you committed it to memory . . . you would have stored in your heart and mind the greatest truths that have impacted the greatest men in the history of the world. Men like Augustine, Luther and Wesley claim that no other writings changed them like this great epistle. Let's dig in and find out why.

# GENERAL INFORMATION

## Author and Context

The man who had previously enjoyed persecuting Christians was now writing to encourage them and teach them the very gospel he had sought to destroy. So how did Paul go from hating this faith and its followers to embracing it and eventually dying for it? Let's take a look at his story.

Paul was born probably a few years after Jesus sometime in the first decade of the first century (roughly A.D. 2-10) in the city of Tarsus of Cilicia. This city was ranked as the third greatest educational center in the empire (after Alexandria and Athens). Tarsus, a very cosmopolitan city, was a major center of trade. It was also the center of a degrading type of Baal worship. With these things in mind, as Paul grew and matured, he was being unconsciously prepared to encounter men of every class, race and religion.

Paul was born into a very orthodox Jewish family. He called himself a "Hebrew of Hebrews." As such, he followed his faith diligently and probably was not of any mixed blood. His father was a Pharisee, belonging to the strictest sect of his religion, and Paul would follow in his father's footsteps.

It is likely that his father, a Roman citizen, was a wealthy businessman since he was able to send his son to Jerusalem to study at the Harvard of his day under Gamaliel, the prestigious Jewish teacher. Leatherworking and tent-making were probably part of his lucrative business.

Young Paul was trained in the synagogue and therefore was educated from an early age in the intricate details of the Mosaic Law. He was most likely sent to Jerusalem around the age of twelve or thirteen to study under Gamaliel. This would have been a tremendous privilege, and Paul must have been a brilliant and highly promising youth to be among the chosen few of Gamaliel's pupils. It is also likely that Paul studied at the University in Tarsus.

## Significance

As mentioned earlier Romans has greatly affected respected men of faith. In the summer of A.D. 386 Augustine read the following words from Romans 13:13b-14, "not in revelry and drunkenness, not in lewdness and lust, not in strife and envy. But put on the Lord Jesus Christ, and make no provision for the flesh, to fulfill its lusts." His response: "No further would I read, nor had I any need; instantly, at the end of this sentence, a clear light flooded my heart and all the darkness of doubt vanished." How significant is this light which illumined the mind of this great saint! After wrestling with Romans 1:17 Martin Luther states that he was "reborn" and that the "whole of Scripture took on new meaning." He explains that "this passage of Paul became to me a gateway into heaven." Finally, John Wesley states that while reading Luther's "Preface to the Epistle to the

Romans," his heart was "strangely warmed" and that he thereafter trusted in Christ alone for his salvation. What precious gems of the faith are these three men! And it was the epistle to the Romans that God used to radically change their lives.

In the worldview section we will explore in more depth why Romans has had such influence on men like these. Here we return to the question in the beginning of our study, "If you were stranded on a deserted island and had *only* Paul's letter to the Romans, what would you have?" Let's look a little more deeply into this question.

Nowhere in the entire Bible is there such a comprehensive explanation of the sinfulness of man. Paul spends no less than three chapters describing the sinfulness of both Gentiles and Jews alike. By the time he is finished, no man can escape the harsh reality that we are all under the wrath of God mentioned in 1:18. Likewise, nowhere in the Bible is there such a thorough explanation of the necessity of faith for salvation and the inability of works to justify the sinner. Again, more on this in the worldview essay.

One of the most significant issues tackled in Romans is the issue of election. If someone wanted to go to one chapter alone to study predestination, Romans 9 would be that chapter. Along with this discussion the apostle gives the most complete answer to the difficult question of the status of Israel. If the Jews are God's chosen people, then why did they reject their Messiah? And where does that leave them now? From the time Paul penned chapter nine of this epistle until the present day, debates have raged over these controversial topics. Nowhere in all of Scripture are these topics addressed in such a complete and systematic manner as they are in the book of Romans. Now we begin to understand the thinking of that New Testament professor who gave "A's" to those who would commit this book to memory!

## Historical Setting

After his Damascus Road conversion and subsequent preparation for the ministry, Paul spent the ten years from A.D. 47–57 evangelizing four areas: Galatia, Macedonia, Achaia, and Asia. He was in the city of Corinth on his third missionary journey when he wrote what we call Romans to the believers in Rome in A.D. 58.

## APPROXIMATE PAULINE CHRONOLOGY

| | |
|---|---|
| A.D. 7 | Paul's birth in Tarsus |
| 20–25 | Rabbinical training in Jerusalem with Gamaliel (age 13–18) |
| 30 | Crucifixion of Christ |
| 33 | Conversion of Paul |
| 47–49 | First Missionary Journey |
| 49 | Paul writes Galatians |
| 50 | Jerusalem Councili |
| 50–52 | Second Missionary Journey (Paul writes 1& 2 Thessalonians from Corinth) |
| 52–57 | Third Missionary Journey |
| 55 | Paul writes 1 Corinthians from Ephesus |
| 56 | Paul writes 2 Corinthians from Macedonia |
| **57–58** | **Paul writes Romans from Corinth** |
| 60–62 | First Roman Imprisonment |
| 61–62 | Paul writes Colossians, Ephesians, Philemon from Rome |
| 62–67 | Release, further travels and 1 Timothy and Titus |
| 66–68 | Paul is arrested, writes 2 Timothy and is martyred |

But what was his ultimate aspiration? What exactly was Paul trying to accomplish? His goals stretched far beyond planting a few churches here and there. Paul would not rest until the world was conquered by the gospel. What was his strategy for such a far-reaching goal? It seems that the apostle's plan involved a two-pronged approach—plant and spread.

PHASE ONE: Plant the gospel in the most influential portion of the Roman Empire, the capital city of Rome. What could have more far-reaching effect than planting a faithful church of stalwart believers in the most powerful city in the world? Tertullian once said, "The blood of the martyrs is the seed of the church." As more and more Christians laid down their lives for the sake of the gospel, the church grew and grew until eventually it was the official religion of the empire. Paul knew that in order for the gospel to conquer the world, it had to invade the heart of all culture, power and influence. The good news must topple Rome!

PHASE TWO: We can further peer into the heart of the apostle by reading Romans 15:23b–24, "... having a great desire these many years to come to you, whenever I journey to Spain, I shall come to you. For I hope to see you on my journey, and to be helped on my way there by you, if first I may enjoy your company for a while." Why Spain? His previous pattern of travel may reveal the underlying reason. Paul had been using the Syrian city of Antioch as a base of operations for his three church-planting journeys. He would launch out from Antioch and begin the journey of spreading the gospel and strengthening the churches (Acts 13:1–3; 15:35–41; 18:22–23). If Paul was keeping with this pattern, he

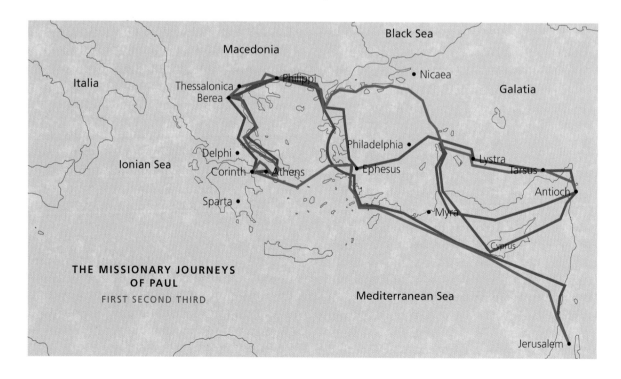

THE MISSIONARY JOURNEYS
OF PAUL
FIRST SECOND THIRD

was planning to use Rome as a similar base of operations to expand westward and reach the ends of the known world with the gospel. "And so I have made it my aim to preach the gospel, not where Christ was named, lest I should build on another man's foundation" (Rom. 15:20). Paul did make it to Rome, but it was not in the manner in which he had planned. While in Jerusalem he was arrested, and he appealed his case to be heard in Rome by Caesar himself. How fitting that the apostle to the Gentiles should appear in the capital of the world.

## Worldview

It has been said that a worldview is a set of eyeglasses through which one views the world. It is the grid through which one interprets all that he experiences. Although he will not always be consistent, an atheist will see the world through atheistic glasses and make judgments based on atheistic presuppositions. Everything he encounters will be viewed through the assumption that there is no God. When we "put on" the book of Romans, how does it change what we see? We have made some dramatic claims about the centrality of Romans, and we have seen how it has effected great change in the lives of some significant men of faith. Let us take a look at four areas in which Romans informs our own worldview: sin, justification by faith, federal headship and election.

### *Sin*

In this section we will go through a basic outline of the book and begin to examine some of the key truths unveiled in the letter. An overview of the book is seen in what is called the "S" Outline:

SIN (1:18–3:20)
SALVATION (3:21–5:21)
SANCTIFICATION (6–8)
SOVEREIGNTY (9–11)
SERVICE (12:1–15:13)

Think about the following quote by Seneca[2]: "Other men's sins are before our eyes, our own are behind our back."[3] One thing is certain—after reading the first three chapters of Romans there is one inescapable conclusion: one cannot ignore that he is a sinner. Paul brings the reality of our own sin "before our eyes."

He begins this section about sin in 1:18 by stating that God has revealed his wrath against all "ungodliness and unrighteousness of men, who suppress the truth..." But how can man be held responsible for sin if he simply did not know any better? Paul says that this is not a valid excuse. He explains how God has "shown it to them. For since the creation His invisible attributes are of the world clearly seen, being understood by the things that are made, even His eternal power and Godhead, so that they are without excuse" (1:19b-20). Paul makes it crystal clear that man's rebellion has been willful and deliberate. He goes on in verse 21 to state that their foolish heart was darkened. When we compare this to 1 Corinthians 2:13-14 and Ephesians 2:1–5 we realize that he is not simply referring to the fact that man commits individual sins; rather, he is getting at something much more profound. Mankind is in a *state* of sin. He *is* a sinner. It is at the core of who he is. No one escapes this indictment. After discussing the sinfulness of Gentile pagans (1:18-32) and then moralist Jews (2:17-29), Paul concludes that both Jews and Greeks are under sin (3:9b). He then provides an abundance of Old Testament verses in 3:10-18 to nail the last nails into the coffin of his argument.

Why, then, are modern psychology, sociology, anthropology and modern philosophies of education based on the premise that man is basically good? They have failed to view reality through the worldview glasses of Romans 1-3. What are the consequences? Which is most important that a doctor do correctly? Diagnose the problem or administer the proper cure? How can a doctor even begin to administer the right medicine if he cannot even acknowledge what the problem is? The failure of modern man to recognize the true nature of the problem has led to disastrous consequences. One example will illustrate the point. How do we confront the rampant sexual promiscuity and teen pregnancy in our country? Modern man, having cast off the worldview glasses of Romans, contends that the problem resides in man's ignorance about an issue, and so therefore the solution must be education. Rather than acknowledge that the real problem is sin and the real solution, repentance, we have chosen to label the problem as a simple lack of knowledge. So we come up with all sorts of wonderful educational programs to "educate" young people about this issue instead of recognizing that the sin is an affront to a holy God and that the solution is confession and repentance. Since modernity has bought into the *Romantic* view of man, that mankind is basically good, his conclusions and solutions will never be consistent with what Paul is asserting in Romans.

## Justification by Faith

We move on now to the second section of the "S" Outline, salvation, as we examine the centrality of the doctrine of justification by faith. After stating the problem of mankind, sin, Paul now reveals the solution. Whereas Paul states in 1:18 that the "wrath of God" was revealed, now in 3:21 he begins to explain that the "righteousness of God" has been manifested as well. Since God cannot simply ignore sin, He chose to display His Son as a "propitiation by His blood" (3:25) in order to demonstrate that God Himself is at the same time both just and the justifier of the sinner who has faith in Jesus (3:26). In this brief passage Paul reveals three glorious perspectives on salvation.

First, he uses the term "justified" in verse 24. This was a legal term common in the law courts of the day. It carried the meaning of being "acquitted," and it suggests an innocence of all charges. It is objective; it cannot be "felt." It is something done for us, not in us. It is an act, not a process. By faith, God justifies us, that is, He declares us "not guilty" because of what Christ accomplished on the cross.

Second, he says that we have "redemption" in Christ. This term was common in the commercial realm and means "to purchase" or "to buy out of." If

you were to go to the slave market in the first century you would hear this word used. The Greek word *lutron* ("ransom") means "price of a slave." We are the "Gomer" in the book of Hosea. Recall from our chapter on the *Minor Prophets* how Gomer was unfaithful to Hosea and left him, and he went and bought her back. Christ was our *lutron* (Mark 10:45), and He bought His people out of the slave market of sin when he died on the cross.

The third perspective Paul gives here centers around the religious term "propitiation." The word means "satisfaction" and refers to an offering so great that it removes both guilt and the anger of God. The only other time this word is used in the New Testament it is translated "mercy seat" and refers to the part of the Ark of the Covenant where the blood was sprinkled once a year by the High Priest (Ex. 25). As God looked down onto the law (the tablets of the Ten Commandments were inside the ark), He saw it through the blood of the sacrifice. In the cross Christ is our propitiation, our satisfaction to appease the wrath of God.

**REDEMPTION →**
THE SALVATION TRIANGLE

But how do we partake of this great salvation offered to us by God? Let us first approach this question through the lenses of other worldview glasses in our quest for the answer.

How is the individual "saved" in other world religions—Islam, Buddhism, Judaism? How do you get to heaven according to these faiths? You do not have to examine these religions for long to realize that the answer is simple and basic—works. All other world religions teach that if you follow some code of ethics, a set of rules, you will be saved. Follow the Eight-Fold Path of Buddhism to reach Nirvana. Live by the Five Pillars and make sure that your good deeds outweigh your bad deeds, and you will go to heaven, according to Islam. Obey the Ten Commandments and live a good moral life, and you will be accepted by God, say the Jews.

How does Romans shape our worldview differently than these religions? Paul is adamant that salvation does not come by obedience to the law. All of chapter four is dedicated to proving that a right standing before God comes, not by works, but rather by faith. Paul uses an ingenious method for accomplishing his goal. He appeals to the common Jewish attitude toward the father of their faith, Abraham. Surely, if it were possible to be saved by good deeds, Abraham fulfilled the requirement. In fact, it was commonly understood that Abraham had indeed done the works necessary for salvation. His faith and circumcision described in Genesis are viewed as good deeds that merited the favor of God. Paul explains that this is a gross misunderstanding of Genesis by pointing out that

In this detail from *Paradise* by Lucas Cranach the Elder, we see Adam committing the act that would doom all of their children to die. Eve was deceived and acted in response to being deceived. Adam was not deceived, so his action was taken in spite of knowing that by doing so, he was acting in opposition to God's command and that he faced punishment. Adam represented all humanity as a federal head, because his sin was intentional, and as such it was a decision made with full awareness of the consequences. When Adam fell, both of the parents of humanity had fallen natures and so passed that nature on to their children.

Abraham was declared righteous by God before he was circumcised, therefore his right standing before God was based on his faith, not any good deeds. In essence, what Paul is saying here is that Abraham is a sinner like all the rest of us and can only be saved by grace through faith.

We saw above how the proper view of sin leads to a better understanding of man's condition and therefore the proper solution to his condition. How does a biblical view of justification change how we view and interpret reality? Instead of working harder and harder to merit God's grace, we rest in Christ and His finished work on the cross. Instead of comparing ourselves to others and trying to make sure we are "more righteous" than they, we realize that we all fall short of God's holy standard and that Jesus fulfilled the law by His perfect life, and we cling to the cross. Living according to a works-based religion is like the hamster in the wheel, spinning and spinning, and going nowhere! It is a self-righteous life that in the end leads to death.

As it is written, "Jacob I have loved, but Esau I have hated." What shall we say then? Is there unrighteousness with God? Certainly not! (Romans 9:13, 14)

## Federal Headship

We come now to the third area in which Romans greatly enriches our worldview, the idea of federal headship. When we think of the word "federal" we usually think of something big like "federal government" or "Federal Savings Bank." We must realize, however, that the meaning of this word has changed. The word "federal" actually comes from the Latin word *foedus* and means "covenant." God makes a covenant with the entire group, but the head is the representative of the group. Federal headship refers to a covenantal arrangement in which the decisions of the head are made for those under his headship. This is an idea that is foreign to the modern American mindset. We say that it would be unfair for the

decision of one to obligate the decision of many. We have more of an individualistic mindset instead of a biblical one. Let us explore this concept further.

Paul explains in chapter five that the Adam's decision to sin brought all of mankind into a state of sin (5:12–21). God was making a covenant with the whole human race, and Adam was our federal head in that he represented us in the test of the forbidden fruit. When he ate, we all ate. How can it be fair that we are all plummeted into sin when we were not even born yet? Are we misreading this text? This is where understanding worldviews is vital. We must take off the glasses of American individualism and put on the glasses of a biblical worldview. In God's eyes we were all "in Adam," and so we sinned in him when he ate of the fruit.

Do we see this concept anywhere else in Scripture? The thread of federal headship runs throughout the Old Testament. Noah's entire family is permitted to enter the ark, because "you (Noah) are righteous before Me" (Gen. 7:1). God makes a covenant with Abraham's descendants based on His dealings with Abraham (Gen. 17:10). In the second commandment God states that He will visit iniquity to the third and fourth generations to those that hate Him and that He will show mercy to thousands of those that love Him and keep His commandments (Ex. 20:5–6). God says to David that He will establish his "seed" after him (Psalm 89:3–4). Achan's entire family is killed because of his sin (Josh. 7:10–26).

We see examples in the New Testament as well. At the end of his famous sermon at Pentecost, Peter states that the promise of the forgiveness of sins and the gift of the Holy Spirit is "to you and to your children" (Acts 2:38–39). Household baptisms in the New Testament make sense in light of the concept of federal headship. In Hebrews 7:4-10, Levi is said to have paid tithes to Melchizedek because his great-grandfather Abraham "gave a tenth of the spoils" (7:4). Levi was not even born yet, and he "paid tithes." How can this be? The writer of Hebrews gives us insight into this profound truth. Verse 10 says that he was "in the loins of his father." Levi committed the act "in Abraham." In God's eyes the father makes decisions and those decisions count for his descendants.

Why is all of this so important to our understanding of Romans and how this epistle shapes our worldview? It provides us with a more profound understanding of the gospel. The latter half of Romans 5 provides us with two significant truths, justification by faith alone and federal headship.

First, Paul is reinforcing that the gospel cannot be earned by works. He states this by explaining that Adam's descendants died as a result of his sin even though they did not sin in the same manner in which he sinned, that is, by transgressing a specific command of God (5:14). Likewise, followers of Christ live even though they have not obeyed as Christ did.

The second truth we see here that enhances our knowledge of the gospel is the idea of federal headship. Having explored this concept and how it is revealed in other portions of Scripture, we can now apply what we know to this passage. Christ took it upon Himself to be our Federal Head when He lived a perfect life and died to be the perfect sacrifice for sin. If we are "in Him," His deed is applied to us! Let's return to the question we asked earlier about the "fairness" of our being in sin because of Adam's decision to eat of the forbidden fruit. Now we have a very different perspective on the matter. Is it "fair" that Jesus died a cruel death even though He lived a sinless life? The fairness argument cuts both ways.

This profound and beautiful truth brings with it both assurance and responsibility. The believer can rest knowing that no amount of good deeds can merit salvation and that no sin can remove the believer from God's favor. Likewise, understanding federal headship brings a greater understanding of our responsibilities as husbands. Marriage is a covenant, and the husband is the federal head (Eph. 5:23). As such he takes upon himself the responsibility of the relationship. Just as Christ took responsibility for His bride, the church, the husband bears the responsibility for the beauty and well-being of his bride.

## Election

Another area in which Romans shapes our worldview concerns the issue of election. Debates have continued through the centuries over the meaning of Paul's words in chapter 9. In the fifth century Augustine wrote against Pelagius[1] on the issue. Luther battled Erasmus in his treatise *On the Bondage of the Will* during the time of the Reformation in the sixteenth century. George Whitefield and John Wesley debated the issue as well. The divide can be seen today in the differences between churches that are Arminian and those that are Calvinistic in their understanding of this chapter.

In chapters 9–11 Paul is dealing with the question of the status of the nation of Israel. They were God's chosen, and He had made specific promises to them in the Old Testament. How are we to understand their rejection of Jesus, their Messiah? In 8:28-30 Paul discusses God's purpose as the assurance of certainty for the believer. But if Israel had a special place in God's purpose, why did they fall into apostasy? Paul was well aware of the fact that his continued references to the Old Testament would lose credibility if he did not address this fundamental question. In chapters 9–11 he appeals to the sovereignty of God and Israel's responsibility in his explanation.

In chapter 9 Paul uses a common method of argumentation. He places a question in the mouth of an imaginary opponent and then proceeds to respond to the argument by proving his point. He begins by responding to what could have been a common solution to the dilemma, the failure of the Word of God. Paul explains that God has kept His promises which were made to spiritual Israel, whom he called according to His purpose in election. God can choose whom he desires.

This raises the next logical argument by his imaginary opponent, "Is God unjust?" Paul's response: "May it never be!" God can show mercy to whom He desires, and He can harden whom He desires. It is up to His sovereign choice.

Finally, Paul poses a third question to be addressed, "Why then does God still blame?" Paul's response: God is the Potter and we are the clay. Who are we to question the choices He makes? Is it not interesting that the same arguments Paul places in the mouth of his imaginary opponent are the same arguments posed today by those who reject the Reformed doctrine of election?

How then is our thinking enriched by grasping the doctrine of election? Can I choose to accept or reject God? Am I in charge or is He in control? Seeing through the lenses of election cause me to see the depths of my own sin (I cannot choose God in a state of sin before He brings about the necessary change of heart—regeneration). Also, I see more of the majesty of God. I bow at His wonderful, divine plan and wonder in amazement that He chose me to be a part of His bride. I rest knowing that if he chose me for salvation, surely He will guide my steps daily. "A man's mind plans his way, but the Lord directs his steps" (Prov. 16:9).

We have chosen to focus on a few of the central truths of Romans here. There are other important issues Paul discusses. Note the third "S" of the "S" outline—sanctification. The life of one justified by faith is a life characterized by peace with God (5:1-11), holy living (6), freedom from the Law's condemnation (7) and the indwelling of the Holy Spirit (8). A dissertation could be written on each of these issues. Paul goes on to explain that the one justified by faith will live a life of obedience, i.e., a life characterized by love (12:10), the "service" portion of the outline. In chapters 13 and 14 he deals with the issues of subjection to the governing authorities and matters of conscience.

After mining the great jewels found in Romans we realize how rich we are to know such glorious truths. The glasses through which we view reality are less tainted with falsehood, and we are free to think more biblically. Our reaction is similar to that of Paul at the end of chapter 11, "Oh, the depth of the riches both of the wisdom and knowledge of God! How unsearchable are His judgments and His ways past finding out!"

—*Bruce Etter*

## For Further Reading

*Veritas Press Bible Cards: Acts through Revelation.* Lancaster, Pa: Veritas Press. 140, 143.

Bruce, F.F. *The Letter of Paul to the Romans (Revised edition).* In *The Tyndale New Testament Commentaries.* Morris, Leon, editor. Grand Rapids, Mich.: Eerdmans, 1986.

Murray, John. *The Epistle to the Romans.* Grand Rapids, Mich.: Eerdmans, 1997.

Stott, John R.W. *The Message of Romans: God's Good News for the World.* Downers Grove, Ill.: InterVarsity Press, 2001.

# SESSION I: PRELUDE

## A Question to Consider

Back to the deserted island! If you had nothing but the book of Romans with you on the island, what would be the most valuable specific truth you possessed? (Several choices include sin, justification, federal headship and election.) Why?

*From the General Information above answer the following questions:*

1. What specific experiences qualify Paul to minister to people of all races, classes and religions?
2. When was Romans written? On which missionary journey? From where?
3. According to Romans 15 it is likely that Paul's desire involved what grand plan?
4. What four areas of the world had Paul focused on during the years 47-57?

5. What is the "S" Outline? List the references and give a brief explanation of each item.

6. Define federal headship. Why is it difficult for many to accept the implications of federal thinking?

7. Name a few of the individuals involved in historic debates over the issue of election.

8. About when did Paul die?

READING
ASSIGNMENT:
Romans 1-7

# SESSION II: RECITATION

Romans 1-7

## Comprehension Questions

*Answer the following questions for factual recall:*

1. List six characteristics of the gospel from 1:1-5.

2. List two words that describe Paul's attitude toward the gospel (1:15-16)

3. What are the consequences of unbelief? What is the just reward?

4. Who is addressed in chapter two?

5. In 3:1-8 Paul answers four objections to his previous teaching and then responds to these objections. List each objection and Paul's response.

6. What is the primary point of chapter four? Explain the significance of Abraham in the argument.

7. What are the results of justification listed in the first four

In the preface to his *Letter of St. Paul to the Romans*, Martin Luther writes, "You must get used to the idea that it is one thing to do the works of the law and quite another to fulfill it. The works of the law are everything that a person does or can do of his own free will and by his own powers to obey the law. But because in doing such works the heart abhors the law and yet is forced to obey it, the works are a total loss and are completely useless. That is what St. Paul means in chapter 3 when he says, 'No human being is justified before God through the works of the law.'" This fourteenth-century illumination shows Moses receiving the law from God.

verses of chapter five?

8. Explain Paul's point in 5:14 (Hint: Verses 15–17 are parenthetical. He resumes the argument in verses 18–19).

9. Why would Paul ask, "Shall we continue in sin that grace may abound?" (6:1)?

10. In chapter 7 Paul explains that, while we are free from the condemnation of the law we nevertheless continue to struggle with our flesh and living a life of obedience. Who is this person in verses 14–25 who is having this struggle? Paul the pre-Christian? Paul the immature Christian? Paul the self-centered Christian? Or Paul the mature Christian?

READING ASSIGNMENT:
Romans 8–16

# SESSION III: DISCUSSION
Romans 8–16

## A Question to Consider

If God is sovereign (in control of all things), including who comes to faith and who does not, then why share my faith with anyone? Where does evangelism fit into the idea that God "has mercy on whom He wills, and whom He wills He hardens" (9:18)?

*Discuss or list short answers to the following questions:*

### Text Analysis

1. Is it true that we are commanded to preach the gospel to all? (Matt. 28:18 – 20)

2. Does the fact that God makes the choice mean that man has no responsibility?

3. Having established the fact that man is without excuse, the question still lingers about evangelism and the sovereignty of God. Why attempt to share the gospel when God has already chosen His elect?

God justified His people through the sacrificial work of Christ on the Cross. This colorful depiction of the Crucifixion is from a Book of Hours.

## Cultural Analysis

1. How is the concept of election understood in our culture?
2. How would election be linked to evangelism in the culture?
3. What exactly is missing in the culture's view?

## Biblical Analysis

1. What does the Old Testament teach about election, especially concerning the people of Israel (Ps. 78)?
2. What did Jesus teach concerning election and evangelism (Matt. 24:22-31, 28:18-20; Mark 13:20, Luke 18:7)?
3. What does Paul say concerning election and evangelism (Eph. 1, Col. 3, 2 Thes. 2:13 – 14)?
4. What about Peter? (1 Pet. 1:1– 4, 2 Pet. 1:10)

## SUMMA

*Write an essay or discuss this question, integrating what you have learned from the material above.*

How do the doctrine of election and the command to preach the gospel to the world fit together?

## OPTIONAL SESSION: RECITATION

Romans 8–16

## Comprehension Questions

*Answer the following questions for factual recall:*

1. What does Paul state is the result of all he has discussed in chapters 1–7 (Hint: look at 8:1)?

2. Count the number of times the word "Spirit" is used in chapter 8. What deductions can be made from Paul's usage?
3. According to chapter 8, what does the Holy Spirit do?
4. An important aspect of biblical interpretation is to consider a text within its immediate context. How shall we then understand 8:28, a frequently quoted verse often used to lend support to unbiblical assertions?
5. In light of this understanding, what does the "all things" of verse 32 refer to?

This aqueduct was built before Paul traveled through the Roman Empire starting churches. Rome's tremendous and various architectural advances were fertile ground for the spread of the gospel.

A painting of the Forum in Rome. Even the grandeur of Rome and all it represents is subject to the lordship of Jesus Christ.

6. In the first three verses of chapter 9 Paul sets the stage for the theme of chapters 9–11. What is that theme?

7. Why do you think Paul suddenly erupts into a doxology in 11:33–36 (*Hint:* look at what precedes it)?

8. In what way does 12:10 summarize what Paul is saying in chapter 12?

9. According to chapter thirteen what attitude does Paul enjoin us to have toward those who govern? Why?

10. Theologians do not agree as to the identity of the "weak" and "strong" in chapters 14 and 15, nor is there agreement as to the precise nature of the situation described there. It is likely that Paul is referring to Jewish Christians whose weakness consisted of a conscience which led them to continue to fulfill Old Testament dietary laws and to observe special days. In any event, what is the charge given to each group?

11. What is the common denominator in chapters 12–15?

12. In the overall context of the book of Romans, what conclusion can be drawn from Paul's emphasis on love after his discussion of the gospel?

13. According to 15:20, 24, 28 what is Paul's ultimate goal?

## ENDNOTES

1 The Jerusalem Council is recorded in Acts 15. It was the first reported meeting of representatives of the entire Christian church and was held to resolve a conflict over the continuing requirement of circumcision for Christians.

2 Seneca (c. 3 B.C.–A.D. 65) was a Roman philosopher, dramatist and statesman. He went to Rome in his childhood, studied rhetoric and philosophy and earned renown as an orator when still a youth. He became the tutor of young Nero. In the first years of Nero's reign Seneca was one of two who virtually ruled of Rome. His influence on the emperor was probably for the best. But the ascendancy of Poppaea, Nero's wife, brought about first the death of Agrippina (A.D. 59), then that of Burrus (A.D. 62). Seneca asked to retire. He had amassed a huge fortune and wanted no more of court life. Accusations of conspiracy were finally leveled at him, who, instructed to commit suicide, slashed his veins. His death scene was considered remarkably noble by the Romans. Seneca was a Stoic, and his writings show a high, unselfish nobility considerably at variance with his own life, in which greed, expediency and even connivance at murder figured.

3 Seneca, Lucius Annaeus, *De Ira* (II, 24).

4 Pelagius was a contemporary of Augustine in the fifth century. His beliefs were called Pelagianism, which denied original sin as well as Christian grace.

5 *This endnote appears only in the teacher's edition.*

# JAMES

Talk is cheap—free, in fact. It is very easy to make statements about who we are or what we believe. Our actions inevitably reveal the truth. The nickname of the state of Missouri reminds us of this truth—"The Show Me State." There are several stories about how this name was derived. The most popular one revolves around a comment made by Willard Duncan Vandiver, a United States Congressman. Mr. Vandiver was speaking to Philadelphia's Five O'Clock Club. Responding to an earlier speaker's remarks and questioning the speaker's accuracy, he concluded, "I am from a state that raises corn and cotton and cockleburs and Democrats, and frothy eloquence neither convinces nor satisfies me. I am from Missouri. You have got to show me." In short, talk is cheap.

James would have made a great resident of the state of Missouri. To those calling themselves followers of Christ whose actions told a different story, he says, "Show me." If you say you are a believer, then your actions should confirm that claim. James was not content to allow an empty profession to suffice. He stands up and boldly challenges us with the reality that faith without works is dead. How do we treat the poor? The hungry? Faith without works is dead. Is our conversation gracious? Or is our tongue "full of deadly poison" (James 3:8)? Faith without works is dead. Are we prideful? Judgmental? Impatient? Do we reveal our trust

Albrecht Dürer captures a plethora of ideas and emotions in his piece called *Praying Hands*. James 5:16b says, "The effective, fervent prayer of a righteous man avails much." James himself was known as a man with an exceptional prayer life.

Rahab watches from the tower as the Israelite army attacks and ultimately prevails against Jericho. James 2:25 demonstrates how Rahab showed her faith in her works.

in our heavenly Father by committing our needs to Him in prayer? James deals with all of these issues, and his response is . . . "Show me."

# GENERAL INFORMATION

## Author and Context

There are four men named James in the New Testament: 1) James, the father of Judas (not Iscariot), is mentioned twice (Luke 6:16; Acts 1:13) as the father of one of the disciples. Otherwise, he is completely unknown. 2) James, the son of Alphaeus (Matt.10:3; Mark 3:18; Luke 6:15; Acts 1:13), also called James the Less (Mark 15:40), was one of the twelve disciples. Apart from the fact that he is listed with the other disciples, he is an obscure figure, and it is unlikely that the early church would have accepted this epistle as authoritative if it came from such an unknown individual. 3) There was also one of the sons of Zebedee, the brother of John (Matt. 4:21, 10:2, 17:1; Mark 3:17, 10:35, 13:3; Luke 9:54; Acts 1:13). It would seem as though this close friend of Jesus would be a prime candidate for the authorship of this epistle,

except that he was martyred by the time the book was written around A.D. 44 (Acts 12:2), making it very unlikely. 4) Finally, there is James, the brother of Jesus (Matt. 13:55; Mark 6:3; Gal. 1:19). He was considered a "pillar" of the church in Jerusalem (Acts 12:17, 15:13-21, 21:18; Gal. 2:9, 12), and there are grammatical similarities between his speech in Acts 15 and the book of James. It is he who most likely penned the book that bears his name.

Other than being the brother of Jesus, what do we know about James? John tells us that while Jesus was performing His earthly ministry, James and his other brothers did not even believe in Him (John 7:5). He was a skeptic, and yet we note a significant change in James after the resurrection of Jesus (1 Cor. 15:7). He was actually among the believers awaiting the coming of the Holy Spirit on the day of Pentecost (Acts 1:14). He played a central role in the Jerusalem Council (Acts 15), and early church tradition describes him as a man of great piety and as someone with a fervent zeal to bring others to the knowledge of Jesus as the Messiah. He was also known as a man with an unusual prayer life. His commitment to Christ eventually led to his death as he was martyred in A.D. 62. James was thrown down from a temple wall, stoned and then beaten by the Christ-rejecting religious leaders of Jerusalem. As he lay dying, he prayed that the Lord would forgive his killers. Eusebius records the moving story of James's violent death. His history is based on the second-century historian Hegesippus, who reports James as stating that Jesus "is about to come on the clouds of heaven." James reportedly said just before his death, "Why do you ask me respecting Jesus the Son of Man? He is now sitting in the heavens, on the right hand of great Power, and is about to come on the clouds of heaven."[1] In less than 10 years, all of Jerusalem would be destroyed along with the Temple, along with perhaps a million people as predicted by Christ in the days of vengeance (Luke 21:6). Many interpreters see James 5:8 ("the coming of the Lord is at hand") in this light.

## Significance

Above all James is about faith, faith that works. While Paul goes to great lengths to make sure his readers know that works cannot save, James stresses the truth that faith that does not result in good works is no faith at all. In the chapter on Romans we considered the question, "If you were stranded on a deserted island, what would you have if you had *only* the book of Romans?" Now we consider the opposite question, "What would be lacking if James were removed from the New Testament?" Without the book of James, the student of the New Testament might conclude that as long as he believes in Jesus, his actions count for little. While Paul himself did not teach the heresy of antinomianism (literally, "against law"), it was a teaching of some in the early church and has continued to plague the church for centuries (and even causes trouble today). It is the idea that, because God's grace is amplified by our sin, our continual sin will reveal more of God's grace that covers that sin. It is a gross perversion of the gospel.

What else would be missing if James were not in the New Testament? We would be missing one of the most practical books in the Bible in terms of living the Christian life. James deals with the importance of taming the tongue. He gives insight into the origin of strife among believers, the sin of pride, the need for humility, the sin of judging others and the reality of the brevity of life. He addresses socio-economic distinctions and challenges the rich and their present attitudes toward the poor. Finally, James stresses aspects of prayer that are vital and exhorts his readers to restore those who have wandered from the faith.

James is a book of action. It is a book that convicts and comforts. It refutes the false claims of the antinomian, and it gives assurance to the one in the midst of trials. In short, if James were not in the New Testament, we would be missing much concerning the will of God and how to live out a vibrant faith.

## Setting

What prompted James to write this epistle? James played a leading role in the church in Jerusalem (Acts 12:17, 15:13, 21:18), and we see his desire to minister to fellow Jews. He writes this letter to his brethren. "To the twelve tribes which are scattered abroad" (1:1) is the designation given to the recipients. While this phrase could refer to Gentile Christians (the church as the new covenant people of God), it is most likely that it refers to Jews who were spread throughout the empire. James is writing to encourage his Jewish brethren and to exhort them in specific areas of the faith.

Who were these Jewish Christians? Why were they "scattered abroad?" Acts 11:19 says that "those who were scattered after the persecution that arose over Stephen traveled as far as Phoenicia, Cyprus, and Antioch, preaching the word to no one but the Jews only." After the stoning of Stephen (Acts 7:54–60) there was a wave of persecution that broke out against Christians, and these new converts to the faith had to flee for their lives. James recognizes their plight and continues to minister to the flock through this letter addressed specifically to them.

These Jews may have been tempted to doubt their decision to follow Christ. There was the threat of individuals like Saul who were looking for Christians to persecute. This would explain the nature of James's opening lines. He does not spend much time in flowery greetings. He immediately gets to the heart of the matter. "My brethren, count it all joy when you fall into various trials" (1:2). James is being a pastor to his flock.

## Worldview

James is significant in that it shapes our thinking in several important areas. First, it provides the perfect balance to the writings of Paul concerning true, saving faith. While some have labeled the difference between the two as a contradiction, it will be observed that James is a necessary complement to the

"Confess your trespasses to one another, and pray for one another, that you may be healed. The effective, fervent prayer of a righteous man avails much. Elijah was a man with a nature like ours, and he prayed earnestly that it would not rain; and it did not rain on the land for three years and six months. And he prayed again, and the heaven gave rain, and the earth produced its fruit." In this eighteenth-century Bulgarian icon are scenes from the life of the prophet Elijah, centered around God's provision for him through the ravens.

emphasis on faith alone in the Pauline epistles. Luther went so far as to ridicule James in comparison to Paul. In the 1522 edition of the German Bible, he wrote,

> In a word, St. John's Gospel and his first Epistle, St. Paul's Epistles, especially Romans, Galatians and Ephesians, and St. Peter's first Epistle are the books that show you Christ and teach you all that is necessary and good for you to know, even though you were never to see or hear any other book or doctrine. Therefore St. James' Epistle is really an epistle of straw, compared to them; for it has nothing of the nature of the Gospel about it.[2]

Second, James's discussion of poverty and wealth is as applicable to our day as the time in which he wrote. Third, we see a unique connection with the Sermon on the Mount in this letter. Fourth, James provides an accurate picture of suffering and trials. Finally, James gives insight into the nature of true wisdom.

To some, it seems like a logical conclusion. Consider the following reasoning:

- God's grace is made evident to sinners when He graciously forgives them of their sins.

- I should sin more and more in order that the grace of God might be made more visible.

What is wrong with this thinking? Is it not logical? James provides the same answer as Paul, only with even more force. His answer would be that the grace of God is not evident in the life of individuals having this mindset, because they have not received faith at all. The man who says that his assent to some set of truths is sufficient, and that he can sin at will and still claim right standing before God, is clearly misguided.

The word *antinomianism* comes from two words: *anti* (against) and *nomos* (law). It refers to the view that the Christian is not bound to obey any kind of moral law at all. He is saved by faith alone, and works play no part in the equation. We are under grace, not law, contends the antinomian

Against this heresy, James shapes our worldview by providing a truly Christian view of faith and life. He states unequivocally that good works must be present in the life of the believer. "But someone will say, 'You have faith, and I have works.' Show me your faith without your works, and I will show you my faith by my works" (2:18). James is refuting the idea that one can simply assent to certain doctrines and then have no concern about this faith being lived out in actions. He continues in that same section, "You believe that there is one God. You do well. Even the demons believe—and tremble!" Having our doctrine right is not enough. If indeed we do have our doctrine right, and we are truly trusting in Christ for our salvation, according to James there will be a visible manifestation of this faith in the way we live.

Some have claimed, however, that James and Paul are in direct contradiction of one another. Consider the following two passages:

> "Therefore we conclude that a man is justified by faith apart from the deeds of the law" (Rom. 3:28).

> "You see then that a man is justified by works, and not by faith only" (James 2:24).

Is this a contradiction in Scripture? Are the two New Testament writers opposed as to how a man obtains salvation? Only a poor understanding of their respective contexts would bring about this false conclusion.

Paul was writing to the church in Rome to explain the heart of the gospel, faith alone in Christ alone. Nothing can merit the favor of God in any way. Jesus, as our Federal Head, took upon Himself the responsibility for His bride, the church. It was His work on the cross alone that accomplishes our salvation. Those who are

chosen in Him are saved, not those who try to earn the favor of God through works of the law. In stressing the core of the gospel, Paul must bring this point out in his letter to those whom he had not visited in person.

James, on the other hand, is writing to a known audience, an audience who needed to hear that, if there was no fruit in the life of the believer, he had better question his standing with God. He writes to an audience who, to some degree, believed that if they simply held to certain facts about God, they were in good stead with God. But is James teaching that salvation is actually obtained by works? Those who claim that he is teaching this form of legalism have not looked closely at the text. James says, "I will show you my faith by my works" (2:18). He is explaining that true faith is revealed by fruit.

James is opposed to dead faith. Paul is opposed to dead works. They are both opposed to death. We must conclude that there are two "levels" of faith. The first is assent to certain facts. This would include believing that God is triune, that Jesus is God, that He was born of a virgin, that He lived a perfect life and died a death to atone for the sins of the church. These are the "facts" of the gospel. James explains, however, that even the demons believe such things and, therefore, simply believing that these things are so is not enough to constitute true, saving faith. Faith must express more than simple agreement with historical events.

The second level of faith as described by James is a faith that shows that it exists as evidenced by works. This is a deeper level of faith and is characterized by trust. It is a faith that trusts in the finished work of Christ for salvation. Is there a contradiction between Paul and James? When these two writers are considered in context, it is clear that they are in hearty agreement. What does Paul say after his discussion of the headship of Christ in our salvation? "What shall we say then? Shall we continue in sin that grace may abound? Certainly not!" (Rom. 6:1). Paul anticipates a likely response to his teaching on faith alone and responds to it. He goes on to explain that the individual who has true faith has "died to sin" (6:2) and has been "united to Christ" (6:5). So Paul directly addresses the antinomian, and his response is definitive. He asks the question again in verse 15, "What then? Shall we sin because we are not under law but under grace? Certainly not! Do you not know that to whom you present yourselves slaves to obey, you are

*Chart 1:* **JAMES AND THE SERMON ON THE MOUNT**

| JAMES | MATTHEW |
|---|---|
| **1:2** | **5:10–12** |
| My brethren, count it all joy when you fall into various trials. | Blessed are those who are persecuted for righteousness' sake, for theirs is the kingdom of heaven. Blessed are you when they revile and persecute you, and say all kinds of evil against you falsely for My sake. Rejoice and be exceedingly glad, for great is your reward in heaven, for so they persecuted the prophets who were before you. |
| **1:4** | **5:48** |
| But let patience have its perfect work, that you may be perfect and complete, lacking nothing. | Therefore you shall be perfect, just as your Father in heaven is perfect. |
| **1:19–20** | **5:22a** |
| So then, my beloved brethren, let every man be swift to hear, slow to speak, slow to wrath; for the wrath of man does not produce the righteousness of God. | But I say to you that whoever is angry with his brother without a cause shall be in danger of the judgment. |
| **1:22** | **7:24** |
| But be doers of the word, and not hearers only, deceiving yourselves. | Therefore whoever hears these things of Mine and does them, I will liken him to a wise man who built his house upon the rock. |
| **2:13** | **6:14–15** |
| For judgment is without mercy to the one who has shown no mercy. Mercy triumphs over judgment. | For if you forgive men their trespasses, your heavenly Father will also forgive you. But if you do not forgive men their trespasses, neither will your Father forgive your trespasses. |
| **4:11** | **7:1–2** |
| Do not speak evil of one another, brethren. He who speaks evil of a brother and judges his brother, speaks evil of the law and judges the law. But if you judge the law you are not a doer of the law but a judge. | Judge not, that you be not judged. For with what judgment you judge, you will be judged; and with the measure you use, it will be measured back to you. |
| **5:2** | **6:19** |
| Your riches are corrupted and your garments are moth eaten. | Do not lay up for yourselves treasures on earth, where moth and rust destroy and where thieves break in and steal. |

that one's slave to obey, whether of sin leading to death, or of obedience leading to righteousness?" (6:15–16). The contradiction, then, is not between Paul and James. Rather, it is found in the life of the individual who says he is a follower of Christ and does not present himself as a slave of righteousness.

But why does James find it necessary to stress works as the evidence of true faith so strongly? He is addressing believers who are undergoing significant trials for their faith (1:2). He wants to encourage them in their difficult times and warn them of becoming apathetic. In the face of persecution it would be much easier to rely on one's assent to certain beliefs rather than be required to show evidence of that faith.

In light of this teaching, according to James, what actions reveal true faith? One issue James confronts is the treatment of the poor. He provides a specific challenge to individuals of varying socio-economic status. Apparently, one of the issues among the original readers of James involved a group of wealthy individuals who were not living out their faith in terms of their attitude toward the poor. It is common in our culture for the affluent to look with disdain upon the poor. There is an air of superiority. James reminds his readers that this is unacceptable for the believer. "Let the lowly brother glory in his exaltation, but the rich in his humiliation, because as a flower of the field he will pass away. For no sooner has the sun risen with a burning heat than it withers the grass; its flower falls, and its beautiful appearance perishes. So the rich man also will fade away in his pursuits" (1:9-11). One way to show our faith, says James, is to change our attitudes about poverty and wealth. But what specifically does this entail?

A common theme of the book is the brevity of life. "Come now, you who say, 'Today or tomorrow we will go to such and such a city, spend a year there, buy and sell, and make a profit'; whereas you do not know what will happen tomorrow. For what is your life? It is even a vapor that appears for a little time and then vanishes away" (4:13-14). The word James uses here for vapor is like a mist. It is like the steam rising from boiling water. As soon as you see it, it is gone. If we have this attitude about our material possessions, we will come closer to living out James's definition of true faith. Riches are here for a time, and then they are gone. Jesus said, "Lay up for yourselves treasure in heaven" (Matt. 6:20). James is writing to saints who were experiencing persecution for their faith. He wanted to make sure they had a truly Christian view of material possessions.

Some have noted that James is lacking in strong theological content, especially concerning the Person and work of Christ. What many have failed to realize, however, is the fact that James is saturated with the teachings of Christ. It is not his purpose to delve into weighty elements of theology. Remember, James is a book about action. Of particular note is the striking similarity of portions of the letter to the Sermon on the Mount. Seven examples are shown in Chart 1.

It makes sense that James, the brother of Jesus, would have been familiar, not only with the content of the Sermon on the Mount, but also the reality of the sermon lived out in the life of the only perfect Man to ever live, Jesus Himself. Imagine, even though James was a skeptic before the resurrection, he would have had the unique opportunity to live day after day with Jesus. He saw how Jesus responded to His mother and father. He saw how Jesus treated others in every kind of setting. He watched Jesus deal with trials. He observed His habits of prayer day after day. In short, he witnessed the Man with the most active faith of anyone ever to live, Jesus, the Son of God. How exciting it is to read a book written by someone who had such a close relationship with Jesus Himself. We have an unusual insight into what is really important to God.

A part of this unique view into the mind of God is how the individual is to respond to trials. James does not simply explain that the believer is to endure trials and make some attempt to survive. He states that trials actually bring about joy. How does this occur? Let's take a look at the progression James discusses in chapter one. In 1:2-3 he says "Count it all joy when you fall into various trials, knowing that the testing of your faith produces patience." What does he mean here? Am I supposed to leap up and down for joy every time I experience a trial? Let's look a little deeper. First, a trial comes along into my life. James is explaining that the response I am to have is obedience in spite of the trial. The end result of the trial, then, will be that patience is worked into my life. I become a more patient person when I respond in obedience to trials. James explains that something special happens when this progression occurs in my life. As a result I become more mature in my faith, and thus, more prepared to handle the next trial. If we were to make a diagram of James 1:2-4, it might look something like this:

Finally, James provides insight into obtaining true wisdom. The story is often told of the young man who approached Socrates in search of wisdom. Socrates took the man to the ocean and asked him what he wanted more than anything. "Wisdom," replied the budding philosopher. Socrates then proceeded to plunge the man's head beneath the water and held it there for a while. Bringing his head back to the surface, Socrates asked again the same question,

"What do you desire more than anything?" The reply was the same, "Wisdom." The great thinker put the man's head under water yet again, only to ask the question again after relieving him. Finally, the third time Socrates held the man's head under the water a long while. The young man was gasping for air, fearing he might die soon if he were not allowed to resurface immediately. When Socrates asked the question, "Now, young man, what did you just now desire more than anything?" The man answered, "Air!" Socrates replied, "When you desire wisdom as much as you just now desired air, come to me, and I will teach you."

James raises the question, "Do any of you lack wisdom?" His response? "Let him ask of God" (1:5). But James is not talking about some casual form of asking here. He goes on to describe a person like the protégé Socrates was seeking, someone who is hungry to petition God with persistence and faith. "But let him ask in faith, with no doubting, for he who doubts is like a wave of the sea driven and tossed by the wind. For let not that man suppose that he will receive anything from the Lord; he is a double-minded man, unstable in his ways" (1:6–8). Even if we do not "feel" like we want wisdom, we should petition God for it. We should believe that as we continue to ask Him for it, He will not only create in us the desire for it, but also that He will give it to us.

In summary, then, James is a book of great practicality. This man whose faith wavered while Jesus was on earth writes an epistle about *true* faith. May we be convicted by its contents and seek ways to apply these truths to our lives to the glory of God.

—*Bruce Etter*

## For Further Reading

Carson, D.A. and Moo, Douglas J. *An Introduction to the New Testament.* Grand Rapids, Mich.: Zondervan Publishing House, 1992.

Tenney, Merrill C. *New Testament Survey Revised.* Grand Rapids, Mich.: Eerdmans, 1985.

# SESSION I: PRELUDE
## A Question to Consider

Do we have to do good works to "prove" we are Christians? Why or why not?

*From the General Information above answer the following questions:*

1. Of the four men named James in the New Testament, why is James, the brother of Jesus, the most likely author of the book of James?
2. List some of the facts we know about James.
3. When was James written?
4. Who were the original recipients of the letter?
5. Why does it make sense that this book would bear similarities to the Sermon on the Mount?
6. What are the two "levels" or ways we understand faith?
7. What does James say is the first step toward gaining wisdom?
8. How and when did James die?

 READING ASSIGNMENT:
James 1–3

# SESSION II: RECITATION
James 1–3

## Comprehension Questions

*Answer the following questions for factual recall:*

1. Explain the progression James describes in 1:2–3 that leads to true joy.
2. What is the image James gives to explain why we should have faith when we pray?
3. Explain how temptation occurs. Where does temptation *not* come from, according to James.
4. What image does James use to describe the person who listens to the word, but does not practice it? What does he mean by this?
5. Why do you think James begins the discussion about showing partiality by appealing to Christ?
6. As discussed in the worldview section earlier, some have asserted that James and Paul contradict one another concerning the role of faith and

works in salvation. How does 2:18 clear up James's position on this issue?

7. James states that individuals who practice a certain profession will receive a stricter judgment because of their involvement in this line of work. What is that profession? Why do you think this is so?

8. What is the main topic of 3:1-12? What is his point?

9. What images does he use to describe the tongue?

10. Make a chart listing the differences between worldly wisdom and heavenly wisdom according to James 3:13-18.

READING ASSIGNMENT:
James 4-5

# SESSION III: DISCUSSION

James 4-5

## A Question to Consider

Should we be living our lives for the present or for the future?

*Discuss or list short answers to the following questions:*

### Text Analysis

1. What advice does James give concerning our planning of the future in 4:13-17 and 5:7-11?

2. What future followed for James and Jerusalem?

3. How does James describe the timing of the "coming of Christ" (James 5:1-9)?

4. Could James be describing the imminent judgment coming of Christ on Jerusalem in A.D. 70 in distinction from the coming of Christ at the end of the world?

5. What does James say is the opposite of trusting in the will of God and patiently awaiting the coming of Christ (4:16)?

6. Why does James mention the prophets (5:10)?

### Cultural Analysis

1. What is the culture's view of patience? (How long are you willing to wait after clicking on a computer icon which opens a program before you start to get angry?)

2. How do people generally view waiting for the Second Coming of Christ? Living for the future and perfection in heaven?

3. What is defective about our culture's views on this issue?

### Biblical Analysis

1. What does Proverbs teach us about living for the future presently (1:7; 9:10; 14:26-27; 23:17)?

2. What did Jesus teach on this subject (Matt. 6:34; 24:44, 25:1-13)?

3. What does Paul teach on this subject (Rom. 8:18, 1 Cor. 15, Phil. 3:13-14, Col. 3:2)?

## SUMMA

*Write an essay or discuss this question, integrating what you have learned from the material above.*
How do we join the teaching in James on perseverance, wisdom, trusting God in light of future judgment?

# OPTIONAL SESSION: RECITATION

James 4-5

## Comprehension Questions

*Answer the following questions for factual recall:*

1. What is the problem of human nature presented in James 4:1-2 and 1:14-15?

2. What is the solution to this problem of human nature (4:7-8)?

3. In the context of what James is saying in chapter 4, how should we understand verse 10?

4. In 4:11 he commands his readers, "Do not speak evil of one another, brethren." Why would James include this?

5. What specific applications could the original readers have made from what James says in 4:13-15?

6. James goes on to tell his readers to await something very special. What is it? What analogy does he give them in this regard? How might this encourage them in their present situation?

7. How might these words in 5:7-8 also challenge them?

8. What examples does James tell his readers to

[T]ake ships as an example. Although they are so large and are driven by strong winds, they are steered by a very small rudder wherever the pilot wants to go. Likewise the tongue is a small part of the body, but it makes great boasts. Consider what a great forest is set on fire by a small spark. The tongue also is a fire, a world of evil among the parts of the body. It corrupts the whole person, sets the whole course of his life on fire, and is itself set on fire by hell. (James 3:4–6)

consider regarding their need to be patient in the face of suffering?

9. In 5:13–14 James gives specific instructions to individuals in different situations. What are their respective situations, and what council does James offer?

10. What two things does James say believers should be doing for one another?

11. What is James's point in using Elijah as an example in 5:17–18?

### ENDNOTES

1    Eusebius. *Ecclesiastical History*. Grand Rapids, Mich.: Baker, 1958. 77–78.

2    It seems that Luther later revised his thinking. This comment is removed from the 1545 edition.

# The Eagle of the Ninth

Admit it. You've done it. It has happened to almost everybody. The majority of us have had a time when we have done something socially wrong to one degree or another and been absolutely clueless that we've done it. There is still a running joke in my family from a time when I committed a social *faux pas* at my aunt's house. I was getting a hot pan out of her oven and grabbed the hot pads hanging next to the stove. There was a screech in the next room and my aunt ran into the kitchen, telling me, "Don't use those!" Evidently, the hot pads hanging next to the stove were for show, but the ones actually meant to be used were in the drawer next to the oven. Silly me.

So what is the big deal about making off with a metal eagle that was on a standard a Roman legion carried into battle? What was so important about this eagle that a father carried, that the son would risk life and limb to get it back? Read and discover.

## General Information

### Author and Context

Rosemary Sutcliff was born in England in 1920. Her father was in the Navy and, as a result, her family moved frequently. When she was a child, she contracted Still's Disease, a type of juvenile arthritis. She had to have many operations and long hospital stays because of this illness. Perhaps because of her illness, her mother read to her a great deal. Sutcliff grew up to love Beatrix Potter, A.A. Milne, Charles Dickens and Rudyard Kipling. Her mother also read her a great deal of historical fiction and Norse, Celtic and Saxon legends.

Sutcliff decided to go to art school at the age of fourteen and made the painting of miniatures her profession. Shortly thereafter, the Second World War broke out. Sometime during the war, she "got the itch" to write. Painting miniatures had become stifling to her. Her first books, *The Chronicles of Robin Hood* and *The Queen Elizabeth Story* were both published in 1950.

Sutcliff developed a method for writing that began with several months of solid historical research. One of the things she is best known for is a good story in a well-researched setting. Though she

The Roman army consisted of legions—the basic unit of their military. Only citizens served in the army, generally serving a term of twenty years.

Hadrian's Wall as we see it today. This wall was erected during the period in which *The Eagle of the Ninth* is set. This defensive fortification along the northern boundary of Roman Britain indicated a different strategic mindset by Hadrian as contrasted with prior Roman leaders. He sought to consolidate holdings rather than expand them.

considered herself primarily a storyteller, not a historian, whenever the historical reality did not get in the way of the story she wanted to tell, she always wanted to get it right—down to the very last detail.

While Sutcliff wrote over fifty books before she died in 1992, *The Eagle of the Ninth* is probably her most famous.

## Significance

How does one go about learning the history of a certain time or place? One way is to study written records and archaeological discoveries from those times. These things give us substantive knowledge. After a history lesson, fiction is like the dessert—it can transport us to those worlds in an entirely different way, using our imagination to flesh out the period,

adding sights, sounds, smells and feelings. In addition, when a student is not yet ready to study original material, fiction can draw them into the time period, spurring them on to further study.

To learn about the early era of Roman Britain, one can (and should) read the recorded history of Plutarch and Suetonius, to name a few. What remains of any stories from this time period are only in legends that were passed and altered from one generation to the next. In steps an author such as Rosemary Sutcliff. Something sparked an idea for a story, and she threw herself into serious study of the time period. She studied this time period so much that she once said, if she were to be sent back in time to Roman Britain, it would take her about a fortnight to get used to it, and then she would feel right at home because she understood what made them tick.

Sutcliff has intertwined fictional figures with historical figures to re-create the era in vivid and accurate detail. *The Eagle of the Ninth* is the first in a series about Roman Britain, whose family connections continue through *The Silver Branch, Frontier Wolf, The Lantern Bearers* and *Dawn Wind*.

## Main Characters

The story centers around Centurion Marcus Flavius Aquila. His journeys through Britain take him to three distinct places, each with their own group of characters. Isca Dumnoniorum is the fort to which Marcus's Auxiliary Cohort is first assigned upon its arrival in Britain. Centurion Drusillus is his *optio*, his second-in-command. While serving there, he befriends a Briton named Cradoc, who lives in the local village.

Calleva is the town where his Uncle Aquila lives and is a magistrate. In his uncle's household there are several servants: Stephanos the body-slave, Sassticca the cook and Marcipor the house-slave. Next door lives a fellow magistrate named Kaeso, whose wife is from a Celtic tribe but is a Roman lady "wannabe," and her niece Cottia. Most important is Esca—who Marcus initially buys to be his personal body-slave.

While traveling north in Valentia and Caledonia, they meet an adopted tribe member whose name is Guern. He is very important to what Marcus is able to discover about his father's lost legion and is able to point Marcus in the right direction. At the farthest point north in Marcus's travels, he comes to stay with a Picti tribe whose chieftain is Dergdian. Dergdian's grandfather Tradui also has a key part to play, as does Liathin, Dergdian's brother.

## Summary and Setting

The Celtic peoples spanned across what is now Germany and France, across the channel into Britain as well. In the first century B.C. and first century A.D., the Celtic tribes in Britain would often incite the tribes on the mainland to rebellion against Rome. In order to suppress these rebellions, Rome decided to quell the resistance at the source. Caesar led his first expedition against the Celtic tribes of Britain in 55 B.C. It was not a success. Caesar learned from the mistakes of the first attack and went back in 54 B.C. This time he was successful in defeating the Celtic tribes, was declared King of Britain and won a yearly tribute for Rome. His conquest resulted in an increase in trade relations between Britain and Rome and thus the gradual Romanization of the Celts. After Caesar's death, the Celts stopped paying their tribute, and in A.D. 43 Claudius began the conquest of Britain. Claudius wanted to make Britain a province of Rome.

Then, between A.D. 77 and 83, the Romans carried out a campaign to wipe out the druids, the Celtic priests. The druids were using their religious, political and social influence to continually incite rebellion against Rome. Rome also considered their animal and human ritualistic sacrifices as barbaric and a huge impediment to their efforts to civilize the tribes, especially the northern tribes.

By the time of Emperor Hadrian, Rome's presence was fairly solid amongst the southern tribes. However, the northern Celtic tribe of the Brigantes, whose area covered most of the northeast of England, continued to ally with the tribes from lowland Scotland against Rome. It was to separate the Brigantes from the Scottish tribes that in A.D. 122 Hadrian decided to build his famous wall that ran from the east to the west coast for over 80 Roman miles.

The above historical information gives you a quick background to the world of Roman Britain around the time of *The Eagle of the Ninth*. In addition to the historical setting, it is also helpful to understand the organization of the Roman legions. Legions were commanded by six tribunes. Over the tribunes were prefects and then legates. The typical Roman legion of this era consisted of ten cohorts, each with 500 men. In addition, each legion had about 120 horsemen, bringing the average number of soldiers for a legion to around 5,500. The cohorts were divided into six centuries of eighty men. Each century was commanded by a centurion. The centurion's second-

Hadrian was considered one of the five good emperors and followed Trajan as Roman emperor. He admired and enjoyed Greek culture. Buildings and public works (aqueducts, bridges, roads and harbor facilities) he had constructed remain to this day, a tribute to his forward thinking and contribution to the land he ruled.

This incredibly detailed carving is found on a sarcophagus from the Imperial Age. The battle it shows illustrates the military spirit that permeated Roman society.

in-command was the optio. The first cohort of the legion had approximately 800 men, divided into five, not six, centuries. The centurions of the first cohort outranked all other centurions in the legion. The primus pilus was the senior centurion of the five centurions in the first cohort. The rank of primus pilus was the ultimate goal for a legionary. This post was held for one year, after which the centurion either retired or moved on to other things. Retirement brought with it a large gratuity.

Each legion had three main types of standard. The *aquila* (eagle), the *signa* (the standard for the individual century) and the *imago* (a portrait of the emperor). The *aquila* was introduced by Marius, was guarded by the first cohort and was the special responsibility of the *primus pilus*. In a fort the standards were kept in a shrine, as the standards were worshiped by the soldiers. The loss of a legion's standard could mean the disbanding of the unit.

The Romans started as a city, and within nine hundred years had become an empire spanning the Mediterranean and reaching as far north as Scotland. Its army was used to hold this empire together. The legions not only defended the frontiers, but also established forts from which these new territories could be civilized. They were to be grafted onto Rome, not just conquered by Rome. Rome learned from, and incorporated cultural aspects of, conquered lands, adopting anything from weaponry to gods, and in turn granted Roman citizenship and all the privileges that went with that citizenship. Resistance was almost futile; all were to be assimilated into Roman culture.

In A.D. 117 the Ninth Legion was sent to quell some unrest in the area known as Valentia. This legion never returned, and mystery and speculation surround its disappearance. Into this historical setting Rosemary Sutcliff writes the story, *The Eagle of the Ninth*. Miss Sutcliff imagines the son of the *primus pilus* of the Ninth coming to Britain as a centurion himself about ten years later to look for his father and to find out what news he can of the fate of the Ninth. An injury he receives forces him to leave his legion and live with his uncle, himself a retired soldier. While there, he makes an opportunity to venture as a spy into the territories beyond the reach of the Roman army to find the true fate of his father's lost legion.

## Worldview

How many times have you bought a book because of its fantastic cover art, only to find that the story on the inside was nowhere close to what you had expected? Perhaps you have bought a bag of chips and been very irritated once you opened it to find out that most of the package was air and not chips. Or maybe you picked up a bright red apple, expecting it to taste wonderfully sweet—only to find the inside to be wormy. There are so many times when something looks great on the outside, but once you look a little further, you realize it is not as great as it seems.

The worldview of *The Eagle of the Ninth* is a little like that. On a quick read through the book, things may look one way. Their world might even be a place where you think you could be content to live—it might seem appealing like the bright red apple. But once you bite into the story and start to chew it up, you find inconsistent theological and moral views and no basis for any judgment of right and wrong. You find a worldview which, if carried through outside of their fictional society, would create havoc. Let's first look at the theological view—the world of their gods.

Eagles were found not only on the standards of legions. Here we see this stately creature on a gold Roman coin. Could it be that the use of eagles in various ways by the United States follows this Roman practice?

Sutcliff presents a world where there are good gods and bad gods, or at least they would appear to be good and bad at first glance. The good gods are presented as being the gods of light—light being a universal symbol of goodness and purity. One of these gods of light is Mithras, a Roman god worshiped by Marcus. Mithras has an aura of goodness because he seems to be a benefactor to Marcus through answered prayer, Marcus is not afraid of him and his worship takes place, not in secret, dark places, but in the open in the presence of the sunlight.

In addition to nightly prayers, Marcus offers several specific requests to Mithras which it would appear are answered. During a battle at the opening of the book, Marcus prays to him for a change of weather that would aid the Romans in their defense of the fort, and the fog lifts as he requested. Later, Marcus offers a sacrifice to Mithras, burning an item which is valuable and very dear to him. He is able to complete his quest, even though faced with appalling odds. Finally, there is an occasion when Marcus finds himself in a cave, in a desperate situation and very afraid. It is dark all around him, and he feels a dangerous presence bearing down on him. He prays for the light from his burning candle to become strong again, and it does, overcoming the darkness.

As stated before, when he prays or offers sacrifices, Marcus is not afraid. Rather he approaches his god with hope in the light open air. All this creates an aura that Mithras is a kind, benevolent god. Esca also worships a god of light, though the name of his god is Lugh. Esca makes evening prayers to Lugh, and in the cave he joins with Marcus in "thinking light" and praying for deliverance. Both gods have the appearance of goodness, an appearance created by our observation of how people interact with them and feel about them. So far the apple looks pretty good. That is, of course, if you ignore the First Commandment.

The bad god is presented as the Horned One. The Horned One is presented as bad, not because he does not answer prayers, but because there is an aura of fear and dread about his worship, he is an overpowering god, unapproachable by anyone but a priest, and the sacrifices to the Horned One are sacrifices of blood. The red apple may look even more appealing when compared to the darkness of the Horned One.

We learn about him at the feast of Saturnalia in the region of Caledonia, when the boys of the tribe go through rites of passage to become men. Rather than taking place in the open air and in the light, the ceremony takes place in darkness, outside of a cave called the "Place of Life." When the priest representing the Horned One appears, all fall down before him, including Marcus and Esca, "as barley going down before the sickle." Marcus unwillingly falls to his knees; Esca covers his eyes. Marcus perceives the presence of a "dark" power. Later, when Marcus and Esca go into the Place of Life, he describes the place as being horrible, with an evil sense of suffocation. It is here that he prays for light to overcome the darkness. This struggle is perhaps the strongest contest of the goodness of Mithras and Lugh pitted against the darkness of the Horned One. Also at the ceremony at the "Place of Life," the priests don animal skins and are perceived as actually being possessed by the spirit of the animal whose skin they wear. The greatest of these is the great stag, the Horned One. This makes him appear bad, because rather than being approachable or having a communal relationship with humans (as is demonstrated by Mithras and Marcus, Lugh and Esca), he is overpowering. And though the priests may invite his presence, the will of all who are present must give way to his.

Two more contrasts which make the Horned One appear bad are the manner in which people are evidently allowed to approach him and the sacrifices presumably demanded by him. Whereas Marcus and Esca approach their gods directly, none of the people of the tribe are seen to pray to the Horned One directly. All approach would seem to be by the priests in secret and in the dark. In addition, the sacrifices offered in the dark are sacrifices of blood— contrasted to Marcus's sacrifice of a small wooden bird. This in combination with the other factors creates the image of a strong, bloodthirsty god who must be appeased. It certainly makes Mithras and Lugh seem like light; bright and shining by comparison. But are they really?

How do we define good and bad within their world? All the judgment of goodness or badness about a god comes from a character's feelings or emotional reaction to a situation. Yet someone's feelings about a god does not make the god's state of goodness or badness necessarily true. Observe two things. First, do the gods say anything about

Three Roman soldiers—a legionary, a signifier and a centurion.

themselves and their nature or even about other gods and their natures? Secondly (though not as important), do people say anything about their gods which indicates goodness or badness?

The answer to both questions is *no*. First, the gods reveal nothing about themselves to the characters in this book. In fact, considering all the talking the humans do to their gods, the gods are remarkably silent. They reveal nothing about themselves, either through a written word, through their priests or to anyone else by any other means. The priests may be able to discern the will of the gods through their many ceremonies. However, it is a very muddy perception— as if to say, "We must have done the right thing because things are going well for us, and therefore our god must be pleased." It goes almost without saying, that if they do not say anything about themselves to people, the gods also say nothing about one another.

Secondly, do the humans say anything about their gods that would indicate that they are good or bad? Again, the answer is *no*. There is a mood the characters create around the worship of their god, or a mood which they perceive about someone else's god—just feelings. Feelings are not a description of character. They could be offering their worship to a leaf on a tree, and there might not be any difference—certainly the leaf would be as well-known to them. The apple is already starting to have less appeal.

In fact, there is no justification for this division of seemingly good gods and bad gods that is presented in the book. Indeed, they seem to have much more in common with one another than they do differences. They all have prayers offered up to them, they all have sacrifices offered to them, and other than perceived circumstantial approval, do not communicate at all to their believers.

In contrast, our God has made Himself known, through his mighty deeds, through the prophets and now in the person and work of Jesus Christ. And what is known about Him is very clear. For we see in His word His glory, holiness, majesty, His righteous judgment of sin and the need for sacrifice as an atonement for sin. But while the gods in *The Eagle of the Ninth* demand sacrifice after sacrifice, and it is never enough, our God has provided for us the fulfillment of His righteous requirement through the perfect offering of His only Son on our behalf. Finally, in *The Eagle of the Ninth* the characters have been given no direction how to pray. They are left to ask only for what they want, what they perceive will be of personal benefit. They have been given no promise that their prayers will be heard. For Christians, the Lord Jesus Christ himself taught us how to pray, first, by giving us numerous examples, most notably The Lord's Prayer (Matt. 6:9–13), and secondly, by giving us His indwelling Holy Spirit who bears testimony to what is true (John 15:26).

So in *The Eagle of the Ninth* the gods provide no basis for right and wrong, truth and falsehood. The gods provide nothing for a moral foundation. So what manner of moral universe have the characters established in the absence of one from their gods? What is important to these characters, what marks them as successful, what drives them, what do they feel makes their existence worthwhile—what saves them, if you will? Is it the pursuit of truth, an attempt to do what is right? There seems to be a goodness of some sort, because we are compelled to root for "the good guys."

Well, once again, when we look below the surface, we find there is no moral compass, no foundation upon which any sense of right and wrong will stand. The characters do not pursue an objective truth, nor is there any awareness that an objective truth exists. Rather, they pursue whatever they have a deep passion for (even if it contradicts a previous passion), and the only evil is to betray it.

There are several battles or contests in the book; one would think there would be a sense of right and wrong there. But we do not find this. In the opening of the book, Marcus has befriended a local Briton named Cradoc. The Britons are in battle because their druid has called them to it, presumably to defend the honor of their gods, who are shamed by the presence of the Romans. Marcus is fighting to fulfill his duty, to defend and win honor for his legion and cohort. Neither man is seen as being right; both men respect one another for giving their lives for what they have given their deepest loyalties to. In another "battle" towards the end of the book, Marcus is being chased by a Picti tribe. Marcus is pursuing his quest, the tribe is trying to protect the honor of their god by not allowing anything to be stolen from him and there is no sense of moral rightness here either. Both respect one another, and in any other case would have been friends. Battles between Romans and the locals just happen; there is neither a good nor bad side.

Esca is seen as a "good" character because of his loyalty to Marcus. What drives him? Well, originally Esca is driven by his desire to kill Romans. As a member of the Brigantes tribe, he rises up along with all his kin to battle with the Romans. If his loyalty to his tribe is anything like Cradoc's, does it make any sense that he would then become best friends with Marcus, a Roman? Either his willingness to die for his tribe was superficial, or something about Marcus compels a greater, deeper loyalty. Even when Marcus asks Esca why he has joined him on his quest, Esca tells him it is to taste freedom with free people, for the pleasure of the hunt. Hmmm. For the pleasure of the hunt and for friendship, he actually helps a Roman against a fellow British tribe? In this case we are to admire Esca for his deep loyalty. Even though what he has been and now is loyal to clash with one another, deep emotion is presented as a good thing.

Cottia is another character who is presented as good, another character who becomes loyal to

Marcus. Cottia comes from a Celtic tribe, the Iceni. Cottia states that she hates things Roman, she hates straight lines, the pervasive Roman order, and she wants to remain loyal to the ways and memory of her tribe. She also hates her Aunt Valerian for trying to make her into a proper little Roman girl. Her tenacity in clinging to her Iceni ways is held up as a noble attribute and contrasted to her Aunt Valerian, who is trying to do everything to appear thoroughly Roman and yet is presented as rather a fool. So what does Cottia do? She falls in love with a Roman and does it with gusto and passion. So it seems her "goodness" lies in the fact that she has deep passions—even though those passions conflict with one another.

Finally, there is Marcus. It is clear that his deepest passion throughout the whole book is to serve Rome. That manifests itself in different ways. First in his service as Centurion, second in his desire to restore the Ninth Legion, and finally to bring the lost Eagle back if he can, so that it can never be used against Rome. In following this passion, he never deviates for the sake of any person, no matter how he may come to feel about them. If his friendship or admiration of someone clashes with his commitment to Rome, Rome will always win. His love for Rome above all things is demonstrated when he expects a former Roman legionary to leave his family and children and return to Roman Britain just so he can be "Roman" again. He never acknowledges true regret or any admission of sin, never acknowledges any sense of right and wrong to judge his own actions. What is right is to pursue his goal with his whole heart. What is wrong is to fail.

In the real world, when everyone follows their passions, when commitment is based only on feelings, when there is no outside sense of right and wrong to guide our actions and feelings, when people respect one another at the same time as they try to kill one another, there is total chaos and anarchy. In the fictional world of *The Eagle of the Ninth*, we do not see chaos—not because there is moral restraint, but because none of the characters decide that they want to conquer the world.

Those who have a moral center do not move. There is a truth outside of themselves they subscribe to, to which they cling. There is an acknowledgement of right and wrong, a recognition that they have done wrong and an attempt to atone for that wrong. To return to our analogy of the bright red apple, the world of *The Eagle of the Ninth* may appear to be attractive and good on the outside, but when we look below the surface, there is no basis for goodness. The gods do not set up a standard of right and wrong, and people do not judge their or others' actions by a moral code either. Goodness in a character is determined entirely by a feeling of loyalty and passion; what that loyalty and passion are given to does not matter.

How wonderful that we have a God Who speaks to us, in Whom there is no change, no shadow of turning, that based on His word, we can judge right and wrong, truth and beauty. We do not have to be subject to emotions, but can be ruled by His law. We can know by that law that we have sinned, and through faith can claim Jesus' death on the cross as the sacrifice that will atone for our sins. We can be like the wise man who built his house upon a rock, so that rain, floods and wind could not make it fall down.

—*Deborah Erb*

## For Further Reading[1]

Spielvogel, Jackson. *Western Civilization*. Fifth Edition. Belmont, Calif.: Wadsworth/Thomson Learning, 2003. 141–154.

*Veritas Press History Cards: New Testament, Greece and Rome*. Lancaster, Pa.: Veritas Press. 32.

*Veritas Press History Cards: Middle Ages, Renaissance and Reformation*. Lancaster, Pa.: Veritas Press. 2.

Connolly, Peter. *The Legionary*. London: Oxford University Press, 1998.

Connolly, Peter. *Greece and Rome at War*. London: Greenhill Books. 1998.

## SESSION I: PRELUDE

### A Question to Consider

Have you ever found yourself in a conversation where you just felt lost? When and why?

*From the General Information above answer the following questions:*

1. What are some of the reasons *The Eagle of the Ninth* may appear to be a "good" story?

2. Why are these reasons not so "good" as they might at first appear?
3. Why did Rome want to conquer the Celtic tribes in Britain?
4. Why did Hadrian want to wipe out the druids?
5. What was so important about the Eagle standard, and whose responsibility was it to protect the Eagle?

 READING ASSIGNMENT:
Chapters 1–4

# SESSION II: DISCUSSION
Chapters 1–4

## A Question to Consider

What would cause you to break a friendship with a close friend? Do you think that forces inside you or outside you would cause this sort of split?

## *Text Analysis*

1. Who does Marcus have friendships with?
2. In what circumstances, if any, do you think Marcus would lay down his life for them?
3. How does Sutcliff allude to problems with Marcus's friendship with Cradoc?
4. Had the druid not come among the tribes, do you think they would have rebelled? Why or why not?
5. Marcus recognizes that, "Cradoc had not broken faith; simply that there had been another and stronger faith that (Cradoc) must keep." Without external intervention, would Cradoc's friendship with Marcus remain strong? What about Marcus's friendship with Cradoc?

## *Cultural Analysis*

1. What do you think the world around you says about friendship in advertising, television, movies, songs, books and magazines?
2. Under what circumstances does the world say we should be faithful to our friends?
3. Can you think of a circumstance when someone would choose principle over friendship, where that decision would be held up to be good? What would make it so?
4. Can you think of a circumstance when someone

"Lugh of the Long Arm" was the leader of the Tuatha De Danaan (the pagan Irish pantheon), the god of light, and was also called Ildánach—which means master of all arts and crafts. He wore the twice-smelted chain mail of Manannan Mac Lir—the Celtic god of the ocean, his foster father—and at his side hung his famous sword, Freagra. He also had a magic spear that was made for him by Goibhniu, a smith god, with which he slayed his evil grandfather, Balor.

would choose principle over friendship, where that decision would be criticized or held up as fanatical? What would make it so?

## Biblical Analysis

1. One of the strongest examples of friendship in the Bible is that of David and Jonathan. What outward circumstances might have pressured David to turn against Jonathan (1 Sam. 20)?

2. What causes their commitment to one another to remain strong?

## SUMMA

 *Write an essay or discuss this question, integrating what you have learned from the material above.*

What should and what should not cause us to break up a close friendship?

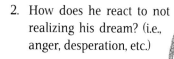 READING ASSIGNMENT: Chapters 5–9

## SESSION III: DISCUSSION
Chapters 5–9

### A Question to Consider

What things have you wanted and not been able to have? What different reactions have you seen from those who have had to give up dreams? Why do you think they react that way?

Cernunnos, the Horned God, was a balding, bearded, elderly god. He was frequently accompanied by a ram-horned snake. He was the guardian of the portal leading to the Otherworld. In his earliest of days he was probably the fertility god to the Gauls. But as time progressed and his legends grew, he became associated with wealth and prosperity. As Herne the Hunter—the British version of the Horned God—he is seen as the leader of the Wild Hunt. As an antlered giant, he is rumored to still survive and live in the forests of Windsor Great Park. His counterpart in Greek myth would be Pan and in Egyptian myth, Osiris—god of the lower world and the judge of the dead.

## Text Analysis

1. There are many characters from today's reading whose lives are not as they want them to be. We are going to take a look at a few of them and their circumstances and how they react to those circumstances. What dream has been taken away from Marcus?

2. How does he react to not realizing his dream? (i.e., anger, desperation, etc.)

3. How does his uncle try to distract him?

4. How has Esca's life changed?

5. How does Esca accept these changes?

6. Does the text tell us or imply how Esca is planning for his future?

7. What does Cottia resent in her life?

8. Though free, Cottia and Marcus both feel trapped. Though a slave, it could be argued that Esca does not feel trapped or helpless. What are their differences?

### Cultural Analysis

1. Name some marketing slogans that tell us to pursue our dreams, seeking to influence what we think is important to do or to have.

2. Is your future in your hands?

### Biblical Analysis

1. Read Jeremiah 29:10–14. Who will bring the Israelites out of Babylon?

2. Who has their future planned as well? What kind of a future is it?

3. What is our responsibility?

## SUMMA

*Write an essay or discuss this question, integrating what you have learned from the material above.*
How should we react when it seems that our dreams are failing to come true?

### Optional Activity

Marcus plays "draughts" with his uncle. Draughts was a precursor to checkers, mentioned as early as the sixteenth century. It is possible that this game of draughts descended from a popular game in the Roman empire called *latrunculi* ("robber-soldiers"). Board games were very popular within the legions because they were so easy to carry. It is known that *latrunculi* was played with two types of pieces: the stones and an extra piece called the *aquila* (eagle). Though the exact rules for the game are not known, a set of proposed rules for the game follows:

**RULES FOR LATRUNCULI**

1. Use a standard checkerboard, 10 black checker pieces and 10 white checker pieces.

2. Each player arranges 8 of his pieces (called stones) along the row closest to him. The eagle is created by placing the remaining 2 pieces on top of each other (like a king in checkers). The eagle is positioned in the second row, on the fifth square from the player's left.

3. Stones and the eagle may move any number of spaces in the horizontal or vertical direction. The black and white spaces of the checkboard have no meaning in *Latrunculi.*

4. Eagles cannot be captured but can be immobilized by being surrounded on all sides.

5. A single stone is captured if it is surrounded on two sides resulting from a move by the opposing player. In other words, a stone is not captured if a player moves his own stone between two opposing pieces. It would be best if the player announced this kind of move as he makes it to avoid any later dispute.

6. The outside walls cannot be used to capture pieces.

7. A stone in the corner can be captured by two stones placed across the corner.

8. To avoid sequences of plays that repeat endlessly, a player may not make the same move with the same piece more than three times in a row.

9. The winner is the first player to immobilize the enemy eagle or capture all his stones.

 READING ASSIGNMENT:
Chapters 10–13

## SESSION IV: RECITATION
Chapters 1–13

## Comprehension Questions

*Answer the following questions for factual recall:*

1. What is Marcus's first dream—the one taken away?

2. For what purpose does Marcus risk his life?

3. Why is the sacrifice of his olive bird such a great sacrifice?

4. How does he react when he finds out the truth about his father's legion?

5. Are these goals imposed upon Marcus, or are they choices he makes?

6. Before Esca became a slave, where were his loyalties? How do we know this?

7. When Esca has an opportunity to escape after the arena, where does he go? Why?

8. Are these duties thrust upon Esca, or are they choices he makes?

9. To what was Guern's loyalty originally given?

10. How did he come to be a member of a Picti tribe?

11. The information that Guern gives to Marcus with regard to the Eagle's location is a betrayal to his tribe. He is not forced to do it. Why does he? (Hint: His situation is similar to Cradoc's.)

**READING ASSIGNMENT:**
Chapters 14–18

# SESSION V: DISCUSSION

Chapters 14–18

## A Question to Consider

What is loyalty? To what or to whom are you loyal?

### Text Analysis

1. Marcus's loyalty to Rome, his father's legion and even the memory of his father have driven him thus far. Now, in the name of loyalty, he has the opportunity to carry out vengeance on the tribe who stole the Eagle. Define "revenge" and "vengeance". (Feel free to use a dictionary.)

2. How is Marcus able to travel safely in Caledonia and Valencia?

3. How can Esca travel safely in Caledonia and Valencia?

4. Does Marcus have any regrets that he is stealing from Dergdian's tribe?

### Biblical Analysis

1. Read Deut 32:39–43. Who takes vengeance in this passage?

2. Who is vengeance taken out on? How do they feel about the Lord?

3. Think of an example where the Lord destroyed his enemies without using people.

4. Think of an example where the Lord did use his people. How did the people know what to do?

5. Think of a time when the people acted in war without or contrary to His direction. What happened?

### SUMMA

*Write an essay or discuss this question, integrating what you have learned from the material above.*

Where should our loyalty be? Should we act vengefully in the name of loyalty?

### Application

There are times when we will want to take vengeance, and times when we may be instructed to take vengeance. Before stepping in to do this, we need to seek the Lord and make sure that it is an action He would have us do, that He is going before us to defeat the enemy and not we by ourselves. Sometimes the answer may not always be clear through Scripture and prayer. We should seek the counsel of those in our families and churches who are more mature in their faith.

**READING ASSIGNMENT:**
Chapters 19–21

# SESSION VI: WORLDVIEW ANALYSIS

## A Question to Consider

A pile of dinosaur bones is discovered somewhere in the desert. A team of scientists gather and with great excitement assemble and prepare the skeleton for exhibit at a museum. If the scientists subscribe to the hypothesis of evolution, how does their museum display look? If the scientists believe that God created the earth, that Genesis is true and that the earth is young, how might their museum display look?

## Rosemary Sutcliff's Beliefs

Some fiction that you read is fairly straightforward. Most of you knew before you started reading *The Chronicles of Narnia* that C.S. Lewis was a Christian. You also saw as you read the books how his beliefs had a dramatic impact on the story he wrote. With other books, such as the *Odyssey*, Homer's beliefs also clearly affect the story he tells.

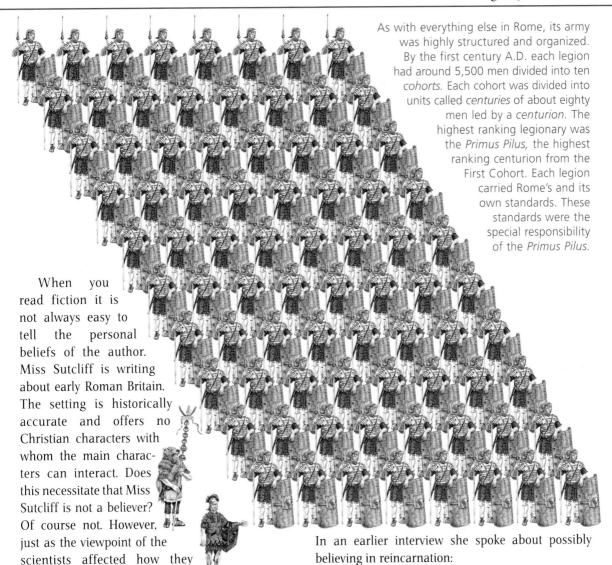

As with everything else in Rome, its army was highly structured and organized. By the first century A.D. each legion had around 5,500 men divided into ten *cohorts*. Each cohort was divided into units called *centuries* of about eighty men led by a *centurion*. The highest ranking legionary was the *Primus Pilus,* the highest ranking centurion from the First Cohort. Each legion carried Rome's and its own standards. These standards were the special responsibility of the *Primus Pilus.*

When you read fiction it is not always easy to tell the personal beliefs of the author. Miss Sutcliff is writing about early Roman Britain. The setting is historically accurate and offers no Christian characters with whom the main characters can interact. Does this necessitate that Miss Sutcliff is not a believer? Of course not. However, just as the viewpoint of the scientists affected how they interpreted and presented the data, so we must recognize that whatever her beliefs are will affect how she interprets historical facts and presents them in her stories. The following quote is taken from an interview with Rosemary Sutcliff given in 1986, six years before she died:

> "The Middle Ages I am not at home in. I am interested in them and love to read about them, but can't write about them, or practically not at all. I think it is because I can't take the all-pervasiveness of religion which has a stranglehold on life. The more level-headed viewpoint of the Romans is nearer to our own way of looking at things."[2]

In an earlier interview she spoke about possibly believing in reincarnation:

Q. What's your attitude to the present, the time from which you look back at these happenings?

A. As I said, I'm never at all certain that I don't believe in reincarnation. I rather think I do. In which case one does know the other times, and one can go back. I think the present—1973—is a very exciting time to be living in, but I don't think it is altogether to my taste.

Q. You've lived another life in Roman Britain?

A. Yes. This is possibly the reason that a lot of writers have this thing, as I was saying just now, about not being able to write about certain periods. Whereas other periods and places one feels completely at home in. This could be explained if they were the places and periods you hadn't experienced yourself, in an earlier life.[3]

*Discuss or write a short answer to the following questions:*

1. Though these are brief quotes, what are some conclusions we can draw about her beliefs with regard to the soul and the place of religion in our lives?

2. Below is a specific passage from Chapter 1:

'[The druids] can preach holy war, and that is ever the most deadly kind, for it recks nothing of consequences.' Hilarion spoke slowly, as though he was thinking the thing out as he went along. 'The frontier tribes are not like those of the south coast, who were half Romanized before ever we landed; they are a wild lot, and superbly brave; but even they have mostly come to think that we are not fiends of darkness, and they have enough sense to see that destroying the local garrison will only mean a punitive expedition and their homes and standing crops burned, and a stronger garrison with a heavier hand thereafter. But let one of their holy men lay hold of them, and all that goes whistling down the wind. They cease to think whether there can be any good come of their rising, cease to think at all. They are keeping faith with their gods by smoking out a nest of unbelievers, and what happens after is no concern of theirs, for they are going West of the Sunset by the warriors' road.'

From Hilarion's point of view, are the druids good or bad? How so?

3. Do you think Sutcliff's beliefs affected how she wrote this passage? How so?

## Writing Assignment

Rewrite Hilarion's passage about the druids with your beliefs having an effect on how you present the information in the story.

This highly decorated broad shield might have been used by a foot soldier in a Roman legion. Note that it was beautifully decorated in addition to being a sturdy means of defense.

# OPTIONAL SESSION A: ACTIVITY

## A Question to Consider

If you were looking for a house, what would it look like? What do you think these things might indicate about you?

*Discuss or list short answers to the following questions:*

1. There are quite a few references to Roman influence both in design and behavior in the book, a few in contrast to Celtic design. As you review the following chapters, what examples can you find?
2. What patterns do you see Miss Sutcliff repeating in her descriptions?
3. Chapter 7 contains the most material that contrasts Roman design work with Celtic work. How would you describe the differences between the two?

## Shield Project

Use your imagination and the illustrated examples to design art work for a Roman shield and a Celtic shield. You may also want to go to your local library to find some historical art books to help you.

The Celtic shields were typically 37" high and 18" wide, 17" in the center to form a very slight peanut shape. The Roman shields were of similar height, but wider—from 20–25" wide. Both shields would have been made out of layers of wood glued together, an early version of plywood. The Roman shields were usually surrounded by a band of leather; the Celtic shields sometimes had razor sharp metal going around the edges. Both shields would have had a small hole in the middle where a hand grip was. Over this hole would have been a metal "shield boss" on the outside, a decorated metal mound used to protect the hand and as a weapon to push against your enemy.

For those of you who are more ambitious, you may want to make your own life-size shield using plywood. There are many re-enactors in Britain who act out the Roman and Celtic soldiers. Some of these groups have posted suggestions on the internet for making your own equipment.

## ENDNOTES

1   At the time of publication, information about the Roman army's presence in Britain can be found at: www.roman-britain.org.
2   At the time of publication, this quote is found at www.lib.rochester.edu/camelot/intrvws/sutcliff.htm.
3   Wintle, Justin and Fisher, Emma. *The Pied Pipers: Interviews with the Influential Creators of Children's Literature.* New York: Paddington Press. 1975. 189.

# THE SCREWTAPE LETTERS

Imagine if you were an American soldier during World War II and you found a Nazi handbook. You would not be able to use it as it was, since you are not a Nazi and probably can't read German. But it would be a great help to your cause. You and your fellow soldiers would probably be able to use it to learn about the enemy. It could even help defeat the Axis power, since discovering how the enemy worked would be very valuable.

*The Screwtape Letters* is very much like an enemy handbook. It is an imaginary collection of letters from a demon, whose name is Screwtape, advising his demonic nephew, Wormwood. The letters contain advice for the young demon on how to tempt men. Screwtape tells Wormwood how to undo the work of God and how to work against Him. It is a demon handbook.

Because *The Screwtape Letters* is a handbook for the enemy, we must be careful when we read it. The advice given is not advice we should follow. But because C.S. Lewis was a Christian, he was trying to help Christians and not demons. We can read *The Screwtape Letters* and not follow its advice, just as we wouldn't want to use a Nazi handbook in the way it was intended. But by looking at what we should not do, it helps us figure out what we should do. Lewis wanted his readers to apply the lessons of these letters in reverse.

## GENERAL INFORMATION

### Author and Context

C.S. Lewis was a Christian apologist and writer during the middle part of the twentieth century. After falling away in his teenage and college years, he was brought back to the Lord later in life. His friend, J.R.R. Tolkien, to whom *The Screwtape Letters* is dedicated, was helpful in his thinking. He spent most of his life as a professor at Oxford and Cambridge Universities, teaching Medieval and Renaissance literature. He was very influential in the Christian world and wrote more

than 30 books, many of which concerned the Christian life. Besides *The Screwtape Letters*, some of his famous books include: *The Chronicles of Narnia* (which you have already read), *Mere Christianity*, *The Great Divorce*, and *The Abolition of Man*. Lewis died in 1963.

*The Screwtape Letters* was originally written as a serial. It was published in the British newspaper *The Guardian* at regular intervals between 1939 and 1941. Readers would read the letter from Screwtape to Wormwood as if it had just arrived to the newspaper. They were not published as a book until 1941.

In this 1998 photo by Karen L. Mulder we see one of the actual typewriters of "Screwtape." Many of Lewis's letters towards the end of his life were typed by his brother Warnie on this formidable machine, which can be seen at the Lewis's home, The Kilns, in Headington, near Oxford, England.

## Significance

The significance of *The Screwtape Letters* lies in two areas. The first was its enormous popularity. Since its publication in 1941, it has sold very well around the world. It is fun and easy to read and understand. Because of this, it is very accessible to many people who might otherwise never pick up a book on theology. It has been influential because of its user-friendliness.

The other significance of *The Screwtape Letters* is its practical nature. Because C.S. Lewis was a great Christian thinker, he had the ability to see sin in our lives very clearly. He provides an excellent way to be convicted of sin and to repent.

In these letters Lewis gives us a look at a point of view we do not often take into account—that of the demons. When we pray the second petition of the Lord's Prayer "Thy kingdom come," we assume that there is another kingdom at work in the world that Christ's kingdom is to replace. That kingdom is the kingdom of Satan, his demonic helpers and those that follow them. Lewis does a great job of showing us the inner workings of that kingdom. By knowing how the enemy is thinking, we as Christians can overcome their evil plots and better understand the temptations that Satan is placing in our path.

"We must picture Hell as a state where everyone is perpetually concerned about his own dignity and advancement, where everyone has a grievance, and where everyone lives the deadly serious passions of envy, self-importance, and resentment."

## Main Characters

The two main characters that we meet in the letters are Wormwood, a demon of low rank that is given the task of leading his "patient" away from Christianity (or at least making him an ineffective Christian), and Screwtape, Wormwood's uncle and superior in the demonic ranks.

*The Screwtape Letters* is a series of letters. It is not written like most books. We read Screwtape's advice to his nephew, though we do not read Wormwood's letters in reply. Wormwood's duty during the course of the correspondence is to tempt a particular human. Screwtape refers to him as "the patient." The patient is never named in the letters, but this is part of the point that Lewis is trying to help us realize. By not naming the patient, it is easier to see how the patient could be us.

## Summary and Setting

The book is set during the early years of World War II, the time when it was actually written. Lewis was living in England during the war. He went through many of the things that the patient goes through in *The Screwtape Letters*. Many of his original readers in *The Guardian* did as well. Nazi Germany instituted a heavy bombing campaign against England during the first part of the war. The war that looms large in the letters is World War II.

Aside from World War II, and the fact that the setting is in the mid-twentieth century, there is very little other historical setting for *The Screwtape Letters*. Lewis chooses to focus on the practical aspects of the Christian life.

Following the actual historical setting, this book sets forth a war. Unlike the great war raging in Europe at the time, this war was fought over one man. It is a war in which the demonic forces seek to tempt and trip their "patient" while the unseen forces of good seek to uphold him.

Almost every one of the letters is very practical. When Screwtape mentions sins that Wormwood should encourage, they are sins that we can see in our own lives. We can look at how the demons would like the sin to be increased. When we see what they want, we can do the opposite. Almost every letter has a practical application to our lives.

## Worldview

Now, imagine again that you, as a soldier in World War II, had come upon a Nazi handbook that told the enemy what to do in every situation. How would you use it? Surely, it would be important to learn and understand, because you could learn how they would react and when to be on special guard against attack. You could know the tactics they might use against you, and you could be ready to counteract any of their schemes. This enemy handbook would be of great value.

In the great war between Christ and Satan, the greatest battle has already taken place. On the cross, Christ purchased His church with His own blood and turned God's wrath away from them. At the resurrection, Christ conquered Satan's greatest weapon, death, and we can see that Christ will undo the kingdom of darkness and bring in the kingdom of light.

Even though Satan is not free now to deceive the nations as he was before Christ was given all authority (Matt. 28), He is still seeking to turn any man that he can away from the truth and toward falsehood. In this task Satan's fallen angels are his servants and helpers. What a find it would be to discover letters written from one demon to another. We could know how they were planning to trip us up and tempt us. We could be ready for them. Though fictional, that is exactly what Lewis does here. By making this communication known, Lewis shows the great difference between the evil and the good.

The distinction between right and wrong is clearly set forth throughout the letters. Of course, we are seeing the contrast from an unusual perspective, a demonic one, but it is still very clear. Screwtape supports Satan and everything he stands for. As he writes to Wormwood, he calls the devil, *our Father*. He is also fully opposed to everything that God stands for. Screwtape's idea of right or wrong is in reverse. Wrong to him is right and right to him is wrong. He cares about hurting God and stealing souls from Him.

As you read *The Screwtape Letters*, it is important to remember that not everything that Screwtape says is true, but neither is everything false. Throughout each letter, he refers to God as the *Enemy*. Of course, God is not our enemy, but our loving Creator and Savior. He is the enemy of demons, but He is our Rock. But Screwtape does get some things about God right.

He rightly points to the glories of heaven when the patient is taken up into heaven, though he does not know why they are offered to men. He acknowledges the importance of Christ's incarnation. Screwtape knows God and trembles, but is still scornful.

There are other aspects of God that come out in *The Screwtape Letters*. God is a mystery to the sinful demons. Just as men who are in sin cannot know God, we also see that Screwtape cannot comprehend the good works of God. There are many things that Screwtape admits to Wormwood that he does not know about his Enemy. They are things that the demon scientists have never been able to discover. Demons cannot understand God's goodness.

God loves and helps his people. Even Screwtape knows this. He finds it impossible to understand love. In Letter 18, Screwtape explains how creatures cannot be selfless and, therefore, cannot love. Because of this, he believes that God must have another, hidden reason to save men. Of course, we know that the Persons of the Triune God love each other perfectly. We are shown something of this love in the Scriptures. This is the love that we are called to imitate. This is the love that the demons cannot understand.

The clearest attribute of God that is seen in *The Screwtape Letters* is God's help to sinners in need.

"The fact that 'devils' are predominantly comic figures in the modern imagination will help you. If any faint suspicion of your existence begins to arise in his mind, suggest to him a picture of something in red tights, and persuade him that since he cannot believe in that (it is an old textbook method of confusing them) he therefore cannot believe in you."

Screwtape is always fearful that God will step in and prevent Wormwood's temptations. Screwtape knows that if the patient prays to God for help in temptation then help will come. We know from the Bible that this is true, and Screwtape confirms that God answers prayer and helps His people.

The God that is portrayed in *The Screwtape Letters* is accurate to a point. The characteristics that Screwtape attributes to God are mostly characteristics that God has. But we must remember that God is still called the Enemy in each letter. Screwtape offers an accurate picture of God only when it helps the demons' cause. But when it is helpful for him to lie, the demon tells his nephew that God cannot actually love us. Of course God does love us, and Screwtape is lying when he says otherwise.

Screwtape is also apparently unaware of the true nature of God. He never makes mention of the Trinity and mentions Jesus Christ only on occasion. He reveals his ignorance of the plan of salvation and the way that God works in human history. He knows that God wants to bring mankind to Himself, but he does not seem to know anything about the Holy Spirit.

While we learn a good deal about God and how He works, we also can see what men are like. This is the most practical part of *The Screwtape Letters*. Lewis shows us sins that are in the patient's life. Sometimes these are sins that we can see in our own lives. We can see in Screwtape's advice how the devil would like us to act, and we can act differently and obey God.

One of the things that we see is the value of repentance. In Letter 12, the demons are delighted because the patient has not repented of his sin. But when he has repented by the next letter, Screwtape is very worried. The patient has come back to God. When man repents, he strikes a blow against sin and its demonic proponents. Repentance renews our commitment to God. We can see the effects of sin and the effects of repentance in the patient's life, because Screwtape recounts them for us.

Throughout the series of letters, we gradually see the patient growing wiser and wiser. At the beginning, Screwtape is much more optimistic about winning his soul back to Hell. But as time goes on, Wormwood makes more and more mistakes. God is gradually winning the battle over the patient's soul. This is also something that we see in our own lives. God is gradually making us more and more like Him in the process we call sanctification. It makes it harder and harder for the devil to gain a foothold.

The demon instructor also gives us a glimpse into what our glorious future life may be like. In the final letter, Screwtape describes the blinding purity of heaven. He thinks that it is horrible that men can look upon God. But because he is a demon, we must remember that it is truly wonderful. This is a breathtaking grace that God bestows on us after our death.

Perhaps the clearest thing that we learn about human beings from this book is how foolish and gullible we are. In almost all of the letters, we can see sins that appear in our own lives. We can see how we are deceived into them. At the base of every sin is deception. It is no accident that Eve sinned because she was deceived by the devil. We deceive ourselves that "this time it is all right." But we are very good at deceiving ourselves. We believe, just as the patient is tempted to believe, that we can save ourselves. We act as if we can be righteous without God. But we are deceived.

The demons also have a backwards view of salvation. Screwtape believes that he can save himself by tempting enough souls away from God. We often act as if we can save ourselves if we simply perform enough good works. But even in *The Screwtape Letters*, the demonic letter writer shows us the true way to God. The only time that the patient is able to step closer to God is when God Himself steps in. The demons can lead the patient away from his Maker, but only God can bring him to Himself. We see this at the beginning of Letter 13, when Screwtape bemoans

the fact that God has interfered.

*The Screwtape Letters* show us a Christian worldview from the perspective of the demons. Lewis is arguing for Christian thinking and living by showing us the futility and foolishness of its opposite. Screwtape tells his nephew that God is the Enemy. He is trying to pull the patient away from God throughout the entire book. But the primary purpose of *The Screwtape Letters* is not to write a "great" work of literature. It does not contain epic similes or a grand setting. The primary purpose is to edify us as Christians. Lewis wrote the letters so that we could better counter temptation. If you read through *The Screwtape Letters* and

"Glubose has this old woman well in hand. She is a positive terror to hostesses and servants. She is always turning from what has been offered her to say with a demure little sigh and a smile 'Oh please, please . . . *all* I want is a cup of tea, weak but not too weak . . .'"

are not better equipped to battle with sin, then Lewis has failed. The entire purpose of the book is to help us to understand how the enemy works so that we might better resist him.

There are other helpful aspects to *The Screwtape Letters* that do not really fall into the category of practical Christian living. Screwtape has a few sections that really should be called philosophy. These sections are not primarily concerned with the distinction between right and wrong (or the *antithesis*). His discussion of laughter in Letter 11 is a good example. Screwtape gives us a straightforward discussion of the causes of laughter. There is no reason to think that he is lying here. When he wants to encourage certain kinds of laughter to cause sin, then we should learn from his advice. Another example of Screwtape thinking in an acceptable worldview is in Letter 15, when he discusses time.

How should we reject temptation? The best example of temptation by a demon in the Bible is that of Jesus Christ in Matthew 4:1–11. When our Lord resists the devil's temptations to sin, He quotes the Bible. He shows the devil from Scripture why the things he is suggesting are sins. This is what we must do when confronted with temptation as well. We should have Bible verses ready at hand to counter temptations. When we are tempted to steal, we should remember Exodus 20:15. When we are tempted to lust, we should remember Jesus' words in Matthew 5:27–28. This is the example set before us by our Lord and Savior. It is there for us to follow.

*The Screwtape Letters* is entertaining to read because C.S. Lewis was such a good writer. But it is helpful to read because he was such a wise Christian man. In nearly every chapter, we learn something about the best ways for us to follow God as Christians. The wisdom that pours out of every letter (though often in reverse) is almost overwhelming.

We can use *The Screwtape Letters* as entertaining reading or even as a devotional. But until we use it as it was designed, it will not be as useful. If we use it like the enemy handbook that it was designed to be, we will be able to better resist temptation.

—*O. Woelke Leithart*

## For Further Reading

Matthew 4 (The Temptation of Christ).

Spielvogel, Jackson. *Western Civilization.* Fifth Edition. Belmont, Calif.: Wadsworth/Thomson Learning, 2003. 771–801.

In his *Preface to Paradise Lost* Lewis wrote, "The door out of Hell is firmly locked, by the devils themselves, on the inside."

# Session I: Prelude
## A Question to Consider
Why do people sin? (What leads us to sin?)

*From the General Information above answer the following questions:*
1. Who was C.S. Lewis?
2. When and where did he live? What did he do for a living?
3. In what form did *The Screwtape Letters* first appear?
4. Who are the letters from? Who are they written to? What is their purpose?
5. Why is the sort of behavior in the letters characteristic of the letter writer?
6. What is the value of a book like *The Screwtape Letters* to the life of a believer?

### Reading Assignment:
Letters 1–10[1]

# Session II: Discussion
Letters 1–10

## A Question to Consider
What should we do when we face trials and temptations?

*Discuss or list short answers to the following questions:*

### Text Analysis
1. What is Wormwood's job with regard to his "patient?"
2. What happens to Wormwood's patient between the first two letters that causes his uncle Screwtape such displeasure?
3. Is Screwtape worried by the church? Explain.
4. Name three of the four ways Screwtape advises Wormwood to exploit the patient's poor relationship with his mother.
5. What is the Law of Undulation?
6. How does Screwtape want the patient to try to recover the feelings of happiness that he experienced at his conversion?

## Cultural Analysis

1. What does our culture believe concerning demons? Is this an accurate picture?
2. Does modern American culture believe (like Screwtape) that it is better to see Christianity as a means to the end of a greater cause? Explain.
3. Screwtape perceives godly prayer as dangerous (Letter 4). Is this attitude shared by America today?

## Biblical Analysis

1. At the beginning of Letter 2, Screwtape says the church is feared by demons. Why would it be this way? Is this a biblical idea (see Matthew 16:18)?
2. Is the Law of Undulation something that God intends? Explain.
3. Is Screwtape right when he says that real Christians do not have such temptations (James 1)?
4. Is God playing a role in Wormwood's patient's life? If so, what role? If not, why not? (Acts 13:48 gives us a view to God's work in salvation.)

## SUMMA

*Write an essay or discuss this question, integrating what you have learned from the material above.*

What should we do when we face trials and temptations?

## Optional Activity: Writing

Classical training in rhetoric included preparatory writing exercises called the *progymnasmata*. These exercises in composition introduced the beginning student to basic forms and techniques that would then be used and combined when practicing more advanced exercises and speeches. One of these progymnasmata was called a *chreia*, or "saying exercise," and was simply a concise exposition of some memorable saying or deed.

A chreia has eight paragraphs. The first is the *Panegyric* which is a paragraph in which you praise the person who uttered the wise saying. The second is called the *Paraphrastic*. In this short paragraph you put the saying into your own words. This paragraph often begins with something like: "When Saint Augustine said that evil was the deprivation of good he meant that . . ." In the third paragraph, called *From the Cause,* you explain the motivation of the person. The fourth paragraph is called *From the Contrary,* and in it you explain what would have happened if the opposite of the saying or action had occurred. For example, "If Diogenes had not struck the inept teacher, bad education would have continued." In the fifth paragraph, called the

> "When he gets to his pew and looks round him he sees just that selection of his neighbours whom he has hitherto avoided. You want to lean pretty heavily on those neighbours. Make his mind flit to and fro between an expression like 'the body of Christ' and the actual faces in the next pew."

*Analogy,* you liken the saying or action to something else, usually something more concrete and easier to understand. The sixth paragraph is similar to the fifth. It is called *Example,* and in it you show the wisdom of the saying or deed by pointing your reader to a specific instance in which this wisdom was demonstrated. The *Analogy* is different from the *Example* in that it is about a general practice (e.g., "Education is like a harvest: you work hard and reap great reward.") whereas the *Example* is about a specific person, place or thing (e.g., "Erasmus studied many things and became a learned man."). The seventh paragraph is called the *Testimony of the Ancients.* Here you quote a sage person from the past who testifies to the truth of the saying. Finally, in the eighth paragraph, called the *Epilogue,* you sum up the chreia.

*Write a chreia on Screwtape's advice in Letter 10: "All mortals tend to turn into the thing they are pretending to be."*

I.  Panegyric
    - Praise the person(s) who uttered the wise saying(s)
II. Paraphrastic
    - Put the saying into your own words
III. From the Cause
    - Explain the motivation of the speaker
IV. From the Contrary
    - Explain the consequences if the opposite of the saying or action had occurred
V.  Analogy
    - Liken the saying or action to something else
VI. Example
    - Point the reader to a specific instance in which the wisdom of the saying was demonstrated
VII. Testimony of the Ancients
    - Quote a sage person from the past who testifies to the truth of the saying
VIII. Epilogue
    - Summarize your previous paragraphs

READING ASSIGNMENT:

Letters 11–19

# SESSION III: RECITATION
Letters 1–19

## Comprehension Questions

*Answer the following questions for factual recall:*

1.  What "abominable advantage" does God have, according to Screwtape? Is Screwtape right?
2.  What sort of pride does Screwtape want to encourage in the patient?
3.  Why is Screwtape afraid of prayer?
4.  What major event disrupts the patient's life in Letter 5? Does Screwtape care about the war?
5.  What general rule does Screwtape offer to his nephew? Is it true?
6.  Do the demons like all extremes? Why or why not?
7.  What does Screwtape say puts the demons' cause in grave danger?
8.  What lack in the church's teaching "for the last few decades" causes Screwtape joy?
9.  According to Screwtape, what causes laughter?
10. Why is Screwtape "almost glad" that the patient is still attending church?
11. What does Screwtape suggest that Wormwood try to make the patient proud of?
12. What two things does Screwtape want to encourage in the patient at this point?
13. Screwtape wishes people to get into parties within the church. Why?
14. According to Screwtape, what is gluttony? Does it simply involve excess?
15. What idea does Screwtape try to encourage in men with regard to their marriage? Is this a true idea?
16. According to Screwtape, is love possible? Why or why not?
17. What part of God's plan for men do demons not understand?
18. Does Screwtape believe that falling in love is good or bad? Why?

READING ASSIGNMENT:

Letters 20–25

# SESSION IV:
# DISCUSSION
Letters 20–25

## A Question to Consider

Why is it important for Christians to marry Christians?

*Discuss or list short answers to the following questions:*

### Text Analysis

1. What is Screwtape angry about in Letter 22?
2. How does Screwtape describe the girl with whom the patient has fallen in love?
3. What does Screwtape say he would have done to this girl in the "old days?"
4. How does Screwtape describe the girl's family and home?
5. What is a hedonist? Is God really one?

### Cultural Analysis

1. In Letter 20, Screwtape speaks of the way that demons have influenced fashion and what makes women appear beautiful. Do you think his description of modern standards of feminine beauty is accurate? Why or why not?
2. How has our culture rejected the virtues evident in the life of the patient's girlfriend?

"Of course war is entertaining. The immediate fear and suffering of the humans is a legitimate and pleasing refreshment for the myriads of our toiling workers. But what permanent good does it do us unless we make use of it for bringing souls to Our Father Below?"

3. How has our culture embraced the noise?

### Biblical Analysis

1. Screwtape is horrified that the patient has chosen to pursue a Christian girl. Should we share his horror? Explain from Scripture.

2. How is the home environment of this girl's house the most disconcerting aspect for Screwtape? (Compare Deut. 6:4 to see what sort of environment God recommends.)

### SUMMA

*Write an essay or discuss this question, integrating what you have learned from the material above.* What sort of a Christian is it good to fall in love with and marry (and thus what sort of Christian should we be ourselves)?

### READING ASSIGNMENT:
Letters 26–31

# SESSION V: RECITATION
Letters 20–31

1. What sort of report does Screwtape want from Wormwood?

2. What sort of attack does Screwtape encourage on the patient? Why?

3. What is wrong with the girl that the patient falls in love with?

4. God has filled the world with something that sickens Screwtape. What is it?

5. As Screwtape describes it, what is the main belief of the "historical Jesus" movement?

6. Has Screwtape begun to be interested in the European war? Why or why not?

7. Which does Screwtape want men to feel: novelty or familiarity? Which does God give us in His world?

8. During what period does Screwtape advocate sowing seeds of discord? Why?

9. What does a woman believe unselfishness means? What does a man believe?

10. Screwtape acknowledges that even sins can be bad for the demons if what happens as a result?

11. What outcome of prayer does Screwtape urge Wormwood to exploit?

12. Does Screwtape want the patient to die? Why or why not?

13. Why is Screwtape encouraging cowardice? Is it a sin?

14. Can the demons tempt men to virtue? Why not?

15. Is courage a virtue? Explain.

16. Why is Screwtape angry at the patient's conduct during the raid?

17. Why is Screwtape angry in Letter 31?

18. Who else does Wormwood see by the patient after his death? How long have they been there?

19. What happens to Wormwood at the end of the series of letters?

# SESSION VI: WRITING

### Essays

*Answer two of the following essays:*

1. In Letter 12, Screwtape says that it does not matter to him how small the sins are, as long as they lead men away from God. Is the idea that one sin is as bad as another

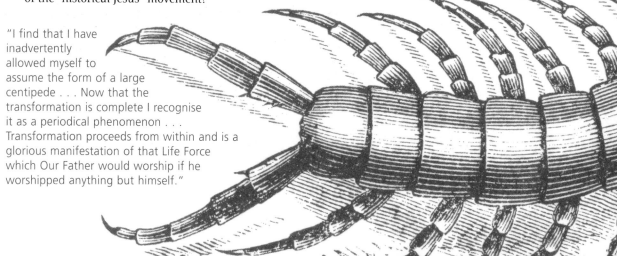

"I find that I have inadvertently allowed myself to assume the form of a large centipede . . . Now that the transformation is complete I recognise it as a periodical phenomenon . . . Transformation proceeds from within and is a glorious manifestation of that Life Force which Our Father would worship if he worshipped anything but himself."

biblical? Explain using Scripture.

2. In Letter 21, Screwtape speaks of the great advantage that demons teach in blurring the differences between various senses of the word "my." We often refer to *our* God. In what sense is He ours? Is it the same sense as our shoes are ours? Explain.

3. Screwtape says that hell is not full of either music or silence but simply Noise (Letter 22). Is this a contrast to heaven? What is heaven full of? Where in the Bible can we see this?

# OPTIONAL SESSION

## Quiz

### Grammar

*(2 points per answer)*

1. What are *The Screwtape Letters?*
2. What is Wormwood supposed to do to the patient?
3. What does Screwtape think of the church?
4. What is the Law of Undulation?
5. Does Screwtape want the patient to attend just one church? Why or why not?
6. Why does Screwtape get a little crazy and turn into a centipede?
7. What is the basic teaching of the "historical Jesus" movement?

8. Does Screwtape want the patient to die in the war? Why or why not?
9. What sort of vice is shown when you are good only when it isn't crucial?
10. What happens to the patient at the end of the series of letters?

### Logic

*Answer 3 of 4 (10 points each) Of course, answers to this can be varied. But the basic answers should more or less follow as suggested.*

1. How does *The Screwtape Letters* teach us?
2. What does *The Screwtape Letters* teach about God?
3. What does it teach about love?
4. What does it teach about the Christian life?

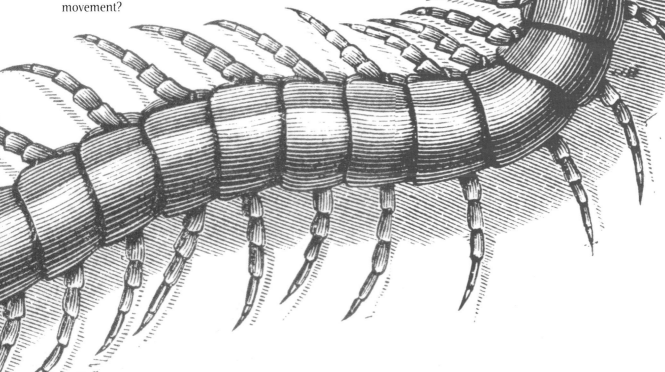

## Lateral Thinking

*Answer 2 of 3 (15 points each)*

1. From the Gospels, show errors of the "historical Jesus" movement?

2. The most detailed temptations we see in the Bible are those of Adam (Gen. 3) and of Jesus (Matt. 4:1-11). How does Adam respond? How does Jesus respond to the temptations of Satan? How should we respond to temptations?

3. Read Luke 18:9–14. How might we answer the temptations that Screwtape advises Wormwood of in Letter 2?

## ENDNOTES

1 Be sure to also read the Prefaces of *The Screwtape Letters*. Most editions include both Lewis's original 1941 preface to the collection as well as the 1961 preface, which he wrote two years before his death.

2 *This endnote appears only in the teacher's edition.*

3 *This endnote appears only in the teacher's edition.*

# THE HOLINESS OF GOD

I could hardly breathe. The ceiling was rushing away from me. It was like nothing that I had ever seen. Each year I go on a field trip with some students and parents to Washington D.C. Many are waiting to see some of the historic buildings of our government: the White House, the Capitol, or the Washington Monument. I, however, never gasped in the Capitol or at the foot of the Lincoln Memorial. But I did, when I went with our fourth graders to the National Cathedral. I will never forget my first sight of it.

Since Washington is the national capital, there are many large churches in the area. Commonly, the fourth graders, having never been on the trip before, see some of these grand churches and cheer, "There it is!" I would look back at my map and shake my head, "That's not it . . . That's not it, either . . . No, we are not there yet!" As the bus chugged through thick traffic, I struck up a conversation with a parent. Just then I heard a gasp from all of the students. I looked back to see who had spilled a drink. All of them were looking to the left in transfixed awe. I turned my head to see what spectacle had so captivated them. I almost fell over. All of the other churches and cathedrals we had passed seemed like tiny chapels. The National Cathedral, or the Cathedral of St. Peter and St. Paul as it is officially named, took ninety years to complete and, although it was built in the twentieth century, its architecture for the most part harkens back to the grand Gothic style (except for the Darth Vader Head gargoyle which I have never been able to find and the moon rock which has found its way into one of the stained-glass windows). It towers above the landscape and dwarfs all else around it. No one on that bus would ever mistake the National Cathedral for any other building again.

This, however, was not when I lost my breath.

We were the first group in line for the tour that morning. We had about a twenty-minute wait outside the building, so I stared up at the towers and the gargoyles (Where is that blasted Darth Vader?). Finally, they let us into the narthex, which is the room between the entrance doors and the sanctuary where worship takes place. As we waited on the docents who would lead the tour, I looked around the narthex.

it was impressive, but lacked the stunning quality of the outside of the church. Notably, it did not offer much of a view of the sanctuary. The students were getting restless and had lost their awe, starting to joke and interact with each other.

Then it happened. The kind docent, ready to lead the tour, led us from the narthex into the nave. The ceiling rushed away from us. Everything drew your eyes upward—toward heaven. Even though every sound we made was amplified by all of the stone, I never had to tell the students to quiet down. The cathedral quieted us all. I felt as if I should just sit down. My head was spinning. I tried to imagine some pagan wandering in. The question that I am sure would be impressed upon him by the architecture is, "What magnificent and grand being is worshiped in this place?"

Unfortunately, the national worship services that our country has pollute this wonderful Cathedral. These services call either upon a "god" (but not on the God and Father of our Lord Jesus Christ) or they beseech every god we can imagine. Watching these events I am always shocked by the obvious contradiction of the service with what I know of the architecture. Behind every speaker at the high altars sits a depiction of Christ holding the orb of the world in His hand. In the right transept, the giant stained glass window shows the Final Judgment. At the center of the window Christ is seated in judgment. The building is so tall that the window looks like it is miles away. Christ looks about three inches tall, but in reality he is the size of a man, six feet.

Perhaps some day we will run the rest of the gods out of this grand building. We may have to scrub the Baal and the Molech off the pulpit. (I would love a turn with that scrub brush.) Some day, perhaps, our nation will worship in the way that the architecture of the

It's been said that people or things can be easily hidden if you hide them up high, because no one ever looks up. Interestingly, typical cathedral architecture, like the engraving of the interior of the cathedral in Milan shown in the background here is designed to do just that—make you look up. The architectural lines and arches all cause you to be drawn up (and in) in awe.

cathedral tells us to. Until then, we will have to soak in all of the majesty and holiness that the building radiates and hear the gospel that at least the stones proclaim.

# GENERAL INFORMATION

## Author and Context

If you were to scan through the radio, chances are you would hear Dr. R.C. Sproul. His radio program, "Renewing Your Mind," can currently be heard in over 50 countries. If you were to browse titles at your local bookstore, chances are you would see several of the many books he has written. If you were to look for Christian books on ethics, prayer, marriage, suffering, and the glory of God or biblical studies, chances are you would see Dr. Sproul's books. What's more, if you were to look at liner notes of the rock music recording, "Van Halen III" (1998), you would also see Dr. Sproul being "thanked." (He has also been known to play golf with "acid" rock star, Alice Cooper.)

He is a kind of statesman of the Reformed faith in our day. Currently, he is the chairman and president of Ligonier Ministries and Senior Minister of Preaching at Saint Andrews Chapel in Sanford, Florida. He has taught at a whole host of seminaries and colleges. With all of this, what is he trying to do? His vision is in his own words, "I dream of a new reformation, a reformation that is not simply a renewal of life but a new vision of life: a vision that yields new forms and structures in society and culture. As long as Christians restrict their Christianity to a religion, a faith that is compartmentalized and isolated from life, they can have revival but never, ever reformation. We need to hear and do the Word of God in all of our lives."

This floorplan is from the cathedral in Milan. This church building has no true narthex—if they had one, it would be a room at the bottom of the diagram —but it does show the nave (1), aisles (2), crossing (3), transept (4), apse/ choir (5) and side chapels (6).

## Significance

The significance of the issue with which this book deals cannot be overestimated. Holiness lies at the center of Who God is. For this reason alone, God's holiness is worthy of constant praise and adoration. In fact, the seraphim in heaven forever sing of this very attribute.

Holiness is a so much a part of God that all of His characteristics take on this description: God's justice is Holy; God's wisdom is Holy; God's love is Holy.

However, as the author aptly points out, the holiness of God is difficult to define. Holiness is that attribute of God whereby we understand that He is "separate" and "above" us. In the face of this mystery we tremble with fear, but also find ourselves drawn in like a moth to a flame. We find that God is a power that we cannot control or comprehend. We find that He sees all of us (even our sin) totally, so we are ashamed before Him. In Him, however, a believer finds the only unchanging love, unfailing power and unflinching goodness.

God's holiness also displays His moral perfection. God is totally pure. This makes Him both unlike us and above all things. Again we are both drawn to the beauty of perfect righteousness and scared because, when we stare into God's moral spotlessness, all our blemishes and cancers are made evident.

In light of the importance of this attribute of God, it is no wonder that Dr. Sproul devoted a book to this subject.

## Historical Setting

Sproul's book is particularly important because the church to which he writes, of which we are members, has lost sight of God's holiness. Instead of trembling with fear and joy before a Holy God, contemporary evangelicalism often seeks to make God our "buddy." Our worship, the architecture of our churches and the preaching of our ministers present a "softer," airbrushed deity whose love flows over and around us like cotton candy. This God does not condemn, does not destroy and does not judge. He exists to make people feel better about themselves.

Unfortunately, this "transformation" has left us with a weak "God." This divine cotton swab is not the God of the Bible, and Dr. Sproul skillfully and adroitly demonstrates the wrongness of this by looking back to the biblical record and setting a humbling picture of an All-Powerful God before us. The God of the Bible strikes down the wicked. Even the proud among His people cannot escape his wrath (Nadab and Abihu will bear witness).

Today, however, by rejecting this God whose actions make us, at times, uncomfortable, we have unwittingly destroyed ourselves. We have become a people who cannot judge, who cannot distinguish and who cannot discern. We act like our idols. By making a god without a backbone, we have become, as C.S. Lewis said in *The Abolition of Man*, "men without chests."

So, in our historical setting Dr. Sproul's book is of great value. A deeper understanding of God's holiness will transform the worship, the preaching and the sacraments of the church. This transformation leads Christians into more holy living and eventually a transformational effect on our culture.

## Worldview

Have you ever been confronted with something that scared you out of your wits, but from which, try as you might, you could not remove your gaze? Once, when I was six, I went fishing with my new rod and reel. My cousin Regina showed up, and I wanted to show her my new rod and reel. So, we scampered to the back of my father's pick-up. That is when it happened. Just as we got to the back of the truck, we were confronted by a huge 30 foot-long snake. (Actually, it was more like six feet long, but I was small, and that is how it seemed). I nearly stepped on it before I saw it.

This snake was a thing of terror and beauty. It was thick and black with white lines that formed diamond

Chartres, Cathedral of Notre-Dame, built c. 1194–1220

In this painting by Raphael displayed in the Vatican Loggias, we see Moses has removed his shoes and hidden his face as the place is holy ground because God is present there.

shapes on its back. We could have hoped that this giant python (I really have no idea what type of snake it was) might have missed the fact that we were about to trample him. He did not, however. He raised his large triangle-shaped head off the ground and drew back as if he were going to strike. His enormous yellow eyes fixed on mine. His tongue flicked in and out, smelling (or was he tasting?) us.

In a moment like that, one hopes to be brave—I was not. I should have been thinking about protecting my cousin Regina. I should have been looking for a stick. I should have at least had the sense to slowly

move away, but I did not. I froze. This snake was the most frightening thing that I had ever seen. I knew that any second he could strike. Still, I was captivated by his glare. I was so afraid, I could not move. Neither could I look away. I was in the face of a power that I feared. I could not fully understand it, yet found it quite impressive.

Losing interest in us, the snake effortlessly slithered into the tall grass. My body went limp. We both started yelling for help (now that we did not need it).

Ironically, this confrontation with the deadly (well, who knows, maybe it was not a poisonous snake) can teach us something about the character of God. Although it is an odd analogy, because the snake represents Satan and the Fall, the incident demonstrated, though imperfectly, what the human reaction is to something holy. Sinners are both repulsed by and drawn to something that is holy. We fear it, but are magnetically drawn to it.

So, what is this "holiness?" Sproul rightly points out and clarifies the aspects of holiness. First and foremost, holiness is being set apart. In India, Hindus wrongly consider cows holy. (This might have been a language problem when some ancients confused the term *tasty* with *holy*.) These cows are allowed go wherever they wish, and if someone kills a cow, he is in deep trouble. Similarly, the emperor of China was formerly believed to be a deity. He was so "set apart" that he had his own color of ink that no one else could legally use. People received the death penalty for looking him in the eyes. Although these examples point to animals and a man who were reckoned holier than they were, God's holiness overwhelms these examples. He is "a cut above" man. He speaks and worlds are created. His plans are never set aside. He speaks and wind and wave obey.

God's holiness is also closely connected with His moral purity. God's law causes sinners to tremble, but not because it consists of moral precepts. All laws do that. God's law terrifies, because it is a reflection of His personal attributes. What is even worse for sinful man, it is the reflection of a morally perfect, all-knowing, all-powerful God Who owns the right to bring judgment on wickedness.

As we consider God's holiness in Dr. Sproul's book, we will see both of these aspects of holiness clearly laid before our eyes. Sproul does an excellent job of laying out this biblical doctrine in all its glory, demonstrating and illustrating the holiness evident in the Father, Son and Holy Spirit. In this he paints a beautiful biblical and helpful picture of God.

But what about the snake? Like the snake, God is both powerful and awe-inspiring. This power can be seen in the life of a college student who was awakened from sleep (as Dr. Sproul relates in the book from his personal experience) and called by some unseen force to a rendezvous with the Almighty, and also in the experience of a prophet who, upon entering into the earthly Temple in Jerusalem, received a vision of the courtroom of heaven. In both cases, fear and trembling were present. This fear results from our sin. Isaiah cries out, "I am a man of unclean lips!" (Isa. 6). The college student wishes to flee the chapel. Both know that they are seen and known by a morally perfect and all-powerful Creator. Both saint and sinner are undone at the thought. For the saint, however, this is not the end of the story. God's children know His power, but also His love for them in Christ. Christians can find true peace and experience exhilarating awe as they stand before God, knowing that the Source of all truth, beauty and goodness knows all of their sins, yet has cleansed them and, through Christ's sacrifice, has accepted them.

In *The Holiness of God*, man is pictured as one who naturally hates God. The reasons for this hatred in the mind of man are many, but they can be reduced to one. Man wants to be God and to control his own destiny and the destinies of others. To be controlled, to be limited, is something that Adam and Eve railed against in the Garden, eating from the one tree forbidden them. Sproul highlights other stories which demonstrate this same point. Nadab and Abihu, sons of Aaron and priests of God, would not be bound by God's word, and instead of offering only the proscribed offerings, they added their own individualized twist—with disastrous results. Uzzah, hoping to steady the Ark of the Covenant which was tottering and ready to fall, was struck down by the Lord for failing to remember that God is holy.

Man is terrified of a holy God. Both men and women, like a little boy and girl faced with a huge snake, tremble before Him. Both saint and sinner recognize holiness and, like Peter in the fishing boat, ask for it to go away. Man finds himself set in his place as a dirty rebel when confronted by a holy God, whether in a vision like Isaiah or in the flesh like Peter.

Our sinfulness becomes powerfully and palpably evident standing before the face of God, yet believers are not only terrified before God, but, like my cousin and I with the snake, they are captivated and drawn to Him. Sproul demonstrates this with stories from his own life as a young Christian, and by drawing out and explaining biblical stories. Although when Christ miraculously filled his nets, the tired fisherman Peter longed for Jesus to leave him, yet, as he later said, he cannot leave Christ because only He "has the words of eternal life."

The rest of the disciples were often confronted with the holiness, or "set-apartness" of Jesus when they were at sea during storms. As Sproul points out, the disciples were more scared after Jesus calmed the waves and wind (Mark 4). This same fear can be seen when Jesus walked out to the disciples on the water (Matt. 14). They believed that Christ was a ghost. They trembled in fear.

Peter's reaction to seeing Jesus walking on the waves, however, shows that believers also experience a deep attraction to holiness. They, like Regina and I, are trapped not only by the fear of the serpent but also by his wondrous glare. We could not take our eyes off its yellow shine. The disciples could not look away from Christ. They left jobs and parents for Him. They hung on His every word. Peter even went into the waves to be with Christ after Jesus called Peter out of the boat. Peter knew that water could not hold him up under normal circumstances. He was convinced that the holiness, or "otherness," of Christ could overcome these circumstances. They did, until Peter looked to the waves and the winds and lost his view of Christ. Still, we see that a view of the holiness of God attracts and transforms believers as they understand and dwell on it.

To that end, this book traces the blessing that the church has consistently received as men in the church were captivated by the holiness of God. This is particularly seen in the life of Martin Luther. Through Luther's experience, Sproul shows how wicked sinners can be reconciled to a holy, perfect God. Luther, as a monk, understood the moral purity of God and the moral perfection that one would have to possess to be in fellowship with Him. He also knew that he did not have this purity. Finally, he knew that God had promised to judge sinners. Luther trembled in fear. He whipped himself; he fasted; he prayed. Still, he had many more sins to repent of the next day. Finally, as he studied Romans, Luther saw that the perfect righteousness the sinner needed was found in Christ and that being united to Christ was a gift of God's grace that could not be earned by works. It could be received by faith. This understanding that "the just shall live by faith" led to the Protestant Reformation and a great flowering of the understanding of the gospel.

Remembrance of the holiness of God is shown to lead to growth in the church and the production of wonderful poetry, literature and music. Augustine, Luther, Bach and Handel are just some of the examples. These men caught a glimpse of the holiness of God, and their works and lives were never the same.

For all of them, their view of God's holiness sprang from and was grounded in the words of the Bible. Dr. Sproul relies extensively on the teaching of the Bible and gives interesting commentary on stories that shed new light on the pages of Scripture. Relying on God's word, Sproul sets before us a fresh view of God's holiness. Discovering God's holiness might almost make stepping on a big, vicious snake seem rather tame.

—*G. Tyler Fischer*

The Ark of the Covenant was a simple, man-made object that represented God's extraordinary holiness so much that even touching it resulted in death.

# Session I: Prelude

## A Question to Consider

Have you ever known something that is one-of-a-kind?

*From the General Information above answer the following questions:*

1. Why is holiness difficult to define?
2. What effect does holiness typically have on sinners?
3. How has the church today sought to change God? What has this caused?
4. What was Isaiah's reaction to God's holiness?
5. What was Luther's initial reaction to God's holiness?
6. What did Luther come to understand?

 Reading Assignment:
Chapters 1–3

# Session II: Discussion

Chapters 1–3

## A Question to Consider

Have you ever felt that you were in the presence of God's holiness? How could you tell?

*Discuss or list short answers to the following questions:*

### Text Analysis

1. What does "separateness" have to do with holiness?
2. How do we see the holiness (or "set apartness") of God in creation?
3. How did holiness affect the prophet Isaiah?
4. Does this effect indicate that he was not a believer?
5. How is holiness related to purity?

### Cultural Analysis

1. If holiness can be seen in having the effect of "undoing" someone, where does our culture find holiness?

Detail from a sixteenth-century painting depicting Jacob's Ladder

2. How does our culture (and sadly the church in general) view the holiness of God?

3. How does our culture connect its version of holiness and moral purity?

### Biblical Analysis

*Review Exodus 3 (Moses at the burning bush) and John 20 (the resurrected Christ returns to the disciples) and answer the following questions:*

1. In what way is God holy or "set apart" in these passages?

2. What do the reactions of Moses and Thomas show us about believers in the presence of the Holy One?

### SUMMA

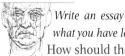 *Write an essay or discuss this question, integrating what you have learned from the material above.* How should the holiness of God affect us?

 READING ASSIGNMENT:
Chapters 4–5

## SESSION III: RECITATION

Chapters 4–5

## Comprehension Questions

*Answer the following questions for factual recall:*

1. What were Sproul's two reactions when he (as a college student and new Christian) reached the chapel?

2. How do people mimic God's creation of the world?

3. What is the extraordinary difference between how God creates and how we create?

4. What does the fact that *Hallowed be Thy Name* is the first petition in the Lord's Prayer teach us about our chief concern as Christians?

5. In the vision of Isaiah, how is God, Israel's true King, contrasted with Uzziah?

6. How are Moses' reaction to God at the burning bush and Isaiah's reaction to his vision of God in the Temple similar?

7. Why do the seraphim cover their faces and feet in the presence of God?

8. What was Isaiah's initial reaction to God?

9. How did God cleanse Isaiah?

10. How was Isaiah changed after the cleansing?

11. What is the meaning of holiness?

12. How is holiness connected to purity?

13. Why did Rudolph Otto call holiness the *mysterium tremendum*?

14. How does Christ's calming of the waves and the winds show that He is *sui generis* (Latin, "of its own kind," "unique")?

15. What does George Bernard Shaw's criticism of Christ tell us about Jesus?

16. Which behaviors of Martin Luther have caused some to accuse him of insanity?

17. What was Luther's ultimate religious experience?

 READING ASSIGNMENT:
Chapters 6–7

## SESSION IV: WRITING

Chapters 6–7

### Progymnasmata

Classical training in rhetoric included preparatory writing exercises called the progymnasmata. These exercises in composition introduced the beginning student to basic forms and techniques that would then be used and combined when practicing more advanced exercises and speeches. One of these progymnasmata was called a *chreia,* or "saying exercise," and was simply a concise exposition of some memorable saying or deed.

A chreia has eight paragraphs. The first is the *Panegyric* which is a paragraph in which you praise the person who uttered the wise saying. The second is called

the *Paraphrastic.* In this short paragraph you put the saying into your own words.

This paragraph often begins with something like: "When Saint Augustine said that evil was the deprivation of good he meant that . . ." In the third paragraph, called *From the Cause,* you explain the motivation of the person. The fourth paragraph is called *From the Contrary,* and in it you explain what would have happened if

the opposite of the saying or action had occurred. For example, "If Diogenes had not struck the inept teacher, bad education would have continued." In the fifth paragraph, called the *Analogy,* you liken the saying or action to something else, usually something more concrete and easier to understand. The sixth paragraph is similar to the fifth. It is called *Example,* and in it you show the wisdom of the saying or deed by pointing your reader to a specific instance in which this wisdom was demonstrated. The Analogy is different from the Example in that it is about a general practice (e.g., "Education is like a harvest: you work hard and reap great reward.") whereas the Example is about a specific person, place or thing (e.g., "Erasmus studied many things and became a learned man."). The seventh paragraph is called the Testimony of the Ancients. Here you quote a sage person from the past who testifies to the truth of the saying. Finally, in the eighth paragraph called the *Epilogue,* you sum up the chreia.

Write a chreia on the statement by Dr. Sproul in The Holiness of God *(p. 110):* "[God] killed Uzzah. He did the same thing to Ananias and Sapphira in the New Testament. These were righteous acts of God's judgment."

I. Panegyric
  • Praise the person(s) who uttered the wise saying(s)
II. Paraphrastic
  • Put the saying into your own words
III. From the Cause
  • Explain the motivation of the speaker
IV. From the Contrary
  • Explain the consequences if the opposite of the saying or action had occurred
 V. Analogy
  • Liken the saying or action to something else
 VI. Example
  • Point the reader to a specific instance in which the wisdom of the saying was demonstrated
   VII. Testimony of the Ancients
    • Quote a sage person from the past

God the Father measuring the Cosmos—an illumination from a twelfth-century French Bible in the National Library, Vienna.

who testifies to the truth of the saying

VIII. Epilogue

  • Summarize your previous paragraphs

READING ASSIGNMENT:
Chapters 8 and 9

# SESSION V: ACTIVITY
Chapters 8 and 9

*Salvation Identification* Game

In chapter nine, you read about three different types of teaching concerning how we are saved (Pelagianism, Semi-Pelagianism and Augustianism). In the following game you will earn points by recognizing these different teachings.

*For individual students:* There are a total of 155 points. Answer each question. Then see how many points you won by checking your answers.

*For a group of students:* Divide the class into three teams. Each team goes in turn and asks for a clue. A characteristic or clue concerning Pelagianism, Semi-Pelagianism and Augustianism will be read. If the team identifies the view correctly, they get points. (Optionally, a wrong answer could result in deducting the points from the team's score.) Each round gets more difficult, and the points for each question rise each round. If a team misses a question, the next team

can answer and steal the points. If all teams miss it, the answer should be revealed before moving on to the next question.

**ROUND 1**

(*2 points per correct answer*)

1. This view is not Christian, but is instead anti-Christian.
2. This view sets grace at the undisputed center of theology.
3. This view says that Jesus was a normal man, but not God.
4. This view says that sinners are helpless and cannot stop hating God.
5. This view does not believe that Christ is coming again.
6. This view claims that we cannot love a holy God without His help.
7. This view claims that sinners are able to bring themselves to God.
8. This view is Christian, but claims that we can decide to be born again.
9. This view could be described as "pious paganism."
10. This view claims that spiritually dead sinners can bring themselves to life spiritually.

**ROUND 2**

(*5 points per correct answer*)

1. This view represents the majority of evangelical churches today.

This engraving shows, from left to right, Melanchthon, Luther, Pomeranus and Cruciger translating the Bible in 1532.

2. This view denies supernatural activity.

3. This view agrees with Augustinianism in many ways.

4. This view maintains that our sin and unrighteousness makes us unable to move toward God by our own power.

5. This view represents a theology of compromise with our natural inclinations.

6. This view claims that we are spiritually impotent without God's help.

7. This view claims that God is sovereign, but claims that we can be persuaded to choose Him without Him doing anything to us first.

8. This view would claim that God's sovereignty means that we are not in control of our own salvation.

9. This view would claim that we cannot decide to be born again.

## ROUND 3

*(10 points per correct answer)*

1. This view is representative of theological liberalism.

2. This view would compare salvation to a dead person being brought to life.

3. This view would deny that Jesus walked on water.

4. Most people who read *The Holiness of God* have this view (according to the author).

5. This view believes that concentrating on God's wrath and justice helps us to see God's grace in its fullness.

6. This view would say that Jesus might have appeared to be dead, but that there is no resurrection.

7. This view implies the need for predestination.

8. This view represents a failure of modern evangelicalism to recognize man's inability and God's holiness.

9. This view would picture salvation as a life preserver thrown out into the ocean to make salvation available to anyone who would swim to it and take hold of it.

## TIE BREAKER

*If playing as a group, to break a tie, the first team to correctly answer the following wins:*

This view is the one held by Dr. Sproul.

READING ASSIGNMENT:
Chapters 10–11

# SESSION VI: DISCUSSION

Chapters 10–11

## A Question to Consider

Can space and time be made holy?

*Discuss or list short answers to the following questions:*

### Text Analysis

1. What is Deism?

2. Why are space and time not holy in the thinking of Deism? (What is God like and what does this imply about His relationship to space and time?)

3. Why was the space surrounding the burning bush sacred?

4. How was the reaction of the child at the St. Louis Cathedral an indication of an understanding of holy space?

5. How has God made each week holy?

6. How does our calendar take into account the coming of Christ?

7. How does the Lord's Supper sanctify time?

### Cultural Analysis

1. How has recent church architecture begun to deny the concept of holy space? (i.e., what are our modern sanctuaries like?)

2. What has our culture turned the Sabbath into?

### Biblical Analysis

1. Why did Aaron have pomegranates sown into his robe? What does this tell us about the holy place (Ex. 28)?

2. What did Aaron's sons wear in the holy place (Ex. 35:19)?

3. What does the holiness of the place in which Joshua was standing imply about the angel speaking to him (Joshua 5:14–15)? (Hint: Remember what made the ground around the burning bush holy.)

4. What are some indications that time can be sanctified (Ex. 23:14–17)?

## SUMMA

*Write an essay or discuss this question, integrating what you have learned from the material above.*

How should we recognize sanctified space and time?

## Optional Activity

Go to a Cathedral: Find the cathedral nearest you and go for a visit. While there, see if you can see what Dr. Sproul was talking about in this chapter. Seek to understand the incredible imagery. Be careful to recognize that not all imagery man has used is necessarily good. If you are on the east coast, try to visit the National Cathedral in Washington, D.C.[6]

## OPTIONAL SESSION: RECITATION
Chapters 6–11

## Comprehension Questions

*Answer the following questions for factual recall:*

1. What problem most consumed Luther and Paul?
2. What happened to Nadab and Abihu?
3. What amazed Hans Küng concerning God's punishment of sinners?
4. When Job questioned God, what answer did God give Job?
5. Is sin pleasurable or is pleasure sinful?
6. What does the phrase *simul justus peccator* mean?
7. How can we know if we are making real progress in our call to be holy?
8. What are three characteristics of God's wrath?
9. What would we do with God if we had the opportunity to have Him in our powers?
10. What is the problem that sinners believe that they have? What problem do we really have?
11. How did John Calvin explain why the natural world does not convince everyone that God exists?
12. How does God relate to truth, beauty and goodness?
13. Why is a church building, like a cathedral, a holy place? Why is it not?

## ENDNOTES

1 The *nave* is the main part of the interior of a church or the long narrow central hall in a cruciform (cross-shaped) church that rises higher than the aisles flanking it (almost all of the great cathedrals, and many other church buildings, follow this cruciform design). The word *nave* comes from the Latin word *navis* or "boat." In this way, we see the architectural, as well as the theological, relationship between the church and Noah's ark.

2 The *transept* is the part of a cruciform church that crosses at right angles to the greatest length between the nave and the

Isaiah 6:1b-3 says, ". . . I saw the Lord sitting on a throne, high and lifted up, and the train of His robe filled the temple. Above it stood seraphim; each one had six wings: with two he covered his face, with two he covered his feet, and with two he flew. And one cried to another and said: 'Holy, holy, holy is the Lord of hosts; The whole earth is full of His glory!'"

*apse* (or choir). Looking toward the front of a church, it is the areas that are at the front of the sanctuary and jut out to the right and left.

3 *This endnote appears only in the teacher's edition.*
4 *This endnote appears only in the teacher's edition.*
5 *This endnote appears only in the teacher's edition.*
6 If you cannot visit the Cathedral, take advantage of the very informative virtual tour at www.cathedral.org/cathedral/discover/highaltar.shtml.

# APPENDIX I: READING SCHEDULE

## Semester 1

|         | PRIMARY                        | RATING* | SECONDARY                          | RATING |
|---------|--------------------------------|---------|------------------------------------|--------|
| Week 1  | Genesis                        | 7.2.1   | Chosen by God                      | 10.0.0 |
| Week 2  | Exodus                         | 7.2.1   | Chosen by God                      | 10.0.0 |
| Week 3  | Epic of Gilgamesh              | 3.2.5   | Till We Have Faces                 | 3.1.6  |
| Week 4  | Code of Hammurabi              | 3.6.1   | Till We Have Faces                 | 3.1.6  |
| Week 5  | First and Second Samuel        | 7.2.1   | Till We Have Faces                 | 3.1.6  |
| Week 6  | First and Second Kings         | 7.2.1   | Magician's Nephew                  | 5.1.4  |
| Week 7  | Odyssey                        | 2.2.6   | Magician's Nephew                  | 5.1.4  |
| Week 8  | Odyssey                        | 2.2.6   | The Lion, the Witch and the Wardrobe | 5.1.4 |
| Week 9  | Odyssey                        | 2.2.6   | The Lion, the Witch and the Wardrobe | 5.1.4 |
| Week 10 | Odyssey                        | 2.2.6   | Horse and His Boy                  | 5.1.4  |
| Week 11 | Histories                      | 1.8.1   | Horse and His Boy                  | 5.1.4  |
| Week 12 | Histories                      | 1.8.1   | Prince Caspian                     | 5.1.4  |
| Week 13 | Histories                      | 1.8.1   | Prince Caspian                     | 5.1.4  |
| Week 14 | Histories                      | 1.8.1   | The Voyage of the *Dawn Treader*   | 5.1.4  |
| Week 15 | Histories                      | 1.8.1   | The Voyage of the *Dawn Treader*   | 5.1.4  |
| Week 16 | Oresteia                       | 3.3.4   | Isaiah                             | 7.2.1  |
| Week 17 | Plutarch's Lives               | 0.8.2   | Jeremiah                           | 7.2.1  |
| Week 18 | Plutarch's Lives               | 0.8.2   | Minor Prophets                     | 7.2.1  |
| Week 19 | F I N A L S                    |         |                                    |        |

## Semester 2

|         | PRIMARY                     | RATING | SECONDARY                | RATING |
|---------|-----------------------------|--------|--------------------------|--------|
| Week 1  | Theban Trilogy              | 3.1.6  | The Silver Chair         | 5.1.4  |
| Week 2  | Last Days of Socrates       | 5.3.2  | The Silver Chair         | 5.1.4  |
| Week 3  | Last Days of Socrates       | 5.3.2  | The Last Battle          | 5.1.4  |
| Week 4  | The Early History of Rome   | 1.8.1  | The Last Battle          | 5.1.4  |
| Week 5  | The Early History of Rome   | 1.8.1  | Best Things in Life      | 5.2.3  |
| Week 6  | The Early History of Rome   | 1.8.1  | Best Things in Life      | 5.2.3  |
| Week 7  | The Early History of Rome   | 1.8.1  | Unaborted Socrates       | 5.2.3  |
| Week 8  | Luke and Acts               | 7.2.1  | Unaborted Socrates       | 5.2.3  |
| Week 9  | Aeneid                      | 2.3.5  | Galatians                | 8.1.1  |
| Week 10 | Aeneid                      | 2.3.5  | Romans                   | 8.1.1  |
| Week 11 | Aeneid                      | 2.3.5  | James                    | 8.1.1  |
| Week 12 | Twelve Caesars              | 1.8.1  | The Eagle of the Ninth   | 0.8.2  |
| Week 13 | Twelve Caesars              | 1.8.1  | The Eagle of the Ninth   | 0.8.2  |
| Week 14 | Twelve Caesars              | 1.8.1  | The Screwtape Letters    | 7.0.3  |
| Week 15 | Julius Caesar               | 0.4.6  | The Screwtape Letters    | 7.0.3  |
| Week 16 | Julius Caesar               | 0.4.6  | The Holiness of God      | 10.0.0 |
| Week 17 | Revelation                  | 6.3.1  | The Holiness of God      | 10.0.0 |
| Week 19 | F I N A L S                 |        |                          |        |

*The books are weighted in the following order: Theology, History and Literature

# TIMELINE

When studying history, different cultures and periods may necessarily be studied in isolation from others. Unfortunately, this sometimes creates the false idea that, for example, Egyptian history ran its course, to be followed sequentially by Greek and then Roman history. This timeline is provided to show how these and other cultures overlapped and how history unfolds as a whole. The timeline can also be printed from the teacher's edition.

EGYPTIAN

GREEK

BIBLICAL

**The Beginning**
Creation

The Fall in
the Garden

The Flood

God's Covenant
with Noah

Tower of Babel

ROMAN

OTHER

2500 B.C.                                    2000 B.C.

Unification of Upper and Lower Egypt by Pharaoh Menes

The Old Kingdom in Egypt

**c. 2200–2050 B.C.**
First Intermediate Period in Egypt

**c. 2050–1800 B.C.**
The Middle Kingdom in Egypt

**c. 2200–1450 B.C.**
Minoan Culture

**c. 2082 B.C.**
God's Covenant with Abraham

**c. 2080 B.C.**
Sodom and Gomorrah

**2000–663 B.C.**
*Gilgamesh*
Shin-eqi-unninni

1800 B.C.  1700 B.C.

## EGYPTIAN

**c. 1800–1570 B.C.**
Second Intermediate
Period in Egypt

## GREEK

## BIBLICAL

**c. 1860 B.C.**
The Twelve
**c. 1878–1871 B.C.** Tribes of
Famine in Egypt Israel

## ROMAN

## OTHER

**c. 1792–1750 B.C.**
*Code of Hammurabi*
Hammurabi

**c. 1792–1750 B.C.**
Code of
Hammurabi

1600 B.C.                          1500 B.C.

**c. 1570–1300 B.C.**
Early New
Kingdom in Egypt

**c. 1450–1200 B.C.**
Mycenaen Culture

**c.1525–
1435 B.C.**
Moses,
author
of          **1500 B.C.**
*Genesis*   *Genesis*
**c. 1525 B.C.**   and         and
Moses' Birth   *Exodus*    *Exodus*
              Moses

**c. 1444–1435 B.C.**   **c. 1440 B.C.**
The Tabernacle   Levitical
and Ark of the   Priesthood   **c. 1446–1406 B.C.**
**c. 1446 B.C.**   **c. 1445 B.C.** Ten   Covenant   Begins   The Wilderness
The Exodus   Commandments                            Wandering

1400 B.C.                                    1300 B.C.

**EGYPTIAN**

c. 1333–1323 B.C.    c. 1300–1090 B.C.
Reign of             Later New
Tutankhamon          Kingdom in Egypt

**GREEK**

**BIBLICAL**

c. 1406 B.C.
Moses Dies,          c. 1400–1350 B.C.    c. 1389–1050 B.C.   c. 1377–1337 B.C.
Joshua Assumes       Israel Given the     The Judges of       Othniel and
Command              Promised Land        Israel              Ehud

**ROMAN**

c. 1300–182
B.C. *Lives*
Plutarch

**OTHER**

1200 B.C.

1000 B.C.

**c. 1200 B.C.**
*Odyssey*
Homer

**c. 1200 B.C.**
Trojan War

**c. 1080 B.C.**
Samson
and Delilah

**c. 1075–990
B.C.** 1 & 2
Samuel

**c. 1050 B.C.**
The Ark is
Taken into
Captivity

**c. 1043
B.C.** Saul,
the First
King of
Israel

**c. 1028 B.C.**
David and
Goliath

**c. 1011–971
B.C.** The
Davidic
Kingdom

**c. 995 B.C.**
David and
Bathsheba

**c.
971–931
B.C.**
Solomon's
Reign

**c. 1200 B.C.**
*Aeneid*
Virgil

**c. 1200–390 B.C.**
*The Early History
of Rome* Livy

**c. 1200–1000 B.C.**
Phoenician
Civilization and
the Alphabet

900 B.C.

**EGYPTIAN**

**GREEK**

**c. 950 B.C.** Life of Lycurgus

**c. 900 B.C.** Life of Homer

**BIBLICAL**

**c. 967–960 B.C.** The Temple is Built

**c. 950 B.C.** The Queen of Sheba Visits Solomon

**c. 931 B.C.** Israel Divides into Two Kingdoms

**c. 870 B.C.** Elijah Destroys the Prophets of Baal

**ROMAN**

**OTHER**

800 B.C.        700 B.C.

**c. 776 B.C.** The Olympics

**c. 750–508 B.C.** Greece Colonized, Democracy Begins

**c. 750–500 B.C.** City-States in Greece

**c. 850 B.C.** Ministry and Miracles of Elisha

**c. 800 B.C.** Jonah and the Great Fish

**c. 760 B.C.** Hezekiah Trusts the Lord

**c. 750–433 B.C.** Minor Prophets

**c. 722 B.C.** Israel Falls to Assyria

**c. 753 B.C.** Founding of Rome

**c. 700 B.C.** Life of Numa Pompilius

**c. 704 –681 B.C.** Reign of Sennacherib

600 B.C.

**EGYPTIAN**

**GREEK**

c. 594–593 B.C. Solon's reforms

**BIBLICAL**

**c. 626–580 B.C.** Ministry of Jeremiah

**c. 626–580 B.C.** *Jeremiah* Jeremiah

**c. 601 B.C.** Daniel Serves in Nebuchadnezzar's Court

**c. 600 B.C.** Shadrach, Meshach, and Abednego

**c. 586 B.C.** Fall of Jerusalem to Babylon

**c. 550–560 B.C.** 1 & 2 King

**ROMAN**

**OTHER**

**c. 559–530 B.C.** Conquests of Cyrus

500 B.C.

**c. 530–522 B.C.**
Cambyses II and
Conquest of
Egypt

**c. 560–546 B.C.** Reign of Croesus

**c. 524–460 B.C.**
Life of
Themistocles

**525–456 B.C.**
Aeschylus, author
of *Oresteia*

**c. 500–480 B.C.**
Persian Wars

**500–338 B.C.**
Golden Age
of Greece

**490 B.C.** Battle
of Marathon

**c. 539 B.C.**
Belshazzar's
Feast

**c. 539 B.C.**
Daniel in the
Lion's Den

**c. 520 B.C.** Jews
Return Under
Zerubbabel, Temple
Restoration Begins

**c. 516 B.C.**
Esther Becomes
Queen

**c. 509–366 B.C.**
Roman Republic
Developed

**c. 500 B.C.**
Life of
Poplicola

**c. 530–522 B.C.**
Cambyses II and
Conquest of
Egypt

**c. 521–486 B.C.**
Reign of Darius

EGYPTIAN

GREEK

**c. 480 B.C.**
Crossing the
Hellespont

**480 B.C.** Battles
of Thermopylae
and Salamis

**461–404 B.C.**
Pericles and the
Peloponnesian
War

**c. 450–322 B.C.**
Greek
Philosophers

**c. 442 B.C.** The
first Sophists
come to Athens

**c. 440 B.C.**
*Histories*
Herodotus

BIBLICAL

**c. 444 B.C.**
Nehemiah
Rebuilds Walls
of Jerusalem

ROMAN

**c. 446–365 B.C.**
Life of Camillus

OTHER

**c. 486–465 B.C.**
Reign of Xerxes

**c. 480 B.C.**
Crossing the
Hellespont

400 B.C.          300 B.C.          200 B.C.

**332 B.C.**
Alexander the
Great conquers
Egypt

**27–347
.C.** Life
f Plato

**c. 400 B.C.**
*Theban Trilogy*
Sophocles

**c. 390 B.C.** *Euthyphro,
Crito, Apology* and
*Phaedo* Plato

**356–323 B.C.**
Alexander the
Great

**c. 250 B.C.**
Architectural
Advances in Rome

100 B.C.

EGYPTIAN

GREEK

BIBLICAL

ROMAN

**146 B.C.** Rome
Rises to World
Power

**133–31 B.C.**
Decline and Fall
of the Roman
Republic

**c. 85 B.C.–A.D. 96**
*The Twelve
Caesars* Seutonius

**75 B.C.–A.D. 14**
Golden Age of
Latin Literature

**70–19 B.C.**
Life of Virgil

**59 B.C.–A.D. 17**
Life of Livy

OTHER

1 B.C.

**30 B.C.** Egypt
Falls to Rome

**4 B.C.** Gabriel
Tells Mary of the
Incarnation

**c. 4 B.C.
–A.D. 67**
Life of Paul
the Apostle

**3 B.C.** Birth of
John the Baptist

**3 B.C.** Birth
of Christ

**c. A.D.
1–62**
Life of
James

**c. A.D.
10–100**
Life of
John the
Apostle

**c. A.D. 27** Twelve
Apostles
Appointed

**47–44 B.C.** Reign
of Julius Caesar

**44 B.C.**
*Julius Caesar*
Shakespeare

**27 B.C.–A.D.14**
Reign of Caesar
Augustus

**A.D. 14–37**
Reign of
Tiberius

EGYPTIAN

GREEK

BIBLICAL

**c. A.D. 27**
The Sermon on the Mount

**c. A.D. 29** Death of John the Baptist

**c. A.D. 30** Crucifixion, Resurrection and Ascension of Christ

**c. A.D. 30** Pentecost

**c. A.D. 33** Conversion of Paul

**c. A.D. 34** First Gentile Converts

ROMAN

**A.D. 37–54** Reign of Caligula

OTHER

A.D. 50

**c. A.D. 45–47**
Paul's First
Missionary
Journey

**c. A.D. 45–48** *Epistle of James* James

**A.D. 47** *Letter to the Galatians* Paul

**c. A.D. 48** The Jerusalem Council

**c. A.D. 50–51**
Paul's Second
Missionary
Journey

**c. A.D. 53–57**
Paul's Third
Missionary
Journey

**c. A.D. 57** *Letter to the Romans* Paul

**c. A.D. 58–60**
Paul in
Rome

**c. A.D. 63** *The Revelation of John*

**A.D. 41–54**
Reign of
Claudius

**A.D. 45–125**
Plutarch,
author of
*Lives*

**A.D. 54–68**
Reign of
Nero

A.D. 70

**EGYPTIAN**

**GREEK**

**BIBLICAL**

**ROMAN**

**A.D. 64** Rome Burns, Nero Persecutes Christians

**A.D. 68–69** Reign of Galba

**A.D. 69** Reign of Otho

**A.D. 69** Reign of Vitellius

**A.D. 69–79** Reign of Vespasian

**c. A.D. 69–140** Life of Seutonius

**A.D. 70** Destruction of Jerusalem

**OTHER**

A.D. 100 A.D. 200 A.D. 300

**A.D. 79**
Pompeii Burns

**A.D. 79–81**
Reign of
Titus

**A.D. 81–96**
Reign of
Domitian

**A.D. 125** *The
Eagle of the Ninth*
Rosemary Sutcliff

**A.D. 286** Split of
the Roman
Empire

**A.D. 313**
Constantine
and the Edict
of Milan

**A.D. 325**
First
Council
of Nicea

**A.D. 367**
Closing of
the Canon

1500  1800  1900

EGYPTIAN

GREEK

BIBLICAL

ROMAN

OTHER

**1564–1603** Life of Shakespeare

**1898–1963** Life of C.S. Lewis

**1920–1992** Life of Rosemary Sutcliff

Peter Kreeft, author of *The Best Things in Life* and *The Unaborted Socrates*

**1951–1956** *The Chronicles of Narnia* C.S. Lewis

**1942** *The Screwtape Letters* C.S. Lewis

**1956** *Till We Have Faces* C.S. Lewis

2000

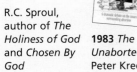
R.C. Sproul,
author of *The
Holiness of God*
and *Chosen By
God*

**1983** *The
Unaborted Socrates*
Peter Kreeft

**1984** *The Best
Things in Life*
Peter Kreeft

**1985** *The Holiness
of God* Sproul

**1986** *Chosen
By God* Sproul

# INDEX

## A

Aaron 27, 29, 35, 567, 573
Abel 9, 16
Abiathar 88, 91
Abihu 567, 574
Abijah 84, 88
Abijam 85
Abner 75
Abraham (Abram) 8, 9, 12–14, 16, 20, 25, 38–39, 44, 50, 54, 69, 76, 82, 157, 238, 240, 242–243, 347, 353, 417, 421, 481, 504, 507
Absalom 71, 73, 75, 78–79
Achilleus (Achilles) 96–97, 103, 108, 187, 252, 261
Achish 71
Adad-nirari III 439
Adam 9, 10, 12, 14–16, 19, 22, 37, 42, 45, 52, 71, 78, 100, 110, 167, 194, 237, 243, 284, 285, 305, 356, 361, 376, 392, 420, 480, 495, 517–519, 562, 567
Adonijah 73
Aegisthus 154, 155, 160, 161
Aeneas 107, 214, 216, 219, 222, 403
Aeschylus 98, 131, 151–159, 161, 306
Agag 71
Agamemnon 121, 151, 153–155, 159–161
Agrippa 504
Agrippina 287
Ahab 83–85, 88, 91, 94
Ahaz 84, 416–417, 423, 441
Ahaziah 84, 100
Ahijah 85, 87–88
Ahoshta 385, 386
Aiolos 95, 113, 117
Alcinous 96
Aldrin, Edwin Eugene Jr 247
Alexander the Great 164, 271
Alexander, son of Amyntas 143
Alfred the Great 393
Allori, Alessandro 97
Alphaeus, 526
Amasa 75
Amata 249, 264–265
Amaziah 84

Ambrose, Saint 491
Amnon 71, 73, 78–79
Amon 84
Amos 438, 440–441
Amoz 416
Amphimedon 121
Amphitrite 111
Amulius 222
Ananias 571
Anat 86
Andromache 252
Angelico, Fra 243, 505
Anna 235, 504
Antigone 181, 184, 186–187, 191–193, 306
Antony, Mark 278, 285, 293, 294, 297–300, 302–305, 307, 308
Anu 37, 40, 48
Anubis 31
Aphrodite 100, 249, 339
Apollo 161, 180, 196, 202, 219, 258
Apsu 11
Apuleius 340, 341, 343, 347, 350
Aquila, Marcus Flavius 537, 539–546
Aquilla 271
Aquinas, Thomas 486
Araunah 85
Aravis 369, 381–386, 389, 390
Aristophanes 98, 125
Aristotle 103, 180, 194, 201, 203, 206, 211, 214
Arminius, James 330, 331
Armstrong, Neil 247
Arsay 86
Arsheesh 381–383, 389
Artemidorus 302
Aruru 37, 40
Asa 84, 85
Ascanius 222, 249
Asherah 86
Aslan 346, 356–359, 361, 362, 365, 366, 368–370, 372, 373, 375–377, 379, 381–386, 390, 392–395, 397–399, 403–407, 412, 414, 450–452, 454–459, 462–466, 468, 469
Assurbanipal 39

Athaliah 84, 87
Athanasius, Saint 373
Athene (Athena) 104, 106, 108, 116, 117, 119, 152–157, 161, 162, 196, 202, 249
Atreus 154
Attila the Hun 492
Augustine, Saint 165, 241, 269, 270, 272–274, 277, 281–283, 285–287, 295, 299, 301, 378, 403, 491, 512, 513, 519, 524, 568
Augustus (Gaius Julius Caesar Octavianus) 248, 249, 251–255, 269, 270, 272–274, 281–283, 285–287
Atum 11
Azariah 84, 416

## B

Baal 83, 86, 87, 93, 513
Baal-Zebub 100
Baasha 84
Bacchus 399
Bach, Johann Sebastian 568
Baggins, Bilbo 10, 13, 14, 16
Bakhuizen, Ludulf 410
Bar 382
Bardia 341, 344, 351
Barnabas 502, 506, 509
Baruch 428
Basil 491
Bathsheba 71, 73, 75, 79
Beaver, Mr. 368, 369, 373, 374, 376, 377
Beaver, Mrs. 368, 369, 370, 373, 376, 377
Beckwith, Francis 495
Bel-Marduk 100
Bezalel 27, 35
Bliss, P.P. 336
Boniface, Saint 132
Botticelli, Sandro 32, 225
Bradley, David 308
Brahma 11
Bree 381, 383, 386
Brown, Harold O. J. 495
Bruce, F.F. 520

Brutus, Lucius Junius 215, 216, 223
Brutus, Marcus 251, 291–308
Bustard, Ned 22
Byron, George Gordon 92

C

Cain 9, 12
Caligula, Gaius Caesar 284, 286
Calpurnia 296, 300
Calvin, John 175, 239, 329–331, 335,
    508, 574
Cambyses 128, 132, 139, 140
Camillus, Marcus Furius 164, 174,
    175, 217, 220, 231–233
Canuleius, Gaius 229
Caravaggio, Michelangelo Merisi 70,
    399, 501
Carson, D.A. 402, 532
Casca 295, 300, 308
Caspian X 392–400, 404, 409, 411,
    450
Cassius Longinus, Gaius 294–300,
    302, 304–307
Castello, Valerio 496
Cato, Marcus Portius 251
Catullus 98
Cebes 198, 212
Cernunnos 539, 540, 544
Champollion, Jean Fancois 33
Charlemagne (Charles the Great) 69,
    79
Charles I 393
Cheops (Khufu) 30
Chesterton, G.K. 359
Chrysostom, John 487, 489, 491
Cicero, Marcus Tullius 164, 248, 261,
    295, 300
Cimber 302
Cincinnatus, Lucius Quinctius 217,
    227, 232, 233
Cinna 302
Circe 96, 103, 109, 112–117, 121
Claudius, Appius 215, 217, 225, 227,
    232
Claudius (Tiberias Claudius Drusus
    Nero) 271, 274, 285, 286, 288,
    537
Clement of Rome 470
Cleopatra 278
Clinton, Bill 420
Cloelia 215, 229
Clytaemnestra 154, 155, 159, 160

Columbus, Christopher 247
Cominus, Pontius 232, 233
Connolly, Peter 542
Cooper, Alice 564
Cor 382, 383
Coriakin 407, 409, 413
Coriolanus, Gaius Marcius 225, 232
Cottia 537, 541, 542, 545
Cowan, Louise 158, 188
Cradoc 537, 541, 543, 546
Cranach, Lucas, the Elder 517
Crassus, Marcus Licinius 295
Creon 181, 186, 190, 191, 193
Crito 198, 208, 212
Croesus 128, 130, 135–137
Cromwell, Oliver 293, 393
Cronos 186
Cruciger 572
Cupid 269, 339, 340
Cyrus (Darius the Mede) 82, 125, 128,
    130, 132, 134, 136, 137, 439

D

Dagon 86
Daniel 130, 137, 145, 428, 434
Dante Alighieri 7, 103, 340, 452
Darius I (the Great) 125, 127,
    130–133, 140–144, 442;
Darius the Mede (see Cyrus)
Darrow, Clarence Seward 162
David 24, 33, 46, 56, 68–79, 82–85,
    87, 94, 132, 168, 169, 223, 238,
    243, 249, 281, 301, 308, 374, 413,
    417, 419, 423, 544
David, Jacques-Louis 166, 205
Davidman, Joy 340
Davies, W. W. 53
DeMar, Gary 319
deMorgan, M. 53
Demosthenes 164
Dergdian, 537, 546
Diana 221
Dickens, Charles 535
Dido 249–251, 253, 254, 258–261,
    264, 265
Dillard, Raymond B. 22
Doctor Cornelius 392–394, 396–398
Domitian (Titus Flavius Domitianus
    Augustus) 271, 289
Doré, Paul Gustave 240, 442, 503
Doyle, Arthur Conan 363
Draco 172

Drinian 404, 409
Drusillus 537
Dumuzi (Tammuz) 54
Dürer, Albrecht 317, 321, 322, 525
Dylan, Jakob 107, 122

E

Ea 40
Eabani 38
Edwards, Jonathan 330
Eglon 301
Ehud 301
Elah 84
Electra 154
Eli 68, 71, 73, 77, 88
Eliakim 84
Elijah 82, 83, 87, 88, 91, 243, 407,
    528
Elisha 82, 83, 87, 88, 91, 440
Elkanah 68
Emeth 462, 465, 467, 469, 470
Emperor-Beyond-the-Sea 466
Enki 54
Enkidu 37, 40–43, 45,46, 49, 50
Enlil 40, 54
Enoch 12, 407
Erasmus, Desiderius 519
Ereshkigal 54
Erickson, Leif 247
Eris 257
Eros 339
Esau 9, 12, 14, 15, 22, 440, 442, 518
Esca 537, 539–541, 545, 546
Esther 130
Eteocles 181, 187, 188
Euripides 98, 125, 131
Euthyphro 197–203, 206, 207, 212
Eusebius of Caesarea 534
Evander 249
Eve 9, 10, 12, 14, 15, 17, 19, 52, 110,
    167, 305, 392, 480, 495, 555, 567
Evil-Merodach 87
van Eyck, Hubert 445
van Eyck, Jan 445
Ezekiel 428, 434, 438
Ezra 439, 440

F

Fabius Dorsuo, Gaius 232
Factor, Fudge 480
Father Christmas 368, 370, 373,
    376, 377

Figulus, Publius Nigidius 283
Finney, Charles 330, 335
Fisher, Emma 549
Flake, Felicia 474–476, 479, 485
Fledge 356, 364, 366
Flora 225
Ford, Paul F. 361, 373, 384, 395, 407, 456, 466
Fox 340, 341, 344–351, 353
Francis of Assisi, Saint 387
Francken, Frans II 90
Freud, Sigmund 24

G
Gaius (see Caligula)
Gamaliel 513, 514
Gentry, Kenneth L. 495
George, Saint 413
Gérard, François 348
Gilgamesh 37–50, 52, 53
Ginger the Cat 469
Giotto di Bondone 327
Glenstorm 398
Glimfeather 450, 456
Glubose 555
Graham, Billy 330. 334
Golg 453
Goliath 85
Gomer 441
Guiness, Os 158, 188
Guern 537, 545, 546
Gumpas 411

H
Habakkuk 428, 433, 438, 441, 445
Hadad 86
Hadad-Rimmon 100
Hades 187
Hadrian 536, 537
Haemon 181, 187
Hagar 9, 504, 507–509
Haggai 438, 442, 445
Ham 9
Hammurabi 51–65
Handel, George Frederick 568
Hannah 68, 72
Hannibal 217, 273
Harding, D.E. 414
Harold II 393
Hector 97, 252
Helen of Troy 257
Hephaestus 261

Hera (see also Juno) 96, 249
Herdonius, Appius 227
Hermes 249
Herod Agrippa 38
Herod the Great 29, 89, 235, 243, 391, 492, 496
Herodotus 123–146, 148, 149, 194, 197, 418, 439, 470
Herrod, Dr. Rex 492, 494, 497, 498, 499, 500
Hesiod 98, 185, 194
Heston, Charlton 308
Hezekiah 84, 87, 88, 94, 130, 416–418, 421, 424, 425, 439, 441
Hiel 88
Hilarion 548
Hilkiah 428
Hill, Paul 499
Hippocrates 125
Hiram 83
Hitler, Adolf 38
Holford, George Peter 319
Holmes, Sherlock 363
Homer 95, 96, 98, 103, 105, 106, 110, 112, 121, 124, 125, 151–154, 197, 219, 546
Hophni 73, 77
Horace (Quintus Horatius Flaccus) 98, 165
Horatius Cocles 232
Hosea 438, 439, 441, 444, 445
Hoshea 84, 87
Huldah 87
Huwawa 40, 41, 48
Hwin 381, 383, 386, 390

I
Irenaeus 236
Isaac 9, 12, 14, 15, 44, 243, 347, 417, 504, 507
Isaiah 87, 415–426, 438, 570
Ishbosheth 69, 71, 78
Ishmael 9, 14, 504, 507
Ishtar 40, 41, 43–45, 48, 50, 54, 55, 418, 425
Ismene 181, 191, 193
Istra 341, 353

J
Jacob 9, 12, 14–16, 21, 25, 28, 44, 88, 243, 417, 422, 440, 442, 518
Jadis (see also White Witch) 356,

358, 359, 361–363, 368
James 387, 502, 506, 525–534
Janson, H.W. 31
Janson, Anthony F. 31
Japheth 9
Jeconiah 84
Jehoahaz 84
Jehoash 84
Jehoiachin (Jeconiah, Coniah) 82, 84, 87
Jehoiada 84
Jehoiakim 87, 428, 429, 433, 434
Jehoikim 84
Jehoram (Joram) 84
Jehoshaphat 84
Jehu 82–84, 87, 88, 93, 94
Jeremiah 92, 427–433, 435, 438
Jeroboam 82–85, 87, 88, 91, 94, 285
Jeroboam II 84, 439, 441
Jerome 491
Jesus Christ 8, 22, 25, 37, 38, 45, 46, 48, 52, 55–61, 68, 69, 72, 82, 83, 87, 94, 100, 101–103, 114, 123, 127, 128, 132–134, 139, 145, 152, 158, 162, 163, 166, 167, 169, 172, 218, 226, 231, 236–245, 249, 253, 255, 256, 270, 272, 273, 277–279, 281, 283, 284, 287–289, 306, 310–323, 356, 358, 367–369, 371–373, 377, 379, 383, 391, 400, 412, 416, 417, 421, 422, 440, 442, 443, 452, 458, 461, 463, 465, 467, 469, 477–479, 480, 481, 490, 493, 495, 497, 502–506, 509, 510, 511–516, 518, 519, 522–533, 540–542, 552–554, 556, 557, 560–563, 567, 568, 570, 572, 573
Jethro 32, 345
Jewel 462, 463, 467–469
Jezebel 83, 84, 88, 91
Joab 71, 75
Joash 84, 87, 88, 94
Job 574
Jocasta 181, 183, 189, 190
Jochebed 25, 28
Joel 438, 440–442, 445
John the Apostle 241, 249, 254, 309, 310, 312–322, 324, 526, 528
John the Baptist 82, 239, 504
John Wesley 513
Jonah 130, 416, 437, 438, 440, 441, 444, 445

Jonathan 46, 69, 71–74, 544
Jones, Peter 279
Jordan, James 16
Joseph, son of Nun 9, 12, 14, 16, 21
Joseph, husband of Mary 235, 239, 504
Josephus, Flavius 241, 288, 290, 322, 324
Joshua 38, 72, 86, 88, 289, 573
Josiah 82–85, 87, 88, 94, 428, 429, 433, 439
Jotham 84, 416, 441
Jove 219
Judah 8, 9, 12
Judas, father of James 526
Judas Iscariot 391
Julius Caesar (Gaius Julius Caesar)164, 248, 251, 252, 261, 265, 271, 274, 279, 280, 281, 285, 286, 537
Juno (see also Hera) 219, 220, 249, 252, 257–259, 261, 399
Jupiter (see also Zeus) 216, 219, 249, 261, 264, 278, 399

K
Kaeso 537
Kalypso 96, 97, 103, 108, 110–112, 114–117, 121
Keats, John 342, 343
Ketterley, Andrew 355–356, 358–363, 366, 374
King Arthur 217, 218
King Frank 356, 392, 393, 398, 463
Kipling, Rudyard 535
Kirke, Digory 355–366, 368–370, 404, 464
Kish 70
Kreeft, Peter 474, 475, 489, 491, 500
Küng, Hans 574
Kushner, Harold 338

L
Laban 9, 15
Ladd, George Eldon 324
Laertes 99, 121
Laius 181, 183, 185, 186, 189, 190, 193
Laocoon 102, 107
Lasaraleen 382, 383, 386, 389
Latinus 249, 261
Lavinia 249, 257

Layard, Austen Henry 39, 40
Leah 9
Leithart, Peter J 16, 76, 89, 104, 162, 188, 444
Leonidas 125, 131
Lepidus 278, 282, 304
Lewis, C.S. 38, 104, 122, 339–341, 343, 345–347, 350, 351–353, 355–357, 359–363, 366–374, 379, 381–387, 392–394, 396, 399, 400, 402–408, 411, 413, 414, 449–454, 456, 458, 459, 461–471, 481, 546, 551–556, 562, 565
Lewis, Warnen 367, 551
Lincoln, Abraham 293
Lindskoog, Kathryn, 414
Livia 282
Livy (Titus Livius) 165, 213–223, 227, 230, 232–234, 271, 287
Longfellow, Henry Wadsworth 399
Longman, Tremper III 22
Lot 9, 12
Louis XVIII 248
Lucifer (see also Satan) 510
Lucretia 215, 220, 221, 223, 226, 233, 234
Lugh 539, 540, 543
Lugulbanda 40
Luke 235–241, 244, 245, 314
Lune 389
Luther, Martin 33, 329, 335, 512, 513, 519, 521, 534, 568, 570, 572, 574
Lycurgus 164, 167, 169, 170, 171, 174
Lygdamis 124

M
Maelius, Spurius 230, 232
Mahershalalhashbaz 416
Malachi 438, 440, 442, 445
el-Malik, Abd 76
Manasseh 84, 85, 416, 418
Mankiewicz, Joseph L. 308
Marcipor 537
Marduk 43, 57, 63, 65
Mark the Evangelist 283, 439
Mary 237, 239, 241, 372, 373, 504
Mattaniah (see Zedekiah)
McGranahan, James 336
McKeon, Richard P. 194
Measurer, Marigold 480
Melanchthon, Philipp Schwarzert 572

Melchizedek 345
Meletus 198
Menahem 84
Meneleos 108, 117, 119, 155
Mercury 249
Messius, Vettius 230, 233
Metis 152
Mettius Fufetius 231
Micah 438, 439, 441, 445
Micaiah 87
Michael the Archangel 510
Michelangelo, Buonarroti 17, 35, 92, 415
Milne, A.A. 535
Milton, John 96, 340
Minerva (see also Athene) 249, 257, 278
Miraz 392–396, 398, 400, 404, 463
Mithras 539, 540
Moo, Douglas J. 532
Moses 8, 9, 12, 19, 22, 24–29, 31, 32, 34–36, 53, 60–62, 65, 69, 72, 74, 82, 86, 169, 173, 199, 235, 240, 243, 521, 570
Mot 86
Moultrie, Gerard 402
Moussorgsky, Modest 397
Mucius, Gaius 215, 225, 232, 233
Mulder, Karen L. 551
Murray, John 520
Mussolini, Benito 293

N
Naaman 470
Nabal 75, 77
Nabopolassar 439, 441
Nabu 57
Nadab 84, 567, 574
Nahum 428, 438, 441, 445
Nanna (Sin) 54
Nathan 68, 71, 79
Nausikaa 97, 110, 117
Nebuchadnezzar 82, 85, 87, 92, 130, 137, 148, 428, 429, 433, 434
Nebuchadnezzar II 439
Nehemiah 439
Neptune (see also Poseidon) 249
Nergal 54
Nero (Nero Claudius Caesar Drusus Germanicus)164, 166, 236, 249, 254, 271, 280, 286, 287, 312
Nesbit, Edith 379

Nestor 108, 117
Nicodemus 249, 412
Nikabrik 392–396, 398, 399
Nike 248
Nimrod 41
Ninsun 40
Ninurta 37
Ninursa 37
Nisus 264
Noah 9, 12–14, 16, 20, 39, 40, 49, 50, 53, 57, 238, 345, 574
Numa Pompilius 164, 170, 171, 174, 232

O
Obadiah 438, 440–442, 445
Octavius (see also Augustus) 297
Odin 100
Odysseus 95–97, 99–101, 103, 104, 106–122, 249, 263, 403
Oedipus 179–191, 193, 194, 306, 382
Ogilvie, Robert 234
Oholiab 35
Omri 82–85, 91, 93, 94
Orestes 153–157, 160–162, 196
Orual 340–353
Osiris 544
Otto, Rudolph 570
Ovid 98, 165, 219
Ozymandias 81

P
Pallas 249, 252, 264, 265
Pan 544
Paris 248, 257
Paul the Apostle 29, 32, 100, 101, 114, 119, 127, 162, 184, 236, 237, 239, 240, 244–246, 271, 274, 276, 277, 289, 290, 372, 391, 417, 421, 422, 501–509, 511–524, 527–530, 532, 533, 574
Paxford, Fred 449
Pekah 84, 417
Pekahiah 84
Pelagius 524
Pelops 154
Penelope 96, 97, 103, 108–110, 114–117, 119–121
Pericles 125, 131, 153
Peter the Apostle 528
Peter the Great 69
Petronius, Gaius 165

Pevensie, Edmund 368–377, 392, 399, 400, 404, 406, 410
Pevensie, Lucy 368–371, 373–375, 392, 398, 399, 404, 407, 409, 410, 413
Pevensie, Peter 239, 240, 368–371, 373, 375, 377, 391, 392, 399, 400, 404, 502, 506–509
Pevensie, Susan 368–371, 373, 375,391–393, 396, 399, 404, 469
Phaedo 197, 198, 208, 212
Phinehas 73, 77
Pidray 86
Pindar 98
Plato 195–201, 203–207, 209, 464, 465, 467, 474, 475
Plutarch 163–168, 171–175, 197, 271, 287, 295, 305, 307
Plummer, Polly 355–359, 361–364, 366, 369
Poggin 462, 467, 469
Pole, Jill 369, 450–453, 455–459, 462–464, 468, 469
Polyneices 181, 186–188, 191, 193
Polyphemos 99, 111, 113, 114, 118
Pomeranus 572
Pompey (Gnaeus Pompeius Magnus) 251, 295, 299, 300
Poplicola (Publius Valerius Publicola) 164, 167, 171–175
Portia 294, 300, 304
Poseidon (see also Neptune) 96, 97, 99, 111, 113, 117, 249
Potter, Beatrix 535
Poussin, Nicolas 180
Pragma, Peter 474–476, 478, 482, 484
Priscilla 271
Prunaprismia 392
Psyche 340–353
Publilius Volero 225
Puddleglum 450, 451, 453–459
Puzzle 462, 467, 468

Q
Queen Helen 356, 392, 393, 398, 463
Quintilian (Marcus Fabius Qunitilianus) 214
Quirinius 241, 270

R
Rabadash 381, 386, 389

Rachel 9, 15
Rahab 526
Ramandu 409
Ramses II 25, 33
Raphael (Raffaello Sanzio) 202, 206, 415, 566
Rawlinson, George 194
Rebekah 9, 15
Redival 341, 344, 347
Regillensis, Marcus Postmius 230, 232
Rehoboam 84, 85, 91
Rembrandt Harmenszoon van Rijn21, 69, 126, 134, 238, 239, 242, 427
Rezin 417
Rhea 399
Rilian 369, 450, 454–459
Robertson, O. Palmer 22
Robinson, Robert 449
Rohl, David 33
Romaine, James 22
Romulus 163, 164, 167, 169, 171, 174, 213, 216, 222, 224, 232, 233
Rubens, Peter Paul 421
Rudolph, Eric 499
Russell, Bertrand 438
Rutherford, Samuel 461

S
Samuel 68–75, 77, 97, 108
Sapphira 571
Sappho 98
Sarah (Sarai) 9, 14, 504, 507–509
Saruman 38
Sassticca 537
Satan 237, 238, 240, 317, 318, 319, 323, 552, 553, 562, 567
Saturn 251
Saul 24, 68–73, 75–79, 84–87, 223
Sayers, Dorothy L. 340
Schliemann, Heinrich 151
Screwtape 551, 553–562
Scrubb, Eustace Clarence 369, 403–406, 409–412, 450–453, 462, 469
de Sélincourt, Aubrey 234
Semele 399
Sempronius Atratinus, Gaius 230
Seneca, Lucius Annaeus 165, 289, 524
Sennacherib 39, 92, 93, 417, 421, 424, 425
Servilius, Publius 224, 225

Servius, Tullius 219, 221
Seti I 25, 33
Shallum 84
Shalmaneser 417, 439
Shamash 40, 44, 50, 53, 54, 56, 65
Shamhat 40
Shasta 369, 381–386, 388–390, 465
Shaw, George Bernard 570
Shearjashub 416
Shelley, Percy Bysshe 81, 414
Shem 9
Sherman, William Tecumseh 336
Shift 462, 467, 468
Shishak 33
Siduri 49
Simeon 235, 238, 504
Simmias 198, 212
Smerdis the Magus 132
Smetana, Bedrich 397
Socrates 125, 131, 195–212, 473–485,
    487, 489, 491–500, 531, 532
Solomon 24, 33, 67, 72, 73, 76, 79,
    82–85, 87–91, 94, 274, 281, 443
Solon 164, 171–175, 197
Sophocles 125, 130, 179, 180, 184,
    185, 188, 189, 191, 306, 382
Spielvogel, Jackson 16, 31, 45, 61, 89,
    104, 158, 164, 168, 175, 188, 194,
    221, 279, 281, 290, 443, 446, 542,
    556
Sproul, R.C. 328, 330, 332, 337, 564,
    565, 567, 568, 570, 571, 573, 574
Spurgeon, Charles Haddon 334, 335,
    384
Stephen 25, 527
Stephanos 537
Stott, John R.W. 520
Strauss 397
Suetonius (Gaius Suetonius
    Tranquillus) 270, 271, 273–279,
    284, 287, 290
Sunday, Billy 334, 335
Sutcliff, Rosemary 535, 536, 538, 539,
    543, 546–549
Syke, "Pop" 492, 493, 498

T
Tacitus, Cornelius 165, 168, 214, 279,
    289, 290
Tallay 86
Tamar 71, 73
Tantalus 154

Tarian, Atilla 490, 492, 498, 500
Tarkaan, Rishda 462, 465, 467, 469
Tarquin (Lucius Tarquinius Superbus)
    216, 220, 223, 226, 232
Tarquinius, Sextus 216, 220
Tash 346, 384, 385, 462, 465, 466,
    469
Tasker, Harold 308
Teiresias 113, 117, 181, 186, 188, 190,
    193, 194
Telemachos 96, 103, 108, 112,
    115–119, 121
Tempanius, Sextus 230
Tenney, Merrill C. 532
Terah 9, 54
Terentillus Arsa, Gaius 227
Tertullian (Quintus Septimius Florens
    Tertullianus) 236
Thales 126
Themistocles 123, 125, 131, 146, 147,
    164, 169, 173–175
Theophilus 236, 238
Theseus 164, 165, 167–169, 171, 174,
    181, 184, 191–193
Thomas the Apostle 570
Thor 100
Thucydides 124, 131, 214, 271
Thyestes 154
Tiamat 43
Tiamut 11
Tiberius (Tiberius Claudius Nero
    Caesar) 282, 283, 284, 286
Tibni 84, 85
Tiglath-pileser III (Pul) 417, 439
Tirian 368, 462–464, 467, 469
Titus (Titus Flavius Sabinus
    Vespasianus) 274, 288
Titus 506
Tolkein, J.R.R. 10, 12, 13, 14, 16, 38,
    340, 551
Tradui 537
Trufflehunter 392–394, 396, 398
Trumpkin 392–398
Tull, Jethro 37
Tullus Hostilius 215
Tumnus 368–371, 373–376
Turnus 249, 251, 252, 262, 264–266
Twain, Mark 95, 405

U
Ulysses (Odysseus) 249
Ungit 339–342, 344, 345, 347,

349–351, 353
Uriah 75
Urshanabi 49
d'Urville, Jules Dumont 248
Utnapishtim 39, 40, 41, 49, 50
Uzzah 567, 571
Uzziah 84, 416, 441, 570

V
Vader, Darth (Anakin Skywalker) 563
Valerius, Manlius 224
van der Land, J.G. 33
Vandiver, Willard Duncan 525
Venus (see also Aphrodite) 269
Verginia 232, 233
Verginius 217, 227
Vespasian (Titus Flavius Sabinus
    Vespasianus) 270, 274, 288
Virgil (Publius Vergilus Maro) 96, 98,
    165, 214, 219
Vivaldi, Antonio 126, 134

W
Walzer, Michael 24
Washington, George 250, 258
Watson, Thomas 335
Whiston, William 241
White Witch (see also Jadis) 356,
    358, 365, 366, 368–377, 463
Whitefield, George 330, 334, 335
William the Conqueror 393
Williams, Ralph Vaughan 402
Wintle, Justin 549
Wittle, Daniel Webster 336
Wordsworth, William 414, 409
Wormwood 551, 553–558, 560–562
Wyatt, William 122

X
Xerxes 125, 131–133, 145–148

Y
Yam 86

Z
Zachariah 84
Zacharias 235, 240, 242, 243
Zebedee 526
Zechariah 438, 442
Zedekiah (Mattaniah) 84, 87, 428,
    429, 434
Zephaniah 428, 433, 438, 441, 445

Zeruiah 75

Zeus (*see also* Jupiter) 96, 97, 100,
    108, 110, 127, 133, 139, 145, 152,
    186, 202, 219, 249

Zimri 84, 85

Zipporah 26

**SELECT ILLUSTRATION CREDITS**

*Illustrations by Matthew Clark are found on the following
pages:* 15, 37, 40, 60, 61, 67, 86, 118, 129, 138, 139, 146,
147, 156, 253, 316, 344, 355 *(with Ned Bustard),* 360, 382,
388, 389, 391, 403, 404, 408, 412, 413, 453–455, 462, 466,
474, 480, 485, 488, 490, 493, 496, 498, 540, 541, 544, 545,
547, 554, 556–558, 562, 568, 574. *More of Matthew's work
can be seen at www.DrawingMatthewClark.com.*

*Illustrations by Ned Bustard are found on the following pages:*
16, 27, 39, 55, 59, 211, 340, 355 *(with Matthew Clark),* 358,
378, 387, 397, 401, 406, 414, 449, 470, 473, 476, 479, 491,
495, 499, 511, 515, 543, 555, 591, 592. *More of Ned's work
can be seen at www.WorldsEndImages.com.*